LEE'S COLONELS

Georgia Dept. of Archives & History

SIMEON B. GIBBONS
10th Virginia

LEE'S COLONELS

A Biographical Register of the Field Officers of the Army of Northern Virginia

4th Edition, Revised

By
ROBERT K. KRICK

Morningside
1992

LIBRARY OF CONGRESS CATALOGING
IN PUBLICATION DATA

Krick, Robert K., 1943-

Lee's Colonels, Lieutenant Colonels and Majors in Army
of Northern Virginia, Virginia, Confederate Army.

ISBN: 0-89029-548-4

Library of Congress Catalog Number 79-52930

Glatfelter Acid Free Paper

Published by Press of

Morningside House, Inc.

260 Oak Street, Dayton, Ohio 45410

Contents

Acknowledgements

The many months and miles consumed by the research which produced this compilation were made successful by a legion of Southerners who helped out in various ways. A couple of pages of the usual acknowledgements cannot adequately pay their freight, but what else is there? Sic transit gloria.

Tom McCall of Raleigh is doubtless the leading purveyor of connectors in the Southern states. Between connections he gave invaluable assistance in my search for North Carolina data, and conducted a considerable volume of North Carolina research himself. Mrs. Julia Martin of VMI has the graduates and eleves of the Institute so well in hand that I frequently found myself wishing that every officer had attended there. The absence of an equivalent person in many other institutions made my task more difficult and less successful. Could Mrs. Martin be cloned, the list of schools needing her attention to the disheveled records of their 19th-century students would be long and hungry.

Anne Minor Baker and Dorothy Barrett, of Richmond's UDC headquarters establishment, were extremely good to me, and good for this book. Michael Musick of the National Archives knows Confederate records so very well, and is anxious to share his knowledge with needy folks like me. It must be added, impolitic though it may be, that the kindly and efficient help of the professional staff at both the National Archives and the Library of Congress is nearly equalled by the unkind and inefficient lack of help displayed by most of the front-line desk people at those places.

George H. S. King of Fredericksburg is unique in any number of ways, some of which had a salutary impact on this register. David Riggs, formerly of the Virginia Historical Society, helped a great deal with the important resources of that organization.

E. P. Walker, of the South Carolina State Library, had a big hand in fleshing out the record of many gray-clad palmettos. Robert J. Younger, who deserves the biggest nod of all as the book's publisher, also used some outstanding favors to get research help in the southwest.

David A. Lilley and Allen W. Greene of Fredericksburg help me with many things each week, and for the past hundred or so weeks that included many things related to Lee's Colonels. Ed Raus and his battered, DLC-bound Pinto fall in the same category. Robert E. L. Krick and William B. Krick regularly light up the life of their father (the compiler of this register); more to the point, they made important contributions to my research by filing and refiling all 2000 cards countless times. Bobby also turned a crank through several miles of microfilm.

Lee A. Wallace deserves a paragraph; Dr. James I. Robertson, Jr., of VPI, is a necessarily close friend of every Confederate researcher; those who think V. H. Davis is the First Lady of the Confederacy have never worked with Eleanor Brockenbrough of the Museum of the Confederacy; Kathy Curtis' Wise Co. vowels penetrated southwestern Virginia sources beyond the reach of this flat-talking Californian.

John E. Devine is a Loudoun Co. oracle; Lucile Portlock of the Norfolk Public Library should be cited as typical of, and perhaps even a bit better than, the countless librarians who helped a stranger through the mails; Lowell Reidenbaugh, of St. Louis, is always anxious to temporarily forswear sweatsock journalism to seek out some post-war Rebel who strayed to the midwestern barrens; Ben Ritter knows the dead of Winchester, Va., better than anyone; Judy Muse made the University of Georgia the best resource in a rather lean state.

Here are a few more, but not all, of the helpful legion: Caroline Killens, Mississippi Dept. of Archives and History; Hyman Schwartzberg, Richmond; Dr. Ronald Heinemann, Hampden-Sydney; Doug Schanz of New Jersey then Philadelphia, then Roanoke, Va.; Ralph Donnelly, CSMC; Mary M. (Mrs. John M.) Bell, Norfolk; Dan Hartzler, New Windsor, Md.; Betty Otto, Sharpsburg Battlefield; Sheila McGarr and Mary Porter, Mary Washington College Library; Deborah Spiller, Fredericksburg; Kenneth Rapp, Robert Schnare and Regina Hanretta, USMA;

Milo B. Howard, Alabama Dept. of Archives and History; Jack Lattimore, Maryland Historical Society; Russell E. Booker, Jr., Virginia Bureau of Vital Records; Jean Jones, New Orleans Public Library; Michael J. Dabrishus, Texas State Library; R. N. Latture, Washington & Lee U.; Doris Hunt, West Virginia Archives and History; Walter Sanford, Alexandria, Va.; Cary Close, Washington, D.C.; Russell K. and Flora P. Krick, who supplied first life, then three days of help at NARS.

Several hundred descendants of Army of Northern Virginia field officers rediscovered birth and death dates for me, with a uniform and gratifying graciousness which made the job practicable. More than one hundred Southern libraries cheerfully pitched in, with less than a half-dozen cranky or unwilling responses in the lot; resort to a few libraries up where all the Southern spoons are stored produced results about as good.

Publication of this biographical register will inevitably result in the appearance of a good bit more information which was missed the first time around. The accrual of such additions, and the existence of much more research data than could be included herein, will leave me well fixed to help any researchers interested in a particular field officer. My clear obligation, incurred by the use of all the good assistance cited above, is to be of help to anyone that I can, and that is my firm intention.

INTRODUCTION TO THE THIRD EDITION

This edition varies from the second by addition of new material on nearly 1,000 of the entries for Lee's Colonels (more than one-half of the total), and on more than 500 of the officers listed in the appendix. The effect of that new material on the tabulations in the preface to the first edition—which already had been revised by second edition additions—is reflected in the appropriate tables, but not necessarily in the prose portion of that introduction.

An important part of the new information for this edition came to me as the result of efforts by four individuals: Raymond Watkins of Northern Virginia; Bruce Allardice of Des Plaines, Illinois; Jim Moody of the Citadel, whose prowess in quest of Palmetto officers is remarkable; and Keith S. Bohannon of Georgia, who is notable both for his historical energy and zeal and for his heroically lovelorn status. I also received assistance from Paul Cooksey of Harrisburg, Pennsylvania; Ed Dallery of Sumter, South Carolina; Jack Dwyer of Fairfax, Virginia; David M. Sherman of Washington, D.C.; and Roger Long of Port Clinton, Ohio. Robert E. L. Krick helped me too, as he always does.

At the suggestion of several interested observers, I will use this space to summarize concisely what *Lee's Colonels* contains and what it does not, in the probably vain hope that confusion over its scope will subside.

—The main portion of this book covers field-grade officers of the line—that is to say, majors, lieutenant colonels, and colonels—from regiments and battalions that served with the Army of Northern Virginia. That includes units that served with the army before R. E. Lee assumed its command. It also includes officers who served with such units only before the units joined Lee's army.

—The appendix contains officers of precisely the same sort who served with units that never were connected with the Army of

Northern Virginia. It also includes some field-grade officers of militia units and other irregular organizations.

—The main portion of this book does *not* include those men who served as field officers in units of the army if those officers eventually achieved the rank of general. An ample body of literature already exists about them.

—This book does *not* include in either of its sections officers of the rank of major, lieutenant colonel, or colonel who served in staff positions, whether with generals in the field, as staff functionaries with field organizations, or in roles subsidiary to the War Department in Richmond. The numbers of such individuals run far into the thousands. The similarities of rank notwithstanding, they represent an entirely different breed of officers than the regimental line commanders. Someone needs to compile a biographical register of the field staff (I have several thousand cards of that sort already myself), but it will run to at least twice the bulk of this book, in the process reporting on individuals who were as a rule less important than Lee's Colonels.

Robert K. Krick
Fredericksburg
December 1990

INTRODUCTION TO THE SECOND EDITION

This new edition differs from the first edition in more ways than just the improved typography and added comeliness of printing and binding. Three hundred sixty-two of the entries have been revised substantially, by means of new information in most cases, but in some few instances by correction of errors or oversights. As a result, occasional changes have been made in the introduction and its appended tables, but without altering the August 1978 signature on the original introduction.

The most substantial alteration from the original edition is addition to the large appendix, which lists 3,510 Confederate field officers who did *not* serve with the Army of Northern Virginia. An explanation of the origins of the list, and of the refinements to which I subjected it, is contained in introductory remarks at that point in the book.

Accumulation of new information over the five years since the appearance of the first edition has been a steady process. Scores of individuals have chipped in from every imaginable vantage point. Two of the most ardent helpers have been my beloved sons. Robert E. L. Krick has become, despite his rather tender sixteen years, a very knowledgeable historical researcher on Virginia Confederate subjects. Anyone in quest of that sort of thing would do far better to wind up in his hands than at the front desk of any university library that comes readily to mind. The advantages of having such a creature in the house have been beyond estimation. William B. Krick is a wonderful little rascal, full of zeal and effervescence, but not much of an after-hours scholar as yet. He was, nevertheless, of considerable help on several days when he corked his ebullience for many more hours than the child-labor laws would countenance, in order to do drudge work at the Library of Congress, the National Archives, and other such places. I'm grateful to them, and thankful for them.

Robert K. Krick
Fredericksburg
November 1983

INTRODUCTION

Marcus Joseph Wright (1831-1922) is a familiar figure to students of Confederate history. He attained the rank of brigadier general late in 1862, but was not exceptionally distinguished during the war. Wright's most important historical contribution began in 1878 when he became an agent of the War Department for collection of Confederate materials as part of the project which produced the published *Official Records*. For almost four decades, General Wright was the key figure in finding, preserving and organizing Confederate records. In the process he produced several listings of Southern officers and units; some of these exist only in manuscript at the National Archives. Among those published—on cheap paper and in a tiny edition of twenty-five copies—was: *List of Field Officers, Regiments, and Battalions in the Confederate States Army, 1861-1865* (Washington, 1891?).

Wright's list of field officers is quite accurate, although he did fail to include most qualifying artillerists. A 1912 publication by one Claud Estes of Macon, Georgia, paid Wright the compliment of pirating his work virtually verbatim, down to typos and asterisks. Wright's simple listing, and Estes' copy thereof, never grew beyond a fleshless column of names. The biographical register published here takes the portion of Wright's field officers who served in the Army of Northern Virginia, adds those he overlooked, then expands them into both civilians and military men of understandable dimensions.

The entries which make up the register are useful individually, but there is also much about the field officers which can only be discerned cumulatively. They were, for instance, a surprisingly young set of men. As can be readily seen on the accompanying chart, more of them were twenty-six years old when they reached field rank than any other age. There are 1765 ages available in this register, for 1968 officers, so the sampling is a more than statistically adequate one. The average age is 32 and the median age is 31. Even those surprisingly low age levels would be noticeably reduced if the statistics did not include a good number of Reserve, Militia and Local Defense officers whose units served with the Army of Northern Virginia for awhile. That breed of officer was generally of an older generation than those in regular field service. Although 76-year-old Richard C. Cotton stands ready to refute the allegation, the Army's field officers can safely be said to have been a youthful lot.

The physical size of Lee's Colonels may not be of lasting moment, but it is interesting enough to warrant a paragraph. Thirty percent of them were 6′0″ or taller. The most common height found was 5′11″, followed by 5′10″ and 6′0″. Towering Royston at 6′7½″ heads the list and diminutive 5′4″ Spengler and Westcott win the Lilliputian Prize. It is widely stated that modern man grows ever taller and stronger. Whether that be so or not, the available height samples for Lee's Colonels reveal an average height of 5′10.4″ and a median height of 5′10½″. The millions of men leaving the U.S. Army at the end of World War II averaged 5′8.4″ in height.

Specific information on the education of the officers is not available in enough volume to allow valid analysis of their educational achievements in general. 947 instances of attendance at or graduation from college level institutions were found. That would be an ample number for the purpose, but for the fact that the absence of evidence of college education is far from conclusive in almost every case. What we can do is learn about the schools which produced the officers, as there is more than enough data to show the schools' status relative to one another. A glance at the educational table will show VMI as a clear leader and the University of Virginia uncontested as runnerup. The Virginia total is somewhat misleading, because a disproportionate number of the men in that column spent relatively brief periods in the University's Law School; fewer of that school's total number were full-fledged long-term students than is the case with any other major school on the educational list.

Despite the caveat, it is impressive to note that about 35% of the time, the institutions found in the officers' backgrounds were either VMI or the University of Virginia. When the other Virginia schools are added in, the sample rises to 48%. Unless there is some reason to believe that Virginia data was more readily retrieved (and the University of Virginia is among the least concerned with ancient alumni, of all the places contacted), it appears that Lee's regimental command was about one-half Virginia educated. It is also worthy of note that precisely 30% of the educational entries were at one of the five military schools on the list.

Forty percent of the men who became field officers in the Army of Northern Virginia were either lawyers or politicians before the war (the distinction being a difficult one). Less than 10% of them had been professional soldiers, despite the military training that 30% of them had enjoyed. In evaluating the prewar occupations enumerated on the accompanying chart, it should be borne in mind that 1275 samples are given, which means that about 60% of the officers do not have an identified occupation; therefore, the number in various professions should be compared with the list, rather than used as raw totals. 114 of the men had identified Mexican War service; twenty-two others served as volunteers in the Creek, Seminole, Texan or other Wars, or filibustered with Walker.

One of the most amazing statistics developed by surveying the data compiled here is the fact that 428 field officers in the Army of Northern Virginia were killed in action. Another 54 were killed in accidents or died of disease during the war. That means that about 24% of the men in the field officer category were lost during the war (using 1968 samples as the total).

At least 156 field officers were dropped at the re-organization of the army in the spring of 1862. The inane notion that troops could best identify the capacity to lead regiments in camp and battle was a product of the Confederate Congress, gathered in sessions of a decidedly non-military nature. Since the Army of Northern Virginia can be loosely said to have had 200 regiments of infantry, it can be easily seen what havoc the spring re-organization wrought. Nearly one field officer per regiment was displaced. There is need for a detailed study, both statistical and analytical, of the course and consequence of those 1862 elections. (cf. Milton Cary's comment, quoted in his sketch, infra.)

There is much of interest in the cumulative statistics concerning post-war occupations and mortality of Lee's Colonels. Only 55 of them, for instance, are known to have emigrated from the ex-Confederate states for any lengthy period. Since death data is available on 1182 of them, it is apparent that the proportion of emigrating ex-officers was negligible. The table of post-war occupations makes it evident that, though pre-war political experience was a good road to an officer's commission, that same commission was an even better road to post-war political office. Nearly 40% of the post-war occupations cited include poltical office on either the state or national levels. The Bloody Shirt of blue, so successfully waved in Presidential elections for years, had a gray counterpart with similarly magical qualities.

The 1497 or so field officers who survived the war lived longer than might have been assumed. Death dates were found for two-thirds of them. It was not until 1898 that half of the veteran field officers were dead, and Hitler was preparing to absorb Poland when Stephen P. Halsey finally died on the eve of an infinitely different war. Using the average age at commission as a basis, it can be estimated that the average age at death for Lee's Colonels was within about one year of 70.

Fife, Hagood and Pate survived a war full of hostile projectiles to meet death in railroad accidents. Ficklin, after adventuring with the Pony Express and serving the Confederacy, ran afoul of a fatal dinner at Willard's Hotel in Washington. Many of Lee's Colonels were caught up in violence quite apart from the sort outlined in Casey's or Hardee's manuals. Berkeley and Falkner were assassinated by outraged competitors. Steedman was murdered by blacks in tumultuous Reconstruction South Carolina; Blair was killed in the same state in apparent retribution for seeking black votes. Styles and Yellowley killed men in pre-war duels; Wright killed a friend in a brawl. Moore fought a post-war duel and absconded to California. Gerald, an august judge, killed two men in an 1897 gunfight. Lowry and Twiggs lost their lives in street fights. Major Henry Burroughs Holliday won less military fame than his son won secular fame as one of the best known of the gunfighter legends.

Before you undertake the use of this biographical register, heed a word of caution about the relative merits of the sources whence it came. The compiled service records which supplied most of the important military data are of good, but occasionally uneven, quality. Although it may not be objectively provable, without some effort, there is a solid suspicion that Louisiana and South Carolina have less adequate records of that sort. Some Virginia units (the 25th and 31st Infantry come to mind) are similarly deficient. Sometimes a particular regiment will have very rough records, for reasons which are not clear.

Some of the Southern states also have much better resources than others for civilian data. Virginia, the Carolinas, Mississippi, Alabama and Texas are strong; Florida, Arkansas, Maryland and Tennessee are middling; Georgia and Louisiana are weak. Doubtless there is some reflection on the author in this analysis, but a strong and equal effort yielded unequal results.

Almost everyone who uses this register will find occasion to note an omission of some fact which it is within their power to supply. Please do supply it, and help me chink up the gaps.

Chancellorsville, Virginia August 1978

Taking the opportunity offered by a new fourth edition printing, I have revised 156 entries in the main section of this book, and added one entirely new entry (that for Meriwether Lewis Clark). In the appendix, this edition contains sixty revised entries and two entirely new names. The statistical tables and textual references in the newly revised original edition introduction reflect the new data that has been added to the individual entries.

Robert K. Krick
Fredericksburg
May 1992

AGES OF LEE'S COLONELS

Age	Number	Age	Number
17	1	40	39
18	2	41	52
19	8	42	31
20	17	43	19
21	47	44	27
22	47	45	22
23	81	46	17
24	61	47	13
25	90	48	14
26	105	49	9
27	96	50	10
28	102	51	8
29	89	52	8
30	96	54	3
31	95	55	4
32	94	56	6
33	76	57	2
34	62	58	1
35	74	60	3
36	70	62	2
37	61	63	1
38	54	65	1
39	44	76	1

Total samples - 1765
Median age - 31
Average age - 32

Ages are at the date on which the individuals first reached field officer status.

MISCELLANEOUS STATISTICS

Total entries in the register - 1968
Number born in the Federal states - 40
Number born outside the United States - 41
Dropped at 1862 unit re-organizations - 156
Emigrated outside the ex-Confederate states for major periods after the war - 60
Killed in action - 428
Died of accidental means, or of disease, during the war - 54
Mexican War veterans - 114

Veterans of volunteer service in other wars - 29
Professional soldiers - 72

HEIGHTS OF LEE'S COLONELS

6′7½″	1	5′9½″	2
6′4″	8	5′9¼″	1
6′3″	7	5′9″	21
6′2″	9	5′8¾″	2
6′1½″	2	5′8½″	6
6′1″	7	5′8″	19
6′0″	31	5′7¾″	1
5′11″¾	1	5′7½″	2
5′11½″	4	5′7″	5
5′11″	35	5′6½″	1
5′10½″	5	5′6″	8
5′10″	33	5′5″	1
5′9¾″	2	5′4″	4

Total number of heights available - 218
Average height - 5′10.5″
Median height - 5′10½″

EDUCATION OF LEE'S COLONELS

VMI	157	Jefferson Medical College	11
U. Virginia	149	U. Mississippi	10
U. N. Carolina	84	Harvard	10
U.S. Military Academy	81	Georgetown	9
U. Georgia	52	Mercer	8
S. C. College	44	Princeton	8
S. C. Military Academy	40	Oglethorpe	6
William & Mary	33	Columbian	6
Washington College	22	Davidson	6
U. Pennsylvania	20	Transylvania	5
Hampden-Sydney	20	U.S. Naval Academy	4
U. Alabama	18	Duke	4
Emory & Henry	18	Maryland	3
Randolph-Macon	18	Jefferson College, Pa.	3
Georgia Military Inst.	16	Washington & Jefferson	3
Yale	14	Lynchburg	2
Wake Forest	12	Medical College of Va.	2
Emory	11	Centenary	2

Allegheny	2	Erskine	2
Nashville	2	Cumberland	2
Amherst	2	Wofford	2
Brown	2	Medical College of S. C.	2

Some of the schools attended by only one officer: Auburn, Indiana, U. Tennessee, Catawba, Roanoke, Dartmouth, Cokesbury, Bethany, St. James, Spring Hill, Gettysburg, Bowdon (Ga.), Cherokee Baptist (Ga.), Clinton (Tenn.), LaGrange Military Academy, Mt. St. Mary's (Md.), NYU.

PRE-WAR OCCUPATIONS OF LEE'S COLONELS

Lawyers and judges	268	Hotel keepers	5
Planters/farmers	231	Carpenters	5
Politicians (state level)	167	Druggists	5
Medical doctors	104	Student	5
Teachers	103	Architects	4
Merchants and businessmen	99	Laborers	4
Professional soldiers	72	Brickmaker	3
Clerks	30	Auctioneers	3
Journalists	28	Railroad manager	3
Law officers	22	Bookkeepers	2
Clergymen	19	Blacksmiths	2
U.S. Congress	17	Grocers	2
Engineers	16	Jewelers	2
Mechanics	8	Justices of the peace	2
Bankers	6	Customs Officers	2
Surveyors	6	Wagon makers	2

Notary public, teamster, barber, cooper, painter, postmaster, miner, saddler, saloon keeper, moulder, coroner, "Gent," gentleman, boatman, canal official, coal dealer, dentist, miller, liquor dealer, land agent, overseer, tailor, tanner, timber measurer, salesman, piano maker, harness maker, iron master—1 each.

(In a few instances, two occupations have been tabulated for one man, primarily when he has Congressional service on record.)

POST-WAR OCCUPATIONS OF LEE'S COLONELS

Politicians (state level)	242
Farmers	91
Merchants	88
Lawyers and judges	79
Teachers	49
Journalists and authors	48
U.S. Congress	45
Law officers	30
Engineers	22
Clergymen	21
Bankers	20
Medical doctors	17
U.S. Civil Service	11
Clerks	8
Mining interests	5
Surveyors	4
Carpenters	4
Millers	3
Druggists	2
Carriage maker, hotel keeper, viticulturist	1 each

POST-WAR MORTALITY AMONG LEE'S COLONELS

1865 - 10	1900 - 31
1866 - 14	1901 - 32
1867 - 12	1902 - 36
1868 - 9	1903 - 25
1869 - 11	1904 - 28
1870 - 10	1905 - 25
1871 - 14	1906 - 28
1872 - 16	1907 - 31
1873 - 15	1908 - 29
1874 - 12	1909 - 19
1875 - 15	1910 - 29
1876 - 20	1911 - 21
1877 - 17	1912 - 24
1878 - 10	1913 - 16
1879 - 15	1914 - 21
1880 - 12	1915 - 20
1881 - 27	1916 - 16
1882 - 8	1917 - 11
1883 - 21	1918 - 11
1884 - 19	1919 - 8
1885 - 22	1920 - 5
1886 - 30	1921 - 4
1887 - 19	1922 - 5
1888 - 19	1923 - 8
1889 - 29	1924 - 3
1890 - 22	1925 - 8
1891 - 24	1926 - 5
1892 - 23	1927 - 1
1893 - 28	1928 - 3
1894 - 22	1929 - 4
1895 - 17	1930 - 2
1896 - 35	1931 - 1
1897 - 27	1932 - 2
1898 - 34	1935 - 1
1899 - 30	1939 - 1

Total number of deaths years available - 1,182.

In 1897, the point was passed at which ½ of the total had died.

Notes and Abbreviations

This biographical register will be somewhat less decipherable to the casual user than it would have been were it practical to make the entries of fully composed prose. Rampant inflation in publishing costs mandates a rather thorough system of abbreviations. Serious students will have no trouble using the register if the subjoined table of abbreviations is consulted—and this work is of esoteric enough nature to be primarily of interest to that archaic sort, in any case.

All units are infantry, unless another designation is included.

In some cases, geographic names are used without inclusion of the state, if an officer's entire civilian entry is composed of places within a single state, and that state is the one shown under his military service. James Theophilus Adams, for instance, was born and lived and died in North Carolina; his entry shows his North Carolina military service and does not reiterate the location of Raleigh, Wake Co. or Holly Springs in the same state.

Marriage and offspring are shown in only a fraction of the instances where that data has been uncovered. If the full outlines of an officer's life are available, his wife's name is usually not included. In sketches which are missing a key point, the wife will be shown to provide additional background.

An effort has been made to make the civilian data appear in appropriate chronology to the military data, obviating the need for "pre-war" or "post-war" when listing an occupation. Thus, information appearing prior to the Confederate record dates from before the war, and post-bellum careers and events are entered after the Confederate record. There will obviously be occasions when data bridges the gap and is applicable for both portions of an officer's life.

It must be noted that in some instances, officers are shown as being in command of units (primarily companies) which did not exist until a later time. The captains of independent companies, which became lettered entitles in a subsequent (and inevitable) regimental organization, are the most common example of this kind of thing. The time span involved was usually short, although sometimes the regimental organization was much delayed. Sometimes, the register also compromises by identifying a unit with its ultimate designation. For instance, the 26th Ga. underwent metamorphosis into the 7th Ga. Bn. and then into the 61st Ga. The register will save its readers the pangs of birth, in most cases, by simply calling the companies and the officers components of the 61st Ga.

A related foible is the not infrequent duality of early war commission dates. An officer enlisting as company commander will have a second date available in his records when he was confirmed at regimental organization. Similarly, state commissioning of the company or regiment, and its officers, will often predate Confederate commissions. These small gaps are sometimes ignored, the rule of thumb being to accept the early date where possible; occasionally both dates are shown in the interest of clarity and at the cost of brevity.

The entries in the register do not normally repeat unit designation at each of the promotion levels. As a result, some officers will be identified by regiment just once, at their lowest grade level. John Harris Baker, for instance, advanced from Captain through Colonel in the 13th Ga., without changing to any other regiment; therefore, the 13th Ga. is only mentioned at the time of the commission as Captain. By contrast, William Todd Robins' restless record shows service in a number of units, and each promotion carries a unit identity because the units kept changing. Artillery officers are excepted from that system, as most promotions in that arm of the service, to the rank of field officers, resulted in postings to unnumbered battalions; as a result, artillery field officers were a corps not unlike staff officers, without the continuing unit affiliation customary in infantry and cavalry. Those of Lee's Colonels who became general officers have not been included in this compilation.

It is imperative for users of the register to understand that the dates of commissions are generally dates from which the appointment *takes rank.* The actual date on which the appointment took place, or was accepted, or was confirmed might be much later than the date from which it took rank. Among the confusions which result is the possibility that a man's rank as Colonel might actually predate his rank as Major, and both ranks might also predate their true time of implementation by as much as two years. The date of rank should coincide with the demise of the last officer to hold the appointment; thus, each field officer post in each regiment would theoretically have an incumbent at all times. Stark evidence of the system can be seen, for example, by looking at the rank dates throughout regiments heavily engaged at Gettysburg. Most of them will have one or more commissions dating from the days in July 1863 when Confederate commissions were vacated by Unionist bullets. Lest this outline of a real point of potential confusion serve to suggest that the commission dates are hollow figures, it should be noted that the large majority of commission dates are not far removed from the date at which they were actually realized.

A few promotions cited in the biographical sketches are shown to have been for "Valor & Skill." They are among the some two hundred men in both the armies and navy of the Confederacy who won promotion under the terms of an April 1862 act which authorized the Confederate President to nominate officers on such a basis.

Virtually all of the military service recorded herein is from official manuscript records, especially the Compiled Service Records in the National Archives. Only a handful of cases fell unanswered in that resource, and left the necessity of recourse to unofficial sources.

The abbreviations clarified below are not the only ones used in the register, but the residue seem to be readily understandable. The abbreviations are not always used, not from sloppiness or caprice, but because they occasionally seemed to render an entry too cryptically.

a.a.g. .... assistant adjutant general
ACS .... assistant commissary of supply
Actg. .... acting
a.d.c. .... aide de camp
adj. .... adjutant
a.i.g. .... assistant inspector general
A.I.G.O. .... Adjutant and Inspector General's Office
A.N.Va. .... Army of North Virginia
AQM .... Assistant Quartermaster
apptd. .... appointed
Appx. .... Paroled at Appomattox in April 1865

att.	attended an institution, but did not necessarily graduate
b.	born
bn.	battalion
bur.	buried
ca.	circa, or approximately
Cav.	Cavalry
Co.	Company or County, as appropriate
CSN	Confederate States Navy
d.	died
gr.	graduated
Immortal 600	A group of Confederate prisoners held under friendly fire by retaliating Federalists; a considerable literature on the group appeared after the war.
Inf.	Infantry
KIA	Killed in action
LDT	Local Defense Troops
legisl.	legislature or legislator, as appropriate
m.	married
MWIA	Mortally wounded in action
OR	Official Records; 128 volumes published by the War Department
org.	the initial organization of a unit
P.A.C.S.	Provisional Army of the Confederate States
POW	Prisoner of war
QM	Quartermaster
re-org.	the re-organization of units, usually in the spring of 1862, involving re-election of officers
res.	resigned
SCMA	South Carolina Military Academy
S.S.	Sharpshooters
U.C.V.	United Confederate Veterans
UNC	University of North Carolina
USMA	U.S. Military Academy, West Point
v.a.d.c.	volunteer aide de camp
Valor & Skill	promotion under an 1862 act (see notes above)
VMI	Virginia Military Institute
wded.	wounded
WIA	Wounded In Action

LEE'S COLONELS

ABNEY, JOSEPH. b. Edgefield Dist., South Carolina, Dec. 2, 1819. Mexican War veteran. Lawyer and in South Carolina legisl. m. Susan Margaret Miller. Capt., Co. A, 22nd South Carolina. Colonel - Jan. 29, 1862. Dropped at May 1862 re-org. Was later Major, 1st Bn. South Carolina Sharpshooters, as of June 21, 1862. Became Major, 27th South Carolina on Oct. 2, 1863. Wded. at Drewry's Bluff. Retired March 6, 1865. d. Edgefield, Feb. 2, 1870, as a result of wound.

ADAMS, CICERO. b. July 1833. gr. SCMA, 1854. Lawyer in Edgefield. Lt., Co. A, 22nd South Carolina - 1861. Captain - Jan. 29, 1862. Major - March 12, 1863, to rank from Feb. 19, 1863, which was the effective date of Heil's resignation. Meanwhile, Adams had been absent sick since Jan. 13, 1863, and spent the rest of the war on conscript duty. Adams' majority held for the 22nd South Carolina for the remainder of the war, however, leaving the regiment with a shortage of officers. d. Jan. 2, 1866. bur. Pioneer Cemetery, Bamberg, South Carolina.

ADAMS, HENRY WARD. Farmer in Campbell Co. in 1860, age 37, worth $26,500. Col., 53rd Virginia Militia, which had only fleeting association with the Army of Northern Virginia. m. Annie P. Floyd. d. 1899 in Campbell Co.

ADAMS, JAMES THEOPHILUS. b. Wake Co., North Carolina, Sept. 7, 1839. Raleigh businessman. Lt., Co. D, 26th North Carolina on May 29, 1861. Capt. - Apr. 21, 1862. Major - July 31, 1863. Lt. Col. - May 6, 1864. Wded. hip at Malvern Hill and lung at Gettysburg. Appx. d. 1918 in Holly Springs.

ADAMS, JOSEPH WARREN. Of Spalding Co. Capt., Co. E, 44th Georgia, March 4, 1862. Major - June 23, 1862. d. of variola at Richmond, March 4, 1863. "A great singer."

ADAMS, PEARSON BERBECK. b. Clarksburg, Virginia, June 20, 1826. gr. VMI 1849. Major, 42nd Virginia - 1861. Dropped at April 1862 re-org. 6′0″. POW in Webster Co. on Feb. 11, 1864, released Feb. 25, 1865. Braxton and Harrison Co. lawyer and farmer. d. Jan. 17, 1893.

AIKEN, DAVID WYATT. b. Winnsboro, South Carolina, Mar. 17, 1828. gr. South Carolina College, 1849. Teacher and planter in Abbeville District. Adj., 7th South Carolina, March 9, 1861. Colonel - May 14, 1862. Wded. in the right lung at Sharpsburg. Commander of post at Macon, Georgia, August 1863 to July 1864. Res. disability - July 14, 1864. Printer and newspaper owner in Charleston. U.S. Congress 1877-1887. d. Cokesbury, Apr. 6, 1887. bur. Magnolia Cemetery, Greenwood, South Carolina. Aiken's extensive war papers are at the University of South Carolina.

AIKEN, HUGH KERR. b. Winnsboro, South Carolina, July 5, 1822. att. South Carolina College. Planter. Pre-war Major General of militia. m. Mary Gayle 1852. Lt. Col., 16th Bn. South Carolina Cav., July 21, 1862. Col., 6th South Carolina Cav., Nov. 1, 1862. Wded. at Trevilian Station. KIA Feb. 27, 1865, near Darlington.

AIKEN, JAMES. b. Aug. 1832, in South Carolina. gr. SCMA, 1851. Moved to Alabama - 1854. 5'11" Capt., Co. D, 13th Alabama, July 19, 1861. Major - June 11, 1862. Lt. Col. - Jan. 4, 1863. Colonel - May 24, 1864. Wded. at Chancellorsville and Bristoe Station. POW at High Bridge. Gadsden lawyer and politician post-war. d. June 22, 1908.

AIKEN, JOHN ALFRED. The 1860 census for Washington Co., Tennessee, shows Aiken as a 29-year-old engineer, living with his parents. Pvt., Co. D, 63rd Tennessee, Apr. 28, 1861 - aged 37? Major - July 30, 1862. Lt. Col. - Nov. 9, 1863. KIA at Drewry's Bluff, May 16, 1864.

AKERS, WILLIAM T. b. Patrick Co., Virginia, 1834. Lt., Co. C, 51st Virginia, 1861. Capt., Co. D, May 5, 1862. Major in fall of 1864. In Virginia legisl. 1870-1874. Militia Brigadier General post-war. Farmer, alive in 1909.

ALLDREDGE, ENOCH, b. Giles Co., Tennessee on May 16, 1807. m. Amelia Pace, 1826. In Alabama legisl. from Blount Co. 1837-1861. Veteran of 1836 Creek War. Appointed Captain July 19, 1861, stationed at Blountsville on commissary duty. Capt., Co. A, 48th Alabama, 1862. Major - May 23, 1862. Wded. at Cedar Mountain, which caused him to resign Sept. 29, 1862. d. Brooksville, Nov. 22, 1879. bur. beside his son, Jesse J.

ALLDREDGE, JESSE J. b. Blount Co., Aug. 16, 1831, son of Col. Enoch Alldredge. Merchant. m. Manila Scott. Lt., Co. A, 48th Alabama, May 27, 1862. (Had served as pvt. in 19th Alabama in 1861.) Capt. - July 15, 1862. Lt. Col. - Oct. 15, 1862. Wded. at Second Manassas. Resigned on disability, June 17, 1863. d. June 7, 1870. bur. family cemetery, Blount Co.

ALLEN, JAMES H. Capt., Co. H, 5th Virginia Cav., June 24, 1861. Lt. Col. - June 6, 1864. Regiment was consolidated with the 15th Virginia Cav. in Nov. 1864. Living in James City Co. in 1870, age 40. Author of SHSP article. Alive in 1896 in Toano, Virginia.

ALLEN, JAMES WALKINSHAW. b. Shenandoah Co., Virginia, July 2, 1829. Lost an eye in childhood. gr. VMI 1849. On VMI faculty pre-war, and farmer. 6′3″ Colonel, 2nd Virginia, Apr. 28, 1861. Wded. at Manassas. KIA Gaines' Mill. bur. Hollywood Cemetery, later moved to Liberty.

ALLEN, ROBERT CLOTWORTHY. b. Shenandoah Co., June 22, 1834. Brother of Col. James W. Allen. gr. VMI 1855. Salem lawyer, as partner of Col. William Watts. Major, 28th Virginia, July 1, 1861. Colonel - Apr. 20, 1862. KIA on third day at Gettysburg. A good account of Allen's dying moments is in *Confederate Veteran*, XXI, 430. Allen is harshly derided in Eppa Hunter's published memoir.

ALLEN, WILLIAM. b. Surry Co., Virginia, July 29, 1828, as William Griffin Orgain, and later changed his name. m. Frances Augusta Jessup in 1852. "One of the strongest men known in his day." Lived at Curl's Neck, and said to have owned 1,000 slaves and 40,000 acres. He later claimed to have lost $450,000 in property during the war: "I am perhaps the largest loser in the southern Confederacy." Capt., Brandon Artillery (Virginia), May 1861. Major at formation of 10th Bn. Virginia Heavy Artillery, Apr. 4, 1862. Res. Aug. 19, 1862, to look after his property. Drowned in the James River, May 19, 1875.

ALLEN, WILLIAM A. b. Wake Co. Lawyer in Duplin Co. Lt., Co. C, 12th North Carolina, April 15, 1861, age 35. Capt., Co. C, 51st North Carolina, Feb. 11, 1862, then Lt. Col. of regiment at its organization on April 30, 1862. Resigned Jan. 19, 1863, during a court martial for drunkenness and insubordination.

ALLISON, WILLIAM BARRY. b. Jan. 28, 1816. Surveyor. Allison appears in the 1860 census for Greenville District as a farmer worth $5,834. Lt., Co. H, 18th South Carolina in 1861, at org. Major - Jan. 2, 1862. Lt. Col. - Aug. 30, 1862. Appx. m. Mary Susan Currence. d. Nov. 13, 1896. bur. Allison Creek Cemetery, York Co.

ALLSTON, BENJAMIN. b. Charleston, South Carolina, Feb. 26, 1833. gr. USMA 1853. Rice planter and Episcopal minister at Georgetown and Union, South Carolina. Many of his letters have been published. Lt., U.S. Cavalry, 1853-1857. Lt., C.S. Artillery, to rank from Mar. 16, 1861. Major, P.A.C.S., June 20, 1862, ordered to 19th Mississippi temporarily. Assigned as Major, 5th Virginia Cavalry, P.A.C.S., but unit never fully formed. Assigned to command 4th Alabama in fall of 1861 while E. M. Law recovered from Manassas wound. Col., a.i.g., May, 1862. Staff officer the rest of war with E. Kirby Smith and others.

ALMON, MOSES TAYLOR. b. Oct. 18, 1832. Of Heard Co. Sgt., Co. G, 7th Georgia, May 31, 1861. Lt. - Sept. 16, 1861. Capt. - May 12, 1862. Major - Feb. 2, 1863. Wded. in the head, spring 1863. Lt. Col. - July 27, 1864. Wded. on Oct. 7, 1864. Appx. d. Feb. 15, 1905. bur. Almon Family Cemetery, Heard Co.

ALSTON, ROBERT WILLIAMS. b. 1837. Of Warren Co., North Carolina. m. Martha Davis. Capt., Co. K, 12th North Carolina, Mar. 13, 1862. Major - May 24, 1863. Wded. mouth at Cedar Creek, and at Ft. Stedman and South Mountain. Claimed to have been wounded a total of 16 times. Paroled at Richmond Apr. 7, 1865. d. Warren Co., Apr. 29, 1901.

ALSTON, THOMAS PINCKNEY. b. Dec. 7, 1832. Capt., Co. F, 1st South Carolina, Aug. 7, 1861. Major - Jan. 4, 1864. WIA at Wilderness. Lt. Col. - May 19, 1864. MWIA at Jericho Ford, May 23, 1864. d. June 19. bur. Magnolia Cemetery, Charleston.

ANDERSON, CHARLES DAVID. b. DeKalb Co., Georgia, May 22, 1827. Capt., Co. C, 6th Georgia, May 27, 1861. Major - Sept.

17, 1862. Lt. Col. - May 15, 1863. Wded. and POW at Sharpsburg. Wded. at Chancellorsville. Res. due to wounds, Jan. 20, 1864. Colonel and Brigadier General of Georgia State Forces in 1864, and in Georgia legisl. late in war. Lived at Fort Valley. d. Feb. 22, 1901. bur. Oaklawn Cemetery.

ANDERSON, DAVID W. b. Louisa Co., Virginia, Sept. 22, 1828. Farmer in Fluvanna Co. Capt., Co. K, 44th Virginia, June 11, 1861. Major - June 16, 1863. Wded. at Sharpsburg and in Oct. 1864. POW at Spotsylvania. In Va. legisl. post-war. d. Fluvanna Co., Apr. 30, 1903. bur. Champion Cemetery, Central Plains.

ANDERSON, EDWARD CLIFFORD, JR. b. Jan. 7, 1838. att. U. Va. m. Jane Margaret Randolph, a great-granddaughter of Thomas Jefferson. Served with Thompson Artillery, 22nd Georgia Battalion. Aide to General Mercer, Nov. 1861. Capt., Co. B, 24th Georgia Cav. Bn., June 1862. Major, 7th Georgia Cavalry, Jan. 12, 1863. Colonel - Dec. 1864. WIA at Trevilian's Station, June 1864. Savannah banker. d. Savannah, Sept. 27, 1876, in a yellow fever epidemic.

ANDERSON, FRANCIS P. Lt. Col., 59th Virginia, July 10, 1861. POW at Roanoke Island, paroled Feb. 21, 1862. Dropped at a Nov. 1862 re-org. POW at Cape Isbel, Florida, May 17, 1865, released Oct. 12, 1865. A subordinate described Anderson as "beastly intoxicated . . . loud and lascivious," fond of "abandoned women," and an "habitual drunkard."

ANDERSON, JAMES W. b. 1835, Coweta Co. Mechanic in Newnan. Lt., Co. A, 1st Georgia, Mar. 18, 1861. Adj. of regiment, Apr. 3, 1861. Major - Dec. 11, 1861. Mustered out, with regiment, Mar. 18, 1862. Later served as Lt. and Capt. with 12th Georgia Battalion Light Artillery. d. 1903.

ANDERSON, LEMUEL B. b. Oct. 2, 1839, Union Dist., South Carolina. Lt., Co. C, 7th Georgia, May 31, 1861. Major - Dec. 27, 1861. Dropped at re-org. early 1862. m. Maggie Sommers 1871. Judge and Georgia legisl. post-war. d. Feb. 1, 1897, at Atlanta Alms House. bur. South View Cemetery.

ANDERSON, RICHARD. Cotton buyer and city alderman in

Columbia. Lt. Col., 15th South Carolina, Sept. 10, 1861. d. Oct. 18, 1861. ". . . He lived an openly immoral life."

ANDERSON, WILLIAM. The 1860 census for Anderson District shows Anderson as a farmer, age 27, born in Scotland. Wife was Rachel Lucretia McFall. Major, Palmetto Sharpshooters, Apr. 16, 1862. MWIA - Frayser's Farm, d. July 4 in Manchester. A contemporary obituary states that Anderson "was for some time in the British Army; passed through the Crimean War." Anderson's war letters are at U. Virginia. bur. First Baptist Church, Anderson.

ANDREWS, CLINTON MILTON. b. Greensboro 1829. att. UNC. Of Iredell Co. Anderson and his brother (John B.) ran a military school in Statesville in the 1850's. Capt., Co. B, 2nd North Carolina cavalry, June 21, 1861. Major - Sept. 6, 1862. Lt. Col. - Feb. 12, 1864. Colonel - Feb. 18, 1864. MWIA at Black and Whites, Virginia, June 23, 1864. Died of effects of amputated leg. bur. Fourth Creek Presbyterian Churchyard, Orange Co., North Carolina.

ANDREWS, HEZEKIAH L. Of Randolph Co. Capt., Co. F, 2nd North Carolina Infantry Battalion, Nov. 30, 1861, age 22. POW at Roanoke Island, Feb. 1862. Major - Oct. 1, 1862. Lt. Col. - June 6, 1863. KIA July 1 at Gettysburg.

ANDREWS, LORENZO DARE, b. Randolph Co. 1829. Teacher there. Lt., Co. H, 38th North Carolina, Nov. 4, 1861. Major - Apr. 18, 1862. Res. Aug. 21, 1862. m. Martha Pemberton. d. 1908. bur. Monroe Cemetery, Union Co., North Carolina.

ANDREWS, RICHARD SNOWDEN. b. Washington, D.C., Oct. 29, 1830. Baltimore architect. Capt., 1st Maryland Light Artillery, May 29, 1861. WIA at Mechanicsville. Major - July 15, 1862. Assigned to Bureau of Ordnance, Oct. 15, 1862, after terrible Cedar Mountain wound. Lt. Col. - Apr. 4, 1863, and back to field duty. WIA at Second Winchester. Ordered to Europe for ordnance duty, Jan. 11, 1864. d. Baltimore Jan. 6, 1903. bur. Rock Creek Cemetery, D.C.

ANTHONY, OLIVER PERRY. b. 1832. gr. Emory College. m. Caroline A. Tennille. Capt., Co. I, 51st Georgia, Mar. 4, 1862.

Major- Mar. 22, 1862. Lt. Col. - May 2, 1863. Res. July 14, 1864. President of Andrew Female College. d. June 11, 1873. bur. New Park Cemetery, Fort Gaines, Georgia.

ARBOGAST, JAMES CRAWFORD. b. 1836. Capt., Co. G, 31st Virginia, May 29, 1861. Major - June 9, 1862. Res. Dec. 20, 1862. d. Pocahontas Co., July 24, 1913. bur. in family cemetery, Greenbank, West Virginia.

ARCHER, FLETCHER HARRIS. b. Petersburg, Feb. 6, 1817. gr. U. Virginia 1841. Mexican War officer. Petersburg lawyer. Capt., Co. K, 12th Virginia, Apr. 1861. Lt. Col. - May 5, 1861, assigned to 3rd Virginia Infantry then to 5th Battalion Virginia Infantry. Dropped at re-org. in May 1862. Practiced law 1862-1864. Lt. Col., 3rd Battalion Virginia Reserves, June 15, 1864. Mayor of Petersburg post-war. d. Aug. 21, 1902. bur. Blandford Cemetery.

ARCHER, ROBERT HARRIS. b. Md., May 20, 1820. Brother of General James J. Archer. m. Ellen Howe Davis, 1853. Lived in Harford Co. Lt., U.S. Army, 1847-1848. Mexican War veteran. Private, Co. K, 1st Virginia Cavalry, April-October 1861. Lt. Col., 55th Virginia, Oct. 1, 1861. Dropped at May 1862 re-org. Capt., a.a.g., Archer's Brigade, June 13, 1862. POW at Gettysburg, exchanged Jan. 1865. d. March 10, 1878, in Richmond.

ARMFIELD, ROBERT FRANKLIN. b. Guilford Co., July 9, 1829. gr. Trinity College. Yadkin Co. lawyer. 6'0". Lt., Co. B, 38th North Carolina, Oct. 16, 1861. Lt. Col. - Apr. 18, 1862. Wded. Shepherdstown, Sept. 20, 1862. Res. Jan. 14, 1863, due to wounds. North Carolina state's attorney - 1863. In North Carolina legisl. post-war. Lt. Gov. of North Carolina, 1875-1876. In U.S. Congress, 1879-1883. d. Statesville, Nov. 9, 1898. bur. Oakwood Cemetery.

ARMSTRONG, JOSEPH. b. 1836 in Putnam Co. gr. Emory & Henry. Capt., Co. I, 18th Georgia, June 22, 1861. Colonel - Jan. 6, 1864. Wded. at Gaines' Mill. Paroled at Petersburg, Apr. 15, 1865. Dooly Co. lawyer and Georgia legisl. post-war. d. Gainesville, July 28, 1901, unmarried. bur. Rose Hill Cemetery, Macon.

Virginia State Library

FLETCHER HARRIS ARCHER
3rd Virginia Infantry

ARNETT, WILLIAM WILEY. b. Marion Co., Oct. 23, 1839. gr. Allegheny College 1860. Pvt., Co. A, 31st Virginia, Apr. 1861. Capt. - April 15, 1863. Later claimed to have commanded the 23rd and 25th Virginia Infantry, though there is no official record of this. Col., 20th Virginia Cavalry, Aug. 14, 1863. Lawyer in St. Louis and Wheeling. d. Feb. 15, 1902, in Wheeling, where he lived at 15th and Chapline.

ARNOLD, JOHN WELLINGTON, SR. b. Walton Co., Dec. 16, 1833. att. U. Georgia m. Florence Holt. Lt., Co. C, 9th Georgia, June 13, 1861. Capt. - Oct. 17, 1863. Major - June 1864. Wded. ankle at Crampton's Gap, chest at Wilderness, and hip at Deep Bottom (Aug. 16, 1864). Appx. Walton Co. editor and lawyer post-war. d. Apr. 24, 1909. bur. Rest Haven Cemetery, Monroe, Georgia.

ARNOLD, ROBERT BOLLING. b. Greenville Dist., 1833. m. Mollie C. Johnson. Lt., Co. E, Hampton Legion, June 12, 1861. Capt. - Sept. 17, 1861. Major - Dec. 13, 1862. Lt. Col. - May 19, 1864. Appx. d. Honea Path, Jan. 19, 1923. bur. at Columbia Baptist Church.

ARNOLD, WILLIAM McINTOSH. m. Elizabeth Rives Brown. Capt., Co. A, 6th Georgia, Apr. 22, 1861. Major - June 16, 1863. Lt. Col. - Jan. 20, 1864. Wded. at Malvern Hill, Sharpsburg, Chancellorsville. KIA at Petersburg, July 7, 1864, by a mortar shell. bur. Sparta City Cemetery. Arnold's papers survive at the Georgia Archives.

ASHCRAFT, JOHN BENJAMIN. b. Union Co., July 15, 1834. Teacher. Capt., Co. D, 37th North Carolina, Sept. 16, 1861. 6'3". Major - July 1, 1862. Lt. Col. - July 30, 1862. Res. due to illness May 29, 1863. First Union Co. Supt. of Schools. m. Sallie Marsh. d. near Monroe, Feb. 11, 1901, bur. in family cemtery at Marshville, North Carolina.

ASHFORD, JOHN. b. Sampson, Sept. 6, 1837. Farmer. 5'10". Capt., Co. D, 38th North Carolina. Major - Aug. 21, 1862. Lt. Col. - Jan. 14, 1863. Colonel - June 18, 1864. Wded. at 2nd Manassas and Gettysburg. Wded. in arm, April 2, 1865. Appx. d. Jan. 1889.

ASHTON, RICHARD WATTS. b. Fauquier Co., Virginia, Nov. 13,

1840. att. Culpeper Military Inst. Mansfield, Louisiana, lawyer. Lt., Co. D, 2nd Louisiana, May 11, 1861. Commissary officer, Aug. 23, 1861. Actg. Adj. - Oct. 8, 1861. Major - May 1, 1862. KIA at Malvern Hill. bur. Hollywood. Died unmarried and childless.

ATKINSON, EDMUND NATHAN b. Marietta, Nov. 14, 1834. 5'9". gr. Georgia Military Inst. Adj., 26th Georgia, 1861. Colonel - May 9, 1862. Wded. in the arm and POW at Fredericksburg. POW at Fisher's Hill, released July 25, 1865. m. Elizabeth Lang - 1868. d. Waycross, June 17, 1884.

ATKINSON, JOHN WILDER. b. Lunenburg Co., May 23, 1830. Educated in Baltimore. Richmond tobacco merchant. Capt., Co. A, 15th Virginia Infantry, Apr. 23, 1861. Dropped at re-org. Capt. and a.d.c. to McLaws at Williamsburg and Seven Pines. Major, 19th Virginia Battalion Heavy Artillery, June 4, 1862. Lt. Col. - Dec. 18, 1862. POW at Sayler's Creek, released May 9, 1865. Merchant in Wilmington, North Carolina post-war. d. there Oct. 26, 1910. bur. Oakdale Cemetery.

AUGUST, THOMAS PEARSON. b. Fredericksburg, Oct. 1821. Richmond lawyer and Virginia legisl. Lt., Richmond Grays, Mexican War. Col., 1st Virginia Volunteers, 1853-1860. Col., 15th Virginia, May 17, 1861. Wded. at Malvern Hill. Assigned to Bureau of Conscription in 1862. Commanded Conscript Camp in North Carolina - Jan. 1863. Retired, disability, Dec. 31, 1864. d. Richmond, July 31, 1869. bur. Hollywood.

AVERETT, CHAPPELL E. Lived in Lunenburg Co. in 1860, age 39. Wife-Mary C. Capt., Co. K, 1st Regiment Virginia Reserves, Apr. 20, 1864. Major - Aug. 12, 1864.

AVERY, CLARKE MOULTON. b. North Carolina Oct. 3, 1819. Of Burke Co. gr. UNC 1839. Capt., Co. G, 1st North Carolina (Bethel), Apr. 25, 1861. Lt. Col., 33rd North Carolina, Sept. 20, 1861. Colonel - Jan. 17, 1862. POW at New Bern, Mar. 14, 1862; exchanged Sept. 1862. MWIA at Wilderness, May 5-6, 1864. d. June 18 at Orange C.H. bur. First Presbyterian Church, Morganton, North Carolina.

AVERY, ISAAC ERWIN. b. Burke Co., Dec. 20, 1828. att. UNC. Yancey Co. farmer and railroad man. Capt., Co. E, 6th North

Carolina, May 16, 1862. Lt. Col. - June 1, 1862. Colonel - June 11, 1862. Wded. at Malvern Hill and Manassas. Mortally wounded at Gettysburg, July 2, d. July 3.

AVERY, JOHN WILLIAM. b. York, South Carolina. Planter there. Lt., Co. F, 17th South Carolina, Nov. 29, 1861. Capt. - May 1, 1862. Major - Aug. 29, 1864. Wded. at 2nd Manassas and Sharpsburg. m. Laura Dinkins. Lawyer, land speculator and oyster farmer in Norfolk County, Virginia, post-war. Alive in 1890. Died May 9, 1892.

AVERY, RICHARD M. b. Alabama. The 1860 census for Kemper Co., Mississippi, shows Avery as a farmer, age 27, worth $14,000. Lt., Co. C, Jeff Davis Legion, Mar. 25, 1861, age 27. Capt. - May 23, 1862. Major - Nov. 14, 1864. This is apparently the same Major Richard M. Avery who is buried in the Guerrant Cemetery near Vincent, Arkansas.

AYLETT, WILLIAM ROANE. b. King William Co., May 14, 1833. att. U. Virginia. Lawyer. m. Alice Brockenbrough, 1860. 5′9″. Capt., Co. D, 53rd Virginia, May 13, 1861. Major - Aug. 29, 1862. Lt. Col. - Feb. 2, 1863. Colonel - Mar. 5, 1863. Wded. at Gettysburg. POW at Sayler's Creek, released July 25 from Johnson's Island. d. Aug. 8, 1900, in King William Co. Aylett's papers are at the Virginia Historical Society and the Northumberland County Historical Society.

AYRES, THOMAS H. b. Buckingham Co. Official of C.S. Ordnance Dept. Capt., Co. A, 1st Virginia Infantry Battalion LDT, May 28, 1863, age 39. Major - Aug. 21, 1864.

BACON, THOMAS GLASCOCK. b. Edgefield, June 24, 1812. Served in Seminole War. Colonel, 7th South Carolina, Apr. 15, 1861. Dropped May 4, 1862, "failing health, declined re-election." In South Carolina legisl. 1863. Hamburg businessman. d. Edgefield Co., Sept. 25, 1876. bur. Baptist Cemetery.

BADHAM, JOHN C. b. Edenton, North Carolina, 1826. gr. Gettysburg College, 1849. Lawyer in Edenton. In North Carolina legisl. Major, 5th North Carolina, May 16, 1861. Lt. Col. - Mar. 6, 1862. KIA at Williamsburg.

Virginia State Library

THOMAS PEARSON AUGUST
15th Virginia Infantry

BAGBY, JOHN ROBERT. b. King and Queen Co., Nov. 13, 1826. Businessman and magistrate there pre-war gr. Columbian College. Capt., Co. K, 34th Virginia (originally 4th Virginia Heavy Artillery Regt.), May 20, 1861. Major - Nov. 3, 1862. Wded. at Petersburg, spring of 1865. Paroled at Richmond, Apr. 15, 1865. d. Mar. 26, 1890.

BAGLEY, EDWARD F. b. Georgia, lived in Alabama. Lt., U.S. Infantry, 1847-1848. Lt., U.S. Artillery, 1856-1861. Major, Infantry Bn. of Cobb's Legion, July 1861. Killed accidentally by his own men, at Yorktown, Nov. 12, 1861. Thomas R. R. Cobb wrote of him: "He is a coarse, ignorant, lazy, stingy, good for nothing fellow." bur. Magnolia Cemetery, Augusta.

BAILEY, ROBERT AUGUSTUS. b. 1839 in Greenbrier Co. Lawyer in Fayette Co. Capt. in 142nd Militia. Capt., Co. C, 22nd Virginia, June 6, 1861. Major - Nov. 23, 1861. Lt. Col., 14th Virginia Cavalry, Sept. 5, 1862. Colonel - Feb. 23, 1863. MWIA at Droop Mountain, Nov. 6, 1863. d. Pocahontas Co., Nov. 12. bur. Old Stone Church Cemetery, Lewisburg.

BAIN, SENECA McNEIL. b. New York. Teacher in Pike Co., Mississippi. Lt., Co. E, 16th Mississippi, Apr. 20, 1861, age 26. Capt. - Apr. 26, 1862. Lt. Col. - May 12, 1864. POW at Weldon R.R., Aug. 21, 1864, exchanged Oct. 31. Physician in Texas post-war. d. there ca. 1900.

BAINE, DAVID WILLIAM. b. Ohio, Aug. 29, 1829. gr. Allegheny College. Teacher and lawyer in Lowndes Co., Alabama. "Slight and slender." Lt. Col., 14th Alabama, at its org. in Aug. 1861, to rank from July 19. KIA at Frayser's Farm.

BAKER, BENJAMIN HURT. b. Georgia, Apr. 1, 1811. Lawyer and state legisl. from Russell Co., Alabama, pre-war. Lt. Col., 6th Alabama, May 17, 1861. Resigned for health reasons by 1863 and died in Crawford, June 4, 1864.

BAKER, BOLLING. Of Florida. Auditor with C.S. Treasury Dept. in Richmond. Capt., Co. F, 3rd Virginia LDT, June 20, 1863. Major - Sept. 23, 1864. Res. Mar. 2, 1865. Paroled at Tallahassee, May 22, 1865.

BAKER, JOHN A. Of New Hanover Co. Lt., Wilmington Light Artillery (North Carolina), May 16, 1861. Res. to serve as a.d.c. on staff of S. G. French. Colonel, 3rd North Carolina Cavalry, Sept. 3, 1862. POW near Petersburg, June 21, 1864. He was among the prisoners who came to be known as "The Immortal Six Hundred," but took the oath and was released on Mar. 6, 1865, under circumstances which caused him to be reviled by his comrades. It was said that he went to the West Indies and never returned home.

BAKER, JOHN HARRIS. b. Aug. 7, 1824. Mexican War vet. Capt., Co. A, 13th Georgia, July 8, 1861. Major - Feb. 1, 1862. Lt. Col. - Sept. 17, 1862. Colonel - Dec. 14, 1863. Wded. 8 times. POW at Gettysburg (Monterey); exchanged May 4, 1864. Paroled Apr. 21, 1865. Zebulon farmer. d. Pike Co., Apr. 7, 1905.

BAKER, SAMUEL E. The 1860 census for Natchez shows Baker as a bookkeeper, age 30. Capt., Co. D, 16th Mississippi, Apr. 25, 1861, age 32. Major - Apr. 28, 1862. Colonel - Dec. 20, 1862. KIA at Spotsylvania, May 12, 1864.

BALDWIN, JOHN BROWN. b. near Staunton, Jan. 11, 1820. Lawyer there. att. U. Virginia. In Virginia legisl. and Virginia Secession Convention. Colonel, 52nd Virginia, Aug. 19, 1861. Dropped at May 1862 re-org. In C.S. Congress, 1862-1865. In Virginia legisl. post-war. Brother of Briscoe G. Baldwin. d. Staunton, Sept. 30, 1873.

BALDWIN, ROBERT FREDERICK. b. Winchester, Aug. 14, 1829. Physician. Col., 31st Virginia Militia. Captured at Romney in Feb. 1862 with Jackson's forces. Later was surgeon, 6th Virginia, and in Valley hospitals. d. Staunton, Nov. 15, 1879. bur. Mt. Hebron Cemetery, Winchester.

BALFOUR, JOHN W. b. Virginia. Farmer in Vernon, Miss. Capt., Co. I, 18th Mississippi, Apr. 18, 1861, age 40. Major - June 3, 1861. Res. Sept. 2, 1861. Raised 6th Bn. Mississippi Infantry, and later served as Colonel, 49th Mississippi.

BALL, EDWARD. b. 1825 in South Carolina. Clerk of court in Randolph Co. Capt., Co. H, 51st Georgia, Mar. 1, 1862. Lt.

Col. - Mar. 22, 1862. Colonel - May 2, 1863. Wounded in the heel at Chancellorsville. MWIA in shoulder at Cedar Creek, d. in Staunton, Nov. 13, 1864. bur. in Cuthbert, Georgia.

BALL, MOTTROM DULANY. b. Fairfax Co., June 23, 1835. gr. Wm. & Mary, 1854. Lawyer and schoolmaster. m. Sallie Lewis Wright, 1860. With Magruder as v.a.d.c. at Yorktown. Capt., Co. I, 11th Virginia Cavalry, 1862. Major - Feb. 15, 1863. Lt. Col. - July 23, 1863. Wded. in Aug. 1863 and Oct. 1864. U.S. District Attorney in Alaska, 1876-1887. d. Sitka, Alaska, Sept. 13, 1887. bur. Old Falls Church Episcopal Graveyard, Virginia.

BALL, WILLIAM BERNARD. b. Chesterfield Co. Physician there in 1860, age 44, worth $18,000. Capt., Co. B, 4th Virginia Cavalry, Apr. 1861. Lt. Col., 15th Virginia Cavalry, Apr. 1862. Colonel - Sept. 11, 1862. Absent beginning Dec. 1862 "on detached service with Navy," as prescribed by the surgeons for his health. Resigned on disability, Feb. 28, 1864.

BALLANTINE, WILLIAM DUNCAN. b. Whitesboro, New York, Feb. 21, 1837. Merchant in Fernandia, Fla. Lt., Co. A, 2nd Florida, May 25, 1861. Capt. - May 1862. Frequently commanded the regiment, and claimed to have been promoted to major then lt. col., but there is no official records of those two actions. Wded. at Seven Pines, Sharpsburg, Chancellorsville, Gettysburg. POW at Gettysburg, released June 12, 1865. On Florida governor's staff post-war. Alive in Fernandia in 1910.

BALLENGER, MARCUS R. b. South Carolina. Physician in Floyd Co., Georgia, in 1860, age 30. Capt., Co. C, 23rd Georgia, Aug. 31, 1861. Major - Sept. 17, 1862. Lt. Col. - Aug. 20, 1864. Colonel - Jan. 5, 1865. Surrendered at Greensboro. In the Georgia legislature, 1868-1872.

BANCROFT, MATTHEW VASSAR. b. Charleston, March 18, 1839. att. SCMA. Lt., Co. C, 23rd South Carolina, Sept. 23, 1861. Capt. - Apr. 16, 1862. Major - Nov. 6, 1862. MWIA at Petersburg, June 18, 1864. d. of wounds in a Petersburg hospital, June 22, 1864.

BANE, JOHN P. b. ca. 1835. Spent early life in Giles Co., Virginia. Farmer and horse breeder. Capt., Co. D, 4th Texas, July 4,

1861. Major - Dec. 29, 1862. Lt. Col. - July 21, 1863. Colonel - Apr. 29, 1864. Wded. arm at Gaines' Mill. "A quiet, dignified man, with rather a sad expression about his face." A humorous story about Baine's flight at Wauhatchie is in M. V. Smith's published memoir. Bane was admitted to the Soldiers' Home in Richmond on Dec. 1, 1885, age 51, "paralized from wounds," and died there on May 14, 1887. bur. Hollywood.

BANKS, RICHARD OLIVER. Capt., Co. H, 44th Georgia, Mar. 4, 1862. Major - Mar. 15, 1862. Resigned, disability, July 23, 1862. Banks moved to Monroe Co. near the end of the war. He was active (but unsuccessful) in Whig politics there, and is buried in Monroe Co.

BANKSTON, THOMAS JEFFERSON. Lt., Co. F, 16th Mississippi, Apr. 27, 1861. Major - June 8, 1861.

BANNING, JAMES W. b. Georgia, May 20, 1836. The 1860 census for Meriwether Co. shows Banning as a married merchant, living at home with his very wealthy Connecticut-born parents. Lt., Co. E, 28th Georgia, Sept. 10, 1861. Capt. - Oct. 15, 1862. Major - Jan. 20, 1864. WIA at Ocean Pond, Feb. 20, 1864, and "severely . . . in hip" at Cold Harbor, June 2, 1864. Judge in Meriwether Co. m. Mary Blalock. d. Greenville, Nov. 10, 1880.

BARBEE, ANDREW RUSSELL. b. Hawsburg, Dec. 9, 1827. gr. U. Pennsylvania in medicine, 1851. Capt., Co. A, 22nd Virginia, May 22, 1861. Lt. Col. - May 2, 1862. Retired to Invalid Corps, Apr. 23, 1864. Paroled at Charleston, May 9, 1865. 5'10" Wded. in right elbow and left hip at White Sulphur Springs, Aug. 1863. Lt. Col. in Invalid Corps and Actg. Chief Surgeon, Dept. SW Va., Jan. 1865. Point Pleasant physician. d. Pruntytown, Aug. 5, 1903. bur. Lone Oak Cemetery, Point Pleasant. Seven of Barbee's war letters survive in RG 393, National Archives.

BARBOUR, THOMAS M. b. Tuscaloosa, Feb. 4, 1830. Pvt. in Mexican War. Capt., Co. D, 43rd Alabama, Apr. 1, 1862. Major - July 21, 1863. Resigned Nov. 2, 1864, to enter the ministry. Farmer and Baptist minister post-war. d. Aug. 19, 1897. bur. Tuscaloosa Cemetery.

BARBOUR, WILLIAM MORGAN. b. Rowan Co., Jan. 24, 1834. gr. St. James College, Maryland. Wilkesboro lawyer. Capt., Co. F, 37th North Carolina, Sept. 24, 1861. Lt. Col. - Nov. 20, 1861. Colonel - July 1, 1862. POW at Spotsylvania. Wded. leg, Aug. 16, 1864. MWIA at Petersburg, Sept. 30, 1864. d. Oct. 3. bur. St. Paul's Episcopal Churchyard, Wilkesboro.

BARCLAY, ELIHU STUART, JR. b. Habersham Co., May 24, 1832. Lawyer. m. Helen Stanford. Capt., Co. C, Infantry Battalion of Phillips' Legion, May 17, 1861. Major - July 6, 1862. Lt. Col. - Dec. 13, 1862. Res. Dec. 31, 1863. Wded. in spine and ankle and POW at South Mountain, paroled Oct. 6, 1862. In Georgia legislature in 1864 and 1867. Timber business in Darien. d. Savannah, March 6, 1879. bur. St. Andrew's Cemetery, Darien.

BARCLAY, WILLIAM P. b. ca. 1828 in Tennessee. Lawyer in Union Co., Georgia. Brother of Elihu S. Lt. Col., 23rd Georgia, at org. on Aug. 31, 1861. Colonel - June 12, 1862. KIA at Sharpsburg.

BARDEN, WILLIAM ALFRED. b. Hamilton, 1842. Clerk in Columbus. Pvt., Co. G, 2nd Georgia, Apr. 16, 1861. Lt., Co. H, 17th Georgia, Aug. 15, 1861. Capt. - June 2, 1862. Major - Jan. 22, 1864. Lt. Col. - Sept. 22, 1864. m. Bessie Miller Hardwick. d. Columbus, Jan. 9, 1880. bur. Linwood Cemetery.

BARHAM, THEOPHILUS G. b. Jan. 1, 1834, at Laxis, Virginia. Of Sussex Co. Lt., Co. F, 5th Virginia Battalion, 1861-1862. Lt., Co. I, 24th Virginia Cavalry, Aug. 1, 1862. Captain - Oct. 15, 1862. Lt. Col. - (Valor & Skill) - Dec. 3, 1864. POW at Sayler's Creek, released July 25. 5′9″. Residence - Heck's Ford. m. Virginia Ann Prince. d. Dec. 31, 1885, in Sussex Co.

BARNES, DIXON. b. Kershaw Dist., Oct. 9, 1816. gr. South Carolina College, 1838. Wealthy planter. Capt., Co. I, 12th South Carolina, Aug. 28, 1861. Lt. Col. - Sept. 1, 1861. Colonel - Apr. 2, 1862. MWIA at Sharpsburg. d. Sept. 27. "A quiet gentleman with a long white beard." bur. Old Camp Creek Church, Lancaster, S.C.

BARRIER, RUFUS ALEXANDER. b. Cabarrus Co., July 28, 1836.

Capt., Co. H, 8th North Carolina, May 16, 1861. Major - Feb. 1, 1864. Lt. Col. - June 7, 1864. Wded. in eye, Aug. 1864. POW at Roanoke Island, Feb. 1862. Paroled at Greensboro. d. Cabarrus Co., Apr. 8, 1876. Barrier's war letters were published in 1989.

BARRINGER, VICTOR CLAY. b. Cabarrus Co., Mar. 29, 1827. gr. UNC, 1848. In North Carolina legisl., and lawyer and legal author at Concord. Major, 1st North Carolina Cavalry, May 16, 1861. Resigned Sept. 30, 1861. Capt. and a.a.g. to Robert Ransom, April 19, 1862. Resigned July 5, 1862. Ransom wrote that on June 26, Barringer had been "guilty of highly disrespectful & insubordinate conduct. He is now in arrest & the service will be benefitted by his leaving it." Professor at Davidson College. On International Court of Appeals in Egypt. d. Washington, D.C., May 27, 1896.

BARRINGER, WILLIAM DAVIDSON. b. North Carolina. Resided in Montgomery Co. Capt., Co. E, 28th North Carolina, Aug. 1, 1861, age 26. Major - Oct. 18, 1862. Lt. Col. - Nov. 1, 1862. Res., ill health, Mar. 11, 1863. POW at Fredericksburg, exchanged four days later. 5′10½″.

BARROW, JAMES. b. Oglethorpe Co., Mar. 26, 1841. att. Georgia Military Institute. att. USMA. Adj., 16th Georgia, July 19, 1861. Capt., a.a.g. to Howell Cobb, Mar. 6, 1862. Severely wounded at Lee's Mill, Apr. 16, 1862. Lt. Col., 64th Georgia, May 26, 1863. KIA at Olustee, bur. Oconee Cemetery, Athens.

BARTON, WILLIAM STONE. b. Sept. 29, 1820. Brother of General Seth Maxwell Barton. gr. U. Virginia. Fredericksburg lawyer. a.a.g. to Daniel Ruggles, May 1861. Apptd. major of 26th Virginia on June 13, 1861, but quickly transferred to the 30th Virginia, to rank from May 17, 1861. Detached as judge advocate in early 1862. Dropped at April 1862 re-org. a.a.g. to Winder later in the war, after being stationed in Ashland. d. Jan. 18, 1898, in Fredericksburg, and is buried there.

BARTOW, FRANCIS STEBBINS. b. Savannah, Sept. 6, 1816. att. Yale and U. Georgia. In Georgia legisl. m. Louisa Greene Berrien, 1844. In C.S. Congress. Capt., Co. B, 8th Georgia, May 21, 1861. Colonel - June 1, 1861. KIA 1st Manassas. A member of Longstreet's staff suggested that Bartow was drunk at Manassas! Bartow is buried in lot 689, Laurel Grove Cemetery, Savannah.

BASINGER, WILLIAM STARR. b. Savannah, Aug. 26, 1827. gr. U. Georgia, 1846. Savannah lawyer, in partnership with General A. R. Lawton. Capt., Co. A, 18th Georgia Battalion, Mar. 1, 1862. Major - May 10, 1863. POW at Sayler's Creek, released July 25. 5′10″. In Georgia legisl. President of North Georgia College, 1886-1893. d. Athens, Apr. 25, 1910. His papers are at U. of Georgia and UNC.

BASS, FREDERICK SAMUEL. b. Brunswick Co., Virginia, June 1829. gr. VMI, 1851. Teacher in Marshall, Texas, military school. Capt., Co. E, 1st Texas, May 28, 1861. Major - Sept. 17, 1862. Lt. Col. - Jan. 5, 1864. Colonel - July 15, 1864. Wded. at Darbytown Road, Oct. 7, 1864. Appx. President of Marshall University (Texas). d. Austin, July 9, 1897.

BASS, MASTON GREEN. m. Mahuldah R. Bradley, 1851. The 1860 census for Fort Gaines shows Bass as a grocer, age 31. Lt., Co. D, 5th Georgia State Troops, Oct. 1861. Capt., Co. E, 59th Georgia, May 10, 1862. Major - July 10, 1863. MWIA in the head, Oct. 7, 1864. Died in Richmond on Oct. 16. bur. Linwood Cemetery, Columbus.

BATTE, PETER VERNON. b. Petersburg, 1841. Pvt., Co. E, 12th Virginia. Lt., Pegram's Battery (Virginia). Major, 44th Virginia Battalion, Nov. 3, 1863. POW at Petersburg, June 15, 1864, released June 20, 1865. Among the "Immortal 600." 5′10″ Clerk and bookkeeper in Stockton, Calif., post-war, where he died "at Asylum" on Dec. 22, 1893.

BAXTER, JAMES M. b. Laurens Dist., Sept. 7, 1825. gr. Erskine College, 1846. Newberry lawyer. Brother-in-law of J. D. Nance. Major, 3rd South Carolina, Feb. 6, 1861. Lt. Col. - early 1862. Dropped at May 1862 re-org. A conscript officer during the rest of the war, and Colonel, 10th South Carolina Reserves. d. Feb. 5, 1881.

BAYA, WILLIAM. b. St. Augustine, Jan. 23, 1834. Moulder in St. Augustine in 1860, living with his parents. 5′8½″. Entered Florida state service Jan. 1861 as a sergeant-major. Lt., C.S. Marines, June 1861. Capt., Co. D, 8th Florida, Nov. 18, 1861. Lt. Col. - Jan. 9, 1863. Wded. and POW at Fredericksburg. Wded. at Bristoe Station and Weldon R.R. POW at Sayler's Creek, released July 25, 1865. Of Jacksonville post-war. d. July 1, 1903. bur. St. Mary's Cemetery.

BAYLOR, WILLIAM SMITH HANGER. b. Augusta Co., Apr. 7, 1831. gr. U. Virginia and Washington College. Staunton Commonwealth's Attorney. Capt., Co. L, 5th Virginia, Apr. 1861. Major - May 28, 1861. Colonel - Apr. 21, 1862. All brigade field officers signed a letter urging that Baylor replace Winder in command of the Stonewall Brigade. KIA at 2nd Manassas. bur. Hebron Presbyterian Church, Rte. 708, Augusta Co.

BEALL, DAVID EDWARD. b. July 25, 1836. Hampshire Co. physician. 5′8½″. Capt., Co. I, 18th Virginia Cavalry, Sept. 1, 1862. Lt. Col. - Dec. 15, 1862. Paroled in Winchester, May 17, 1865. d. Feb. 27, 1880. bur. Mt. Hebron Cemetery, Winchester. Judging from contemporary letters, his name must have been pronounced "Bell."

BEALL, JAMES FRANKLIN. b. Davidson Co., Sept. 1, 1837. att. U. Virginia and UNC. gr. Jefferson Medical College. Davidson Co. physician. Sgt., Co. A, 21st North Carolina, May 8, 1861. Lt. - July 8, 1861. Captain - May 25, 1862. Major - Oct. 19, 1864. Wded. 4 times. d. Davidson Co., Dec. 7, 1907. bur. there in Jersey Baptist Churchyard. Beall wrote the sketch of his regiment in Clark's North Carolina compendium.

BEARD, JAMES H. Of Shreveport. Major, 1st Louisiana Battalion, Aug. 16, 1861. Present on regimental returns through Feb. 1862. Later was Major, 11th Louisiana Battalion (to rank June 19, 1862), and then Colonel, Crescent Regiment Louisiana Infantry. Killed Apr. 8, 1864, at Mansfield, Louisiana.

BECK, BENJAMIN. b. Sparta, Georgia. Merchant, age 33, worth $6,500 in 1860 Baldwin Co. census. Capt., Co. F, 9th Georgia, June 12, 1861. Colonel - Aug. 1, 1862. Wded. at 2nd Manassas. Resigned, disability, Mar. 16, 1864. Moved from Milledgeville postwar, and died by 1890.

BECK, JAMES W. Sgt., Co. B, 2nd Georgia, July 12, 1861. Capt., Co. K, 44th Georgia, Mar. 4, 1862. Major - May 26, 1863. Lt. Col. - Sept. 11, 1863. Wded. at Malvern Hill. m. Margaret Wells. Baptist preacher and educator. Alive in Milner, Georgia in 1903.

BECKHAM, ROBERT FRANKLIN. b. Culpeper, Virginia, May 6, 1837. gr. USMA, 1859. Lt., U.S. Engineers, 1859-1861. Lt., C.S. Artillery, Mar. 16, 1861. Lt. on G. W. Smith's staff, Jan. 14, 1862. Elected Capt., Jeff Davis Artillery, Mar. 31, 1862, but did not accept. Major and ordnance officer to G. W. Smith, Aug. 30, 1862. Assigned command of Stuart Horse Artillery (vice Pelham), on Stuart's request, Apr. 8, 1863. Transferred west on Feb. 16, 1864, as Colonel, to command Army of Tennessee artillery. MWIA at Franklin, Nov. 29, 1864, d. Dec. 5. bur. St. John's Churchyard, Ashwood, Tennessee.

BECKHAM, THOMAS CHISHOLM. b. Landsford, June 8, 1832. att. SCMA. Lived in Florida. m. Martha Hinkle. Private, Co. B, 5th South Carolina, 1861. Captain at Apr. 1862 re-org. Promoted major between Sept. 1863 and Aug. 1864. Wded at Chattanooga. Appx. d. Rock Hill, Sept. 30, 1911.

BECKLEY, HENRY M. Of Montgomery Co. 5′11″. Capt., Co. B, 36th Virginia, May 1861. Lt. Col., 1st Virginia State Line, 1863. Lt. Col., 45th Virginia Battalion, Dec. 21, 1863. Wded. at Piedmont. POW at Winchester, Sept. 19, 1864.

BELL, JAMES RAIFORD. b. Holmes Co., Dec. 5, 1831. Married planter worth $32,550 in 1860 Yazoo Co. census. 5′8″. Lt., Co. I, 12th Mississippi, Apr. 24, 1861. Capt. - Apr. 28, 1862. Major - Mar. 19, 1864. Wded. at Seven Pines. POW on Aug. 21, 1864, released June 21, 1865. d. Yazoo Co., Feb. 12, 1906.

BELO, ALFRED HORATIO, b. Salem, North Carolina, May 27, 1839. att. UNC. Capt., Co. D, 21st North Carolina, May 22, 1861. Defeated at re-org., Apr. 1862. Capt. and AQM, 55th North Carolina, Nov. 1, 1862. Major, 55th North Carolina, May 1863. Lt. Col. - July 3, 1863. Fought a wartime duel with Mississippi rifles, against John Cussons. Wded. in leg and lung at

Gettysburg, and at Cold Harbor. Galveston, Texas, newspaperman in 1865. Established Dallas *News* in 1885. d. Asheville, North Carolina, Apr. 19, 1901. bur. in Winston-Salem.

BELSCHES, BENJAMIN W. b. Sussex Co., Apr. 26, 1817. att. U. Va. Capt., Co. C, 5th Virginia Cavalry, 1861. Major, 16th Virginia Cavalry Battalion, June 26, 1862. Unit became 13th Virginia Cavalry Regiment on July 29, 1862. Res., Feb. 20, 1863. m. Anna C. Harrison. d. Oct. 13, 1872. bur. in family cemetery in Sussex Co.

BENBOW, HENRY LAURENS. b. Sumter District, Oct. 25, 1829. att. Cokesbury College. Pvt., Hampton Legion, 1861. Capt., Co. I, 23rd South Carolina, Nov. 15, 1861. Colonel - Apr. 16, 1862. Commanding Evans' Brigade in Oct. 1863. Wded. at 2nd Manassas and Petersburg. Severely wounded and POW at Five Forks, released June 15. Summerton planter. d. there, Dec. 21, 1907.

BENNETT, MATTHEW DAVIS. b. Montgomery Co., Mar. 9, 1836. Lt., Co. E, 4th Virginia, Apr. 18, 1861. Captain - Apr. 22, 1862. Major - Sept. 15, 1863. Wded. at 2nd Manassas and Winchester (9-19-64). Resigned, Feb. 23, 1865. Farmer near Blacksburg. d. Montgomery Co., Dec. 22, 1896.

BENNETT, RISDEN TYLER. b. Wadesboro, North Carolina, June 18, 1840. gr. Cumberland U. (Tennessee). Anson Co. lawyer. Cpl., Co. C, 14th North Carolina, Apr. 22, 1861. Capt. and A.C.S., Sept. 28, 1861. Lt. Col. - Apr. 27, 1862. Colonel - July 5, 1862. Wded. at Gettysburg, Spotsylvania, Cold Harbor, and Sharpsburg. POW at Winchester (9-19-64). Judge of North Carolina Superior Court, 1880. In U.S. Congress, 1883-1887. d. Wadesboro, July 21, 1913, and buried there in family cemetery.

BENTLEY, WILLIAM WELDON. b. Montgomery Co., June 27, 1839. gr. VMI. Capt., Co. E, 24th Virginia, May 27, 1861. Major - May 29, 1864. Wded. at Williamsburg. Commanding Terry's Brigade at Appomattox. Of Pulaski Co. post-war. d. Richmond, July 23, 1924. Bentley led the 1913 reenactment of Pickett's charge.

BERKELEY, EDMUND. b. Feb. 7, 1824. m. Mary Lawson Williams. Capt., Co. C, 8th Virginia, May 11, 1861. Major - June 3, 1862. Lt. Col. - Aug. 9, 1863. Paroled at Fairfax C.H., Apr. 29, 1865. Lived in Prince William Co. d. Dec. 1, 1915. bur. St. Paul's Episcopal Church, Haymarket.

BERKELEY, NORBORNE. b. Mar. 31, 1828. gr. VMI, 1848. Major, 8th Virginia, Apr. 1861. Lt. Col. - Apr. 27, 1862. Colonel - Aug. 9, 1863. POW at Gettysburg and wded. in foot, exchanged Mar. 18, 1864. Frequently absent with chronic rheumatism and finally resigned Mar. 2, 1865. Paroled at Richmond, Apr. 24, 1865. m. Lavinia Hart Berkeley (a cousin). Lived in Oregon awhile post-war. Prince William Co. farmer. d. Jan. 16, 1911. bur. St. Paul's Episcopal Church, Haymarket.

BERKELEY, WILLIAM NOLAND. b. Feb. 28, 1826. Brother of two preceding men. Capt., Co. D, 8th Virginia, May 13, 1861. Major - Aug. 9, 1863. Wded. and POW at Gettysburg, exchanged Mar. 3, 1864. POW at Sayler's Creek, released June 27, 1865. d. Charlottesville, Apr. 25, 1907. bur. Sharon Cemetery, Middleburg.

BERKELEY, WILLIAM RANDOLPH. b. Farmville, Sept. 21, 1838. att. U. Virginia. gr. Hampden-Sydney. School teacher in Milton, North Carolina. Capt., Co. K, 21st Virginia, May 28, 1861. Major - Apr. 20, 1862. Resigned Mar. 25, 1863, because he despised Col. Witcher, then tried in vain to withdraw his resignation. Farmville lawyer. Killed there, Dec. 27, 1877, "by a man he was opposing in a law case."

BERRY, THOMAS J. b. Georgia, Sept. 1835. 5'10". Lived in Coweta Co. gr. USMA, 1857. Lt., U.S. Cavalry, 1857-1861. Lt. of Arty., CSA, March 16, 1861. Served on Lawton's staff. Major, 60th Georgia, Sept. 19, 1861. WIA at Second Manassas. Lt. Col. - Sept. 8, 1862. Acted as Colonel, 7th Virginia Cavalry during the fall of 1864. Retired, Jan. 3, 1865. d. Oct. 16, 1865. "Could not help sometimes taking a little too much whiskey."

BEST, EMORY FISKE. b. March 28, 1840, in Maryland. 1860 occupation—"gentleman." Lt., Co. C, 23rd Georgia, Aug. 31, 1861. Major - Aug. 31, 1861. Lt. Col. - Aug. 16, 1862. Colonel - Nov. 25, 1862. Wded. at Sharpsburg. Dismissed by court-martial

Chevis Clarke, Sr.

HENRY LAURENS BENBOW
23rd South Carolina

Dec. 23, 1863, as a result of his performance at Chancellorsville. m. Mrs. Mary Hill. Clerk in various D.C. government offices postwar. d. Apr. 23, 1912. bur. Macon.

BETSILL, ROBERT JEFFERSON. b. Sept. 12, 1838. Lt., Co. C, 18th South Carolina, Dec. 13, 1861. Capt. - May 5, 1862. Major - Aug. 30, 1862. Appx. Of Union Co. post-war. m. Catherine Van Wert. d. Feb. 8, 1902.

BETTS, WILLIAM H. Macon farmer. Capt., Co. B, 13th Alabama, July 19, 1861, age 22. Major - Jan. 10, 1862. Lt. Col. - June 11, 1862. Resigned, disability, Jan. 14, 1863.

BILLUPS, ROBERT S. b. Mathews Co. Farmer there in 1860, age 23. Major, 61st Virginia Militia, July 1861. Unit disbanded in May 1862.

BIRD, FRANCIS WILDER. b. Apr. 6, 1830. Lived in Bertie Co. att. Brown U. and Wake Forest. Lt., Co. L, 1st North Carolina (Bethel), May 1, 1861. Capt., Co. C, 11th North Carolina, Jan. 22, 1862. Major - July 1, 1863. Lt. Col. - Apr. 27, 1864. MWIA at Ream's Station, Aug. 25, 1864. Died the next day.

BIRD, PICKENS BUTLER. b. Edgefield Dist., South Carolina. Planter in Jefferson Co., Florida, net worth $41,000 in 1860. Capt., Co. K, 10th Florida, then Major, 6th Florida Battalion, which merged into the 9th Florida Regiment. Major, 9th Florida, Apr. 6, 1863. MWIA at Cold Harbor, June 3, 1864. d. June 6. bur. Hollywood Cemetery.

BLACK, HARVEY HANNIBAL. b. Kentucky, 1833. Moved to Texas ca. 1851. Raised stock in Hopkins Co., Texas. Capt., Co. A, 1st Texas, May 16, 1861. Major - Nov. 30, 1861. Lt. Col. - Jan. 2, 1862. KIA at Eltham's Landing, May 7, 1862. bur. on the battlefield.

BLACK, JOHN LOGAN. b. York Dist., July 12, 1830. att. USMA. Lt. Co., 1st South Carolina Cavalry, Oct. 31, 1861. Colonel - June 25, 1862. WIA at Upperville and Brandy Station. Present into 1865. Mining magnate and planter in Blacksburg, South Carolina, post-war. d. there Mar. 25, 1902.

BLACKFORD, EUGENE. b. Virginia, Apr. 11, 1839. att. U. Va. m. Rebecca Chapman Gordon. Capt., Co. K, 5th Alabama, May 15, 1861. Major - July 17, 1862. Cashiered by a court-martial for "misbehaviour before the enemy at . . . Cedar Creek." After a flood of petitions from peers, subordinates and superiors, he was reinstated by President Davis on Feb. 11, 1865. Teacher and dairy farmer in Maryland. d. Pikesville, Maryland, Feb. 4, 1908.

BLACKFORD, WILLIAM WILLIS. b. Mar. 23, 1831. att. U. Va. m. Mary Robertson, 1856. Lt., 1st Virginia Cavalry, May 14, 1861. a.d.c. to J.E.B. Stuart, July 1861. Capt., Corps of Engineers and on Stuart's staff, May 26, 1862. Major, 1st Engineers, Jan. 19, 1864. Lt. Col. - Apr. 1, 1864. Appx. Author of famous cavalry memoir. d. May 1, 1905.

BLACKNALL, CHARLES CHRISTOPHER. b. Granville Co., Dec. 4, 1830. Brother of Major T. H. Blacknall, 37th Arkansas. Capt., Co. G, 23rd North Carolina, June 11, 1861. Major - May 31, 1862. Lt. Col. - July 17, 1863. Colonel - Sept. 1, 1863. POW at Chancellorsville. Wded. in mouth and POW at Gettysburg, exchanged Mar. 1864. MWIA at Winchester, Sept. 19, 1864, d. near there Nov. 6. bur. in Winchester.

BLAIN, JAMES SIMEON. b. Augusta, July 23, 1838. Glynn Co. physician. att. Mercer U. and Augusta Medical College. Lt., Co. K, 26th Georgia, May 29, 1861. Capt. - Aug. 1, 1861. Major - Dec. 3, 1862. Lt. Col. - Aug. 12, 1863. Wded. shoulder, Aug. 25, 1864, in the Valley. d. Brunswick, Dec. 24, 1886.

BLAIR, JOHN ALAN. b. Hardeman Co., Tennessee, Aug. 23, 1835. gr. U. of Mississippi, 1860. Pvt., Co. K, 2nd Mississippi, Apr. 1861, later became regimental sgt. major. Major - Apr. 16, 1862. Lt. Col. - July 3, 1863. Wded. at 1st Manassas. POW at Gettysburg, exchanged Mar. 1864. POW at Hatcher's Run. 5′10″. Lawyer, in Mississippi legisl. d. Tupelo, Nov. 1, 1898. Blair's Civil War diary was the subject of a 1948 dissertation at the University of New Mexico.

BLAIR, LOVICK WILLIAM ROCHELLE. b. South Carolina, 1821. att. U. Virginia. Capt., Co. A, 7th South Carolina Battalion, Nov. 14, 1861. Major - July 10, 1862. Resigned due to "typhoid fever," Mar. 5, 1863. A huge and "dangerous" man, of "imposing figure and of ugly temper." Cultivated the Negro vote in Reconstruction South Carolina, and ran for governor in 1880. Camden newspaper editor. Murdered in a political row on July 4, 1882.

BLAKE, JULIUS AUGUSTUS. m. Julia Amelia Lewis. Age 34 in May 1864. Commanded the 17th South Carolina Militia in 1861. Capt., Co. I, 27th South Carolina, Feb. 17, 1862. Lt. Col. - Oct. 2, 1863. Wded. May 7, 1864, near Petersburg. POW at Weldon R.R., Aug. 21, 1864, exchanged Oct. 31. Dropped Jan. 27, 1865. Declared by Hagood to be ineffective. Coal and commission merchant in Charleston. d. April 11, 1903, age 73. bur. Magnolia Cemetery.

BLAND, ELBERT. b. Edgefield Dist., Apr. 29, 1823. gr. Medical College of New York. Asst. Surgeon, Palmetto Regiment, Mexican War. Surgeon, 1st South Carolina, 1861. Capt., Co. H, 7th South Carolina, Apr. 15, 1861. Lt. Col. - May 14, 1862. Bland fought a duel with Major Seibels during the winter of 1861-1862 near Manassas. Wded. at Savage Station, Fredericksburg and Gettysburg. KIA at Chickamauga. bur. Willowbrook Cemetery, Edgefield.

BLANDFORD, MARK HARDEN. b. Warren Co., July 13, 1826. att. Mercer U. Sgt. during Mexican War. Capt., Co. K, 12th Georgia, June 15, 1861. Lt. Col. - Jan. 24, 1863. Lost arm at McDowell. Resigned June 9, 1863, to enter C.S. Congress. Col. of Cavalry, July 24, 1863, but resigned Oct. 31, 1863. Georgia Supreme Court Justice post-war. d. Columbus, Jan. 31, 1902.

BLANDING, JAMES DOUGLASS. b. Columbia, June 26, 1821. Officer in Palmetto Regiment, Mexican War. Mayor of Sumter, 1852-1856. Married, lawyer worth $55,000 in 1860 Sumter District census. Lt. Col., 9th South Carolina, Apr. 8, 1861. Colonel - July 12, 1861. Regiment ceased to exist at April 1862 re-org. Later sought to raise a bn. of partisan rangers. d. Heriot, South Carolina, Oct. 24, 1906. bur. Sumter Cemetery.

BLESSING, WILLIAM. Farmer in Smyth Co. in 1860, age 33. Capt., Co. A, 23rd Virginia Battalion, Aug. 6, 1861. Major - Mar. 5, 1863. Present at least until Nov. 1864.

Mrs. Mary Wallace Day

ELBERT BLAND
7th South Carolina

BLOUNT, JOSEPH GRAY. b. Putnam Co., Georgia, Dec. 12, 1837. att. Georgia Military Institute and USMA. Lt., C.S. Infantry, Mar. 16, 1861, and with 6th South Carolina Infantry. Served in Dept. of South Carolina, Georgia and Florida. Lt. in Dearing's Lynchburg Battery (Virginia), May 1862. Became Captain of the Battery, now known as Blount's, Jan. 23, 1863. Major of Artillery, Stribling's Bn. (also known as the 38th Bn. Virginia Artillery), Oct. 27, 1864. Merchant in Columbus, Georgia. d. Talbotton, Georgia, Dec. 22, 1875, and bur. there.

BLOW, GEORGE, JR. b. Sussex Co., May 5, 1813. att. Hampden-Sydney, Wm. & Mary, and U. Va. Emigrated to Texas in 1840, and served in Texas legisl. Settled in Norfolk in 1845. In Virginia Secession Convention. Lt. Col., 41st Virginia, July 8, 1861. Dropped at May 1862 re-org. Norfolk judge post-war. d. Norfolk, May 2, 1894.

BOARD, FRANCIS HOWARD. b. Bedford Co., Virginia, Feb. 10, 1832. gr. Baltimore Medical College. Merchant. m. Buena Vista Arnold. Capt., Co. I, 58th Virginia, July 24, 1861. Lt. Col. - May 1, 1862. Colonel - Oct. 30, 1862. Wded. at Gaines' Mill. KIA at Winchester, July 20, 1864. bur. Stonewall Cemetery, Winchester.

BOGGAN, WALTER JONES. b. Anson Co. Lt., Co. C, 14th North Carolina, Apr. 20, 1861. Capt., Co. H, 43rd North Carolina, Feb. 24, 1862, age 21. 6′2″. Major - Mar. 24, 1862. Resigned Dec. 6, 1864, having been charged with "intoxication while on duty."

BOGGS, FRANCIS JOHNSTON. b. Greencastle, Pennsylvania, Nov. 28, 1821. Pastor of Union Station Methodist Church, Richmond, Virginia, in 1861. Capt., Co. H, 1st Virginia Infantry, May 4, 1861. Res. Sept. 6, 1861. Major, 12th Battalion Virginia Light Artillery, May 15, 1862. Became Chief of Artillery to Genl. James A. Walker, commanding in the Richmond defenses, Oct. 21, 1864. Served as pastor of many Virginia Methodist congregations after the war, including at Suffolk. d. Ashland, Jan. 3, 1894.

BOGGS, THOMAS HAMILTON. b. Liberty, South Carolina, May 6, 1823. m. Martha Ann Hamilton. Farmer in Pickens District in 1860. Capt., Co. E, 2nd South Carolina Rifles, Oct. 24, 1861. Major - Dec. 10, 1861. Lt. Col. - May 12, 1862. d. at home in Pickens Dist., of fever, July 6, 1862. bur. Carmel Presbyterian Churchyard.

BOHANNAN, JOHN G. b. Mathews Co. Physician in Mathews Co. in 1860, age 32. Colonel, 61st Virginia Militia, Sept. 25, 1858. Commanded this militia unit at Yorktown, until it was disbanded ca. May 1862. State legisl. from Mathews Co., 1886-1887.

BOMAR, THOMAS HAYNE. b. Macon, Nov. 4, 1842. att. Georgia Military Institute. Capt., Co. L, 38th Georgia, Oct. 13, 1861. Major - July 2, 1863. POW at Cedar Creek, released July 24, 1865. Civil engineer with railroads post-war. m. Mary Wilson. John B. Gordon: "One of the bravest men I ever saw." d. Pecos, Texas, Mar. 11, 1927. bur. El Paso.

BONAUD, AUGUSTUS. b. Marseilles, France. Liquor merchant in Savannah in 1860, age 38. Major, 28th Battalion Georgia Artillery, Aug. 6, 1863. Also served as Captain, 1st Georgia Infantry (Olmstead's); Captain, 22nd Battalion Georgia Heavy Artillery; and Drill Master, C.S.A. Professor of dancing in Savannah. d. Feb. 16, 1892, age 70. bur. Catholic Cemetery, Savannah.

BOND, THOMAS H. b. Petersburg, Sept. 22, 1824. Capt., Co. C, 12th Virginia, Apr. 1861 (had commanded the company since 1859). Resigned 1862. Became captain of a company of Va. reserves formed of men detailed to the Petersburg & Weldon R.R. Major, Hood's Battalion Virginia Reserves, Aug. 6, 1864. Grocer and tax collector in Petersburg post-war. d. there, of erysipelas, Feb. 5, 1901. bur. Blandford.

BONDURANT, JAMES WILLIAM. b. Buckingham Co., Virginia. Sgt., Jeff Davis Artillery, July 23, 1861. Lt. - Jan. 28, 1862. Captain - early 1862. Major of artillery - May 8, 1863. Lt. Col. - Aug. 11, 1863. Chief of Artillery, D. H. Hill's Division, 1863. Chief of Artillery Hindman's Corps, Army of Tennessee, Jan. 1864.

Assigned at Andersonville in 1864, then back to D. H. Hill. Lived in Marengo Co., Alabama. Lived in Baltimore post-war, then in Perry Co., Alabama.

BOOKER, GEORGE EDWARD. b. Buckingham Co., Feb. 13, 1827. gr. Randolph-Macon. Capt., Co. H, 58th Virginia, Sept. 28, 1861. Major early in 1862, but dropped at May 1862 re-org. Became chaplain in the 48th Virginia. Methodist minister at Richmond, Suffolk, Lexington and Petersburg. d. Cumberland C.H., Feb. 12, 1899. bur. at "Wardside" near there.

BOOKER, RICHARD ANDERSON. b. Nov. 15, 1817. In Virginia legisl. in 1861. Capt., Co. F, 18th Virginia, Apr. 1861. Wded. at 2nd Manassas and resigned. Capt., Co. D, 3rd Virginia Reserves, Apr. 20, 1864. Colonel - Sept. 30, 1864. Paroled at Farmville between Apr. 11 and 21, 1865. d. Farmville, Apr. 30, 1904, and bur. there.

BOOKTER, EDWIN FAUST. b. Richland Dist., Nov. 11, 1837. att. South Carolina College. In South Carolina legisl., 1860-1861. Capt., Co. D, 12th South Carolina, Aug. 20, 1861. Major - Feb. 27, 1863. Lt. Col. - Nov. 17, 1863. Colonel - May 6, 1864. Wded. at Gaines' Mill, 2nd Manassas and Wilderness. KIA at Jones' Farm Sept. 30, 1864. bur. Mt. Pleasant Methodist Church near Columbia.

BOONE, BARTLEY BARRY. b. Lincoln Co., Tennessee, Apr. 6, 1831. Capt., Co. A, 2nd Mississippi, Apr. 30, 1861 (had been captain since Feb. 20). Lt. Col. - May 10, 1861. POW at 1st Manassas. Resigned, "ill health," Jan. 31, 1862. m. Lou Petty. Established Booneville, Mississippi. Prentiss Co. judge. d. Booneville, Sept. 19, 1905.

BOONE, FRANCIS MARION. b. Tennessee, Jan. 19, 1822. Planter at Booneville, Mississippi. 6'0". Age shown variously as 40 or 42 in 1861, and 44 in July 1862. Elected Lt. Col. 26th Mississippi, Sept. 10, 1861, though it was not finally confirmed until Apr. 1863. POW at Ft. Donelson, Feb. 1862; released July 31, 1862. On detached service, June 1863-Feb. 1864. KIA at Wilderness, May 6, 1864.

Virginia State Library

LOUIS J. BOSSIEUX
25th Virginia Battalion

BOSSIEUX, LOUIS J. b. New York, Sept. 24, 1817, son of a French officer on tour. Family moved to Richmond from France ca. 1820. Lt., Co. G, 12th Virginia Infantry, 1861. He had belonged to this unit, the Richmond Grays, since 1844. Capt., Co. B, 25th Battalion ("Richmond City Battalion"), July 21, 1862. Major - July 25, 1863. Paroled at Richmond, Apr. 24, 1865. Richmond candy manufacturer. d. Richmond, of heart disease, June 15, 1886. bur. Shockoe Hill.

BOST, JACKSON LAFAYETTE. b. Jan. 31, 1832, Bost's Mills, North Carolina. gr. U. Pennsylvania Medical School. Lt., Co. D, 37th North Carolina, Sept. 16, 1861. Captain - Aug. 1862. Major - July 24, 1863. Wded. at Chancellorsville and Gettysburg. POW at Slash Church. Appx. d. Olive Branch, North Carolina, Oct. 27, 1909.

BOSTON, REUBEN BEVERLEY. b. Fluvanna Co., Apr. 21, 1834. att. U. Virginia. Lt., Co. I, 5th Virginia Cavalry. Captain - May 2, 1862. Colonel - June 16, 1864. POW at Aldie, June 17, 1863 (exchanged Mar. 10, 1864), and at Trevilian's. KIA Apr. 7, 1865.

BOSTON, WILLIAM JAMES. b. Jan. 16, 1834. Lt., Co. A, 23rd Georgia, Aug. 31, 1861. Captain - Apr. 22, 1862. Major - Aug. 1864. Paroled at Greensboro. Lived in Resaca, Georgia. d. Dec. 23, 1910. bur. Resaca Cemetery.

BOSWELL, THOMAS TAYLOR. b. Virginia. Lived in Mecklenburg Co. Capt., Co. A, 56th Virginia, 1861. Capt., Co. A, 1st Virginia Reserves, Apr. 20, 1864. Lt. Col. - Aug. 12, 1864. Paroled May 13, 1865, by U.S. Sixth Corps. m. Martha Nelson. Living in Halifax Co. in 1870, age 46.

BOTTS, LAWSON. b. Fredericksburg, July 25, 1825. gr. VMI, 1844. m. Sarah Elizabeth Bibb Ranson, 1851. Charlestown lawyer, defended John Brown. Capt., Co. G, 2nd Virginia, Apr. 18, 1861 (had commanded this volunteer company since Nov. 4, 1859). Major - June 12, 1861. Lt. Col. - Sept. 11, 1861. Colonel - June 27, 1862. MWIA through cheek and ear at 2nd Manassas, d. Sept. 16 near Middleburg. bur. Charleston Episcopal Church. Some of Botts' papers are at Duke University.

BOTTS, WALTER BROWNE. b. Fredericksburg, Virginia, Sept. 7, 1835. Brother of Col. Lawson Botts. gr. VMI, 1854. Lawyer in Houston, Texas. Capt., Co. A, 5th Texas, July 19, 1861. Major - Nov. 4, 1861. Lt. Col. - June 1, 1862. Wded. at Seven Pines, and resigned due to "shattered health" which resulted, July 17, 1862. m. Martha E. McIlheny. d. Houston, Texas, Mar. 7, 1894.

BOWEN, HENRY S. b. Tazewell Co., Aug. 3, 1820. m. Mary E. Miller, 1854. Colonel, 188th Virginia Militia - 1861. Major and Commissary, summer 1862. Colonel, 22nd Virginia Cavalry, Aug. 1, 1863. Present into 1865. Paroled at Charleston, June 12, 1865. 6′4″. Farmer in Wythe Co. in 1884.

BOWEN, ROBERT ESLI. b. Pickens Dist., Sept. 8, 1830. Lt., Co. E, 2nd South Carolina Rifles, Oct. 24, 1861. Captain - Dec. 19, 1861. Lt. Col. - Nov. 13, 1863. Colonel - Jan. 22, 1864. Wded. at Wauhatchie. In South Carolina legisl. during and after the war. Appx. Pickens Co. farmer and railroad man, and Clemson U. trustee. d. Fairforest, South Carolina, Jan. 11, 1909.

BOWEN, THOMAS PEERY. b. Maiden Spring, Virginia, Aug. 2, 1838. Lt., Co. H, 8th Virginia Cavalry, July 25, 1861. Captain - fall of 1861. Major - May 15, 1862. m. Hannah Augusta Stuart, 1866. d. Maiden Spring, Oct. 6, 1911. bur. Maplewood Cemetery, Tazewell Co.

BOWLES, JOHN SAMUEL. (known as "Johnsam") b. Goochland Co., Dec. 17, 1844. Capt., Co. H, 22nd Virginia Battalion, Feb. 4, 1862. Major - Nov. 18, 1862. Injured by falling tree, Dec. 1862. Wded. in May 1864. Paroled at Columbia, Virginia, May 8, 1865. m. Eddie Rutherford. d. Belzoni, Mississippi, Apr. 11, 1914.

BOWLES, PINCKNEY DOWNIE. b. Edgefield Dist., South Carolina, July 7, 1835. att. SCMA. Capt., 4th Alabama, Apr. 1, 1861. Major - Aug. 22, 1862. Lt. Col. - Sept. 30, 1862. Colonel - Oct. 3, 1862. gr. U. Virginia. Evergreen, Alabama, judge. d. Tampa, Florida, July 25, 1910.

BOYD, ANDREW JACKSON. b. Rockingham Co., Feb. 24, 1836.

Brother of Samuel H. Boyd. att. Emory & Henry. Lawyer. Lt., Co. L, 21st North Carolina, June 3, 1861. Captain - Sept. 3, 1861. Major, 45th North Carolina, Apr. 3, 1862. Lt. Col. - Sept. 30, 1862. Resigned due to chronic bronchitis, Jan. 8, 1863. In North Carolina legisl., 1864. Rockingham Co. banker and lawyer post-war. d. Aug. 18, 1893.

BOYD, SAMUEL HILL. b. Rockingham Co. Resident of Troublesome, North Carolina. Capt., Co. E, 45th North Carolina, Feb. 27, 1862, age 28. Occupation - merchant. 6'4". Lt. Col. - Jan. 31, 1863. Colonel - June 26, 1863. POW at Hagerstown, July 4, 1863; paroled Mar. 3, 1864. KIA at Spotsylvania. bur. Wentworth Methodist Cemetery, Rockingham Co.

BOYD, WALLER MASSIE. b. in Arkansas, Aug. 21, 1843. att. VMI. Resided at Massie's Mill, Virginia. 5'10". Lt., Co. G, 19th Virginia, May 1, 1861. Captain - Apr. 28, 1862. Major - Oct. 24, 1864. Wded. and POW at Gettysburg, paroled Mar. 3, 1864. POW at Sayler's Creek, released July 25, 1865. Apple grower at Roseland, Virginia. d. May 6, 1917.

BOYD, WILLIAM WADE. b. Union District, South Carolina, Jan. 19, 1819. m. Harriet Adaline Brem. Tailor in Marietta. Lt. in pre-war militia company. Colonel, 19th Georgia, at org., June 11, 1861. Resigned, due to rheumatism, Jan. 12, 1862. Boyd's home was torched by Sherman's men. d. July 9, 1878, in Atlanta. bur. Oakland Cemetery.

BOYKIN, EDWARD MORTIMER. b. May 17, 1820. Physician. gr. Medical College of South Carolina. Lt., Co. H, 7th South Carolina Cavalry, Sept. 21, 1861. Capt., Co. K, Sept. 5, 1862. Major - Sept. 7, 1864 (an earlier appointment had not been confirmed). Of Camden, South Carolina, post-war. Author of a Civil War memoir and a family genealogy. m. Mary Chestnut Lang. d. Nov. 10, 1891.

BOYKIN, FRANCIS MARSHALL, JR. b. Isle of Wight Co., Mar. 1, 1837. gr. VMI, 1856. Major, 31st Virginia, Dec. 14, 1861. Lt. Col. - early 1862. Dropped at May 1862 re-org. Nearly killed by a mob in Grafton early in the war. Became Capt., Co.

E, 25th Virginia Battalion, in 1862. Richmond tobacco merchant post-war. d. Richmond, May 5, 1906. bur. Hollywood.

BOYKIN, STEPHEN MADISON. b. Sumter Dist., Dec. 10, 1817. A surveyor. Capt., Co. A, 20th South Carolina, Dec. 24, 1861. Major - Apr. 1, 1862. Colonel - June 2, 1864. Wded. by saber in the head and POW at Cedar Creek, released July 24, 1865. 5′11″. d. Sumter Co., Sept. 25, 1897. bur. in family cemtery.

BRABBLE, EDMUND CREY, b. Jan. 5, 1835. Lived in Tyrrell Co., North Carolina. gr. Dartmouth, 1857 (as valedictorian). Capt., Co. L, 12th North Carolina (which became Co. A, 1st Battalion North Carolina Infantry), on May 16, 1861. Major, 1st Battalion North Carolina, Nov. 29, 1861. Colonel, 32nd North Carolina, Mar. 17, 1862. KIA at Spotsylvania. bur. Albemarle Cemetery, near Columbia, North Carolina.

BRADFORD, CHARLES M. b. Dec. 1826 in Pennsylvania. att. USMA. Capt., Co. A, 1st Louisiana, Jan. 7, 1861. To major, Feb. 6, 1861. Lt. Col., 15th Louisiana, Sept 4, 1861. Court-martialed for disrespect to a superior. Resigned June 5, 1862. Also served as Lt. Col., 3rd Louisiana Battalion and Colonel, Bradford's Regiment Texas Cavalry. Lawyer in New Orleans. d. New Orleans, Sept. 26, 1867.

BRADFORD, TAUL. b. Talledega, Jan. 20, 1835. gr. U. Alabama, 1854. Major, 10th Alabama, July 8, 1861. Resigned Aug. 21, 1861. Later became Lt. Col., 30th Alabama. In Alabama legisl., 1871-1872. In U.S. Congress, 1875-1877. d. Talladega, Oct. 28, 1883. bur. Oak Hill Cemetery.

BRADLEY, JOHN M. b. North Carolina. The 1860 census for Louisville, Mississippi, carries Bradley as a 33-year-old merchant, living in a hotel. Capt., Co. B, 13th Mississippi, Mar. 16, 1861. 6′0″. Major - Aug. 12, 1862. Lt. Col. - July 2, 1863. Wded. at Sharpsburg. Wded. at Gettysburg and left at Williamsport. d. July 28, 1863. Age at death - 36.

BRADSHAW, CHARLES W. Capt., Co. A, 42nd North Carolina, Feb. 27, 1862, aged 28. Major - Nov. 20, 1862. Lt. Col. - Jan. 7, 1864. Paroled at Greensboro. Living in Charlotte in 1901.

BRADY, ANDREW. Clerk in New Orleans. Capt., Co. A, 15th Louisiana, June 3, 1861. Major - Aug. 30, 1862. On detached service in Louisiana, summer of 1864, then ordered to Trans-Mississippi Dept. in Aug. 1864. Paroled at Alexandria, Louisiana, June 4, 1865. d. Feb. 22, 1889. bur. Metairie Cemetery, New Orleans.

BRAILSFORD, EDWARD DuBOSE. b. Oct. 15, 1834, in Clarendon District. att. SCMA. Wife - Columbia Hill of Virginia. Lt., Co. I, 1st South Carolina (Gregg's), July 1861. Captain - June 27, 1862. Major - June 19, 1864. Present in Feb. 1865. d. Charleston Sept. 23, 1879. bur. St. Mark's Episcopal Church, Sumter Co.

BRANCH, JAMES READ. b. Prince George Co., July 28, 1828. gr. Randolph-Macon in 1848, with second honors. Petersburg merchant. Capt., Co. K, 16th Virginia, May 1861. This unit was assigned as artillery in Mar. 1862. Major - May 2, 1863. Lt. Col. - Aug. 25, 1863, and assigned to First Corps. Wded. at Plymouth, North Carolina, in what one officer described as a drunken equestrian accident. Retired, Mar. 28, 1865. Richmond broker and banker post-war. Killed in Richmond by a bridge collapse, July 2, 1869. E. P. Alexander called him "an excellent officer & a fine fellow."

BRANDER, THOMAS ALEXANDER. b. Richmond, Dec. 12, 1839. Member of Richmond's famed "Company F" at outset of the war. Lt., Co. A, 20th Virginia, 1861. Lt., Letcher Artillery (Virginia), Feb. 15, 1862. Major - Feb. 18, 1865, assigned to Poague's Battalion. Wded. at Fredericksburg. Appx. Richmond insurance man. Commander of R. E. Lee Camp #1, U.C.V. d. Richmond, Jan. 28, 1900. bur. Hollywood Cemetery.

BRANDON, NATHAN. b. Stewart Co., Jan. 20, 1820. Lawyer in Dover in 1860, net worth $54,000. Capt., Co. E, 14th Tennessee, May 17, 1861. Major - June 6, 1861. Lt. Col. - Nov. 1, 1861. Dropped at Apr. 1862 re-org. Paroled at Ft. Donelson surrender, where he was wounded seven times, while ostensibly at home on furlough. In Tennessee legisl. post-war. d. Dover, Tennessee, Apr. 20, 1891. Brandon was married four times.

National Park Service

CARTER MOORE BRAXTON
Virginia Artillery

BRAXTON, CARTER MOORE. b. Norfolk, Sept. 5, 1836. Grandson of a signer of the Declaration. Lived in Fredericksburg. Capt. of Engineers, State of Virginia, Apr. 1861. Capt., Fredericksburg Artillery (Virginia), May 1861. Major - Mar. 2, 1863, assigned to Carter's Battalion. Lt. Col. - Feb. 27, 1864. Civil engineer for R. F. & P. Railroad and C & O Railroad and others. Lived in Newport News late in life. d. May 27, 1898.

BREATHED, JAMES. b. Maryland, Feb. 13, 1838. Educated in Baltimore. 5′11″. Pvt., Co. B, 1st Virginia Cavalry, Aug. 31, 1861. Lt., Pelham's Battery (Virginia), Mar. 23, 1862. Captain - Aug. 9, 1862. Major - Feb. 27, 1864, assigned to Horse Artillery Battalion. Wded. at Yellow Tavern. Paroled at Winchester, Apr. 24, 1865. Physician in Hancock, Maryland, post-war. d. there Feb. 14, 1870. bur. in Hancock.

BRECKINRIDGE, CARY. b. Botetourt Co., Oct. 5, 1839. gr. VMI, 1860. m. Virginia Calwell. Lt., Co. C, 2nd Virginia Cavalry, May 17, 1861. Captain - Jan. 30, 1862. Major - Apr. 25, 1862. Lt. Col. - Dec. 7, 1864. POW at Kelly's Ford. Wded. Aug. 21, 1864. In Virginia legisl. Fincastle mayor, banker, farmer and Botetourt Supt. of Schools. d. Fincastle, May 11, 1918.

BRENAN, PETER. b. Ireland. Merchant in Quitman Co., age 49, in 1860. Capt., Co. F, 61st Georgia, Aug. 15, 1861. Major - Mar. 1, 1863. KIA at Gettysburg, July 1. bur. Laurel Hill Cemetery, Savannah.

BRENT, GEORGE WILLIAM. b. Alexandria, Aug. 1821. gr. U. Virginia. In Virginia legisl. and the Secession Convention. Fauquier Co. lawyer. Major, 17th Virginia, May 2, 1861. Dropped at Apr. 1862 re-org. Colonel and a.a.g. to Beauregard and Bragg later in the war. d. Alexandria, Jan. 2, 1872. bur. St. Mary's Cemetery.

BREWER, SEPTIMUS LENIAL. b. Georgia. Farmer in Taylor Co. in 1860, age 43. Married, with 11 children. Capt., Co. F, 27th Georgia, Sept. 9, 1861. Lt. Col. - Sept. 11, 1861. Resigned in Nov. 1861.

BRIDGFORD, DAVID B. Son of a British officer (1792-1868) in the militia of Upper Canada, distinguished in the War of 1812.

Ship's broker and commission merchant in New York City before and after the war. Merchant in Richmond in 1860, age 29. Capt., Co. B, 1st Virginia Battalion Regulars ("Irish Bn."), May 17, 1861. Major - Oct. 11, 1862. Detached as Provost Marshal of Second Corps, then of entire Army of Northern Virginia from the fall of 1862 onward. He was with Jackson at Guiney Station in May 1863 and escorted the general's corpse to Richmond and Lexington. Bridgford was involved in a Cuban revolution post-war. d. in New York City "many years ago" before 1904. An officer of the 1st Virginia Battalion wrote that Bridgford had "the gift of attracting the notice of superior officers, but . . . did not measure up. . . ."

BRIEN, LUKE TIERNAN. b. Urbana, Maryland, Dec. 22, 1827. gr. Georgetown U. Lived in Baltimore and Frederick. Capt., P.A.C.S., and a.a.g. to Stuart, Sept. 24, 1861. Lt. Col., 1st Virginia Cavalry, Apr. 23, 1862. Resigned Oct. 1862. Major and a.a.g. to Rooney Lee in 1864. Appx. With Illinois Central R.R. post-war. Lived in the building in Urbana, Maryland, made famous by J.E.B. Stuart's 1862 dance there. d. Frederick, Maryland, Nov. 25, 1912. bur. St. Ignatius-Loyola Catholic Church, Urbana.

BRIGGS, BENJAMIN F. Of Gaston Co., North Carolina. Capt., Co. M, 16th North Carolina. Major - June 17, 1861. Defeated at Apr. 1862 re-org.

BROCKENBROUGH, JOHN BOWYER. b. Apr. 6, 1836. Known as "Beau." att. Washington College. gr. U. Virginia. Lawyer, lived in Lexington, Virginia. Lt., Rockbridge Artillery, Apr. 1861. Wded. at 1st Manassas. Capt., Baltimore Light Artillery (Maryland), Mar. 2, 1862. Major - Mar. 2, 1863. Chief of Artillery of Taliaferro's Division (as a captain), fall 1862. Second in command of Hilary P. Jones' Battalion. Suffered disabling wound at Fredericksburg. Retired Mar. 23, 1864. m. Lucy Alice Murrell, 1864. m. 2nd time and went West to Oregon, California and Wyoming, where he was a federal land inspector. d. Nov. 15, 1901. bur. Loudon Park Cemetery, Baltimore, Maryland.

BROCKENBROUGH, JOHN MERCER. b. Richmond Co., Aug. 1, 1830. Farmer there. gr. VMI, 1850. m. Austina Brockenbrough (a cousin), 1856. m. 2nd, Kate Cornelia Mallory, 1877 (she's a sister of Col. Francis Mallory, q.v.). Colonel, 40th Virginia, May 25, 1861. Resigned Jan. 21, 1864, because H. H. Walker, his inexperienced Lt. Col., was made Brigadier General over him. Col., 2nd Virginia Reserves, in late 1864. Lived in Norfolk and Richmond. d. Richmond, Aug. 24, 1892. bur. Hollywood.

BROCKETT, EDGAR LONGDEN. b. Alexandria, Mar. 9, 1821. Merchant in Petersburg. Colonel, 39th Virginia Militia, at outset of war. Major, 12th Virginia, May 9, 1861. Dropped at May 1862 re-org. Applied for a C.S. Treasury Dept. clerkship. d. Mar. 7, 1887, in Alexandria. bur. Presbyterian Cemetery.

BROCKMAN, BENJAMIN THOMAS. b. Greenville Dist., South Carolina, Dec. 11, 1831. Spartanburg merchant. Capt., Co. B, 13th South Carolina, Aug. 31, 1861. Major - June 19, 1862. Lt. Col. - late 1862. Colonel - June 21, 1863. Wded. at 2nd Manassas. MWIA in arm and head at Spotsylvania, May 3, 1864. d. in Richmond, June 8. bur. Hollywood.

BRONAUGH, WILLIAM NAYLOR. b. Fauquier Co., Virginia, Feb. 9, 1833. gr. U. Virginia. m. Evelyn Taliaferro. Taught in Little Rock, Arkansas. Adj., 1st Arkansas, 1861. Major, 2nd Arkansas Battalion, at re-org. in spring of 1862. KIA at Mechanicsville. bur. Hollywood.

BROOKS, JOHN STANLEY. b. Greenville, North Carolina, Oct. 20, 1840. Brunswick Co. farmer. Capt., Co. G, 20th North Carolina, May 25, 1861. Major - May 10, 1863. Lt. Col. - Nov. 2, 1863. Wded. at Gaines' Mill and Gettysburg. KIA at Spotsylvania. bur. Spotsylvania Confederate Cemetery.

BROOME, JAMES ANDREW. b. LaGrange, Ga., Nov. 27, 1839. att. VMI. Capt., Co. I, 14th Alabama, July 20, 1861. Major - June 30, 1862. Lt. Col. - July 8, 1862. Lost a leg in service. Retired to Invalid Corps, Mar. 25, 1865. Farmer and merchant in LaGrange. d. May 7, 1917.

BROUN, THOMAS LEE. b. Dec. 26, 1823, in Loudoun Co. gr. U. Va. Lawyer in Kanawha and Boone Co. Law partner of

George S. Patton. Edited *Kanawha Valley Star.* Pvt., Co. I, 22nd Virginia Infantry, April 1861. Major of 60th Virginia Infantry by appointment of H. A. Wise from Aug. 13 to Nov. 22, 1861, when supplanted by Major Sweeney on orders of the War Dept. Major and QM to Heth, Feb. 1862. QM of post at Dublin's Depot, 1862-1864, then in Augusta, Georgia, and Columbia, South Carolina. m. Mary M. Fontaine, June 1866 and moved to New York City. Back to West Virginia in 1870. Edited Neale book about his brother. Living in Putnam Co. in 1910. d. March 1914.

BROUN, WILLIAM LeROY. b. Loudoun Co., Virginia, Oct. 1, 1827. gr. U. Virginia. m. Sallie J. Fleming, 1859 (she was half-sister of Col. Lewis Minor Coleman, and full sister of Vivian Minor Fleming). C.S. ordnance officer, commanding arsenal at Richmond. Lt. Col., 5th Virginia Battalion LDT (the "Arsenal Bn."), June 24, 1863. Resigned May 15, 1864 (accepted Aug. 11), because his duties as commander of the arsenal were too pressing to allow him time for this infantry sidelight. Faculty member of Vanderbilt, U. Georgia, U. Texas, Auburn U., etc. post-war. Author of noteworthy Neale book. d. Auburn, Alabama, Jan. 23, 1902. bur. Pine Hill Cemetery.

BROWN, HAMILTON ALLEN. b. Sept. 25, 1837. att. U. Virginia. Lived in Wilkes Co. Capt., Co. B, 1st North Carolina, May 16, 1861. Major - Apr. 21, 1862. Lt. Col. - July 8, 1862. Colonel - Dec. 14, 1863. Wded. at Mine Run. POW at Ft. Stedman, released July 24, 1865. Farmer at Columbia, Tennessee in 1900. d. Apr. 9, 1917. bur. St. Paul's Episcopal Churchyard, Wilkesboro, North Carolina. Brown stuttered violently when in battle.

BROWN, JOHN CANTY. Of Coffee Co., Alabama. Capt., Co. D, 12th Alabama, May 23, 1861. Major - Nov. 9, 1861. Resigned Mar. 6, 1862. Died in Florida.

BROWN, JOHN EDMUNDS. b. Caswell Co., 1830. Mecklenburg Co. lawyer. att. Hampden-Sydney. Brother of Major Thomas Jethro Brown. m. Laura T. Morrison. Lt., Co. D, 7th North Carolina, May 16, 1861. Adj., 7th North Carolina, Aug. 26,

1861. Lt. Col., 42nd North Carolina, Apr. 22, 1862. Colonel - Jan. 7, 1864. Paroled at Greensboro. Charlotte lawyer post-war.

BROWN, JOHN THOMPSON. b. Petersburg, Feb. 6, 1835. gr. U. Virginia. m. Mary Martha Southall, 1858 (she later married Charles S. Venable of Lee's staff). Lt., Richmond Howitzers, Apr. 21, 1861. Captain - May 1861. Major - Sept. 1861. Lt. Col. - spring 1862. Colonel - June 2, 1862. Commanded Second Corps artillery reserve. KIA at Wilderness.

BROWN, JOSEPH NEWTON. b. Anderson, South Carolina, Dec. 16, 1832. Laurens lawyer. m. Lizzie Louisa Bruce. Pvt., Co. D, 1st South Carolina, Jan. 1861. Capt., Co. E, 14th South Carolina, Aug. 16, 1861. Lt. Col. - Feb. 20, 1863. Colonel - Sept. 17, 1863. Wded. at Gaines' Mill and Gettysburg. POW at Noel Station, North Anna, May 23, 1864; exchanged Aug. 3, 1864. Author of a fine book on Spotsylvania and Gettysburg. In South Carolina legisl. post-war. d. Jan. 24, 1920.

BROWN, OWEN NEIL. b. Fayetteville, North Carolina. Lived in Mecklenburg Co. att. UNC. Teacher. Pvt., Co. C, 37th North Carolina, Sept. 16, 1861, aged 24 or 26. 5′11″. Lt. - Feb. 25, 1862. Captain - June 28, 1862. Major - May 29, 1863. MWIA at Gettysburg, d. July 24.

BROWN, RIDGELY. b. Montgomery Co., Maryland, Nov. 12, 1833. Lt., Co. K, 1st Virginia Cavalry, 1861-1862. Capt., Co. A, 1st Maryland Cavalry Battalion, early 1862. Major - Nov. 12, 1862. Lt. Col. - Aug. 20, 1863. Wded. at Greenland Gap, Apr. 25, 1863. KIA at South Anna River, June 1, 1864. Reburied in 1866 at "Elton" in eastern Montgomery Co., Maryland.

BROWN, SHERIDAN RAGLAND. b. Jasper Co., Dec. 21, 1831. Farmer in Henry Co. Sgt., Co. F, 53rd Georgia, May 2, 1862. Captain - June 11, 1862. Major - Dec. 19, 1863. Wded. at Gettysburg. Resigned, disability, Sept. 23, 1864. d. McDonough, Georgia, Oct. 2, 1902. bur. McDonough.

BROWN, THOMAS JETHRO. b. Aug. 3, 1833. Brother of Col. John E. Brown. Lt., Co. G, 4th North Carolina, May 16, 1861. Capt., Co. E, 42nd North Carolina, May 10, 1862. Major - Jan. 7, 1864.

Paroled at Greensboro. m. Dalphine Hall, 1868. Attorney and tobacco businessman in Winston. d. July 17, 1914.

BROWN, WILLIAM A. JACKSON. Known almost inevitably, even in official documents, as simply "Jack" Brown. b. Georgia, 1830. gr. U. Georgia, 1850 (entering from Washington, D.C.). m. Margaret Shelton. Capt., Co. G, 10th Georgia State Troops, Dec. 16, 1861. Capt., Co. H, 59th Georgia, May 6, 1862. Colonel - June 16, 1862. Wded. and POW at Gettysburg, exchanged Mar. 10, 1864. Wded. in the leg, Aug. 14, 1864. Appx. Talbotton lawyer post-war. d. 1900.

BROWNE, WILLIAM HENRY. b. Tazewell Co., Virginia, Nov. 9, 1838. Lived at Jeffersonville. att. USMA, 1857-1861, and resigned Apr. 22, 1861. Capt., Co. G, 45th Virginia, May 29, 1861. Colonel - May 14, 1862. KIA at Piedmont, June 5, 1864. bur. Maplewood Cemetery, Tazewell Co.

BRUCE, JAMES DOUGLAS. b. Winchester, July 1833. gr. VMI, 1853. Civil engineer. m. (1) Angie Brooke. m. (2) Claiborne Hubard. Capt., Co. I, 47th Virginia, Apr. 21, 1861. Major - Nov. 14, 1862. Lt. Col. - Dec. 19, 1864. Lost arm at Mine Run. POW at Sayler's Creek, released June 20. d. near Boyce, Virginia, Jan. 18, 1922. bur. Mt. Hebron Cemetery, Winchester.

BRUMBY, ARNOLDUS VANDERHORST. b. South Carolina, Dec. 12, 1808. gr. USMA. m. Annie E. Wallis. Faculty of U. Alabama and founder of Georgia Military Institute. Col., 14th Georgia, July 17, 1861. Resigned, Nov. 21, 1861. Lt. Patterson of Co. E accused Brumby of being "drunk often" and incompetent. d. Cartersville, Georgia, Nov. 2, 1887. bur. Oak Hill Cemetery.

BRUSTER, EBENEZER. Farmer in Tazewell Co. in 1860, age 33. Capt., Co. H, 29th Virginia, Apr. 2, 1862. Major - June 2, 1864. Paroled at Charleston, West Virginia, June 12, 1865. 5′4″. Living in Tazewell in 1870.

BRYAN, DAVID F. Dentist and surgeon in Fayette Co. in 1860, age 31. Capt., Co. A, 3rd Alabama Bn., 1861. POW at Fort Donelson. Major, 26th Alabama, Dec. 4, 1862.

BRYAN, JOHN G. Of Alexander Co. Capt., Co. G, 37th North Carolina, Oct. 9, 1861, aged 53. 5'6½". Major - Nov. 20, 1861. Resigned, due to health, Mar. 14, 1862. Wife - Mary. Had six children.

BRYAN, KING. Full first name is variously given as Kendellia or Kindallis, but he always used the shortened version as shown. b. Berwicks Bay, Louisiana, Jan. 20, 1818. Moved to Texas in 1834, and served in state legisl. pre-war. Farmer. Served in the Texas War of Independence. Sheriff of Liberty Co., 1848-49 and 1852-54. Capt., Co. F, 5th Texas, July 11, 1861. Major - Aug. 30, 1862. Lt. Col. - Nov. 1, 1862. Wded. at Gettysburg and Wilderness. Latter wounds, in both arms, disabled Bryan and he retired Mar. 8, 1865. Member of the 1865 Texas Convention. d. Oct. 8, 1866, in Liberty.

BRYSON, SAMUEL C. Of Haywood Co. Lawyer. Capt., Co. A, 25th North Carolina, June 31, 1861, aged 30. Major - Apr. 30, 1862. Lt. Col. - May 21, 1862. Res. Dec. 24, 1864. In North Carolina legisl. during war. Wded. June 17, 1864. m. Margaret Francis. Moved to Texas after the war and became a judge.

BUCHANAN, FELIX GRUNDY. b. Lincoln Co., Mar. 23, 1838. att. Emory and Henry. Lt., Co. G, 1st Tennessee, Apr. 29, 1861. Captain - Apr. 27, 1862. Major - June 27, 1862. Wded. at Gaines' Mill, Fredericksburg, Gettysburg, Wilderness, and Weldon R.R. Appx. m. Kate McClellan, 1874. d. Lincoln County, Mar. 16, 1907.

BUCHANAN, JOHN H. b. York District, South Carolina, Aug. 4, 1819. Mexican War veteran. Capt., Co. B, 2nd Mississippi, May 1, 1861, aged 41. Major on July 13, 1864, to rank from July 3, 1863. Wded. and POW at Gettysburg, paroled Mar. 3, 1864. Wded. in hand, Aug. 18, 1864. Resigned Jan. 16, 1865, having been elected sheriff of Tippah Co. d. May 5, 1886. bur. Blue Mountain Cemetery, Tippah Co., Mississippi.

BUCKNER, THOMAS ROY. b. Caroline Co., 1836. Entered U. Virginia in 1855 from Fredericksburg. One of 18 children in his family. Living in Buckingham Co. in 1860. Capt., Co. C, 44th Virginia, June 6, 1861. Lt. Col. - June 16, 1863. Wded. at Port Republic. KIA at Spotsylvania, May 8, 1864.

Irwin Rider

THOMAS M. BURKE
55th Virginia

BULGER, MICHAEL JEFFERSON. b. Richland Dist., South Carolina, Feb. 13, 1806. Moved to Montgomery, Alabama, in 1823. In Alabama legisl. before and after the war. Brigadier General of militia. Capt., Co. A, 47th Alabama, Mar. 20, 1862. Major - Aug. 23, 1862. Lt. Col. - Sept. 13, 1862. Colonel - July 10, 1863. Wded. twice at Cedar Mountain. Wded. and POW at Gettysburg, exchanged Mar. 10, 1864. One of his captors called Bulger a "small bald headed man . . . pleasant and courteous." Retired to Invalid Corps, Feb. 14, 1865. d. Tallapoosa Co., Sept. 11, 1900.

BULL, GUSTAVUS ADOLPHEUS. b. Mar. 18, 1835. Of Troup Co. gr. U. of Georgia as valedictorian. Lt., Co. B, 4th Georgia, Apr. 26, 1861. Res. Oct. 17, 1861. Lt. Col., 35th Georgia, Oct. 17, 1861. MWIA at Seven Pines. May 31, 1862. d. June 1. Bull has a memorial shaft in Hillview Cemetery, LaGrange, Georgia, which says he's buried in an unknown grave.

BURGWYN, HENRY KING, JR. (pronounced Bur-GWINN') b. Oct. 3, 1841. gr. VMI, 1861. att. UNC. Lt. Col., 26th North Carolina, Aug. 27, 1861. Colonel - Aug. 19, 1862. KIA at Gettysburg. Buried on the battlefield in a gun case, and reburied in Raleigh in 1867 in Oakwood Cemetery.

BURKE, ROSS E. b. New York. Bookkeeper. Resident of Natchitoches. Lt., Co. A, 2nd Louisiana, May 11, 1861, age 30. Captain - Aug. 7, 1861. Major - June 26, 1862. Wded. and POW at Gettysburg, exchanged May 3, 1864. Promoted Colonel by death of Col. Williams, but never again served with the regiment.

BURKE, THOMAS MUNDIE. b. Essex Co., Apr. 20, 1829. Farmer. att. VMI. Capt., Co. F, 55th Virginia, May 21, 1861 (he had raised the company in 1859). Major - June 24, 1862. Wded. in left arm at Mechanicsville. KIA at Frayser's Farm.

BURKS, JESSE SPINNER. b. Bedford Co., Mar. 20, 1823. att. Washington College. gr. VMI, 1844. Farmer. In Virginia legisl. 1853-1854 and 1874-1877. Colonel, 42nd Virginia, July 1861. Disabled by Kernstown wound. Res. July 21, 1862. d. Bedford Co., June 15, 1885.

BURKS, RICHARD HORSELEY. b. Botetourt Co., Nov. 1826. att. VMI. Farmer. Lt. Col., Virginia Militia, pre-war. Served in the Mexican War. Adjutant, 2nd Virginia Cavalry, and aide to McCausland. Lt. Col., 12th Virginia Cav., June 20, 1862. Resigned Mar. 2, 1863. Also was Colonel, Botetourt Regiment Virginia Home Guards. d. Washington, D.C., Nov. 24, 1899.

BURROUGHS, EDGAR. Methodist Minister in Princess Anne Co. in 1860, age 37, worth $19,150. Capt., Co. I, 5th Virginia Cav., June 20, 1861. Major, 14th Virginia Cav. Bn., May 2, 1862. Major, 15th Virginia Cav., Sept. 11, 1862, but resigned Oct. 18, 1862.

BURT, ERASMUS R. His granddaughter said that Burt's middle name was "Arthmala," but he always signed as "E. R. Burt." It is possible that he used the "R." as a phonetic initial for the peculiar middle name. b. in South Carolina. State auditor of Mississippi. Owned 54 acres and one slave near Jackson. "Father of the Deaf and Dumb Institute of Mississippi." In Mississippi legisl. Capt., Co. K, 18th Mississippi, Apr. 22, 1861. Colonel - June 7, 1861. MWIA in abdomen at Leesburg, Oct. 21, 1861, d. Oct. 26. It was claimed that he personally killed Edward D. Baker at Ball's Bluff with his pistol. bur. Greenwood Cemetery, Jackson.

BURT, WILLIAM GIROUD. The 1860 Richland District census shows a William Burt (no middle name), born in Ireland, age 32, stone cutter. Sgt., Co. A, 22nd South Carolina, Dec. 1861. Lt. - Mar. 12, 1863. Lt. Col. - Aug. 18, 1864. Colonel - July 30, 1864 (the confusing dates being the result of appointments "to rank from . . ."). Appx. m. Mary F. Belcher. Living in Bossier Parish, Louisiana, in 1872.

BURTON, AUGUSTUS WALLER. Cleveland Co. lawyer, age 34 in 1860 census. Capt., Co. E, 12th North Carolina, Apr. 23, 1861, aged 32. Major - May 14, 1861. Defeated at May 1862 re-org.

BUSSEY, HEZEKIAH. b. Talbotton, Georgia, Apr. 18, 1840. gr. U. Georgia, 1861. Lt., Co. K, 27th Georgia, Sept. 10, 1861. Captain - Sept. 11, 1861. Major - Apr. 1, 1864. Lt. Col. - June 24, 1864. POW Sept. 13, 1862, exchanged Nov. 10, 1862. Paroled at

Greensboro. Lawyer and Primitive Baptist minister in Columbus. d. Nov. 5, 1917. bur. Linwood Cemetery, Columbus.

BUTLER, ANDREW PICKENS. b. Pebble Hill, South Carolina, Dec. 15, 1826. Hamburg planter. Capt., Co. G, 1st South Carolina (Gregg's), Aug. 16, 1861. Major - May 12, 1864. Lt. Col. - June 19, 1864. In South Carolina legisl., 1876-1879. d. Aiken Co., May 4, 1902. bur. Clearwater Church.

BUTLER, SAMUEL F. Butler is in the 1860 Lowndes Co. census as a 24-year-old planter worth $50,000. (The 1850 census had listed his age as 16.) Major, 11th Mississippi, May 5, 1861. Lt. Col. - Apr. 21, 1862. MWIA in abdomen at Sharpsburg, d. Oct. 3 at Frederick. bur. Friendship Cemetery, Columbus.

BUTT, EDGAR M. b. Georgia. 25-year-old lawyer in Buena Vista in the 1860 census. Major, 2nd Georgia, June 1, 1861. Colonel - Apr. 28, 1862. Wded. and disabled at Malvern Hill. m. Mary Rutherford. In Georgia legisl. post-war. d. June 26, 1893. bur. Buena Vista Cemetery.

BYNUM, WILLIAM PRESTON. b. Stokes Co., June 16, 1820. gr. Davidson, 1842. Rutherfordton lawyer. Lt. Col., 2nd North Carolina, May 8, 1861. Colonel - Sept. 17, 1862. Resigned Mar. 21, 1863, to become Solicitor of Lincolnton, North Carolina, Circuit. In state legisl., and North Carolina Supreme Court justice. d. Charlotte, Dec. 30, 1909.

BYRD, STEPHEN DECATUR MILLER. b. Cartersville, South Carolina, Nov. 18, 1832. gr. Wake Forest and Oglethorpe Medical College. C.S. surgeon in 1861. Capt., Co. I, 26th South Carolina, Jan. 13, 1862. Major - Sept. 9, 1862. Resigned Apr. 23, 1863, due to "difficulty with the Lt. Col.," apparently Hudson. In South Carolina legisl., 1860-1864 and 1879-1880. d. Scranton, Jan. 21, 1901.

CABELL, GEORGE CRAIGHEAD. b. Danville, Jan. 25, 1836. att. U. Virginia. Lawyer and newspaper editor. Brother of Genl. William L. Cabell. Major, 18th Virginia, May 25, 1861. Lt. Col. - July 21, 1864. Wded. at Drewry's Bluff, May 16, 1864. In U.S. Congress post-war. d. Baltimore, Maryland, June 23, 1906. bur. Greenhill Cemetery, Danville.

CABELL, HENRY COALTER. b. Feb. 14, 1820. gr. U. Virginia, 1842. Lawyer in Richmond. Capt., Richmond Fayette Artillery, Apr. 25, 1861. Lt. Col. - Sept. 12, 1861. Colonel - July 4, 1862. Chief of Artillery, McLaws' Division for most of the war. Took the oath at Richmond, July 26, 1865. d. Richmond, Jan. 31, 1889. bur. Hollywood. E. P. Alexander said of Cabell: ". . . the old man was not only a superb soldier, but a delightful gentleman also."

CABELL, JOHN GRATTAN. b. June 17, 1817. att. Washington College and U. Virginia. gr. U. Maryland as M.D. in 1841. Physician in Nelson Co. and Richmond. Capt., Co. I, 4th Virginia Cav., 1861 (had been commanding the company since 1860). Major, 6th Virginia Cav., Sept. 11, 1861. Lt. Col. - Apr. 15, 1862. Superintendent of Richmond's Jackson Hospital, 1862-1865. d. Richmond, Mar. 26, 1896.

CABELL, JOSEPH ROBERT. b. May 28, 1840. Brother of Genl. William L. Cabell. m. Mary Elizabeth Irby, 1863. Capt., Co. E, 38th Virginia, May 28, 1861. Major - May 12, 1862. Lt. Col. - July 3, 1863. Colonel - Nov. 15, 1863. KIA at Drewry's Bluff, May 10, 1864. bur. Old Grove Street Cemetery, Danville.

CAIN, JAMES GRANBERRY. b. Jefferson Co., Jan. 20, 1835. gr. Mercer College, 1856. Capt., Co. I, 28th Georgia, Sept. 10, 1861. Major - Nov. 13, 1861. Lt. Col. - May 3, 1862. Wded. leg at Malvern Hill. Res., disability, Jan. 28, 1863. In state legisl. post-war. Lawyer in Louisville, Georgia. d. there, Jan. 12, 1910. bur. Louisville Cemetery.

CALAHAN, WILLIAM G. The 1860 census for Jackson Co. carries Calahan as a 20-year-old wagon maker. Lt., Co. C, 18th Georgia, Apr. 30, 1861. WIA at Sharpsburg. Captain - Mar. 27, 1863. Major - Feb. 19, 1864, for "Valor and Skill." KIA at Sayler's Creek.

CALDWELL, JOHN HENRY. b. Huntsville, Apr. 4, 1826. m. Mary Greer, 1846. In Alabama legisl. pre-war. Capt., Co. A, 10th Alabama, June 4, 1861. Major - Mar. 14, 1862. Lt. Col. - June 27, 1862. Wded. in head at Frayser's Farm. Resigned June

10, 1863, to become State's Attorney for the 10th Judicial Circuit of Alabama. In U.S. Congress, 1873-1877. Lawyer in Jacksonville, Alabama. d. there Sept. 4, 1902. Caldwell's war letters are in the hands of a descendant in Florida.

CALHOUN, PATRICK LUDLOW. b. Abbeville Dist., 1813. Laurens planter. In South Carolina legisl., 1844-1854. Lt. Col., 13th South Carolina, Sept. 4, 1861. Resigned due to "pleurisy" on June 19, 1862. Enlisted as a private in the 5th South Carolina Reserves, Nov. 10, 1862. d. June 8, 1863. bur. at Huntsville Church near Clinton.

CALL, GEORGE WILLIAM. b. Kentucky. In Florida legisl. Railroad man and lawyer at Fernandia, Florida. m. Sarah Stark Mays. Capt., Co. K, 2nd Florida, July 8, 1861, age 36. Major - May 11, 1862. KIA at Seven Pines. bur. Hollywood, reburied in Old City Cemetery, Jacksonville.

CALLCOTE, ALEXANDER DANIEL. b. Isle of Wight Co., June 1830. gr. VMI, 1851. Teacher and farmer. m. Mrs. Harriet Hancock Land. Capt., Co. K, 3rd Virginia, June 23, 1861. Major - Apr. 27, 1862. Lt. Col. by Mar. 1863. KIA at Gettysburg.

CALLOWAY, ABNER SYDENHAM. b. Wilkes Co., North Carolina, Sept. 6, 1838. gr. UNC, 1859. Capt., Co. B, 55th North Carolina, and was elected Lt. Col. at May 1862 org. of the regiment. Resigned within a few months. In North Carolina legisl. in 1864. d. 1873.

CALMES, FIELDING HELMS. b. Clarke Co., June 17, 1832. Farmer. 5′6″. m. (1) - Margaret Moore. m. (2) - Mildred Meetze. Cpl., Co. D, 1st Virginia Cav., Apr. 18, 1861. Unit became Co. D, 6th Virginia Cav., and Calmes was made Sgt. in 1862. Capt., Co. D, 23rd Virginia Cav., Sept. 7, 1863. Major - Apr. 28, 1864. Wded. at Charlestown, Nov. 1863. POW at Strasburg, May 3, 1864. d. at "Helmsley," Clarke Co., Dec. 12, 1901. bur. there.

CAMAK, THOMAS. b. Sept. 13, 1829. gr. U. Ga., 1848. m. Laura Raglan. Cotton factor. Capt., Co. D, Inf. Bn. of Cobb's Georgia Legion, Sept. 5, 1861. Major - Sept. 15, 1862. Wded. and POW at Crampton's Gap, Sept. 14, 1862; paroled Oct. 12. KIA at Gettysburg. The hypercritical T. R. R. Cobb said of Camak: "a poor officer . . . drinks excessively."

CAMDEN, GIDEON DRAPER, JR. b. Harrison Co., Virginia, Jan. 1838. Son of a prominent jurist. Major, 9th Bn. Virginia Inf., at June 1861 org. Unit was merged into the 25th Virginia in May 1862, at which point Camden actively sought a clerkship in the C.S. Treasury Dept. d. Oct. 7, 1881. bur. I.O.O.F. Cemetery, Clarksburg, West Virginia.

CAMDEN, J. D. Assigned as Major, 23rd Virginia, by Special Order 297/11, dated Oct. 5, 1861. There is no further record of Camden's service.

CAMPBELL, JAMES CHARLES. gr. U. Mississippi, 1858. Secretary to the governor of Mississippi in 1860, at age of 22. Lt., Co. K, 18th Mississippi, May 24, 1861. Captain - Oct. 5, 1861. Major - Apr. 26, 1862. Wded. at Sharpsburg. MWIA and captured at Second Fredericksburg, May 3, 1863. Escaped, but "died in a few days."

CAMPBELL, JAMES CUMMINGS. b. Nov. 1830, in Washington Co. Farmer there. m. Ellen Kernan, 1853. Capt., Co. E, 48th Virginia, June 18, 1861. Major - Apr. 21, 1862. Res. Jan. 28, 1863, due to chest wound received at McDowell. Clerk of Courts in Washington Co. d. Apr. 1896. bur. in Washington Co.

CAMPBELL, JAMES McDONALD. b. McMinn Co., Tennessee, Oct. 8, 1830. Methodist preacher in Florida. Chaplain of 1st Georgia in 1861. Capt., Co. E, 47th Alabama, Apr. 30, 1862. Major - Aug. 23, 1862. KIA at Spotsylvania, May 12, 1864, when shot through head by sharpshooter. Campbell's letters and a superb photo of him in uniform have been published by his descendants in an obscure publication.

CAMPBELL, JOHN ARTHUR. b. Washington Co., Va., Oct. 3, 1823. att. Emory and Henry, VMI, and U. Va. Lawyer in Nashville and Abingdon. In Virginia Secession Convention. Colonel, 48th Virginia, Sept. 1861. Wded. at Winchester, May 1862. Resigned Oct. 16, 1862, due to dismay over appointment of a new

Brigadier General to the brigade he'd been commanding. d. June 17, 1886, in Abingdon.

CAMPBELL, REUBEN PHILANDER. b. Iredell Co., North Carolina, Apr. 16, 1818. gr. USMA, 1840. Lt. and Capt., U.S. Army, 1840-1861. Mexican War vet. Colonel, 7th North Carolina, May 16, 1861. KIA at Gaines' Mill.

CAMPBELL, ROBERT. b. Aug. 20, 1838. gr. SCMA, 1857. Lawyer in Charleston. Lt. Col., 11th South Carolina, Sept. 10, 1861. Dropped at May 1862 re-org. Private in 3rd South Carolina Cav. Became Lt., Co. I, 11th South Carolina, Jan. 1863. Retired to Invalid Corps, Dec. 15, 1864. d. Jan. 26, 1876. bur. Live Oak Cemetery, Walterboro.

CANTWELL, EDWARD PAYNE. b. Charleston, South Carolina, Dec. 22, 1825. Raleigh, North Carolina, lawyer. Lt. in Mexican War. Lt. Col., 12th North Carolina, May 14, 1861. Defeated in May 1862 re-org. Served briefly as a.d.c. to General Clingman in 1862. Lt. Col., 4th North Carolina Cav., Sept. 28, 1862. POW at Middleburg, June 19, 1863, exchanged Mar. 10, 1864. Colonel, to serve on Second Corps military court, Oct. 15, 1864. m. Ellen Denning. d. Apr. 11, 1891.

CANTWELL, JOHN LUCAS. b. Dec. 29, 1828, in Charleston, South Carolina. Cotton broker. Mexican War vet. Capt., Co. D, 13th North Carolina Infantry Bn., Dec. 1861. Colonel, 51st North Carolina, at Apr. 1862 org. Resigned during the fall of 1862. Capt., Co. F, 3rd North Carolina, Nov. 13, 1863. POW at Spotsylvania, May 12, 1864; released May 26, 1865. d. Dec. 21, 1909. bur. Oakdale Cemetery, Wilmington, North Carolina.

CAPERS, HENRY DICKSON. b. Columbia, South Carolina, June 2, 1835. att. SCMA. gr. Medical College of South Carolina, 1857. m. Mary Elizabeth Means. Lived in Oxford, Georgia. Resigned as Chief Clerk and Disbursing Officer, C.S. Treasury, Feb., 1862. On Magruder's staff, Mar. 1862. Major, 12th Georgia Artillery Bn., May 29, 1862 (the bn. was created from disbanding companies of the 1st Georgia Inf.). Lt. Col. - Nov. 6, 1862. Wded. at Cold Harbor. Retired Dec. 23, 1864, and served in Ordnance Bureau thereafter. Lawyer in Atlanta, Georgia, and West Union,

South Carolina, after the war. Author of Memminger biography. d. Apr. 18, 1912, in Atlanta.

CAPERS, JAMES HICKSON. b. South Carolina. Merchant in Berlin, Arkansas. Coroner of Union Co. Capt., Co. B, 3rd Arkansas, June 9, 1861, aged 46. Major - Mar. 11, 1862. Res. Apr. 23, 1862, to do staff duty (which is not traceable).

CARMICAL, GEORGE H. b. Coweta Co., Jan. 23, 1842. Lt., Co. A, 7th Georgia, May 31, 1861. Captain - Dec. 16, 1861. Major - July 1, 1862. Lt. Col. - Sept. 1, 1862. Colonel - Sept. 1, 1862. Wded. at 2nd Manassas, Knoxville (four times within one minute) and Fussell's Mill. Appx. m. Florence Robinson. Coweta Co. sheriff. d. Newnan, Oct. 31, 1929. bur. Oak Hill Cemetery.

CARMICHAEL, ABNER BYNUM. Of Wilkes Co. Capt., Co. C, 26th North Carolina, June 12, 1861. Major - Aug. 27, 1861. KIA at New Bern, Mar. 14, 1862. bur. Wilkesboro Presbyterian Churchyard.

CARPENTER, JOSEPH HANNAH. b. Alleghany Co., July 24, 1834. gr. VMI, 1856. Rarely used middle name or initial. Lt., Co. A, 27th Virginia, Apr. 22, 1861. Adj. of regt., June 2, 1861. Captain, Co. A, 27th Virginia, Aug. 26, 1861. Lt. Col. - May 28, 1862, but "Declined." MWIA at Cedar Mountain, d. Feb. 5, 1863.

CARR, GEORGE WATSON. b. Albemarle Co., June 1823. A "near relative" of Thomas Jefferson. att. U. Virginia. Lawyer in Kanawha Co. Lt., U.S. Army, 1847-1861. Said to have fought in the Crimean War. Capt., C.S. Infantry, Mar. 16, 1861. Lt. Col., 57th Virginia, Sept. 25, 1861. Colonel - Apr. 24, 1862. Dropped two weeks later at re-org. Capt. and a.a.i.g. in Army of Southwest Virginia, then under Bragg, then with Breckinridge to rank as Major from March 5, 1864. Described by one Lt. as a "red tape" officer. A. G. Jenkins said that Carr was "rather too fond of gun-powder." Farmer near Roanoke. d. Apr. 19, 1899. bur. on Watts Farm near Roanoke.

CARRINGTON, HENRY. b. Halifax Co., Feb. 7, 1836. att. Hampden-Sydney. Lt., Co. H, 3rd Virginia Cav., May 25, 1861. Captain - Apr. 25, 1862. Major - Nov. 14, 1862. POW at Aldie, June 17, 1863; returned May 3, 1864. Res. Feb. 4, 1865. Halifax Co. farmer. d. Hampden-Sydney, Feb. 11, 1893.

CARRINGTON, HENRY ALEXANDER. b. Charlotte Co., Sept. 13, 1832. gr. U. Virginia and VMI. m. Charlotte E. Cullen, 1856. Lt. Col., 18th Virginia, May 25, 1861. Colonel - July 2, 1864. Wded. at Seven Pines. Wded. and POW at Gettysburg, exchanged Mar. 3, 1864. Paroled at Burkeville, Apr. 27, 1865. d. Jan. 22, 1885. bur. Shockoe Hill Cemetery, Richmond.

CARRINGTON, ISAAC HOWELL. b. Richmond, Mar. 7, 1827. att. U. Virginia and UNC. Pittsylvania Co. lawyer. Major, 38th Virginia, June 1861. Dropped at spring 1862 re-org. Chief of Staff to Gen. Floyd, 1862-1863. Commissioner of Prisoners of War, in Richmond, appointed July 1863. Served in Provost Marshal's office in Richmond, Mar. 1864 until the end of the war. Appointed Superintendent for raising black troops late in the war. Participated in effiorts to spirit away the Confederate treasury. Post-war Yankee accusations of theft of money from prisoners were dismissed. d. Richmond, Jan. 30, 1887. bur. Hollywood. Carrington's war letters are in the Langhorne Scruggs Papers at Duke.

CARSON, JOHN THOMAS. b. Nov. 11, 1825. Farmer in Macon Co. Lt., Co. C, 12th Georgia, June 15, 1861. Captain - May 8, 1862. Major - June 9, 1863. POW in May 1864, exchanged in July. MWIA at Winchester, Sept. 19, 1864, d. Sept. 30. bur. Carson Family Cemetery, Reynolds, Georgia.

CARSON, ROBERT PRESTON. b. Washington Co., July 10, 1832. gr. VMI, 1854. School teacher in Lee Co. Capt., Co. F, 37th Virginia, Apr. 1861. Lt. Col. - later in 1861. Res. June 28, 1862. Abingdon Supt. of Schools post-war. d. Oct. 20, 1924.

CARSWELL, REUBEN W. b. Jefferson Co., Sept. 26, 1828. gr. Emory, 1850. Lawyer in Louisville, Georgia. Lt., Co. C, 20th Georgia, June 14, 1861. Capt., Co. E, 48th Georgia, Mar. 1862. Lt. Col. - Mar. 22, 1862. Res. Nov. 12, 1864. In Georgia legislature, 1863-1865. Became General of Georgia Militia. Judge in Jefferson Co. post-war. d. 1886.

CARTER, BENJAMIN F. b. Maury Co., Tennessee, ca. 1831. gr. Jackson College, Columbia, Texas. Mayor of Austin, and lawyer there. m. Louisa O. Rust. Capt., Co. B, 4th Texas, July 11, 1861. Major - June 27, 1862. Lt. Col. - July 10, 1862. MWIA at Gettysburg. d. July 21 at Chambersburg, Pa. An enlisted man said that no officer in the Texas Brigade "was more universally loved."

CARTER, DAVID MILLER. b. Hyde Co., Jan. 12, 1830. gr. UNC, 1851. Lived in Moore Co. Capt., Co. E, 4th North Carolina, May 16, 1861. Lt. Col. - June 19, 1862. Military Judge in Second and Third Corps. Resigned Dec. 23, 1862, citing a bad Seven Pines wound. In North Carolina legisl. during and after the war. d. Jan. 7, 1877.

CARTER, HILL. b. April 14, 1796. Planter at "Shirley." War of 1812 midshipman. Colonel, 52nd Virginia Militia, which served in conjunction with the Army of Northern Virginia around Williamsburg in the spring of 1862. Unit was disbanded about May 1862. d. May 20, 1875.

CARTER, JAMES W. Capt., Co. C, 13th Mississippi, Apr. 13, 1861, aged 30. Lt. Col. - Apr. 26, 1862. Colonel - Aug. 12, 1862. Wded. at Malvern Hill. KIA at Gettysburg.

CARTER, JAMES W. Capt., Co. C, 45th Georgia, Mar. 4, 1862. Major - May 2, 1863. Lt. Col. - Mar. 17, 1864. KIA on June 22, 1864, near Petersburg. A war letter by a lieutenant in the 45th described Carter: "Gentle & unassuming in his manner to everyone, he had endeared himself to all who knew him."

CARTER, RICHARD WELBY. b. Fauquier Co., Mar. 11, 1837. att. VMI, where he was steadily in trouble. Capt., Co. H, 1st Virginia Cavalry, Apr. 27, 1861 (had commanded the company since 1859). Major - July 24, 1862. Lt. Col. - 1862. Colonel - July 16, 1863. POW at Upperville, Dec. 17, 1863; exchanged Aug. 4, 1864. Cashiered for cowardice at Tom's Brook. POW at home, Feb. 21, 1865; released July 19, 1865. 6′1″. m. Sophia DeButts Carter, 1867. Loudoun Co. farmer. Carter was widely disliked by men and officers: "fat and looked greasy"; "a coward"; "white livered." d. Dec. 18, 1888.

CARTER, THOMAS HENRY. b. June 13, 1831. gr. VMI, 1849. gr. U. Virginia. m. Susan Roy. Capt., King William Artillery (Virginia), June 1, 1861. Major - Dec. 12, 1862, and Chief of Artillery, D. H. Hill's Division. Lt. Col. - Mar. 2, 1863, commanding an artillery bn. Colonel - Feb. 27, 1864. Chief of Artillery, Early's Valley Army. Appx. Farmer and physician. d. June 2, 1908.

CARTER, WILLIAM INGRAM. b. Jan. 21, 1823. Farmer in Darlington District. Capt., Co. A, 14th South Carolina, Aug. 19, 1861. Major - Apr. 11, 1862. WIA at Gaines' Mill. Resigned Feb. 20, 1863, due to chronic disease (to avoid being cashiered.) Served from Oct. 1863 as a private on QM duty. d. July 19, 1881. bur. Cartersville Cemetery.

CARTER, WILLIAM RICHARD. b. Nottoway Co., Apr. 22, 1833. gr. Hampden-Sydney, 1852, with 1st honors. Richmond lawyer. Pvt., Co. G, 3rd Virginia Cav., May 27, 1861. Lt., Co. E, 3rd Virginia Cav., Nov. 23, 1861. Captain - Apr. 25, 1862. Major - Oct. 21, 1862. Lt. Col. - Nov. 18, 1862. MWIA at Trevilian's, June 11, 1864, d. July 8 at a Gordonsville hospital.

CARY, GEORGE WALTON. b. LaGrange, Alabama, 1839. Sgt., 10th Alabama, 1861. Capt., Co. E, 44th Alabama, May 16, 1862. Major - June 18, 1863. Wded. Aug. 16, 1864. Appx. m. Virginia Paxton. Merchant in New York City and New Orleans. d. New York City, Mar. 16, 1909.

CARY, JOHN BAYTOP. b. Hampton, Oct. 18, 1819. gr. William and Mary, 1839. Principal of Hampton Military Academy. m. Columbia H. Hudgins, 1844. Lt. Col., 32nd Virginia, July 1, 1861. Acting Provost Marshal at Yorktown, early 1862. Dropped at May 1862 re-org. Inspector-general and a.a.g. to Magruder, 1862. When Magruder went west, Cary "was put on duty in the pay department in Richmond" until the end of the war. Insurance official in New York City and Richmond. Supt. of Richmond schools. d. Richmond, Jan. 13, 1898. bur. Hollywood.

CARY, NATHANIEL ROBERT. b. Elizabeth City Co., Virginia, June 3, 1822. att. William and Mary. Physician in Pontotoc, Miss. Capt. in 1st Mississippi Bn. during the Mexican War. Farmer and physician in Northampton, Virginia. Major, 39th

City of Austin

BENJAMIN F. CARTER
4th Texas Infantry

Virginia, 1861. 39th Virginia was disbanded Jan. 1862. Served as surgeon in Virginia field hospitals. Major, 19th Virginia Bn. Heavy Artillery, May 23, 1863. Present into 1865. d. in Pensacola, Florida, yellow fever epidemic, Sept. 6, 1874.

CARY, RICHARD MILTON. b. ca. 1824. gr. William and Mary. Lived at Hampton, Virginia. Richmond lawyer. m. (1) Anne Dunbar. m. (2) Lucy Willson. Captain of Richmond's famous "F" Company, and went into the 1st Virginia with it. Author of Confederate imprint drill manual. Colonel, 30th Virginia, June 13, 1861. Declined re-election in Apr. 1862, opposing the principle. He was elected nonetheless, but refused to accept, due to "unwillingness to hold position conferred by those subject to his control." Ordnance officer the rest of the war, commanding Bellona Arsenal, and at Macon and Salisbury. Ranks in that service were: Lt. of Artillery, June 4, 1862; Captain - Mar. 26, 1863; Major - Sept. 10, 1863. Cotton and tobacco merchant in England post-war. Died March 15, 1886, in Falmouth District, County of Cornwall, of Albuminuria and Morbus Cordis.

CASH, ELLERBE BOGGAN CRAWFORD. b. Anson Co., North Carolina, July 1, 1823. att. South Carolina College. In South Carolina legisl. Colonel, 8th South Carolina, Mar. 20, 1861. Dropped at May 1862 re-org. Colonel, 2nd South Carolina Reserves, 1862. Lawyer and planter in Chesterfield Co. Involved in noted South Carolina duels with DePass and Shannon in 1880. d. Mar. 10, 1888. bur. at Cash's Depot, South Carolina. "A tall, stalwart fellow . . . red headed, red faced. . . ."

CASKIE, ROBERT ALEXANDER. b. Richmond, July 12, 1830. att. U. Virginia. m. Amanda Wallace Gregory, 1859. Capt., Co. A, 10th Virginia Cav., May 15, 1861. Major - Aug. 8, 1863. Lt. Col. - Sept. 11, 1863. Colonel - late in the war, but apparently never confirmed. Appx. Tobacco merchant in Missouri postwar. d. Merion, Pa., Aug. 31, 1928.

CASKIE, WILLIAM HENDERSON. b. 1834. m. Mary Augusta Ambler, a great-niece of Thomas Jefferson. Richmond merchant. Lt., Hampden Artillery (Virginia), 1861. Captain - Apr. 21,

1862. Major - Apr. 9, 1864, assigned to Moseley's Bn. Took the oath at Richmond, May 15, 1865. Noted cartoonist on a Texas newspaper post-war. Also an actor and painter. d. 1900.

CECIL, WILLIAM PRESTON. b. Tazewell Co., Apr. 9, 1820. In Virginia Secession Convention. Capt., Co. D, 23rd Virginia Bn., Aug. 22, 1861 (this unit was originally in the 51st Virginia). Major - May 26, 1862. Res. due to health, Mar. 5, 1863. Giles Co. farmer after two years in California. In Virginia legisl. d. Tazewell Co., July 12, 1899.

CHAMBERS, PINCKNEY BROWN. b. Iredell Co., Jan. 28, 1821. Farmer. 5′8½″. Capt., Co. C, 49th North Carolina, Feb. 25, 1862. Major - Nov. 1, 1862. Resigned on Sept. 16, 1863, to go home, because he was the "owner of 115 Negroes," and there were 700 more Negroes in the neighborhood. d. Statesville, Feb. 18, 1905.

CHANDLER, JOSEPH NEWTON. b. Oconee Dist., South Carolina, 1824. Farmer in Banks Co., Georgia. Capt., Co. A, 24th Georgia, Aug. 24, 1861. Lt. Col. - Jan. 9, 1864. Res. Sept. 10, 1864. Moved to Texas post-war. d. 1909 in Granbury, Texas, where he was a preacher.

CHAPMAN, WILLIAM HENRY. b. Madison Co., Apr. 17, 1840. att. U. Virginia. Lived in Fauquier Co. Lt., Booton's Battery (Virginia), June 21, 1861. Captain - Dec. 8, 1861. Battery was disbanded in Oct. 1862. Conscript officer in Fauquier Co., 1862-1863. Capt., Co. C, 43rd Virginia Cav. Bn., Dec. 7, 1863. Lt. Col., Mosby's Cav. Regt., Dec. 7, 1864, at expansion of the bn. into a regt. Paroled at Winchester, Apr. 22, 1865. 5′11″. m. Josephine Macrae Jeffries, 1864. U.S. Revenue Service employee in St. Louis, Alexandria, Gordonsville and Richmond. d. Greensboro, North Carolina, Sept. 13, 1929.

CHARLTON, WILLIAM WYATT. b. 1827 in Washington Co. Merchant and law student in Clarksville. Lt., Co. A, 2nd Georgia, Apr. 20, 1861. Capt. - Apr. 20, 1862. Major - July 2, 1863. Res. Jan. 15, 1864. d. Oct. 1, 1897, in Habersham Co.

CHASTAIN, ELIJAH WEBB. b. Pickens, South Carolina, Sept. 25, 1813. Officer in Seminole War. In Georgia legisl., 1840-1850. In U.S. Congress, 1851-1855. In Georgia Secession Convention.

Lt. Col., 1st Georgia Regulars, Mar. 21, 1861. Res. June 18, 1861. Colonel, 8th Georgia State Troops, Dec. 14, 1861. d. Dalton, Apr. 9, 1874. bur. near Morganton, Georgia, in family cemetery. Chastain "truckled to no man and his regiment loved him," but he "lost his sword" for calling a staff officer "a d--- flop-eared Jew."

CHEEK, WILLIAM HAYES. b. Warren Co., Mar. 18, 1835. att. Wake Forest. gr. Randolph-Macon. Warren Co. lawyer. Capt., Co. E, 1st North Carolina Cav., May 16, 1861. Lt. Col. - Sept. 28, 1863. Colonel - Oct. 17, 1863. Wded. at Yellow Tavern, Virginia, May 11, 1864. POW at Burkesville, Apr. 5, 1865, released July 25. In North Carolina legisl. Lived in Henderson, North Carolina. d. there March 1901.

CHENOWETH, JOSEPH HART. b. Beverly, Apr. 8, 1837. gr. VMI, 1859. On faculty of VMI and Maryland Agricultural College. Pvt., Co. F, 31st Virginia, Feb. 1862. Major - May 1, 1862. KIA at Port Republic. His papers are at Virginia Historical Society.

CHERRY, GWEN REYNALDS. b. Pontotoc Co., Mississippi, May 21, 1836. Said to have been the first white child born in the county. Saltillo lawyer. Lt., Co. C, 17th Mississippi, June 1, 1861. Captain - Apr. 26, 1862. Major - Jan. 26, 1864. Lt. Col. - Feb. 26, 1864. Wded. at Savage Station, Sharpsburg, Gettysburg and Knoxville. Appx. d. Jan. 23, 1898. bur. Saltillo.

CHEW, ROBERT STANARD. b. Oct. 3, 1828. Clerk of Court in Fredericksburg. Physician. Capt., Co. B, 30th Virginia, Apr. 22, 1861. Lt. Col. - Apr. 19, 1862. Colonel - Nov. 5, 1864. Commanded Corse's Brigade for a time in 1864. WIA at Sharpsburg. d. Aug. 17, 1886. bur. Fredericksburg Confederate Cemetery.

CHEW, ROGER PRESTON. b. Loudoun Co., Apr. 9, 1843. att. VMI. Captain, Chew's Battery (Virginia), Sept. 1861. Major - Feb. 27, 1864. Lt. Col. - Feb. 18, 1865. Chief of Horse Artillery, A.N.Va. m. Louise Fontaine Washington, 1871. In Virginia legisl., 1884-1890, from the lower Valley. d. Charlestown, West Virginia, Mar. 16, 1921. bur. Zion Episcopal Church.

CHRISTIAN, BARTHOLOMEW DANDRIDGE. b. New Kent

Co., Apr. 1, 1828. Clerk at New Kent C.H. Major, 52nd Virginia Militia, 1861 (cf. Hill Carter, q.v.). d. Jan. 24, 1873. bur. St. Peter's Churchyard, New Kent Co.

CHRISTIAN, CHARLES BURKS. b. Amherst Co., Feb. 15, 1834. gr. Washington College. Amherst Co. lawyer. Capt., Co. B, 49th Virginia, Apr. 23, 1861. Major, in a contested election, Jan. 31, 1863. Lt. Col. - Jan. 31, 1863 (actually done on Oct. 27, 1863, with rank from Jan.). Wded. in both shoulders and POW at Cold Harbor, May 30, 1864, released July 15, 1865. 5'8". Among the "Immortal 600." d. Walker Ford, Virginia, Jan. 2, 1916. bur. Christian family cemetery, Amherst Co.

CHRISTIAN, EDMUND J. b. Montgomery Co., North Carolina, 1834. Farmer. Lt., Co. C, 23rd North Carolina, May 27, 1861. Major - Apr. 16, 1862. MWIA at Seven Pines, d. June 3.

CHRISTIAN, WILLIAM STEPTOE. b. Middlesex Co., Dec. 26, 1830. gr. Columbian College, 1848. gr. Jefferson Medical College, 1851. Capt., Co. C, 55th Virginia, June 2, 1861. Major - May 1, 1862. Lt. Col. - June 23, 1862. "Severe wounds" during the Seven Days. Colonel - May 2, 1863. POW at Falling Waters, July 14, 1863, exchanged Mar. 1864. Retired Mar. 14, 1865, to seek a medical post. Middlesex Co. physician and druggist and Supt. of Schools. President of Medical Society of Virginia. d. Urbanna, Dec. 10, 1910. bur. Hewic Cemetery, Urbanna. An important letter by Christian on Gettysburg is at U. Virginia.

CHRISTIE, DANIEL HARVEY. b. Frederick Co., Virginia, Mar. 28, 1833. Established Henderson Military Institute in North Carolina. Major, 23rd North Carolina, July 12, 1861. Colonel - Apr. 16, 1862. Wded. at Seven Pines and Gaines' Mill. MWIA at Gettysburg, d. July 17 in Winchester and bur. there.

CHRISTY, GEORGE WILLIAM. b. New Orleans, Nov. 22, 1818. gr. Harvard, 1839. Lawyer and notary public in New Orleans. Lt., Co. G, 6th Louisiana, May 9, 1861. Major - Nov. 22, 1861. Did not stand for re-election in spring 1862 re-org. Became a major of artillery and ordnance officer. POW at Sayler's Creek, released June 25. d. New Orleans, Feb. 7, 1891.

CLAIBORNE, JAMES ROBERT. b. Franklin Co., Virginia, Aug.

5, 1839. Farmer there. Pvt., Co. D, 2nd Virginia Cav., 1861. Capt., Co. A, 37th Virginia Cav. Bn., Aug. 1, 1862. Major - Feb. 13, 1863. Paroled at Franklin C.H., June 6, 1865. Prosecuting attorney and judge in St. Louis post-war. In Missouri legisl. d. St. Louis, Apr. 22, 1911. bur. Bellefontaine Cemetery.

CLARK, GEORGE McINTOSH. b. Montgomery Co., 1838. att. UNC. 6'0". Lt., Co. K, 34th North Carolina, Sept. 9, 1861. Captain - July 1, 1862. Major - May 6, 1863. KIA at Gettysburg.

CLARK, MERIWETHER LEWIS. 1809-1881. See page 412.

CLARKE, CHARLES HAMMETT. b. 1827 in Henrico Co. Pvt., Co. G, 15th Virginia, Apr. 22, 1861. Lt. - Sept. 18, 1861. Capt. - Apr. 25, 1862. Major - Jan. 24, 1863. Wded. at Drewry's Bluff, May 16, 1864. Appx. Lived in North Carolina, 1865-1897. Alive in 1900, as a member of Richmond's R. E. Lee Camp, No. 1, U.C.V. Pension application in June 1902 showed him as a farmer, age 75.

CLARKE, JAMES O. b. Augusta. Mexican War veteran. Master mason. Capt., Co. D, 1st Georgia, Mar. 18, 1861. Lt. Col. - Apr. 3, 1861. Colonel - Dec. 11, 1861. After disbandment of the regt., Clarke was a Lt. and drillmaster in Georgia. d. Dec. 6, 1889, in Augusta, age 64. bur. Magnolia Cemetery.

CLARKE, JOHN LYLE. b. Richmond, Virginia, Dec. 16, 1833. Lived in Gloucester Co., Virginia, as a youth. Baltimore businessman. Capt., Co. B, 21st Virginia, May 1861. Company was disbanded in May 1862. On Loring's staff, 1862. Lt. Co., 30th Bn. Virginia S.S., Oct. 5, 1862. A bad injury from a falling tree limb, near Staunton in late 1864, sent Clarke home for the duration, though he remained on the rolls. d. Jan. 5, 1898. bur. Loudon Park. Clarke's papers are at Maryland Historical Society.

CLARKE, ROBERT. Of Adams Co. Capt., Co. I, 16th Mississippi, May 25, 1861 (had commanded the company since 1838!). Lt. Col. - June 8, 1861. Dropped at May 1862 re-org., missing re-election "by a few votes."

CLARKE, THOMAS ERSKINE. b. Alabama. Town marshal of Marianna, Florida, in 1860, age 28. Enlisted in 1st Florida, Mar. 1861. Capt., Co. E, 8th Florida, May 6, 1862. Major - Oct. 2,

1862. Wded. in head at Fredericksburg, Dec. 11, 1862. Appx. m. Sara Bell Von Tillingham.

CLARKE, WILLIAM JOHN. b. North Carolina, 1821. gr. UNC, 1841. Capt. and Major, Mexican War. 5′7″. m. Mary Bayard Devereux. North Carolina State Comptroller, 1851-1855. Colonel, 24th North Carolina, July 18, 1861. Wded. at Petersburg, May 15, 1864. POW at Dinwiddie C.H., Feb. 5, 1865, released July 24. New Bern and Raleigh businessman in lumber, iron and railroads. Judge and state legisl. d. New Bern, 1886. bur. Cedar Grove Cemetery.

CLAYBROOK, RICHARD ANDERSON. b. Middlesex Co., June 23, 1817. att. U. Virginia and Columbia College. In Virginia House of Delegates, 1856-1858; lost Senate bid in 1860. Lt. Col., 40th Virginia, about July 1861. Resigned "the following winter," but still reported himself in the position when taken prisoner in Apr. 1863. He was practicing law in Northumberland Co. until Northern soldiers burned down his property in Dec. 1864. d. Nov. 11, 1873 at The Hague.

CLEMENT, ADAM. b. Campbell Co., Jan. 1826. Capt., Co. C, 11th Virginia, May 16, 1861. Wded. at Seven Pines and Boonsboro. Major - May 23, 1862; commission was accepted Aug. 2, 1862, but was never confirmed due to a seniority squabble. Clement resigned Oct. 12, 1864, to become Campbell Co. sheriff. In state legisl. d. July 8, 1915. One of his men called him "a true man, among the bravest of the brave."

CLEMENT, WILLIAM BAILEY. b. Franklin Co., Virginia. Lived in North Carolina. 5′11″. Capt., Co. H, 10th Virginia Cavalry (a North Carolina company), Oct. 29, 1861, aged 36. Major - Sept. 25, 1863. Lt. Col. commission was "suspended."

CLEVELAND, WILDE CLAYTON. b. Crawford Co., Apr. 9, 1836. att. U. Georgia. Lawyer in Knoxville, Georgia. Capt., Co. E, 6th Georgia, May 27, 1861. Wded. at Sharpsburg. Major - 1862. Lt. Col. - Mar. 26, 1863. Resigned due to disability, June 16, 1863. Lawyer and Baptist preacher in Culloden. d. Oct. 31, 1904. bur. Culloden Cemetery.

CLOPTON, ALBERT GALLATIN. b. 1828 near Eatonton, Georgia. Lived in Alabama as a youth. Served in the Mexican War. Capt., Co. D, 1st Texas, June 6, 1861. Major - Jan. 2, 1862. Lt. Col. - May 7, 1862. Physician in Jefferson, Texas. d. 1916.

CLOUD, ABEL S. Of Burke Co. Sgt., Co. E, 16th North Carolina, May 10, 1861, aged 20. Student. Lt. - Apr. 26, 1862. Captain - May 31, 1862. Lt. Col. - Jan. 27, 1864. POW at Gettysburg, exchanged Mar. 1864. Appx. A little man, noted for his fancy clothes. Cloud's father was a full-blooded Cherokee.

CLYBURN, BENJAMIN R. b. 1840. Of Butler, South Carolina. att. SCMA. Lt., Co. H, 2nd South Carolina, Apr. 28, 1861. Captain - May 13, 1862. Major - May 6, 1864. Wded. in leg and face, June 2, 1863. Wded. at Gettysburg. Wded. (leg amputated) and POW at Cedar Creek. m. Clara Mittag. d. sometime before 1896. bur. Lancaster Presbyterian Churchyard.

CLYBURN, THOMAS FRANKLIN. b. Lancaster Dist., May 12, 1843. Lt., Co. E, 12th South Carolina, Aug. 26, 1861. Captain - Nov. 20, 1861. Major - Nov. 17, 1863. Lt. Col. - May 6, 1864. Severely wounded, May 23, 1864. Lancaster Co. planter and county auditor. In South Carolina legisl., 1868-1870 and 1882-1886. d. Douglas, South Carolina, Oct. 21, 1896. bur. Presbyterian Churchyard there.

COBB, JOHN PROBERT. b. Wayne Co., Nov. 23, 1834. gr. UNC, 1854. Lt., Co. H, 2nd North Carolina, May 16, 1861. Captain - May 10, 1862. Colonel - Aug. 30, 1864. Wded. at Malvern Hill, Chancellorsville and Cold Harbor. Wded. (leg amputated) and POW at Winchester, Sept. 19, 1864, exchanged Mar. 1865. Moved to Florida in 1883, became a county court clerk. d. Tallahassee, Mar. 13, 1923.

COBB, NORVELL. b. Buckingham Co. Farmville militia officer pre-war. Hotel Keeper in Farmville in 1860, age 36. Capt., Co. G, 44th Virginia, June 1, 1861. Major - May 1, 1862. Colonel - June 16, 1863. Wded. at Chancellorsville and Gettysburg. POW at Spotsylvania, May 10, 1864, exchanged Aug. 3. Paroled at Burkeville, Apr. 15, 1865. Banker and insurance man in Prince Edward Co. and Richmond post-war. Cobb's papers are at UNC.

COCHRAN, JAMES. b. 1828 in Augusta Co. att. U. Virginia, from Staunton. Farmer at Loch Willow. Lt., Co. I, 14th Virginia Cavalry, May 13, 1861. Captain - May 15, 1862. Colonel - Feb. 12, 1863. Applied for retirement, Oct. 1864. Lawyer and postmaster and newspaper editor in Culpeper C.H. post-war. d. Aug. 17, 1883, in Culpeper. bur. Masonic Cemetery, Rte. 229.

COFFEE, JOHN A. b. Telfair Co., April 26, 1838. Farmer in Telfair Co. in 1860, living with his parents. Lt., Co. H, 20th Georgia, June 6, 1861. Captain - Oct. 3, 1861. WIA at Chickamauga in knee. Major - May 6, 1864, but the promotion was later said to have been made "erroneously," and Coffee was retired to the Invalid Corps as a Captain on Oct. 14, 1864. Brother of Joshua Coffee of Co. H, 20th Georgia. d. March 11, 1901, in Hawkinsville. bur. Orange Hill Cemetery.

COFFMAN, ISAAC GORE. b. Jan. 1827. Lt., Co. B, 10th Virginia, Apr. 18, 1861. Captain - Apr. 23, 1862. Major - May 3, 1863. m. Magdalene McDowel Smith. POW at 2nd Fredericksburg, May 3, 1863, paroled 15 days later. MWIA at Wilderness, d. May 10 at Orange C.H.

COIT, JAMES CAMPBELL. b. Marlboro Dist., South Carolina, Oct. 4, 1832. gr. Princeton, 1854. Capt., Chesterfield Artillery (South Carolina), 1861, served in the Blackwater region. Major - Sept. 12, 1863, assigned to Branch's Bn. Present into 1865. In South Carolina legisl. (the "Wallace House") in 1878, and a judge. d. Washington, D.C., Apr. 11, 1908.

COKER, JAMES LIDE. b. Darlington Dist., Jan. 3, 1837. att. Harvard and SCMA. m. Susan Armstrong Stout. Capt., Co. G, 9th South Carolina, 1861. Capt., Co. E, 6th South Carolina, 1862-1864. Badly wounded at Wauhatchie. Made Major while off in prison, 1864. In South Carolina legisl. in 1864 and post-war. Darlington banker and merchant. d. June 25, 1918. bur. Hartsville Baptist Church.

COLE, CHRISTOPHER COLUMBUS. b. Stokes Co., Feb. 12, 1834. gr. Trinity College, 1854. Editor, Greensboro *Times.* Capt., Co. E, 22nd North Carolina, May 23, 1861. Major - June

13, 1862. Lt. Col. - Mar. 16, 1863. KIA at Chancellorsville. bur. Green Hill Cemetery, Greensboro.

COLEMAN, CLAYTON GLANVILLE, JR. b. Roxbury, New Kent Co., Virginia, 1840. att. VMI. Capt., Co. G, 23rd Virginia, Apr. 24, 1861. Major - Dec. 16, 1861. Lt. Col. - Apr. 15, 1862, then dropped a week later at re-org. Appointed asst. surgeon to rank from Sept. 30, 1862. Served at Winchester, Goldsboro, Howard's Grove, and with the 24th Virginia. In Virginia legisl., 1865 and 1867, from Louisa Co. Became civil engineer and U.S. Civil Service employee. d. Little Rock, Arkansas, Oct. 7, 1908.

COLEMAN, HENRY EATON. b. Halifax Co., Virginia, Jan. 5, 1837. att. William & Mary and VMI. Granville Co., North Carolina, farmer. Capt., Co. B, 12th North Carolina, Apr. 26, 1861. Defeated at May 1862 re-org. V.a.d.c. to Iverson, 1863. Appointed Colonel, 12th North Carolina, Aug. 11, 1863, to rank from May 4, 1863. Wded. at Spotsylvania in the head. Played a gallant role at Staunton River Bridge while wded. d. June 25, 1890.

COLEMAN, LEWIS MINOR. b. Hanover Co., Virginia, Feb. 3, 1827. gr. U. Virginia, and on the faculty there. m. Mary Ambler Marshall. Principal of Hanover Academy. Capt., Morris Artillery (Virginia), Aug. 1861. Major - May 12, 1862. Lt. Col. - June 2, 1862. MWIA at Fredericksburg, d. Mar. 21, 1863.

COLEMAN, THOMAS K. b. Sept. 1836. att. Georgia Military Institute. Of Perry Co. Lt., Co. D, 4th Alabama, Apr. 25, 1861. Captain - Apr. 21, 1862. Major - Oct. 3, 1862. MWIA at Chickamauga, d. Oct. 3 in Marietta. bur. Rosemont Cemetery, Uniontown, Alabama.

COLLINS, CHARLES READ. b. Pennsylvania, Dec. 7, 1836. gr. USMA, 1859 (having entered from Pa.). Lt. of engineers, U.S. Army, 1859-1861. m. Augusta Mason. Lt. of artillery, PACS, July 23, 1861. Capt. of engineers, PACS, Oct. 7, 1861. Aide to Field and Whiting, 1862. Engineer officer to McLaws, Mar. 1863. Major, 15th Virginia Cavalry, Apr. 29, 1863. Colonel - Feb. 28, 1864. KIA at Todd's Tavern, May 7, 1864. bur. St. John's Episcopal Churchyard, King George C.H., Virginia. E. P. Alexander said of Collins: "He was superb and admirable, both in person and character, and universally popular."

COLSTON, RALEIGH THOMAS. b. Richmond, Feb. 18, 1834. Farmer in Hedgesville. att. VMI. Capt., Co. E, 2nd Virginia, Apr. 19, 1861 (had commanded this company since Oct. 1859). Lt. Col. - Sept. 16, 1862. Wded. at Seven Pines and Winchester (May 1862). MWIA at Mine Run (lost leg), Nov. 27, 1863, d. Dec. 23 at Charlottesville. bur. at U. Virginia Chapel on Christmas.

CONN, CHARLES AUGUSTUS. b. 1836 in Milledgeville. Merchant. Capt., Co. G, 45th Georgia, Mar. 4, 1862. Major - June 22, 1864. Lt. Col. - Dec. 2, 1864. m. Lucia Griswold, 1864. Wded. at Wilderness. KIA at Petersburg, Mar. 25, 1865. A contemporary obituary described Conn as "a self-made man who rose to his rank . . . without the assistance of fortune or friends." Conn's war letters were published in 1962 in the *Georgia Historical Quarterly.*

CONNALLY, JOHN KERR. b. Jackson, Tennessee, Sept. 3, 1839. Lived in Yadkin Co., North Carolina. att. U.S. Naval Academy. Capt., Co. B, 21st North Carolina, May 12, 1861. Colonel, 55th North Carolina, May 19, 1862. Wded. at Gettysburg and Cold Harbor and in Sept. 1864. POW at Gettysburg, exchanged Mar. 1864. Res. Mar. 7, 1865. Paroled at Richmond, Apr. 26, 1865. Texas lawyer and Virginia legisl. post-war. m. Alice Thomas. d. Asheville, North Carolina, Jan. 31, 1904. bur. there in Riverside Cemetery. Dorsey Pender called him "a most conceited fellow."

CONNER, WILLIAM GUSTINE. b. Adams Co., Mississippi, Apr. 5, 1826. gr. Yale, 1845. m. Eliza Wood, 1846. Lt., Co. A, Jeff Davis Legion Cavalry, May 18, 1861. Captain - Oct. 28, 1861. Major - Dec. 2, 1862. POW at Williamsburg, May 4, 1862, returned to duty Aug. 9. KIA at Gettysburg, July 3.

CONNER, ZEPHANIER TURNER. b. Jan. 30, 1807, in Virginia. Land agent in Macon, Georgia. m. Louisa Godwin. Pvt., Co. A, 1st Georgia, Mar. 15, 1861. Left the regt., May 19, 1861. Lt. Col., 12th Georgia, July 2, 1861. Colonel - Dec. 3, 1861. Cashiered in 1862, as a result of Jackson's displeasure with Conner's comportment in the lower Valley during Jackson's famous campaign there. d. Macon, April 30, 1866. bur. Rose Hill Cemetery. A lieutenant in the 12th called Conner an "arrogant fop." The unusual spelling of Zephanier comes from the tombstones of both the colonel and his son.

CONYERS, WILLIAM DENISON, JR. b. 1838. gr. Georgia Military Institute. Lawyer in Covington. m. Virginia Bates, 1861. Lt., Co. A, Infantry Battalion of Cobb's Georgia Legion, Aug. 1, 1861. Captain - Dec. 14, 1861. Major - July 3, 1863. Wded. and POW at Crampton's Gap, exchanged Oct. 12, 1862. KIA at Spotsylvania, May 12, 1864. bur. family cemetery between Oxford and Covington.

COOK, ALPHONSO F. b. Buchanan, Apr. 10, 1830. Trader in New Mexico before the war. Sgt., U.S. Army, 1856-1861. Lt., Co. A, 8th Virginia Cavalry, May 27, 1861. Lt. Col. - May 15, 1862. Wded. and POW at Buchanan, Virginia, Aug. 30, 1862. Wded. and POW at Beverly Ford, left leg amputated, Jan. 11, 1865. 5'11". Smyth Co. farmer. d. Abingdon, Feb. 11, 1900. bur. Sinking Spring Cemetery.

COOK, EDWARD B. b. Maryland. Auctioneer and merchant in Richmond in 1860, age 42. Capt., Co. D, 2nd Battalion Virginia Reserves, May 16, 1864. Major - July 6, 1864.

COOK, HATCH. b. Sept. 23, 1827. Of Columbus, Georgia. Farmer. m. Fredonia Elizabeth Brown. Major, Hilliard's Alabama Legion, June 25, 1862. Major, 60th Alabama, Nov. 25, 1863. KIA at White Oak Road, Virginia, Mar. 31, 1865.

COOK, ROBERT THOMAS. Capt., Co. B, Infantry Battalion of Phillips' Georgia Legion, June 11, 1861. Major - July 1, 1862. Lt. Col. - July 6, 1862. KIA at Fredericksburg, "before the engagement was fairly commenced." bur. Presbyterian Cemetery, Dalton.

COOKE, OLIVER HUGH. b. 1831. m. Rebecca Antoinette Wilcox. Capt., Co. F, 49th Georgia, Mar. 4, 1862. Lt. Col. - July 29, 1863. Resigned Feb. 23, 1864, to enter Georgia legisl. d. Thomasville, 1887.

COOPER, JAMES FAIRLIE. b. New York, Sept. 1814. gr. USMA

1834. Lt., U.S. Army, 1834-1837. Lt. Col., 7th Georgia, May 31, 1861. Res. Dec. 6, 1861. d. Atlanta, Georgia, Oct. 14, 1869.

COOPER, JOHN FREDERIC. b. July 27, 1834. gr. U. Georgia, 1854. Lawyer. m. Harriet Cornelia Smith. Capt., Co. H, 8th Georgia, May 13, 1861. Major - July 21, 1861. MWIA (knee) at 1st Manassas, d. Sept. 6. bur. Rome, Georgia. Cooper's wartime photo and papers are at Georgia Archives. Brother of Colonel Thomas L.

COOPER, THOMAS LACKINGTON. b. Oct. 8, 1831. gr. U. Georgia, 1850, as valedictorian. m. Mary Pope. Atlanta lawyer. Capt., Co. F, 8th Georgia, May 22, 1861. Major - June 1, 1861. Lt. Col. - July 21, 1861. Killed in a fall from his horse, Centerville, Virginia, Dec. 23, 1861. Brother of Major John F.

COOPER, WILLIAM POPE. b. Virginia, July 26, 1825. 5′11″. Lt., Co. C, 31st Virginia, July 1, 1861. Captain - May 1, 1862. Major - Aug. 1, 1863. WIA on May 12, 1864, and at Cedar Creek. Appx. Editor of Fairmont, West Virginia, *Index*. d. Sept. 17, 1880. bur. Woodlawn Cemetery in Fairmont.

COPPENS, GEORGES AUGUSTE GASTON. Came to the U.S. from Martinique in 1853. m. Miss Bellocq. Lt. Col., 1st Louisiana Zouave Battalion, Mar. 27, 1861, having raised the bn. under authorization from Jefferson Davis. KIA at Sharpsburg, where he'd been given temporary command of the 8th Florida.

COPPENS, MARIE ALFRED. Brother of Lt. Col. Georges Coppens. b. France, came to U.S. with his brother. m. Miss Pizzini of Richmond, Virginia. Capt., Co. F, 1st Louisiana Zouave Battalion, May 9, 1861. Lt. Col. - Sept. 18, 1862. Retired due to wounds, Nov. 17, 1864. Fought with France against Prussia, according to one source. Drowned in Galveston Bay, Texas, in 1868, according to another.

CORLEY, JAMES LAWRENCE. b. South Carolina, Oct. 5, 1829. gr. USMA, 1850. Lt., QM and Adj., U.S. Army, 1850-1861. Capt. and QM on R. S. Garnett's staff, July 1861. Lt. Col., 60th Virginia, Oct. 13, 1861. Res. Mar. 10, 1862. Assigned to Adj. Genl. Dept. as Judge Advocate in Dept. of South Carolina, Georgia and Florida. QM on staff of R. E. Lee from 1862 through most of the war. Insurance agent in Norfolk post-war. d. there Mar. 28, 1883. bur. Elmwood Cemetery.

CORMIER, CHARLES EMILE. b. Louisiana. New Orleans clerk. m. Fannie J. Meeks, 1857. 5'11". Capt., Co. I, 1st Louisiana, May 4, 1861. Major - July 3, 1863. Wded. at Seven Days. POW at 2nd Fredericksburg, May 3, 1863. POW at Fisher's Hill, Sept. 20, 1864, released July 24, 1865. d. Feb. 22, 1873 in New Orleans, age 40 years, 2 months. bur. St. Louis Cemetery. Cormier's war letters are at Tulane.

CORNS, JAMES M. Architect. 5'11". 35 years old in March 1865. Married twice. Capt., Co. E, 8th Virginia Cavalry, May 28, 1861. Colonel - May 15, 1862. Surrendered at Charleston, West Virginia, Mar. 1865, having resigned the previous month. Alive in 1880 in Kilgore, Texas.

CORPREW, THOMAS JEFFERSON. b. Norfolk, July 4, 1830. Captain of Norfolk Light Artillery Blues pre-war. Lt. Col., 6th Virginia, May 1, 1861. Colonel - Dec. 14, 1861. Dropped at May 1862 re-org. Norfolk businessman and railroad executive. d. Norfolk, May 24, 1873.

COTTON, RICHARD CARNEY. Farmer in Chatham Co., North Carolina. In North Carolina legisl. for 20 years between 1816 and 1858. Capt., Co. E, 44th North Carolina, Mar. 17, 1862. Lt. Col. - Mar. 28, 1862. Resigned May 30, 1862. Cotton's records state his age at enlistment to be 76 years, and repeat that fantastic figure three times elsewhere!

COUNCELL, EDWARD C. Lt., Co. D, 16th Mississippi, June 1, 1861, aged 28. Captain - Apr. 26, 1862. Major - Dec. 20, 1862. Colonel - May 12, 1864. MWIA and POW at Weldon R.R., Aug. 21, 1864. d. in enemy hands at Alexandria, Sept. 10.

COUNCILL, JAMES CALVIN. b. Southampton Co., Virginia, Dec. 10, 1825. gr. VMI, 1848. Resided in King & Queen Co. Taught at VMI. Founded Aberdeen Academy before the war, and ran it for four decades. 5'5". m. Mary Ellen Smith, 1853. Capt., Co. I, 26th Virginia, June 23, 1861. Lt. Col. - May 13,

Georgia State Archives

JOHN F. COOPER
8th Georgia

1862. POW at Jordan's Farm, Virginia, June 15, 1864, released July 21, 1865. Among the "Immortal 600." d. King & Queen Co., Jan. 22, 1904. bur. St. Stephen's Church.

COURTNEY, ALFRED RANSON. b. King & Queen Co., Va., Nov. 17, 1833. Capt., Henrico Artillery (Virginia), July 8, 1861. Major - July 14, 1862. Chief of Artillery of Ewell's Division. Relieved of A.N.Va. duty, at his own request, and assigned to A.I.G.O., Apr. 20, 1863. He had been court-martialed for dereliction of duty at Sharpsburg, having failed to go into battle with the batteries, and found guilty on most counts. In July 1863, Courtney was ordered west to report to Gen. Buckner. Served in Virginia legisl. post-war, and was Grand Master of Virginia Masons. d. Richmond, Nov. 4, 1914.

COWAN, ROBERT HARPER. b. Wilmington, North Carolina, Aug. 3, 1824. gr. UNC, 1844. Lt. Col., 3rd North Carolina, May 16, 1861. Colonel, 18th North Carolina, Apr. 26, 1862. Res., illness, Nov. 11, 1862. Railroad president and North Carolina legisl. post-war. d. Nov. 11, 1872. bur. Oakdale Cemetery, Wilmington.

COWAN, ROBERT V. b. May 26, 1840. Lived in Iredell Co., North Carolina. att. USMA; resigned Apr. 21, 1861. Capt., Co. A, 33rd North Carolina, May 1861. Major - Apr. 25, 1862. Lt. Col. - Aug. 5, 1862. Colonel - June 18, 1864. POW at Fredericksburg. Appx. d. Mar. 5, 1877, at Statesville.

COWAND, DAVID G. Of Tyrrell Co., North Carolina. Sgt., Co. A, 32nd North Carolina, May 16, 1861. Sgt.-Major of regt., Oct. 1861. Major - July 23, 1862. Lt. Col. - June 18, 1863. Colonel - May 10, 1864. Wded. at Spotsylvania. A weak administrator. Commanded his brigade from Dec. 1864 to Mar. 1865. Appx. Aged 29 in 1861.

COWARD, ASBURY. b. Berkeley Dist., South Carolina, Sept. 19, 1835. gr. SCMA. m. Eliza Larimore Blum, 1856. Established King's Mountain Military Academy, with Micah Jenkins, and ran it for many years. Captain and Major, a.d.c. to D. R. Jones, 1861-1862. Colonel, 5th South Carolina, Aug. 12, 1862. Wded. at Wilderness. Appx. Supt. of the Citadel post-war. d. Rock Hill, South Carolina, Apr. 28, 1925. An enlisted man described Coward as "very unpopular with his reg't and I think he should be so."

COWLES, WILLIAM HENRY HARRISON. b. Hamptonville, North Carolina, Apr. 22, 1840. Lt., Co. A, 1st North Carolina Cavalry, May 16, 1861. Captain - Mar. 1, 1862. Major - Oct. 17, 1863. Lt. Col. - June 1, 1864. Wded. in abdomen at Mine Run, and in head at Petersburg (Mar. 31, 1865). Paroled at Point of Rocks, Virginia, Apr. 23, 1865. In U.S. Congress, 1885-1893. d. Wilkesboro, North Carolina, Dec. 30, 1901. bur. Presbyterian Cemetery, Wilkesboro.

COX, DANIEL LIVINGSTON. Shown as 39-year-old married farmer, worth $10,000, in 1860 Anderson County census. Capt., Co. D, 2nd South Carolina Rifles, Nov. 27, 1861, aged 41. Major - Sept. 3, 1862. Res., "physical disability," Jan. 22, 1864.

COX, FLEET WILLIAM. b. Westmoreland Co., Virginia, Oct. 15, 1824. gr. VMI, 1849. Teacher at Hague, lawyer at Northumberland C.H. att. U. Virginia. Capt., Co. A, 40th Virginia, May 25, 1861. Major - Apr. 23, 1862. Lt. Col. - Aug. 26, 1862 (actually done 6 months later, to rank from Aug.). Retired to Invalid Corps, Feb. 2, 1865. Had been in Virginia legisl. for some time. Lost an eye at Chancellorsville. Made prisoner in Westmoreland Co., May 12, 1865, released June 28. Farmer, teacher, lawyer, politician in Westmoreland. d. Kinsale, Mar. 17, 1888. bur. Yeocomico Church, Westmoreland Co. Cox's war letters are at U. Virginia.

CRAIG, WILLIAM. b. Ireland. Merchant in Augusta, age 33, in 1860. Lt., Co. K, 20th Georgia, Aug. 8, 1861. Captain - Jan. 10, 1862. Major - May 8, 1864. Paroled in Augusta, Georgia, May 20, 1865.

CRAIGE, JAMES ALEXANDER. b. Jan. 1842. Lived in Rowan Co., North Carolina. att. Charlotte Military Inst., Davidson, and USMA. Capt., Co. G, 6th North Carolina, May 16, 1861. Major, 57th North Carolina, July 17, 1862. Wded. knee, Aug. 1864. Paroled at Salisbury, May 3, 1865. Planter, living in Maury Co., Tennessee, 1900.

CRANE, JAMES PARRAN. b. 1838. att. U. Virginia. Lived in St. Mary's Co., Maryland. Capt., Co. B, 2nd Maryland Battalion, Aug. 27, 1862. Major, 2nd Maryland Battalion, June 3, 1864.

Wded. Aug. 18, 1864, resulting in "partial paralysis . . . from injury to spine caused by blow from a musket." Lawyer in Leonardstown, Maryland, d. 1916. An unpublished memoir by a Maryland soldier is harshly critical of Crane for cowardice at Cold Harbor.

CRATON, MARSHALL DAVID. b. June 1829. Of Wayne Co., North Carolina. att. USMA. Lt. Col., 35th North Carolina, Nov. 8, 1861. Colonel, 50th North Carolina, Apr. 15, 1862. Resigned Dec. 1, 1862, due to diarrhea and dysentery. Businessman in Goldsboro. d. May 27, 1866. bur. Rutherfordton City Cemetery.

CRAWFORD, GIBSON M. Schoolteacher in Coffee Co., Tennessee in 1860, age 24. Capt., Co. C, 44th Tennessee, Dec. 1861. Major - May 1, 1863. MWIA at Petersburg, June 16, 1864, d. June 23.

CRAWFORD, JOHN P. b. 1831. Capt., Co. G, 51st Georgia, Mar. 4, 1862. Major - Jan. 14, 1864. Lt. Col. - Nov. 12, 1864. POW at Sayler's Creek.

CRAWFORD, ROBERT ASHTON. Lt., Co. A, 1st Georgia Regulars, Feb. 1, 1861. Res. Nov. 23, 1861. Elected Lt. Col., 2nd Georgia Battalion, 1862.

CRAWFORD, WILLIAM PETER. att. U. Georgia. m. Nelie Richmond. Lived in Belair, Georgia. Capt., Co. C, 28th Georgia, Sept. 10, 1861. Lt. Col - Jan. 20, 1864. Severely wded. in leg at Ocean Pond, Feb. 20, 1864. d. 1889.

CRAWLEY, WILLIAM JAMES. b. 1833. gr. SCMA, 1855. Farmer in Barnwell District in 1860. Capt., Co. D, Holcombe Legion (South Carolina), Dec. 8, 1861, aged 28. Lt. Col. - Dec. 5, 1862. Colonel - Sept. 28, 1864. Wded. June 29, 1864. Retired to Invalid Corps, Mar. 8, 1865. Teacher and farmer in McDuffie Co., Georgia. d. 1902.

CRENSHAW, JAMES H. Lt. Col., 23rd Virginia Infantry. This man has no Compiled Service Record at all, but he was present at this rank in the summer of 1861. He remains a sizable enigma.

CRENSHAW, JAMES RICHARD. b. Richmond, Apr. 15, 1830. Richmond lawyer. In Co. "F" pre-war. Acting Commissary General of Virginia Forces, Apr. 26, 1861. Lt. Col., 15th Virginia, July 1, 1861. Dropped at Apr. 1862 re-org. Became a C.S. commissary agent, sent to Nassau. Served briefly as Lt. Col., 20th Virginia, during the summer of 1861, for some unknown reason. Ran post-war cotton business in Brazil, New York City, and Richmond. d. Richmond, in his home at 104 N. 7th St., July 25, 1891. bur. Hollywood.

CRITCHER, JOHN. b. Westmoreland Co., Virginia, Mar. 11, 1820. gr. U. Virginia. Studied in France. Lawyer and Virginia legisl. pre-war. Lt. Col., 15th Virginia Cavalry Battalion, spring 1862. Lt. Col., 15th Virginia Cavalry Regiment, Sept. 11, 1862 (when the bn. was expanded to regimental strength). POW in Westmoreland Co., May 23, 1863. Resigned June 21, 1864, because of promotion to others over him. A Yankee cavalry guidon captured by Critcher personally is on display at Chancellorsville Museum. In U.S. Congress post-war. d. Alexandria, Sept. 27, 1901. bur. Ivy Hill Cemetery.

CRITTENDEN, CHARLES THOMAS. b. Feb. 17, 1836. His home was a landmark on Cedar Mountain battlefield. Lt., Co. B, 13th Virginia, Apr. 17, 1861. Captain - May 31, 1861. Major - May 15, 1863. Wded. at Gaines' Mill and "through the breast" at Cold Harbor. d. in Richmond Soldiers' Home, Jan. 20, 1907. bur. at All Saints' Church, at the foot of Cedar Mountain.

CROFT, EDWARD. b. Greenville, South Carolina, Jan. 4, 1835. gr. SCMA, 1856. Capt., Co. H, 14th South Carolina, Aug. 16, 1861. Major - Feb. 24, 1863. Lt. Col. - Sept. 10, 1863. Wded. at Seven Days and Gettysburg. Appx. Greenville lawyer and planter. d. May 9, 1892. bur. Christ Church Cemetery, Greenville.

CROMWELL, ELISHA. b. Oct. 9, 1821. Of Edgecombe Co. Capt., Co. B, 44th North Carolina, Jan. 14, 1862. Major - Mar. 28, 1862. Lt. Col. - May 3, 1862. Res. due to kidney disease, July 24, 1862. d. May 15, 1884. bur. Edgecombe Co.

CROW, JAMES McCULLOUGH. b. Florence, Alabama, Mar. 16, 1836. Lived in Lauderdale Co. Lt., Co. D, 9th Alabama, May 27, 1861. Captain - 1862. Major - Sept. 11, 1863. Wded. at

Gaines' Mill. Ran a steamboat line at Saltillo, Tennessee, postwar. U.S. Marshal at Birmingham, Ala., in 1880's. d. Madisonville, Kentucky, Oct. 1922. Crow is mentioned frequently in the published memoirs of E. D. Patterson.

CROWDER, JOHN TERRELL. b. Jan. 8, 1820, in Monroe Co. The 1860 census for Monroe Co. shows Crowder living alone, a farmer, worth $30,000. Capt., Co. D, 31st Georgia, Oct. 14, 1861. Lt. Col. - May 13, 1862. Wded. at Sharpsburg. Res. Aug. 19, 1863. In Georgia legisl. postwar. Grew cotton on more than 1,000 acres. d. Dec. 22, 1895. bur. Crowder family cemetery near Boxankle.

CRUDUP, ARCHIBALD D. b. Franklin Co., North Carolina, ca. 1816. Granville Co. farmer. 5'8". Capt., Co. B, 47th North Carolina, Feb. 22, 1862. Major - Apr. 5, 1863. Lt. Col. - Mar. 3, 1864. Wded. in arm and hip, and POW, at Gettysburg, exchanged Mar. 10, 1864. Res. due to health, Aug. 30, 1864. d. Kittrell, North Carolina, June 7, 1896, in his 84th year. Unmarried. bur. family cemetery.

CRUMP, CHARLES ALFRED. b. Powhatan Co., Virginia, Aug. 16, 1822. att. VMI. Colonel in Nottoway Co. Militia pre-war. In Virginia legisl. from Amelia and Nottoway. Principal of male school in Burkeville. Lt. Col., 16th Virginia, May 1861. Colonel, 26th Virginia, July 1861. Dropped at spring 1862 re-org. Rejoined 16th Virginia as its Colonel near Salem, Virginia, Aug. 28, 1862, and was killed two days later at 2nd Manassas. bur. Haymarket.

CRUMP, SAMUEL HOWARD. b. Augusta, Aug. 22, 1823. Mexican War veteran. Capt., Co. I, 1st Georgia, Mar. 18, 1861. Capt., Co. B, 12th Georgia Artillery Battalion, May 1, 1862. Major - Jan. 27, 1863. Transferred to the staff of W. H. T. Walker, May 3, 1863. Apptd. Capt. and AIG, Sept. 20, 1863. Returned to the 12th Georgia Artillery Battalion late in the war, with the rank of Captain, and surrendered at Appx. Deputy sheriff, clerk of court in Richmond Co. d. Sept. 19, 1883. bur. Magnolia Cemetery, Augusta.

CRUMPLER, LEWIS HENRY. b. Coosa Co., Alabama, Dec. 27, 1843. Pvt., Co. F, 8th Alabama, 1861. Capt., Co. C, 59th Alabama, Mar. 26, 1862. Major - May 16, 1864. Wded. Dec. 14,

1863. Appx. m. Nettie Oden, 1865. Farmer at Sylacauga. d. there Feb. 14, 1910. bur. Marble City Cemetery.

CRUMPLER, THOMAS NEWTON. Ashe Co. lawyer and state legisl. att. UNC. Capt., Co. A, 1st North Carolina Cavalry, May 16, 1861, aged 26. Major - Mar. 1, 1862. MWIA during Seven Days, d. July 11.

CRUTCHFIELD, STAPLETON. b. Spotsylvania Co., Virginia, June 21, 1835. gr. VMI, 1855, with first honors. Major, 9th Virginia, at Craney Island, July 1861. Major, 58th Virginia, Oct. 1861. Promoted to Lt. Col., 58th Virginia, but dropped at May 1862 re-org. Elected Colonel, 16th Virginia, but declined. Colonel of Artillery, May 5, 1862. Chief of Artillery, Jackson's Valley District and later of Jackson's Corps. Lost a leg at Chancellorsville. Assigned to duty with the AIGO, inspecting seacoast batteries, Mar. 16, 1864. Ordered back to A.N.Va., Jan. 18, 1865. KIA at Sayler's Creek.

CULP, JOHN RIPLEY. b. Chester Dist., South Carolina, Oct. 19, 1829. Militia colonel pre-war. Capt., Co. A, 17th South Carolina, Mar. 26, 1861. Major - Sept. 1, 1862. Lt. Col. - Aug. 29, 1864. Wded. at 2nd Manassas and Five Forks. POW on Apr. 1, 1865, released July 25. Rossville postmaster and county supervisor. d. Chester Co., June 3, 1907.

CULPEPPER, JAMES MONROE. b. Aug. 28, 1838, in Monroe Co. Sgt., Co. C, 6th Georgia, May 27, 1861. Lt. - June 1861. Captain - Sept. 17, 1862. Major - Jan. 1865. Surrendered at Greensboro. Councilman and state senator postwar. m. (1) Martha Kemp. m. (2) Nancy Kemp. d. June 29, 1901, at Fort Valley, Georgia. bur. Oakland Cemetery.

CULVER, ISAAC FRANKLIN. b. Hancock Co., Georgia, Oct. 20, 1830. Farmer in Henry Co., Alabama, in 1860, worth $44,000. Pvt., Co. B, 6th Alabama, May 18, 1861. Sgt. - Aug. 26, 1861. Capt., Co. K, 6th Alabama, May 1862. Major - May 7, 1863. Wded. at Malvern Hill, South Mountain and Gettysburg. Appx. In Alabama legisl., 1878-1882. Bullock Co., Alabama, Supt. of Education. d. after 1900.

CUMMING, JOHN B. Mexican War veteran. City Marshal of Macon in 1860, age 37. Capt., Co. A, 20th Georgia, May 17, 1861. Lt. Col. - Sept. 5, 1861. Colonel - Mar. 7, 1862. Res. May 29, 1863. Colonel, 5th Georgia Reserves, 1864. Paroled at Macon, Apr. 1865. Doorkeeper of the Georgia Senate, 1873-1877. Died before 1890. A Confederate officer wrote of him: "an easy going, reckless fellow, sociable with privates as with his equals in rank, often entertaining us with his cock fighting reminiscences." Cumming's war papers are at UNC.

CUMMINGS, ARTHUR CAMPBELL. b. Washington Co., Virginia, Oct. 1, 1822. gr. VMI, 1844. m. Elizabeth Preston, 1854. Capt. and Brevet Major, Mexican War. Colonel, 33rd Virginia, July 1, 1861. Dropped at 1862 re-org. In Virginia legisl. during the war. Lawyer and farmer in Abingdon. d. Mar. 19, 1905.

CUNNINGHAM, ARTHUR SINCLAIR. b. Norfolk, Virginia, Apr. 1835. gr. USMA, 1857. Lt., U.S. Infantry, 1857-1861. Capt., a.a.g. to G. B. Crittenden, Sept. 1861. Major, same duty, Nov. 16, 1861. Assigned to temporary command of 10th Alabama during Seven Days, with rank as Lt. Col., and was wounded. Then became an ordnance officer at Richmond. In 1864, Cunningham commanded the 40th Virginia for a time, then reported again to the A.I.G.O. Wded. at Pegram's Farm, Sept. 30, 1864. Employed by Wells Fargo post-war. d. Eureka, Calif., July 26, 1885.

CUNNINGHAM, GEORGE ALFRED. b. Georgia, July 1834. gr. USMA, 1857 (entering from Alabama). Lt., U.S. Cav., 1857-1861. Major and Lt. Col., 51st Virginia, 1861. The absence of a Compiled Service Record makes his service obscure. During the last three years of the war, he reported mostly to Hoke or Whiting in North Carolina, generally in artillery posts. d. May 13, 1904.

CUNNINGHAM, JOHN WILSON. b. Person Co., North Carolina, Feb. 6, 1820. att. UNC. Major, 2nd North Carolina, May 16, 1861. Declined appointment, never served. Democratic Party leader in Person Co., served in North Carolina legisl. d. July 15, 1887.

CUNNINGHAM, RICHARD HOOPE, JR. b. Goochland Co.,

Virginia, 1834. Richmond merchant. In Co. "F" pre-war. Lt., Co. F, 21st Virginia, Apr. 21, 1861. Captain - May 1861. Lt. Col. - Apr. 21, 1862. KIA at Cedar Mountain.

CURLIN, MARTIN W. b. 1828. Entered CSN construction work at Gosport Navy Yard, Apr. 1861. Moved to Naval Ordnance Works in Richmond. Capt., Co. A, 4th Virginia Bn. LDT ("Naval Bn."), June 20, 1863. Major - Feb. 13, 1864. Present into 1865. d. Jan. 19, 1890. bur. Oak Grove Cemetery, Portsmouth.

CURRY, DUNCAN. b. Mar. 6, 1818, in Telfair Co. Farmer. m. Mary J. Love. Capt., Co. F, 50th Georgia, Mar. 4, 1862. Major - Oct. 8, 1862. Res. Feb. 24, 1863. d. Apr. 26, 1886.

CURTIS, GEORGE WASHINGTON. Of Bethany, Virginia. Mexican War vet. Brother of Union Genl. William B. Curtis. Lt. Col., 23rd Virginia, Apr. 21, 1862. KIA at Cedar Mountain, two days after leaving a Charlottesville hospital. Family papers are at West Virginia University. Age at death - 35.

CUTSHAW, WILFRED EMORY. b. Harpers Ferry, Virginia, Jan. 25, 1828. gr. VMI. Lt., C.S. Inf., Oct. 31, 1861. Captain of artillery, Mar. 1862, commanding Jackson Artillery (Virginia). Major - Feb. 27, 1864. Wded. and POW in May 1862 in the Valley, released Apr. 1863. On VMI staff in 1863, then AIG of Second Corps artillery in Sept. 1863. Commanded artillery bn. after promotion to majority. Wded. at Spotsylvania. Lost leg at Sayler's Creek. Richmond City Engineer. d. Richmond, Dec. 19, 1907. bur. Hollywood.

CUTTS, ALLEN SHERROD. b. Pulaski Co., Ga., Dec. 4, 1827. Artillery pvt. in Mexican War. Americus planter. Capt., Sumter Flying Artillery (Georgia), July 6, 1861. Major - May 22, 1862. Lt. Col. - May 26, 1862. m. Fannie O. Brown. Mayor, sheriff and Georgia legisl. in Americus. d. Nov. 1896. bur. Oak Grove Cemetery, Americus.

DALE, MATT. b. Nashville, Tennessee. Moved to Palestine, Texas, 1852. In Texas legisl., 1859. Lt., Co. G, 1st Texas, June 23, 1861. Major - May 19, 1862. KIA at Sharpsburg. ca. 30 years old at his death.

DALTON, JAMES SAMUEL. b. Rockingham Co., North Carolina, Aug. 1, 1835. Farmer. 5′8½″. m. Maggie Reid. Lt., Co. D, 45th North Carolina, Mar. 11, 1862. Captain - Aug. 21, 1862. Lt. Col. - May 19, 1864, while a POW, which occurred May 10, 1864, at Spotsylvania; he was released June 14, 1865. d. Reidsville, North Carolina, ca. 1907.

DANCE, WILLIS JEFFERSON. b. Powhatan Co., Virginia, June 20, 1821. Lawyer there. att. U. Virginia and Hampden-Sydney. Capt., Powhatan Artillery (Virginia), July 16, 1861. Major - Feb. 18, 1865. Wded. at Fort Harrison. Paroled at Farmville, Apr. 1865. In Virginia legisl. Powhatan Commonwealth's Attorney for 30 years. d. Powhatan Co., Feb. 13, 1887, of apoplexy.

DANIEL, JOHN WILHITE LEWIS. b. LaGrange, Georgia, Aug. 1, 1831. Lawyer in Midway, Alabama. In Alabama Secession Convention. Capt., Co. B, 15th Alabama, but elected Major at org., July 27, 1861. Res., ill health, Jan. 25, 1862. Later served in 1st Alabama Cav., and in post command at Greenville, Tennessee. d. Midway, Aug. 31, 1876.

DANTZLER, OLIN MILLER. b. St. Matthews, South Carolina, Jan. 14, 1825. gr. Randolph-Macon, 1846. m. Caroline Ann Glover, 1852. In South Carolina legisl., 1852-1862. Orangeburg planter. Lt., Co. F, 25th South Carolina, 1861. Lt., Co. D, 1st South Carolina, July 20, 1861. Lt. Col., 20th South Carolina, Jan. 11, 1862. Colonel, 22nd South Carolina, Apr. 29, 1864. KIA at Bermuda Hundred, June 2, 1864. bur. Tabernacle Methodist Churchyard, St. Matthews.

DARGAN, ALONZO TIMOTHY. b. Darlington, South Carolina, 1839. att. Wake Forest. Darlington lawyer. Lt., Co. B, 21st South Carolina, Dec. 23, 1861. Lt. Col. - Jan. 25, 1862. KIA at Port Walthall Junction, May 7, 1864. bur. Darlington Baptist Cemetery.

DAVANT, PHILLIP EDWIN. b. Mar. 22, 1839, in Crawfordsville. Lawyer in Hart Co. att. Mercer U. Capt., Co. B, 24th Georgia, June 9, 1861. Maj., 3rd Bn. Georgia S.S., June 8, 1863. Lt. Col., 38th Georgia, Sept. 18, 1863. POW at Spotsylvania, exchanged June 1864. Appx. m. Hortense Moore. d. Oct. 9, 1906, in Butler, Georgia. bur. Butler.

DAVIDSON, WILLIAM LEE. b. Mecklenburg Co., North Carolina, Feb. 10, 1825. Charlotte merchant. Capt., Co. D, 7th North Carolina, May 16, 1861. Major - Feb. 24, 1863. Lt. Col. - May 3, 1863. Colonel - Nov. 28, 1864. Wded. at Chancellorsville and Wilderness. POW at Wilderness, exchanged Aug. 3, 1864. Paroled at Charlotte, May 15, 1865. d. Aug. 13, 1899.

DAVIES, JOHN NESBITT. b. Augusta, Georgia, Dec. 7, 1838. att. U. Virginia. Capt., Co. C, 7th Georgia Cav., Jan. 12, 1863. Major sometime in 1864. Res. Mar. 14, 1865. POW after resignation, released July 25, 1865. 5′11″. d. Dec. 27, 1887. bur. Summerville Cemetery, Richmond Co.

DAVIS, ALEXANDER MATHEWS. b. Wythe Co., Virginia, Jan. 17, 1833. gr. Emory and Henry. 5′10″. Lawyer in Wytheville and Independence. Capt., Co. C, 45th Virginia, May 29, 1861. Major - May 14, 1862. Lt. Col. - May 1864. Genl. Wise disliked Davis, and ordered him out of the army, but the War Dept. rescinded Wise's order. POW at Piedmont, released July 25, 1865. In U.S. Congress for a year until unseated in a credentials contest. d. Independence, Sept. 25, 1889. bur. in family cemetery there.

DAVIS, BENJAMIN F. The 1860 census for Marion Co. (p. 261) has a 30-year-old overseer of this name. Lt., Co. E, 5th Florida, Feb. 26, 1862. Major - Feb. 6, 1862 (a backdating for ranking purposes). Wded. at Chancellorsville. "Cashiered" - Apr. 11, 1864.

DAVIS, CHAMPION THOMAS NEAL. b. Virginia. Lawyer in Rutherford Co., North Carolina. m. Eliza C. Nixon. Served in state legislature. Capt., Co. G, 16th North Carolina, May 9, 1861, aged 34. Colonel - Apr. 26, 1862. KIA at Seven Pines. bur. Oakdale Cemetery, Wilmington, North Carolina.

DAVIS, DAVID SYLVESTER. b. Lenoir Co., North Carolina, Feb. 7, 1840. att. Wake Forest. Sgt., Co. H, 1st North Carolina Cav., June 20, 1861. Capt., Co. B, 8th Bn. North Carolina Partisan Rangers, July 1862. Capt., Co. C, 66th North Carolina, July 23, 1863. Major - July 14, 1864. Paroled at Greensboro. m. Anna Lightner. d. Mar. 31, 1913.

DAVIS, HENRY CAMPBELL. b. Columbia, South Carolina, Aug. 6, 1823. gr. South Carolina College, 1844. In South Carolina legisl., 1858-1860 and 1864-1865. In South Carolina Secession Convention. Capt., Co. C, 12th South Carolina, Aug. 20, 1861. Major - Feb. 9, 1863. Lt. Col. - Feb. 27, 1863. Wded. at Sharpsburg. Res. on surgeon's certificate, Nov. 17, 1863. d. Aug. 27, 1886. bur. Ridgeway, South Carolina.

DAVIS, JAMES C. Of Marshall Co., Tennessee. Lt., Co. C, 17th Tennessee, May 15, 1861. Captain - Dec. 30, 1861. Major - June 21, 1862. Promoted Asst. Commissary, but declined. POW at Murfreesboro. Documents at his capture show him to have been 28 years old, 5′11½″; exchanged Mar. 3, 1864. POW at Chickamauga. d. of disease Dec. 15, 1864, at Lewisburg, Tennessee.

DAVIS, JAMES LUCIUS. b. Virginia, Feb. 1813. gr. USMA, 1833. Lt., U.S. Artillery, 1833-1836. Author of a Confederate imprint cavalry manual. Col., 46th Virginia, June 24, 1861. Lt. Col., 8th Virginia Cav. Bn., early 1862. That short-lived unit became the 10th Virginia Cav. Regt., and Davis became Colonel of the 10th, Sept. 24, 1862. Wded. and POW near Hagerstown, July 6, 1863; exchanged Mar. 10, 1864. Res. Feb. 2, 1865. d. Buckingham Co., Virginia, May 11, 1871. Davis was described by an infantry officer as "very sensitive and very courteous."

DAVIS, JAMES TAYLOR. b. Mecklenburg Co., North Carolina, 1836. Lawyer there. 5′11¾″. Pvt., Co. B, 1st North Carolina, June 1861. Capt., Co. F, 49th North Carolina, Apr. 21, 1862. Major - Sept. 16, 1863. Lt. Col. - July 30, 1864. MWIA in stomach at Ft. Stedman, Mar. 25, 1865. bur. in Sharon Presbyterian Churchyard, Mecklenburg Co.

DAVIS, JOHN BUNYAN. b. Fairfield Dist., May 10, 1826. att. USMA. Fairfield Dist. physician. Capt., Co. E, 15th South Carolina, Aug. 30, 1861. Colonel - Jan. 19, 1864. Paroled at Greensboro. d. Nov. 26, 1899. bur. Episcopal Cemetery, Fairfield Co.

Museum of the Confederacy

JAMES LUCIUS DAVIS
10th Virginia Cavalry

DAVIS, MATTHEW L., JR. b. North Carolina, Aug. 1829. Lived in Rutherford Co. gr. USMA, 1852. Lt., U.S. Army, 1852-1861. Major and AQM when apptd. Colonel, 2nd North Carolina Cav., to rank from Apr. 12, 1862. d. 11 days later of pneumonia at Goldsboro.

DAVIS, WILLIAM SMITH. b. Warren Co., North Carolina, Jan. 9, 1840. att. U. Virginia and Randolph-Macon. m. Elizabeth Ann Jones. Lt., Co. C, 12th North Carolina, Apr. 30, 1861. Captain - May 1, 1862. Lt. Col. - May 24, 1863. Lost arm at Cedar Creek. Res. due to wounds, Feb. 10, 1865. Had temporarily commanded the 23rd North Carolina at one time. Methodist minister. d. Nov. 23, 1910, at Warrenton, North Carolina. bur. Fairview Cemetery, Warrenton.

DAVIS, ZIMMERMAN. b. Fairfield Dist., Oct. 8, 1834. gr. Charleston College. m. Cornelia McIver. Charleston businessman. Pvt., Washington Light Inf., Dec. 1860 to Apr. 1861. Lt., same company, 1861-1862. Capt., Co. D, 5th South Carolina Cav., Apr. 12, 1862. Served as a.i.g. on Butler's staff, 1863-64. Col., 5th South Carolina Cav., Oct. 27, 1864. U.C.V. leader and orator post-war. d. Charleston, Mar. 30, 1910. bur. Magnolia Cemetery.

DAWSON, GEORGE OSCAR. b. 1825. gr. U. Georgia. Planter and lawyer in Greensboro. State legisl. Capt., Co. I, 8th Georgia, May 16, 1861. Major - Dec. 16, 1862. Wded. at 2nd Manassas and Gettysburg. Assigned at Columbus, Georgia, June 1864. A fellow officer described Dawson as: "a droll genius, but withal a very clever fellow—a bachelor of about 40 years and moderately wealthy." d. June 1865. bur. family cemetery near Greensboro.

DAWSON, REGINALD HEBER. b. Mar. 19, 1838. att. U. Alabama. Capt., Co. A, 13th Alabama, Aug. 19, 1861. Major - Nov. 27, 1861. Lt. Col. - Jan. 10, 1862. Wded. at Seven Pines. Resigned June 11, 1862, citing typhoid and dysentery. Lawyer and prison official in Selma and Camden. d. Flat Top Mines, Alabama, July 11, 1906.

Alabama State Archives

REGINALD H. DAWSON
13th Alabama

DEAN, ROBERT AARON. b. Marshall Co., Mississippi, Dec. 29, 1836. Farmer. Sgt., Co. I, 19th Mississippi, May 25, 1861. Lieutenant - July 17, 1861. Captain - Apr. 16, 1863, to rank from July 15, 1862. Major - May 12, 1864. Paroled at Memphis, May 1865. m. Lucy Ann Langston in 1864. In Mississippi legisl. Alive in 1912.

DEAN, WILLIAM T. m. Margaret Nelson, 1849. Capt. and Adj. of a New Orleans militia unit, 1856-1860. Cuban adventurer pre-war. Major, 5th Louisiana, May 1861. Lt. Col. - July 31, 1862. Absent sick in late 1862, and then disappeared from rolls. Deputy constable in New Orleans in 1871. Dean's papers are at Tulane.

DEARING, ST. CLAIR. b. Georgia, June 1833. Lt., U.S. Army, 1855-1861. Lt. Col., 25th North Carolina, Aug. 15, 1861. Declined re-election in Apr. 1862 with what he later called "petulance." Lt. of Cavalry, Nov. 1864. In April 1865, Dearing was endeavoring to raise colored troops in Georgia.

DeBLANC, ALCIBIADES. b. Louisiana, 1820. St. Martinville lawyer. Capt., Co. C, 8th Louisiana, June 19, 1861. Major - Oct. 15, 1862. Lt. Col. - Apr. 6, 1863. Colonel - July 2, 1863. POW at Banks' Ford, Chancellorsville, May 4, 1863. Wded. at Gettysburg, and never returned to duty. Retired Aug. 15, 1864. d. Nov. 8, 1883. bur. St. Martinville Cemetery.

DeBORDENAVE, FULGENCE. b. Jan. 26, 1830. Frenchman, unable to speak English in 1861. He had served in Algiers and the Crimean War. Capt., Co. B, 1st Louisiana Zouave Bn., Apr. 4, 1861. Major - Sept. 15, 1862. Commanded the bn. after Nov. 1864 retirement of Coppens. m. Mattie Ki Pipkin. Settled in Franklin, Virginia, post-war and died there Dec. 19, 1904. bur. Poplar Springs Cemetery.

DeCHOISEUL, CHARLES. b. 1818. Lt. Col., 7th Louisiana, May 1861. MWIA at Port Republic, d. June 19. bur. St. John's in the Wilderness Cemetery, Flat Rock, North Carolina. A Virginia woman called him "particularly pleasant."

DeGRAFFENRIED, FRANCIS H. b. Decatur Co. Merchant, age 21, in Dougherty Co. 1860 census. Sgt., Co. E, 4th Georgia,

Apr. 28, 1861. Lieutenant - Sept. 30, 1861. Captain - Aug. 1, 1862. Major - Aug. 5, 1864. Wded. in jaw at Chancellorsville. MWIA at Ft. Stedman, Mar. 25, 1865, d. next day.

DeLAGNEL, JOHNSTON. Stationed at Jamestown Island, without rank, Sept. 1861. Temporary rank of Captain, Oct. 7, 1861. Captain, to report to Hardy's Bluff Battery on the James, Dec. 6, 1861. It is informally recorded that DeLagnel was elected Colonel of the 9th Virginia in May 1862, but declined. Major, 20th Bn. Virginia Heavy Artillery, July 3, 1862, but the Senate later rejected the nomination. Captain and ordnance officer in South Carolina, 1863-64. d. Charleston, South Carolina, Apr. 8, 1864. The Virginia Historical Society owns some interesting Civil War drawings by DeLagnel.

DELONY, WILLIAM GASTON. b. Sept. 8, 1826. gr. U. Georgia, 1846, with first honors. Lawyer. m. Rosa Eugenia Huguenin. Capt., Co. C, Cav. Bn. of Cobb's Georgia Legion, Aug. 1, 1861. Major - May 23, 1862. Lt. Col. - Nov. 1, 1862. Wded. in the face at Gettysburg. MWIA near Brandy Station, Sept. 23, 1863, d. in U.S. hospital in D.C. on Oct. 2. T. R. R. Cobb wrote of Delony that he was "an excellent officer," though he was "drinking a great deal." bur. Oconee Hill Cemetery, Athens. Delony's very detailed letters to his wife (379 of them) are at U. Georgia.

DeMARIGNY, ANTOINE JAMES. (known as Mandeville DeMarigny). b. Nov. 21, 1811, in Louisiana. gr. from a French military school. New Orleans merchant. m. Sophronia Claiborne. A "tall commanding figure." Colonel at enlistment of 10th Louisiana into C.S. service, July 22, 1861 (had commanded it since Mar. 1861). Res. July 1862. Later raised some cavalry. d. June 3, 1890 in New Orleans. Another source renders this officer's full name as Antoine Jacques Philippe de Mandeville de Marigny.

DENDY, STILES PLUMER. b. Pickens Dist., South Carolina, May 28, 1839. att. U. Virginia and South Carolina College. Lt., Co. C, 2nd South Carolina Rifles, Nov. 2, 1861. Captain - Feb. 13, 1862. Major - Jan. 22, 1864. m. Alice E. Sitton, 1871. Walhalla judge. In South Carolina legisl., 1880-82 and 1899-1900. d. Nov. 11, 1907. bur. Westview Cemetery, Walhalla.

DENIS, JULES CHARLES. b. New Orleans, Oct. 7, 1829. Merchant. Lt. Col., 10th Louisiana, May 1861. Resigned Dec. 1861. Later served on Polk's staff and on recruiting duty in Mississippi. Became Colonel of the 32nd Louisiana and the 1st Mississippi Cav. Reserves. New Orleans police commissioner and bank president. d. Nov. 24, 1904.

DENNIS CHARLES J. Farmer in Knoxville, Georgia, in 1860, age 20. Capt., Co. C, 27th Georgia, July 6, 1861. Major - Sept. 17, 1862. Res. Jan. 2, 1863.

DERBY, CHARLES ALEXANDER. b. Dinwiddie Co., Virginia, Sept. 12, 1828. gr. VMI, 1848. Math professor at Georgia Military Institute. Episcopal clergyman at St. Peter's Church, Lowndes Co., Alabama. Wife - Charlotte. Lt. Col., 44th Alabama, May 16, 1862. Colonel - Sept. 1, 1862. Wded. at 2nd Manassas. KIA at Sharpsburg, body not recovered.

DeROSSET, WILLIAM LORD. b. Wilmington, North Carolina, Oct. 27, 1832. att. UNC. Major, 3rd North Carolina, May 16, 1861. Lt. Col. - Apr. 26, 1862. Colonel - July 1, 1862. Wded. hip and thigh at Sharpsburg. Res. due to wounds, Oct. 3, 1863. Iron magnate and U.C.V. official. d. Wilmington, Aug. 14, 1910. bur. Oakdale Cemetery.

DERRICK, CLARENCE. b. Washington, D.C., Oct. 1837. gr. USMA. Lt. of artillery, P.A.C.S., Mar. 16, 1861. A.a.g. to Genl. Floyd, Sept. 1861 to April 1862. Lt. Col., 23rd Virginia Bn., May 26, 1862. POW at Winchester, Sept. 19, 1864, released June 14, 1865. 6′0″. Lived in West Chester, Pennsylvania, and Greensboro, Alabama. Lawyer. d. Greensboro, Dec. 9, 1907. bur. St. Paul's Church there.

DeRUSSY, LEWIS GUSTAVUS. b. June 1795. gr. USMA, 1814. Lt., U.S. Artillery, 1814-1842. Colonel of Louisiana regt. in Mexican War. Colonel, 2nd Louisiana, May 1861. Served on Polk's staff later in 1861. d. Dec. 17, 1864.

DeSAUSSURE, WILLIAM DAVIE. b. Columbia, South Carolina,

Dec. 12, 1819. gr. South Carolina College. Lawyer. Mexican War veteran. In State legislature. Capt., U.S. Army, 1846-1848 and 1855-1861. Capt., P.A.C.S., Mar. 16, 1861. Colonel, 15th South Carolina, Sept. 9, 1861. KIA at Gettysburg. Reburied in Columbia after the war at the 1st Presbyterian Church.

DEVANE, DUNCAN JAMES. b. May 1, 1834. att. Davidson. Lawyer and planter in Sampson Co. m. Vivian Faison. Lt., Co. I, 20th North Carolina, June 10, 1861. Captain - Apr. 28, 1862. Major - May 12, 1864. Wded. arm at Spotsylvania, and at Sharpsburg and Gettysburg. Appx. d. Apr. 9, 1884. bur. Oakdale Cemetery, Wilmington.

DEVANE, WILLIAM STEWART. b. Mar. 4, 1828. Brother of Duncan J. Lawyer in Sampson Co. m. Laura Murphy. Pvt., Co. A, 61st North Carolina (though regiment wasn't formed until 9/62), Apr. 1861. Captain - Oct. 9, 1861. Lt. Col. - Sept. 5, 1862. Colonel - Oct. 11, 1864. Wded. shoulder, June 18, 1864. Paroled at Salisbury, May 2, 1865. d. Feb. 24, 1879. bur. Oakdale Cemetery, Wilmington.

DEWEY, GEORGE STANLEY. b. Sept. 20, 1841. Resided in Craven Co. Pvt., Co. H, 1st North Carolina Cavalry, June 29, 1861. Commissary Sgt. of regt., June 16, 1862. Returned to original post as pvt., Oct. 1862. Lt. and Adj. of regt., July 23, 1863. Lt., Co. H, Aug. 29, 1864. Captain - Aug. 30, 1864. Made Maj., 1st North Carolina Cavalry, in the last days of the war. KIA at Chamberlain Run, Mar. 31, 1865. bur. New Bern.

DEYERLE, ANDREW JACKSON. b. Montgomery Co., Virginia, Apr. 24, 1823. Capt., Co. E, 42nd Virginia, June 4, 1861. Colonel - June 19, 1863 (backdated from the end of 1863). Severe hip wound at Cedar Mountain. In Virginia legisl., 1864. Roanoke County farmer. d. Elliston, Virginia, June 18, 1907. bur. East Hill Cemetery, Salem.

DEYERLE, JOHN SCOTT. b. Montgomery Co., Virginia, June 1, 1835. Brother of Andrew J. Deyerle, above. att. Roanoke College, Hampden-Sydney and U. Virginia. Capt., Co. K, 54th Virginia, Oct. 10, 1861. Major - Nov. 13, 1862. Resigned to take surgeon's exam, Apr. 27, 1863. Became Surgeon, 21st Virginia

Cavalry. Salem physician. Roanoke Co. Treasurer. d. July 5, 1890. bur. East Hill Cemetery, Salem.

DICKEY, JAMES. b. 1823 in South Carolina. Farmer in Calhoun Co., Georgia, in 1860, worth $27,000. Capt., Co. E, 51st Georgia, Mar. 4, 1862. Major - July 2, 1863. Lt. Col. - Jan. 14, 1864. Colonel - Nov. 12, 1864. POW at Frederick, Maryland, Sept. 1, 1862, exchanged Apr. 1863. POW at Sayler's Creek.

DICKEY, STEPHEN MILES. Hotel keeper and real estate man in Grayson Co., Virginia. Farmer in 1860, age 35. Capt., Co. A, 51st Virginia, June 24, 1861. Major - May 26, 1862. Resigned July 4, 1863, to enter Virginia legisl. d. 1903.

DICKINS, JOHN R. b. North Carolina. The 1860 census for Panola Co. shows Dickins as a farmer, married, age 38, worth $63,175. Capt., Co. E, 12th Mississippi, Feb. 1861, aged 39. Major - May 20, 1861. Disappeared, without explanation, into the Army of Mississippi, spring of 1862.

DINGLE, JAMES HERVEY, JR. The 1860 census for Clarendon District identifies Dingle as a married farmer, age 36, worth $22,670. Lt., Co. C, Hampton Legion, June 12, 1861, aged 37. Major - June 20, 1862. Much lauded for bravery at Second Manassas. KIA at Sharpsburg, "with the flag of the Legion in his hand."

DIXON, EDWARD. b. Cleveland Co., North Carolina Farmer. Capt., Co. D, 14th North Carolina, Apr. 26, 1861, aged 30. Major - Apr. 27, 1862. d. of disease in Richmond, July 8, 1862.

DOCKERY, OLIVER HART. b. Richmond Co., North Carolina, Aug. 12, 1830. gr. UNC. att. Wake Forest. Planter. 5′9″. Capt., Co. E, 38th North Carolina, Oct. 30, 1861. Lt. Col. - Jan. 17, 1862. Defeated at re-org. in Apr. 1862, but later, in a fit of Republican zeal, claimed that he "withdrew and advocated sustaining the Federal govt." In North Carolina legisl. as a scalawag post-war. Unsuccessful candidate for governor. In U.S. Congress. d. Baltimore, Maryland, Mar. 21, 1906. bur. Mangum, North Carolina.

DONALD, DAVID LEWIS. b. Donalds, South Carolina, Jan. 25, 1825. Lt., Palmetto Regiment, Mexican War. Lt., Co. F, 2nd

South Carolina Rifles, Oct. 29, 1861. Captain - Dec. 19, 1861. Lt. Col. - Jan. 22, 1864. Wded. leg at Wilderness. Wded. thigh, Aug. 14, 1864. Appx. d. April 25, 1872.

DONALD, GEORGE LAVALLE. b. Sumter Co., Alabama, Sept. 29, 1838. gr. U. Mississsippi, 1859. Lt., Co. I, 13th Mississippi, May 23, 1861. Capt., Co. G, 13th Mississippi, Apr. 26, 1862. Major - July 29, 1863. Clarke Co. Sheriff. In Mississippi legisl. m. Mary Eliza Hicks, 1867. d. 1911. bur. Quitman, Mississippi.

DOOLEY, JOHN. b. Ireland, ca. 1810. Came to U.S. in 1832. m. Sarah Dooley (a cousin), 1836. Capt., Co. C, 1st Virginia, Apr. 21, 1861 (state commission is dated June 12, 1859). Major - Nov. 18, 1861. Dropped at April 1862 re-org. Served in Richmond ambulance corps later in the war. His son and namesake wrote a notable Confederate memoir. d. Richmond, Feb. 11, 1869.

DORSEY, EDWARD R. Of Howard Co., Md. Capt., Co. C, 1st Maryland, May 17, 1861. Major - July 21, 1861. Lt. Col. - Mar. 18, 1862. Wded. in shoulder and disabled at Winchester, May 25, 1862.

DORSEY, GUSTAVUS WARFIELD. Of Montgomery Co., Md. Pvt., Co. K, 1st Virginia Cavalry, 1861, aged 22. Sergeant - later in 1861. Lieutenant - May 1862. Captain - Oct. 1, 1863. This company was transferred to the 1st Md. Cav., Aug. 1864. Dorsey became Lt. Col. for "Valor & Skill," Feb. 17, 1865. Wded. at Fredericksburg and Fisher's Hill. Said to have caught J. E. B. Stuart when the General was mortally wounded. d. Brookville, Maryland, Sept. 6, 1911. bur. near Brookville in Owens Family Cemetery.

DORSEY, JASPER NEWTON. b. Oct. 19, 1825. Of Hall Co., Georgia. m. Junius Cornelia Tucker. Capt., Co. D, 27th Georgia, Aug. 10, 1861. Lt. Col. - Jan. 10, 1863. Dismissed in Feb. 1864 for drunkenness on duty. Later was Captain, 11th Georgia Cavalry. d. Gainesville, Georgia, Dec. 5, 1883. bur. Alta Vista Cemetery.

DORTCH, WILLIAM THEOPHILUS. b. Rocky Mount, North Carolina, Aug. 23, 1824. Lt. Col., 6th North Carolina, May 16,

1861. Resigned July 11, 1861, to become Speaker of the House in the North Carolina legisl. Later in C. S. Congress. Goldsboro lawyer. d. there Nov. 21, 1889.

DOUGLAS, BEVERLY BROWNE. b. New Kent Co., Virginia, Dec. 21, 1822. att. Yale U. and U. of Edinburgh, Scotland. gr. William & Mary. Norfolk and King William Co. lawyer. In Virginia legisl. Capt., Co. H, 9th Virginia Cav., July 1861. Maj., 5th Virginia Cav., June 24, 1862. Res. Jan. 8, 1863, to return to Virginia legisl. In U.S. Congress post-war. d. Washington, D.C., Dec. 22, 1878.

DOUGLASS, MARCELLUS. b. Thomaston, Georgia, Oct. 5, 1820. gr. U. Georgia m. Menla Davis. In Georgia Secession Convention. "Small, fair-skinned man with light blue eyes and blonde curly hair." Capt., Co. E, 13th Georgia, June 19, 1861. Lt. Col. - July 8, 1861. Colonel - Feb. 1, 1862. KIA at Sharpsburg. bur. Rosedale Cemetery, Cuthbert, Georgia. An Alabamian reported seeing Douglass' corpse stripped of clothes the day after the battle.

DOWD, HENRY AUSTIN. b. Jan. 5, 1833. Lived in Edgecombe Co. Lt., Co. I, 15th North Carolina, May 22, 1861. Adj. of regt., Oct. 7, 1861. Colonel - Apr. 20, 1862. Wded. at Malvern Hill, and resigned due to wounds, Feb. 27, 1863. Capt. and AQM later. d. May 12, 1902. bur. Edgecombe Co.

DOWNER, WILLIAM S. Supt. of Richmond Armory. Maj., 1st Virginia Bn. LDT, briefly in 1863 ("Armory Bn.").

DOWNS, GEORGE. b. Monongalia Co., Apr. 17, 1820. m. Elizabeth Parish in Harrison Co., 1840. Miller in Calhoun Co. in 1860. Capt. of Virginia Troops, July 15, 1861. Capt., Co. A, 19th Virginia Cav., Mar. 1, 1863. Major - Feb. 26, 1864. Wded. June 17, 1864. Downs' early war experience was as Captain of a company in the 3rd Regt. Virginia State Line; many members of the company went with him to form the 19th Virginia Cav. company he commanded in early 1863. Farmer in Calhoun Co. d. Mar. 18, 1899. bur. Sturm Cemetery.

DOYAL, LEONARD T. b. Columbia Co., Georgia, 1816. Lawyer in Culloden, then in McDonough. Served in 1850 Georgia Convention. Lawyer in Griffin in 1860, worth $44,500. Capt., Co. D, 2nd Georgia Bn., Apr. 20, 1861. Col., 53rd Georgia, May 12, 1862. Resigned Oct. 8, 1862. Died before 1893. A member of the 53rd wrote in August 1862 that Doyal "is idolized unanimously by the whole regt., and is a perfect gentleman."

DOYLE, ROBERT L. b. Augusta Co., Virginia, ca. 1812. att. Washington College. Capt., Co. C, 5th Virginia, Apr. 1861. Lt. Col., 62nd Virginia, Sept. 9, 1862. Res. Nov. 10, 1863, to become Augusta Co. Commonwealth's Atty. KIA at Piedmont, "while acting as Captain of reserves."

DRAKE, JAMES HENRY. b. Newtown, Frederick Co., Virginia, June 9, 1822. Plasterer, mechanic and militia officer. Wife - Sarah Ann. Capt., Co. A, 1st Virginia Cav., Apr. 19, 1861. Major - Apr. 22, 1862. His service record mentions promotions to Lt. Col. and Colonel, but does not date them. KIA near Shepherdstown, July 16, 1862. A member of the regiment declared that Drake was a good curser and was "much beloved by his men"—who despised Drake's successor. Drake's papers are at the Library of Congress. bur. Lutheran Churchyard, Mulberry Street, Stephens City, Va., in an unmarked grave.

DRAUGHON, WALTER. b. Sampson Co., North Carolina, 1811. Of Cumberland Co. Lt. Col., 30th North Carolina, Sept. 26, 1861. Dropped at May 1862 re-org. d. before 1880. bur. Fayetteville.

DREUX, CHARLES DIDIER. b. New Orleans, May 11, 1832. att. Amherst College and Kentucky Mil. Inst. gr. Transylvania U. m. Amanda Mollie Haynes. Louisiana lawyer and state legisl. Lt. Col., 1st Louisiana Bn., Apr. 1861. KIA near Newport News, July 5, 1861. bur. Metairie Cemetery, New Orleans.

DUFF, WILLIAM LEWIS. b. Lafayette Co., Mississippi, Aug. 25, 1843. att. U. Mississippi. Lived at Sarepta. Lt., Co. K, 17th Mississippi, Apr. 23, 1861. Captain - May 28, 1861. Major - Nov. 1, 1862. Wded. at 2nd Fredericksburg, May 3, 1863. Dropped, Jan. 1, 1864. Commanded 8th Misissippi Cav. later. Moved to Eureka, California, in 1881. Lawyer. Alive in San Francisco, 1909.

DUFFIELD, CHARLES B. Major, 8th Virginia Cav. Bn., at org., early 1862. Resigned, Apr. 24, 1862, aged 20. 5′9″.

DUFFY, PATRICK B. b. Nicholas Co., 1838. gr. Mt. St. Mary's College, Maryland. Capt., Co. C, 9th Virginia Bn., May 1861. This unit became Co. Co, 25th Virginia, May 1862. Lt. Col. - May 1, 1862. Resigned Oct. 8, 1862. Later became Capt. and A.C.S. m. Fannie E. McConihay, 1867. Merchant in Braxton Co. "Died in the seventies" . . . whether referring to the decade or his age is unclear.

DUGGAN, JAMES BARNES. b. Washington Co., Georgia, Nov. 1, 1833. Lt., Co. A, 49th Georgia, Mar. 4, 1862. Captain - Sept. 9, 1862. Major - June 11, 1864. Appx. In Georgia legisl. d. Dudley, Georgia, Sept. 29, 1915.

DUKE, RICHARD THOMAS WALKER. b. Albemarle Co., Virginia, June 6, 1822. gr. VMI, 1845. gr. U. Virginia. Charlottesville lawyer. Capt., Co. B, 19th Virginia, Apr. 1861. Col., 46th Virginia, May 24, 1862. Res. Mar. 28, 1864. Lt. Col., 1st Virginia Bn. Reserves, 1864, in the trenches at Ft. Harrison. POW at Sayler's Creek, released July 25. In U.S. Congress. d. Charlottesville, July 2, 1898. bur. Maplewood Cemetery.

DULANY, RICHARD HENRY. b. Loudoun Co., Virginia, Aug. 10, 1820. Capt., Co. A, 6th Virginia Cav., June 1861. Lt. Col., 7th Virginia Cav., June 20, 1862. Wded. at Greenland Gap, Apr. 25, 1863. Colonel - Mar. 23, 1865. d. Loudoun Co., Oct. 31, 1906.

DUMONTEIL, FELIX (De la Greze). b. France. New Orleans merchant. Maj., 10th Louisiana, July 22, 1861. Resigned Dec. 1861. Later was Colonel, 14th Confederate Cavalry.

DUNCAN, DAVID ROBINSON. b. Mecklenburg Co., Virginia, Sept. 27, 1836. gr. Randolph-Macon, 1855. Spartanburg, South Carolina, lawyer. Lt., Co. C, 13th South Carolina, Aug. 27, 1861. Captain - Sept. 4, 1861. Major - June 8, 1864. POW at Petersburg, Apr. 2, 1865, released May 18. 5′9″. In South Caroline legisl., 1865-1867 and 1870-1876. d. Spartanburg, Jan. 28, 1902. bur. Oakwood Cemetery there.

DUNCAN, JAMES HENDERSON. b. Mt. Pleasant, Tenn., March 15, 1839. Merchant in Oxford, Miss. Lt., Co. E, 19th Mississippi, May 15, 1861. Captain - 1863. Major - Jan. 20, 1864. Lt. Col. - May 12, 1864. Temporary duty as Lt. Col. of 16th Mississippi in Nov. 1864. Wded. and POW at Ft. Gregg, Apr. 2, 1865; released on June 18. d. Sept. 16, 1871. bur. Clear Creek Baptist Church, Lafayette Co., Miss. Earlier editions of this book erroneously used military service details of Capt. James H. Duncan of the 16th Mississippi.

DUNCAN, WILLIAM HANSFORD. b. Barnwell, South Carolina, Aug. 22, 1835. Farmer near Barnwell. Capt., Co. G, 1st South Carolina (Hagood's), Dec. 7, 1861. Capt., Co. E, Apr. 12, 1862. Major - May 16, 1862. Lt. Col. - July 12, 1862. Acted as Colonel from Sept. 1862 to Jan. 1863, under orders from Genl. Micah Jenkins, but the War Dept. rejected this, and Duncan resigned his commission as Lt. Col., Jan. 10, 1863. m. Harriet M. Hurley. Auditor of Barnwell Co. and school trustee. d. Dec. 14, 1889. bur. Seven Pines Church.

DUNGAN, ROBERT H. b. Sept. 18, 1834. att. Emory & Henry. Founded Jonesboro Male Inst., Jonesboro, Tennessee. Lt., Co. A, 48th Virginia, May 18, 1861. Captain - Apr. 21, 1862. Lt. Col. - Oct. 16, 1862. Colonel - May 3, 1863. Commanded his brigade, summer of 1864. Wded. at Cedar Mountain, Chancellorsville, and Kernstown (July 1864 . Appx. m. Susan Virginia Baker, 1865. d. Bristol, Nov. 6, 1903. bur. East Hill Cemetery.

DUNHAM, JOHN WHITTIER. b. Pitt Co., North Carolina, Mar. 6, 1842. Lived in Wilson Co. att. UNC. Lt., Co. F, 4th North Carolina, May 16, 1861. Captain - May 31, 1862. Wded. thigh at Seven Pines. Resigned due to that wound, Mar. 9, 1863. Apptd. Major at some later date, but apparently never served at that rank, although he did serve as Major in the Home Guards. In North Carolina legisl. d. Wilmington, Jan. 27, 1889. bur. Oakdale Cemetery.

DUNN, AMBROSE C. b. Randolph Co., Georgia, Aug. 10, 1835. Capt., Co. A, 60th Georgia, Aug. 21, 1861. Dismissed by court-martial, Nov. 20, 1861. Lt. Col., 37th Virginia Cav. Bn., Aug. 2,

1862. "Cashiered" on Nov. 6, 1863, on charges of disobedience of orders brought by William L. Jackson. Reinstated by the President, June 24, 1864. Resigned Mar. 31, 1865. Paroled at Lynchburg, May 29, 1865. Alive in New York City in 1914. Another source asserts that Dunn was born Feb. 13, 1840; it is more reliable than that from which the 1835 date came.

DUNOVANT, RICHARD GILL MILLS. b. Chester, South Carolina, May 18, 1821. att. South Carolina College. Physician. Edgefield planter. Colonel during Mexican War. In South Carolina Secession Convention. Col., 12th South Carolina, Sept. 1, 1861. Res. Apr. 2, 1862. In South Carolina legisl., 1864-1865. Author of a Mexican War regimental history. d. Edgefield, May 12, 1898. Brother of the South Carolina general.

DUNWODY, HENRY MACON. b. Georgia, Mar. 13, 1826. gr. U. Georgia, 1846. m. Matilda Maxwell. Roswell planter. Capt., Co. A, 51st Georgia, Mar. 4, 1862. Major - May 2, 1863. KIA at Gettysburg. bur. Presbyterian Cemetery, Roswell, Georgia.

DUNWODY, JOHN. b. Hartford, Connecticut, Nov. 6, 1818. att. USMA. Mexican War veteran. Government surveyor in Kansas. Major, 7th Georgia, May 31, 1861. Lt. Col. - Dec. 23, 1861. Dropped at re-org. Major in A.I.G.O. Served in C.S. Nitre and Mining Bureau, 1862-1864. d. Sept. 2, 1903 in Atlanta. bur. Oakland Cemetery.

DURHAM, JOHN A. b. 1826 in South Carolina. Farmer at Crawfordsville, Georgia. Lt., Co. D, 49th Georgia, Mar. 1862. Captain - Aug. 30, 1862. Major - Mar. 24, 1864. MWIA at Jericho Ford, May 23, 1864, d. June 11. bur. Hollywood. Durham has a marker at Raytown Baptist Church, Taliaferro Co., Georgia.

DYER, DAVID. Farmer in Pittsylvania Co. in 1860, age 36. Capt., Co. D, 57th Virginia, June 22, 1861. Major - May 23, 1862. Lt. Col. - 1862. Colonel - July 30, 1862. Res. Jan. 12, 1863.

EAKLE, BENJAMIN FRANKLIN. b. Augusta Co., Virginia, Aug. 7, 1826. Lewisburg merchant. 5′10″. Lt., "Greenbrier Cavalry," 1861. Capt., Co. A, 14th Virginia Cavalry, Jan. 22, 1862. Major - Feb. 12, 1863. Wded. at Gettysburg and Monocacy. Wded.

and POW at Nineveh, Virginia, Nov. 12, 1864, released July 24, 1865. Greenbrier Co. farmer. d. July 22, 1898. bur. Old Stone Church, Lewisburg. Eakle's photo was published in a 1906 Greenbrier veterans pamphlet. Some of his correspondence is at West Virginia University.

EASLEY, WILLIAM KING. b. Pickens Dist., South Carolina, Jan. 28, 1825. Lawyer there and in New Orleans. m. Carolina Sloan. In South Carolina Secession Convention. Lt. Col., 2nd South Carolina Cavalry, sometime in 1862. Absence of a Compiled Service Record leaves Easley indistinct. Resigned Aug. 20, 1862, due to yellow fever. Became Major, 4th South Carolina Cavalry Battalion. Died in Atlanta, Georgia, July 1872. bur. Crosswell, South Carolina.

ECTOR, WALTON. b. Georgia, Sept. 1820. Planter in Columbus. att. USMA. Volunteer in 1836 Creek War. Captain in Mexican War. General of Georgia Militia. Farmer in Meriwether Co., owned 39 slaves. Capt., Co. B, 13th Georgia, May 1, 1861. Colonel - July 8, 1861. d. Feb. 1, 1862.

EDELIN, THOMAS BOYD. b. and lived in Md. Lt., U.S. Army, 1855-1861. Aide to Hampton and Butler. Transferred from staff of P. M. B. Young, where he was Capt. and a.i.g., to the temporary rank of Lt. Col., with the 16th North Carolina Cavalry Battalion, on Dec. 7, 1864. POW at Dinwiddie C.H., Mar. 30, 1865, released Apr. 12. d. Feb. 8, 1902, in Culpeper, Virginia, age 67.

EDGAR, GEORGE MATHEWS. b. Union, Virginia, Mar. 1, 1837. gr. VMI, 1856, and on the faculty there. Drillmaster of 1st Florida early in war. Capt., Co. D, 26th Virginia Battalion, Aug. 1861. Major - May 23, 1862. Lt. Col. - Nov. 1862. POW at Lewisburg, May 23, 1862. Wded. by bayonet at Cold Harbor. POW at Winchester, Sept. 19, 1864, exchanged Oct. 31. Educator at U. Alabama and U. Arkansas post-war. d. Paris, Kentucky, Oct. 18, 1913.

EDMONDS, EDWARD CLAXTON. b. Paris, Virginia, Jan. 21, 1835. gr. VMI, 1858. Principal, Danville Military Academy. Colonel, 38th Virginia, June 12, 1861. Wded. at Seven Pines. KIA at Gettysburg.

EDMONDSON, HENRY ARCHER. b. Halifax Co., Oct. 20, 1833.

Pvt., Co. A, Montague's Virginia Battalion (became part of 53rd Virginia, Nov. 1861), Apr. 24, 1861. Sergeant - 1861. Lt., Co. A, 53rd Virginia, May 5, 1862. Captain - May 27, 1862. Major - Oct. 22, 1864. South Boston tobacco merchant. In Virginia legisl. Halifax Co. sheriff, 1869-1887. d. Dec. 29, 1918.

EDMONDSON, JAMES KERR. b. Rockbridge Co., Feb. 11, 1832. m. Emily Taylor, 1857. Lexington lawyer. Lt., Co. H, 27th Virginia, Apr. 18, 1861. Captain - Oct. 7, 1861. Lt. Col. - July 24, 1862. Colonel - Nov. 19, 1862. Lost left arm at Chancellorsville, amputated at the shoulder, and resigned Dec. 12, 1863. Rockbridge Co. judge, 1870-1881. Mayor of Lexington. d. Mar. 31, 1898.

EDMONDSTON, PATRICK MUIR. b. Charleston, South Carolina, Aug. 1, 1819. Planter in Halifax Co., North Carolina. Capt., Co. G, 3rd North Carolina Cavalry, Apr. 23, 1861. Major, P.A.C.S., Sept. 24, 1861. Lt. Col., 8th Virginia Cavalry, Feb. 5, 1862. No further record was found. Later served as a.a.g. with North Carolina Militia. Fell into bankruptcy after the war. d. Aug. 19, 1871. His wife's very extensive journal was published in 1979.

EDMUNDSON, DAVID. b. Montgomery Co., Apr. 11, 1829. att. VMI. m. Mary B. Richardson. Lt. Col., 5th Virginia State Line, for a brief period in 1861. Capt., Co. B, 4th Virginia, Apr. 1861. Wded. at 1st Manassas. Capt., Co. B, 21st Virginia Cavalry, Apr. 1, 1863. Lt. Col. - Aug. 31, 1863. POW at Fisher's Hill, exchanged Feb. 1865. Montgomery Co. farmer. d. Sept. 24, 1893.

EDMUNDSON, HENRY ALONZO. b. Blacksburg, June 14, 1814. gr. Georgetown U. Salem farmer. In U.S. Congress, 1849-1861. A.d.c. to Gov. Letcher, June 18, 1861. Lt. Col., 54th Virginia, Sept. 4, 1861. Dropped at May 1862 re-org. Lt. Col., 27th Virginia Cavalry Battalion, Sept. 1, 1862. This unit, supplemented, became the 25th Virginia Cav. Regt., July 1864. Edmundson resigned Oct. 8, 1864. Montgomery Co. lawyer and farmer. d. there Dec. 16, 1890. bur. Fotheringay Cemetery.

EDWARDS, JOHN CUBBAGE. Capt., Co. A, 5th South Carolina Cavalry, Dec. 24, 1861. Service records show Edwards as a captain through the end of 1864, but other documents report him as Colonel of the regt. at war's end.

EDWARDS, OLIVER EVANS. b. Spartanburg Dist., South Carolina, Nov. 9, 1819. Raised in Cass Co., Georgia. Spartanburg C.H. lawyer and militia colonel. Mexican War officer. In South Carolina legisl. A "pious Baptist" who declined a duel during the war for religious reasons. Colonel, 13th South Carolina, Sept. 4, 1861. Wded. at 2nd Manassas. MWIA at Chancellorsville, d. June 21 at Goldsboro, North Carolina.

EDWARDS, WILLIAM POSEY. b. Talbot Co., Nov. 9, 1835. Pvt., Co. F, 27th Georgia, Sept. 9, 1861. Lieutenant - June 27, 1862. Captain - Jan. 7, 1863. Elected Lt. Col. later in the war, but there is some question about the finality of that promotion. Wded. and POW at Sharpsburg. Wded. at Olustee. In U.S. Congress, 1868-1869. Lawyer in Butler, Georgia. d. there June 28, 1900. bur. Methodist Cemetery.

EELLS, JOHN. b. New York City. Moved from N.Y. to Gloucester Co., Virginia, about three years before the war. Corporal in 9th Virginia Cav., 1861. Capt., Co. F, 5th Virginia Cavalry, Mar. 24, 1862. Major - Apr. 11, 1863, "Valor & Skill." KIA June 22, 1863, in a charge at Upperville. bur. Stonewall Cemetery, Winchester. Aged 23 at death. Eells was described as "well educated and courteous."

ELIASON, WILLIAM ALEXANDER. b. Jan. 28, 1831, at Old Point Comfort, Virginia. att. VMI. Civil engineer in Danville, Virginia. Lt., Co. A, 4th North Carolina, May 16, 1861. Capt. and AQM, 7th North Carolina, Feb. 18, 1862. Maj., 11th North Carolina, Mar. 31, 1862, but declined. Lt. Col., 49th North Carolina, Apr. 12, 1862. Res. June 19, 1862, due to bad health. Mayor of Statesville, North Carolina. d. Statesville, Feb. 19, 1902.

ELLIOTT, WYATT MOSELEY. b. Campbell Co., Feb. 25, 1823. gr. VMI, in its first class ever. Richmond journalist. Captain of the Richmond Grays for many years pre-war, and entered C.S. service as their Captain when the unit became Co. A, 1st Virginia, Apr. 19, 1861. Maj., 25th Virginia Battalion ("Richmond City Bn."), Aug. 15, 1862. Lt. Col. - July 20, 1863. POW at Sayler's Creek, released June 25. In Virginia legisl. U.S. Circuit Court clerk in Lynchburg. d. Lynchburg, Feb. 25, 1897.

ELLIS, ANDERSON. b. Davidson Co. Lived at Salisbury. Capt., Co. A, 54th North Carolina, May 26, 1862, aged 33. 5′10″. Planter. Major - Sept. 3, 1862. Lt. Col. - May 8, 1863. POW at Rappahannock Station, Nov. 7, 1863, exchanged Apr. 1864. Wded. Sept. 19, 1864.

ELLIS, DANIEL HIX. b. Beaufort Dist., Aug. 16, 1824. In South Carolina legisl., 1852-1856 and 1862-1865. Colonel, 11th South Carolina, May 3, 1862. Resigned Nov. 27, 1862, which move was accepted with delight by Gen. W. T. Walker. In South Carolina legisl. and a tax collector the rest of the war. d. Dec. 13, 1873. bur. near Hampton.

ELLIS, JOHN THOMAS. b. Amherst Co., Mar. 16, 1827. Merchant there. gr. VMI, 1848. Capt., Co. H, 19th Virginia, July 1, 1861. Major - Apr. 29, 1862. Lt. Col. - Sept. 14, 1862. Wded. thigh at Gaines' Mill. KIA at Gettysburg, when he was beheaded by a cannonball.

ELLIS, WILLIAM L. A. Capt. of Georgia State Troops, Oct. 1861. Capt., Co. C, 62nd Georgia, May 10, 1862. Major - July 25, 1864. The unit turned into the 8th Georgia Cavalry just about concurrently with Ellis' promotion. Living in Dallas, Texas, in 1890.

EMANUEL, WILLIAM PLEDGER. b. May 9, 1828. m. Frances Meng. Of Marlboro Dist. Major, 12th Battalion South Carolina Cavalry, early 1862. Major, 4th South Carolina Cavalry, Dec. 16, 1862. Under arrest by Beauregard for months. POW at Louisa C.H., June 11, 1864, paroled Dec. 15, 1864. Planter. Marlboro Co. sheriff, 1876-1879. d. 1879. bur. Bennettsville, South Carolina.

EMRICH, JOHN P. b. Germany. Mechanic in Mobile, Alabama. Capt., Co. G, 8th Alabama, May 25, 1861. Major - June 16, 1862. Lt. Col. - Nov. 2, 1864. Wded. at Gaines' Mill and Petersburg. "A gallant Prussian." d. in Mobile after the war.

ENNETT, WILLIAM THOMAS. b. Onslow Co., Nov. 19, 1839,

att. UNC. Lt., Co. E, 3rd North Carolina, May 16, 1861. Captain - Dec. 12, 1861. Major - Oct. 3, 1863. Wded. at Sharpsburg and Chancellorsville. POW at Spotsylvania, May 12, 1864, exchanged Aug. 3. Appx. Physician and President of the North Carolina Medical Society. d. June 24, 1889. bur. Oakdale Cemetery, Wilmington.

ENNIS, PHILIP J. Of Washington, D.C. Capt., Co. F, 5th Virginia Battalion LDT ("Arsenal Bn."), June 16, 1863. Lt. Col. - Sept. 21, 1864. Present into 1865.

ERSON, ERIC. Of Lincolnton, North Carolina. Pvt., Co. K, 1st North Carolina (Bethel), Apr. 25, 1861, aged 21. Cpl. - July 25, 1861. Capt., Co. H, 52nd North Carolina, Apr. 28, 1862. His commission shows him to have been born in Sweden, occupation merchant, height 5′10″. Major - July 3, 1863. Lt. Col. - Aug. 30, 1864. Wded. hand at Gettysburg. Wded. thigh on Aug. 25, 1864. Appx.

ERWIN, MARCUS. b. June 28, 1826 in Burke Co. gr. Transylvania U. Mexican War veteran. Maj., 2nd North Carolina Battalion, Aug. 7, 1861. POW at Roanoke Island, Feb. 1862. Dropped at Sept. 1862 re-org. Asheville newspaperman. In North Carolina legisl. d. July 9, 1881 in Morganton.

ESHLEMAN, BENJAMIN FRANKLIN. b. Lancaster Co., Pennsylvania, Mar. 9, 1830. Capt., 4th Company, Washington Artillery (Louisiana), May 26, 1861. Major - Mar. 26, 1862. Lt. Col. - Feb. 22, 1864. Paroled in Richmond. New Orleans merchant and President of the Board of Trade. d. July 6, 1909.

ESTES, JOHN BAYLUS. b. Anderson Dist., South Carolina, June 4, 1835. Jonesboro, Georgia, teacher. 6′0″. Capt., Co. D, 44th Georgia, Mar. 1862. Lt. Col. - Mar. 17, 1862. Colonel - June 26, 1862. Wded. at Ellerson's Mill, Seven Days. Res. due to wounds, May 26, 1863. In Georgia legisl. post-war, and circuit judge. d. Gainesville, Sept. 16, 1903.

ETHERIDGE, WILLIAM HENRY. b. Norfolk Co., July 27, 1820. Farmer and blacksmith. Capt., Co. F, 41st Virginia, Apr. 22, 1861 (he'd actually been commanding this unit for sometime before the war). Major - July 29, 1862. Appx. d. Norfolk, June 3, 1908. bur. Magnolia Cemetery. An article by him is in *Confederate Veteran*, XVI, p. 167. An officer in the 41st said of Etheridge: he "is always afraid of doing wrong. . . . The fact is, he is the wrong man in the wrong place."

EVANS, DUDLEY. b. Morgantown, Virginia, Jan. 27, 1838. gr. Washington & Jefferson College, 1859. 5'10". School teacher. In Virginia legisl., 1862. Capt.. Co. A, 20th Virginia Cavalry, Apr. 15, 1863. Lt. Col. - Aug. 14, 1863. Res. Nov. 22, 1864. m. Nellie Seelye, 1878 Wells Fargo agent in Oregon, then president of company in New York. d. Mar. 27, 1910, in New York City.

EVANS, JOHN WESLEY. m. Lucy Aurelia Beck, 1849. Lawyer in Early Co., age 32, in 1860, worth $34,000. Capt., Co. G, 1st Georgia, Mar. 18, 1861. Colonel, 64th Georgia, May 26, 1863. Wded. at Olustee. KIA at the Crater.

EVANS, JONATHAN. b. 1838. att. UNC. Of Cumberland Co. Capt., Co. G, 24th North Carolina, June 1, 1861. Major - July 16, 1861. Dropped at May 1862 re-org. m. Elizabeth Smith. Planter and journalist. d. Mar. 5, 1892. bur. in family cemetery near Cape Fear River in Cedar Creek Township.

EVANS, MOSES FORD THOMAS. b. South Carolina, June 1820. gr. U. Pennsylvania. Physician in Amelia Co., Virginia. Lt., Co. A, 14th Virginia, Apr. 22, 1861 (had held this rank since Dec. 1859). Adj. of regt., May 14, 1861. Lt. Col. - May 6, 1862. Wded. at Seven Pines and Malvern Hill. Res., health, Aug. 26, 1862. Amelia Co. Supt. of Schools. d. Jan. 16, 1877.

EVANS, PETER GUSTAVUS. b. Chatham Co., North Carolina, 1822. att. UNC. Planter. m. Ann Eliza Morehead, daughter of North Carolina governor. Capt., Co. E, 3rd North Carolina Cavalry, Oct. 7, 1861. Dropped at April 1862 re-org. Colonel, 5th North Carolina Cavalry, Oct. 1, 1862. MWIA at Middleburg, June 21, 1863. d. in enemy hands in Washington, D.C., July 24. bur. in Presbyterian Cemetery. Greensboro, North Carolina. Evans' daughter married General R. D. Johnston.

EVANS, STEPHEN B. b. Pitt Co., North Carolina. Farmer in Craven County. Lt., Co. E, 3rd North Carolina Cavalry, Oct. 7,

1861. Dropped at Apr. 1862 re-org. Capt., Co. B, 5th North Carolina Cavalry, June 12, 1862. Lt. Col. - Oct. 1, 1862. Retired to Invalid Corps, Jan. 28, 1865.

EVANS, TALIAFERRO SIDNEY. (A grandniece of Evans gave his name as Thomas Sidney, but the weight of evidence points strongly toward Taliaferro S. as his correct name). b. Abbeville Dist., South Carolina, Jan. 1827. Lawyer. Traveled from Miss. to Harpers Ferry on his own to join Co. H, 11th Mississippi. Major -Apr. 26, 1862. Wded. at Gaines' Mill. KIA at Sharpsburg.

EWELL, BENJAMIN STODDERT. b. Washington, D.C., June 10, 1810. gr. USMA, 1832. Instructor at USMA until 1836. Educator at Hampden-Sydney, Washington College and William & Mary. Colonel, 32nd Virginia, July 1, 1861. Dropped at May 1862 re-org., and joined J. E. Johnston's staff. Resigned, disability, Mar. 20, 1865. President of William & Mary. d. June 19, 1894 in Williamsburg. bur. on the grounds of the college.

EWERS, WILLIAM M. b. Amherst Co. Clerk in a Nelson Co. store in 1860, age 41. Capt., Co. H, 3rd Virginia Reserves, Apr. 16, 1864. Major - Sept. 30, 1864. Reported as absent without leave, Feb. 1865.

FAIN, RICHARD GAMMON. b. May 1811. Of Hawkins Co., Tennessee. gr. USMA, 1832. Lt. of Artillery, U.S. Army, for a few months in 1832. Teacher at a military institute. Major and Commissary, 1861. Colonel, 63rd Tennessee, July 30, 1862. Res. Nov. 3, 1863. d. Sept. 12, 1878. General Humphrey Marshall called Fain "a very smart fellow."

FAIR, ROBERT ANDERSON. b. Abbeville Dist., South Carolina, Dec. 12, 1820. Lawyer there. An 1854 address of his, urging distribution of Bibles to South Carolina slaves, was published. Lt. Col., 7th South Carolina, Apr. 15, 1861. Dropped at May 1862 re-org. In South Carolina legisl., 1862-1865. Pastor of Aveleigh Presbyterian Church, Newberry, South Carolina. Living in Richmond, Virginia, in 1890. d. Apr. 11, 1899, at Savannah, Georgia. bur. Upper Long Cane Presbyterian Church, Abbeville, South Carolina.

FAISON, FRANKLIN J. Planter in Sampson Co. b. Jan. 1, 1824. Capt., Co. A, 20th North Carolina, 1861. Lt. Col. - June 18,

1861, at org. KIA at Gaines' Mill, "manning a captured artillery piece . . . when the piece exploded." Wife - Ida M.

FAISON, PAUL FLETCHER. b. May 4, 1840. Of Northhampton Co., North Carolina. att. Randolph-Macon and USMA. Major, 14th North Carolina, May 28, 1861. Defeated at Apr. 1862 re-org. Colonel, 56th North Carolina, July 31, 1862. Appx. m. Annie Haywood (Bryan). In 1893 Faison was "Coordinator for Indian Affairs" at some unidentified location. d. March 3, 1896.

FALKNER, WILLIAM CLARK. b. Virginia, July 6, 1825 (this is the best of four different birth dates offered by various sources). Great-grandfather of noted literary figure William Faulkner, the family name spelling having altered since. m. Holland Pearce, 1847. Lt., 1st Mississippi, during the Mexican War. Author of three books. Railroad builder and entrepeneur. Capt., Co. F, 2nd Mississippi, Mar. 4, 1861. Colonel - May 10, 1861. Wded. at 1st Manassas. Dropped at Apr. 1862 re-org. Later raised the 7th Mississippi Cavalry. Assassinated Nov. 5, 1889, having just been elected to the state legisl. bur. Ripley Cemetery.

FARIBAULT, GEORGE H. Wake Co. planter. Capt., Co. E, 14th North Carolina, May 1, 1861, aged 31. Lt. Col., 47th North Carolina, Mar. 24, 1862. Colonel - Apr. 5, 1863. Wded. at Gettysburg. Res. Jan. 5, 1865, in ill health.

FARINHOLT, BENJAMIN LINES. b. Yorktown, Virginia, May 26, 1839. att. Randolph-Macon. Lived at West Point, Virginia. Capt., Co. E, 53rd Virginia, July 8, 1861. Lt. Col., Farinholt's Battalion Virginia Reserves, July 18, 1864. Colonel, 1st Virginia Reserves, Aug. 12, 1864. Wded. and POW at Gettysburg. Escaped from Johnson's Island, Feb. 22, 1864. A hero of the Battle of Staunton River Bridge. Merchant in Baltimore and West Point. d. West Point, Dec. 24, 1919.

FARIS, WILSON. b. Smyth Co., Virginia, Dec. 30, 1840. m. Mary Jane Durman, 1863. Sgt., Co. A, 48th Virginia, May 18, 1861. Lt., Co. D, 48th Virginia, Apr. 21, 1862. Captain - Oct. 16, 1862. Major - May 3,1863. Wded. at Sharpsburg, Chancellorsville and

C. J. Devett

GEORGE M. FERNEYHOUGH
35th Virginia Cavalry Battalion

Spotsylvania. Present into 1865. Smyth Co. farmer. d. Apr. 3, 1911, at Seven Mile Ford, Virginia. bur. there.

FARROW, THOMAS STOBO. b. Laurens Dist., South Carolina, Oct. 12, 1832. att. South Carolina College. m. (1) - Laura Henry, 1854. m. (2) - Jeannie Bedon, 1861. Spartanburg lawyer. Lt., "Spartan Rifles," Apr. 1861. Capt., Co. C, 13th South Carolina, Aug. 27, 1861. Major - Sept. 4, 1861. Lt. Col. - June 19, 1862. Wded. at 2nd Manassas. Res. to become Commissioner of Equity, Spartanburg Dist., Jan. 6, 1863. Lawyer in Atlanta and Spartanburg. Moved to Washington, D.C., in 1885 and became U.S. War Dept. auditor. Living there in 1900. Dead by 1910.

FAUNTLEROY, ROBERT BRUCE. b. 1832. gr. U. Maryland Medical School. Lt., Co. C, 55th Virginia, June 2, 1861. Captain - May 17, 1862. Major - Aug. 19, 1864. Wded. at Chancellorsville. In Virginia legisl., 1863-1865. Farmer and physician in Middlesex Co. d. 1907.

FEAGIN, ISAAC BALL. b. Jones Co., Georgia, July 17, 1833. Merchant in Midway, Alabama. Barbour Co., Alabama, deputy sheriff. Capt., Co. B, 15th Alabama, July 26, 1861. Lt. Col. - Apr. 28, 1863. Wded. at Shepherdstown, Sept. 19, 1862. Lost leg and POW at Gettysburg, exchanged Mar. 10, 1864. Acquitted of D. H. Hill's charges of cowardice at Sharpsburg. Retired to Invalid Corps, Dec. 7, 1864. Barbour Co. sheriff and judge. d. May 2, 1900.

FEENEY, WILLIAM A. Saddler in Senatobia, Mississippi. UDC Chapter there named for him. Lt., Co. I, 9th Mississippi, 1861-1862. Capt., Co. B, 42nd Mississippi, May 14, 1862. Major in Sept. 1862 (rank back-dated to May 14). Colonel - Dec. 18, 1863. KIA at Wilderness.

FEILD, EVERARD MEADE. b. Greensville Co., July 18, 1831. Feild attended a military school run by Maghee and Bryan. Capt., Co. F, 12th Virginia, June 6, 1861. Major - Aug. 30, 1862. Lt. Col. - Oct. 3, 1862. Colonel - July 30, 1864. Wded. three times. Petersburg merchant. d. Petersburg, July 17, 1915. Virginia Historical Society has his papers.

FEILD, WILLIAM MEADE. b. Brunswick Co., May 15, 1837. att. Hampden-Sydney and William & Mary. Lt., Co. I, 3rd Virginia Cavalry, May 29, 1861. Captain - Apr. 25, 1862. Lt. Col. - Feb. 4, 1865. Wded. at Haw's Shop and Five Forks. Appx. Treasurer of Dinwiddie Co. for decades. d. Dinwiddie Co., June 17, 1895.

FELTUS, ABRAM MORRELL. b. Woodville, Mississippi, Oct. 6, 1833. gr. U. Pennsylvania, 1854. Lt., Co. K, 16th Mississippi, Apr. 21, 1861. Captain - June 6, 1861. Lt. Col. - Dec. 20, 1862. KIA at Spotsylvania, May 12, 1864.

FEREBEE, DENNIS DOZIER. b. Currituck Co., Nov. 9, 1815. Camden Co. lawyer and planter. In North Carolina legisl. gr. UNC, 1839. Colonel 4th North Carolina Cavalry, Aug. 10, 1862. Wded. foot at Bristoe Station. Res. Mar. 24, 1865, to serve on Gov. Vance's staff. d. Apr. 26, 1884, in Camden Co. bur. family cemetery.

FERGUSON, MILTON J. b. Wayne Co. about 1833. Colonel, 167th Virginia Militia, 1861. Capt., Co. H, 16th Virginia Cavalry, Sept. 1862. This company and six others formed a bn. commanded by Captain Ferguson and known informally as Ferguson's Bn. The bn. was united with Caldwell's Bn. Virginia Cav. in Jan. 1863 to form the 16th Virginia Cav. Ferguson was made its Colonel, Jan. 15, 1863. POW at Wayne Co., Feb. 15, 1864. Wded. in head at 3rd Winchester, and several other times. Paroled at Charleston, West Virginia, May 22, 1865. Ferguson wore a military hat "covered . . . with gold bands and acorns hanging down on each side." Lawyer in Louisa, Kentucky. d. Apr. 22, 1881. bur. in family plot in Wayne Co., West Virginia.

FERGUSON, THOMAS B. b. Apr. 5, 1839. Sgt., Co. E, 6th South Carolina Cavalry, May 1, 1862. Major - Jan. 1, 1863. Wded. Mar. 10, 1865. d. Jan. 31, 1886. bur. Springwood Cemetery, Greenville.

FERNEYHOUGH, GEORGE M. b. Albermarle Co., 1839. att. U. Virginia. Lived in Washington, D.C. Capt., Co. F, 35th Virginia Cavalry Battalion, summer 1862. Major - Feb. 4, 1863. Res. Sept. 21, 1864. Albermarle Co. farmer. d. at the age of 36 years and 4 months.

FERRELL, MICKLEBERRY P. b. Ga. Farmer in Chambers Co., Alabama in 1860, age 25, worth $43,750. Capt., Co. F, 14th Alabama, June 27, 1861. Major - July 16, 1861. Res. Dec. 2, 1862, due to chronic diarrhea.

FICKLIN, BENJAMIN FRANKLIN. b. Dec. 18, 1827, in Albermarle Co. gr. VMI, 1849. Cpl. in the Mexican War. An organizer of the Pony Express Line. Lt. Col., 45th Virginia, June 17, 1861, but never joined the regt. nor accepted, and was thus dropped. Served in QM Dept. in Richmond, and as a "Foreign Commissioner." d. Georgetown, D.C., Mar. 10, 1871, from choking over dinner at the Willard Hotel.

FICKLING, WILLIAM HAMPTON. b. Crawford Co., 1834. Farmer in Taylor Co. m. Caroline Elisabeth Walker. Capt., Co. C, 59th Georgia, May 8, 1862. Major - Oct. 16, 1864. d. in Taylor Co., 1907.

FIELD, GEORGE. b. Greene Co., Alabama. Deputy sheriff there. Age 32 in 1860. Capt., Co. B, 11th Alabama, May 27, 1861. Major - May 7, 1862. Wded. at Frayser's Farm. Resigned Sept. 11, 1862, declaring himself "unfitted for the position." d. Eutaw, Alabama, 1866.

FIELDER, JAMES MONROE. b. Morgan Co., Nov. 24, 1816. m. Roxana Williamson. Farmer in Cherokee Co. in 1860. Capt., Co. D, 14th Georgia, July 9, 1861. Major - Oct. 23, 1862. Lt. Col. - Nov. 8, 1862. MWIA at Chancellorsville, d. May 10. bur. Hollywood.

FIFE, WILLIAM ESTILL. b. Charleston, Virginia, Feb. 7, 1834. gr. VMI, 1855. 5'10". Capt., Co. A, 36th Virginia, May 13, 1861. Major - Mar. 30, 1864. Lt. Col. - May 18, 1864. Wded. thigh Oct. 19, 1864. Charleston lawyer and judge. Killed in railroad accident, July 4, 1897.

FINNEY, WILLIAM WOOD. b. "Prospect Hill," Powhatan Co., Virginia, May 16, 1829. gr. VMI, 1848. Taught school in North Carolina. Went to Calif. for gold in 1850. Associated with B. F. Ficklin (q.v.) in establishing Pony Express Line, and ran its Sacramento office. Lt. Col., 50th Virginia, July 3, 1861. Dropped at May 1862 re-org. Lt. Col., 189th Virginia Militia, 1862. Be-

Alabama State Archives

ISAAC B. FEAGIN
15th Alabama

came purser on the blockade runner *Robert E. Lee.* Powhatan farmer and civil engineer. Ran Old Point Comfort Hotel. d. Petersburg, Jan. 26, 1910. bur. St. Luke's Churchyard.

FISHER, CHARLES FREDERICK. b. Salisbury, Dec. 26, 1816. att. Yale. Planter and railroad president. Editor, *Western Carolinian.* In North Carolina legisl. Colonel, 6th North Carolina, May 16, 1861. KIA at Manassas. bur. Old Lutheran Cemetery, Salisbury, North Carolina.

FITE, JOHN AMENAS. b. DeKalb Co., Tennessee, Feb. 10, 1832. gr. Cumberland U., 1855. Lawyer. Capt., Co. B, 7th Tennessee, May 20, 1861. Major - May 23, 1862. Lt. Col. - July 9, 1862. Colonel - Apr. 8, 1863. Wded. at Mechanicsville, Cedar Mountain and Chancellorsville. POW at Gettysburg, held until 1865. Smith Co. banker, judge, state legisl. Adjutant General of Tennessee. d. Lebanon, Tennessee, Aug. 23, 1925. bur. Cedar Grove Cemetery.

FITZGERALD, JOHN PATERSON. b. Nottoway C.H., May 15, 1837. gr. Hampden-Sydney, 1857. att. U. Virginia. Lawyer. Lt., Co. I, 23rd Virginia, May 21, 1861. Captain - July 28, 1861. Major - June 10, 1863. Lt. Col. - Nov. 27, 1863. POW at Spotsylvania. Appx. Treasurer of Hampden-Sydney. d. Farmville, June 10, 1898. bur. Westview Cemetery.

FITZGERALD, WILLIAM HENRY. b. Wilmington, North Carolina, Sept. 29, 1830. Lawyer. 6′0″. m. Frances Wilmoth Harvey, 1862. Capt., Co. F, 21st Mississippi, June 25, 1861. Major - Oct. 30, 1863. Lt. Col. - Oct. 19, 1864. POW at Sayler's Creek, released June 18. In Mississippi legisl. d. Friars Point, Mississippi, June 18, 1904.

FITZHUGH, HENRY, JR. b. Fauquier Co., Virginia, Jan. 10, 1830. Charleston banker and lawyer. Maj., 8th Virginia Cavalry, Mar. 1, 1862. Lt. Col. - Mar. 22, 1862. Not re-elected at re-org. Major, a.a.g. to Loring, 1862. Went to England on Confederate business, 1864. New York City banker and Chicago gas businessman. d. New York City, Apr. 10, 1891 (the last digit of the death year is blurred and uncertain).

FITZHUGH, PATRICK HENRY. b. 1818. Lived on Virginia's Eastern Shore, moved to Gloucester Co. and farmed there. m. (1) a Miss Clark. m. (2) Mary Steptoe Christian. Capt., Co. B, 26th Virginia, Apr. 23, 1861. Major - Oct. 15, 1863. MWIA at Taylor's Farm, June 18, 1864, died in enemy hands.

FIZER, JOHN CALVIN. b. Dyer Co., Tennessee, May 4, 1838. Lived with an uncle in Panola Co., Miss. Lt., Co. H, 17th Mississippi, May 27, 1861. Adj. of regt., June 7, 1861. Lt. Col. - Apr. 26, 1862. Colonel - Feb. 26, 1864. Wded. at Gettysburg. Lost right arm at Knoxville. Retired, disability, June 12, 1864. Memphis merchant. d. there June 15, 1876. A member of the regiment described Fizer as "a great favorite with the souldiers." McLaws urged Fizer's promotion to brigadier general on the basis of his "good cool judgement in a fight inspiring his men & taking care of them."

FLEMING, DAVID GEORGE. b. Columbia, Apr. 1832. gr. SCMA. Civil engineer in the West. Lt. and Capt., 1st South Carolina Artillery. Colonel, 22nd South Carolina, June 2, 1864. KIA at the Crater, July 30, 1864. Body never found. Died unmarried.

FLEMING, WILLIAM OLIVER. b. Liberty Co., Apr. 2, 1835. att. Franklin College. Lt., Co. G, 1st Georgia, Mar. 18, 1861. Lt., Co. F, 50th Georgia, Mar. 4, 1862. Captain - Oct. 8, 1862. Major - Feb. 24, 1863. Lt. Col. - July 31, 1863. Res. to enter Georgia legisl., Dec. 22, 1863. Judge. d. Bainbridge, Nov. 4, 1881. Fleming's papers are at UNC. A subordinate called him "a fine Georgia gentleman, but a little timid."

FLEMMING, JOHN A. b. McDowell Co. Farmer. 5′9″. Pvt., Co. E, 1st North Carolina, April 1861. Capt., Co. A, 49th North Carolina, Feb. 15, 1862, aged 25. Major - June 19, 1862. Lt. Col. - Nov. 1, 1862. KIA at the Crater.

FLETCHER, RICHARD J. b. Uniontown, Alabama, 1834. att. VMI, 1856 class, from Hicks Ford, Virginia. Teacher in Washington Co., Ala. Capt., Co. E, 11th Alabama, June 11, 1861. Major - Sept. 11, 862. Lost leg at Gettysburg. Retired to Invalid Corps, Sept. 7, 1864. d. ca. 1895 or 1896 in Calif.

FLOURNOY, CABELL EDWARD. b. June 30, 1840, in Halifax Co. att. Washington College. Lived in Pittsylvania Co. Capt., Co. E, 6th Virginia Cavalry, May 27, 1861. Major - July 15, 1862. KIA at Cold Harbor, May 31, 1864. Buried in family cemetery near Rte. 729, Halifax Co. Son of Colonel Thomas S. Flournoy.

FLOURNOY, THOMAS STANHOPE. b. Prince Edward Co., Dec. 15, 1811. gr. Hampden-Sydney, 1831. Lawyer. m. (1) Susan Ann Love, 1835. m. (2) Mildred H. Coles, 1852. U.S. Congressman. Capt., Co. G, 6th Virginia Cavalry, Aug. 19, 1861. Colonel - July 16, 1862. Res. Oct. 15, 1862. Lawyer in Danville. d. Halifax Co., Mar. 12, 1883. bur. family cemetery.

FLOWERREE, CHARLES CONWAY. b. Fauquier Co., Virginia, Oct. 26, 1842. att. VMI. 5′11″. Actg. Adj., 7th Virginia, summer 1861. Major - Apr. 27, 1862. Lt. Col. - June 3, 1862. Colonel - July 21, 1863. Wded. at 2nd Manassas. POW at Sayler's Creek, released July 28. Moved to Vicksburg, Mississippi, in 1866. President, Vicksburg Ice Co. d. Sept. 16, 1929 in Vicksburg, and is buried there. One soldier writing in 1863 called Flowerree "the most immodest obscene profane low flung blackguard on this earth."

FLOWERS, GEORGE WASHINGTON. b. Alexander Co., North Carolina, Apr. 25, 1842. Teacher. 5′11″. Lt., Co. G, 38th North Carolina, Nov. 21, 1861. Captain - Apr. 18, 1862. Major - Feb. 16, 1864. Lt. Col. - June 18, 1864. Wded. at Mechanicsville and Wilderness. Appx. m. Sallie J. Haynes, 1870. Taylorsville merchant. d. Durham, 1918.

FLOWERS, JOHN Y. b. July 6, 1815. Large farmer at Doraville. Sheriff of DeKalb Co. Capt., Co. A, 38th Georgia, Sept. 26, 1861. Major - Feb. 14, 1862. Resigned due to hernia, July 15, 1862. d. Aug. 6, 1887. bur. Nancy Creek Baptist Church, Atlanta.

FLOYD, RICHARD FERNADINA. b. July 7, 1810, in Georgia. m. Mary Ann Chevalier, 1831. Farmer in St. Johns Co., Florida, in 1860, worth $40,200. Floyd had served as Colonel then Brigadier General of State Troops in 1861-1862. Colonel, 8th Florida, July 15, 1862. Resigned due to "severe illness," Oct. 2, 1862. d. Green Cove Springs, June 27, 1870.

FLOYD, WATT W. AQM, 17th Tennessee, June 1861. Lt. Col. - May 16, 1862. KIA at Drewry's Bluff, May 16, 1864.

FLYNT, TILGHMAN WILLIS. b. Monroe Co., Feb. 24, 1827. McDonough lawyer. m. Martha Jane Turner. Capt., Co. G, 19th Georgia, July 2, 1861. Lt. Col. - Aug. 20, 1863. Wded. leg at Sharpsburg. Retired to Invalid Corps, Sept. 17, 1864. Griffin lawyer and farmer. d. Aug. 1, 1908. bur. McDonough.

FOLSOM, ROBERT WARREN. b. Aug. 28, 1835. Physician. Unmarried. Capt., Co. B, 14th Georgia, July 9, 1861. Major - Aug. 1, 1861. Lt. Col. - Sept. 1, 1861. Colonel - Oct. 23, 1862. MWIA through the body at Wilderness, d. in Richmond May 24. bur. Hollywood.

FONTAINE, CLEMENT R. b. Buckingham Co., 1832. att. U. Virginia. Lt., Co. A, 57th Virginia, May 29, 1861. Captain - Apr. 24, 1862. Major - Feb. 4, 1863. WIA at Gettysburg. Colonel - July 5, 1863. Paroled at Columbia, Virginia, May 3, 1865. Wytheville teacher. d. Wythe Co., Apr. 8, 1906. A member of the 57th wrote in 1863 that Fontaine "does not possess . . . great interlectual [sic] endowments."

FORBES, WILLIAM ARCHIBALD. b. May 31, 1824. gr. VMI, 1842. President, Clarksville College, Tennessee. Capt., Co. A, 14th Tennessee, 1861. Colonel - June 6, 1861. MWIA at 2nd Manassas, Aug. 30, 1862. d. Sept. 2.

FORD, CHARLES HENRY. "An experienced English officer." "Said to be an ex-cavalry officer of the English army." Clerk and Assistant Master Armorer at the Richmond Armory. "Over six feet high." Maj., 1st Virginia Battalion LDT ("Armory Bn."), Aug. 6, 1863. Resigned July 26, 1864.

FORD, FRANCIS MARION. b. Dickson Co., Tennessee, 1832. m. Fanny Barber. Capt., Co. H, 18th Georgia, June 13, 1861. Lt. Col. - Mar. 25, 1864. Paroled at Kingston, Georgia, May 12, 1865. In Georgia legisl. Cartersville merchant and mayor. d. there Sept. 21, 1903.

FORNO, HENRY. b. Louisiana, 1797. Louisiana officer in Mexican War. New Orleans police chief in 1850's. Wife - Maria. Lt. Co., 5th Louisiana, May 10, 1861. Colonel - July 31, 1862. Wded. at 2nd Manassas. Present at least into 1864. On recruiting service at Mobile late in the war. d. Jan. 31, 1866 in railroad accident at Amite City, Louisiana.

FORSBERG, AUGUSTUS. b. Stockholm, Sweden, Jan. 13, 1832. Swedish Army engineer, came to America in 1850's on an engineering contract. m. Mrs. Mollie Otey. 5'9". Lt. of infantry, P.A.C.S., Nov. 11, 1861. Served on Floyd's staff. Lt. Col., 51st Virginia, May 26, 1862. Colonel - July 8, 1863. POW at Waynesboro, Mar. 2, 1865, released July 24. Lynchburg engineer. d. Lynchburg, July 15, 1910. A descendant of Forsberg says his name was actually Ludwig August Forsberg. He is buried under that name in Presbyterian Cemetery, Lynchburg. Forsberg's papers are at Washington and Lee.

FORSYTH, CHARLES. b. Alabama. Clerk in Mobile in 1860, age 24. Lt., Co. A, 3rd Alabama, Apr. 23, 1861. Adj. of regt., Apr. 28, 1861. Major - Aug. 15, 1861. Lt. Col. - May 31, 1862. Colonel - Aug. 20, 1863. Wounded in ankle at Gettysburg. Wounded in thigh, May 12, 1864.

FOSTER, BARHAM BOBO. b. Spartanburg Dist., Jan. 22, 1817. m. Mary Ann Perrin, 1837. In South Carolina Secession Convention. Lt. Col., 3rd South Carolina, Feb. 6, 1861. Resigned Jan. 30, 1862, "health failed." Glenn Springs farmer. d. Jonesville, South Carolina, June 9, 1897.

FOSTER, WILLIAM MOULTRIE. b. Spartanburg Dist., July 28, 1825. m. Sarah Lettice Surratt. In South Carolina legisl. Maj., 5th South Carolina, Apr. 23, 1862. Resigned Dec. 24, 1862. Baptist preacher. d. Spartanburg Co., Apr. 1915.

FOSTER, WILLIAM R. b. Dinwiddie Co. Farmer there in 1860, unmarried, age 26. Lt., Co. B, 5th Virginia Battalion, May 1, 1861. Major - May 22, 1862. Died June 1862.

FOWLE, DANIEL GOULD. b. Washington, North Carolina, Mar. 3, 1831. att. Princeton. Major and Commissary, 1861. Lt.

Col., 31st North Carolina, Sept. 19, 1861. POW at Roanoke Island, Feb. 8, 1862. Dropped at spring 1862 re-org. Became Adjutant General of North Carolina. In North Carolina legisl. during the war. Governor post-war. d. Raleigh, Apr. 7, 1891. bur. Oakwood Cemetery.

FRANCIS, JOHN W. b. Roane Co., Tennessee, June 24, 1813. Of Cherokee Co., North Carolina. Capt., Co. D, 25th North Carolina, Aug. 20, 1861. Major - May 21, 1862. Resigned Dec. 6, 1862, for family reasons. Wded. at Seven Days. In North Carolina legisl. late in war. Merchant in Rusk, Texas, post-war. d. Rusk, May 9, 1902. bur. Cedar Hill Cemetery there.

FRANKLIN, ALEXANDER H. b. Georgia. Farmer in Neshoba Co. in 1860, worth $4,900. Capt., Co. D, 11th Mississippi, Apr. 24, 1861, aged 36. Lt. Col. - Jan. 12, 1863. "Dismissed," Feb. 1863.

FRAZER, PHILIP FOUKE. b. Greenbrier Co., Dec. 22, 1844. att. VMI. Lt., Co. E, 27th Virginia, Aug. 25, 1861. Captain - Apr. 23, 1862. Major - Sept. 4, 1863. KIA at Wilderness, well short of his 20th birthday.

FREDERICK, JAMES DANIEL. b. South Carolina, June 3, 1827. gr. U. Georgia, 1850, entering from Marshallville, Georgia. Planter. Capt., Co. A, 10th Georgia Battalion, Mar. 4, 1862. Major - June 1864. In Georgia legisl. d. June 24, 1899. bur. Marshallville Cemetery.

FRENCH, WILLIAM HENDERSON. b. Giles Co., 1812. Lived in Princeton, Virginia. In Virginia legisl. Sheriff of Giles Co. Capt., Co. D, 8th Virginia Cavalry (later became Co. A, 17th Virginia Cavalry), July 31, 1861. Colonel, 17th Virginia Cavalry, Jan. 28, 1863. Res. Sept. 3, 1864. d. Mercer Co., July 16, 1872. Never married.

FROBEL, BUSHROD WASHINGTON. b. 1826 near Alexandria, Virginia. Civil engineer. In the U.S. Revenue Service pre-war. Apptd. to C.S. Navy from Virginia. Transferred from the Navy as Captain of Artillery, Oct. 7, 1861, and served along the Potomac under Whiting. Chief of Artillery, Hood's Division. Major -

July 24, 1862. Lt. Col. - June 15, 1863. Served in North Carolina with Whiting, 1863-1864. On duty with C.S. Engineers in Aug. 1864, at Army of Tennessee headquarters. m. Mary Compton, 1868. Supt. of Public Works in Georgia and railroad executive. d. July 12, 1888, in Monticello, Georgia.

FRY, HUGH WALKER, JR. b. Fredericksburg, Virginia, Apr. 14, 1826. Richmond merchant. Maj., 46th Virginia, June 24, 1861. POW at Roanoke Island, Feb. 1862. Maj., Fry's Battalion Virginia Volunteers (a temporary organization) in 1862. d. Richmond, Oct. 22, 1875.

FRY, WILLIAM HUGH (middle name sometimes given as Henry, though with slightly less authority). b. Fredericksburg, Virginia, Oct. 8, 1821. m. Jane Margaret Watson, 1841. Merchant in Richmond. Capt., Richmond Light Infantry Blues prewar. Lt. Col., 1st Virginia, Sept. 18, 1861. Res. Nov. 11, 1861. Served later at Charlottesville camp of military instruction, and then in the Bureau of Conscription at Richmond. d. Coyner's Springs, Virginia, Sept. 8, 1902. bur. Hollywood Cemetery, Richmond.

FULKERSON, ABRAHAM. b. Washington Co., Virginia, May 13, 1834. gr. VMI. 6′1″. Teacher at Rogersville, Tenn. Captain then Major, 19th Tennessee. Lt. Col., 63rd Tennessee, July 20, 1862. Colonel - Nov. 9, 1863. Wded. at Chickamauga. POW at Petersburg, June 17, 1864, released July 21, 1865. In U.S. Congress post-war. d. Bristol, Virginia, Dec. 17, 1902. bur. East Hill Cemetery.

FULKERSON, SAMUEL VANCE. b. Washington Co., Virginia, Oct. 31, 1822. Brother of Col. Abraham Fulkerson. Mexican War officer. Estellville lawyer, and circuit court judge, Colonel, 37th Virginia, May 28, 1861. KIA at Gaines' Mill. bur. Abingdon. Fulkerson was "a great favorite" of Stonewall Jackson, who cried when told of his death.

FULKERSON, WILLIAM H. Of Claiborne Co., Tennessee. Showed residences at Rogersville and in Hawkins County. Capt., Co. A, 63rd Tennessee, Apr. 15, 1862. Major - Nov. 9,

Ben Ritter

JOHN HENRY STOVER FUNK
5th Virginia Infantry

1863. Lt. Col. - May 16, 1864. Aged 34 in Apr. 1864. Wded. at Chickamauga. Retired Oct. 24, 1864.

FULTON, JOHN S. b. Fayetteville, Tennessee, Mar. 31, 1828. Lawyer. Pvt., Co. F, 44th Tennessee, Mar. 27, 1862. Captain - Apr. 14, 1862. Major - Apr. 19, 1862. Colonel, May 5, 1862. Wded. at Murfreesboro. Commanding Johnson's Brigade in late 1863. MWIA near Petersburg, June 30, 1864, d. July 4.

FULTON, SAUNDERS F. Of Stokes Co. Lt., Co. G, 21st North Carolina, May 30, 1861, aged 24. Major - Apr. 26, 1862. Lt. Col. - May 25, 1862. KIA at 2nd Manassas. Fulton was described as being "a man . . . absolutely without fear."

FUNK, JOHN HENRY STOVER. b. Winchester, June 28, 1837. gr. Winchester Medical College, 1860. Practiced in Marion Co. Capt., Co. A, 5th Virginia, Apr. 28, 1861. Lt. Col. - Apr. 21, 1862. Colonel - Aug. 29, 1862. MWIA on Sept. 19, 1864, died in enemy lines at Winchester on Sept. 21. bur. Mt. Hebron Cemetery, Winchester.

FUNSTEN, DAVID. b. Clarke Co., Oct. 14, 1819. gr. Princeton. Alexandria lawyer. In Virginia legisl. Lt. Col., 11th Virginia, May 16, 1861. Colonel - May 23, 1862. Severe foot wound at Seven Pines led to Funsten's resignation, Sept. 24, 1863. In C.S. Congress. d. near Alexandria, Apr. 6, 1866. bur. Ivy Hill Cemetery.

FUNSTEN, OLIVER RIDGEWAY, SR. b. Clarke Co., Virginia, Apr. 15, 1817. gr. U. Pennsylvania, 1837. In Virginia legisl. Clarke Co. physician. m. (1) Mary Catherine Meade. m. (2) May Bowen. Captain and a.d.c. at Harpers Ferry, May 3, 1861. Major, 7th Virginia Cavalry, July 17, 1861. Lt. Col., 17th Virginia Cavalry Battalion, Oct. 14, 1862. Colonel, 11th Virginia Cavalry, July 23, 1863. Res. Feb. 21, 1865. d. near Winchester, July 14, 1871.

GADBERRY, JAMES M. b. North Carolina, ca. 1818. A tinworker, with little education, but in South Carolina legisl. Lawyer. Mexican War veteran. Very tall. Capt., Co. E, 1st South Carolina 1861. Pvt., Co. B, 18th South Carolina, Dec. 17, 1861. Colonel, 18th South Carolina, Jan. 2, 1862. KIA at 2nd Manassas. bur. in Union, South Carolina, in Presbyterian Churchyard.

GAILLARD, FRANKLIN. b. Pineville, Apr. 26, 1829. gr. South Carolina College, 1849. Editor at Columbia and Winnsboro. m. Catherine C. Porcher, 1853. Went to California during the gold rush. Lt., Co. A, 2nd South Carolina, Apr. 8, 1861. Major - May 14, 1862. Lt. Col. - June 3, 1863. Wded. at Fredericksburg. KIA at Wilderness. bur. Fredericksburg Confederate Cemetery. Gaillard's papers are at UNC.

GAILLARD, PETER CHEVES. b. South Carolina, Dec. 29, 1812. gr. USMA, 1835. Lt., U.S. Army, 1835-1838. Major, Charleston Battalion (South Carolina) Infantry, Apr. 1862. Colonel, 27th South Carolina, Oct. 1863. Retired to Invalid Corps, Mar. 6, 1865, having been disabled by a shell wound at Battery Wagner. d. Jan. 11, 1889. bur. Magnolia Cemetery, Charleston. Several sources render Gaillard's middle name as Charles.

GAINES, JAMES LUTTRELL. b. Knoxville, Tennessee, Dec. 3, 1839. att. UNC. Lived in Buncombe Co., North Carolina. Lt., Co. G, 1st North Carolina Cavalry, Aug. 15, 1861. Lt. and Adj. of regt., Apr. 15, 1862. Wded. June 29, 1862. Capt. and a.a.g. on staff of L. S. Baker, Sept. 2, 1863. Lt. Col. on Baker's staff, July 23, 1863, then on Barringer's staff in 1864. Transferred to command of 2nd North Carolina Cavalry, as Lt. Col., Mar. 1, 1865. Lost arm at Chamberlain Run, Mar. 31, 1865. State Comptroller of Tennessee post-war. Manager of Tennessee C.I. Railroad Company.

GALLAWAY, JOHN MARION. b. Rockingham Co., Dec. 13, 1835. gr. UNC, 1854. Farmer. Capt., Co. D, 5th North Carolina Cavalry, Aug. 1, 1862. Major - Mar. 1865. Wded. at Plymouth, Dec. 10, 1862, and at Weldon R.R., Aug. 21, 1864. Paroled at Greensboro, May 12, 1865. Lumberman in Tennessee. m. Mary Haviland Lawson, 1873. In North Carolina legisl. Rockingham Co. Commissioner, 1885-1895. Madison, North Carolina, mayor and banker. d. July 21, 1909, in Madison. bur. family cemetery.

GALLOWAY, THOMAS SPRAGGINS, JR. b. June 18, 1840. att. UNC. gr. VMI, 1861. Major, 22nd North Carolina, July 11,

1861. Wded. at Seven Pines. Defeated at June 1862 re-org. Became Capt., 45th North Carolina, Feb. 27, 1863. Colonel, 22nd North Carolina, Sept. 21, 1863. Appx. Lawyer in Somerville, Tennessee. m. Minerva Allison Greenlee. d. May 23, 1903. bur. Old Episcopal Church Cemetery, Arlington, Shelby Co., Tennessee.

GAMBLE, ROGER LAWSON. b. Jefferson Co., April 27, 1829. Planter in Louisville, worth $210,000 in 1860. m. Martha R. Gobert. Capt., Co. C, 20th Georgia, June 14, 1861. Major - Mar. 7, 1862. Res. June 14, 1862. d. March 6, 1893. bur. Louisville Cemetery.

GANTT, FREDERICK HAY. b. Oct. 10, 1833. att. SCMA. Lived in Barnwell District. Lt., Co. K, 11th South Carolina, Sept. 7, 1861. Lt. Col. - May 3, 1862. Colonel - Nov. 27, 1862. Paroled at Augusta, May 18, 1865. "A good drill officer." South Carolina State Solicitor, 1876-1885. d. Nov. 10, 1885. Never married.

GANTT, HENRY. b. 1831. gr. VMI, 1851, from Scottsville, Virginia. m. Pattie Eppes. Major, 19th Virginia, May 17, 1861. Lt. Col. - Apr. 29, 1862. Colonel - Sept. 14, 1862. Wded. at 2nd Manassas and Gettysburg. Paroled at Columbia, Virginia, Apr. 1865. Farmer. d. Albermarle Co., 1884.

GARDNER, JAMES. Law student in Talbotton, Georgia, in 1860, age 21. gr. U. Georgia, 1860. m. Virginia Persons. Sgt., Co. A, 4th Georgia, Apr. 26, 1861. Discharged Nov. 16, 1861. Adj., 27th Georgia, Dec. 24, 1861. Severely wded. at Malvern Hill. Major - May 2, 1863, "Valor & Skill." Lt. Col. - Apr. 1, 1864. MWIA in left eye at Petersburg, June 18, 1864. d. June 25.

GARDNER, ROBERT DAVISON. b. Dec. 22, 1830. Served with Virginia Regt. in Mexican War. Lt., Co. C, 4th Virginia, Apr. 17, 1861. Captain - July 25, 1861. Lt. Col. - Apr. 22, 1862. Wded. at Sharpsburg. Wded. in jaw and lung at Fredericksburg. Retired Apr. 9, 1864. Clerk of Pulaski Co. Courts. d. Dublin, Virginia, July 12, 1906. bur. Newbern Cemetery.

GARDNER, THOMAS N. b. North Carolina. Lawyer in Brunswick, Georgia, in 1860, age 41. Lt., Co. K, 26th Georgia, May 29, 1861. Major - Aug. 24, 1861. Retired May 8, 1862.

GARLINGTON, ALBERT CRESSWELL. b. Oglethorpe Co., Georgia, June 9, 1822. gr. U. Georgia, 1842, with first honors. In South Carolina legisl., 1854-1867. Major, Holcombe Legion (South Carolina), Dec. 19, 1861. Res. May 21, 1862. Adj. Genl. of South Carolina during the war. Brigadier General of South Carolina State Troops. d. Newberry, Mar. 25, 1885. bur. Rosemont Cemetery.

GARLINGTON, BENJAMIN CONWAY. b. Laurens Court House, South Carolina, Nov. 4, 1836. att. South Carolina College and U. Virginia. Capt., Co. A, 3rd South Carolina, Apr. 14, 1861 (had been Capt. of South Carolina Troops since Jan. 7). Major - early 1862. Lt. Col. - May 14, 1862. KIA at Savage Station.

GARNETT, JOHN JAMESON. b. Westmoreland Co., Virginia, May 1839. att. USMA. Lt. of artillery, P.A.C.S., Mar. 16, 1861. Lt., 3rd Co., Washington Artillery (Louisiana), June 20, 1861. Resigned June 16, 1862, to accept appt. as Major of Artillery in D. R. Jones' Division. Apptd. "Inspector of Ordnance and Artillery of Longstreet's Corps," Nov. 14, 1862. Lt. Col., commanding artillery bn., Apr. 4, 1863. "Suspended" by R. E. Lee, Feb. 18, 1864. Relieved from duty with A.N. Va., Apr. 1, 1864. Commanded post at Hicksford, Virginia, 1864. Inspector of artillery, Army of Tennessee, Nov. 1864. Wrote a Gettysburg Cyclorama guide, and biographical sketches of Lee and Grant. New York newspaper editor, living at Baldwin, Long Island. Committed suicide in New York City, Sept. 10, 1902.

GARNETT, THOMAS STUART. b. Westmoreland Co., Virginia, Apr. 19, 1825. att. VMI. gr. U. Virginia. Physician in New Kent Co. and Bowling Green. m. Emma L. Baber, 1848. Lt. in Mexican War. Capt., Co. C, 9th Virginia Cavalry, May 1861. Soon thereafter became Lt. Col., 48th Virginia. Colonel - Oct. 16, 1862. Wded. at Cedar Mountain. MWIA at Chancellorsville, May 3, 1863, d. 10:30 a.m. May 4, 1863. bur. Hollywood. Garnett also has a marker in a family cemetery on the Northern Neck at "Spy Hill," King George Co. His war letters are at the Virginia State Library.

GARRETT, JOSHUA LEIGH. b. Gloucester Co., Virginia, Jan. 31, 1831. gr. Wm. & Mary. Capt., Co. A, 26th Virginia, Apr. 20, 1861. Major - May 13, 1862. Res. Oct. 15, 1863, due to deafness from shell explosion. Did some chaplain service. m. Sallie Hays. Methodist minister and farmer. d. Harrellsville, North Carolina, while fighting a fire, May 1883.

GARRETT, THOMAS MILES. b. Hertford Co., June 13, 1830. gr. UNC. Bertie Co. lawyer. Capt., Co. F, 5th North Carolina, May 16, 1861. Colonel - Jan. 16, 1863. Wded. at Sharpsburg and Chancellorsville. POW at Sharpsburg. Arrested by D. K. McRae on several petty charges, but cleared. KIA at Spotsylvania, May 12, 1864.

GARVIN, JOHN SPRINGER. Attorney and editor in Tuscaloosa in 1860, age 33. Adj., 26th Alabama, Sept. 26, 1861. Major - Nov. 16, 1861. Lt. Col. - Apr. 23, 1862. Wded. at Chancellorsville and Franklin. POW at Ft. Donelson, returned Oct. 28, 1862. bur. City Cemetery, West Point, Mississippi.

GAYLE, BRISTOR B. b. Portsmouth, Virginia, Apr. 19, 1839. gr. Virginia Military and Collegiate Institute in Portsmouth. Teacher at Summerville, Alabama. Capt., Co. H, 12th Alabama, July 8, 1861. Colonel - June 1, 1862. KIA at South Mountain, Sept. 14, 1862. bur. Washington Confederate Cemetery, Hagerstown, Maryland.

GEE, BOLIVAR HOPKINS. b. 1824 in South Carolina. m. Margaret Susan McElveen, 1856. Farmer in Decatur Co., Georgia, in 1860, worth $23,000. In Georgia Secession Convention. Lt., Co. K, 1st Georgia State Troops, 1861. Capt., Co. A, 59th Georgia, May 3, 1862. Major - Dec. 22, 1862. Lt. Col. - July 10, 1863. Wded. severely in the arm at Wilderness. Appx. d. Mitchell County, Georgia, 1888.

GEE, JOHN HENRY. b. 1819. Physician. Major, 4th Florida Battalion, May 2, 1863. Major, 11th Florida, June 11, 1864, but declined. Commanded at Salisbury POW Camp, 1864-1865. Tried by the Yankees post-war on the basis of camp operations, but acquitted. Killed while fighting a fire in Quincy, Florida, Aug. 13, 1876.

H. E. Howard

ROBERT DAVISON GARDNER
4th Virginia Infantry

GEORGE, FORNEY. b. Columbus Co., North Carolina, Jan. 8, 1830. gr. UNC. Lawyer and planter at Whiteville. Capt., Co. C, 18th North Carolina, Apr. 26, 1861, aged 32. Major - Mar. 6, 1862. Lt. Col. - Nov. 11, 1862. Resigned May 11, 1863, to serve in North Carolina legisl. Wded. at Cedar Mountain and Chancellorsville. Trustee at UNC in 1879.

GEORGE, NEWTON J. Of Lincoln Co., Tennessee. Lt., Co. H, 1st Tennessee, Apr. 29, 1861, aged 21. Capt., Co. H, 1st Tennessee, at re-org., Apr. 27, 1862. Lt. Col. - June 27, 1862. POW at Gettysburg, paroled June 19, 1865. Minister to a South American country during Cleveland's administration.

GERALD, GEORGE BRUCE. b. Yazoo Co., Mississippi, 1836. att. Indiana U. m. Omega Melton, 1857. Capt., Co. F, 18th Mississippi, Apr. 27, 1861. Major - May 5, 1863. Wded. at Cedar Creek. County judge and postmaster of Waco, Texas, moving there in 1869. In Texas legisl. Edited Waco newspaper. In 1897 Gerald engaged in a gunfight in Waco with two Harris brothers, one of whom was a rival newspaper editor; he killed both Harrisses. d. Jan. 21, 1914. His cremated ashes were spread over the Gulf of Mexico.

GHOLSON, MILTON G. b. Cumberland Co., Ky., Mar. 11, 1814. Planter in Montgomery Co., Tennessee. Capt., Co. B, 14th Tennessee, 1861. Lt. Col. - June 6, 1861. Res. Oct. 1861. Brig. Genl. of Tennessee Militia later in war. d. Montgomery Co., Jan. 18, 1883.

GHOLSTON, JAMES S. b. Madison Co., Georgia. Farmer at Danielsville in 1860, age 48, worth $19,000. m. Mary Daniel. State Senator. Member of Secession Convention. Capt., Co. A, 16th Georgia, July 11, 1861. Major - Feb. 1, 1862. Lt. Col. - Aug. 16, 1864. Retired to Invalid Corps, Aug. 24, 1864. Paroled at Athens, May 8, 1865. Georgia legislator and judge post-war. d. 1888.

GIBBES, WADE HAMPTON. b. Columbia, Apr. 3, 1837. gr. USMA, 1860. Lt., U.S. Cavalry, 1860-1861. m. Jane Allen Mason. Served in western Virginia with Wise, got typhoid fever. Went west on Heth's staff. Got more typhoid while at Wilmington with Whiting. Major, 13th Bn. Virginia Artillery, Apr. 1864. Disabled at the Crater. Businessman and public official in Richland Co., South Carolina. d. June 12, 1903, in South Carolina. bur. Trinity Episcopal Church, Columbia.

GIBBONS, SIMEON BEAUFORD. b. Page Co., May 25, 1833. gr. VMI. Colonel, 10th Virginia, July 1, 1861. KIA at McDowell. bur. Woodbine Cemetery, Harrisonburg. Copies of Gibbons' war letters are at the Georgia Archives.

GIBBS, GEORGE COOPER. b. St. Simons Island, Georgia, Apr. 7, 1822. Planter in Quincy, Florida. Mexican War officer from Louisiana. Capt. of infantry, apptd. from Florida, May 20, 1861. Commandant at Salisbury POW camp, 1861. Colonel, 42nd North Carolina, Apr. 22, 1862. Res. Jan. 7, 1864. Later was Col., 2nd Georgia Reserves, and served at Andersonville. Paroled at Washington, D.C., June 16, 1865. Subpoenaed to appear in Wirz trial. m. Julia Williams. d. St. Augustine, Florida, Feb. 18, 1873.

GIBSON, AURELIUS W. Farmer in Knoxville, Georgia, in 1860, age 27, married, worth $20,000. Capt., Co. K, 45th Georgia, Mar. 4, 1862. Major - Dec. 2, 1864. Wded. at Frayser's Farm and Wilderness. POW at Petersburg, Mar. 25, 1865, released July 24.

GIBSON, JOHN ALEXANDER. b. Rockbridge Co., Sept. 5, 1833. att. Washington College. 6'0". Lt., Co. H, 14th Virginia Cav., Apr. 1861. Captain - Apr. 1862. Lt. Col. - Feb. 12, 1863. Wded. at Monocacy. Wded. and POW at Nineveh, Virginia, Nov. 12, 1864, released July 24. m. George Anna Lackey, 1864. Postmaster, farmer and distiller in Rockbridge Co. d. Rockbridge Co., Aug. 2, 1906. bur. Timber Hill.

GIBSON, JONATHAN CATLETT. b. Culpeper Co., 1835. att. U. Virginia. Capt., Co. D, 49th Virginia, June 8, 1861. Lt. Col. - May 1, 1862. Colonel - Jan. 3, 1863, back-dated from Oct. 27, 1863. Wded. at Seven Pines, Seven Days, 2nd Manassas, Sharpsburg and Fredericksburg. Lawyer in New York, briefly. Lawyer, U.S. Attorney, and Virginia legisl. from Culpeper Co. m.

Mary George Shackelford. It was in Gibson's home (called the Shackelford House from his wife's connections) that John Pelham died. Gibson died in Culpeper, Jan. 29, 1907. bur. Fairview Cemetery.

GIBSON, WILLIAM. b. Warren Co., Mar. 10, 1822. m. Martha Mitchell Rogers, 1843. Augusta lawyer and judge. Pvt., Co. C, 48th Georgia for one day before being elected Colonel on Mar. 4, 1862. Wded. at Malvern Hill, 2nd Manassas, and Sharpsburg. Wded. and POW at Gettysburg. Res. Nov. 12, 1864. A. P. Hill considered Gibson "entirely unfitted" for brigade command. President of Georgia Senate post-war. d. Macon, Apr. 5, 1893. bur. Magnolia Cemetery, Augusta.

GILES, JAMES. b. Danville, June 2, 1831. Lived in Portsmouth. gr. VMI, 1851. 5′8″. Major, 29th Virginia, Nov. 4, 1861. Lt. Col. - May 13, 1862. Colonel - Apr. 10, 1863. In Nov. 1862 Giles wrote a fight-filled letter to the Secretary of War, demanding transfer to the scene of some serious action. A Nov. 1864 inspection report declared Giles to be completely inept, displaying "total indifference" to his duties. POW at Dinwiddie C.H., Apr. 1, 1865, released June 6. Teacher and civil engineer. d. Mar. 22, 1887.

GILES, JOHN ROBERT RUSSELL. b. 1838. Of Union Co. Lt., Co. D, 5th South Carolina, Apr. 13, 1861. Captain - May 25, 1861. Colonel - Apr. 23, 1862. KIA at Seven Pines.

GILHAM, WILLIAM. b. Vincennes, Indiana, Jan. 13, 1818. gr. USMA, 1840. Lt., U.S. Artillery, 1840-1846. m. Cordelia Adelaide Hayden. On the VMI faculty. Author of noted drill and tactics manual. Colonel, 21st Virginia, July 1861. Ordered back to VMI staff, Jan. 20, 1862, and dropped from 21st Virginia rolls Apr. 21, 1862. After the war, when VMI faculty had to serve without pay, Gilham (who had 8 children) had to take a position as chemist for a large fertilizer company, though his name stayed on VMI faculty lists. Died in Brandon, Vermont, where he'd gone for his health, on Nov. 16, 1872. bur. Lexington, Virginia. Tom Munford described Gilham as having "a twinkling, quick, mischief-making eye."

GILLETTE, JOSEPH EZRA. b. near Franklin, Virginia, June 26,

1827. Southampton Co. planter, owned 22 slaves in 1860. m. Edith Emmaline Worrell, 1849. Capt., Co. H, 5th Virginia Cav., May 7, 1861. Capt., Co. A, 13th Virginia Cav., May 7, 1862. Major - Feb. 20, 1863. MWIA in legs at Brandy Station, Oct. 11, 1863. d. Oct. 21. bur. on Gillette farm, Rte. 58 near Franklin.

GILLIAM, HENRY AUGUSTUS. b. 1819. Lawyer in Windsor, North Carolina. Capt., Co. H, 17th North Carolina, May 3, 1861. Major - July 27, 1861. POW at Ft. Hatteras, Aug. 1861. Regt. disbanded, Mar. 1862.

GILLIAM, JAMES SKELTON. b. Apr. 13, 1806, according to best evidence. Major, 9th Virginia, May 20, 1862. Lt. Col. - May 24, 1862. Res. June 19, 1863, "dropsy and debility." The woods are full of James Skelton Gilliams in Southside and Tidewater Virginia. Confusion reigns in relating them. The Capt., Co. C, 41st Virginia, by the same name was aged 22 in 1861. The 1806 birthdate above is from a 1904 newspaper genealogy which identifies that date as belonging to the Lt. Col., 9th Virginia. A 9th Virginia officer reported that the Colonel was called "Castor Oil" in the regiment, and that he resigned because he didn't want to face a board of examiners.

GILLIAM, WILLIAM ADDISON. b. Botetourt Co., 1837. att. U. Virginia. Capt., Co. K, 60th Virginia, June 18, 1861. Lt. Col. - May 9, 1864. POW at Cloyd's Farm, May 9, 1864. Farmer and postmaster at Covington, Virginia. m. Martha Elizabeth Fudge, 1869. d. Buchanan, Virginia, 1903.

GILMER, JOHN ALEXANDER, JR. b. North Carolina, Apr. 22, 1838. att. UNC. Nephew of Genl. J. F. Gilmer. Lived in Greensboro. Lt., Co. B, 27th North Carolina, Apr. 20, 1861. Adj. of regt., Nov. 1861. Major - Jan. 6, 1862. Lt. Col. - Nov. 1, 1862. Colonel - Dec. 5, 1862. Wded. leg at Fredericksburg and again at Bristoe Station. Commandant of Salisbury POW Camp, 1864. Retired Jan. 11, 1865. In North Carolina legisl., and on state supreme court. d. Mar. 17, 1892. bur. Green Hill Cemetery, Greensboro.

GILMOR, HARRY W. b. Baltimore, Jan. 24, 1838. m. Mentoria

Strong. Lived in Wisconsin and Nebraska pre-war. Gilmor signed his name "H. W. Gilmor," but dropped the middle initial later. Pvt., Co. G, 7th Virginia Cav., Aug. 31, 1861. Capt., Co. F, 12th Virginia Cav., Mar. 27, 1862. Major, 2nd Maryland Cav. Bn., May 27, 1863. POW at Moorefield, Virginia, Feb. 4, 1865, paroled July 24. Author of a famous, if somewhat adventurous, cavalry memoir. Baltimore Police Commissioner, 1874-1879. d. Baltimore, Mar. 4, 1883. bur. Loudon Park Cemetery. In Dec. 1861, "Stonewall" Jackson complained to Gilmor's captain that Gilmor had been drunk and disorderly in Shepherdstown.

GIST, JOSEPH FINCHER. b. Union Dist., Oct. 11, 1818. att. South Carolina College. Militia general. In South Carolina legisl., 1846-48 and 1856-60. Lawyer, planter and judge at Union, South Carolina. Never married. Major, 15th South Carolina, Sept. 10, 1861. Lt. Col. - Oct. 19, 1861. Colonel - July 2, 1863. Wded. at Chickamauga. Res., disability, Jan. 5, 1864. d. Union, Oct. 6, 1890. bur. Fair Forest Cemetery.

GIST, WILLIAM MURENA. b. Union Dist., Oct. 3, 1840. gr. South Carolina College. Sgt., 1st South Carolina (Gregg's), early 1861. Capt., Co. B, 15th South Carolina, Aug. 22, 1861. Major - Dec. 14, 1861. KIA Nov. 18, 1863 at Knoxville. Son of Gov. W. H. Gist. A fine photo of Gist has been published recently in W. C. Davis' multi-volume photographic history of the war. bur. family cemetery, Union Co., South Carolina.

GLENN, LUTHER JUDSON. b. McDonough Co., Georgia, Nov. 26, 1818. gr. U. Georgia, 1841. Lawyer. m. sister of T. R. R. Cobb. In Georgia Secession Convention. Capt., Co. C, Inf. Bn. of Cobb's Legion (Georgia), Aug. 1, 1861. Major - July 18, 1862. Lt. Col. - Sept. 15, 1862. Wded. at Chancellorsville. Retired, Jan. 11, 1865. Mayor of Atlanta, and in Georgia legisl. d. Atlanta, June 9, 1886. Although his sister-in-law called Glenn "thriftless and intemperate," and T. R. R. Cobb was very critical of him, Cobb eventually referred to Glenn as "the best officer I have in the legion." bur. Oconee Hill Cemetery, Athens.

GLOVER, JOHN VINYARD. b. Sept. 5, 1831. Capt., Co. A, 1st South Carolina (Hagood's), July 29, 1861. Major, 25th South

Carolina, July 22, 1862. MWIA at Cold Harbor. d. in Richmond June 19, 1864.

GLOVER, THOMAS COKE. b. Augusta Co., Jan. 28, 1826. m. Elizabeth Camp. Physician in Campbell Co. Member of the Georgia Secession Convention (voted yes). Capt., Co. A, 21st Georgia, June 6, 1861. Major - July 27, 1862. Lt. Col. - Apr. 18, 1864. Wded. at Sharpsburg. KIA at Winchester, Sept. 19, 1864. bur. Mt. Hebron Cemetery, Winchester.

GLOVER, THOMAS JAMISON. b. Orangeburg, July 30, 1830. gr. South Carolina College, 1849. In South Carolina legisl. Lt. Col., 1st South Carolina (Hagood's), Jan. 8, 1861. Colonel - July 12, 1862. MWIA in knee, calf and abdomen at 2nd Manassas, Aug. 29, 1862. d. Aug. 31.

GODWIN, DAVID E. "Col., Camp of Conscripts," in April 1863. Major, 4th Bn. Virginia Reserves, Aug. 27, 1864, at org. of that unit.

GODWIN, DAVID JEREMIAH. b. Suffolk, Virginia, 1829. Portsmouth lawyer. m. (1) Lucrece P. Wilson. m. (2) Miss Osprey of South Carolina. Lt. Col., 3rd Virginia, pre-war. Lt. Col., 14th Virginia, May 17, 1861. Defeated at May 1862 re-org. Lt. Col., 9th Virginia, May 20, 1862. Colonel - May 24, 1862. Disabled by riding injury and Seven Pines wound, and resigned Oct. 30, 1862. Soon thereafter he sought, in vain, to have his resignation rescinded. Norfolk judge. Went to Washington, D.C., in the 1880's to work on compilation of the Official Records set. bur. Cedar Grove Cemetery, Portsmouth.

GOGGANS, ELIJAH JEREMIAH. b. Sept. 30, 1834. Merchant in Edgefield District in 1860. m. Adela M. Bouknight. Lt., Co. E, 7th South Carolina, Apr. 15, 1861. Capt., Co. M, 7th South Carolina, May 9, 1862. Remained as Captain until late 1864, when he was promoted to Lt. Col., apparently backdated to Sept. 1863. His record is unclear. Living at Clouds Creek in 1901.

GOLDSBOROUGH, WILLIAM WORTHINGTON. b. Oct. 6, 1831 in Frederick Co., Maryland. Lived in Baltimore. 5′11″.

Capt., Co. G, 2nd Maryland Bn., June 29, 1861. Major - Jan. 26, 1863. Wded. at 2nd Manassas. Dangerously wounded in the left side at Gettysburg, and taken prisoner. Released June 13, 1865. Author of two fine Maryland Confederate books. Newspaper shop foreman in Philadelphia and Washington state. d. Philadelphia, Dec. 25, 1901. bur. Loudon Park Cemetery, Baltimore. Goldsborough was a cousin of Bradley T. Johnson. As he lay dying, Goldsborough told his wife: "don't bury me among the ---- Yankees here, send my body to . . . Baltimore."

GOLDSBY, THOMAS JEFFERSON. b. Georgia, 1831. Of Dallas, Alabama. m. Mary Agnes Winston. gr. Princeton. Planter. Capt., Co. A, 4th Alabama, Apr. 26, 1861. Lt. Col. - Nov. 8, 1861. Wded. at Gaines' Mill. Lived in Mobile post-war. d. 1884.

GOLDSMITH, WASHINGTON LaFAYETTE. b. July 15, 1837, in South Carolina. att. Cherokee Baptist College, Cassville, Georgia. Lt., Co. K, 14th Georgia, July 9, 1861. Captain - Oct. 25, 1861. Major - May 5, 1863. Lt. Col. - May 6, 1864. Paroled at Macon, Georgia, Apr. 25, 1865. Comptroller General of Georgia, 1872-1878. Lived in New Orleans post-war. d. Berryville, Virginia, July 3, 1925. Author of an interesting memoir published in 1896.

GOLLADAY, JACOB BURNER. b. Virginia, Mar. 1838. Lived at Strasburg and Woodstock. 5'10". Lt., Co. B, 33rd Virginia, June 1861. Captain - Apr. 21, 1862. Major - Mar. 21, 1864. Wded. at Malvern Hill and Sharpsburg. POW at Woodstock, Virginia, Sept. 23, 1864, released July 24. d. July 3, 1874. bur. Lutheran Churchyard, Woodstock. (There is some confusion about Golladay's middle name, which may have been Benjamin.)

GOODE, CHARLES THOMAS. b. Upson Co., Georgia, Oct. 26, 1835. gr. U. Georgia. m. Cornelia Warren. Major, 11th Georgia, July 2, 1861. Resigned Jan. 20, 1862. Major, 19th Georgia Cav. Bn., Oct. 14, 1862. Colonel, 10th Confederate Cavalry, Dec. 27, 1862. Retired June 20, 1864. Americus lawyer, in Georgia legisl. Died in Americus, Jan. 15, 1875.

John T. Bland

JOHN THOMAS GOODE
34th Virginia

GOODE, EDMOND. b. Bedford Co., Virginia, May 4, 1825. gr. VMI, 1846. Teacher and farmer. Brother of Hon. John Goode. Adj., 28th Virginia, early 1861. Colonel, 58th Virginia, Sept. 27, 1861. d. Mar. 8, 1862.

GOODE, JOHN THOMAS. b. Mecklenburg Co., Virginia, July 21, 1835. att. VMI. Lt., U.S. Artillery, 1855-61; fought Seminoles and was stationed in Utah and Kansas. Capt. of artillery, P.A.C.S., Mar. 16, 1861. Major - Oct. 1861. Lt. Col. - Apr. 1862. Col., 4th Virginia Heavy Artillery (later became 34th Virginia Infantry), May 15, 1862. This appt. was initially called "temporary rank." Goode's service record is an extremely confusing one. He commanded Wise's Brigade a good bit in 1864. Appx. Farmer and in Virginia legisl. Married four times. d. Chase City, Virginia, Apr. 13, 1916. bur. St. James Church, Boydton.

GOODE, THOMAS FRANCIS. b. Roanoke Co., June 28, 1825. Mecklenburg Co. lawyer. In Virginia Secession Convention. m. Rosa C. Chambers. Capt., Co. A, 3rd Virginia Cav., May 14, 1861. Major - ca. Oct. 1861. Lt. Col. - Oct. 4, 1861. Colonel - Apr. 26, 1862. Resigned due to ill health, Nov. 18, 1862. In Virginia legisl., 1863-64. Mecklenburg lawyer and businessman post-war. d. Jan. 6, 1905, at Boydton, Virginia.

GOODGAME, JOHN CHAPMAN. b. Fayetteville, Alabama, Sept. 18, 1835. Teacher in Coosa Co. m. Elverena Thomas, 1858. Capt., Co. B. 12th Alabama, June 17, 1861. Major - June 1, 1862. Lt. Col. - Sept. 14, 1862. Wded. at Spotsylvania, May 12, 1864. 6′0″. Sheriff and tax collector in Henderson Co., Texas, post-war. Murdered in Texas, June 8, 1876.

GOODING, JOHN JACOB. b. May 10, 1841. Lt., Co. D, 11th South Carolina, July 15, 1861. Captain - May 3, 1862. Major - Nov. 27, 1862. Paroled at Augusta, Georgia, May 25, 1865. m. Deborah Terry. Auditor of Hampton Co., South Carolina, for 34 years post-war. d. July 26, 1911. bur. Hampton Cemetery.

GOODLETT, SPARTAN DAVID. b. Apr. 20, 1831. m. Mary Lyles, 1860. Lt. Col., 22nd South Carolina, Jan. 29, 1862. Colonel - May 15, 1862. "Cashiered" by court-martial, Apr. 28, 1864, on charges brought by Genl. Evans that Goodlett left his post in the face of the enemy. Lawyer in Pickens and Greenville. d. May 16, 1874.

GOODMAN, GEORGE AUGUSTUS. b. Albemarle Co., Apr. 16, 1828. gr. VMI, 1852. Louisa Co. farmer and teacher. 6'0". Lt., Co. C, 12th Virginia, Apr. 17, 1861. Captain - Apr. 26, 1862. Major - Oct. 30, 1862. Lt. Col. - May 15, 1863. Wded. at Gaines' Mill. POW at Winchester, Sept. 19, 1864, released July 15. d. June 24, 1884. He was called "Old Gus" by his men, or "Aunt Sally," or "Old Granny," according to two diarists.

GOODNER, JOHN FITE. b. July 6, 1822. Mexican War captain. Farmer in DeKalb Co. Capt., Co. A, 7th Tennessee, May 20, 1861. Lt. Col. - May 27, 1861, at org. Colonel - May 23, 1862. Res. Apr. 8, 1863, "ill health." d. August 1871. bur. West View Cemetery, Alexandria, Tennessee. Goodner's war letters have been published.

GOODWYN, ARTEMAS DARBY. b. 1827. gr. South Carolina College. Married farmer at Gadsden in 1860, age 32, worth $38,000. Major, 2nd South Carolina, Apr. 9, 1861. Lt. Col. - May 14, 1862. Wded. ankle at Savage Station, which led to his resignation, June 3, 1863. d. Aug. 11, 1898.

GOODWYN, McGAVOCK. b. Louisiana, Nov. 23, 1841. att. VMI. Lived in Rosedale, Louisiana. Capt., Co. C, 7th Louisiana Bn., June 8, 1861. Capt., Co. K, 15th Louisiana, 1861. Major - June 24, 1862. Lt. Col. - 1862. Wded. at Seven Pines, Chancellorsville and Cedar Creek. Never married. d. June 21, 1875.

GORDON, AUGUSTUS MANLY. b. 1842 in Georgia. att. La Grange Military Academy, Alabama. Of Jackson Co., Alabama. Lt., Co. I, 6th Alabama, May 15, 1861. Major - May 30, 1862. Lt. Col. - May 7, 1863. KIA at Chancellorsville. bur. Linwood Cemetery, Columbus, Georgia. He was the brother of General John Brown Gordon.

GORDON, GEORGE T. "Formerly of the British Army." A big man, with red whiskers, fond of gambling. Gave his residence as Rockbridge Alum Springs, Virginia. V.a. d. c. to A. P. Hill; also aide to Whiting, Winder and Bragg. Major, 34th North

Carolina, Dec. 14, 1862. Lt. Col. - May 6, 1863. Wded. leg at Gettysburg, leg again in June 1864 and foot in Sept. 1863. Retired to Invalid Corps, Nov. 25, 1864.

GORDON, WILLIAM WESTMORELAND. b. Essex Co., Aug. 1831. gr. VMI, 1850, with first honors. gr. U. Virginia. On VMI faculty. m. Fannie Brockenbrough. Colonel, 27th Virginia, May 30, 1861. Resigned Oct. 14, 1861. Richmond lawyer post-war. d. Dec. 5, 1893.

GOSS, JOHN WESLEY. b. Nov. 24, 1825. Capt., Co. A, Palmetto Sharpshooters (South Carolina), Apr. 13, 1862. Major - July 4, 1862. Lt. Col. - July 22, 1862. d. Apr. 15, 1866. bur. Presbyterian Cemetery, Union Co., South Carolina.

GOULDIN, JOHN MILTON. b. Sparta, Virginia, 1839. att. U. Virginia and VMI. gr. U. Maryland. m. Susan Jones Wright. Capt., Co. H, 30th Virginia, Apr. 24, 1861. Major - Apr. 19, 1862. Lt. Col. - Nov. 5, 1864. Wded. knee at Cold Harbor. Under arrest in Oct. 1862. Appx. Physician in Essex Co., Virginia and Peytona, W. Virginia. d. Essex Co., Sept. 20, 1878. Local tradition reported Gouldin as a heavy drinker.

GOULDING, EDWIN ROSS. m. Sarah Searcy Owen. Mexican War officer. Age 37 in 1860. Ran railroad lumber business. Capt., Co. E, 9th Georgia, June 11, 1861, and elected Colonel on that same date. Died of disease, Apr. 4, 1862. bur. Old Ephesus Presbyterian Church, Woodland, Georgia.

GRACE, BENJAMIN F. b. Tattnall Co. "Timber measurer" at Reidsville in 1860, age 22. Sgt., Co. M, 26th Georgia, Aug. 13, 1861. Lt. - Sept. 9, 1861. Captain - May 8, 1862. Major - Aug. 12, 1863. KIA at Hatcher's Run, Feb. 6, 1865.

GRACE, PHILIP THOMAS. b. Hampshire Co., Feb. 9, 1832. Capt., Co. A, 33rd Virginia, June 6, 1861. Promoted to Major on Aug. 28, 1862, and resigned about Jan. 1863, citing "declining health." Grace's record is sketchy and full of anomalies. He was alive in Hennessey, Oklahoma, in 1900. d. Jan. 21, 1907, in Oklahoma.

GRADY, WILLIAM SAMMONS. b. June 10, 1821. Lived in North Carolina in 1840's. Merchant in Athens, Georgia. Capt., Co. G, 25th North Carolina, July 8, 1861, aged 40. Major - Dec. 18, 1862. MWIA at the Crater, July 30, 1864. d. Oct. 20 in Greenville, South Carolina. His son was Henry W. Grady, the orator and journalist of "New South" fame.

GRAHAM, DAVID PEIRCE. b. Wythe Co., Virginia, Oct. 24, 1838. att. VMI. Capt., Co. B, 51st Virginia, July 31, 1861. Major - July 8, 1863. Res. Apr. 23, 1864. Later served on Wharton's staff. Farmer, miner and iron manufacturer in Bluefield, West Virginia. d. Nov. 5, 1898.

GRAHAM, JOHN WASHINGTON. b. Hillsboro, North Carolina, July 22, 1838. Orange Co. lawyer. Son of a governor and U.S. Senator. Lt., "Orange Guards," Apr. 28, 1861. A.d.c. to Genl. Gatlin, Sept. 1861. Capt., Co. D, 56th North Carolina, Mar. 25, 1862. Major - Sept. 1, 1863. Wded. spring of 1864. Severely wded. at Ft. Stedman, Mar. 25, 1865. Paroled from a Petersburg hospital, May 6, 1865. In North Carolina legisl. d. Hillsboro, Mar. 24, 1928. bur. there in St. Matthews Episcopal Churchyard.

GRAHAM, ROBERT FLADGER. b. Marion, South Carolina, Nov. 12, 1833. gr. South Carolina College. Marion lawyer. m. Harriett Ellen Harllee. Lt., 1st South Carolina, 1861. Colonel, 21st South Carolina, Jan. 26, 1862. Wded. at Port Walthall Junction, May 7, 1864. Paroled at Greensboro, May 1, 1865. Judge and state legisl. in South Carolina post-war. d. Charleston, Nov. 5, 1874. bur. Old Town Cemetery, Marion, South Carolina.

GRAHAM, WILLIAM LEANDER. b. Smyth Co., Virginia, Oct. 2, 1820. Mexican War officer. Lived in Tazewell Co. m. Louise Bowen Thompson. Lt. Col., 16th Virginia Cav., Jan. 15, 1863. POW at Moorefield, Aug. 7, 1864. 5′9″. Described post-war as "the most powerful man in Tazewell Co." d. Apr. 16, 1908, at Wittens Mills, Virginia.

GRAMMER, JOHN JR. b. Dinwiddie Co., Virginia, June 1, 1833. att. U. Virginia. gr. New York Medical College, 1856. Captain,

Halifax Co. Volunteers, 1859. Capt., Co. A, 53rd Virginia, Apr. 24, 1861. Major - May 22, 1862. Lt. Col. - Aug. 29, 1862. Colonel - Jan. 6, 1863. Res. Mar. 5, 1863, and became Surgeon, 26th Virginia Bn. and 62nd Virginia. Wded. arm at Seven Pines. Halifax Co. physician. d. there, Mar. 27, 1900.

GRAVES, BAZILLIA YANCEY. b. Surry Co., North Carolina, Oct. 10, 1835. att. Wake Forest. Capt., Co. C, 21st North Carolina, May 20, 1861. Major - May 25, 1862. Lt. Col. - Aug. 28, 1862. Wded. at Seven Days and Ox Hill. Resigned due to latter wound, Feb. 24, 1863. Surry Co. Collector of Revenue. Postmaster of Mt. Airy. Living in Surry Co. in 1895. d. ca. 1900.

GRAVES, GEORGE AZARIAH. Of Morganton, North Carolina. gr. Wake Forest, 1859. Capt., Co. G, 22nd North Carolina, Apr. 20, 1861. Lt. Col. - May 3, 1863, but declined the appt. (aged 24 at this point). Wded. arm and POW at Gettysburg. Retired to Invalid Corps, as Captain, Nov. 2, 1864. Farmer. m. Minerva Isabelle Williamson. d. July 5, 1907.

GRAVES, JOHN AZARIAH. b. Nov. 18, 1822, in Yanceyville. Lived in Caswell Co., North Carolina. Capt., Co. A, 13th North Carolina, Apr. 29, 1861. Major, 47th North Carolina, Mar. 24, 1862. Lt. Col. - April 5, 1863. POW at Gettysburg. Died while imprisoned at Johnson's Island, Mar. 2, 1864, of a stroke. His body was sent to friends in Philadelphia. bur. First Baptist Church, Yanceyville, North Carolina.

GRAVES, WILLIAM FOUNTAIN. b. Pittsylvania Co., Virginia, Sept. 26, 1832. m. Mary Jane Johnson, 1856. Sgt., Co. F, 2nd Virginia Cav., May 28, 1861. Lt. - Aug. 1, 1861. Captain - Sept. 17, 1861. Major - Dec. 7, 1864. Wded. at Todd's Tavern, May 7, 1864, and at Nance's Shop, June 24, 1864. Bedford Co. farmer and miller. In Virginia legisl. Vinton city official. d. July 3, 1923. An article by Graves was published in a Richmond paper in 1906, and several of his letters to Tom Munford are at Duke University.

GRAY, HARVEY. Capt., Co. E, 64th Virginia (initially part of the 21st Virginia Bn.), Apr. 6, 1862. Major - Feb. 5, 1864.

GRAY, ROBERT HARPER. b. Jan. 10, 1831. m. Martha Horney. Capt., Co. L, 22nd North Carolina, June 18, 1861. Lt. Col. - June

13, 1862. d. of disease, near Frederickburg, Mar. 16, 1863. bur. Hopewell M.E. Churchyard, Randolph Co., North Carolina. Although a history of the regiment says that Gray was "always a man of delicate health," Dorsey Pender's letters state bluntly that Gray drank himself to death. A July 1862 letter written by Gray is at the Museum of the Confederacy. Strong compliment to Gray by one of his officers would seem to offset the criticisms by Pender, who was often pompous and overly judgemental.

GRAYBILL, TULLY. b. June 2, 1821. Physician in Sandersville in 1860, worth $23,000. Capt., Co. A, 28th Georgia, Sept. 10, 1861. Major - May 3, 1862. Colonel - Nov. 3, 1862. POW at Seven Pines, exchanged Sept. 1, 1862. Wded. at Sharpsburg. d. Oct. 2, 1883. bur. Oconee, Washington Co., Georgia.

GREEN, ALLEN JONES. b. Jan. 1819. Physician in Columbia in 1860, married, worth $80,000. Mayor of Columbia. Lt. Col., 23rd South Carolina, Nov. 11, 1861. Dropped at re-org. Major, to report to Conscript Bureau for service in South Carolina, Apr. 14, 1864. d. Mar. 1879 in Alabama.

GREEN, CHARLES JONES. b. Falmouth, Aug. 3, 1839. gr. VMI, 1859. Capt., Co. A, 47th Virginia, Apr. 23, 1861. Major - Dec. 19, 1864. Paroled at Ashland, Apr. 29, 1865. Farmer and merchant. Lived in Dallas, Texas, post-war. d. Sept. 7, 1909 in Culpeper of stomach cancer. bur. Greenwood Cemetery, Dallas.

GREEN, FRANCIS MARION. b. Fauquier Co., Virginia, Nov. 7, 1823. Lawyer at Oxford, Mississippi. Capt., Co. G, 11th Mississippi, Feb. 23, 1861. Major - Oct. 3, 1862. Colonel - Sept. 25, 1862 (backdated), but appt. was not confirmed. Reappointed Colonel, Feb. 19, 1864. MWIA at Spotsylvania, May 12, 1864, d. May 15. bur. Sharon Cemetery, Middleburg, Virginia. Green's war letters are at Mississippi Department of Archives and History.

GREEN, JOHN SHACKLEFORD. b. Rappahannock Co., June 19, 1817. Farmer there. Capt., Co. B, 6th Virginia Cav., Apr. 22, 1861. Major - Apr. 30, 1862. Severely wded. near Harrisonburg, June 6, 1862. Lt. Col. - July 16, 1862. Res. May 4, 1864. Lived in Norfolk post-war. d. there, Jan. 1, 1891. bur. Cedar Grove Cemetery, Norfolk.

GREEN, WHARTON JACKSON. (Always referred to as "Jack.") b. St. Mark's, Florida, Feb. 28, 1831. att. Georgetown U. and U. Virginia. att. USMA. Author of an autobiographical memoir which includes much Civil War material. Pvt., Co. F, 12th North Carolina, Apr. 18, 1861. Warren Co., North Carolina, farmer at enlistment. "Apptd. Colonel in Wise's Legion," but the organization was not completed. Lt. Col., 2nd North Carolina Bn., Dec. 9, 1861. Paroled at Roanoke Island, Feb. 1862. Dropped at Sept. 1862 re-org. V.a. d. c. to Junius Daniel, June 1863. Viticulturist. In U.S. Congress, 1883-1887. d. near Fayetteville, North Carolina, Aug. 6, 1910. bur. Cross Creek Cemetery.

GREEN, WILLIAM EDWIN. b. Greenwood, Virginia, Feb. 5, 1827. gr. Hampden-Sydney and U. Virginia. m. Jennie Elliott Boylan. Large farmer in Charlotte Co. Capt., Co. I, 56th Virginia, July 18, 1861. Major - Sept. 17, 1861. Lt. Col. - July 31, 1863. Colonel - June 13, 1864. d. Greenwood, Dec. 12, 1891.

GREEN, WILLIAM FURNIFOLD. Of Franklin Co. att. Wake Forest, 1847-48. att. U. Virginia. gr. Washington and Jefferson, 1850. Lawyer and planter. In North Carolina legislature. Capt., Co. L, 15th North Carolina, May 20, 1861. Major - June 11, 1861. Defeated at May 1862 re-org. d. Aug. 10, 1898.

GREEN, WILLIAM JAMES. b. Falmouth, Nov. 25, 1825. gr. VMI, 1846. Lt. Col., 47th Virginia, May 2, 1861 (was briefly attached to 30th Virginia). Dropped at May 1862 re-org. KIA at Seven Days while v.a.d.c. to General Pender. Green's tombstone is right under the water tower at Stafford High School.

GRESHAM, THOMAS ROBERT. b. Essex Co. Farmer in King & Queen Co. in 1860, age 35, worth $37,741. gr. William & Mary. Lawyer. Lt. Col., 9th Virginia Militia, 1861-1862 (this unit was in A.N.Va. at Gloucester Pt. in early 1862). Later became Colonel 87th Virginia Militia.

GRICE, WASHINGTON LEONIDAS. b. Carroll Co., Feb. 22, 1832. Sgt., Co. G, 6th Georgia, May 27, 1861. Lt. - Feb. 27, 1862. Major, 45th Georgia, May 15, 1862. Lt. Col. - Oct. 13, 1862. Res. Mar. 17, 1864. Apptd. Orderly Sgt. of Pruden's

Battery, May 1864. Paroled at Milledgeville, May 12, 1865. m. Martha Virginia Warren, 1870. Macon judge. d. Mar. 9, 1925.

GRIEVE, MILLER, JR. b. Milledgeville, Sept. 22, 1834. att. Oglethorpe College. Son of a Milledgeville newspaper owner. Lawyer. Capt., Co. H, 1st Georgia Regulars, Feb. 1, 1861. WIA at Second Manassas. Major - Aug. 3, 1864. Lt. Col. - Sept. 3, 1864. "Lawyer, architect and dramatist." d. Milledgeville, Aug. 5, 1897. bur. City Cemetery.

GRIFFIN, ELI SHORTER. b. 1829. Farmer in Twiggs Co. Served in state legisl. both before and after the war. Capt., Co. E, 26th Georgia, Sept. 25, 1861. Major - May 8, 1862. Lt. Col. - Dec. 3, 1862. Wded. at 2nd Manassas. Res. Aug. 12, 1863. In Georgia legisl. late in war. m. Avarila Nash. d. March 15, 1891. bur. Jeffersonville, Georgia, Cemetery.

GRIFFIN, JAMES BENJAMIN. b. Oct. 10, 1825, in South Carolina. Married farmer in Edgefield District in 1860, worth $81,530. South Carolina Militia General pre-war. Major, Hampton Legion (South Carolina), June 12, 1861, having "declined Col." Lt. Col. - July 21, 1861. Injured by lightning, Oct. 1861. Dropped at re-org. Lt. Col. of State Troops the remainder of the war. Owned brickyards in Waxahachie, 1872-1876, then Fort Worth, 1877-1881. d. Fort Worth, Texas, June 25, 1881.

GRIFFIN, JOEL R. b. South Carolina. att. Georgia Military Institute. Lawyer in Macon in 1860, age 24. Capt., Co. E, 3rd Georgia, Apr. 27, 1861. Major, 1st Battalion Georgia Partisan Rangers, June 18, 1862. Lt. Col., 15th Battalion Georgia Partisan Rangers, July 1, 1862. Colonel, 62nd Georgia, Aug. 1, 1862. Transferred to 8th Georgia Cavalry, July 11, 1864. Present through early 1865. Superintendent of Andersonville cemetery in 1865, by appointment of U.S. Army. Edited a Fort Valley newspaper in the 1870's.

GRIFFIN, THOMAS M. b. Jan. 7, 1816. Lt. Col., 18th Mississippi, June 7, 1861. Colonel - Nov. 18, 1862. Wounded at Malvern Hill and Gettysburg. Retired due to wounds, Nov. 18, 1864, and commanded the post at Newnan, Georgia. d. of yellow fever, Oct. 2, 1878. bur. Cayuga, Miss., Methodist Church.

GRIFFIS, JOHN C. b. Marietta, Georgia, July 15, 1834. att. Georgia Military Institute. m. Susan B. Bowie. Adjutant, 18th Georgia, June 14, 1861. Elected Major, Apr. 7, 1862. WIA at 2nd Manassas. Major and Commissary Officer, Feb. 17, 1863. Appx. Merchant in Americus. Moved to Texas in 1872. d. Sept. 27, 1901. bur. Greenwood Cemetery, Dallas. The first edition of this work used personal data supplied by a descendant which now seems to be spurious (b. 1828 in Ohio, m. Clara Dewson).

GRIGGS, GEORGE KING. b. Henry Co., Sept. 12, 1839. att. VMI. Capt., Co. K, 38th Virginia, June 2, 1861. Major - July 3, 1863. Lt. Col. - Nov. 15, 1863. Colonel - May 16, 1864. Wded. several times, including at Gettysburg. Appx. Danville businessman. d. Oct. 15, 1914. The colonel's diary and a photograph are at the Museum of the Confederacy. bur. Greenhill Cemetery, Danville.

GRIGSBY, ANDREW JACKSON. b. Rockbridge Co., Virginia, Nov. 2, 1819. Brother of Colonel John Warren Grigsby of the 6th Kentucky Cavalry. att. USMA, resigned Mar. 20, 1838. A member of Doniphan's Regt. Missouri Cav. during the Mexican War. Major, 27th Virginia, June 12, 1861. Lt. Col. - Oct. 14, 1861. Colonel - May 28, 1862. Wded. at Malvern Hill "in the left breast." Resigned Nov. 19, 1862, feeling overslaughed in the promotion sequence. "A bluff soldier much given to swearing." Two prominent Confederates, in written correspondence, concluded that the devout T. J. Jackson denied Grigsby promotion due to his speech. "I verily believe," wrote one man, that Jackson denied Grigsby's promotion because he was "such an awful swearer." d. Dec. 23, 1895. bur. near Stony Point, Virginia.

GRIMES, GEORGE MARTIN. b. May 24, 1832. Farmer in Bamberg, South Carolina. Capt., Co. F, 1st South Carolina (Hagood's), July 20, 1861. Capt. Co. G, same regt., Apr. 12, 1862. Major from Sept. 1, 1862, until Feb. 7, 1864, by order of Genl. Micah Jenkins, but the War Dept. rejected this long-standing promotion and ordered Grimes back to company command. Wded. at Wilderness. MWIA at Ft. Harrison. d. Oct. 1, 1864.

GRIMSLEY, DANIEL AMON. b. Rappahannock Co., Apr. 3, 1840. Sgt., Co. B, 6th Virginia Cavalry, Apr. 22, 1861. Captain

- Apr. 20, 1862. Major - June 4, 1864. Culpeper lawyer and circuit judge. In Virginia legisl. m. Bettie Browning. d. Feb. 5, 1910. bur. Culpeper Cemetery, Route 522. A memoir by Grimsley is at Virginia Historical Society.

GROGAN, MICHAEL A. b. Ireland. Machinist. Lt., Co. B, 2nd Louisiana, May 9, 1861, age 26. Major - July 1, 1862. Lt. Col. - May 12, 1864. Wded. Nov. 12, 1864.

GRONER, VIRGINIUS DESPEAUX. b. Norfolk, Virginia, Sept. 7, 1836. Fought Indians in Texas pre-war. Capt. and a.a.g. at Montgomery and Richmond, in central govt. departments. Colonel, 61st Virginia, Oct. 1, 1862. Wded. at Spotsylvania. Appx. Some accounts cite brief service as Lt. Col., 4th North Carolina Cavalry in the summer of 1862, but the official service records shed no light on this. Norfolk shipping magnate. m. Katherine Campbell, 1866. d. Nov. 25, 1903. bur. Cedar Grove Cemetery, Norfolk.

GROVES, WILLIAM LUCAS. b. Nov. 1, 1820, in Madison Co. m. Jane Scott. Farmer in Chattooga Co. Capt., Co. I, 35th Georgia, Sept. 25, 1861. Major - Nov. 1, 1862. Resigned, having been elected to Georgia legisl., Dec. 21, 1863. d. Chattooga Co., May 17, 1873.

GUERRY, THEODORE LeGRAND. b. Dec. 5, 1812, in Sumter District, South Carolina. Moved to Twiggs Co., Georgia, in 1816. m. Martha Harrison, 1837. Lawyer. In Georgia legisl., 1845, 1853-1860, and 1863-1864. Quitman Co. judge. Capt., Co. I, 11th Georgia, July 2, 1861. Lt. Col. - July 3, 1861. Res. May 12, 1862. d. Dec. 12, 1895. bur. Baptist Cemetery, Quitman.

GUNNELS, GEORGE M. Physician in Laurens District in 1860, age 43. Capt., Co. D, 3rd South Carolina Battalion, Dec. 1, 1861. Major - Sept. 15, 1862. Res. Apr. 27, 1863, chronic rheumatism.

GUY, JOHN HENRY. b. Louisa Co., Virginia, 1833. gr. Randolph-Macon, 1851. Capt., Goochland Artillery (Virginia), June 1861. POW at Fort Donelson. Dropped at re-org. Lt. Col., 2nd Battalion Virginia Reserves, July 6, 1864. Paroled at Richmond,

May 9, 1865. In Virginia Senate, 1863-1865, from Goochland. m. Mary Ranson, 1871. d. June 1890.

GUY, WILLIAM SCOTT. b. Caroline Co., Va., Nov. 2, 1835. gr. VMI, 1856. Teacher in Granville Co., North Carolina. m. Lizzie Bouldin Williams. Lt. Col., 13th North Carolina, May 27, 1861. Defeated at April 1862 re-org. Became Pvt., Co. E, 3rd Virginia Cavalry, Oct. 1862. Lt. - Dec. 1862. Lost eye at Shepherdstown, July 16, 1863. d. Nov. 29, 1907.

HADDEN, WILLIAM M. Unmarried lawyer at Pickens C.H. in 1860, age 28(?). Lt., Co. A, 1st South Carolina Rifles, July 20, 1861, aged 34. Captain - Feb. 1, 1862. Major - Aug. 28, 1863. Lt. Col. - Apr. 7, 1864. KIA July 28, 1864.

HAGOOD, JAMES ROBERT. b. Nov. 26, 1844. att. SCMA. Brother of Genl. Johnson Hagood. Pvt., Co. C, 1st South Carolina (Hagood's), summer 1862. Sgt.-Major of regt., Aug. 1862. Adj. of regt. - 1862. Capt., Co. K, 1st South Carolina, Jan. 2, 1863. Colonel - Nov. 16, 1863, while still short of his 19th birthday. Appx. d. Nov. 15, 1870, as the result of a train wreck. Hagood's feisty unpublished war memoir is at the University of South Carolina.

HAIRSTON, PETER, JR. b. Henry Co., June 20, 1835. m. Miss Jones, of Appomattox, in 1858. Lt. Col., 24th Virginia, May 24, 1861. Wded. at Williamsburg and 2nd Manassas. Res. Apr. 9, 1863. In Virginia legisl. Lived at Martinsville. U.S. Revenue Collector. d. Mar. 13, 1915. bur. Oakwood Cemetery, Martinsville.

HALE, STEPHEN FOWLER. b. Ky., Jan. 31, 1816. Moved to Greene Co., Alabama, late 1830's. Lawyer in Eutaw. In Alabama legisl. and C.S. Congress. Lt. in Mexican War. Lt. Col., 11th Alabama, June 11, 1861. Temporarily and briefly commanded the 9th Alabama, as Lt. Col., in the spring of 1862. MWIA at Gaines' Mill. d. in Richmond July 18, 1862. A contemporary described Hale as "tall and lank, with a large and knotty head. He was somewhat eccentric in his manners."

HALL, BOLLING, JR. b. Georgia, Sept. 17, 1837. gr. U. Alabama, 1858. Clerk of Montgomery City Court, 1860. Colonel, 59th

Alabama, Nov. 25, 1863. Before that time he had been Lt. Col., 2nd Infantry Battalion, Hilliard's Alabama Legion. Wded. at Chickamauga and lost leg at Drewry's Bluff, May 16, 1864. Paroled at Augusta, May 18, 1865. d. of wounds Feb. 3, 1866.

HALL, EDWARD DUDLEY. b. Wilmington, Sept. 27, 1823. m. Sallie Landon Green. In North Carolina legisl., pre-war and post-war. Sheriff of New Hanover County, 1852-1861. Capt., Co. H, 3rd North Carolina Artillery, May 16, 1861. Major, 7th North Carolina, Aug. 17, 1861. Colonel, 46th North Carolina, Apr. 4, 1862. Res. Dec. 31, 1863, to resume post as Sheriff of New Hanover Co. Mayor and Chief of Police in Wilmington. d. there June 11, 1896.

HALL, GEORGE ALEXANDER. b. 1825. att. U. Virginia and U. Georgia. m. Martha Dixon. Lived in Greenville, Georgia. In Georgia legisl. Major, 8th Georgia Battalion, Sept. 5, 1861. Lt. Col., 28th Georgia, Nov. 13, 1861. d. Yorktown, Virginia, May 3, 1862, "of typhoid pneumonia."

HALL, JOSEPHUS MARION. b. Alabama. m. Eliza Erin. Resident of Eutaw. Capt., Co. A, 5th Alabama, May 6, 1861. Lt. Col. - Apr. 27, 1862. Colonel - July 17, 1862. WIA on May 10, 1864, arm amputated. Retired on Nov. 29, 1864.

HALL, MATTHEW ROBERT. b. Warren Co., Georgia, Mar. 15, 1836. gr. N.Y.U., 1857. m. Miss F. I. Latimer, 1857. Capt., Co. B, 48th Georgia, Mar. 1862. Major - July 17, 1863. Lt. Col. - Dec. 24, 1863. Colonel - Nov. 12, 1864. Wded. at Wilderness. On detail at Danville at war's end. Physician in Warrenton, Georgia, alive in 1899. Served in Georgia legisl. d. Jan. 28, 1905. bur. Warrenton City Cemetery.

HALL, SAMUEL HOUSTON. b. Staunton, Apr. 18, 1836. 5′9″. Entered service in Apr. 1861 in Co. C, 25th Virginia. Capt., Co. A, 62nd Virginia, 1862. Major - Nov. 10, 1863. POW at Woodstock, Virginia, Sept. 23, 1864; released July 19, 1865. m. Emma Moseley, 1868. Lived at Iron Gate, Virginia. d. Oct. 2, 1923, in Augusta Co. The major usually dropped his first given name, and was known simply as Houston Hall.

HALSEY, STEPHEN PETERS. b. Lynchburg, Nov. 13, 1843. Nephew of Col. William E. Peters. att. Emory & Henry. Pvt., Co. G, 2nd Virginia Cavalry, 1861. Capt., Co. A, 21st Virginia Cavalry, Apr. 1, 1863. Major - Aug. 31, 1863. Wded. at Woodstock on Oct. 9, 1864, and twice at the Battle of Lynchburg. m. Rebecca Emily Holmes, 1870. In tobacco, coal and banking in Lynchburg. d. there Mar. 1, 1939.

HAM, JOSEPH HUTCHINSON. b. Hampton, June 6, 1838. gr. VMI, 1859. m. Anna Gambol. Lt., Provisional Army of Virginia, May 23, 1861. Capt., Co. F, 16th Virginia, Aug. 17, 1861. Lt. Col. - May 3, 1862. Colonel - Aug. 30, 1862. Wded. at 2nd Manassas, and in May and Oct. 1864. Clerk of Court and Supt. of Schools in Hampton. d. Apr. 26, 1912.

HAMBRICK, JOHN TURNER: b. Halifax, North Carolina, Dec. 1, 1823. Mexican War veteran. Caswell Co. merchant. Capt., Co. D, 13th North Carolina, May 1, 1861. Major - Apr. 26, 1862. Res. due to illness, Oct. 15, 1862. d. Apr. 26, 1872. bur. Fairgrove M.E. Churchyard, Davidson Co. (A descendant supplies the birthyear of 1826, which does not agree with either his age of enlistment or his tombstone.)

HAMBRICK, JOSEPH ADAM. b. Franklin Co., Virginia, Apr. 17, 1833. gr. VMI, 1857. gr. U. Virginia. Lawyer. Capt., Co. B, 24th Virginia, Apr. 25, 1861. Major - summer 1863. Wounded at Gettysburg. MWIA in chin and legs at Drewry's Bluff, May 16, 1864, d. May 29.

HAMILTON, DANIEL HEYWARD, SR. b. May 2, 1816. att. U. Virginia. m. Rebecca Matte Middleton. Mexican War veteran U.S. Marshal pre-war. Lt. Col., 1st South Carolina (Gregg's), July 1861. Colonel - Dec. 14, 1861. Res. Jan. 4, 1864. Assigned to duty on South Carolina coast. His actual departure was dated Aug. 27, 1863, when he was "permanently detached from the regiment" by appt. as enrolling officer. A. C. Haskell said of Hamilton: "The Brigade had no confidence in him, for he had never shown any capacity." Others were similarly critical. d. Dec. 29, 1868.

HAMILTON, DANIEL HEYWARD, JR. b. Charleston, South

Preston Satterfield III

JOHN TURNER HAMBRICK
13th North Carolina

Carolina, Mar. 19, 1838. Son of last man listed above. att. SCMA. Lived in Orange Co., North Carolina. m. Frances Gray Roulhac, 1859. Instructor at Hillsboro Military Institute. Major, 13th North Carolina, May 26, 1861. Defeated at Apr. 1862 re-org. Served on Genl. Ripley's staff, and as Adj., 1st South Carolina (Gregg's). Disabled by a Shepherdstown wound. d. Hillsboro, North Carolina, Sept. 18, 1908. bur. St. Matthew's Episcopal Church.

HAMILTON, JOSEPH. b. County Tyrone, Ireland. Emigrated to Rutherfordton, North Carolina, then to Dahlonega and Dalton, Georgia. att. Wofford College. Capt., Co. E, Infantry Battalion of Phillips' Georgia Legion, July 9, 1861. Major - Dec. 13, 1862. Lt. Col. - Dec. 31, 1863. Wded. at South Mountain and Cold Harbor. Wded. Nov. 29, 1863, at Ft. Sanders. POW at Sayler's Creek (5′8″, aged 25), released July 25, 1865. Teacher in Dalton, then in Los Angeles, California. d. Oct. 22, 1932. bur. Marietta Confederate Cemetery.

HAMILTON, SAMUEL PRIOLEAU. b. 1826. Brother of Col. D. H. Hamilton, Sr. Capt., Co. M, 1st Georgia Regulars, Feb. 1, 1861. Capt., Co. A, 1st Georgia, July 24, 1861. Major of artillery - July 1, 1862. Commanded an artillery bn. at Sharpsburg and Fredericksburg. Chief of Artillery, McLaws' Division, fall 1862 (soon supplanted by Cabell). Assigned as a Judge Advocate, Jan. 1863. In 1864 was serving in the field again as Major in Cabell's Battalion. Lawyer in Chester, South Carolina. d. 1897.

HAMILTON, WILLIAM F. Sgt., Co. F, 19th Georgia, June 11, 1861. Lt. - Apr. 12, 1862. Captain - June 14, 1862. Major - Sept. 21, 1864. Paroled at Greensboro.

HAMMERSKOLD, CHARLES J. b. Lincoln Co., North Carolina. Lt., Co. E, 34th North Carolina, Oct. 25, 1861. Major - 1862. Lt. Col. - Apr. 18, 1862. Res. July 17, 1862, citing "near-sightedness," presumably of the ocular variety.

HAMMET, JAMES PRESTON. b. Christiansburg, Sept. 26, 1832. gr. VMI, 1853. M.D. from Jefferson Medical College. m. Katherine Markham Spiller, 1856. Major, 24th Virginia, May 1861.

Resigned Aug. 1861. Became C.S. Surgeon. d. Radford, Aug. 13, 1879.

HAMMOND, GEORGE WILSON. b. Fincastle, Virginia, July 24, 1828. att. U. Virginia. gr. U. Pennsylvania as M.D., 1851. Covington physician. Capt., Co. D, 60th Virginia, July 1, 1861. Major - Aug. 6, 1862. Lt. Col. - July 24, 1863. KIA at Cloyd's Mountain, May 9, 1864.

HAMMOND, GRAY WILLIS. b. Franklin Co., Oct. 22, 1829. Lived in Edgecombe Co. Lt., Co. K, 15th North Carolina, Apr. 24, 1861. Captain - May 24, 1861. Major - Feb. 27, 1863. Lt. Col. - Nov. 4, 1864. Appx. Mayor, merchant and farmer in Rocky Mount post-war. d. July 1879.

HAMPTON, FRANK. b. June 19, 1829 in New York. Farmer in Richland District in 1860, worth $215,000. Brother of General Wade Hampton. m. Sally Baxter, 1855. Lt. Col., 2nd South Carolina Cavalry, Aug. 22, 1862. KIA at Brandy Station, by a saber cut across the face and head. bur. Trinity Church, Columbia, South Carolina.

HANCE, JAMES WASHINGTON. b. 1828. att. South Carolina College. Lived in Laurens Dist., South Carolina. Lt., Co. D, 19th Georgia, June 11, 1861. Capt., Co. D, 53rd Georgia, May 6, 1862. Lt. Col. - Oct. 27, 1862. KIA at Gettysburg.

HANCOCK, JOHN M. Of Asheboro. Lt., Co. F, 2nd North Carolina Battalion, Nov. 30, 1861, aged 23. Served with the 54th North Carolina, May through Sept. 1862. Capt., Co. F, 2nd North Carolina Battalion, Sept. 26, 1862. Major - June 6, 1863. Wded. and POW at Gettysburg, exchanged Mar. 22, 1865.

HANES, GARLAND BROWN. b. about 1831. Capt., Co. A, 57th Virginia, May 29, 1861. Major - Apr. 24, 1862. Dropped at May 1862 re-org. Later became clerk in C.S. Treasury Dept. Lawyer and college professor. Living in Buckingham Co. in 1875.

HANLON, JOSEPH. b. Ireland. Newspaper reporter. Lived in Orleans Parish. 5′7″. Lt., Co. I, 6th Louisiana Infantry, May 3, 1861, age 28. Lt. Col. - June 4, 1861. POW at Winchester (June 1, 1862), Chancellorsville, and Strasburg (Oct. 19, 1864), released from last imprisonment on July 21, 1865. Wded. at Winchester, May 25, 1862.

HANSBROUGH, GEORGE WOODSON. b. Aug. 16, 1828. att. U. Virginia. Lawyer in Taylor Co. and Salem, Virginia. Lt. Col., 9th Virginia Battalion, June 1861. Wded. at Alleghany Mountain, Dec. 13, 1861. The bn. was merged into the 25th Virginia in May 1862, but the merger was declared invalid by the War Dept. When Hansbrough failed to re-organize the bn., however, the merger was finally completed. He became Lt. Col. of "Hansbrough's Roanoke Bn. Va. Detailed Conscripts and Reserves" in 1864. d. July 26, 1896. bur. East Hill Cemetery, Salem.

HANVEY, GEORGE McDUFFIE. b. 1828 in Abbeville, South Carolina. Mexican War veteran. Capt., Co. A, 1st Georgia (Ramsey's), Mar. 18, 1861. Capt., Co. A, 12th Georgia Artillery Battalion, May 1, 1862. Major - Nov. 6, 1862. Wded. in arm and lung, and POW, at Monocacy, released July 1865. 5′7″. Clerk in Atlanta. Died there Nov. 7, 1900. bur. Oakland Cemetery. Hanvey's papers are at U. Georgia.

HARD, JOHN STEWART. b. Dec. 2, 1842. Of Graniteville, South Carolina. Capt., Co. F, 7th South Carolina, June 4, 1861. Major - Sept. 17, 1862. KIA at Chickamauga.

HARDAWAY, ROBERT ARCHELAUS. b. Morgan Co., Georgia, Feb. 2, 1829. gr. Emory, 1847. Of Chambers Co., Alabama. m. Rebecca Hunt, 1857. Capt., Hardaway's Battery (Alabama), May 1, 1861. Major - Dec. 3, 1862. Lt. Col. - Feb. 27, 1864. Wded. at Spotsylvania, May 12, 1864. Appx. Civil engineer, and professor at U. Alabama and Auburn. d. Columbus, Georgia, Apr. 27, 1899. Stapleton Crutchfield declared that Hardaway was "not at all fitted" for battalion command.

HARDEMAN, ISAAC. b. Clinton, Georgia, Aug. 29, 1834. Sgt., Co. B, 12th Georgia, June 19, 1861. Lt. - Aug. 10, 1861. Captain - Nov. 8, 1861. Major - Jan. 22, 1863. Lt. Col. - June 9, 1863. POW at 2nd Manassas and Spotsylvania, released from latter imprisonment on July 24, 1865. Macon lawyer. d. Macon, Sept. 20, 1914. bur. Riverside Cemetery.

HARDEMAN, THOMAS, JR. b. Putnam Co., Jan. 12, 1825. gr. Emory, 1845. In Georgia legisl. In U.S. Congress, 1859-1861 and 1883-1885. Capt., Co. C, 2nd Georgia Battalion, Apr. 20, 1861. Major - May 15, 1861. Colonel, 45th Georgia, Mar. 15, 1862. Res., Oct. 13, 1862. d. Macon, Mar. 6, 1891. bur. Rose Hill Cemetery.

HARDEN, EDWARD RANDOLPH. att. U. Georgia, 1829-30. Lawyer. In Georgia legisl. Judge in Nebraska Territory, 1854-56. Major, 1st Georgia Regulars, Feb. 1, 1861. Resigned Mar. 15, 1861. d. June 12, 1884. Duke U. has Harden's ms. papers.

HARDIN, MARK BERNARD. b. Alexandria, Virginia, Aug. 14, 1838. gr. VMI, 1858, then on the faculty there. Fought at 1st Manassas with the 33rd Virginia, as Captain of the Provisional Army of Virginia. Major, 9th Virginia Infantry, Oct. 16, 1861. Dropped at May 1862 re-org. Major, 18th Battalion Virginia Heavy Artillery, June 1862. Commanded this unit in the Richmond defenses until the end of the war. Wounded twice. POW at Sayler's Creek. Chemistry professor at Clemson College, and on VMI faculty again. d. Apr. 26, 1916.

HARDIN, THOMAS JOSEPH. b. July 27, 1829 in Monroe Co., Kentucky. Farmer in Marshall Co., Mississippi. Capt., Co. I, 19th Mississippi, May 25, 1861. Major - May 5, 1863. Lt. Col. - July 17, 1863. Colonel - Jan. 20, 1864. KIA at Spotsylvania, May 12, 1864. bur. Spotsylvania Confederate Cemetery. Hardin also has a stone at Hill Crest Cemetery, Holly Springs, Mississippi.

HARDING, CYRUS, JR. b. Northumberland Co., Nov. 12, 1834. att. VMI. Served in the 40th Virginia, 1861-1862. Capt., Co. D, 15th Virginia Cavalry, Mar. 28, 1862. Major, 5th Virginia Cavalry, Nov. 8, 1864. Wded. hip at Wilderness. Paroled at Nottoway C.H., May 8, 1865. Farmer. m. (1) Laura Eugene Blackwell. m. (2) Judith Gertrude Blackwell (his sister-in-law). d. Mar. 23, 1893. bur. Farnham Baptist Church, Richmond Co.

HARDING, HENRY. b. Beaufort Co., North Carolina, May 8, 1836. Capt., Co. B, 61st North Carolina, Nov. 6, 1861. Major - Sept. 5, 1862. Res. Aug. 10, 1864. Lived in Greenville, North

Carolina. m. Susan Elizabeth Sugg, 1867. d. Aurora, North Carolina, Apr. 12, 1912. bur. Cherry Hill Cemetery, Greenville.

HARDING, RICHARD JAMES. b. Lynchburg, Virginia, Apr. 24, 1842. att. VMI. Moved to Texas with his family, 1852. Sgt., Co. B, 1st Texas, May 16, 1861. Lt. - Oct. 10, 1861. Captain - May 16, 1862. Major - Jan. 5, 1864. Lt. Col. - July 15, 1864. Wded. shoulder at Cold Harbor, resulting in his retirement on Nov. 9, 1864. An Aug. 13, 1862, A.N.Va. general order announced Harding guilty of the specification but not of the charge of "Deserting his command upon the march." Sheriff of Hinds Co., Mississippi. President of the Hood's Texas Brigade Association in 1905. d. Jackson, Mississippi, Sept. 21, 1917.

HARDWICK, WILLIAM MACK. b. Feb. 10, 1834. Of Eufala. 5′10″. Lt., Co. H, 48th Alabama, May 27, 1862. Captain - Sept. 17, 1862. Major - Oct. 15, 1862. Lt. Col. - July 17, 1863. POW at Sharpsburg, and in Alabama while on furlough in June 1864. Released July 25, 1865. m. Lucy Searcy, 1868. Lived in Henry Co. post-war. d. there May 16, 1919. bur. Adaniron Cemetery.

HARGROVE, TAZEWELL LEE. b. Granville Co., North Carolina, Apr. 6, 1830. Lived in Oxford. gr. Randolph-Macon. 6′0″. Lawyer. In North Carolina Secession Convention. Capt., Co. A, 44th North Carolina, Mar. 10, 1862. Major - May 3, 1862. Lt. Col. - July 28, 1862. Wded. and POW at South Anna, June 26, 1863, where he commanded with great distinction. Released July 24, 1865, after being among the "Immortal 600." In North Carolina legisl. Attorney General of North Carolina. d. Dec. 16, 1889, "a victim to wounds received in battle and to disease contracted in a Northern prison." bur. Townsville Cemetery. Hargrove's papers are at UNC.

HARMAN, ASHER WATERMAN. b. near Waynesboro, Virginia, Jan. 24, 1830. Went to Cincinnati briefly as a youth. Operated a stage line in Staunton. 5′9″. Capt., Co. G, 5th Virginia, Apr. 1861. Quartermaster of post at Staunton in 1862. Colonel, 12th Virginia Cavalry, June 21, 1862. Wded. at Brandy Station. POW near Harpers Ferry, July 14, 1863, released ca. Feb. 1865. Paroled at Staunton, Apr. 30, 1865. Staunton Railroad executive post-war. d. Richmond, Apr. 9, 1895. bur. Thornrose Cemetery, Staunton.

HARMAN, AUSTIN. b. Floyd Co., June 3, 1835. Lt., Co. D, 54th Virginia, Oct. 1, 1861. Captain - May 13, 1862. Major - Apr. 27, 1863. Paroled at Greensboro. m. Sarah Harter, 1864. Lived in Floyd Co. post-war. d. Sept. 15, 1914.

HARMAN, EDWIN HOUSTON. b. Tazewell Co., Feb. 13, 1835. att. Emory & Henry. m. Jennie King, 1861. Capt., Co. H, 45th Virginia, May 29, 1861. Lt. Col. - May 14, 1862. MWIA at Cloyd's Mountain.

HARMAN, MICHAEL GARBER. b. Staunton, Aug. 22, 1823. Ran a Staunton hotel and stage business. m. Caroline V. Stevenson. Major and QM of Virginia forces at the outset of the war. Lt. Col., 52nd Virginia, Aug. 19, 1861. Colonel - May 1, 1862. Wded. arm at McDowell. Res., disability, June 6, 1863. Did QM duty at Staunton the rest of the war. He was exonerated by court-martial of charges of impropriety in the duties he discharged as QM. President of Valley Railroad. d. on a train, Dec. 18, 1877.

HARMAN, WILLIAM HENRY. b. Waynesboro, Feb. 17, 1828. Mexican War veteran. m. Margaret Singleton Garver. Commonwealth's Attorney for Augusta Co., 1851-61. Lt. Col., 5th Virginia, May 7, 1861. Colonel - Sept. 11, 1861. Dropped at Apr. 1862 re-org. V.a.d.c. to Genl. Edward Johnson, 1862. KIA on Mar. 2, 1865, near Gallaher's Mill in Waynesboro, during Early's disaster there. bur. Thornrose Cemetery, Staunton.

HARMAN, WILLIAM NEEL. b. Hollybrook, Virginia (Bland Co.), Dec. 11, 1822. gr. Emory & Henry. Teacher in Kentucky and Texas, then lawyer in Bland Co. Sgt., Co. F, 45th Virginia, 1861. Capt., Co. F, 8th Virginia Cavalry, Aug. 1861. Major, 47th Virginia Cavalry Battalion, Apr. 4, 1864. Res., Sept. 20, 1864. d. Bonanza, Arkansas, July 30, 1905.

HARNESBERGER, STEPHEN ZELLARS. b. Lincoln Co., Georgia, Sept. 4, 1834. Farmer. Lt., Co. G, 15th Georgia, July 15, 1861. Captain - Dec. 3, 1861. Lt. Col. - March 4, 1863. POW at

Gettysburg. Caught tuberculosis at Johnson's Island "from which he eventually died." Exchanged Mar. 22, 1865. Moved to Upson Co. postwar. "Over six feet tall and of commanding presence." m. Ann Brooks, 1866. d. Feb. 21, 1871.

HARNESS, WILLIAM HENRY. b. Moorefield, Virginia, 1834. att. Georgetown and U. Virginia. 5'7½". Farmer. Colonel, 14th Virginia Militia, 1861. Capt., Co. B, 17th Virginia Cavalry Battalion (this unit was originally attached to the 7th Virginia Cav.), Mar. 10, 1862. In Feb. 1863 the 17th Bn. became part of the 11th Virginia Cav. Harness was apptd. Major, 11th Virginia Cavalry, July 23, 1863, but the promotion was "revoked." He resigned Nov. 5, 1863, after having been formally charged with cowardice. Lived in Wardensville post-war. d. Apr. 8, 1915 in Frederick Co. bur. Stonewall Cemetery, Winchester.

HARPER, HENRY HOLCOMBE. b. Oct. 10, 1827. Farmer in Lowndesville, worth $44,000 in 1860. Capt., Co. I, 14th South Carolina, at July 1861 org. Major - late 1863. Wded. four times, and imprisoned at Fortress Monroe for "several months." The absence of a Compiled Service Record on Harper makes his traces indistinct. Lowndesville farmer. In South Carolina legisl., 1858-61 and 1878-80. d. Mar. 4, 1886. bur. family cemetery in Lowndesville.

HARPER, KENTON. b. Pennsylvania 1801. Moved to Staunton, Virginia, from Chambersburg, Pennsylvania, in 1823. Published a Staunton newspaper, and was mayor of the town. General of Virginia Militia. Mexican War officer. In Virginia legisl. Colonel, 5th Virginia, May 7, 1861. Resigned Sept. 1861, by AIGO Special Order dated Sept. 5. d. Augusta Co., of pneumonia, Dec. 25, 1867. Harper's papers are at UNC. bur. Thornrose Cemetery, Staunton.

HARPER, WILSON. b. Port Republic, July 19, 1833. Teacher in Kansas and in Pendleton Co., Virginia, pre-war. Lt., Co. B, 31st Virginia, May 18, 1861. This unit became Co. K of the 25th Virginia at May 1862 re-org., with Harper as Captain. Major - Aug. 20, 1863. Wded. at Cedar Mountain and Wilderness. Appx. Rockingham Co. farmer. d. there Feb. 17, 1914.

HARRELL, GEORGE A. The 1860 census for Clarksville offers a possible match in G. A. Harrell, age 38, a lawyer born in Kentucky. Capt., Co. A, 14th Tennessee, May 14, 1861. Major - Nov. 1, 1861. Lt. Col. - Apr. 26, 1862. MWIA at Cedar Mountain, d. in Charlottesville, Aug. 15, 1862, aged 46. bur. Maplewood Cemetery, Charlottesville.

HARRELL, JARRETTE NORFLEET. b. Murfreesboro, North Carolina, Jan. 24, 1824. m. (1) Susan Ruffin. m. (2) Ellen O. Lawrence. Capt., Co. F, 1st North Carolina, May 16, 1861. Major - July 29, 1863. Lt. Col. - Dec. 14, 1863. Wded. at Chancellorsville. POW at Wilderness, released July 24, 1865. Murfreesboro merchant. d. Murfreesboro, Nov. 4, 1892.

HARRIS, CHARLES JENKINS. b. Milledgeville, Nov. 26, 1833. m. Mary C. Wiley, 1857. Capt., Co. K, 59th Georgia, May 15, 1862. Major - June 16, 1862. Lt. Col. - Dec. 22, 1862. Res. July 10, 1863. Colonel, 3rd Georgia Reserves, 1864. Macon judge. d. Jan. 22, 1893. bur. Rose Hill Cemetery.

HARRIS, JAMES GILMER. b. Mecklenburg Co., North Carolina, Nov. 10, 1841. Cabarrus Co. farmer. att. North Carolina Military Institute. Capt., Co. H, 7th North Carolina, May 16, 1861. Major - Nov. 28, 1864. Wded. in groin and hip at Jones' Farm, Sept. 30, 1864. Paroled at Greensboro. d. 1902.

HARRIS, JOHN L. b. 1828. Trader in Person Co. Capt., Co. H, 24th North Carolina, June 6, 1861. Lt. Col. - May 16, 1862. Wded. at Fredericksburg and at Ft. Stedman.

HARRIS, MERRIE B. (Harris' daughter spelled his given name "Merrie," but all official records use "Merry.") b. Copiah Co., Miss., ca. 1829. Lived at Gallatin. Capt., Co. D, 12th Mississippi, 1861. Lt. Col. at sometime prior to May 1863. Subsequently became Colonel, 12th Mississippi. The unfortunate absence of a service record on Harris leaves his career sadly obscured. A severe head wound at Weldon R.R. on June 24, 1864, disabled him. Harris died Aug. 15, 1865, "from four wounds." His widow, the former Emmaline Allen (m. 1850), survived him.

HARRIS, ROBERT A. Capt., Co. A, 1st Special Battalion Louisiana Infantry ("Wheat's Tigers"), Apr. 22, 1861. Major - ca. early

1862. Last roll showing Harris present is June 30, 1862. Paroled at Meridian, Mississippi, May 9, 1865.

HARRIS, SAMPSON WATKINS. b. Wetumpka, Alabama, Mar. 1838. gr. U. Georgia, 1857. m. Lucy W. Todd. Lt., Co. K, 6th Georgia, May 28, 1861. Captain - Nov. 1, 1862. Lt. Col. - July 7, 1864. Colonel - Feb. 14, 1865. Wded. at Bentonville. Adjutant General of Georgia. Carrollton lawyer and judge. d. Carrollton, May 31, 1912. bur. West Point (Georgia) Cemetery.

HARRIS, SKIDMORE. b. Rockingham Co., North Carolina, Aug. 29, 1832. Mined gold and copper in Georgia pre-war. m. Anne Donaldson. Of Cherokee Co., Georgia. Lt., Co. F, 2nd Georgia, Apr. 18, 1861. Lt. Col. - May 14, 1861. WIA at Sharpsburg. Colonel, 43rd Georgia, Mar. 20, 1863. MWIA at Baker's Creek, Mississippi, May 16, 1863, died the next day. bur. First Methodist Church, Canton, Georgia. The grave marker shows Harris' full given name as James Alpheus Skidmore.

HARRIS, WILLIAM AUGUSTUS. b. Milledgeville, Nov. 18, 1826. Mexican War pvt. att. Oglethorpe College. Lawyer in Irwin Co., Georgia. Frequently in Georgia legisl. Capt., Co. G, 14th Georgia, July 9, 1861. Major - Dec. 9, 1861. Lt. Col. - Oct. 23, 1862. Suffered a broken leg in a fall from his horse at Seven Pines. Resigned Nov. 8, 1862. Captain, 5th Georgia Militia, 1864. Major, 10th Georgia Militia, 1864-65. m. Gussie Ford, 1868. Georgia Secretary of State. Lawyer in Isabella. d. Aug. 17, 1894. bur. in Milledgeville.

HARRIS, WILLIAM TERRELL. b. Sparta, Georgia, Nov. 29, 1829. gr. U. Georgia, 1849. m. Martha L. Chambers. Lawyer, planter, state legisl. Capt., Co. B, 2nd Georgia, July 12, 1861. Major - Apr. 28, 1862. Lt. Col. - Sept. 17, 1862. KIA at Gettysburg. bur. Linwood Cemetery, Columbus, Georgia.

HARRISON, ARCHIBALD TAYLOR. b. Goochland Co., Oct. 28, 1829. att. VMI. Lt. Col., 30th Virginia, June 13, 1861. Colonel - Apr. 19, 1862. Absent frequently because of an injury, and retired Nov. 5, 1864. Paroled in Richmond, July 21, 1865. Lived on Cary Street in Richmond, then farmed in Prince George

County. m. Mary Montgomery Orgain, 1864. Died in Richmond, May 5, 1889. bur. Shockoe Hill.

HARRISON, CARTER HENRY. b. July 9, 1831. gr. VMI. Farmer. m. Alice B. Williams, 1852. Capt., Co. E, 11th Virginia, Apr. 22, 1861. Major - May 7, 1861. KIA at Blackburn's Ford, Virginia, July 18, 1861.

HARRISON, FRANCIS EUGENE. b. Andersonville, South Caroline, Apr. 29, 1821. att. U. Virginia. Planter. m. (1) Anna Elizabeth Ross, 1842. m. (2) Elizabeth Perrin Cotchran. Capt., Co. D, 1st South Carolina Rifles, July 20, 1861. Major - Nov. 12, 1862. Lt. Col. - Mar. 25, 1863. Wded. at Gaines' Mill. Colonel - May 5, 1863. Retired to Invalid Corps, Apr. 8, 1864. d. Nov. 19, 1874. His papers are at UNC.

HARRISON, ISHAM, JR. b. Jefferson Co., Alabama, Mar. 3, 1821. Lived in Lowndes Co., Alabama. Major, 13th Mississippi, May 23, 1861. Dropped at Apr. 1862 re-org. Was later Colonel, 6th Mississippi Cavalry. Spent much time seeking appointment to military courts, and did some commissary duty in Mississippi. KIA at the Battle of Harrisburg, Mississippi, July 14, 1864. He was a twin of Colonel Richard Harrison of the 43rd Mississippi.

HARRISON, JOHN J. Farmer in Beaufort District in 1860, age 28, worth $13,150. Capt., Co. D, 11th South Carolina, July 15, 1861. Major - May 5, 1862. KIA Oct. 22, 1862, at Coosawhatchie. Widow - Mary S. Harrison.

HARRISON, JULIEN. b. Richmond, Feb. 6, 1827. m. (1) Lavinia Heth. m. (2) Lillie Johnston. Lt. Col., 6th Virginia Cavalry, Sept. 11, 1861. Colonel - Apr. 15, 1862. Harrison resigned on July 28, 1862, but was reappointed colonel on Sept. 19, 1863. Wded. at Brandy Station, Oct. 11, 1863. Retired Mar. 6, 1865. d. July 17, 1877.

HARRISON, RANDOLPH. b. Cumberland Co., Sept. 26, 1829. att. U. Virginia. Cumberland Co. farmer. Lt., Co. E, 18th Virginia, 1861, then became Captain of the same company. Lt. Col., 4th Virginia Heavy Artillery, June 3, 1862. This unit became the 34th Virginia Inf. in 1864. Harrison was present into

1865 and lost a leg at Petersburg in 1865. Farmer and state official post-war. d. Cumberland Co., Sept. 13, 1900.

HARRISON, RANDOLPH. b. Richmond, Feb. 12, 1831. Brother of Colonel Julien Harrison (q.v.). att. William & Mary. gr. U. Pennsylvania in medicine, 1853. m. Elizabeth Williamson, 1853. 6′0″. Capt., Co. H, 46th Virginia, May 19, 1862. Lt. Col. - May 24, 1862. Colonel - 1864. Wded. severely in the neck at Petersburg, June 15, 1864. POW at Petersburg, Oct. 26, 1864, released June 13. Harrison escaped en route to Fort Delaware, but was recaptured in Baltimore. Williamsburg physician. d. there June 14, 1894. bur. Bruton Parish Church.

HARRISON, SAMUEL R. Lt., Co. I, 1st Louisiana, Apr. 25, 1861, aged 28. Elected Major, but resigned before the regiment was ever engaged.

HART, ALEXANDER. b. New Orleans, Oct. 1, 1839. Clerk. m. Leonora Levy. Lt., Co. E, 5th Louisiana, May 10, 1861. Captain - Oct. 16, 1861. Major - Jan. 1863. Wded. at Sharpsburg and Gettysburg. POW at Winchester, Sept. 19, 1864, exchanged Nov. 16. Merchant in Richmond, Staunton, Norfolk and elsewhere post-war. d. Norfolk, Va., Sept. 21, 1911.

HART, JAMES FRANKLIN. b. Union Dist., South Carolina, Feb. 13, 1837. gr. SCMA. Teacher in Union Dist. Lt., C.S. Engineers, 1861. Lt., Hampton Legion Artillery, June 15, 1861. Captain, Hart's Horse Artillery Battery (South Carolina), Nov. 27, 1861. Lost a leg at Burgess' Mill, Oct. 27, 1864, which ended his war service, but promotion was made to Major, ca. Feb. 1865. m. Margaret Jane Ratchford, 1863. Lawyer in Yorkville. In South Carolina legisl., 1882-84. d. York, South Carolina, Apr. 20, 1905. bur. Rose Hill Cemetery.

HART, ROBERT D. b. North Carolina. Marengo Co. lawyer in 1860, age 30. Capt., Co. B, 43rd Alabama, Mar. 18, 1862. Major - Dec. 16, 1862. Res. July 20, 1863.

HARTSFIELD, WILEY F., Jr. b. Georgia. Miller in Zebulon, age 23, in 1860. Pvt., Co. A, 1st Georgia, Mar. 1861. Lt., Co. H, 53rd Georgia, May 5, 1862. Major - Nov. 8, 1863. Lt. Col. - Dec. 3, 1863. Wded. at Wilderness. KIA at Sayler's Creek.

HASKELL, ALEXANDER CHEVES. b. Abbeville Dist., South Carolina, Sept. 22, 1839. gr. South Carolina College. Pvt., Co. D, 1st South Carolina, Jan. 1861. Adj. of the regt. - Feb. 1861. Lt. and a.d.c. to Maxcy Gregg, Dec. 14, 1861. Capt. and a.a.g., Jan. 18, 1862. Lt. Col., 7th South Carolina Cavalry, Apr. 1864. Colonel - June 1864. Wded. at Fredericksburg, Chancellorsville, Cold Harbor and Darbytown Road. Appx. m. (1) Rebecca Singleton, 1861. m. (2) Alice Van Yeveren Alexander, 1870 (she was a sister of Genl. E. P. Alexander). d. Columbia, Apr. 13, 1910. bur. Elmwood Cemetery.

HASKELL, JOHN CHEVES. b. Oct. 21, 1841. Lt., Co. A, 1st South Carolina Artillery, May 18, 1861. Major and Commissary, Dec. 21, 1861, serving with G. W. Smith and then D. R. Jones. Wded. at Gaines' Mill and lost right arm. Major of Artillery, Apr. 13, 1863. Lt. Col. - Feb. 18, 1865. m. (1) Sally Preston Hampton, daughter of General Wade Hampton. m. (2) Lucy Hampton, daughter of Lt. Col. Frank Hampton. In S. C. legisl. Columbia lawyer and Mississippi planter. d. Columbia, June 26, 1906.

HATCH, LEWIS M. b. Salem, New Hampshire, Nov. 28, 1815. m. Emily E. Bell. Farmer near Charleston. Veteran of Seminole War. Colonel and AQM, Beauregard's Command, Aug. 1861. Colonel, 23rd South Carolina, Nov. 11, 1861. Hatch soon returned to South Carolina State Commands, however, and remained in South Carolina service. d. Jan. 12, 1887. bur. Magnolia Cemetery, Charleston.

HATCHER, DANIEL COOKE. b. 1837. Clerk in a Middleburg store in 1860. Lt., Co. A, 7th Virginia Cavalry, Apr. 19, 1861. Captain - May 23, 1862. Major - Feb. 4, 1865. Court-martialed in 1864. Paroled at Winchester, May 8, 1865. 5'11". d. Jan. 8, 1912, at Rectortown. bur. Sharon Cemetery, Middleburg.

HATELEY, JOHN C. b. Georgia. Lawyer in Jasper, Florida, in 1860, age 37, worth $20,609. Colonel, 5th Florida, Apr. 8, 1862. Wded. at Sharpsburg. Res. due to those wounds, July 6, 1863. A later effort at re-instatement failed. d. 1869. bur. Evergreen Cemetery, Jasper.

HAWES, RICHARD RANDOLPH. b. Apr. 17, 1829. Capt., Co. A, 10th Georgia, May 10, 1861. Major - Sept. 25, 1861. Res. on disability, Aug. 4, 1862. In Georgia legisl., 1863. d. Oct. 4, 1866, in Lumpkin. bur. Linwood Cemetery, Columbus.

HAWKINS, WILLIS ALSTON. b. Morgan Co., Jan. 15, 1825. Americus lawyer. m. (1) Terinda Smith, 1847. m. (2) Mary Finn, 1854. In Georgia Secession Convention. Capt., Co. A, 12th Georgia, June 15, 1861. Major - Apr. 10, 1862. Lt. Col. - Jan. 22, 1863. Res. Jan. 24, 1863. Hawkins apparently was disgraced along with Z. T. Conner at Front Royal. One of Jackson's staff spoke of Hawkins' "cowardice." Georgia Supreme Court Justice. d. Americus, Nov. 28, 1886.

HAYES, GEORGE EVERARD. b. Georgia, March 28, 1835. att. U. Georgia. Druggist, educated in Philadelphia. Lt., Co. K, 3rd Georgia, Apr. 25, 1861. Major - Aug. 15, 1864. KIA at Weldon R.R., Aug. 21, 1864. Hayes weighed about 120 pounds, but had "an iron will."

HAYNES, ALEXANDER. b. Patrick Co., late 1839 or early 1840. Capt., Co. E, 29th Va., Aug. 6, 1861. Major - Apr. 10, 1863. MWIA (leg amputated), May 14, 1864, apparently at Drewry's Bluff. d. May 30. Posthumously promoted lieutenant colonel.

HAYNES, CHARLES LEWIS. b. Clifton Forge. Farmer in Craig Co. Lt., Co. C, 27th Virginia, May 10, 1861, aged 27. Captain - Apr. 23, 1862. Lt. Col. - Sept. 4, 1863. Wded. groin at Gettysburg. POW at Spotsylvania, May 10, 1864. Among the "Immortal 600" as a prisoner. Exchanged Aug. 3, 1864. Commanding the tiny Stonewall Brigade in Feb. 1865. Farmer and carpenter at Clifton Forge. d. June 18, 1881.

HAYWOOD, EDWARD GRAHAM. Wake Co. lawyer. Lt. Col., 7th North Carolina, May 16, 1861, aged 30. Colonel - June 27, 1862. Wded. at 2nd Manassas and Chancellorsville. Retired to Invalid Corps, Nov. 28, 1864, due to partial blindness resulting from his wounds. Haywood was cashiered for drunkenness on Dec. 26, 1863, but obviously the judgment was suspended.

HECK, JONATHAN McGEE. b. Monongalia Co., Virginia, May 5, 1831. Lawyer there. m. Mattie A. Callendine, 1859. Lt. Col.,

25th Virginia, July 1861. Dropped at May 1862 re-org. Mining magnate in N. C. post-war. d. Feb. 10, 1894. bur. Oakwood Cemetery, Raleigh. North Carolina Department of Arichives and History has Heck's papers.

HECKMAN, DAVID P. Physician in Franklin Co., Virginia. 5'9". Lt., Co. C, 57th Virginia, June 21, 1861. Acting surgeon of 57th Virginia, Oct. 1861. Captain - May 7, 1862. Major - July 5, 1863. Wded. at Gettysburg. POW at Dinwiddie C. H., April. 1, 1865, released July 25, age 34.

HENAGAN, JOHN WILLIFORD. b. Marlboro Dist., Nov. 22, 1822. In S. C. legisl. Sheriff of Marlboro. Lt. Col., 8th South Carolina, Apr. 13, 1861. Colonel - May 14, 1862. Wded. at South Mountain. POW near Winchester, Sept. 13, 1864. d. Johnson's Island Prison, Apr. 26, 1865. bur. there.

HENDERSON, WILLIAM GASTON. b. Milton, N. C., Aug. 3, 1828. Lawyer in Okolona, Miss. m. Dona Hubbard, 1855. Lt., Co. B, Jeff Davis Legion Cavalry (Mississippi), Feb. 1861. Captain - later in 1861. Shattered ankle at Upperville, Virginia, June 21, 1863. Subsequently promoted Major, but never again served with Jeff Davis Legion. A similar rank in the 5th Mississippi Cavalry was never filled by him. Postmaster of Biloxi post-war. Alive there in 1899.

HENLEY, JOHN A. b. Williamsburg, Virginia. att. William & Mary, 1834-35. Clerk of Circuit Court in Williamsburg in 1860, worth $28,000. Capt., Co. C, 32nd Virginia, April 1861. Became a C. S. War Dept. official. Capt., Co. A, 3rd Virginia Battalion LDT ("Clerk's Bn."), June 13, 1863, aged 42. Major - June 29, 1863. Resigned, illness, March 29, 1864. Paroled at Richmond, Apr. 21, 1865.

HENNINGSEN, CHARLES FREDERICK. b. Brussels, Belgium, Feb. 21, 1815. m. Williamina Belt Connelly. Fought with Carlists in Spain and with Kossuth in Hungary. Came to America in 1851. Filibusterer with William Walker. Author of six books on European things. Colonel, 59th Virginia, Aug. 1, 1861. Dropped at Nov. 1862 re-org. d. Washington, D. C., June 14, 1877. bur. Congressional Cemetery.

HENRY, ELI G. b. South Carolina. Lawyer and judge in Madison Co., Mississippi, in 1860, age 40, worth $30,000. Lt., Co. C, 18th Mississippi, Apr. 17, 1861, aged 46. Major- Sept. 13, 1861. Dropped back to Capt., Co. C, Apr. 26, 1862, at re-org. KIA at Malvern Hill.

HENRY, MATHIS WINSTON. b. Kentucky, Nov. 28, 1838. Lived in Russellville, Kentucky. gr. USMA, 1860. Lt., U.S. Army, 1860-61. 5′10″. Lt., Confederate States Cavalry, Feb. 15, 1862 (to rank from Mar. 1861). Acting on J. E. B. Stuart's staff, Mar. 1862. Captain of a Virginia Horse Artillery Battery named for him, Aug. 9, 1862. Major - Feb. 21, 1863. Commanded an artillery battalion in Hood's Division. Transferred to the western army in 1864. POW at Salisbury, North Carolina, Apr. 12, 1865, released July 25. m. Susie R. Burwell, 1874. Held Nevada silver mining interests post-war. d. Brooklyn, New York, Nov. 28, 1877. bur. Old Chapel, Clarke Co., Virginia.

HENRY, PATRICK MILLER. b. Cumberland Co., 1815. m. Susan Toby Robertson. Colonel, Henry's Regiment Virginia Reserves. Lt. Col., 5th Battalion Virginia Reserves, May 28, 1864. This unit, briefly designated as Henry's Regt., was posted on the Richmond and Danville R.R. d. Washington, D.C., 1873.

HENRY, SAMUEL. b. Sevier Co., Tennessee, July 17, 1825. m. Charity E. Fennell, 1856. Merchant at Gunter's Landing, Alabama. Capt., 9th Alabama, July 1861. Lt. Col. - July 3, 1861. Colonel - Oct. 21, 1861. "Cashiered," Mar. 19, 1863, for cowardice. Gadsden merchant. d. Gadsden, Mar. 20, 1893. bur. Forrest Cemetery.

HENSLEY, JAMES O. b. 1837. "Promising young lawyer" of Bedford Co., 1861. Lt., Jordan's Battery (Virginia), Apr. 18, 1861 (the Bedford Artillery). Capt., Co. B, 19th Battalion Heavy Artillery, Mar. 10, 1862. Major - Aug. 19, 1862. d. 1878. bur. Longmount Cemetery, Bedford.

HERBERT, ARTHUR. b. Alexandria, Virginia, July 27, 1829, in the Carlyle House, which was opened to the public in 1978. Capt., Co. H, 17th Virginia, Apr. 17, 1861. Occupation at enlistment shown as "Barber." Major - Apr. 27, 1862. WIA in foot at Seven Pines. Lt. Col. - Nov. 1, 1862. Colonel - July 8, 1864. Herbert commanded the 7th Virginia at South Mountain; the 29th Virginia in Apr.-May 1863, and Corse's Brigade at Appomattox. Herbert was a founder of Burke & Herbert Bank & Trust, which is still located in Alexandria. d. Alexandria, Feb. 23, 1919. bur. Ivy Hill Cemetery.

HERBERT, HILARY ABNER. b. South Carolina, Mar. 12, 1834. att. U. Alabama and U. Virginia. Capt., Co. F, 8th Alabama, May 20, 1861. Major - Mar. 20, 1862. Lt. Col. - June 16, 1862. Colonel - 1864. Retired for disability, Nov. 2, 1864. Wded. at Wilderness. m. Ella Bettie Smith, 1867. In U.S. Congress, 1877-93. Secretary of the Navy, 1893-97. Author of several books. His fine mss. memoirs are at UNC. d. Tampa, Florida, Mar. 5, 1919. bur. Oakwood Cemetery, Montgomery, Alabama.

HERBERT, JAMES R. b. Woodstock, Maryland, Aug. 18, 1833. As a youthful sailor, Herbert was said to have been one of only two cholera survivors on a stricken ship. Lt., Co. A, 1st Maryland, early 1861. Capt., Co. D, 1st Maryland, June 1861. Capt., Co. C, 2nd Maryland Battalion, Sept. 11, 1862. Major - Oct. 2, 1862. Lt. Col. - Jan. 26, 1863. Wded. in leg, arm, and abdomen, and POW at Gettysburg. Paroled at Greensboro. General of Maryland National Guard post-war. m. Elizabeth Coleman Alexander. Baltimore Police Commissioner. d. Aug. 5, 1884. bur. Loudon Park, Baltimore.

HERRING, CALVIN. b. North Carolina. Of Lenoir Co. Lt., Co. D, 27th North Carolina, Apr. 27, 1861. Captain - Feb. 21, 1862. Major - Jan. 11, 1865. Wded. chest, Aug. 25, 1864. Appx. m. Martha Rouse. Moved to Texas.

HEYWARD, WILLIAM CRUGER. b. New York, July 1808. gr. USMA, 1830. Lt., U.S. Army, 1830-32. Colonel, 11th South Carolina, July 1861. Dropped at May 1862 re-org. d. Sept. 1, 1863. bur. St. Michael's Episcopal Church, Charleston.

HICKERSON, CHARLES NAPOLEON. b. Wilkes Co., North Carolina, 1829. Farmer. 5′10½″. Pvt., Co. F, 37th North Carolina, Sept. 24, 1861. Captain - Nov. 20, 1861. Major - Apr. 17,

1862. Lt. Col. - June 30, 1862. Resigned for health reasons, July 30, 1862. m. three times. d. 1915.

HIGGINBOTHAM, JOHN CARLTON. b. Nov. 11, 1842. att. Lynchburg College. Capt., Co. A, 25th Virginia, May 27, 1861. Major - May 1, 1862. Lt. Col. - Oct. 8, 1862. Colonel - Jan. 28, 1863. Wded. at McDowell (leg) and 2nd Manassas (thigh). KIA at Spotsylvania, May 10, 1864. bur. Spotsylvania Confederate Cemetery.

HILL, ALBERT A. b. Iredell Co., ca. 1827. Davidson Co. physician. 6'3". Capt., Co. B, 48th North Carolina, Feb. 2, 1862. Major - Oct. 20, 1862. Lt. Col. - Dec. 4, 1863. Wded. at Fredericksburg in shoulder. Appx.

HILL, ALONZO ALEXANDER FRANKLIN. b. Oglethorpe Co., Georgia, Dec. 4, 1826. gr. U. Georgia, 1845. gr. Jefferson Medical College. Surgeon, USN, and lawyer. Capt., Troup Artillery (Georgia), Apr. 26, 1861. Resigned quite soon. Capt., Co. A, 1st Georgia Regulars, June 18, 1861. Also Captain of Co. L and Co. M during 1861. Major - Sept. 3, 1864. d. Jan. 9, 1872. bur. Oconee Hill Cemetery, Clarke Co., Georgia. Had "the longest beard of any man" in Athens.

HILL, DANIEL PIKE. b. July 18, 1824. Living in Harris Co. in 1860, a lawyer, worth $92,641. Member of the Secession Convention (voted yes). Lt. Col., 31st Georgia, Nov. 19, 1861. Resigned May 13, 1862. d. Aug. 3, 1900. bur. Oakland Cemetery, Atlanta.

HILL, JAMES CHRISTIAN. b. Charles City Co., May 29, 1831. Pvt., Co. E, 46th Virginia, May 1861. Captain - June 5, 1861. Major - Mar. 28, 1864. Wded. June 17, 1864, arm amputated. Albermarle Co. businessman. In Virginia legisl. d. Scottsville, Sept. 21, 1906. bur. Baptist Cemetery there.

HILL, JUNIUS LEROY. b. Iredell Co., Mar. 12, 1836. Capt., Co. A, 7th North Carolina, May 16, 1861. Major - Apr. 4, 1862. Lt. Col. - June 27, 1862. KIA at Chancellorsville.

HILL, LEWIS H. b. South Carolina. Merchant in Coosa Co., Alabama, in 1860, age 27. Lt., Co. I, 3rd Alabama, 1861. Major, 59th Alabama, summer 1863. Lt. Col., 61st Alabama, backdated to May 2, 1863. POW at Petersburg, Apr. 2, 1865, released July 25, 1865. At release, aged 32, 5′10″.

HILL, ROBERT CLINTON. b. Iredell Co., North Carolina, Aug. 1833. gr. USMA, 1855. Lt., U.S. Army, 1855-61. Lt. of Confederate States Artillery, Mar. 16, 1861. Major and a.a.g. to Genl. Branch, Jan. 1862. Colonel, 48th North Carolina, Apr. 9, 1862. d. at his home in North Carolina, Dec. 4, 1863, of disease. Hill is criticized sternly and accused of cowardice in a manuscript memoir by Col. Walkup. He was known in the old Army as "Crazy Hill" because of his excitable manner.

HILL, WILLIAM J. b. Virginia. Lived at Gatesville, North Carolina. Capt., Co. B, 5th North Carolina, May 16, 1861. Major - May 5, 1862. Lt. Col. - Dec. 3, 1862, but declined appt. Lt. Col. - May 12, 1864, while in prison. Wded. leg at Chancellorsville. POW at Gatesville, North Carolina, while on wounded furlough, June 5, 1863, exchanged Feb. 1865. Paroled at Charlotte, May 13, 1865.

HILTON, MIEL. Farmer at Hickory Head, South Carolina, in 1860, age 34, married, worth $2,800. Capt., Co. E, 22nd South Carolina, Jan. 9, 1862. Major - 1862. Resigned Feb. 19, 1863, citing a "Mexican War wound" which was acting up.

HINES, JAMES STEPHEN. b. 1830. Lived in New Hanover Co. Capt., Co. C, 1st North Carolina, May 16, 1861. Major - July 8, 1862. Resigned July 29, 1863, due to "partial paralysis . . . great nervous derangement." d. 1904. bur. Old Town Cemetery, Faison, North Carolina.

HINTON, JAMES W. b. Pasquotank Co., North Carolina, 1827. Elizabeth City lawyer. 5′10″. Capt., Co. A, 8th North Carolina, May 16, 1861. Major - Oct. 25, 1862. Lt. Col. - Feb. 20, 1863. Colonel, 68th North Carolina, July 8, 1863. POW at Roanoke River, Dec. 12, 1864, released July 21. Lawyer in Norfolk, Virginia. Died there, Jan. 23, 1875.

HOBSON, ALEXANDER M. b. Richmond, 1831. att. U. Virginia. Farmer. Capt., Co. F, 4th Virginia Cavalry, May 10, 1861. Major - June 13, 1862. d. Oct. 24, 1863.

HOBSON, CALEB BOND. b. Yadkin Co. Merchant in Duplin Co. Lt. in 26th N. C. Militia in 1861. Capt., Co. B, 51st North Carolina, Apr. 1862, age 31. Lt. Col. - Jan. 1863. KIA at Ft. Harrison, Sept. 30, 1864.

HOBSON, EDWIN LAFAYETTE. b. Greensboro, Alabama, Oct. 13, 1835. att. U. Virginia. Capt., Co. I, 5th Alabama, Apr. 13, 1861. Lt. Col. - July 15, 1862. Colonel - Nov. 29, 1864. Wded. thigh at Chancellorsville and right arm at Spotsylvania. Married Frances Anderson, daughter of Genl. Joseph R. Anderson. Official of Tredegar works in Richmond. d. Richmond, Nov. 9, 1901.

HODGES, JAMES GREGORY. b. Portsmouth, Dec. 28, 1829. Physician there, and Mayor of Portsmouth. Colonel, 14th Virginia, May 17, 1861. KIA at Gettysburg, July 3. bur. in unknown grave. Widow - Sallie W. Hodges. (N.B. - An equally reliable source gives Hodges' birth as Dec. 25, 1828, and his education as U. of Pennsylvania. The latter item, at least, is inaccurate.)

HODGES, JOHN JACKSON. b. Georgia. m. Nellie Coleman. Lawyer in Bossier Parish, Louisiana. Capt., Co. D, 9th Louisiana, July 7, 1861. Major - July 4, 1863. Lt. Col. - Oct. 8, 1863. Wded. and POW at Monocacy, exchanged Nov. 15, 1864. Paroled at Natchitoches, June 6, 1865.

HODGES, WESLEY C. b. 1822 in Milledgeville. att. Emory. Mexican War veteran. Cotton merchant in Columbus. Lt., Co. G, 2nd Georgia, Apr. 16, 1861. Lt. Col., 17th Georgia, Aug. 9, 1861. Colonel - Jan. 4, 1863. Wded. at Wilderness, and absent thereafter. d. Columbus, Sept. 19, 1874. bur. Linwood Cemetery. Hodges wrote a Mexican War novel, but later destroyed most copies. None are recorded at DLC.

HOFFMAN, JOHN STRINGER. b. Weston, Virginia, 1821. Clarksburg lawyer. Cousin of Gideon D. Camden, Jr. (q.v.). "Distinguished for his great physique, his bachelorhood and his fondness for a game of euchre or whist." Hoffman wore eyeglasses to compensate for acute nearsightedness. A member of the regiment called Hoffman "a hard, brave fighter, but a dull and slow man, unsuited to command . . . a brigade." Sgt., Co. C, 31st Virginia, May 21, 1861. Major - Dec. 14, 1861. Colonel -

May 1, 1862. Wded. Feb. 5, 1865. Clarksburg judge. d. Nov. 1887. bur. I.O.O.F. Cemetery, Clarksburg, West Virginia. Hoffman's papers are at WVU.

HOGAN, RIDGEWAY BOLIVAR. Lt., Co. C, 19th Georgia, June 11, 1861. Captain - June 3, 1862. Lt. Col. - Sept. 21, 1864. m. Cathaline Barkman Stern.

HOGE, EDWARD FOSTER. b. 1840. Lt., Co. G, 9th Georgia, June 12, 1861. Captain - Aug. 28, 1861. Lt. Col. - Aug. 17, 1863. Colonel - Mar. 1, 1864. Wded. at Gettysburg. Speaker of Georgia House. Founded the Atlanta *Journal*. m. Julia Clayton. d. Aug. 10, 1885, "in 46th year." bur. Oakland Cemetery, Atlanta.

HOKE, JOHN FRANKLIN. b. Lincoln Co., May 8, 1820. gr. UNC, 1841. Lawyer. Mexican War officer. Adj. Genl. of North Carolina in 1861. Colonel, 23rd North Carolina, July 15, 1861. Failed at spring 1862 re-org. Later served as Colonel, 4th North Carolina Senior Reserves. m. Catherine Wilson Alexander. d. Oct. 27, 1888, while viewing a political parade from his porch.

HOKE, WILLIAM JAMES. b. 1826. Of Lincoln Co., North Carolina. Capt., Co. K, 1st North Carolina (Bethel), Apr. 25, 1861. Colonel, 38th North Carolina, Jan. 17, 1862. Wded. at Mechanicsville and Gettysburg. Retired to Invalid Corps, June 18, 1864. Merchant in Lincoln Co. m. Georgianna T. Sumner. d. Oct. 11, 1870 in Columbia, South Carolina. Dorsey Pender called Hoke "the greatest old granny." Hoke's letters are in the W. G. Childs Papers, University of South Carolina, and at UNC.

HOLDER, WILLIAM DUNBAR. b. Franklin Co., Tennessee, Mar. 6, 1824. Planter and U.S. Marshal in Birmingham and Pontotoc, Mississippi. In Mississippi legisl. m. Catharine T. Bowles. Capt., Co. C, 17th Mississippi, June 1, 1861. Colonel - Apr. 26, 1862. Wded. at Malvern Hill (absent eight months) and in groin at Gettysburg. Resigned Feb. 26, 1864. Served in C.S. Congress, 1863-65. d. Jackson, Mississippi, Apr. 26, 1900. bur. Greenwood Cemetery.

HOLLADAY, FRANCIS DAVID. b. Suffolk, June 8, 1817. m. Emily Susan Pinner. Hotel keeper. Capt., Co. B, 16th Virginia,

Apr. 17, 1861. Major - Jan. 6, 1862. POW at Crampton's Gap, exchanged Nov. 10, 1862. Resigned Mar. 16, 1863, to the delight of William Mahone. d. July 3, 1868. bur. Cedar Hill Cemetery, Suffolk.

HOLLIDAY, FREDERICK WILLIAM MACKEY. b. Winchester, Feb. 22, 1828. gr. Yale U. and U. Virginia. Frederick Co. Commonwealth's Attorney. Capt., Co. D, 33rd Virginia, May 10, 1861. Major - Apr. 22, 1862. Lt. Col. - Nov. 15, 1862. Colonel - Feb. 1, 1863. Lost right arm at Cedar Mountain. Retired to Invalid Corps, Mar. 21, 1864. In C.S. Congress. Elected governor of Virginia in 1877, vigorously opposing Readjustors. d. Winchester, May 29, 1899. bur. Mt. Hebron Cemetery. Holliday's fine and extensive papers are at Duke.

HOLLIDAY, HENRY BURROUGHS. b. Laurens Dist., South Carolina, Mar. 11, 1819. m. Alice Jane McKey, 1849. Father of John Henry Holliday, famous as a western gunfighter under the name "Doc" Holliday. Served in Cherokee and Mexican Wars. From the latter war, he brought home an adopted Mexican son who became a Confederate soldier in the 30th Georgia. AQM, 27th Georgia, Sept. 2, 1861. Major - Dec. 25, 1861. Res. Aug. 24, 1862. Valdosta, Georgia, pecan farmer and merchant. d. Valdosta, Feb. 23, 1893.

HOLMAN, DANIEL WILSON. b. Oct. 2, 1832, Mulberry, Tennessee. Major, 1st Tennessee, Apr. 27, 1861. Not re-elected in Apr. 1862 re-org. Went on to become Colonel of the 11th Tennessee Cavalry in the western theater. Lawyer in Fayetteville, Tennessee. d. there Sept. 22, 1885. bur. Rose Hill Cemetery.

HOLMAN, JAMES HARDY. b. Lincoln Co., Tennessee, Mar. 7, 1836. Lt., U.S. Army, 1857-61. Lt. Col., 1st Tennessee, Apr. 27, 1861. Not re-elected in Apr. 1862 re-org. In Jan. 1863 was Lt. commanding a conscript camp in Knoxville. Aide to Genl. T. H. Taylor. Lawyer and prohibition leader in Fayetteville, Tennessee. d. there Mar. 27, 1910. bur. Rose Hill Cemetery.

HOLMES, JAMES CLINTON. b. 1826. Farmer and merchant in Sampson Co. Lt., Co. A, 30th North Carolina, Apr. 20, 1861.

Captain - Aug. 3, 1861. Major - Sept. 3, 1863. Retired to Invalid Corps, with paralysis, Aug. 19, 1864. bur. Clinton Cemetery.

HOLMES, WILLIAM R. b. 1821. Physician in Burke Co., Georgia. Capt., Co. D, 2nd Georgia, Apr. 19, 1861. Lt. Col. - Apr. 28, 1862. KIA at Sharpsburg. Unmarried. Holmes has a marker in Waynesboro Confederate Cemetery, Burke Co., but his body was not recovered.

HOLT, BOLLING HALL. b. Nov. 10, 1840. att. U. Virginia (from Ohio). Pvt., Co. G, 2nd Georgia, Apr. 16, 1861. Major, 35th Georgia, Oct. 14, 1861. Lt. Col. - June 1, 1862. Colonel - Nov. 1, 1862. Appx. d. Sept. 27, 1867. bur. Linwood Cemetery, Columbus, Georgia.

HOLT, WILLIS COX. Druggist and lawyer. Mexican War sergeant. m. Susannah Busey, 1850. Capt., Co. C, 10th Georgia, May 18, 1861, age 31. Major - Aug. 4, 1862. Lt. Col. - Oct. 29, 1862. Colonel - May 19, 1864. Wded. in head at Sharpsburg. MWIA at Cedar Creek, Oct. 19, 1864. bur. Massanutten Cemetery, Woodstock, Virginia.

HOOD, WILLIAM HENRY. b. near Berlin, Southampton Co., Virginia, July 22, 1832. gr. VMI, 1856. Capt., Co. D, 3rd Virginia, June 1861. Major then Lt. Col., Hood's Battalion Virginia Reserves, 1864. This unit served in the Petersburg trenches. POW June 1864, exchanged Dec. 1864. In the "Immortal 600." Farmer and civil engineer. d. Henderson, North Carolina, Jan. 19, 1908.

HOOLE, AXALLA JOHN. b. Darlington Dist., Oct. 12, 1822. Farmer. Militia officer. m. Elizabeth G. Brunson, 1856. Capt., Co. A, 8th South Carolina, Apr. 13, 1861. Lt. Col. - May 14, 1862. KIA at Chickamauga. bur. Brunson Graveyard, near Darlington.

HOOPER, GEORGE WILLIAM. b. Lafayette, Alabama, July 27, 1839. Russell Co. lawyer. Lt., Co. I, 6th Alabama, May 2, 1861. Capt., Co. F, 6th Alabama, 1862. Major - May 2, 1863. Lt. Col. - May 11, 1863. Wded. near Richmond, June 12, 1862. Wded. June 1, 1863. "Disabled by accident," which apparently means that one of those two wounds was by friendly accident. Retirement papers were lost, and as a result Hooper was dropped from the rolls for prolonged absence without leave, on Mar. 23, 1865. d. Opelika, 1883.

HOOPER, JOHN WORD, JR. b. Oct. 13, 1833. Of Bartow Co., Georgia. m. Frances Stuart. Capt., Co. K, 19th Georgia, June 11, 1861. Major - Jan. 1863. Res., disability, June 23, 1863. In Georgia legisl., 1863-65. d. Clarendon, Arkansas, July 31, 1886.

HOOPER, THOMAS WILLIAM. b. Jan. 7, 1840. Resigned from U.S. Navy to become Adj., 21st Georgia, July 20, 1861. Major - Sept. 27, 1861. Lt. Col. - Mar. 30, 1862. Colonel - Apr. 18, 1864. Wded. in arm at Gaines' Mill. POW at Winchester, Sept. 19, 1864, released July 24, 1865. Lawyer in Atlanta and Arkansas. m. Martha Trippe. Died in Arkansas, 1886.

HOPKINS, CHARLES RINALDO FLOYD. b. Camden Co., Georgia, Dec. 1, 1824. gr. U.S. Naval Academy. Resigned from U.S. Navy, Nov. 1851. St. Augustine, Florida, civil engineer. m. Frances Humphreys. Major, 1st Florida Battalion, Feb. 12, 1862. Lt. Col. - May 18, 1862. The 1st Florida Battalion later merged into the 10th Florida Regiment. Hopkins became Colonel, 10th Florida, June 11, 1864. Wded. arm and thigh at Olustee. Appx. d. Jacksonville, Florida, Jan. 17, 1898. bur. Old City Cemetery.

HOPKINS, WARREN MONTGOMERY. b. Powhatan Co., June 1, 1839. Farmer. Sgt., Co. D, 1st Virginia Cavalry, Apr. 1861. Adj., 1st Virginia Cavalry, 1862. Served on W. E. Jones' staff. Colonel, 25th Virginia Cavalry, Dec. 31, 1864. m. Mary H. Baltzell, 1862. d. Dec. 9, 1875. bur. Singing Spring Cemetery, Abingdon, Virginia.

HORNE, WILLIAM R. B. b. Virginia. Tanner in Smyth Co. in 1860, age 30. Capt., Co. B, 29th Virginia, July 23, 1861. Major - Oct. 18, 1862. Resigned Nov. 11, 1862, "to pursue my regular avocation."

HOUCK, WILLIAM A. Capt., Co. D, 34th North Carolina, Sept. 9, 1861, aged 35. 5′11″. Farmer. Lt. Col. - Oct. 25, 1861. Dropped at April 1862 re-org. Paroled at Salisbury, June 7, 1865.

HOUNSHELL, DAVID STUART. b. Wytheville, Virginia, Nov. 4, 1835. att. VMI. Maj., 23rd Virginia Battalion, Jan. 15, 1862. Dropped at May 1862 re-org. Lt. Col., 5th Virginia State Line, 1863. Colonel, 4th Virginia State Line, 1863. Lt. Col., Hounshell's Battalion Virginia Cavalry Partisan Rangers, 1865. d. Dayton, Ky., July 11, 1901.

HOWARD, JAMES. b. Baltimore, Md., Oct. 23, 1832. Brother of McHenry Howard, noted author and staff officer. Lt., U.S. Artillery, 1857-61, serving on the Plains and in the far west. 6′0″. Lt. of C.S. Artillery, Apr. 16, 1861, assigned as artillery instructor at Ft. Pickens. On staff of Genl. G. W. Smith, Sept. 1861 to Sept. 1862. Lt. Col. - Aug. 30, 1862. Served as such in the defenses of Richmond throughout the war, commanding the 18th and 20th Battalion Virginia Heavy Artillery. The Lt. Col. rank seems to have been designated as "temporary" throughout the entire period. POW at Sayler's Creek, released May 26. Adj. Genl. of Maryland post-war. d. Baltimore, Nov. 1, 1910.

HOWARD, JOHN. b. Tarboro, North Carolina. att. U. Pennsylvania. m. Marinda Brown. Lived in Wilson Co. Capt., Co. B, 2nd North Carolina, May 16, 1861, aged 27. Major - Sept. 17, 1862. MWIA on same date as promotion, at Sharpsburg, d. Oct. 4, 1862. bur. Calvary Episcopal Church, Tarboro.

HOWARD, JOHN K. Clerk and magistrate of court in Wilson Co., Tennessee in 1860, age 33, married, worth $35,085. Capt., Co. H, 7th Tennessee. Elected Major at May 27, 1861, organization of the regiment. Lt. Col. - May 23, 1862. MWIA at Gaines' Mill, d. July 9, 1862. bur. Cedar Grove Cemetery, Wilson Co., Tennessee.

HOYLE, ELI W. b. 1828. Merchant. Pvt., Co. B, 7th Georgia, May 31, 1861. Adj., 7th Georgia, Sept. 1861. Lt., Co. B, 7th Georgia, Oct. 18, 1861. Major - May 12, 1862. KIA at Malvern Hill.

HUBARD, JAMES LENAEUS. b. Feb. 27, 1835. att. VMI, from Cumberland Co. gr. U. Va. m. Isaetta C. Randolph, 1860. Planter in Buckingham Co. Lt. Col., 44th Virginia, June 14, 1861. Dropped at May 1862 re-org. Lawyer, author, farmer in Nelson

Co. d. Dec. 4, 1913. A letter from Hubard to John Warwick Daniel, recounting experiences with the 44th Virginia, is at U. Virginia.

HUDGENS, THOMAS ALLISON. b. Laurens Dist., June 19, 1831. gr. South Carolina College, 1858. gr. Jefferson Medical College. Lt., Co. B, 7th South Carolina, Apr. 15, 1861. Captain - May 13, 1862. Wded. at Wilderness. Lt. Col., 7th South Carolina, Apr. 9, 1865, near Greensboro, North Carolina (says his compiled service record). Paroled at Greensboro, May 2, 1865. In South Carolina legisl. Physician at Honea Path, South Carolina. d. there Feb. 25, 1892.

HUDGINGS, LEMUEL TILLMAN. b. Pickens Co., July 20, 1825. Lived in Tuscaloosa. Capt., Co. G, 41st Alabama, Apr. 3, 1862. Major - Feb. 18, 1864. m. Lucretia Isabelle Latham. MWIA near Richmond, d. June 20, 1864.

HUDSON, JOSHUA HILARY. b. Chester, Jan. 29, 1832. gr. South Carolina College, 1852, with 1st honors. m. Mary Miller, 1854. Enrolled in 26th South Carolina as Pvt., Jan. 1862. Became adj. of regt., then Major. Lt. Col., 26th South Carolina, Sept. 9, 1862. Some early service was with the 9th South Carolina Bn., which merged into the 26th Regt. Lawyer and judge. In South Carolina legisl., 1905-1906. d. Greenville, July 22, 1909. bur. Bennettsville.

HUGER, FRANK. b. Fortress Monroe, Virginia, Sept. 29, 1837. gr. USMA, 1860. Lt., U. S. Army, 1860-61. Son of Genl. Benjamin Huger. Capt., Huger's Battery (Va.), June 1861. Capt. and a.d.c. to his father, Feb. 1862. Major of Artillery, Mar. 2, 1863. Lt. Col. - Feb. 27, 1864. Colonel - Feb. 18, 1865. m. Julia Trible. Railroad president. d. Roanoke, Virginia, June 11, 1897.

HUGGINS, JAMES HOWARD. b. Franklin, North Carolina, Aug. 7, 1828. m. Mary Jones. Member of the Georgia Secession Convention (and voted no!). Capt., Co. B, 23rd Georgia, Aug. 31, 1861. Major - Aug. 16, 1862. Lt. Col. - Sept. 17, 1862. Colonel - Dec. 15, 1863. Wded. in both legs at South Mountain. Resigned Aug. 13, 1864. d. Lula, Georgia, Mar. 8, 1900.

HUGHES, ABNER A. b. Kentucky. Lived in Cherokee Co., Alabama, then farmer in DeKalb Co. Aged 45 in 1861. Lt. Col., 48th Alabama, May 22, 1862. Res. Oct. 15, 1862, due to "fatigue and exhaustion."

HUGHES, HENRY. b. Port Gibson, Apr. 17, 1819. gr. Oakland College. Widely known sociologist who was labeled "The First American Sociologist." Author of numerous publications. A slavery apologist. Capt., Co. H, 12th Mississippi, Mar. 14, 1861. Colonel - Nov. 13, 1861. d. Port Gibson, Oct. 3, 1862, of inflammatory rheumatism.

HUGHES, JOHN M. (Last name is frequently given as Hughs, and may actually be spelled in that fashion.) Farmer in Overton Co., Tennessee. Lt., Co. D, 25th Tennessee, Aug. 1, 1861, aged 29. Major - summer 1862. Colonel - July 21, 1862. Wded. slightly in head at Murfreesboro. Res. Mar. 17, 1865. Bushrod Johnson stated that Hugh[e]s was found incompetent by a board of examiners—a finding with which Johnson heartily agreed.

HUGULEY, GEORGE WHITFIELD. b. Osanippa, Alabama, Aug. 1, 1938. Very large planter in Chambers Co. Married Rebecca Lucinda Gaines. Capt., "Osanippa Rangers" (a 6 mos. coast defense unit), 1861. Capt., Co. C, 1st Bn., Hilliard Legion (Alabama), May 12, 1862. Major, 59th Alabama, Nov. 25, 1863. Lt. Col. - May 16, 1864. d. Osanippa, Aug. 17, 1889.

HUMPHREYS, DAVID W. Lt., Co. B, 2nd Mississippi, Mar. 4, 1861, at Ripley. Major - May 10, 1861. Lt. Col. - Apr. 16, 1862. KIA at Gettysburg, July 3.

HUMPHREYS, WILLIAM WIRT. b. Anderson Dist., Oct. 30, 1837. gr. Center College, Danville, Kentucky. Lt., Co. B, 4th South Carolina, Apr. 1861. Capt., Co. C, Palmetto Sharpshooters (South Carolina), 1862. Major - Jan. 30, 1863. Wded. at Frayser's Farm. Mayor of Anderson, South Carolina. d. Oct. 6, 1893.

HUNT, ISAAC FOSTER. b. Newberry Dist., Nov. 16, 1833. att. SCMA. m. Harriet Austin, 1860. Pvt., Co. B, 1st South Carolina, 1861. Capt., Co. D, 13th South Carolina, Aug. 23, 1861. Major - Jan. 6, 1863. Lt. Col. - June 21, 1863. Colonel - June 8, 1864.

Wded. at Gaines' Mill, Fredericksburg and Fussell's Mill. Distinguished at Spotsylvania's Bloody Angle, and wrote an account of that fight. Appx. Hunt's uniform jacket is on display at Fredericksburg. Greenville merchant post-war. d. Apr. 13, 1900.

HUNT, THEODORE GAILLARD. b. Charleston, South Carolina, Oct. 23, 1805. Lawyer there. Moved to Louisiana in 1830. In Louisiana legisl. New Orleans judge. In U.S. Congress, 1853-55. Colonel, 5th Louisiana, May 10, 1861. Res. July 31, 1862. d. New Orleans, Nov. 15, 1893. bur. Metairie Cemetery.

HUNT, WILLIAM HENRY. b. Cobb Co., Oct. 31, 1837. att. Georgia Military Institute. Taught at La Grange Military Academy, Alabama. Capt., Co. C, 3rd Alabama Bn., 1861. Capt., Co. B, 35th Alabama, 1861. Later was Major, 35th Alabama. Lt. Col., 26th Alabama, Mar. 27, 1862. d. Marietta, Georgia, June 20, 1862, of typhoid fever while en route to Virginia. bur. Episcopal Cemetery.

HUNTER, GEORGE R. Judge and lawyer in Crawford Co. In Georgia legisl., 1839-1843. Age 48 in 1860, net worth $43,530. Colonel, Georgia State Troops, 1861. Lt. Col., 59th Georgia, July 16, 1862. Res. Dec. 22, 1862.

HURTT, DANIEL WASHINGTON. b. New Bern, June 9, 1825. Lived in Craven Co. Capt., Co. I, 2nd North Carolina, May 16, 1861. Major - Mar. 21, 1863. Wded. and POW at Sharpsburg. Wded. wrist at Gettysburg. Res. as a result, Aug. 30, 1863. d. Mar. 18, 1905. bur. Cedar Grove Cemetery, New Bern.

HUSKE, BENJAMIN ROBINSON. b. Oct. 28, 1829. gr. UNC, 1850. Lived in Cumberland Co. m. Anna Bella Giles Norwood. Lt., Co. H, 1st North Carolina (Bethel), Apr. 17, 1861. Capt., Co. D, 48th North Carolina, Feb. 24, 1862. Major - Apr. 9, 1862. MWIA at Seven Days, June 25, 1862. d. in Manchester, Virginia, July 15, 1862. bur. Presbyterian Churchyard, Hillsboro, North Carolina.

HUSTON, GEORGE. b. Virginia, ca. 1829. Farmer in Harrisonburg in 1860, age 30, worth $21,000. Lt., Co. I, 33rd Virginia,

Lee A. Wallace, Jr.

ISAAC FOSTER HUNT
13th South Carolina Infantry

June 22, 1861. Capt. - Apr. 21, 1862. Under arrest from May to Aug. 1862. Major - sometime prior to May 1863. Lt. Col. - Mar. 21, 1864. Wded. at Chancellorsville. KIA near Petersburg, Feb. 6, 1865. bur. Woodbine Cemetery, Harrisonburg.

HUTCHERSON, THOMAS. b. Virginia. Farmer in Cherokee Co. in 1860, worth $14,000, age 42. Colonel, 23rd Georgia, Aug. 31, 1861. Res. due to chronic rheumatism, June 12, 1862.

HUTCHINS, ANDREW JACKSON. Major, 19th Georgia, May 1, 1861. Lt. Col. - June 26, 1862. Colonel - Jan. 12, 1863. Res. Aug. 20, 1863. Later served as a commissary officer in Georgia. Hutchins was called "Jack."

HUTCHINS, NATHAN LOUIS, JR. b. Gwinnett Co., Oct. 4, 1835. gr. Emory. Lawyer. Capt., Co. I, 16th Georgia, Mar. 6, 1861. Lt. Col., 3rd Bn., Georgia Sharpshooters, Apr. 1863. POW at Sayler's Creek, released July 25. m. Carrie Orr. In Georgia legisl. Gwinnett Co. judge. d. June 8, 1905. bur. Old Lawrenceville Methodist Cemetery.

HUTTER, JAMES RISQUE. b. Lynchburg, Oct. 22, 1841. gr. VMI, 1860. gr. U. Virginia. 5'9". Capt., Co. H, 11th Virginia, May 15, 1861. Major - Sept. 24, 1863. Wded. and POW at Gettysburg, released early 1865. POW at Five Forks, released July 25. Campbell Co. farmer and surveyor. m. Lottie Hutter (a cousin). d. June 15, 1923. Hutter's diary is at U. Virginia.

HUTTON, ELIHU. b. Randolph Co., Virginia, Dec. 31, 1837. On "militia and scout" duty in the first two years of the war. Capt., Co. C, 20th Virginia Cav., Apr. 23, 1863. Major - Nov. 22, 1864. Late war reference to a commission as Lt. Col. is undated and indistinct. m. Sophronia E. Woodford, 1872. In West Virginia legisl. Large landowner in Randolph Co. d. Apr. 19, 1916.

HYLLESTED, WALDEMAR V. Served in the French Foreign Legion, 1839-1845; in the Palmetto Regiment during the Mexican War; and in the Danish Army, 1848-1859. Hyllested's papers at Tulane University, all in foreign languages, cover this service. His middle initial is from the Tulane papers; he used none at all in Civil War records. Major, 1st Louisiana Zouave

Battalion, Apr. 4, 1861. On Magruder's staff as volunteer aide during Seven Days. POW at Second Manassas; exchanged November 8, 1862. Major and provost in Texas, 1863-1864.

HYMAN, JOSEPH HENRY. b. Mar. 24, 1835. Lived in Edgecombe Co., North Carolina. gr. UNC, 1855. Capt., Co. G, 13th North Carolina, May 1, 1861. Major - Oct. 15, 1862. Lt. Col. - Mar. 2, 1863. Colonel - June 13, 1863. Wded. foot at Gettysburg. Appx. Real estate broker. d. Mar. 1902.

IHRIE, ROSS R. b. Easton, Pennsylvania, Mar. 24, 1828. gr. U. Pennsylvania, M.D., 1850. m. Mary Anne Williams Houghton. Physician in Chatham Co., North Carolina. Capt., Co. M, 15th North Carolina, Apr. 15, 1861. Lt. Col. - June 11, 1861. Defeated at May 1862 re-org. Later was Colonel of a Home Guards regt. d. Pittsboro, North Carolina, June 28, 1889. bur. St. Bartholomew's Episcopal Church.

IMBODEN, GEORGE WILLIAM. b. Augusta Co., June 25, 1836. Staunton lawyer. Brother of Genl. John D. Imboden. Sgt., Staunton Artillery, Apr. 1861. Lt. - May 1861. Capt., Co. A, 62nd Virginia, July 3, 1862. Major - Sept. 9, 1862. Colonel, 18th Virginia Cav., Dec. 15, 1862. Wded. severely in the face late in 1864. Present into 1865. Lawyer and in coal and mercantile businesses in Ansted, West Virginia. In West Virginia legisl. m. (1) Mary Frances Tyree, 1859. m. (2) Angia Mildred Dickinson, 1889. d. Ansted, Jan. 8, 1922. bur. West Lake Cemetery, near Stonewall Jackson's mother.

IRBY, THOMAS EVANS. b. Marlboro Dist., South Carolina, Dec. 17, 1823. att. U. Alabama. Mexican War veteran. Planter in Wilcox Co. and Dallas Co., Alabama. In Alabama legisl. Major, 8th Alabama, June 9, 1861. Lt. Col. - Mar. 20, 1862. KIA at Williamsburg.

IREDELL, JAMES JOHNSTON. b. Feb. 3, 1828. gr. UNC, 1848. Major, 53rd North Carolina, May 6, 1862. Transferred as Major to 2nd North Carolina Bn., Aug. 10, 1863. KIA at Spotsylvania, May 10, 1864. bur. Raleigh City Cemetery.

IRVING, CHARLES ROBERT. b. Amelia Co., Feb. 25, 1835. gr. M.D. at Medical College of Virginia, 1855. m. Ann Maria

Archer. Lt., Co. G, 1st Virginia Cav., 1861. Captain - July 21, 1861. Major - July 16, 1863. Recommended for Lt. Col. commission, but service record shows him as a Major at Appx. d. Amelia C.H., May 3, 1914. bur. Green Hill Cemetery.

IZARD, ALLEN CADWALLADER. b. Chester, South Carolina, July 13, 1834. att. South Carolina College. gr. U.S. Naval Academy, 1856. Resigned from U.S. Navy, May 1857. Capt., Co. I, 11th South Carolina, Feb. 25, 1862. Major - Oct. 22, 1862. Lt. Col. - Nov. 27, 1862. Resigned Dec. 10, 1864, being "desirous of returning to the Navy, which is my old profession." Postmaster at Walterboro, South Carolina. d. there Feb. 28, 1901.

JACKSON, ALFRED HENRY. b. McConnelsville, Ohio, Jan. 1, 1836. gr. Washington College, 1857. m. Mary Blair Paxton, 1858. Lawyer and deputy U.S. Marshal, Lewis Co., Virginia, Capt., Co. I, 31st Virginia, June 21, 1861. Resigned Dec. 10, 1861. Major and a.a.g. to Stonewall Jackson, Nov. 1861 to May 1862. Lt. Col., 31st Virginia, May 1, 1862. MWIA at Cedar Mountain and died in Lexington just eight days short of one year later—Aug. 1, 1863. bur. in Lexington. Jackson's papers are at West Virginia University.

JACKSON, ANDREW. b. Petersburg, Virginia, Oct. 29, 1828. att. VMI. Lt., U.S. Army, 1847-61. Capt., Co. B, 5th South Carolina, Apr. 13, 1861. Lt. Col. - Apr. 1862. Wded. at Gaines' Mill (arm amputated), and resigned as a result. Unmarried. d. July 21, 1870.

JACKSON, GEORGE. b. Clarksburg, Jan. 25, 1833. Brother of Genl. William L. Jackson. gr. USMA, 1856. Lt., U.S. Cavalry, 1856-61, and served on the Mormon expedition. Major of C.S. Cavalry, early 1861. Served with Garnett as such in western Virginia at Laurel Hill. Then stationed at Franklin, Virginia. A command of Jackson's was absorbed into the 14th Virginia Cav., and he is shown as that regiment's Major briefly. He later served with Whiting in North Carolina and gave "faithful service, but had little opportunity for distinction." A subordinate wrote that Jackson "drinks hard." Jackson was also on Genl. B. H. Robertson's staff for a time. Parkersburg mineral oil businessman postwar. d. there May 27, 1883.

JACKSON, JAMES W. Of Tallapoosa. Lt. Col., 47th Alabama, May 22, 1862, aged 30. Colonel - Aug. 11, 1862. Wded. at Sharpsburg. Res. July 10, 1863. Official documents indicate that Jackson resigned because he was disgraced at Gettysburg.

JACKSON, WILLIAM A. b. Fredericksburg, ca. 1807, son of William and Elizabeth Minor Jackson. m. Emma Cassandra Riely (1815-1889). Coal dealer near Charleston in 1860. His daughter, Emma Catherine, married Col. L. W. Reid (q.v.). Lt. Col., 22nd Virginia, Dec. 21, 1861. Dropped at May 1862 re-org. Lt. Col., 4th Virginia State Line. Served in the Nitre and Mining Bureau later in the war. d. at son's home in Pulaski Co., Jan. 15, 1875. bur. Fredericksburg Confederate Cemetery.

JAMES, GEORGE SHOLTER. b. Laurens Dist., 1829. Teacher in South Carolina, Texas, and Arkansas. Lt., U.S. Artillery, 1856-61. Served in Palmetto Regt., Mexican War. att. South Carolina College and Erskine College. Capt., South Carolina Artillery, 1861. Lt. Col., 3rd South Carolina Bn., Feb. 2, 1862. KIA at South Mountain, Sept. 14, 1862. bur. on the battlefield. (An obituary in the Charleston *Courier* uses this information which contradicts the other sources: George Strother James, b. Jan. 1828).

JAMES, LEMUEL. b. June 10, 1827. Of Mathews Co. Lt. Col., 61st Virginia Militia, Oct. 10, 1859. Present into May 1862, during which month the unit was disbanded. d. June 21, 1899.

JAMES, SAMUEL L. b. Louisiana. New Orleans engineer. Capt., Co. I, 6th Louisiana, June 4, 1861, aged 35. Apptd. Major immediately upon org. Res. Dec. 1861.

JAMES, WADDY THOMPSON. b. Aug. 12, 1836. Lived in Franklin Co. m. Mary Jane Warren. Capt., Co. B, 57th Virginia, June 15, 1861. Lt. Col. - May 7, 1862. Resigned July 23, 1862, citing "physical imbecility." In Virginia legisl., 1874-1882. d. May 14, 1926.

JAMISON, SANDERS GLOVER. b. Orangeburg, South Carolina, June 27, 1830. m. Annie Sydnor of Virginia. Chief, Confederate States Treasury Note Bureau. Capt., Co. C, 3rd Virginia LDT,

June 8, 1863, aged 33. Major - Apr. 20, 1864. Resigned May 26, 1864, his office having been transferred to Columbia, South Carolina. Lived postwar in Roanoke, Virginia. Alive in 1900 in Frederick Co., Virginia.

JARVIS, WILLIAM H. b. Feb. 15, 1824. Of Petersburg. 5′10″. Capt., Co. F, 3rd Virginia Bn. Reserves, May 5, 1864. Major - June 17, 1864. Chief Engineer of Petersburg Volunteer Fire Dept. Danville merchant. d. Danville, Nov. 30, 1877. bur. Blandford Cemetery, Petersburg.

JAYNE, JOSEPH McAFEE. b. Covington Co., Mississippi. m. Melissa McRae. Farmer in Rankin Co. in 1860, age 37, worth $65,600. 5′8″. Capt., Co. A, 18th Mississippi, 1861. Colonel, 48th Mississippi, Jan. 17, 1863. Wded. at Chancellorsville. POW at Sayler's Creek, released June 18, 1865, aged 38.

JEFFORDS, ROBERT JOSIAH. b. May 1, 1834. Commission merchant in Charleston. Lt. Col., 5th South Carolina Cav., Jan. 18, 1863. Wded. at Cold Harbor (thigh). KIA at White Oak Rd. or Burgess' Mill, Oct. 27, 1864. bur. Magnolia Cemetery, Charleston, South Carolina.

JEFFRIES, JOHN MILLER. Of Pickens Co. Lt., Co. I, 41st Alabama, May 3, 1862, aged 27. Captain - Dec. 16, 1862. Major - Nov. 17, 1864. Wded. June 30, 1864 (lost a finger). Appx.

JENIFER, WALTER HANSON. b. St. Mary's Co., Maryland, Aug. 1823. att. USMA. Lt. and Capt., U.S. Cavalry, 1847-48 and 1855-61. Merchant in California. Capt. of Cav., CSA, Mar. 15, 1861. Colonel P.A.C.S., Sept. 24, 1861. Assigned to command 8th Virginia Cav. in Jan. 1862. Dropped at May 1862 re-org. Served in western Virginia, 1862-63; in Richmond, 1863; and around Mobile late in the war. Served the Khedive of Egypt after the war. d. Apr. 9, 1878, in Richmond. Jenifer was a celebrated horse trainer. He was a groomsman at the wedding of W. H. F. "Rooney" Lee.

JENKINS, CHARLES S. Lawyer in Paulding Co. in 1860, age 33. 6′0″. Capt., Co. K, 64th Georgia, Feb. 26, 1863. Promotions to Major and Lt. Col. are mentioned but not specified. POW at Deep Bottom, Virginia, Aug. 16, 1864, released June 10, 1865.

JENKINS, WILLIAM ALEXANDER. b. Warrenton, North Carolina, 1829. gr. UNC. Wife - Della M. In North Carolina legisl. Attorney General of North Carolina. Capt., Co. C, 46th North Carolina, Feb. 1862. Lt. Col. - Apr. 4, 1862. Res. Jan. 21, 1863, citing family matters. He later sought reinstatement, in vain. d. 1869.

JEROME, ROBERT P. b. 1840. Lived in Union Co. Lt., Co. B, 15th North Carolina, May 11, 1861. Captain - May 2, 1862. Major - Nov. 4, 1864. Paroled at Greensboro. d. 1913. bur. Edgewood Cemetery, Apopka, Florida.

JOHNSON, BENJAMIN JENKINS. b. Beaufort, South Carolina, Mar. 18, 1817. gr. William & Mary. In South Carolina legisl., 1838-40 and 1844-61. Almost successful candidate for South Carolina governor, 1860. m. Caroline Ann Johnson, 1842. Lt. Col., Hampton Legion, June 12, 1861. KIA at 1st Manassas. bur. Magnolia Cemetery, Charleston. A subordinate called Johnson "brave, large, [and] awkward."

JOHNSON, JAMES CHRISTOPHER. b. King William Co., 1823. Farmer at Aylett's. att. U. Virginia. Capt., Co. G, 22nd Virginia Bn., Jan. 31, 1862. Lt. Col. - June 16, 1862. Resigned Nov. 8, 1862.

JOHNSON, JAMES HICKMAN. b. Oct. 8, 1840. att. Cumberland U. Lived in Montgomery Co., Tennessee. Lt., Co. G, 14th Tennessee, May 22, 1861. Captain - Apr. 26, 1862. Major - Aug. 12, 1864. Badly wded. at Cedar Mountain, captured while recuperating. Appx. Lawyer postwar. m. Mary Boyd, 1867. d. Clarksville, Tennessee, Oct. 28, 1880. bur. Greenwood Cemetery.

JOHNSON, JAMES THEODORE. b. Catawba Co., North Carolina, Mar. 31, 1836. gr. U. Pennsylvania, M.D., 1861. 5′11″. Lived in Burke Co. Lt., Co. K, 35th North Carolina, Oct. 29, 1861. Captain - Dec. 1861. Major - Dec. 1862. Lt. Col. - June 15, 1863. Colonel - June 18, 1864. POW at Dinwiddie C.H., Apr. 1, 1865, released June 19, 1865. Physician at Hickory, North Carolina. Died there Dec. 24, 1914.

JOHNSON, JEFFERSON. Farmer in Floyd Co. in 1860, age 31, worth $20,000. Major, 18th Georgia, Apr. 25, 1861. Res., disability, Mar. 29, 1862, with "Chronic Hepatitis & Dysentery." According to a subordinate, Johnson was "a burden to his horse." He was a brother of Col. Abda Johnson, 40th Georgia.

JOHNSON, JOHN EVANS. b. Virginia, Sept. 1814. Lived at Wilkinsonville, Chesterfield Co., Virginia. Entered USMA, July 1830; dismissed Sept. 1832; restored that Oct. and resigned Dec. 1832. Colonel, 9th Virginia Cav., Jan. 1862. Dropped at April 1862 re-org. Became v.a.d.c. to Genl. Ewell, May 1863. Living in Charlotte Co., Virginia, in 1877. d. King William Court House, June 11, 1905.

JOHNSON, LEWIS W. b. Wilkes Co., North Carolina, Oct. 1, 1832. Sgt., Co. E, 10th Alabama, June 4, 1861. Lt. - Sept. 15, 1861. Captain - July 9, 1863. Major - Nov. 26, 1864. Wded. foot, Sept. 17, 1863. m. Malissa Brown, 1881. Talladega businessman. d. Holt, Alabama, Dec. 8, 1909.

JOHNSON, LUCIUS JUNIUS. b. Chowan Co. gr. UNC. Lawyer in Perquimans Co. Capt., Co. I, 17th North Carolina, May 8, 1861, aged 40. Capt., Co. L, 17th North Carolina, May 1, 1863. Major - May 27, 1864. POW at Ft. Hatteras, Aug. 1861. POW at Kinston, Mar. 10, 1865, released in July. d. 1865.

JOHNSON, MARMADUKE. b. Chesterfield Co., Aug. 8, 1826. att. U. Virginia. Renowned Richmond lawyer and orator. Capt., Jackson Flying Artillery (Virginia), Mar. 17, 1862. Engaged in a street fight in Richmond in 1862. Major - Feb. 27, 1864, assigned to McIntosh's Bn. Lt. Col. - Feb. 18, 1865. Appx. Ran the "Davis House" Hotel in Richmond post-war. Died at his Clay St. home in Richmond, Nov. 20, 1871.

JOHNSON, THOMAS COKE. b. Feb. 10, 1835. att. Emory and Georgia Military Institute. Lt. Col., 19th Georgia, May 1, 1861. KIA at Mechanicsville. bur. family cemetery near Palmetto, Georgia.

JOHNSTON, GEORGE WASHINGTON. Of Pitt Co. Capt., Co. C, 17th North Carolina, Apr. 26, 1861, aged 35. Lt. Col. - July 27, 1861. POW at Ft. Hatteras, Aug. 29, 1861, exchanged Feb. 1862. Regt. was disbanded Mar. 1862.

Dr. C. Cooper Bell, Jr.

THOMAS C. JOHNSON
19th Georgia

JOHNSTON, JOHN Y. Physician in Tallapoosa Co. Major, 47th Alabama, at org., May 22, 1862, aged 30. Res. Aug. 1863.

JOHNSTON, PHILIP PRESTON. b. King George Co., Virginia, Apr. 4, 1840. Pvt., 1st Maryland Inf., May 17, 1861. Pvt., Breathed's Battery (Virginia Horse Artillery), spring 1862. Promoted corporal then sergeant. Lt. - Oct. 3, 1862. Captain - Feb. 27, 1864. "Major by endorsement of Gen. Jubal A. Early from Feb. 8, 1865." Assigned to Stuart Horse Artillery. Paroled in South Carolina, May 1865. gr. Transylvania U., 1868. m. Sallie Chiles, 1870. Judge and horse breeder in Lexington, Kentucky, post-war. In Kentucky legisl. d. Lexington, Feb. 10, 1925. bur. there in family cemetery. U. Kentucky Library owns Johnston's papers.

JOHNSTON, ROBERT. b. Richmond, Virginia, July 3, 1830. gr. USMA, 1850. Lt., U.S. Cavalry, 1850-61. Capt., P.A.C.S., Mar. 16, 1861. Colonel, 3rd Virginia Cav., June 20, 1861. Was sometimes styled "Commander in Chief of Cavalry, Army of the Peninsula." Dropped at May 1862 re-org. On Pickett's staff as a.a.g., Sept. 1862. Educator at DeVeaux College in New York post-war. d. Geneva, New York, July 8, 1902. bur. Albany Rural Cemetery near Albany, New York. Johnston's letterbook is at the Museum of the Confederacy.

JOHNSTON, WILLIAM A. Of Halifax Co. Capt., Co. A, 14th North Carolina, Mar. 20, 1861, aged 26. Lt. Col. - July 5, 1862. Wded. at Sharpsburg. Wded. arm at Chancellorsville. Wded. at Petersburg. Appx.

JOLLY, JOHN JEFFERSON. b. Mar. 18, 1838. att. U. Alabama. gr. Franklin College, Tennessee, 1856. Capt., Co. C, 43rd Alabama, Mar. 8, 1862. Lt. Col. - Dec. 16, 1862. In Alabama legisl., 1876-1877. Birmingham lawyer. d. Gainesville, May 2, 1881.

JONES, ALEXANDER CALDWELL. b. near Moundsville, Marshall Co., 1830. gr. VMI, 1850. Judge and militia officer in Minnesota, 1854-1861. Major, 44th Virginia, June 1861. Lt. Col. at unspecified date. Ordered to report to A.I.G.O., Dec. 22, 1862. Inspector General and Chief of Staff to Genl. Magruder, 1864. Lawyer in D.C. and West Virginia. U.S. Consul in Japan and China. d. there Jan. 1898. Evidence that Jones may have been a late-war general is in his papers at Virginia Historical Society.

JONES, ALLEN CADWALLADER. b. Everetts, North Carolina, Nov. 7, 1811. m. Catherine Erwin, 1845. Planter in Greene Co., Alabama. In Alabama legisl. Lt. Col., 5th Alabama, May 11, 1861. Colonel - Nov. 20, 1861. Dropped at re-org. Lived in Greensboro, Alabama post-war.

JONES, BUEHRING HAMPDEN. b. Clifton, Kanawha Co., Virginia, May 12, 1823. Lawyer in Palmyra, Missouri. 5′11″. Capt., Co. C, 60th Virginia, June 26, 1862. Lt. Col. - Apr. 27, 1862. Colonel - Aug. 6, 1862. POW at Piedmont, June 5, 1864, released June 19, 1865. Compiled an article concerning his Johnson's Island prisoner experiences, and a book of prison poetry. Secretary of 1872 West Virginia Convention. d. Charleston, West Virginia, Mar. 18, 1872.

JONES, CADWALLADER. b. Halifax, North Carolina, Aug. 17, 1813. gr. UNC, 1832. m. Annie Isabella Iredell, 1836. Wrote a family genealogy. In North Carolina legisl. Jones' son and namesake was a Capt. in the 12th South Carolina. Jones, Sr., became Capt., Co. H, 12th South Carolina, Aug. 13, 1861. Major - Aug. 30, 1861. Lt. Col. - Apr. 2, 1862. Colonel - Sept. 27, 1862. Res. in ill health, Feb. 27, 1863. In South Carolina legisl. 1864-1865. d. Columbia, Dec. 1, 1899. bur. Elmwood Cemetery.

JONES, EGBERT J. b. Limestone Co., Alabama, 1820. gr. U. Virginia. Lived at Madison. 6′3″. In Alabama legisl. On U. Alabama Board of Trustees. Described by a contemporary as "the most diffident young man I ever knew . . . as bashful as a timid young lady." Capt., 4th Alabama, Apr. 26, 1861. Colonel - May 7, 1861. MWIA in both hips at 1st Manassas, died at Orange Court House, Sept. 2, 1861.

JONES, ERVINE P. Lawyer in Greenville, South Carolina. Lt. Col., 2nd South Carolina, May 16, 1861, age 46. Dropped at May 13, 1862, re-org. Jones' file is full of letters from his wife to sundry officials, seeking a post on a military court for him.

JONES, FRANCIS BUCKNER. b. Frederick Co., June 14, 1828. gr. VMI, 1848. m. Susan Peyton Clark, 1853. Frederick Co.

farmer. Aide to "Stonewall" Jackson in 1861. Major, 2nd Virginia, Aug. 26, 1861. MWIA at Gaines' Mill, and died July 9 in great suffering described as a "shattered nervous condition." bur. Stonewall Cemetery, Winchester. Jones' diary covering March-June 1862 is at Handley Library, Winchester.

JONES, GEORGE H. Living in Glascock Co. in 1860, age 22, worth $6,455. Justice of an inferior court. Capt., Co. B, 22nd Georgia, Sept. 3, 1861. Colonel - Nov. 14, 1863. Wded. and POW at Gettysburg, exchanged Mar. 22, 1865.

JONES, HAMILTON CHAMBERLAIN, JR. b. Salisbury, Nov. 3, 1837. gr. UNC, 1858. Capt., Co. K, 5th North Carolina, May 16, 1861. Wded. at Williamsburg. Lt. Col., 57th North Carolina, July 17, 1862. Colonel - Feb. 1865. POW at Rappahannock Station, Nov. 7, 1863, exchanged Feb. 20, 1865. Wded. Mar. 25, 1865. Paroled at Salisbury, May 12, 1865. In North Carolina legisl. U.S. District Attorney. m. Connie Meyers, 1873. d. Charlotte, Aug. 23, 1904.

JONES, HILARY POLLARD. b. Fluvanna Co., Virginia, July 13, 1833. Lived in Hanover Co. att. U. Virginia. m. Claudia Hamilton Marshall, 1861. Teacher at Taylorsville. Lt., Morris Artillery (Virginia), Aug. 1861. Captain - Feb. 1862. Major - May 28, 1862. Lt. Col. - Mar. 2, 1863. Colonel - Feb. 27, 1864. Commanded an artillery bn., 1862-63. Acted as Chief of Artillery, 2nd Corps, after Chancellorsville. Chief of Artillery, Dept. of North Carolina and Southern Virginia, 1864. Chief of Artillery, Anderson's Corps, Dec. 1864 to Appx. Principal of Hanover Academy. Jones' son and namesake was a prominent 20th-century U.S. Navy Admiral. Colonel Jones died at his son's home in Washington, D.C., in 1913. Stapleton Crutchfield said of Jones: "a moderately good officer; no very strong points, nor yet any objectionable ones."

JONES, JAMES. b. Oct. 3, 1805. gr. South Carolina College. Edgefield lawyer. m. Catherine Louisa Creyon. Seminole War officer. First chairman of the Board of Visitors, SCMA. Colonel, 14th South Carolina, Sept. 9, 1861. Resigned Apr. 11, 1862, feeling slighted by appointment of Gist ahead of him. QM General of South Carolina thereafter. d. Oct. 20, 1865.

JONES, JOHN ARCHIBALD. b. Apr. 14, 1831. gr. U. Alabama, 1855. Teacher at Tuskegee. m. Mary Vincent Sott, 1856. Capt., Co. B, 44th Alabama, Mar. 15, 1862. Major - Sept. 1, 1862. Lt. Col. - Sept. 17, 1862. Appx. Educator in several Alabama institutions, and at Central College in Lexington, Missouri, postwar. d. Mar. 20, 1896.

JONES, JOHN AUGUSTUS. b. 1820 in Columbus. Son of Hon. Seaborn Jones. Captain in Mexican War. m. Mary Louisa Leonard, 1843. Lived in Columbus, Georgia. att. Georgetown U. Lawyer and politician. Capt., Co. I, 20th Georgia, May 23, 1861. Major - Aug. 30, 1861. Lt. Col. - Apr. 3, 1862. Colonel - May 29, 1863. KIA at Gettysburg. bur. Linwood Cemetery, Columbus, Georgia. The Linwood grave marker is only a memorial, as Jones' body was lost at sea. Strong new evidence suggests that Jones' middle name actually was Abraham; three sources use Abraham, two use Augustus.

JONES, JOHN F. b. Aug. 23, 1840, in Covington. gr. Georgia Military Institute. Merchant. Lt., Co. H, 3rd Georgia, Apr. 25, 1861. Captain - May 18, 1861. Major - July 1, 1862. Lost right arm at Chancellorsville. Retired to Invalid Corps, Aug. 4, 1864. Chief Clerk to Georgia Secretary of State. In Georgia legisl. d. Atlanta, Sept. 4, 1888. bur. Oakland Cemetery.

JONES, JOHN G. b. Person Co. att. Wake Forest. Baptist preacher. 5'11". Capt., Co. E, 35th North Carolina, Oct. 29, 1861, aged 26. Major - Apr. 15, 1862. Lt. Col. - July 1, 1862. Colonel - June 15, 1863. KIA at Petersburg, June 17, 1864.

JONES, JOHN THOMAS. b. Caldwell Co., North Carolina, Jan. 21, 1841. gr. UNC, 1861. Pvt., Co. D, 1st North Carolina (Bethel), Apr. 6, 1861. Lt., Co. I, 26th North Carolina, July 26, 1861. Captain - Apr. 21, 1862. Major - Sept. 27, 1862. Lt. Col. - July 2, 1863. KIA at Wilderness. bur. in family cemetery, Cadwell Co. His papers are at UNC.

JONES, JOSEPH. b. Brunswick Co., Aug. 1814. Farmer there. Capt., Co. I, 20th Virginia, June 3, 1861. This unit became Co. D, 46th Virginia, in May 1862 and then was converted to Co. B, 59th Virginia, in Oct. 1862. Jones became Lt. Col., 59th

Virginia, Nov. 1, 1862. Wded. at Nottoway Bridge, May 8, 1864. Unmarried. d. Brunswick Co., Sept. 18, 1865, of "dropsy of heart."

JONES, JOSEPH PICKETT. b. North Carolina, June 1833. att. USMA. Anson Co. lawyer. Lt., U.S. Artillery, 1856-61. Lt. Col., 5th North Carolina, May 16, 1861. Resigned Oct. 24, 1861. Later was temporarily assigned as Colonel, 17th Alabama. Lived in Pensacola, Florida, post-war. d. 1894. bur. Trenton Cemetery, Trenton, Jones Co., North Carolina. (Note–Jones' middle name is sometimes given as "Peck," but without as much credence as "Pickett.")

JONES, RICHARD WASHINGTON. b. Feb. 22, 1821, in Virginia. att. Emory & Henry. gr. U. Pennsylvania. Mexican War officer. Physician in Penhook, Louisiana. Capt., Co. I, 14th Louisiana, May 20, 1861. One soldier called Jones "a whining methodist class leader." Resigned as Lt. Col., 14th Louisiana (promotion date not available), on Aug. 10, 1862. Physician in Hawkins Co., Tennessee, post-war. d. Jan. 11, 1886.

JONES, RICHARD WATSON. b. Greensville Co., Virginia, May 16, 1837. gr. Randolph-Macon, 1857, and University Virginia, 1861. Capt., Co. I, 12th Virginia, Feb. 22, 1862. Major - July 30, 1864. Appx. m. Bettie Sue Spratley, 1864. Wrote widely. Professor at Randolph-Macon and U. Mississippi. President of Mississippi Industrial Institute and of Martha Washington College. Drew a pension in Florida. d. Laurel, Mississippi, Dec. 18, 1914.

JONES, ROBERT HARRIS. b. South Carolina, Sept. 22, 1828. m. Lucintha Elizabeth Cotton. Methodist preacher. Carriage maker in Alabama then in Cartersville, Georgia. Colonel, 22nd Georgia, at Aug. 31, 1861, organization. Wded. at Sharpsburg in head and stomach and resigned as a result on Apr. 22, 1863. d. Sept. 1, 1899. bur. Oak Hill Cemetery, Cartersville.

JONES, ROBERT TIGNALL. b. Mecklenburg Co., Virginia, Oct. 8, 1815. gr. USMA, 1837. Lt., 3rd U.S. Artillery, 1837-38, fighting Seminoles. Lived in Perry Co., Alabama, in 1860, farmer, worth $100,360. Colonel, 12th Alabama, July 17, 1861. KIA at Seven Pines.

JONES, SAMUEL W. Lt., Co. F, 13th Georgia, July 8, 1861. Captain - Oct. 29, 1861. Major - Dec. 14, 1863. Lt. Col. - Mar. 24, 1864. KIA at Spotsylvania, May 12, 1864. bur. Spotsylvania Confederate Cemetery.

JONES, SEABORN, JR. Nephew of a U.S. Congressman from Columbus, Georgia. b. Oct. 5, 1825. att. Emory. Gold miner. Farmer in Polk Co. in 1860, worth $95,000. Lt. Col., Infantry Bn. of Phillips' Legion (Georgia), Aug. 2, 1861. Resigned on July 4, 1862, due to "permanent physical infirmity." d. Feb. 13, 1891. bur. Rose Hill Cemetery, Polk Co.

JONES, THOMAS L. Warren Co. medical student in 1861, aged 21. Capt., Co. C, 12th North Carolina, May 4, 1861. Major - May 1, 1862. Lt. Col. - May 24, 1862. Resigned, disability, Oct. 20, 1862.

JONES, WARNER THROCKMORTON. b. "Lowland Cottage," Gloucester Co., Virginia, Oct. 19, 1819. gr. William & Mary. Lawyer, judge and state legisl. Colonel, 21st Virginia Militia, 1861. In Virginia legisl. during the war. d. Gloucester Co., Nov. 5, 1891.

JONES, WATERS BURRAS. b. 1825. Sheriff of Troup Co., Georgia. Capt., Co. B, 60th Georgia, July 17, 1861. Major - Aug. 17, 1863. Wded. at Wilderness. His troops called Jones "Old Red." Colonel commanding 60th and 61st Georgia at Appomattox, but date of promotion is not clear. d. May 28, 1898. bur. Hillview Cemetery, La Grange. According to an obituary, Jones "often entered a battle smoking his pipe, having it shot from his mouth repeatedly."

JONES, WILLIAM HOGAN. b. Raleigh, Mar. 4, 1826. gr. UNC. Chatham Co. lawyer. Capt., Co. G, 48th North Carolina, Mar. 11, 1862. Major - Dec. 4, 1862. Resigned, due to chronic diarrhea, Aug. 30, 1864. d. Aug. 5, 1865.

JONES, WILLIAM M. Capt., Co. B, 9th Georgia, June 12, 1861. Major - Apr. 18, 1862. Wded. at Spotsylvania, May 12, 1864. Died of wounds, Oct. 26, 1864. bur. Hollywood Cemetery, Richmond. 24 years old at death.

JORDAN, JOHN THOMAS. b. Washington Co., Georgia, Nov. 9, 1839. gr. U. Georgia, 1861. Lawyer. Pvt., Co. E, 1st Georgia, Mar. 1861. Lt., Co. C, 49th Georgia, Mar. 4, 1862. Captain - July 31, 1862. Lt. Col. - Feb. 23, 1864. Colonel - Mar. 24, 1864. Wded. at Petersburg, Apr. 2, 1865. m. Mrs. Elizabeth Rives Arnold, widow of the colonel of the 6th Georgia. In Georgia legisl. d. Mar. 10, 1895. bur. Sparta City Cemetery.

JORDAN, JOHN V. b. 1822. Of Craven Co. Colonel, 31st North Carolina, Sept. 19, 1861. POW at Roanoke Island, Feb. 1862. Wded. thigh near Petersburg, May 16, 1864. Lived at High Point. Wife - Julia L. Jordan. d. Sept. 5, 1895. bur. Cedar Grove Cemetery, New Bern.

JORDAN, TYLER CALHOUN. b. Bedford Co., Virginia, 1835. att. U. Virginia. Capt., Bedford Light Artillery (Virginia), May 8, 1861. Major - Mar. 14, 1864, assigned to Huger's Bn. Commanded Huger's Bn. at Appx. m. Annie R. Lewis, 1869. Lawyer and judge in Dallas, Texas. Manufacturer in Glen Rose, Texas. Jordan was deeply involved in a 1902 railroad project in Mexico, then moved to California. d. Long Beach, California, Nov. 24, 1913.

JORDAN, WILLIAM FLEMING. b. Aug. 10, 1832. gr. U. Georgia, 1854. m. Orpha J. Goolsby. Farmer at Monticello, worth $34,775. Lt., Co. G, 4th Georgia, Apr. 25, 1861. Captain - Apr. 26, 1862. Major - Apr. 28, 1862. Lt. Col. - May 22, 1862. Resigned Aug. 15, 1862. In Georgia legisl. d. Jasper Co., Mar. 23, 1901. bur. Monticello, Georgia.

JUDGE, THOMAS JAMES. b. Richland Dist., South Carolina, Nov. 1, 1815. Newspaper editor in Greenville, Alabama. In Alabama legisl., 1844-53. Lowndes Co. lawyer. Twice a candidate for U.S. Congress. Went to Washington in Feb. 1861 as Alabama's commissioner to negotiate concerning U.S. forts and property. Served briefly as a volunteer private at Pensacola. Colonel, 14th Alabama, July 19, 1861. Resigned July 10, 1862, due to injuries received in a military railroad accident in Virginia. Judge of a Military Court at Mobile. On Alabama Supreme Court post-war. d. Butler Co., Mar. 3, 1876.

KASEY, JOHN G. b. Bedford Co., 1839. m. Elvira F. Lumpkin. 5′10″. Lived at Chamblissburg, Virginia. Capt., Co. B, 58th Virginia, July 23, 1861. Major - May 1, 1862. Lt. Col. - Oct. 30, 1862. Wded. at Cedar Mountain and Spotsylvania. POW at Petersburg, Mar. 25, 1865, released July 24. Sheriff post-war. d. Bedford, ca. Jan. 19, 1902. bur. Longwood Cemetery, Bedford Co.

KAVANAUGH, JAMES R. Capt., Co. K, 9th Louisiana, July 7, 1861. Major - Nov. 20, 1861. POW at Huntsville, Alabama, Apr. 11, 1862; paroled Sept. 1, 1862. Reported then to Vicksburg.

KEARNEY, WALTER GUSTON. b. Maury Co., Tennessee, Feb. 28, 1827. gr. Centenary College. Planter at Vernon and Flora, Mississippi. m. Susannah Owens, 1851. His daughter, Belle Kearney, became a noted suffragette and author. In Mississippi legisl., 1858-60 and 1892-94. Pvt., Co. I, 18th Mississippi, Apr. 18, 1861, but promoted Lt. within a few days. Captain - May 23, 1861. Lt. Col. - Nov. 17, 1861. Dropped at April 1862 re-org. Suffered from a hand badly mangled by a railroad car while in service. d. Madison Co., Mississippi, Apr. 3, 1908.

KEARSE, FRANCIS. b. 1837. Pvt., Co. E, 50th Georgia, Mar. 4, 1861. Lt. Col. - Mar. 22, 1862. KIA at Gettysburg. bur. Laurel Hill Cemetery, Savannah.

KEEBLE, RICHARD H. b. 1831. Lt., Co. K, 23rd Tennessee, Aug. 22, 1861. Colonel - Dec. 16, 1862. KIA at Petersburg, June 30, 1864. bur. Evergreen Cemetery, somewhere in Tennessee.

KEEN, ELISHA FORD. b. July 25, 1825. Partner in the Danville firm that manufactured Confederate carbines. m. Mary Anne Perkins. Keen's granddaughter was the famous Lady Astor, of prominence in English politics and society in the 20th century (by way of Keen's daughter who married a Langhorne). He served in the Virginia legisl., 1857-61 and 1863-67. Major, "Keen's Infantry Battalion," 1861. The battalion merged into the 57th Virginia. Lt. Col., 57th Virginia, Apr. 24, 1862. Colonel - May 7, 1862. Resigned July 31, 1862, citing a "frail and feeble constitution." d. Dec. 8, 1868. bur. in a family cemetery on Route 58 west of Danville.

KEITT, LAURENCE MASSILLON. b. Orangeburg Dist., Oct. 4, 1824. gr. South Carolina College. m. Susanna Sparks. In U.S. Congress, 1853-60. Raised the 20th South Carolina, and was commissioned its Colonel, Jan. 11, 1862. Served in C.S. Congress. MWIA at Cold Harbor, June 2, 1864, d. in Richmond June 4. bur. family cemetery, St. Matthews, South Carolina. His papers are at Duke.

KELL, JAMES T. b. Mecklenburg Co., Jan. 19, 1834. Major, 30th North Carolina, Sept. 26, 1861. Lt. Col. - May 2, 1862. Wded. by a piece of shell and disabled at Gaines' Mill. Resigned Sept. 3, 1863. d. May 4, 1910.

KELLEY, ALFRED. Lt., Co. G, 21st Virginia, July 2, 1861. Captain - Apr. 21, 1862. Major - June 10, 1863. Wded. at Cedar Mountain. Resigned Mar. 7, 1865, to search for a new unit with which to serve.

KELLY, CHARLES C. b. 1840. Occupation—"collector." m. Malinda Solomon. Lt., Co. B, 14th Georgia, July 9, 1861. Captain - Sept. 1, 1861. Resigned Dec. 23, 1862. Enlisted again as a private in Jan. 1863, and was restored as Captain, Co. B, Jan. 27, 1863. Major - May 8, 1864. POW at Richmond, Apr. 3, 1865, released May 30. bur. Ramah Church, Wilkinson County.

KELLY, HENRY BROOKE. b. Maryland. Lawyer. Lt., U.S. Army, 1847-1861. Colonel, 8th Louisiana, June 10, 1861, age 46. Frequently absent sick. Transferred to Military Court of Genl. Pemberton's Corps, Apr. 6, 1863. d. June 16, 1894. bur. Metairie Cemetery, New Orleans. Kelly wrote a small book on Port Republic.

KELLY, JOHN McDONALD. b. Carthage, North Carolina, Feb. 9, 1837. att. UNC. Capt., Co. C, 35th North Carolina, Nov. 6, 1861. 6′1½″. Major - July 1, 1862. KIA at Fredericksburg. Never married.

KEMPER, DELAWARE. b. Culpeper Co., Virginia, Aug. 24, 1833. att. U. Virginia. Teacher. Captain, Alexandria Artillery (Virginia), Apr. 1861. Major - June 25, 1862. Lt. Col. - Mar. 2, 1863. Severely wounded shoulder at 2nd Manassas. Ordered to Beauregard in South Carolina on Apr. 7, 1863, and remained in the Dept. of South Carolina, Georgia and Florida into 1865. m. Frances Snowden Hay, 1871. d. June 29, 1899. bur. St. Paul's Cemetery, Alexandria, Virginia. A Confederate soldier wrote that Kemper had a big nose and resembled Beauregard.

KENAN, THOMAS STEPHENS. b. Duplin Co., Feb. 12, 1838. gr. UNC. Lawyer. 5′10½″. Capt., Co. C, 12th North Carolina, Apr. 15, 1861. Capt., Co. A, 43rd North Carolina, Mar. 6, 1862. Lt. Col. - Mar. 20, 1862. Colonel - Apr. 21, 1862. Wded. and POW at Gettysburg, paroled Mar. 14, 1865. m. Sallie Dortch, 1866. Lived in Kenansville. Mayor of Wilson. Attorney General of North Carolina. d. Raleigh, Dec. 12, 1911. bur. Oakwood Cemetery.

KENDALL, JAMES S. b. New Hanover Co. Lived in Anson County. Lt., Co. K, 26th North Carolina, July 1, 1861, aged 23. Major - Apr. 21, 1862. Resigned Aug. 1, 1862, stating that his relations with other field officers of the 26th North Carolina made his remaining "incompatible with my honor as a gentleman and Soldier." Died of yellow fever during 1862. bur. Eastview Cemetery, Wadesboro, North Carolina.

KENDRICK, HENRY F. b. Russell Co., Virginia, Jan. 7, 1832. Became Captain of an independent Virginia Cavalry Co., which was joined to "Baldwin's Squadron Virginia Partisan Rangers" in early 1863. Major, 22nd Virginia Cavalry, Oct. 27, 1863. Wded. and POW at Monocacy (hip wound). Kendrick was imprisoned until exchanged in Feb. 1865, although in Oct. 1864 he petitioned to take the Federal oath and then go to Cincinnati where his mother lived, claiming that he was "never a rebel in principle," having been forced into service by conscription. His plea apparently failed. Lived in Washington Co., Virginia, post-war. d. Jan. 29, 1907. bur. Aston Cemetery, Washington County.

KENNEDY, JOHN THOMAS. b. 1826. Farmer in Wayne Co., N. C. Lt., Co. I, 35th N. C. Cavalry, Oct. 1861. Capt., 1st Battalion Georgia Partisan Rangers, June 16, 1862. Major, 62nd Georgia, Aug. 1, 1862. Lt. Col. - July 24, 1863. Wded. in back and POW at Petersburg, June 9, 1864, exchanged Aug. 8. Transferred with some of his troops and took command of the 16th North Carolina Cavalry Battalion, July 11, 1864, while in prison. Paroled at Greensboro, May 15, 1865. Sheriff of Wayne Co. and in state legislature. d. 1913.

KENT, JAMES. b. Petersburg, Virginia, Jan. 8, 1830. gr. William & Mary. gr. U. Pennsylvania, M.D. Physician in Dallas Co., Alabama. Capt., Co. D, 8th Alabama, 1861. Colonel, 44th Alabama, May 12, 1862. Resigned due to heart trouble, Sept. 1, 1862. m. Mary Grey. In Alabama legisl., 1880-81. d. Birmingham, May 5, 1881.

KENT, JOSEPH FERDINAND. b. Montgomery Co., Mar. 6, 1820. att. USMA. Capt., Co. A, 4th Virginia, Apr. 17, 1861. Major - May 4, 1861. Refused a commission as Lt. Col., from Gov. Letcher, and resigned Jan. 31, 1862. Later was Colonel, Wythe Reserves, a Home Guard unit from Wytheville. Wytheville postmaster, and manufacturer of woolen goods. d. Max Meadows, Sept. 4, 1886.

KESSLER, JOSEPH R. Capt., Co. D, 3rd Virginia State Line, 1862. Capt., Co. C, 19th Virginia Cavalry, Mar. 15, 1863. Major - Apr. 11, 1863. Lt. Col., 46th Virginia Cavalry Battalion, Feb. 26, 1864. Lt. Col., 26th Virginia Cavalry, Jan. 1865. POW at Fisher's Hill, Oct. 8, 1864; released July 24, 1865. Residence—Covington. 5′6″.

KEY, JOHN CALHOUN. b. Jasper Co., Feb. 25, 1826. In Georgia legisl., 1859-61 and after the war. m. Phoebe Allen, 1857. Capt., Co. B, 44th Georgia, Mar. 1862. Major - Sept. 11, 1863. Wded. at Chancellorsville and Gettysburg (thigh). Retired to Invalid Corps, May 13, 1864. On duty in Augusta in 1865. Newspaper editor postwar. d. Monticello, Georgia, June 1, 1902. bur. Monticello Methodist Churchyard. Key detailed his war experiences in some 30 newspaper columns in the Jasper County *News* during 1898-1899.

KEY, JOHN COTLETT GARRETT. b. South Carolina, 1809. Lawyer in Sparta and Belview, Louisiana, then in Gonzalez, Texas, moving to the latter place in 1854. Capt., Co. A, 4th

Texas, July 11, 1861. Major - Mar. 3, 1862. Lt. Col. - June 27, 1862. Colonel - July 10, 1862. Wded. at Gaines' Mill and Gettysburg. Retired due to ill health, Apr. 29, 1864. d. in Gonzalez in 1866 and buried there.

KIBBEE, CHARLES CARROLL. b. Macon, Georgia, Aug. 20, 1839. gr. Princeton. Sgt., Co. G, 10th Georgia, May 20, 1861. Lt. - Aug. 21, 1861. Captain - Jan. 2, 1862. Lt. Col. - Feb. 20, 1865, for "Valor & Skill." In Georgia legisl., 1870-76. Judge. d. Morrow's Station, Georgia, Oct. 17, 1905.

KILPATRICK, FRANKLIN WHITNER. b. Pendleton Dist., South Carolina, Sept. 30, 1837. att. U. Virginia. Pvt., 1st South Carolina, early 1861. Capt., Co. E, 4th South Carolina, June 7, 1861. Capt., Co. B, Palmetto Sharpshooters, Apr. 14, 1862. Major - July 22, 1862. Colonel, Palmetto Sharpshooters, Aug. 12, 1862, but declined. Colonel, 1st South Carolina (Hagood's), Jan. 31, 1863, on application of the regiment's officers. KIA at Wauhatchie, Oct. 28, 1863. bur. Taylor Cemetery, Anderson, South Carolina.

KING, BARRINGTON SIMERAL. b. Liberty Co., Georgia, Oct. 17, 1833. m. Sarah Elizabeth Macleod, 1859. Physician in Columbia, South Carolina. Pvt., Co. C, Cavalry Battalion, Cobb's Legion (Georgia), Aug. 1, 1861. Acting as surgeon for the company, Nov. 1, 1861. Captain - Mar. 22, 1862. Lt. Col. - Oct. 9, 1863. Transferred to the 9th Georgia Cavalry in 1865. KIA Mar. 10, 1865, near Averasboro, North Carolina. bur. Presbyterian Cemetery, Roswell, Georgia.

KING, JOHN FLOYD. b. Monticello, Georgia, Apr. 20, 1842. gr. U. Virginia. Lt., Co. M, 1st Georgia Regulars, Mar. 28, 1861. Transferred to Co. L and Co. A, same unit. Major of Artillery - 1862. Commanded 13th Battalion Virginia Artillery. Lt. Col. by 1864. Appx. Louisiana planter and lawyer. In U.S. Congress, 1879-1887. d. Washington, D.C., May 8, 1915. bur. Arlington Cemetery.

KING, JOSEPH HORACE. b. Alabama. Merchant in Morgan Co. Capt., Co. E, 9th Alabama, June 4, 1861. Major - June 5, 1861.

Colonel - Mar. 19, 1863. Wded. in Seven Days and at Gettysburg. Died "a few years after the war" in Decatur.

KING, PORTER. b. Perry Co., Alabama, Apr. 30, 1824. gr. U. Alabama. att. Brown U. In Alabama legisl. Circut Court judge. m. Callender McGregor Lumpkin, daughter of Georgia's Chief Justice. Capt., Co. G, 4th Alabama, 1861. Lt. Col., 41st Alabama, May 16, 1862, but dropped from the rolls almost immediately. Perry Co., Alabama, judge post-war. d. Atlanta, Jan. 3, 1890.

KINLOCH, JOHN MILLAR. b. Charleston, Mar. 31, 1834. m. Mary Lawson Simms, daughter of William Gilmore Simms. Lt., Co. A, 23rd South Carolina, Sept. 23, 1861. Captain - Jan. 1862. Lt. Col. - Nov. 6, 1862. An April 1863 letter by Col. Benbow declares that Kinloch has missed battles because of "a disease contracted by his own imprudence." Appx. Clerk of Courts for Charleston Co. d. Jan. 26, 1898, in Charleston. bur. Magnolia Cemetery.

KIRKLAND, BENJAMIN BROWN. b. Buford's Bridge, South Carolina, Aug. 22, 1838. m. Margaret A. Dunbar. Lt., Co. I, 1st South Carolina (Hagood's), Sept. 1, 1861. Capt., Co. C, 1st South Carolina, Apr. 12, 1862. Major - Feb. 7, 1864. Lt. Col. - Mar. 19, 1864. Barnwell Co. planter post-war. d. Cohens Bluff, Oct. 20, 1885. bur. Smyrna Baptist Church near Allendale.

KIRKPATRICK, THOMAS JELLIS. b. Cumberland Co., Virginia, July 31, 1829. att. Washington College. m. Fortunata Sydnor, 1852. Capt., Amherst Artillery (Virginia), July 1861. Major of artillery - Feb. 1865, assigned to Nelson's Bn. Paroled at Lynchburg, May 22, 1865. Lynchburg lawyer and state legisl. d. Lynchburg, Oct. 17, 1897. bur. Presbyterian Cemetery, Lynchburg.

KISER, JOHN F. b. Campbell Co., Mar. 27, 1836. Clerk at Powder Springs. Lt., Co. D, 7th Georgia, May 4, 1861. Captain - May 12, 1862. Wded. at 2nd Manassas (hand) and Wilderness (lung). Major - July 27, 1864. Appx. Prominent merchant. d. Atlanta, July 30, 1882. bur. Oakland Cemetery.

KNIGHT, CHARLES W. Of Edgecombe Co. Capt., Co. F, 31st North Carolina, Oct. 8, 1861, aged 26. Lt. Col. - June 7, 1863. POW at Roanoke Island, Feb. 1862.

KNIGHT, GAZAWAY LAMAR BUGG. b. Augusta, Apr. 11, 1825. att. Mercer University. Physician at Madison. Capt., Co. G, Infantry Battalion of Cobb's Legion (Georgia), July 29, 1861. Lt. Col. - May 5, 1862. Resigned July 18, 1862, and blamed a "kidney affliction." m. Isabelle Reid Hill. T. R. R. Cobb was displeased with Knight, among other reasons being a fist fight Knight had with a subordinate. d. Jan. 2, 1902. bur. Westview Cemetery, Madison.

KNOTT, JOHN LOCHER. b. Jefferson Co., Feb. 6, 1834. m. Mary Virginia Reinhart. Lived at Moler's Cross Roads. Boatman on the C.&O. Canal. Capt., Co. D, 12th Virginia Cavalry, Mar. 1, 1862. Major - Mar. 2, 1863. Wded. Nov. 1862. KIA at High Bridge. bur. Elmwood Cemetery, Shepherdstown, West Virginia.

KNOX, ROBERT LEON. b. Mt. Pleasant, Mississippi, 1833. Physician. 5'7". Pvt., Co. F, 17th Mississippi, Jan. 1, 1863. "Druggist - extra duty," says his service record. Promoted to Asst. Surgeon, 17th Mississippi, July 14, 1864. Records indicate that Knox served as Major of the 17th Mississippi in a temporary assignment, at an unspecified time. m. Fanny Steger. Memphis, Tennessee, physician. d. Oct. 17, 1919.

KOINER, ABSALOM. b. Augusta Co., Aug. 5, 1824. att. U. Virginia. Staunton attorney. m. Virginia M. Koiner (a cousin), 1850. In Virginia legisl. before and after the war. Capt., Co. H, 5th Virginia, Apr. 1861. Major - Sept. 11, 1861. Dropped at April 1862 re-org. Fishersville farmer. d. Dec. 31, 1920. bur. Bethlehem Lutheran Church.

LACKLAND, FRANCIS. b. Jefferson Co., May 20, 1830. gr. VMI, 1849. Lived in Jefferson Co., and engineer in Alabama. Lt. Col., 2nd Virginia, July 1861. d. Sept. 4, 1861, of pnenmonia and heart disease. bur. Zion Episcopal Church, Jefferson Co.

LADY, JOHN BUFORD. Lt., Co. G, 27th Virginia, 1861-62. Lt., Co. D, 36th Virginia Cavalry Battalion, early 1863. Major, 20th Virginia Cavalry, Aug. 14, 1863. Lt. Col. - Nov. 22, 1864. Wded. at 2nd Manassas. Paroled at Staunton, May 16, 1865. Farmer in Rockbridge Co. in 1870, age 29, worth $26,000. m. Helen White. d. June 8, 1883, in Lexington.

LALLERSTEDT, LAWRENCE D. Lawyer in Richmond Co. in 1860, age 41, owned 14 slaves. Capt., Co. A, 22nd Georgia, Aug. 31, 1861. Major - June 2, 1862. Wded. at Sharpsburg. Resigned on disability, July 16, 1863.

LAMAR, CHARLES AUGUSTUS LAFAYETTE. b. Savannah, Apr. 1, 1824. A godson of Lafayette. m. Caroline Agnes Nicoll, 1846. Slave ship owner and Savannah official pre-war. Colonel, 26th Georgia, Oct. 10, 1861. Resigned Mar. 12, 1862. Killed at Columbus near the end of the war (apparently on Apr. 16, 1865). bur. Savannah.

LAMAR, JEFFERSON MIRABEAU. b. Jan. 3, 1835. Brother of L. Q. C. Lamar. att. U. Virginia. gr. U. Mississippi. m. Mary Ann Lamar (a cousin), 1861. Covington, Georgia, lawyer. Capt., Co. A, Infantry Battalion of Cobb's Legion (Georgia), Aug. 1, 1861. Major - Nov. 16, 1861. Lt. Col. - Jan. 18, 1862. MWIA at Crampton's Gap, Sept. 14, 1862, d. Sept. 15 at Burkettsville. T. R. R. Cobb, though normally querulous in the extreme, called Lamar "a first rate man."

LAMAR, JOHN HILL. att. U. Georgia. Planter in 1860 near Macon, age 20. "Very profane." m. Mrs. Jane A. Carter in Orange Co., Virginia. Pvt., Co. B, 2nd Georgia Battalion, Apr. 20, 1861. Major, 61st Georgia, Oct. 11, 1861. Lt. Col. - Mar. 15, 1862. Colonel - June 1, 1862. WIA in hand at Fredericksburg. KIA at Monocacy. bur. Rose Hill Cemetery, Macon.

LAMAR, LUCIUS MIRABEAU. b. Bibb Co., June 25, 1834. gr. U. Georgia. m. Mary Frances Rawls. Capt., Co. C, 8th Georgia, Apr. 15, 1861. Major - Sept. 12, 1861. Lt. Col. - Dec. 24, 1861. Colonel - Jan. 28, 1862. Wded. and POW at Savage Station. Resigned Dec. 1862. Later appointed member of a military court. Planter in Pulaski Co. post-war. Georgia state senator and Speaker of the Georgia House. d. Macon, Feb. 25, 1889. bur. Rose Hill Cemetery.

LAMAR, LUCIUS QUINTUS CINCINNATUS. b. Eatonton, Georgia, Sept. 17, 1825. gr. Emory, 1845. m. Virginia Longstreet, 1847. m. (2) Henrietta Dean, 1887. In U.S. Congress both before and after the war. Lt. Col., 19th Mississippi, June

11, 1861. Colonel - May 5, 1862. Resigned Nov. 24, 1862. Paroled at Appomattox as Colonel (commission dated Dec. 3, 1864) on a 3rd Corps Military Court. U.S. Secretary of the Interior. d. Vineville, Georgia, Jan. 23, 1893. bur. St. Peter's Cemetery, Oxford, Mississippi.

LAMAR, THOMPSON BIRD. b. Jan. 27, 1828 in Georgia. Gave occupation as "Gent" in 1860 census; worth $51,000. Brother of L. Q. C. Lamar. Lt. Col., 5th Florida, Apr. 8, 1862. Colonel - July 6, 1863. Wded. at Sharpsburg. KIA at Petersburg, Aug. 30, 1864.

LAMB, JOHN CALHOUN. b. Camden Co., Dec. 21, 1836. Martin Co. merchant. Unmarried. Capt., Co. F, 17th North Carolina, May 1, 1861. Lt. Col. - May 16, 1862. MWIA at Bermuda Hundred, May 20, 1864, d. May 27.

LAMBETH, JOSEPH HARRISON. b. Apr. 3, 1840. Clerk in Davidson Co. Lt., Co. B, 14th North Carolina, May 26, 1861. Captain - Apr. 25, 1862. Major - July 5, 1862. POW at Winchester, May 19, 1864, exchanged Nov. 1864. Paroled at Greensboro. Thomasville banker post-war. d. Mar. 10, 1914. bur. Fairgrove Cemetery, Davidson Co.

LAND, CETH SMITH. b. Edgecombe Co., North Carolina, Dec. 9, 1833. Moved to South Carolina in 1855. m. Jane Thigpen, 1860. Pvt., 1st South Carolina, 1861. Lt., Co. I, 26th South Carolina, Jan. 13, 1862. Captain - May 24, 1862. Major - Dec. 9, 1864, for "Valor & Skill." Appx. Dealer in pine stores and naval products in Clarendon and Williamsburg counties. d. Dec. 26, 1899. bur. Foreston, South Carolina.

LANDIS, ABSALOM LOWE. b. Bedford Co., Tennessee, Aug. 31, 1823. Shelbyville merchant. m. Nancy Carter. Major, 17th Tennessee, by Sept. 1861. Served throughout most of the war years. POW at Knoxville, May 21, 1865, released June 16. Nashville banker and railroad man. In Tennessee legisl. d. Nashville, June 5, 1896.

LANE, ANDREW JACKSON. b. June 6, 1822, in Virginia. Planter in Hancock Co., Georgia, worth $80,600 in 1860. m. Frances

Brooking. Capt., Co. I, 49th Georgia, Mar. 1862. Colonel - Mar. 22, 1862. Wded. at Seven Pines and Mechanicsville. Resigned May 8, 1863. Railroad magnate and in Georgia legisl. d. Sparta, Jan. 2, 1886. bur. Rose Hill Cemetery, Macon.

LANE, HENRY. b. Warren Co., Virginia, Jan. 9, 1826. Lawyer in Patrick and Floyd counties. Editor of Floyd newspaper. Capt., Co. B, 42nd Virginia, June 15, 1861. Major - Apr. 21, 1862. Wded. above right eye by shell fragment near Winchester, May 1862. KIA at Cedar Mountain.

LANE, JOHN. Son of Senator Joseph Lane of Oregon. Lived in Winchester, Oregon. att. USMA but ranked very low in his class. Captain, Sumter Artillery (Lane's Georgia Battery), June 11, 1861, age 23. Major - Mar. 2, 1863, assigned to Cutts' Bn. Lt. Col. - Feb. 18, 1865. Lived in Idaho postwar and died there about 1915. Seven Lane letters are at Indiana University. A fellow officer described Lane as "so disgusting in his habits, and so prodigal and vagabondish in his principles that . . . the Battn. is much dissatisfied." The published memoir by Mills of the 16th North Carolina, by contrast, comments favorably on Lane.

LANE, JOHN RANDOLPH. b. Chatham Co., July 4, 1835. Corporal, Co. G, 26th North Carolina, June 10, 1861. Captain - Sept. 2, 1861. Lt. Col. - Oct. 11, 1862. Colonel - July 2, 1863. Wded. in head at Gettysburg; wded. in thigh at Wilderness; wded. in the side by a shell, Aug. 25, 1864. Paroled at Greensboro. Chatham Co. businessman. d. North Carolina, Jan. 7, 1909.

LANE, WILLIAM AUGUSTUS. Brooks Co. lawyer. Capt., Co. I, 26th Georgia, July 23, 1861. Lt. Col. - Aug. 17, 1861. Retired May 10, 1862. Brooks Co. surveyor post-war. In Georgia legisl.

LANG, DAVID. b. Camden Co., Georgia, May 9, 1838. gr. Georgia Military Institute, 1857. Surveyor in Suwannee Co., Florida. Pvt., Co. H, 1st Florida, 1861. Promoted to sergeant, and mustered out, Apr. 1862. Capt., Co. C, 8th Florida, May 10, 1862. Colonel - Oct. 2, 1862. Badly wded. in the head at Fredericksburg, Dec. 11, 1862. Commanded Perry's Brigade at Gettysburg. Commanded Finegan's Brigade late in the war. Adjutant Gen-

Indiana University

JOHN LANE
Artillery

eral of Florida. Private secretary to two Governors of Florida, 1893-1901. d. Tallahassee, 1917. bur. Tallahassee city cemetery.

LANG, DAVID BERKELEY. b. Harrison Co., Virginia, Jan. 31, 1831. Farmer and physician in Barbour Co. 6′1″. m. Elizabeth Powell, 1851. Lang was possessed of hair as "red as a fox's tail." Served in western Virginia as a volunteer scout, 1861-1862. Major, 62nd Virginia, Feb. 1, 1863. Lt. Col. - Nov. 10, 1863. MWIA near Bunker Hill, Sept. 5, 1864. d. Sept. 6. bur. Stonewall Cemetery, Winchester.

LANGHORNE, DANIEL ALLEN. b. Cumberland Co., July 25, 1825. gr. VMI, 1845. gr. U. Pennsylvania, M.D., 1848. Lt. Col., 42nd Virginia, July 1861. Dropped at April 1862 re-org. Did local duty in Lynchburg the rest of the war. m. Virginia P. Kent. d. Lynchburg, Feb. 10, 1908.

LANGHORNE, JOHN SCAISBROOKE. b. Cumberland Co., June 1, 1817. m. Elizabeth Dabney. Capt., Co. B, 2nd Virginia Cavalry, May 13, 1861. Major - Aug. 21, 1861. Retired in late 1861, and ran a flour mill in Lynchburg for the C.S. govt. His own mill went bankrupt in 1870. d. Lynchburg, Aug. 29, 1886. bur. Spring Hill Cemetery.

LANGHORNE, MAURICE SCAISBROOKE. b. Cumberland Co., Mar. 27, 1823. Lynchburg tobacco businessman. m. 3 times. Capt., Co. A, 11th Virginia, Apr. 22, 1861 (this unit had existed for some years). Major - Aug. 21, 1861. Lt. Col. - May 7, 1862. Colonel - Sept. 24, 1863. Seriously wded. at Seven Pines. Retired Dec. 20, 1864, after spending some time in reserve commands at and near Lynchburg. Paroled at Lynchburg, Apr. 15, 1865. Ran insurance and tobacco businesses in Lynchburg postwar. d. there Mar. 27, 1908.

LANGLEY, FRANCIS H. b. Maryland, 1830. Carpenter in Richmond, Virginia. 5′9″. Sgt., Co. G, 1st Virginia, Apr. 21, 1861. Lt. - May 4, 1861. Captain - Apr. 27, 1862. Major - May 2, 1863. Lt. Col. - July 3, 1863. POW at Sayler's Creek, released July 25. Served on the Richmond police force. d. at Richmond Soldiers' Home, Mar. 5, 1908. bur. Oakwood Cemetery.

LANKFORD, WILLIAM C. b. Franklin Co., North Carolina, 1833. att. U. Virginia. gr. U. New York, M.D., 1854. 6'0". Franklin Co. physician. Capt., Co. F, 47th North Carolina, Feb. 4, 1862. Major - Mar. 3, 1864. Postmaster of Wake Forest post-war, and a county commissioner. Died in 1902.

LATHAM, LOUIS CHARLES. b. Plymouth, Sept. 11, 1840. gr. UNC, 1859. Capt., Co. G, 1st North Carolina, May 16, 1861. Major - Dec. 14, 1863. Wded. at Sharpsburg and Wilderness (side). In North Carolina legisl., 1864-65. Appx. Lawyer in Greenville, North Carolina. In North Carolina legisl. post-war. In U.S. Congress, 1881-83 and 1887-89. d. Baltimore, Maryland, Oct. 16, 1895. bur. Greenville.

LATIMER, JOSEPH WHITE. b. Prince William Co., Aug. 27, 1843. att. VMI. Served as cadet drillmaster for Hampden Light Artillery (Virginia) in early 1861. Lt., Courtney Artillery (Virginia), Sept. 15, 1861. Captain - summer 1862. Major - Mar. 2, 1863, assigned to Andrews' Bn. Acting Chief of Artillery, Ewell's Division, Dec. 1862. MWIA at Gettysburg. d. Aug. 1, 1863, in Harrisonburg, Virginia. bur. there in Woodbine Cemetery. A subordinate wrote of Latimer: "I believe he is the *very best* Arty. Capt. in Genl. Lee's Army and would make the best Maj. and I know we have worse Generals by far than he wd. make."

LATTA, JOSEPH W. Of Wake Co. Capt., Co. A, 66th North Carolina, Nov. 20, 1861 (although this regiment was not formed until Oct. 1863, the company was organized in 1861). Major - June 3, 1864, but "Appt. Revoked." Resigned July 14, 1864.

LAWSON, CHARLES NICHOLAS. b. White Stone, Jan. 21, 1821. Lancaster Co. planter. m. Catherine Ann Brent, 1855. Major, 92nd Virginia Militia, 1861. Capt., Co. L, 55th Virginia, Mar. 25, 1862. Major - May 2, 1863. POW at Fredericksburg. Suspended without pay for 15 days by sentence of a court-martial, Apr. 1864 (execution of the sentence was later cancelled). KIA Aug. 19, 1864, at Weldon R.R.

LAWSON, JOHN. b. Fredericksburg, Dec. 28, 1828. gr. VMI, 1849, and on VMI faculty. Major, 59th Virginia, Aug. 13, 1861. Paroled POW at Roanoke Island, Feb. 21, 1862. Dropped at

Nov. 1862 re-org. Became Pvt., Co. C, 15th Virginia. Later applied for position as a Treasury Clerk. Civil engineer post-war. d. Aug. 31, 1870 "from effects of wounds." bur. Cave Hill Cemetery, Louisville, Ky.

LAY, LOUIS. b. France. New Orleans "cotton classer." Lt. Col., 6th Louisiana, June 4, 1861, aged 40. Resigned in 1861.

LEA, JOHN WILLIS. b. Sept. 16, 1838, in South Carolina. att. USMA. Lived in Caswell Co., North Carolina. Capt., Co. I, 5th North Carolina, May 16, 1861. Lt. Col. - Feb. 2, 1863. Colonel - May 12, 1864. Wded. and POW at Williamsburg, exchanged Nov. 1862. Wded. at Chancellorsville and at Winchester (Sept. 19, 1864). Lea commanded R. D. Johnston's Brigade from Fort Stedman to Appomattox. The Museum of the Confederacy has Lea's uniform.

LEACH, JAMES MADISON. b. Randolph Co., North Carolina, Jan. 17, 1815. Lived in Davidson Co. gr. USMA, 1838. In U.S. Congress, 1859-61 and 1871-75. Capt., Co. A, 21st North Carolina, May 8, 1861. Lt. Col. - July 3, 1861. Resigned Dec. 23, 1861. In C.S. Congress, 1864-65, and maintained a strong anti-administration stance. In North Carolina legisl. post-war. Died in Lexington, June 1, 1891. bur. Hopewell Cemetery, Trinity, North Carolina. A lieutenant in his regiment wrote that Leach was "kind and obliging," but "would make a better politician than military commander."

LEAK, JOHN WALL. b. Richmond Co., North Carolina, Mar. 16, 1816. gr. Randolph-Macon, 1838. m. Ann Cole. Lt. Col., 23rd North Carolina, July 15, 1861. Dropped at April 1862 re-org. Rockingham Co. cotton merchant. d. May 6, 1876. Buried in family cemetery, Richmond Co.

LEDBETTER, DANIEL ALEXANDER. b. near Pendleton, South Carolina, July 18, 1828. Millwright at Townville. Stood 6′4″ and possessed a noteworthy stentorian voice. Capt., Co. A, 1st South Carolina Rifles, 1861. Major - July 23, 1861. Lt. Col. - Jan. 29, 1862. Colonel - Aug. 29, 1862. MWIA at 2nd Manassas, d. Sept. 1, 1862. bur. on Bushy Park Farm, Route 676, Prince William Co., Virginia.

LEE, AUGUSTUS H. b. Georgia. Lawyer at Covington in 1860, age 32, worth $92,985. Capt., Co. H, 3rd Georgia, Apr. 25, 1861. Major - May 8, 1861. Retired Apr. 28, 1862.

LEE, BAKER PERKINS, JR. b. York Co., Mar. 13, 1830. gr. U. Virginia. m. Mary Esther Simkins, 1855. Lt., Co. E, 32nd Virginia, May 14, 1861. Captain - Apr. 30, 1862. Major - Jan. 5, 1863. Paroled at Richmond, Apr. 24, 1865. Lawyer and politician on Virginia Eastern Shore, then in Richmond, then Hampton. Author of SHSP article and various memorial tracts. d. Hampton, Sept. 2, 1901. bur. St. John's Episcopal Church.

LEE, CHARLES COCHRANE. b. South Carolina, Jan. 1834. Lived in Mecklenburg Co., North Carolina. gr. USMA, 1856. Lt., U.S. Army, 1856-59. Instructor at Charlotte Military Academy. Lt. Col., 1st North Carolina (Bethel), May 11, 1861. Colonel - Sept. 1, 1861. Colonel, 37th North Carolina, Nov. 20, 1861. KIA at Frayser's Farm.

LEE, GEORGE WASHINGTON. b. ca. 1830. Saloon keeper in Atlanta. Pvt., Co. M, 38th Georgia, Sept. 26, 1861. Lt. Col. - Oct. 11, 1861. Colonel - Feb. 18, 1862. Resigned in July 1862. Was later a field officer in the 25th Battalion Georgia Provost Guard and the 3rd Battalion Georgia State Guards.

LEE, HENDERSON LEWIS. b. Lunenburg Co., Oct. 23, 1826. att. William & Mary. gr. Hampden-Sydney. m. Lucy Scott. Lt., Co. G, 38th Virginia, Dec. 11, 1861. Captain - 1862. Major - Nov. 15, 1863. Lost an arm at Gettysburg. Retired Dec. 2, 1864. Lunenburg lawyer. d. Soldiers' Home in Richmond, Mar. 5, 1894. bur. Lunenburg Co.

LEE, HERBERT D. Lawyer in Rutherford Co., North Carolina. Capt., Co. D, 16th North Carolina, May 1, 1861, aged 30. Major - May 31, 1862. Wded. knee at Fredericksburg. Resigned Jan. 27, 1864, due to "atrophy of the thigh" from that wound. Alive in Cleveland Co., North Carolina, in 1881.

LEE, LEVI C. Physician in Yalobusha Co. in 1860, age 37. Capt., Co. D, 2nd Mississippi Battalion, Aug. 14, 1861. Major - Nov. 3, 1862. Wded. in thigh and arm at Fredericksburg. 2nd Bn.

merged into the 48th Mississippi in early 1863. Paroled Apr. 17, 1865.

LEE, STEPHEN. b. Charleston, South Carolina, June 7, 1801. att. USMA. m. Caroline Lee (a cousin), and had 14 children. Master of a boys' school in Asheville, North Carolina. Colonel, 15th and 16th North Carolina on June 17, 1861; chose to accept the 16th North Carolina appt. Resigned Feb. 13, 1862, due to old age and illness. Later was a captain of Local Defense Troops. d. Asheville, Aug. 2, 1879. bur. Riverside Cemetery.

LEE, WILLIAM FITZHUGH. b. April 27, 1833. gr. VMI, 1853. Lt., 2nd U.S. Infantry, 1855-1861. Several sources identify Lee as Lt. Col. of the 33rd Virginia when he was MWIA at 1st Manassas (d. July 29). He has no official service record at all extant with that unit. A&IGO correspondence synopses show Lee as Lt., CSA, July 1, 1861, and applying for rank of Lt. Col. on July 8. The 33rd Va. itself only mustered into CSA service on July 1, and the colonel's rank (Cummings) dates from then. It would be a close call whether Lee could have had a commission back from Richmond within thirteen days, even if it were handled very promptly. bur. Elmwood Cemetery, Shepherdstown.

LEFTWICH, JOEL BRECKINRIDGE. b. June 29, 1816. m. Lucy Frances Moorman, 1842. Capt., Co. D, 42nd Virginia Infantry, May 1861. Capt., Co. F, 3rd Virginia Reserves, Apr. 16, 1864. Lt. Col. - Sept. 30, 1864. In Virginia legisl. post-war. d. Campbell Co., Jan. 6, 1890.

LEGETT, JOHN M. b. Scotland, 1835. New Orleans lawyer. Capt., Co. F, 10th Louisiana, July 22, 1861. Major - July 28, 1862. Lt. Col. - Aug. 30, 1862. Killed in action at Chancellorsville. bur. Hollywood Cemetery.

LEGG, GEORGE WASHINGTON HAMILTON. b. Spartanburg Dist., South Carolina, Nov. 26, 1814. m. Clemantine S. Kennedy, 1840. Postmaster of Spartanburg. Lt. Col., 5th South Carolina, Apr. 13, 1861. Dropped in 1862 due to age, became militia officer. Railroad agent and trial justice. d. Spartanburg Co., May 15, 1880.

LEIGH, JOHN WICKHAM. b. Richmond, Virginia, 1825. Lt. in Voltigeurs Regiment, Mexican War. Major, 4th Virginia Heavy Artillery, May 15, 1862. Resigned Oct. 28, 1862.

LEIGH, WILLIAM. Lt. Col., 29th Virginia, Nov. 1861. Dropped at May 1862 re-org. Leigh is also shown as Major, 53rd Virginia, but no supporting records of any sort have been located. General Humphrey Marshall called Leigh "precise and strict, brave, urbane, intelligent, well instructed, of good habits."

LESESNE, HENRY HILTON. Farmer in Clarendon District in 1860, age 20, worth $63,000. Lt., Co. I, 23rd South Carolina, Nov. 15, 1861. Captain - Apr. 16, 1862. Major - June 22, 1864. Appx. m. Letitia Margaret Wells. Sheriff after the war. d. 1901.

LESTER, GERMAN ALBERT. b. Pulaski, Tennessee, Feb. 21, 1834. gr. U. Mississippi, 1855. Lawyer in Winnsboro, Louisiana. Capt., Co. E, 8th Louisiana, June 19, 1861. Major - sometime before summer 1863. Lt. Col. - date unknown. Wded. at Chancellorsville. KIA at Cold Harbor, June 1, 1864. bur. Hollywood Cemetery.

LESTER, RICHARD PAUL. b. Gwinnett Co., Nov. 30, 1832. m. Mary Jane Waddell. Lawyer in Cummings. Capt., Co. E, 14th Georgia, July 4, 1861. Major - Nov. 8, 1862. Lt. Col. - May 10, 1863. Colonel - May 8, 1864. Appx. d. Nov. 29, 1902 in Covington. bur. South View Cemetery.

LESTER, WILLIAM. b. Newberry Dist., Oct. 9, 1819. m. (1) Sarah Hunter. m. (2) Hannah Young. 6′2″. Capt., Co. G, 13th South Carolina, Aug. 26, 1861. Major - Nov. 4, 1863. Lt. Col. - June 8, 1864. Wded. at Fredericksburg. Appx. Newberry farmer. d. Nov. 11, 1886. bur. Prosperity, South Carolina.

LETCHER, SAMUEL HOUSTON. b. Rockbridge Co., Feb. 23, 1828. Brother of Virginia's war governor, John Letcher. att. Washington College. Lexington lawyer. Capt., Co. B, 5th Virginia, Apr. 1861. Lt. Col., 58th Virginia, Oct. 1861. Colonel - May 1, 1862. Letcher demanded a court of inquiry concerning his experiences at Gaines' Mill and resigned Sept. 21, 1862, when its proceedings were delayed. His resignation was accepted Oct. 30, 1862. Lexington newspaper editor post-war. Died in Lexington, unmarried, Nov. 10, 1868, and buried there.

LEVY, WILLIAM MALLORY. b. Isle of Wight Co., Virginia, Oct. 31, 1827. gr. William & Mary. Lt., Virginia Volunteers, in Mexican War. Moved to Natchitoches, Louisiana, in 1852. In Louisiana legisl. Capt., Co. A, 2nd Louisiana, May 11, 1862. Became Colonel, 2nd Louisiana, prior to Oct. 1861. Dropped at May 1862 re-org. Major on Richard Taylor's staff, July 1862. Lt. Col. and a.i.g. to Taylor, Spring 1864. In U.S. Congress, 1875-1877. d. Saratoga, New York, Aug. 14, 1882. bur. Natchitoches.

LEWELLEN, JOHN RICHARD. b. 1821 in Campbell Co. Mexican War veteran. Farmer, politician and newspaperman. "Over 6 feet in height, fine personal appearance, made venerable by white hair and beard." Capt., Co. K, 12th Virginia, May 4, 1861. Major - Oct. 3, 1862. Lt. Col. - July 30, 1864. Wded. at 2nd Manassas and Crampton's Gap. Absent detailed on conscript duty frequently. Paroled in Richmond, Apr. 17, 1865. Lived in Norfolk post-war, and edited the Danville *Register*. d. Danville, Dec. 4, 1886. bur. Blandford Cemetery, Petersburg.

LEWIE, FREDERICK SIMS. b. Lexington Dist., South Carolina, Aug. 13, 1831. Educated in medicine in Paris, France. m. Rachel Leaphart, 1851. Planter and physician in Lexington Dist. Sgt., 1st South Carolina (Gregg's), early 1861. Capt., Co. C, 15th South Carolina, Aug. 16, 1861. Major - Nov. 18, 1863. Lt. Col. - Jan. 5, 1864. Temporarily commanded the 20th South Carolina. Paroled at Augusta, May 7, 1865. In South Carolina legisl., 1864-67. d. Summit, South Carolina, June 20, 1873. bur. St. James Lutheran Churchyard.

LEWIS, ABNER McCOY. b. 1834 in Upson Co. Lt., Co. B, 2nd Georgia, July 12, 1861. Wded. at Garnett's Farm. Captain - Apr. 28, 1862. Major - Jan. 15, 1864. Wded. at Chickamauga, leg amputated. Retired on disability, Dec. 23, 1864. Married three times. Moved in about 1903 from Upson Co. to Dawson. d. Nov. 4, 1918. bur. Thomaston, Georgia.

Hattie Belle Lester

WILLIAM LESTER
13th South Carolina Infantry

LEWIS, HENRY G. Of Tyrrell and Edgecombe Counties. Lt., Co. A, 32nd North Carolina, May 16, 1861. Captain - Jan. 23, 1862. Major - June 18, 1863. Lt. Col. - shown on Nov. 1864 roll, without details. Wded. in face and POW at Gettysburg, released July 24, 1865. 5′10″. Lived in Scuppernong, North Carolina.

LEWIS, IVEY FOREMAN. b. 1833. att. UNC. Lt., Co. E, Jeff Davis Legion (Mississippi), Sept. 24, 1861. Captain - Mar. 1, 1862. Major - July 3, 1863. Paroled at Demopolis, Alabama, June 8, 1865. d. 1884.

LEWIS, JOHN REDMAN COXE. b. 1833. In U.S. Navy pre-war. Served in Bedford Light Artillery (Virginia) early in the war. Major of artillery, July 21, 1862. Second in command of an A.N.Va. artillery bn. in 1862-1863. "Transferred to another arm of the service" in 1863. Lt. Col. and a.i.g. at the Mobile post in 1864. Returned to the A.N.Va. in Jan. 1865. Paroled at Manchester, Apr. 30, 1865. Lived in Berryville, Virginia, post-war. d. Dec. 11, 1898. bur. Hollywood Cemetery, Richmond.

LEWIS, MERIWETHER. b. Essex Co., Feb. 17, 1827. att. U. Virginia. m. Julia Ann Sanders. Northumberland Co. physician and Virginia legisl. Capt., Co. D, 9th Virginia Cavalry, June 16, 1861. Major - Apr. 28, 1862. Lt. Col. - Oct. 18, 1862. Wded. lung at Upperville, June 22, 1863, caused his resignation on May 9, 1864. Lived at "Litwalton," Northumberland County. d. July 25, 1883. bur. St. Mary's White Chapel, Lancaster Co.

LEWIS, TREVANION D. b. Baton Rouge clerk. Lt., Co. A, 8th Louisiana, June 19, 1861, aged 24. Adj. of 8th Louisiana, 1861-62. Major - May 7, 1862. Lt. Col. - summer 1862. Colonel - Oct. 1862. Wded. at Sharpsburg. POW at 2nd Fredericksburg, May 4, 1863, paroled May 18. KIA at Gettysburg, July 2, 1863.

LEYDEN, AUSTIN. b. Pennsylvania, May 1826. Manufacturer in Atlanta, Georgia. Lt., Co. F, 1st Georgia, Mar. 18, 1861. Resigned Nov. 5, 1861. Major, 9th Georgia Artillery Battalion, Apr. 1862. Present into 1865. Member of Atlanta City Council. Invented "a revolving rifle" and patented a U.S. mail bag fastening device. d. Atlanta, Feb. 14, 1900. bur. Oakland Cemetery (unmarked grave).

LIDDELL, PHILIP FRANK. Captain in the 2nd Mississippi during the Mexican War. Capt., Co. K, 11th Mississippi, Feb. 26, 1861. Lt. Col. - May 4, 1861. Colonel - Apr. 21, 1862. MWIA at Sharpsburg, d. Sept. 25, 1862.

LIGHTFOOT, CHARLES EDWARD. b. Culpeper, Virginia, Apr. 18, 1834. gr. VMI, 1854. 5′6″. Faculty member at Hillsboro, North Carolina, Military Academy. Major, 6th North Carolina, May 16, 1861. Wded. at 1st Manassas. Lt. Col. - July 11, 1861. Colonel, 22nd North Carolina, Mar. 29, 1862. Defeated at June 13, 1862, re-org., while absent in enemy hands, having been captured at Seven Pines (exchanged Aug. 5, 1862). He became the "bitter enemy" of Genl. Dorsey Pender. Lt. Col. of Artillery, Aug. 18, 1862. Served in command of a bn. of light artillery in the Richmond defenses the rest of the war. Paroled in Richmond, Apr. 24, 1865. Professor at Bethel Military Academy (Culpeper Co., Virginia) post-war. d. July 3, 1878.

LIGHTFOOT, JAMES NEWELL. b. Early Co., Georgia, Aug. 14, 1839. Lt., Co. A, 6th Alabama, May 11, 1861. Captain - Nov. 30, 1861. Lt. Col. - May 30, 1862. Colonel - May 7, 1863. Wded. at Seven Pines, Sharpsburg, Gettysburg, Spotsylvania. Retired Mar. 11, 1865. m. Mrs. Mary Elizabeth Gordon McAllister in 1862. Farmer in Henry Co., Alabama. d. Eufaula, Sept. 18, 1885.

LILES, EDWARD RUTLEDGE. b. 1833. Anson Co. farmer. att. UNC. Capt., Co. B, 31st North Carolina, Oct. 3, 1861. Lt. Col. - Sept. 17, 1862. Resigned Apr. 22, 1863. m. (1) Helen Bennett. m. (2) Fannie Fladger. d. 1883.

LILLEY, JOHN DOAK. b. Greenville, Virginia, Sept. 5, 1841. att. VMI. Lt., Co. H, 52nd Virginia, July 23, 1861. Captain - Nov. 23, 1861. Major - Dec. 19, 1863. Lt. Col. - May 30, 1864. Wded. at 2nd Manassas. Served as enrolling officer in Rockbridge Co., 1862-63. Paroled at Staunton, May 23, 1865. Augusta Co. surveyor and farmer. d. June 13, 1913. bur. Bethel Presbyterian Church.

LILLY, WILLIAM H. b. Louisiana. Lawyer in Natchez. Pvt., Co. B, 12th Mississippi, Apr. 25, 1861, aged 24. Major - spring of 1862. Wded. in Seven Days. d. Feb. 17, 1863, in a railroad accident. bur. near Hickory Station, Mississippi.

LINKOUS, BENJAMIN R. Raleigh Co., Virginia. Mexican War veteran. Lived in Beckley. Doorkeeper of Virginia Secession Convention. Capt., Co. C, 36th Virginia, June 3, 1861, aged 37. Lt. Col. - May 15, 1862. Resigned Mar. 30, 1864, to return to the Virginia legisl., but was wded. at Cloyd's Mountain, May 9, 1864, and paroled at Blacksburg three days later. Lived in Montgomery Co. d. 1877. bur. Christiansburg Municipal Cemetery.

LIPSCOMB, THOMAS JEFFERSON. b. Asheville Dist., Mar. 27, 1833. gr. South Carolina Medical College. Nephew of General M. L. Bonham. att. U. Virginia. gr. Jefferson Medical College. Newberry planter. Lt., Co. B, 3rd South Carolina, 1861. Capt., Co. G, 2nd South Carolina Cavalry, June 20, 1862.. Major - Aug. 22, 1862. Lt. Col. - June 10, 1863. Colonel - Sept. 1, 1863. Lipscomb seems to have served as an a.d.c. to Bonham, Early and Kershaw briefly in 1861. m. Hattie Harrington, 1868. Burned out of his home by Reconstruction radicals. In South Carolina legisl. Newberry cotton merchant. Mayor of Columbia. d. Nov. 4, 1908.

LITTLE, BENJAMIN FRANKLIN. b. Richmond Co., North Carolina, 1830. Farmer. 5′9¾″. Capt., Co. E, 52nd North Carolina, Apr. 28, 1862. Lt. Col. - July 3, 1863. Wded. and POW at Gettysburg. Resigned Aug. 30, 1864. d. 1879.

LITTLE, FRANCIS HAMILTON. gr. U. Georgia, 1861. Lawyer in Lafayette, Georgia. Lt., Co. G, 11th Georgia, July 3, 1861, age 22. Major - July 11, 1862. Colonel - Nov. 8, 1862. Wded. at Gettysburg. Wded. severely at Reams's Station. Returned to duty in mid-October. Commanded G. T. Anderson's Brigade at times late in the war. Died before 1890.

LIVINGSTON, DANIEL. b. North, Orangeburg Dist., South Carolina, Nov. 17, 1827. m. Narcissa Fleming. Capt., Co. B, 1st Carolina (Hagood's), July 20, 1861. Major - July 12, 1862. Lt. Col. - Sept. 1, 1862. Resigned Mar. 19, 1864. Wded. at 2nd Manassas and Sharpsburg. d. North, South Carolina, Oct. 28, 1881.

LIVINGSTON, JAMES WILLIAM. b. Abbeville Dist., Aug. 12, 1832. gr. South Carolina College, 1852. Abbeville lawyer. m. Clara Kilpatrick, 1858 (she was a sister of Colonel Franklin W. Kilpatrick, q.v.). Capt., Co. A, 1st South Carolina Rifles, July 20, 1861. Major - Jan. 29, 1862. Colonel - Sept. 1, 1862. Livingston "fainted from heat" during the Battle of Sharpsburg. Resigned due to ill health, Nov. 12, 1862. In South Carolina legisl. postwar. Farmer and newspaper editor in Seneca. d. Aug. 25, 1886.

LOCKE, ROBERT WEAKLEY. b. Tennessee, Feb. 22, 1829. m. Elizabeth Cathey. Farmer in Thyatira, Mississippi. Sgt., Co. D, 42nd Mississippi, at org. Captain - Apr. 27, 1862. Major - Dec. 18, 1863. Badly wded. at Gettysburg, retired May 1864. Paroled at Grenada, Mississippi, May 19, 1865. d. Senatobia, June 17, 1904. Locke's sizable war diary has survived.

LOCKERT, JAMES WILLIAM. b. Montgomery Co., June 11, 1828. m. (1) Serepta Wilson, 1852. m. (2) Sarah Miles, 1867. Capt., Co. K, 14th Tennessee, May 27, 1861, age 35(?). Major - Aug. 15, 1862. Lt. Col. - Sept. 2, 1862. Wded. and POW at Gettysburg, released June 21, 1865. 5′6″. Farmer and sawyer in Montgomery and Robertson Counties. d. Aug. 13, 1912, in Todd County.

LOFTON, JOHN T. b. Nov. 11, 1827. gr. U. Georgia, 1850. m. Lizzie Johnson. Elbert Co. lawyer. Capt., Co. K, 6th Georgia, May 28, 1861. Colonel - Sept. 17, 1862. KIA at Ft. Fisher, Jan. 15, 1865. bur. Elmhurst Cemetery, Elbert Co.

LOGAN, ROBERT HENRY. b. Salem, Virginia, July 10, 1839. att. USMA. Adj., 42nd Virginia, 1861. Served on Floyd's staff, Dec. 1861 and into 1862. Commanded a mountain howitzer detachment in 1863. On Wharton's staff, 1864. Commanded Wharton's Brigade, while ranking as Captain, Sept. 1864. Although official records are lacking, Wharton later confirmed that Logan was commissioned Lt. Col., 45th Virginia, late in 1864. Wded. and POW at Waynesboro. Salem mayor and attorney, and in Virginia legisl. m. Anna Clayton. d. Dec. 26, 1900. bur. East Hill Cemetery, Salem.

LOMAX, TENNENT. b. Abbeville, South Carolina, Sept. 20, 1820. gr. Randolph-Macon. Editor of Columbus *Times*. m. Mrs. Carrie Billingslea Shorter, 1857. Mexican War officer. 6′4″. Lt. Col., 3rd Alabama, Apr. 28, 1861, at Montgomery. Colonel - July 31, 1861. KIA at Seven Pines. bur. Oakwood Cemetery, Montgomery.

LONG, JAMES A. b. 1828. Physician in Troup Co., Georgia. Capt., Co. K, 13th Georgia, July 8, 1861. Wded. in arm at Sharpsburg. Major - Dec. 13, 1862. Resigned Mar. 1, 1864, being disabled by a wound. In Georgia legisl., 1863-65. Physician in LaGrange and at Sherman, Texas. d. Aug. 25, 1879. Long's recollections are at the Georgia Archives.

LONG, JOHN OSMOND. b. Illinois, Nov. 1832. gr. USMA, 1854. Lt., U.S. Army, 1854-1861. 5′6″. Lt. of artillery, Mar. 16, 1861. Lt. Col., 22nd North Carolina, July 11, 1861. POW at Seven Pines, and defeated at June 13, 1862, re-org. while in enemy hands. Became Lt. Col. in the Trans-Mississippi, and served on Magruder's staff. d. Apr. 3, 1875.

LOUD, PHILOLOGUS H. b. London, England, in 1800. Piano maker in Philadelphia. Professor of chemistry in Madison, Georgia in 1860. m. Sarah Elizabeth Williams. Capt., Co. H, 10th Georgia, May 20, 1861. Wded. in the head at Sharpsburg. Major - Oct. 29, 1862. Retired Feb. 13, 1865, having been absent on disability since Apr. 1863. Loud was living in Williston, S. C., in 1898.

LOVE, JAMES ROBERT. b. Jackson Co., North Carolina, in 1832. gr. Emory & Henry. In North Carolina legisl. before and after the war. Lt., Co. A, 16th North Carolina, Apr. 1861, age 27. Capt., Co. A, Thomas' North Carolina Legion, May 31, 1862. Lt. Col. - Sept. 27, 1862. m. Julia Reagan. Merchant in Monroe Co., Tennessee. d. Sweetwater, Tennessee, Nov. 10, 1885.

LOVE, MATTHEW NORRIS. Resident of Henderson Co. Lt., Co. A, 25th North Carolina, June 30, 1861, aged 30. Captain - Apr. 30, 1862. Major - Nov. 5, 1864. Lt. Col. - Jan. 1, 1865. Wded. wrist at Fredericksburg. Appx.

LOVE, ROBERT GUSTAVUS ADOLPHUS. b. Jan. 4, 1827, in Waynesville, North Carolina. Lived in Haywood Co. In North Carolina legislature pre-war. m. Mary Ann Dillard. Capt., Co. L, 16th North Carolina, May 4, 1861. Lt. Col. - June 17, 1861. Defeated at re-org. Later was Colonel, 62nd North Carolina. d. May 24, 1887.

LOVE, THADDEUS DELANO. b. Dec. 21, 1839. m. Lillian Marie Robeson. Lived at St. Pauls, North Carolina. 5'10". Capt., Co. G, 24th North Carolina, June 4, 1861. Major - May 16, 1862. Wded. and POW at Petersburg, Mar. 25, 1865, released July 24. d. Wilmington, North Carolina, Jan. 6, 1892. bur. Beth-Car Presbyterian Cemetery, near Tar Heel, North Carolina.

LOVEJOY, GEORGE STEPTOE. b. Aug. 1839. att. USMA. Lived in Wake Co. Lt. Col., 14th North Carolina, June 3, 1861. Defeated at April 1862 re-org. d. July 20, 1862.

LOWE, JOHN GREEN. b. Hartsville, Tennessee, Feb. 1831. Lt., Co. G, 23rd Tennessee, Aug. 23, 1861. Captain - May 8, 1862. Major - Dec. 16, 1862. POW at Petersburg, June 17, 1864, released June 8, 1865. 5'11". d. Hartsville, Dec. 1909.

LOWE, JOHN HOLLINGER. b. Stewart Co., Georgia, May 5, 1833. m. Lucy Haynes, 1855. Capt., Co. G, 31st Georgia, Nov. 10, 1861. Major - May 13, 1862. Lt. Col. - Aug. 19, 1863. Colonel - May 19, 1864. Wded. at Winchester, June 13, 1863. Appx. Stewart County Supt. of Schools post-war. Moved to Buena Vista, Georgia, 1884. d. May 30, 1911. bur. Buena Vista Cemetery.

LOWE, SAMUEL D. b. North Carolina. Lived in Lincoln Co. 5'10". Lt., Co. C, 28th North Carolina, Aug. 13, 1861. Captain - Sept. 26, 1861. Major - Apr. 12, 1862. Lt. Col. - June 11, 1862. Colonel - Nov. 1, 1862. Wded. at Gettysburg. POW at Slash Church, May 27, 1862, exchanged Nov. 8. Retired to Invalid Corps, July 8, 1864. Commanded the post at Asheville. Merchant in Iron Station, North Carolina, post-war. Moved out of the state in 1873. d. Buena Vista, Virginia, May 30, 1891.

LOWE, THOMAS LAFAYETTE. b. Catawba Co., Apr. 27, 1831. gr. Catawba College, 1852. m. Anna D. Coulter, 1854. Lincolnton school teacher and surveyor. Capt., Co. C, 28th North Carolina, Aug. 13, 1861. Lt. Col. - Sept. 21, 1861. Died of pneumonia, near Richmond, June 11, 1862. bur. Grace Church, Catawba Co.

LOWRANCE, WILLIAM LEE JOSHUA. (The name Joshua was frequently omitted.) b. Mooresville, July 26, 1836. att. Davidson College. Lt., Co. D, 34th North Carolina, Sept. 9, 1861. Captain - Oct. 25, 1861. Colonel - Feb. 10, 1863. Merchant in Oxford, Mississippi. In Mississippi legisl. Moved to Texas and entered the ministry in 1880. Pastor of Oakcliff Presbyterian Church in Dallas. d. Forestville, Texas, Mar. 24, 1916.

LOWRY, WILLIAM BENJAMIN. b. Sept. 3, 1843, near Crawfordsville, Mississippi. att. U. Mississippi, class of 1862. Lived in Lowndes Co. Capt., Co. A, 11th Mississippi, Apr. 26, 1861. Major - Sept. 17, 1862. Lt. Col. - Sept. 26, 1862. Apptd. Colonel, but was rejected by the President. Wded. in face at Seven Pines, which led to his resignation Dec. 1, 1864. Lowry was killed in a gunfight in Texas late in the 19th century.

LOWTHER, ALEXANDER A. b. Nov. 29, 1826. Of Russell Co. Mexican War veteran. Capt., Co. A, 15th Alabama, July 26, 1861. Major - Jan. 25, 1862. Colonel - Apr. 28, 1863. Lowther was repeatedly accused of craven cowardice by William C. Oates of the 15th Alabama and others. Oates also widely denounced Lowther as incompetent. Lowther was wded. Aug. 16, 1864, and surrendered at Appx. d. Sept. 4, 1889. bur. Linwood Cemetery, Columbus, Georgia.

LUCAS, THOMAS EPHRAIM. b. Kershaw, Feb. 28, 1836. gr. SCMA, 1855. Physician. m. Dorothy Craig Hanna. Major, 8th South Carolina, Apr. 13, 1861. Dropped at May 1862 re-org. Later became an officer in the 15th Battalion South Carolina Heavy Artillery. In South Carolina legisl., 1864. d. Chesterfield Co., June 12, 1920.

LUFFMAN, WILLIAM. b. Nov. 1, 1820, in Guilford Co., North Carolina. Mexican War veteran. Lawyer in Surry Co., North Carolina, then in Spring Place, Georgia. In Georgia legisl. Capt., Co. C, 11th Georgia, July 3, 1861. Major - Jan. 27, 1862. Lt. Col. - May 26, 1862. Wded. in both legs at Second Manassas. Wded. at Gettysburg. Severe hip wound at Wilderness. In Georgia legisl. from Murray Co., 1878-1879. d. Dec. 13, 1893. bur. Old Spring Place Cemetery.

LUKE, GRANVILLE GRATIOTT. b. Portsmouth, Virginia, Oct. 19, 1833. att. Partridge's Military Academy in Virginia. 5′8″. m. Mary Wright. Teacher in Camden C.H. and Elizabeth City, North Carolina. Capt., Co. A, 56th North Carolina, Apr. 23, 1862. Lt. Col. - July 31, 1862. POW at Dinwiddle C.H., Apr. 1, 1865, released July 25. Lived in Norfolk, Virginia, post-war. d. there 1895. bur. Elizabeth City.

LUMPKIN, SAMUEL P. b. Dec. 5, 1833. gr. Jefferson Medical College. Physician in Clarke Co. Capt., Co. C, 44th Georgia, Mar. 4, 1862. Lt. Col. - June 28, 1862. Colonel - May 26, 1863. Wded. at Malvern Hill and Chancellorsville. MWIA and POW at Gettysburg, July 1, 1863 (lost leg). d. near Hagerstown, Sept. 11, 1863. bur. Hagerstown Confederate Cemetery.

LUNDY, WILLIAM T. Major, 6th Virginia, May 25, 1861, aged 34. Lt. Col. - Dec. 14, 1861. Dropped at May 3, 1862, re-org. In Virginia legisl. later in the war.

LUSE, WILLIAM HENRY. b. Mississippi, Sept. 23, 1837. Farmer at Benton. 6′2″. att. U. Mississippi. Capt., Co. B, 18th Mississippi, Apr. 27, 1861. Lt. Col. - Apr. 26, 1862. POW at 2nd Fredericksburg, May 3, 1863. POW at Gettysburg. Escaped from Johnson's Island Jan. 6, 1864, but was recaptured in Newark, Ohio, Jan. 7. Released June 20, 1865. d. Mar. 25, 1904. bur. Black Jack Baptist Churchyard, Yazoo Co., Mississippi.

LYELL, JOHN WARNER. b. Westmoreland Co., 1838. gr. VMI, 1859. Capt., Co. D, 47th Virginia, June 6, 1861. Lt. Col. - May 1, 1862. Lost arm Aug. 19, 1864, at Weldon R.R. Retired to Invalid Corps, Dec. 19, 1864. On VMI faculty. Merchant in Washington, D.C. d. Oct. 16, 1902, in Eckington, Virginia. bur. Oak Hill Cemetery, D.C.

LYLES, JOHN M. b. South Carolina. Aged 37 in 1860 census. Physician at Sarepta, Mississippi. Capt., Co. K, 17th Mississippi, Apr. 23, 1861. Major - June 5, 1861. Dropped at spring 1862 re-org.

LYNCH, MICHAEL. b. 1835. Lived in Stewart Co. m. Margaret Hennessee. Capt., Co. I, 21st Georgia, July 17, 1861. Major - Apr. 18, 1864. Wded. at Chancellorsville. Retired Nov. 18, 1864. Ran a dairy business. Alive in DeKalb Co. in 1903. J. C. Nisbet said of Lynch: "Like most Irishmen [he] was a born soldier and a very efficient officer."

McAFEE, LEROY MANGUM. (McAfee normally signed himself Lee M.) b. Dec. 17, 1837. gr. UNC, 1858. Lawyer in Shelby. Major, 49th North Carolina, Apr. 12, 1862. Lt. Col. - June 19, 1862. Colonel - Nov. 1, 1862. Wded. at Drewry's Bluff, May 16, 1864. Wded. Mar. 25, 1865, and again in the hand, Apr. 1, 1865. In North Carolina legisl. post-war. d. 1873.

McALISTER, ALEXANDER CARY. b. Cumberland Co., Nov. 7, 1838. gr. UNC, 1858. Lived in Randolph Co. Capt., Co. F, 46th North Carolina, Apr. 16, 1862. Major - Mar. 21, 1863. Lt. Col. - Dec. 31, 1863. m. Adelaide Worth. Merchant in Burlington and Asheboro. d. Asheboro, Dec. 8, 1916.

McALLISTER, JOSEPH LONGWORTH. b. Bryan Co., Georgia, Oct. 9, 1820. att. Amherst College. Capt., "Hardwick Mounted Rifles," Apr. 1862. Lt. Col., 7th Georgia Cavalry, Jan. 1864. KIA at Trevilian's Station, June 11, 1864. bur. Oatland Cemetery, on Ellisville Road, Louisa Co., Virginia.

McALPINE, CHARLES ROBERT. b. Princess Anne Co., Virginia, Apr. 9, 1827. att. William & Mary. gr. U. Pennsylvania, M.D., 1847. m. Mrs. Elizabeth Anne Land, 1852. Portsmouth physician. Capt., Co. I, 61st Virginia, June 16, 1861. Major - May 12, 1864. Wded. in right side, June 13, 1864. d. Feb. 14, 1876.

McANERNEY, JOHN, JR. b. Providence, R.I., Aug. 10, 1838. Lived in New Orleans pre-war. Sgt., Co. F, 3rd Alabama, 1861. Capt., Co. B, 3rd Virginia LDT, June 18, 1863. Lt. Col. - Apr. 20, 1864. Colonel - Sept. 23, 1864. Wded. at Green's Farm (during the Kilpatrick Raid on Richmond, in which McAnerney was one of the heroes). Paroled at Chester, South Carolina, May 5, 1865. Owner of railroad supply firm, and president of the 7th National Bank, in New York City. d. there Mar. 22, 1928.

McARTHUR, ARTHUR, JR. b. 1830, in Connecticut. Painter in Union Parish, La. Capt., Co. A, 6th Louisiana, June 4, 1861. Major - spring of 1862. KIA at Winchester, May 25, 1862. A moving account of McArthur's death and burial is in Cornelia McDonald's published diary.

McARTHUR, CHARLES W. b. 1836. Farmer. Unmarried. Capt., Co. E, 61st Georgia, July 10, 1861. Major - Nov. 29, 1862. Lt. Col. - Feb. 18, 1863. KIA at Spotsylvania, May 12, 1864, by a shell fragment while in reserve. McArthur's war letters are at Kennesaw Mountain National Battlefield Park. bur. Confederate Cemetery, Spotsylvania Court House.

McBRIDE, ANDREW JACKSON. b. Fayetteville, Georgia, Sept. 29, 1836. Lawyer in Atlanta. Lt., Co. E, 10th Georgia, May 20, 1861. Captain - Oct. 16, 1861. Colonel - Feb. 20, 1865. Wded. at Crampton's Gap, Wilderness and Cold Harbor. McBride was in an Augusta, Georgia, hospital at the close of the war. m. (1) Malinda Carroll. m. (2) Frances Johnson. Atlanta crockery manufacturer. d. Atlanta, Mar. 4, 1922. bur. Oakland Cemetery. McBride's papers are at Duke and Atlanta Historical Society.

McCARVER, SAMUEL HANNAH. b. Highland, Tennessee, May 25, 1842. Student in Jackson Co. Lt., Co. G, 25th Tennessee, Sept. 24, 1861. Captain - July 13, 1862. Major - Jan. 8, 1863. KIA at Drewry's Bluff, May 16, 1864.

McCLAMMY, CHARLES WASHINGTON, JR. b. Pender Co., May 29, 1839. gr. UNC, 1859. Lived in New Hanover Co. Pvt., Co. A, 3rd North Carolina Cavalry, Oct. 1, 1861. Lt. - Oct. 18, 1861. Captain - Sept. 12, 1863. Major - Dec. 9, 1864. m. Margaret Fennell. In North Carolina legisl. In U.S. Congress, 1887-1891. d. Scott's Hill, North Carolina, Feb. 25, 1896.

McCLELLAN, JAMES F. b. Bristol, Tennessee, Aug. 1824. Judge in Jackson Co., Florida. m. Addie McKenzie Yonge, 1848. Capt., Co. F, 2nd Florida, July 13, 1861. Retired, May 10, 1862. Lt. Col., 4th Florida Battalion, May 2, 1863. Colonel, 11th Florida, 1864 (the 4th Bn. was merged into the 11th Regt.). Resigned, Feb. 27, 1865. Compiled a standard legal digest of Florida's laws, published in 1879. d. Pensacola, Apr. 16, 1890.

McCONNELL, SYLVESTER PATTON. b. Mar. 16, 1829. m. Emeline Tolbert, 1859. Pvt., Co. E, 48th Virginia, 1861-62. Capt., Co. A, 25th Virginia Cavalry, Aug. 16, 1862. Major - Nov. 1, 1862. Resigned Aug. 8, 1864, having been elected clerk of the Scott Co. court. McConnell held that same post for decades, and also owned a printing firm. d. Apr. 23, 1918. bur. Estill Cemetery, Gate City.

McCORD, ROBERT A. b. Georgia. Farmer in Tallapoosa Co., Alabama, in 1860, age 24. Lt., Co. G, 14th Alabama, July 13, 1861. Captain - May 22, 1862. Major - Oct. 3, 1862. Court-martialed in spring 1863. MWIA at Salem Church, May 3, 1863, d. May 26.

McCORKLE, WILLIAM HART. b. Ebenezer, York Dist., South Carolina, Aug. 25, 1821. m. Margaret L. Robinson, 1849. Capt., Co. A, 12th South Carolina, Aug. 20, 1861. Major - Apr. 2, 1862. Lt. Col. - Sept. 27, 1862. Wded. at 2nd Manassas. Resigned Feb. 4, 1863, citing "rheumatism of heart." York Co. judge, and mayor of Yorkville for 8 terms. d. Feb. 13, 1904. bur. Rose Hill Cemetery, Yorkville.

McCRADY, EDWARD, JR. b. Charleston, South Carolina, Apr. 8, 1833. gr. Charleston College, 1853. McCrady was involved in the capture of Castle Pinckney as Captain of the "Meagher Guards." Capt., Co. K, 1st South Carolina (Gregg's), June 25, 1861. Major - Dec. 14, 1861. Lt. Col. - June 27, 1862. Severe head wound at 2nd Manassas. In Jan. 1863, McCrady was "injured in camp by a falling tree, and incapacitated for further duty on the field." Resigned, disability, Jan. 1, 1864. Commanded a camp of instruction in Madison, Florida, Mar. 1864. Charleston lawyer. In South Carolina legisl. Author of many things, and very busy in veterans' affairs. d. Charleston, Nov. 2, 1903.

McCREARY, COMILLUS WYCLIFFE. (McCreary's given name is sometimes shown as Charles W., but he always signed as "C. W." and family records declare him to be named as shown above.) b. June 1836 at Williston. gr. SCMA. Never married. Lived in Barnwell Dist. Professor at Aiken Classical and Military Academy. Capt., Co. A, 1st South Carolina (Gregg's), July 13, 1861. Major - July 1, 1862. Colonel - Jan. 4, 1864. Wded. at Spotsylvania on May 10, 1864; at Jones farm on Sept. 30, 1864; and at Pegram House, Oct. 10, 1864. KIA March 31, 1865, at White Oak Road. bur. in family graveyard near Williston, South Carolina. In 1977, plans were afoot to move the stone (but not any remains) into the Williston City Cemetery.

McCULLOHS, WILLIAM HENRY. b. Talbot Co., Nov. 1839. Lived in Harris Co. Capt., Co. K, 35th Georgia, July 4, 1861. Major - July 3, 1862. Lt. Col. - Nov. 1, 1862. On the rolls, though absent sick, into early 1865. m. Martha Maria Lowe. d. Waverly Hall, Harris Co., July 18, 1912.

McCURRY, BENJAMIN C. Clergyman in Paulding Co. in 1860, age 35. Capt., Co. C, 22nd Georgia, Aug. 31, 1861. Lt. Col. - July 16, 1863. Died of fever at Dallas, Georgia, Nov. 14, 1863.

McCUTCHEN, JAMES SAMUEL KERR. b. Augusta Co., June 6, 1830. Teacher in Gilmer Co. 6′0″. Capt., Co. D, 31st Virginia, Aug. 2, 1861. Major - Dec. 20, 1862. Lt. Col. - Aug. 1, 1863. Wded. at Cedar Mountain. In Virginia legisl. in 1865. Died unmarried on Sept. 27, 1915, in Exeter, California.

McDANIEL, HENRY DICKERSON. b. Monroe, Georgia, Sept. 4, 1836. gr. Mercer U. In Georgia Secession Convention. Lt., Co. H, 11th Georgia, July 3, 1861. Lt. and AQM, 11th Georgia, July 15, 1861. Capt. and AQM, Aug. 29, 1862. Major - Nov. 8, 1862. Wded. at Funkstown, Md., July 10, 1863. POW at Hagerstown, July 12, 1863, released July 25, 1865. m. Hester Felker, 1865. Governor of Georgia, 1883-86. d. July 25, 1926. McDaniel's fine war letters were published in 1977.

McDANIEL, WILLIAM WALKER. b. Henry Co., Georgia, June 7, 1838. gr. Bowdon College, Bowdon, Georgia. Lt., Co. B, Infantry Battalion of Cobb's Legion (Georgia), July 30, 1861. Captain - Mar. 17, 1862. Major - May 12, 1864. Retired Feb. 4, 1865, due to leg wounds. Married Frances Marion Horne. d. Henry Co., Alabama, July 10, 1892.

McDONALD, ANGUS WILLIAM, SR. b. Winchester, Virginia, Feb. 14, 1799. gr. USMA, 1817. Lt., U.S. Artillery, 1817-1819.

6'0". m. (1) Leacy Anne Naylor, 1827. m. (2) Cornelia Peake, 1847. Lawyer in Romney and Winchester. A frontiersman and partner in the Missouri Fur Company. Colonel and v.a.d.c. at Harpers Ferry, May 3, 1861. Col., 7th Virginia Cavalry, June 5, 1861. Disabled by rheumatism, fall of 1861. Relieved from field duty, Nov. 1861. Did post duty until 1864. POW in Rockbridge Co., July 13, 1864. Died in Richmond, Dec. 1, 1864, after having suffered a succession of indecencies at the hands of his captors, notably David Hunter. bur. Hollywood Cemetery.

McDONALD, EDWARD HITCHCOCK. b. Romney, Oct. 26, 1832. Son of Colonel Angus W. McDonald. 5'10½". Merchant at New Creek. Pvt., 13th Virginia Inf., Apr. 1861. Colonel, 77th Virginia Militia, July 14, 1861. Capt., Co. D, 11th Virginia Cavalry, Mar. 7, 1862. Major - July 23, 1863. Severely wded. on retreat to Appx. m. Julia Yates Leavell, 1869. Ran a Kentucky land title business; returned to West Virginia in 1892. d. Sept. 20, 1912. bur. Zion Episcopal Churchyard, Charlestown.

McDONALD, JAMES. b. Telfair Co., July 15, 1812. In Georgia legisl. Veteran of Indian wars. m. Serena Swain. Gunmaker. Capt., Co. C, 26th Georgia (which unit became the 61st Georgia after McDonald had resigned), Sept. 7, 1861. Lt. Col. - Oct. 9, 1861. Resigned on the basis of disability and age, 1862. d. Thomasville, Mar. 14, 1877. bur. in family cemetery near Pavo.

McDONALD, JAMES R. b. Fayetteville, North Carolina. Merchant in Cumberland Co. enl. Co. F, 1st North Carolina (Bethel), Apr. 17, 1861, as a private, age 35. Served there until Nov. 1861. Capt., Co. D, 51st North Carolina, Apr. 1862. Major - Jan. 1863. POW at Cold Harbor; released July 24, 1865. d. 1905. bur. Forest Hill Cemetery, Memphis, Tennessee.

McDONALD, JOHN CLAIBORNE. b. Mar. 14, 1831, in Montgomery Co. Giles Co. merchant. Lt., Co. K, 22nd Virginia, June 6, 1861. Captain - Dec. 24, 1861. Major - Nov. 12, 1863. Lt. Col. - May 15, 1864. Paroled at Charleston, West Virginia, May 25, 1865. Building contractor in Hinton, West Virginia, and Craig Co., Virginia, post-war. d. Craig City, Dec. 22, 1914.

McDONALD, WILLIAM ANGUS. b. Bulloch Co., Feb. 11, 1817. Ware Co. planter. Member of the Georgia House 1842-43, 1847-51, 1877, 1888-89, and 1894-95; and of the Georgia Senate 1855-58 and 1882-83. In Georgia Secession Convention. Capt., Co. H, 26th Georgia, Oct. 1, 1861. Lt. Col. - May 10, 1862. Resigned Dec. 3, 1862, to enter Georgia legisl. m. 3 times. Minister postwar. d. Ware Co., June 4, 1896. McDonald had 22 children, 20 of whom lived to maturity.

McDOWELL, JAMES CHARLES SHEFFIELD. b. Burke Co., Feb. 6, 1831. Farmer there. 6′2″. Lt., Co. G, 1st North Carolina (Bethel), Apr. 25, 1861. Lt. Col., 54th North Carolina, May 16, 1862. Colonel - Sept. 3, 1862. MWIA in face at Chancellorsville, May 4, 1863, d. May 9. Widow - Julia M. bur. New Bern Ave., Raleigh City Cemetery.

McDOWELL, JOHN A. b. June 20, 1826. Bladen Co. businessman. Major, 1st North Carolina, May 16, 1861. Lt. Col. - Apr. 21, 1862. Colonel - July 8, 1862. Wded. at Mechanicsville. Resigned Dec. 14, 1863. d. Jan. 11, 1899. bur. in family cemetery, Bladen County.

McDOWELL, JOHN LEWIS. b. Rutherford Co. Farmer. 5′9½″. Lt., Co. I, 34th North Carolina, Oct. 6, 1861. Captain - Apr. 18, 1862. Lt. Col. - Sept. 3, 1862. Resigned, Dec. 4, 1862.

McDUFFIE, JAMES Y. Served in Georgia legisl. 1839-40, from Irwin Co. Capt., Co. A, 61st Georgia, Aug. 27, 1861. Lt. Col. - May 31, 1862. Resigned, ill health, Nov. 1862. McDuffie's will, which showed him to have been wealthy, was probated in Mar. 1863.

McELROY, JOHN SMITH. b. Feb. 28, 1835, in Yancey Co. Lawyer in Yancey Co. and Madison Co. m. Mary Josephine Carter. Capt., Co. C, 16th North Carolina, May 1, 1861. Lt. Col. - Apr. 26, 1862. Colonel - June 1, 1862. Wded. in the mouth at Chancellorsville. Resigned Dec. 8, 1863. Served in the state legislature. d. Madison Co., June 3, 1919. bur. West Memorial Cemetery, Weaverville.

McELROY, KENNON. gr. U. Mississippi, 1861. Farmer from Lauderdale, Mississippi. Capt., Co. G, 13th Mississippi, Mar. 30,

1861, aged 21. Major - Apr. 26, 1862. Lt. Col. - Aug. 12, 1862. Colonel - July 3, 1863. Wded. at Sharpsburg and Gettysburg. KIA at Knoxville, Nov. 29, 1863.

McELVANY, JAMES THOMAS. b. Gwinnett Co., Dec. 3, 1834. Farmer. Lt., Co. F, 35th Georgia, Sept. 23, 1861. Captain - May 9, 1862. Major - May 19, 1864. Wded. at Cedar Run. Sheriff of Gwinnett Co. and State legislator postwar. d. Feb. 3, 1901. bur. Bay Creek Church.

McEWEN, JOHN LAPSLEY. b. Williamson Co., Jan. 1822. gr. U. Nashville. Lawyer. Capt., Co. I, 44th Tennessee, Dec. 21, 1861. Lt. Col. - Apr. 18, 1862. MWIA at Drewry's Bluff, May 16, 1864. d. May 27.

McFARLANE, JOHN A. b. 1839. Lived in Russell Co. Lt., Co. I, 34th Virginia Cavalry Battalion, Apr. 7, 1862. Major - July 28, 1864. Farmer near Honaker. m. Lou A. Hurt. d. 1889.

McGEE, JOSEPH B. b. Gaston, North Carolina. Farmer in Mecklenburg Co. 5′11″. Sgt., Co. G, 34th North Carolina, Oct. 25, 1861, aged 32. Lt. - Jan. 1862. Captain - Apr. 18, 1862. Major - Dec. 13, 1862. Resigned Dec. 14, 1862, citing "weak lungs."

McGILL, JOHN W. b. Sampson Co., North Carolina. Student in Bladen Co. Lt., Co. B, 18th North Carolina, May 3, 1861, aged 18. Captain - May 27, 1862. Lt. Col. - May 3, 1863. Wded. at Frayser's Farm and Gettysburg. McGill was in a Danville hospital on Apr. 4, 1865.

McGLASHAN, PETER ALEXANDER SELKIRK. b. Edinburgh, Scotland, May 16, 1831. Moved to Savannah in 1848. Went West with the gold rush, and to Nicaraugua with Walker's filibusterers. Lt., Co. E, 50th Georgia, Mar. 4, 1862. Captain - Oct. 1, 1862. Colonel - July 31, 1863. POW at Sayler's Creek, released July 25 at Johnson's Island. Mayor of Thomasville. Active and important in veterans' affairs. d. Savannah, June 13, 1908. bur. Laurel Grove Cemetery.

McGRAW, JOSEPH. Lived in Sharpsburg, Md. Occupation - teamster. Sgt., Purcell Artillery (Virginia), May 15, 1861. Lt. - Mar 31, 1862. Captain - spring of 1863. Major - Feb. 27, 1864, assigned to Pegram's Battalion. Wded. in Seven Days. Lost arm at Spotsylvania, May 18, 1864. Commanding an artillery bn. at Appx. Moved to Brooklyn, New York, post-war, and disappeared after trauma over the death of his son.

McGREGOR, WILLIAM MORRELL. b. Talladega Co., Alabama, Nov. 18, 1842. att. Auburn. Pvt., Co. E, 10th Alabama, 1861. Lt., Stuart's Horse Artillery (Virginia), May 1, 1862. Seriously wounded in Nov. 1862. Captain, McGregor's Horse Artillery (Virginia), Feb. 15, 1863. Major - Feb. 18, 1865. Acted as Chief of Artillery to W. H. F. Lee. Appx. Talladega lawyer post-war. Moved to Texas in 1873. m. Emma Rosa Cousins, 1865. d. Cameron, Texas, Dec. 28, 1907. bur. Oak Hill Cemetery.

McGRUDER, ZACHARIAH S. Physician in Richmond in 1860, age 30, worth $12,000. Capt., Co. I, 10th Virginia Cavalry, May 8, 1861 (had been commanding this unit since Nov. 1860). Lt. Col. - May 27, 1862. Resigned Sept. 11, 1863. d. 1896.

McGUIRK, JOHN. b. New York, June 24, 1827. Druggist in Holly Springs, Mississippi. Capt., Co. B, 17th Mississippi, May 8, 1861. Lt. Col. - June 6, 1861. Dropped at May 1862 re-org. Later served as v.a.d.c. to Joseph Wheeler, and as Colonel, 3rd Mississippi Cavalry. d. Oct. 16, 1871. bur. Hill Crest Cemetery, Holly Springs.

McINTOSH, DAVID GREGG. b. Society Hill, South Carolina, Mar. 16, 1836. gr. South Carolina College. Lawyer. Capt., Co. D, 1st South Carolina, July 29, 1861. Capt., Pee Dee Artillery (South Carolina), Mar. 1862 (this was the same company, now converted to artillery service). Major - Mar. 2, 1863. Lt. Col. - Feb. 27, 1864. Colonel - Feb. 18, 1865. Wded. Aug. 18, 1864. Commanded an A.N.Va. artillery bn., and acted as Chief of Artillery for the 2nd Corps at the end of the war. m. Virginia J. Pegram, sister of two prominent C.S. officers. Lawyer in Towson, Maryland, and President of the Maryland Bar Association. Author of a good pamphlet on Chancellorsville. d. Towson, Oct. 6, 1916. bur. Hollywood Cemetery, Richmond, Virginia. McIntosh's papers at the Virginia Historical Society include a detailed diary for Apr. 1865.

McINTOSH, WILLIAM MacPHERSON. b. Feb. 14, 1815. In Georgia legisl. Lawyer and planter in Elbert Co. m. Maria Louisa Allen, 1842. Major, 15th Georgia, July 15, 1861. Lt. Col. - Dec. 21, 1861. Colonel - Mar. 29, 1862. KIA at Garnett's Farm, Virginia, June 27, 1862, during the Seven Days.

McIVER, GEORGE WILLIAMS. b. Cheraw, Jan. 1, 1825. m. Harriet LaCosta. Lt., Co. D, 21st South Carolina, Jan. 1, 1862. Major - Jan. 26, 1862. Lt. Col. - May 7, 1864. Paroled at Cheraw, South Carolina, Mar. 5, 1865. d. Charleston, July 31, 1896.

McKAY, JOHN A. D. b. Mar. 11, 1841. Of Harnett Co. Capt., Co. I, 31st North Carolina, Oct. 30, 1861. Major - June 7, 1863. POW at Roanoke Island, Feb. 1862. Wded. at White Hall, North Carolina, Dec. 1862. Court-martialed for cowardice at Petersburg, in an incident of June 17, 1864. Resigned July 25, 1864. d. Sept. 5, 1891. bur. Fayetteville.

McKETHAN, HECTOR McALLISTER. (He never used the middle name.) b. Sept. 15, 1834. Lived in Cumberland Co. Unmarried. Lt., Co. H, 1st North Carolina, April 17, 1861. Capt., Co. I, 51st North Carolina, March 19, 1862. Major - April 30, 1862, at org. Lt. Col. - fall 1862. Colonel - Jan. 19, 1863. Wded. June 17, 1864, at Petersburg. Fayetteville carriage maker. Died in Fayetteville, Nov. 6, 1881. bur. Cross Creek Cemetery No. 2.

McKINNEY, ROBERT M. b. Lynchburg, Virginia, Feb. 12, 1835. Lived in Lynchburg, and was a pre-war member of the Lynchburg Home Guard. Professor at North Carolina Military Institute in Charlotte, North Carolina. gr. VMI, 1856. Capt., Co. A, 6th North Carolina, May 16, 1861. Colonel, 15th North Carolina, June 24, 1861. KIA at Lee's Mill, Virginia, Apr. 16, 1862. bur. Lynchburg Presbyterian Cemetery.

McKISSICK, ISAAC GOING. b. Union Dist., Dec. 16, 1825. m. Sarah Foster. Clerk of court at Unionville. Capt., Co. C, 7th South Carolina Cav., Dec. 5, 1861. Lt. Col. - Apr. 20, 1864. Wded. at Williamsburg and Cold Harbor. Appx. d. June 8, 1896. bur. Presbyterian Cemetery, Union, South Carolina.

McLAUCHLIN, MURDOCK McRAE. b. Cumberland Co., North Carolina. att. Davidson College. Capt., Co. K, 38th North Carolina, Nov. 9, 1861, aged 28. Major - Jan. 14, 1863. Wded. in jaw at Chancellorsville. Resigned Feb. 16, 1864. Teacher. 5′9″. d. Dec. 15, 1913.

McLAUGHLIN, MARTIN V. Lawyer in Lincoln Co. Lt., Co. H, 1st Tennessee, Apr. 29, 1861, aged 27. Major - Apr. 27, 1862. KIA at Gaines' Mill.

McLAUGHLIN, WILLIAM. b. Jan. 6, 1828, in Rockbridge County. gr. Washington College. Lt., Rockbridge Artillery (Virginia), May 1861. Captain - July 1861. Supplanted by Poague at Apr. 1862 re-org. Major and Judge Advocate - Apr. 10, 1862. Major and AQM - July 28, 1862, with Echols. Major of Artillery - Oct. 9, 1862. Chief of Artillery to Echols. Commanded a bn. of artillery in Early's 1864 Valley Campaign. Rockbridge Co. lawyer and judge. In Virginia legisl. d. Aug. 18, 1898. Sandy Pendleton called McLaughlin "very incompetent" and "very worthless."

McLEMORE, OWEN KENAN. b. Alabama, Nov. 1835. gr. USMA, 1856. Lt., U.S. Infantry, 1856-61. Major, 14th Alabama, Nov. 20, 1861. Lt. Col., 4th Alabama, May 2, 1862. Wded. at Seven Days. MWIA at South Mountain, Sept. 14, 1862, d. Sept. 30.

McLENNAN, JOHN D. Of Barbour Co. Lt. Col., 59th Alabama, Nov. 25, 1863. KIA at Drewry's Bluff, May 16, 1864.

McLEOD, DONALD McDAIRMED. b. Dec. 18, 1823. gr. South Carolina College, 1847. Farmer at Bennettsville. 6′4″. m. Margaret C. Alford. Lived at Hunt's Bluff, South Carolina. Capt., Co. K, 8th South Carolina, Apr. 13, 1861. Major - May 14, 1862. MWIA at Gettysburg, d. July 5 at Cashtown. bur. Parnassus Methodist Church, Marlboro Co.

McLEOD, HUGH. b. New York, New York, Aug. 1, 1814. gr. USMA in 1835, finishing dead last in a class of 56. He entered the USMA from Georgia. McLeod fought in the Texas Army in the 1830's and 1840's, and was its Adjutant General. He was in several Indian fights. Major, 1st Texas, Aug. 20, 1861. Lt. Col. - Sept. 2, 1861. Colonel - Oct. 21, 1861. Died of pneumonia at Dumfries, Virginia, Jan. 2, 1862. A funeral was held in Galveston two months and two days later, and McLeod was buried in Austin.

McLEOD, MARCUS D. L. Of Mecklenburg Co. Lt. and Acting Commissary of 1st North Carolina Cavalry, Oct. 23, 1861. Capt., Co. C, 1st North Carolina Cavalry, Feb. 6, 1862. Major - June 1, 1864. Wded. at Culpeper, Sept. 13, 1863. Wded. near Petersburg, Mar. 31, 1865, in the face.

McLURE, EDWARD CONRAD. b. New Jersey, Aug. 19, 1834. gr. Harvard, 1854. Lawyer at Chester, South Carolina in 1860. Capt., Co. F, 6th South Carolina, Apr. 11, 1861. Major - June 30, 1863. Elected to South Carolina legisl. from Chester Dist., 1864. m. (1) Louise Neely. m. (2) Jane Wylie. Owner and publisher of two Chester newspapers, 1867-1884. Moved then to Dallas, Texas. d. Feb. 28, 1889, in Washington, D.C.

McMASTER, FITZ WILLIAM. b. Winnsboro, South Carolina, Mar. 26, 1826. gr. South Carolina College, 1847. Married Mary Jane McFie in 1852, and she went about producing 15 children. 5′11½″. Lt. Col., 17th South Carolina, Dec. 18, 1861. Colonel - Sept. 1, 1862. Wded. at 2nd Manassas and Sharpsburg. POW at Petersburg, Mar. 25, 1865, released July 24. In South Carolina legisl. Mayor of Columbia. d. Sept. 10, 1899. bur. 1st Presbyterian Churchyard, Columbia.

McMICHAEL, PAUL AGABUS. b. Mar. 20, 1820. Orangeburg planter. m. Margaret Tyler, 1844. Capt., Co. B, 20th South Carolina, Dec. 30, 1861. Lt. Col. - June 2, 1864. POW at Strasburg, Virginia, Oct. 19, 1864, released July 24, 1865. 6′0″. d. Jan. 12, 1869, said to be the result of "hardships of prison life."

McMILLAN, ROBERT. b. Antrim, Ireland, Jan. 7, 1805. m. Ruth Ann Banks, 1833. In Georgia legisl. from Elbert Co. Colonel, 24th Georgia, Aug. 30, 1861. Resigned Jan. 9, 1864. d. May 6, 1868. bur. Old Cemetery, Clarksville, Habersham Co., Georgia.

McMILLAN, ROBERT EMMETT. b. Nov. 20, 1835. Son of Colonel Robert McMillan. Lived in Elbert Co. Major, 24th Georgia,

Georgia Dept. of Archives & History

ARCHIBALD P. McRAE
61st Georgia

Aug. 24, 1861. Wded. leg at Sharpsburg, caused him to resign Jan. 8, 1864. d. Mar. 26, 1890. bur. beside his father.

McNEILL, JAMES HIPKINS. b. May 23, 1825, in Cumberland Co., North Carolina. att. Harvard and Princeton. Presbyterian clergyman. Capt., Co. A, 5th North Carolina Cavalry, June 19, 1862. Major - Oct. 26, 1862. Colonel - Nov. 24, 1864. Wded. at Middleburg, June 17, 1863. KIA at Chamberlain Run, Mar. 31, 1865. bur. Cross Creek Cemetery, Fayetteville, North Carolina.

McNEILL, NEILL McKAY. b. Moore Co., North Carolina, June 10, 1825. Farmer. 6′1½″. m. Jane Johnson Pegues. Capt., Co. H, 46th North Carolina, Mar. 6, 1862. Major - Dec. 31, 1863. Appx. Ran a turpentine business in Moultrie, Georgia, post-war. d. Moultrie, Dec. 29, 1902.

McPHAIL, JOHN BLAIR, JR. b. Nov. 1, 1835. Lived in Mecklenburg Co. 5′10″. gr. Hampden-Sydney, 1856. Lt., Co. A, 56th Virginia, July 18, 1861. Captain - May 3, 1862. Major - June 13, 1864. POW at Hatcher's Run, Mar. 30, 1865, released July 25. Lived in Charlotte and Halifax counties. Farmer and railroad president. Never married. d. July 23, 1904, at "Mulberry Hill," Charlotte Co.

McRAE, ARCHIBALD PHILIP. b. Montgomery Co. about 1832. Merchant in Reidsville. Capt., Co. B, 26th Georgia (which later became the 61st Georgia), Aug. 3, 1861. Major - May 3, 1862. KIA at Sharpsburg. His body was burned in a Sharpsburg building.

McRAE, DUNCAN KIRKLAND. b. Fayetteville, North Carolina, Aug. 16, 1820. att. UNC and William & Mary. In North Carolina legisl. Unsuccessful candidate for North Carolina governorship in 1858. U.S. Consul General in Paris pre-war. Colonel, 5th North Carolina, May 16, 1861. Wded. at South Mountain. Resigned Nov. 13, 1862 (accepted Dec. 12), in anger over being passed over for promotion. Went to Europe for the C.S. government concerning cotton. Raleigh newspaper editor, 1864-65. Lived in North Carolina, Tennessee and Illinois post-war. d. Brooklyn, New York, Feb. 12, 1888.

MacRAE, HENRY. b. Wilmington, May 8, 1829. Lived in New Hanover Co. Brother of General William MacRae. Capt., Co. C, 8th North Carolina, May 16, 1861. POW at Roanoke Island, Feb. 1862. Major - Feb. 20, 1863. Died of typhoid in Charleston, South Carolina, Apr. 22, 1863. Married, with two daughters. bur. Oakdale Cemetery, Wilmington.

McRAE, JOHN HENRY DUNCAN. b. Walton Co., Feb. 15, 1831. Teacher in Jackson Co. Capt., Co. F, 16th Georgia, July 19, 1861. Ran in vain for Georgia legisl. in 1863. Colonel - 1864. POW at Sayler's Creek, released June 19, 1865. Moved to Florida in 1881. d. Jacksonville, Florida, Nov. 5, 1911. bur. Evergreen Cemetery.

MacRAE, ROBERT BURNS. b. New Hanover Co., Dec. 15, 1832, and resided there. Capt., Co. C, 7th North Carolina, May 16, 1861. Major - Jan. 6, 1863. Wded. in neck at Chantilly, which caused his retirement, Feb. 24, 1863. d. Dec. 28, 1864. bur. Wilmington. MacRae's war letters are at Duke U. Brother of Henry.

MABRY, CHARLES W. b. Georgia, Aug. 22, 1819. Heard Co. attorney. In Georgia Secession Convention (voted no!). Wife - Sarah B. Capt., Co. E, 19th Georgia, June 26, 1861. Major - July 1, 1863. Resigned Sept. 21, 1864, having been elected to Georgia Senate. d. Apr. 9, 1884. bur. Hillview Cemetery, LaGrange.

MAFFETT, ROBERT CLAYTON. b. Newberry Dist., about 1832. Capt., Co. C, 3rd South Carolina, Apr. 14, 1861. Major - July 1, 1862. Lt. Col. - May 6, 1864. Wded. at Savage Station and Fredericksburg. For a time, Maffett commanded the 7th South Carolina in the Valley in 1864. POW at Halltown, Virginia, Aug. 26, 1864. Died in prison at Fort Delaware, Feb. 14, 1865.

MAGILL, WILLIAM JOSEPH. b. Georgetown, South Carolina, Mar. 10, 1827. gr. SCMA. Served in Mexican War. Commandant of Georgia Military Institute. Capt., Co. A, 1st Georgia Regulars, Feb. 1, 1861. Lt. Col. - June 8, 1861. Colonel - Feb. 6, 1862. Lost arm at Sharpsburg. Retired Aug. 3, 1864. Ran an Atlanta insurance business, then moved to Florida in 1876 and raised oranges. d. Jacksonville, Florida, Sept. 17, 1890. bur. Evergreen Cemetery.

MAGRUDER, EDWARD JONES. b. Fluvanna Co., Virginia, May 14, 1835. Lived in Gordonsville. gr. VMI, 1855. City official in Rome, Georgia. m. Florence Fouchi. Capt., Co. A, 8th Georgia, May 18, 1861. Major - Jan. 28, 1862. Lt. Col. - Dec. 16, 1862. Wded. June 21, 1864. d. Rome, Georgia, Feb. 27, 1892.

MAGRUDER, JOHN BOWIE. b. Scottsville, Nov. 24, 1839. Lived at Keswick Depot. att. VMI. gr. U. Virginia. Culpeper teacher. Capt., Co. H, 57th Virginia, July 22, 1861. Major - 1862. Lt. Col. - July 31, 1862. Colonel - Jan. 12, 1863. MWIA at Gettysburg, July 3, 1863, d. July 5. Magruder's war letters are at the Virginia State Library.

MALLETT, EDWARD. b. Cumberland Co., Feb. 14, 1827. gr. UNC. Cumberland Co. farmer. m. Mary Hunter. Capt., Co. C, 61st North Carolina, Mar. 1, 1862. Major - Aug. 10, 1864. Lt. Col. - Oct. 11, 1864. Killed in action at Bentonville. bur. Chapel Hill Cemetery.

MALLORY, CHARLES KING. b. Norfolk, Feb. 20, 1820. gr. William & Mary. Judge and lawyer in Oxford, Mississippi, and Hampton, Virginia. In Virginia Secession Convention. Colonel, 115th Virginia Militia, early 1861. Mallory's slaves were among the very first confiscated by Beast Butler as contraband. The 115th Militia served on the Peninsula in 1861 and 1862 under Magruder and Johnston. Hampton planter post-war. d. Hampton, May 7, 1875.

MALLORY, FRANCIS. b. Norfolk, May 28, 1833. gr. VMI, 1853. Mallory was a groomsman at "Rooney" Lee's wedding. Lt., U.S. Infantry, 1856-61. Engineer, Norfolk & Petersburg R.R. Lt., Confederate States Infantry, Mar. 16, 1861. Colonel, 55th Virginia, Sept. 12, 1861. KIA at Chancellorsville. Reburied in 1866 at Elmwood Cemetery, Norfolk.

MALTBIE, RICHARD. b. Georgia, 1837. att. U. Georgia. Lt., Co. H, 13th Georgia, July 8, 1861. Captain - Nov. 17, 1861. Major - Mar. 14, 1864. Lt. Col. - May 12, 1864, and wounded "through the shoulder" the same day. Commanded the 13th Georgia at Appomattox. Lawyer and judge in McKinney, Texas, post-war. d. Collin Co., Texas, July 5, 1888.

Pamela Manning Fein

VANNOY HARTROG MANNING
3rd Arkansas Infantry

MANLOVE, THOMAS B. Of Vicksburg. Lt., Co. G, 2nd Mississippi Battalion, May 1861. Captain - June 3, 1861. Lt. Col., 2nd Mississippi Battalion, Nov. 3, 1862. The 2nd Bn. was merged into the 48th Mississippi Regt. in early 1863. Wded. at Sharpsburg. Wded. in abdomen, Feb. 7, 1865, and taken prisoner. Paroled at Varona, Virginia, Mar. 22, 1865.

MANLY, BASIL CHARLES. b. Raleigh, May 9, 1839. att. UNC. Pvt., Ellis Light Artillery (North Carolina), May 9, 1861. Lt. - May 16, 1861. Captain - backdated to rank from May 8, 1861. Major of artillery - Feb. 18, 1865. Mayor of Raleigh. m. Lucy Haywood. d. May 16, 1882.

MANNING, SEABORN M. b. 1824 in Georgia. Merchant in Pulaski Co. in 1860, worth $103,000. Capt., Co. K, 49th Georgia, Mar. 4, 1862. Lt. Col. - Mar. 22, 1862. MWIA at Cedar Mountain, d. Sept. 9, 1862.

MANNING, VANNOY HARTROG. b. Edgecombe Co., North Carolina, July 26, 1839. att. U. Tennessee. 5′7″. Capt., Co. K, 3rd Arkansas, June 20, 1861. Major - July 9, 1861. Colonel - Mar. 11, 1862. Wded. at Sharpsburg. Wded. in right thigh at Wilderness, and POW, released July 24, 1865. Among the "Immortal 600." Lawyer in Hamburg, Arkansas. In U.S. Congress, 1877-1883. Washington, D.C., lawyer. d. Branchville, Maryland, Nov. 3, 1892. bur. Glenwood Cemetery, D.C.

MANNING, WILLIAM HENRY. b. Poughkeepsie, New York, Aug. 14, 1837. Cooper in New Orleans. Capt., Co. K, 6th Louisiana, June 4, 1861. Major - fall 1862. Wded. at Winchester, June 14, 1863. POW at Wilderness. Appx. m. Mary Ann Cunningham. d. New Orleans, 1880.

MANNING, WILLIAM R. b. 1817 in Georgia. Colonel of militia, 1846-1852. Large landholder near Valdosta. Colonel, 50th Georgia, Mar. 22, 1862. Resigned July 31, 1863. d. Oct. 11, 1871. bur. Sunset Cemetery, Valdosta.

MARKS, SAMUEL BLACKBURN. b. June 7, 1820. att. U. Virginia and U. Alabama. Planter in Montgomery Co., Alabama. Major, 13th Alabama, July 19, 1861. Lt. Col. - Nov. 27, 1861. Resigned Jan. 10, 1862. Served as an ordnance officer later.

MARSH, EDWARD STANLEY. b. Washington, North Carolina, Oct. 9, 1838. Lived in Belhaven. Sgt., Co. I, 4th North Carolina, June 25, 1861. Lt. - Aug. 29, 1861. Resigned Sept. 1861, for an unknown reason. Lt. again - Sept. 11, 1862. Captain - Sept. 24, 1862. Major - May 19, 1864. Wded. in lung at Chancellorsville. Resigned as a result, Feb. 9, 1865. m. Elizabeth Bonner Eborn, 1866. d. Belhaven, Oct. 20, 1906.

MARSHALL, JAMES KEITH. b. Fauquier Co., Virginia, Apr. 17, 1839. gr. VMI, 1860. Teacher at Edenton, North Carolina. Capt., Co. M, 1st North Carolina (Bethel), Apr. 29, 1861. Colonel, 52nd North Carolina, Apr. 23, 1862. KIA at Gettysburg, July 3.

MARSHALL, JEHU FOSTER. b. South Carolina, Aug. 28, 1817. gr. South Carolina College, 1837. Abbeville lawyer. Capt., Palmetto Regiment, Mexican War. m. Elizabeth Ann DeBrull. In South Carolina legisl., 1848-1862. Lt. Col., 1st South Carolina Rifles, July 20, 1861. Colonel - Jan. 29, 1862. KIA at 2nd Manassas. bur. Abbeville.

MARSHALL, JOHN. b. Charlotte Co., Virginia, ca. 1825. Moved to Mississippi as a youth and edited a newspaper there. Went to Texas in 1854, became an Austin journalist and protegé of Louis T. Wigfall. 5′4″. Lt. Col., 4th Texas, Oct. 2, 1861. Colonel - Mar. 3, 1862. KIA at Gaines' Mill. bur. Hollywood. A member of the 4th Texas reported that Marshall "failed to come up to the standard as a military man," and blamed his appointment on "political favoritism." (Earlier editions of this book showed Marshall as born ca. 1812, but both the 1860 census and an article based on family sources suggest birth about 1825. The earlier date, based on Marcus J. Wright's *Texas in the War*, seems to gain support from Val C. Giles' published description of Marshall.)

MARSHALL, THOMAS. b. Fauquier Co., Jan. 17, 1836. Grandson of Chief Justice John Marshall. att. U. Virginia. Volunteer a.d.c. to T. J. Jackson, 1861. Capt., 7th Virginia Cavalry, Mar. 11, 1862 (the company later became Co. C, 12th Virginia Cav., but Marshall stayed with the 7th). Major - June 20, 1862.

Lt. Col. - Oct. 30, 1862. POW near Orange C.H. on Aug. 7, 1862, exchanged in Sept. KIA on Nov. 12, 1864. bur. Stonewall Cemetery, Winchester.

MARTIN, GEORGE ALEXANDER. b. Norfolk Co., Sept. 3, 1833. att. U. Virginia. m. Georgia Alice Wickens, 1857. Capt., Co. B, 20th Battalion Virginia Heavy Artillery, July 6, 1861. This company, known as the St. Bride's Artillery, became Co. I, 28th Virginia Inf., Apr. 1864. Martin became Lt. Col., 38th Virginia, on Dec. 2, 1864. The appointment was never confirmed, though it was actually in force until the end of the war. Martin went into Georgia with Jefferson Davis' retreating party in 1865. Lawyer in New York City. In Virginia legisl. d. Norfolk, Jan. 1915.

MARTIN, JAMES BENSON. b. Habersham Co., Georgia, Sept. 27, 1825. Lawyer in Talladega and Jacksonville, Alabama. m. Miss Nesbit. In Alabama legisl. Judge. Lt. Col., 10th Alabama, June 4, 1861. KIA at Dranesville, Virginia, Dec. 20, 1861. bur. Jacksonville.

MARTIN, JOHN MARSHALL. b. Edgefield Dist., South Carolina, Mar. 18, 1832. att. SCMA. 6′0″. Capt., Marion Light Artillery (Florida), 1861. Served in C.S. Congress. Lt. Col., 6th Florida Battalion, Sept. 5, 1863. Colonel, 9th Florida, Apr. 28, 1864. Surrendered at Madison, Florida. Ocala orange planter post-war. d. Ocala, Aug. 10, 1921.

MARTIN, RAWLEY WHITE. b. Pittsylvania Co., Virginia, Sept. 20, 1835. att. U. Virginia. gr. U. of New York, M.D. Lt., Co. I, 53rd Virginia, Apr. 22, 1861. Captain - May 5, 1862. Major - Feb. 4, 1863. Lt. Col. - Mar. 5, 1863. Severely wounded at Gettysburg, near Genl. Armistead's mortal wounding, and taken prisoner; exchanged Apr. 27, 1864. Paroled at Bowling Green, May 4, 1865. Lynchburg physician post-war. m. Ellen Johnson, 1867. d. Apr. 20, 1912. bur. Chatham, Virginia. Martin's papers are at UNC and Duke U.

MARTIN, THOMAS A. Of Franklin Co. Corporal, Co. E, 13th North Carolina, May 9, 1861, aged 20. Sgt. - July 12, 1861.

Lt. - Apr. 26, 1862. Captain - Nov. 17, 1862. Major - Jan. 19, 1865. Wded. hip at Gettysburg. Appx.

MARTIN, WILLIAM. b. Jones Co., Feb. 3, 1812. m. Martha Caroline Davis. Lawyer, judge and scholar. Owned land in Florida and Arkansas. In Georgia legisl. Capt., Co. B, 1st Georgia Regulars, Feb. 1, 1861. Lt. Col. - Feb. 3, 1862. Died at home on sick leave Oct. 16, 1864, in Dahlonega of tuberculosis.

MARTIN, WILLIAM. Lawyer in Henry Co. in 1860, age 46. Lt. Col., 42nd Virginia, Apr. 21, 1862. Resigned Aug. 2, 1862, due to lung disease. Living in Henry Co. in 1870.

MARTIN, WILLIAM FRANCIS. b. Pasquotank Co., 1821. Elizabeth City lawyer. Brother of Genl. James G. Martin. gr. UNC, 1842. Capt., Co. L, 17th North Carolina, May 4, 1861. Colonel - July 27, 1861. POW at Ft. Hatteras, Aug. 29, 1861, exchanged Feb. 1862. Present with the 17th North Carolina into 1865. d. 1880.

MARTIN, WILLIAM HARRISON. (nicknamed "Howdy") b. Eufala, Alabama, May 3, 1823. Moved to Texas in 1850. Lawyer and in Texas legisl. 5′11″. Capt., Co. K, 4th Texas, July 15, 1861, in Henderson Co., Texas. Major - Apr. 29, 1864. In U.S. Congress. d. Hillsboro, Feb. 3, 1898. A member of the 4th Texas called Martin "a man we all loved and could approach . . . gruff in manner, homely in appearance . . . [but] a nobleman pure and simple."

MARTIN, WILLIAM JOSEPH. b. Richmond, Virginia, Dec. 11, 1830. att. U. Virginia. Professor at UNC and at Washington College, Pennsylvania. Capt., Co. C, 28th North Carolina, 1861. Major, 11th North Carolina, Apr. 28, 1862. Lt. Col. - May 6, 1862. Colonel - Apr. 27, 1864. Wded. head and arm at Bristoe Station. Wded. leg at Jones' Farm, Sept. 30, 1864. Appx. Teacher at Columbia, Tennessee. d. Mar. 23, 1896.

MARTZ, DORILAS HENRY LEE. b. Rockingham Co., May 23, 1837. m. Mary Nicholas Carter, 1860. Sgt., Co. G, 10th Virginia, Apr. 18, 1861. Lt. - Aug. 15, 1861. Captain - Nov. 7, 1861. Lt. Col. - May 3, 1863. Wded. at Chancellorsville. POW at

Wilderness. Appx. Clerk of the Rockingham Circuit Court post-war. d. Harrisonburg, Oct. 20, 1914. bur. Woodbine Cemetery.

MARYE, MORTON. b. "Brompton," Fredericksburg, Virginia, Sept. 1, 1831. Lawyer and merchant. 5′9½″. "The Colonel was a very heavy man." m. Homassel Voss. Capt., Co. A, 17th Virginia, Apr. 17, 1861. Lt. Col. - Apr. 27, 1862. Colonel - Nov. 1, 1862. POW at Frayser's Farm. Lost leg at 2nd Manassas. Retired July 8, 1864. Clerk of Courts in Alexandria. State Auditor of Virginia for many years. d. Dec. 22, 1910.

MASSIE, JAMES WOODS. b. Augusta Co., May 28, 1826. gr. VMI, 1849. Lawyer in Lexington. On VMI faculty before and after the war. m. (1) Sophonisba McDowell. m. (2) Susanna Smith Preston. Lt. Col., 51st Virginia, July 17, 1861. Dropped at May 1862 re-org. Returned to VMI staff in 1862. Served in Virginia legisl. d. Jan. 16, 1872.

MASSIE, THOMAS BENJAMIN. b. near Upperville, Dec. 16, 1820. Warren Co. farmer. m. Eliza Anderson. Capt., Co. B, 7th Virginia Infantry, Apr. 20, 1861. Capt., Co. I, 12th Virginia Cavalry, Apr. 25, 1862. Major - June 21, 1862. Lt. Col. - Mar. 2, 1863. Wded. at Port Republic and in May 1864. POW in Warren Co., Feb. 18, 1865; Sheridan ordered, "Guerrilla: not to be exchanged." Member of Rappahannock Co. Board of Supervisors for 25 years. d. Rappahannock Co., Apr. 29, 1908.

MATHEWS, CHARLES W. Farmer at Lumpkin in 1860, married, age 29. Capt., Co. I, 17th Georgia, Aug. 30, 1861. AQM, 17th Georgia, June 5, 1862. Lt. Col. - Feb. 14, 1863. KIA at Chickamauga.

MATHEWS, JAMES DAVANT. b. Aug. 27, 1827. gr. Mercer University. Lawyer and Georgia legisl. m. 4 times. Capt., Co. E, 38th Georgia, Sept. 29, 1861. Major - June 1862. Lt. Col. - July 15, 1862. Colonel - Dec. 13, 1862. Wded. at Gaines' Mill. Retired to Invalid Corps, Oct. 31, 1864. Lawyer in Lexington, Georgia. Elected to U.S. Congress, but denied his seat by Reconstruction radicals. d. White Sulphur Springs, Georgia, Aug. 23, 1878.

MATHEWS, JOHN J. b. Feb. 14, 1827. gr. SCMA, 1848. Agent for Atlanta & West Point R.R. Physician in Troup Co. Capt., Co. D,

4th Georgia, Apr. 26, 1861. Lt. Col. - May 9, 1861. Resigned, disability, May 22, 1862. d. Mar. 13, 1864. bur. Troup Co.

MATTISON, CHARLES STARKE. b. May 26, 1831. m. Mary Lewis. Lt. Col., 4th South Carolina, Apr. 14, 1861. He became Major of the 4th South Carolina Battalion, into which the 4th South Carolina Regt. was consolidated. Severely wounded at Seven Pines. Resigned Nov. 28, 1862. In South Carolina legisl., 1860-64 and 1878-80. d. Feb. 17, 1882. bur. Mattison family cemetery near Anderson.

MAURIN, VICTOR. b. Ascension Parish, Louisiana, Oct. 2, 1818. Businessman. m. Lise Vives, 1851. Capt., Donaldsonville Artillery (Louisiana), Sept. 13, 1861. Major of artillery - Feb. 27, 1864, assigned to Richardson's Bn. POW at Erwinville, Georgia, May 10, 1865. d. Ascension Parish, Mar. 19, 1875.

MAURY, JOHN MINOR. Son of Richard B. Maury. Became the ward of his father's cousin, the renowned Virginian, Matthew Fontaine Maury, on the death of his father in 1838. Apptd. 3d Asst. Engineer, USN, Mar. 1848. Served in the USN for years. Early during the war, young Maury worked with his famous guardian's torpedo effort. Captain of artillery, Oct. 7, 1861, transferred from C.S. Navy. Lt. Col. - Aug. 6, 1862. Commanded at Chaffin's Bluff and environs. POW at Ft. Harrison, Sept. 29, 1864, released July 24, 1865. d. New Orleans, Sept. 13, 1868, aged 43.

MAURY, RICHARD LAUNCELOT. b. Fredericksburg, Oct. 9, 1840, son of Matthew Fontaine Maury. Pvt. in Virginia army, Apr. 28, 1861. Lt., Virginia State Troops - June 1861. Major, 24th Virginia, Sept. 6, 1861. Lt. Col. - Apr. 9, 1863. Maury was still writing in search of Colonel's rank in Feb. 1865. Wded. at Seven Pines and Drewry's Bluff. Appx. Prominent Richmond lawyer. Wrote a monograph on the Battle of Williamsburg, and an article on his father. m. Susan Elizabeth Crutchfield, 1862. d. Oct. 14, 1907. bur. Hollywood Cemetery. A soldier under Maury called him "a strict disciplinarian and not very popular. . . ." Maury's war letters are at the Library of Congress.

MAY, JOHN PEGRAM. b. Petersburg, Sept. 17, 1829. Wife -

Mary D. Petersburg lawyer. Capt., Co. A, 12th Virginia, Apr. 18, 1861. Major - May 3, 1862. KIA at 2nd Manassas.

MAYHEW, THOMAS WILLIAM. b. Dec. 14, 1838. Of Hyde County. Capt., Co. B, 33rd North Carolina, Sept. 20, 1861. Major - Aug. 5, 1862. POW at New Bern, Mar. 1862. MWIA at Chancellorsville, d. May 12, 1863, in Richmond. bur. Cedar Grove Cemetery, New Bern, North Carolina.

MAYO, JAMES MICAJAH. b. 1841. att. U. Virginia. Lived at Tarboro, North Carolina. Capt., Pimlico Artillery (North Carolina), Oct. 9, 1861. Dropped at spring 1862 re-org. Major, 4th North Carolina Cavalry, Sept. 11, 1862. POW at Upperville, June 21, 1863, exchanged Feb. 24, 1865. Whitakers, North Carolina, planter post-war.

MAYO, JOSEPH, JR. Feb. 5, 1834. Lawyer. m. Mary Armistead Tyler. gr. VMI, 1852. Major, 3rd Virginia, May 3, 1861. Lt. Col. - Nov. 6, 1861. Colonel - Apr. 27, 1862. Wded. at Sharpsburg. Treasurer of Virginia. d. Apr. 11, 1898. bur. Yeocomico Church, Westmoreland Co.

MAYO, ROBERT MURPHY. b. Westmoreland Co., Apr. 28, 1836. att. William & Mary. gr. VMI, 1857. On VMI staff pre-war. Major, 47th Virginia, May 8, 1861. Colonel - May 1, 1862. Mayo was found guilty of drunkenness on duty, by a court-martial, stemming from an incident of July 8, 1863. Present into 1865. Paroled at Ashland, Apr. 27, 1865. Wded. arm at Seven Days. In Virginia legisl. In U.S. Congress for a year before being unseated in a credentials dispute. d. Mar. 29, 1896. bur. Yeocomico Church, Westmoreland County. Mayo's wife, Lucy Claybrook, was a daughter of Lt. Col. Claybrook, 40th Virginia.

MEANS, JOHN HUGH. b. Fairfield Dist., South Carolina, Aug. 18, 1812. gr. South Carolina College, 1832. Governor of South Carolina, 1850. m. Susan Rebecca Stark. Colonel, 17th South Carolina, Dec. 18, 1861. KIA at 2nd Manassas.

MEANS, ROBERT STARK. b. Dec. 10, 1833. Son of Colonel John H. Means. Planter and physician in Fairfield Dist. m. Ann Emily Preston, 1856. Major, 17th South Carolina, Apr. 29, 1862.

David M. Sherman

JOHN THOMAS MERCER
21st Georgia

Lt. Col. - Sept. 1, 1862. Wded. at South Mountain and disabled. Retired to Invalid Corps, Aug. 29, 1864. Became enrolling officer at Columbia, South Carolina. d. Blacksburg, South Carolina, June 20, 1874. Means' war letters are at the University of South Carolina.

MEARES, OLIVER PENDLETON. b. Wilmington, Feb. 24, 1828. gr. UNC, 1848. Wilmington lawyer. Capt., Co. I, 18th North Carolina, Apr. 15, 1861. Lt. Col. - July 20, 1861. Defeated at April 1862 re-org. Later was Capt. and AQM, 61st North Carolina, and served with Clingman. New Hanover Co. judge. d. Wilmington, Nov. 22, 1906. bur. Oakdale Cemetery.

MEARES, WILLIAM GATSON. (He normally did not use his first name.) b. 1821. Settled in Arkansas, and served in the Mexican War from that state. Lawyer and businessman in New Hanover Co., North Carolina. Brother-in-law of W. L. DeRosset (q.v.). Colonel, 3rd North Carolina, May 16, 1861. KIA at Malvern Hill. bur. Oakdale Cemetery, Wilmington.

MENGER, BRUCE. Capt., Co. I, 5th Louisiana, May 22, 1861. Major - sometime between Feb. and Aug. 1862. Lt. Col. - date unknown. Wded. at Sharpsburg and 2nd Fredericksburg. KIA at Spotsylvania, May 12, 1864. Buried in Spotsylvania Confederate Cemetery.

MERCER, JOHN THOMAS. b. Crawfordville, Feb. 7, 1830. att. Mercer U. Colonel of Georgia militia. gr. Columbian College, 1850. gr. USMA, 1854. Lt., U.S. Army, 1854-61, with service in Missouri, New Mexico, and California. Lt. of C.S. Cavalry, Apr. 27, 1861. Lt. Col., 4th Georgia Battalion, July 19, 1861. Colonel, 21st Georgia, Sept. 27, 1861. Captain Nisbet of the 21st Georgia stated that Mercer had trouble with "booze." KIA at Plymouth, North Carolina, Apr. 18, 1864. bur. Calvary Episcopal Churchyard, Tarboro, North Carolina. Mercer never married.

MILLEN, JOHN MACPHERSON. b. Chester Co., Delaware, 1828. Lawyer and judge in Savannah. m. Elizabeth A. Hayward. Lt., Co. K, 10th Georgia Infantry, May 18, 1861. Major, Millen's (20th) Battalion Georgia Partisan Rangers, May 15,

1862. Lt. Col. - Sept. 16, 1863. KIA at Haw's Shop, May 28, 1864. bur. Hollywood. The battalion was merged into the 8th Georgia Cavalry in July 1864.

MILLER, ALEXANDER. Of Forsyth Co. Lt., Co. K, 21st North Carolina, June 11, 1861, aged 28. Captain, Co. D, 21st North Carolina, Apr. 26, 1862. Major - Mar. 12, 1863. MWIA and POW at Gettysburg, d. Aug. 2, 1863.

MILLER, DANIEL BYRD. Clerk of the Columbia City Council in 1860, age 34. Capt., Co. F, 3rd South Carolina Battalion, Jan. 30, 1862. Major - Apr. 27, 1863. POW at South Mountain, exchanged Oct. 6, 1862. Resigned Dec. 5, 1864, having been elected Clerk of Court in Richland Dist., South Carolina. d. 1885. bur. Elmwood Cemetery, Columbia.

MILLER, ELI H. b. Cleveland Co., North Carolina, Jan. 10, 1837. gr. Wofford. Teacher. 5′9″. Sgt., Co. F, 34th North Carolina, Oct. 25, 1861. Regimental Commissary, Nov. 1, 1861. Major - Apr. 18, 1862. MWIA at Ox Hill, died Sept. 3, 1862. bur. Sunset Cemetery, Shelby, North Carolina. Never married.

MILLER, GEORGE McDUFFIE. b. Aug. 2, 1830. Capt., Co. G, 1st South Carolina Rifles, July 20, 1861. Major - Mar. 25, 1863. Lt. Col. - May 4, 1863. Colonel - Apr. 7, 1864. Wded. at Chancellorsville. POW on April 3, 1865; released July 25. m. Virginia Griffin, 1865. Became a prominent U.C.V. official. d. Ninety-Six, South Carolina, July 12, 1899.

MILLER, HUGH REID. b. South Carolina, May 14, 1812. Moved to Pontotoc, Mississippi, in 1840. Circuit judge. In Mississippi legisl., and Mississippi Secession Convention. Captain at 1st Manassas. Colonel, 42nd Mississippi, May 14, 1862. MWIA at Gettysburg, d. July 19. Miller's funeral was held in Richmond's 1st Presbyterian Church on July 29. His wife, nee Susan Gray Walton, was buried with him on Jan. 23, 1864.

MILLER, JOHN LUCAS. b. York Dist. Sept. 5, 1829. gr. Davidson. m. Mary Green Sadler. Yorkville lawyer and newspaper editor. In S.C. legisl. Capt. Co. B, 12th South Carolina, Aug. 13, 1861. Major - Sept. 27, 1862. Lt. Col. - Feb. 9, 1863. Colonel -

Feb. 27, 1863. MWIA in bowels at Wilderness, May 5, 1864, d. May 6. bur. Hollywood Cemetery, Richmond.

MILLER, LOVICK PIERCE. b. Dec. 9, 1832. gr. College of Charleston, 1855. Teacher. Capt., Co. A, 23rd South Carolina, Sept. 23, 1861. Major - Dec. 28, 1861. Dropped at spring 1862 re-org. Enlisted as a Pvt., Co. G, 6th South Carolina Cavalry, June 29, 1862. Lt. Col. - Dec. 4, 1863, to rank from Dec. 13, 1862. Lived in Georgetown then in Ocala, Florida, post-war. m. Hattie Keitt. In South Carolina legisl. d. March 30, 1921, in Newberry, S. C. bur. Rosemont Cemetery.

MILLER, MERRITT BUCHANAN. b. New York, ca. 1826. Lived in New Orleans. Capt., 3rd Company, Washington Artillery (Louisiana), Mar. 26, 1861. Major - Feb. 27, 1864, assigned to Garnett's Bn. Paroled in Richmond, July 20, 1865. In New Orleans sugar business. He was known as "Old Buck," and was reputed to have been "a hard, stern officer." "His voice . . . was about the loudest and harshest there was in the army." d. New Orleans, Feb. 26, 1880.

MILLICAN, WILLIAM TERRELL. b. Jan. 7, 1823, in Jefferson, Georgia. Lawyer in Jackson Co. att. U. Georgia. m. Lucinda Elizabeth Weld. Capt., Co. B, 15th Georgia, July 14, 1861. Lt. Col. - May 1, 1862. Colonel - July 22, 1862. MWIA and POW at Sharpsburg. bur. Hagerstown Confederate Cemetery.

MILLS, JULIUS. b. Sept. 17, 1839 in Chester District. att. SCMA. Adjutant of 6th South Carolina in 1861. Private, Co. A, 17th South Carolina, 1861. Major, 17th South Carolina, Dec. 19, 1861. Dropped at re-org., April 29, 1862. Later served as Lieutenant and Captain of Co. F, 23rd South Carolina. m. Patience Amelia Stringfellow. Planter and miller in Chester Co. d. Jan. 5, 1889. bur. Evergreen Cemetery, Chester.

MIMS, ALFRED. b. Nov. 13, 1828, in Clay Co., Alabama. Teacher and farmer near Lexington. Major, 20th South Carolina, Jan. 11, 1862. Resigned Mar. 27, 1862. Later on ordnance duty at Augusta and Macon. d. Dec. 2, 1894. bur. Lewiedale Lutheran Church, Lexington Co.

Lee Joyner

WILLIAM T. MILLICAN
15th Georgia

MIMS, WILLIAM JEMISON. b. Autauga Co., Alabama, Apr. 10, 1834. att. Emory & Henry and U. Alabama. Jefferson Co. tax collector. Capt., Co. G, 43rd Alabama, May 10, 1862. Major - Nov. 2, 1864. Wded. arm at Meadow Bridge, May 1864. Appx. Jefferson Co. farmer and official post-war. d. Aug. 25, 1891. Buried in Birmingham.

MINETREE, JOSEPH POWHATAN. b. Petersburg, Mar. 20, 1839. gr. VMI, 1859. Adj., 41st Virginia, July 12, 1861. Major - May 3, 1862. Lt. Col. - July 29, 1862. Wded. at Wilderness. Appx. m. Virginia Elizabeth Eppes, 1866. Purchasing agent, Southern Railway Co. d. Washington, D.C., Jan. 25, 1907. bur. Rock Creek Cemetery. (The surname was pronounced Min'-uh-tree.)

MINOR, ROBERT DABNEY. b. Fredericksburg, Virginia, Sept. 27, 1827. Lived in Fauquier Co. m. Ladonia Randolph. In U.S. Navy. The Virginia Historical Society owns Minor's papers, which include photos of him in uniform from his time in the U.S.N. as well as during his Confederate service. Lt., CSN, 1861. Superintendent of Naval Ordnance Works in Richmond. Major, 4th Virginia Battalion LDT, June 30, 1863 (the "Naval Bn."). Resigned Feb. 13, 1864, having been ordered away to superintend ironclad construction in North Carolina. Also assigned to the James River Squadron. After the war, Minor built gunboats in Chile, and worked as an engineer on the James River. d. Richmond, Nov. 25, 1871.

MITCHELL, JULIUS CAESAR BONAPARTE. b. 1819. m. Rebecca Murdock. Planter near Montgomery. Lt. Col., 13th Alabama, July 19, 1861. Resigned Nov. 27, 1861. Later became Colonel, 34th Alabama. d. Oct. 4, 1869.

MITCHELL, RUSH J. b. North Carolina. Of Granville Co. Captain in the Mexican War. Major, 46th North Carolina, Apr. 4, 1862. Resigned, citing rheumatism, Aug. 4, 1862.

MITCHELL, WILLIAM L. Of Alleghany Co. Pvt., Co. F, 22nd North Carolina, May 27, 1861, aged 33. Captain - May 15, 1862. Lt. Col. - May 3, 1863. Appx.

MOFFETT, CHARLES JACKSON. b. Muscogee Co., May 29, 1834. att. U. Georgia. gr. Jefferson Medical College, M.D. m. Sarah C. Threewits. Farmer and druggist. Lt., Co. A, 2nd Georgia Battalion, Apr. 20, 1861. Captain - Mar. 1862. Major - Aug. 2, 1863. Wded. at Chancellorsville and Ream's Station. Lived in St. Louis for awhile post-war. d. Mar. 7, 1907. bur. Linwood Cemetery, Columbus, Georgia.

MONAGHAN, WILLIAM. b. Ireland. Notary public in New Orleans. Capt., Co. F, 6th Louisiana, June 4, 1861, aged 44. Lt. Col. - Sept. 1862. Colonel - fall 1862. Wded. at Ox Hill. POW at Strasburg, June 2, 1862, exchanged Aug. 5. KIA Aug. 25, 1864. bur. Elmwood Cemetery, Shepherdstown, West Virginia.

MONIER, HENRY D. b. Assumption Parish, Louisiana, Oct. 23, 1836. New Orleans clerk and merchant. Lt., Co. I, 10th Louisiana, July 22, 1861. Captain - Jan. 17, 1862. Major - Dec. 1862. Lt. Col. - May 1863. Colonel - sometime after Aug. 1864. Wded. at Chancellorsville. Paroled at Lynchburg, Apr. 14, 1865. Monier's war journal is quoted at length in Napier Bartlett's Louisiana book. m. Adelaide LeBon, 1868. New Orleans deputy sheriff and tax collector. d. March 24, 1911.

MONROE, ALEXANDER. b. Romney, Virginia, 1817. Hampshire Co. teacher and lawyer. 5′11″. m. (1) Sarah A. French. m. (2) Margaret Pugh. Colonel, 114th Virginia Militia, 1861. Major, 18th Virginia Cavalry, Dec. 15, 1862. In Virginia legisl. during the war. Paroled at Winchester, May 6, 1865. d. near Romney, Mar. 22, 1905. bur. Indian Creek Cemetery, Romney.

MONTAGUE, EDGAR BURWELL. b. Essex Co., Aug. 2, 1832. att. VMI and William & Mary. Lived in Middlesex Co. m. Virginia Eubank. Montague's Bn. was temporarily attached to the 32nd Virginia in Aug. 1861, then merged into the 53rd Virginia in Sept. 1861. Lt. Col., 53rd Virginia, Nov. 9, 1861. Colonel, 32nd Virginia, May 21, 1862. Present to the end of the war and paroled at Richmond, Apr. 24, 1865. Judge and merchant in King & Queen Co. d. Feb. 21, 1885 in King & Queen Co. Montague was a great-grandfather of the wife of the noted 20th-century Marine, "Chesty" Puller.

MONTGOMERY, ALEXANDER B. Born May 19, 1831, and raised in Augusta, Georgia. Lt., U.S. Artillery, 1857-61. Lt., Co. D, 1st Georgia Regulars, Mar. 16, 1861. Apptd. to temporary rank of Major, Aug. 1, 1862. Elected Major, 3rd Georgia, Aug. 5, 1862. Wded. in thigh at 2nd Manassas. Relieved as Major, Dec. 23, 1862. Elected Lt. Col., 3rd Georgia, May 12, 1863. It seems that the elections were never approved. Montgomery was assigned as Commandant of Prisoners, Charleston, South Carolina, Sept. 15, 1864. He was also posted in Florida. Planter in Floyd Co., Georgia, post-war. d. Feb. 2, 1904. bur. Myrtle Hill Cemetery, Rome.

MONTGOMERY, WILLIAM JAMES. b. Aug. 14, 1834. Of Stanley Co. gr. UNC, 1855. m. (1) Mary G. Cottrell, 1859. m. (2) Lucy M. Richmond, 1871. Capt., Co. D, 28th North Carolina, July 29, 1861. Major - June 12, 1862. Resigned, ill health, Oct. 17, 1862. Judge and teacher. d. June 28, 1912.

MOODY, DANIEL N. b. Connecticut. Jeweler in Vicksburg. Capt,. Co. A, 21st Mississippi, May 15, 1861, at Vicksburg, aged 36. Major - Nov. 2, 1861. Lt. Col. - July 2, 1863. Colonel - Oct. 28, 1863. Wded. in Sept. 1862 and Nov. 1864. Paroled at Jackson, Mississippi, May 15, 1865.

MOORE, ALEXANDER DUNCAN. b. Apr. 1838. Of New Hanover Co., North Carolina. att. USMA. Lt., Wilmington Light Artillery (North Carolina), Mar. 16, 1861. Captain - May 16, 1861. Colonel, 66th North Carolina, Aug. 3, 1863. MWIA in neck at Cold Harbor by a sharpshooter on June 3, 1864.

MOORE, ALFRED CLEON. b. Patrick Co., Virginia, Dec. 12, 1805. m. Ann Frances Kent, 1830. In North Carolina legisl., 1829-31. Colonel, 29th Virginia, Nov. 4, 1861. Resigned due to "advanced age . . . failing health" on Apr. 8, 1863. Later was an officer of reserves in Wythe Co. Wytheville physician. d. Mar. 16, 1890. bur. McGavock Cemetery, Ft. Chiswell.

MOORE, EDWIN LYTTLETON. b. Feb. 14, 1831. Jefferson Co. banker. Lt., Co. G, 2nd Virginia, Apr. 18, 1861. Captain - June 16, 1861. Major - Sept. 16, 1862. Acting a.i.g., Trimble's Division, 1862-63. Apptd. a.a.g. to John B. Gordon, 1864. d. Dec.

11, 1881. bur. Zion Episcopal Churchyard, Shepherdstown, West Virginia.

MOORE, JAMES BENJAMIN. b. Girard, Alabama, Dec. 23, 1840. Reared in Columbus, Georgia. Pvt., Co. C, 17th Georgia, Aug. 14, 1861. Captain - June 9, 1862. Major - July 12, 1864. Appx. Moved to Cameron, Texas, where he was a druggist and insurance agent. Mayor of Cameron. Alive in 1907.

MOORE, JOHN BROWN. b. South Carolina, Mar. 22, 1835. att. U. Virginia. m. Clara J. Jones. Lawyer at Anderson, South Carolina. Capt., Co. L, 1st South Carolina Rifles, July 20, 1861. Major - May 5, 1863. Resigned Aug. 28, 1863, in ill health. In South Carolina legisl., 1868-70 and 1882-86. Moved to Colusa, California, after fighting a duel with E. B. Murray, his successor in the South Carolina legisl. Justice of the peace in Colusa. d. there Nov. 22, 1926.

MOORE, JOHN L. b. Georgia, 1837. Farmer in Griffin in 1860, married, worth $23,000. Capt., Co. C, 13th Georgia, July 8, 1861. Major - Sept. 17, 1862. Resigned, disability, Dec. 13, 1862. Lt. Col., 3rd Georgia Reserves, May 1864. d. 1881. bur. Umatilla Cemetery, Umatilla, Florida.

MOORE, JOHN VINRO. Lawyer at Anderson C.H. Editor of the *True Carolinian*. Capt., Co. F, 2nd South Carolina Rifles, Oct. 29, 1861, aged 35. Colonel - May 12, 1862. MWIA at 2nd Manassas. d. Sept. 3, 1862. bur. Haymarket, Virginia.

MOORE, JOHN WHEELER. b. Hertford Co., North Carolina, Oct. 23, 1833. gr. UNC, 1853. m. Ann Ward, 1853, and had 12 children. Lived in Hertford Co. Captain and A.C.S., 2nd North Carolina Cavalry, June 18, 1861. Major of artillery, Feb. 24, 1862. He was assigned to an artillery bn. which served with A.N.Va., designated as the 2nd Bn. North Carolina Light Artillery, or as Moore's Bn. Present into 1865, and paroled at Greensboro. Moore wrote a roster of North Carolina troops; he also wrote two histories of his state, and several novels. d. Hertford Co., Dec. 8, 1906.

MOORE, LEWIS TILGHMAN. b. Loudoun Co., Virginia, Feb. 25, 1816. Winchester lawyer. Pre-war militia colonel. Colonel of a Winchester regiment of Virginia Troops, Apr. 18, 1861. Lt.

Col., 4th Virginia, June 1, 1861. Badly wded. knee at 1st Manassas disabled him. Although Moore seems not to have returned to duty after 1st Manassas, no official resignation document can be found. T. J. Jackson used Moore's Winchester home as his headquarters during the first year of the war. d. Winchester, Dec. 28, 1897. bur. Mt. Hebron Cemetery.

MOORE, PATRICK HENRY. Major, 22nd Virginia Inf., June 13, 1861. Resigned Aug. 1, 1861; accepted by Gov. Letcher on Aug. 10. Moore was a son of the editor of the Wheeling *Union*.

MOORE, ROGER. b. Wilmington, North Carolina, July 19, 1838. Served in Co. H, 7th Confederate Cavalry, 1862. Captain and A.C.S., 3rd North Carolina Cavalry, Jan. 4, 1863. Major - Aug. 18, 1863. Lt. Col. - Aug. 10, 1864. m. (1) Rebecca Scott Smith. m. (2) Mrs. Eugenie Berry Atkins, 1871. Ku Klux Klan division chief at Wilmington, 1868. d. Apr. 21, 1900. Buried in Oakdale Cemetery, Wilmington.

MOORE, SYDENHAM. b. Rutherford Co., Tennessee, May 25, 1817. gr. U. Alabama, 1836. Married a sister of Col. E. L. Hobson. Lawyer in Greensboro, Alabama. Fought in the Mexican War and against Cherokees. In U.S. Congress, 1857-61. Colonel, 11th Alabama, June 11, 1861. MWIA in the leg and spine at Seven Pines, d. Aug. 20, 1862. bur. Greensboro.

MOORE, WALTER RALEIGH. b. Florida. Merchant in Columbia Co. Capt., Co. C, 2nd Florida, May 22, 1861, aged 26. Major - May 31, 1862. Colonel - July 12, 1864. (Promotion to Lt. Col. occurred sometime during 1863, it seems.) Wded. at Seven Pines and Chancellorsville. Wded. and POW at Gettysburg, exchanged Oct. 11, 1864. Appx.

MOORE, WILLIAM HUDSON. b. Sept. 14, 1829 in Alabama. Farmer at Aberdeen, Mississippi. m. Sarah Adeline Timms. Capt., Co. I, 11th Mississippi, Feb. 20, 1861. Colonel - May 4, 1861. Resigned Apr. 4, 1862, having wounded himself in the foot with a pistol. Became Colonel, 43rd Mississippi, and was mortally wounded at Corinth, Oct. 4, 1862, d. Nov. 9.

MOORMAN, MARCELLUS NEWTON. b. Campbell Co., Virginia, Mar. 13, 1835. gr. VMI, 1856. Captain, Beauregard Rifles

Ben Ritter

LEWIS TILGHMAN MOORE
4th Virginia Infantry

Horse Artillery (Virginia), May 1861. Major of artillery, Feb. 27, 1864, assigned to Braxton's Bn. m. Ellen Grace Moorman (a cousin), 1863. Campbell Co. tobacconist. d. there May 29, 1904.

MOREHEAD, JAMES TURNER, JR. b. 1838. Guilford Co. farmer. gr. UNC. 6'0". Lt., Co. B, 27th North Carolina, Apr. 1861. Captain, 45th North Carolina, 1862. Lt. Col., 53rd North Carolina, May 6, 1862. Colonel - July 19, 1864. Wded. at Gettysburg, and in the leg, Sept. 1864. POW near Petersburg, Mar. 25, 1865, released June 7, 1865. In North Carolina Senate, 1872-1876. d. Greensboro, North Carolina, Apr. 1, 1919. bur. Presbyterian Cemetery.

MOREHEAD, JOHN HENRY. b. Guilford Co., North Carolina, Dec. 11, 1833. att. UNC. gr. Princeton, 1853. Wife - Susan L. Capt., Co. E, 2nd North Carolina, May 16, 1861. Lt. Col., 45th North Carolina, Apr. 3, 1862. Colonel - Sept. 30, 1862. Died of disease at Martinsburg, Virginia, June 26, 1863. bur. Presbyterian Cemetery, Greensboro, North Carolina.

MORGAN, JOSEPH HARGROVE. Farmer and physician in Orangeburg District in 1860, age 44, worth $121,086. m. Narcissa Catherine Salley. Major, 5th South Carolina Cav., Jan. 18, 1863. Wded. at Gravelly Run (foot amputated), Aug. 23, 1864.

MORGAN, WILLIAM AUGUSTINE. b. Fairfax Co., Mar. 30, 1831. m. Anna J. Smith, 1854. Capt., Co. F, 1st Virginia Cav., Apr. 18, 1861. Major - Oct. 2, 1862. Lt. Col. - July 16, 1863. Colonel - 1865. Commanded his brigade in 1864. Paroled at Winchester, Apr. 21, 1865. Deputy sheriff of Jefferson Co. postwar. d. near Shepherdstown, West Virginia, Feb. 14, 1899. bur. Elmwood Cemetery. Morgan was much admired by his men, who had loathed his predecessor.

MORGAN, WILLIAM Y. b. Jan. 31, 1836. Of Buncombe Co. Lt., Co. I, 25th North Carolina, July 22, 1861. Captain - Apr. 28, 1862. Major - Jan. 1, 1865. Appx. d. Mar. 1, 1935.

MORRIS, NATHANIEL MILTON. Of Stewart Co., Tennessee. Salesman. Lt., Co. E, 14th Tennessee, May 18, 1861, aged 26. Captain - July 30, 1861. Major - Sept. 2, 1862. Disabled by a bad wound at 2nd Manassas, which left him with a fractured skull and partial paralysis. Morris never returned to the field, but he was not officially retired until Aug. 12, 1864.

MORRIS, WILLIAM GROVES. b. Loudoun Co., Va., Nov. 20, 1825. Farmer in Gaston Co., N. C. 5'11½". Lt., Co. H, 37th North Carolina, October 6, 1861. Captain - Mar. 29 1862. Major - July 30, 1862. Lt. Col. - May 29, 1863. POW at Gettysburg. Carpenter and millwright. d. Gaston Co., Nov. 29, 1918.

MORRISON, EMMETT MASALON. b. Smithfield, Aug. 21, 1841. gr. VMI, 1861. 5'8". Capt., Co. C, 15th Virginia, Apr. 25, 1862. Major - Aug. 19, 1862. Lt. Col. - Jan. 24, 1863. Wded. shoulder and POW at Sharpsburg, exchanged Apr. 1863. POW at Sayler's Creek, released July 25, 1865. Smithfield teacher and postmaster. m. Sarah A. Wilson, 1872. Died June 8, 1932. bur. St. Luke's Church, Isle of Wight Co.

MORRISON, JAMES J. b. Hopkinsville, Kentucky, Oct. 31, 1829. att. U. Georgia. Planter in Cedartown, Georgia. m. (1) Athey Janes, 1850. m. (2) Hattie Cox, 1863. Served with the 3rd U.S. Dragoons in the Mexican War. Major, 4th Georgia Bn., July 19, 1861. Lt. Col., 21st Georgia, Sept. 27, 1861. Resigned Mar. 30, 1862. Acting Lt. Col., 1st Georgia Cav., 1862. Colonel, 1st Georgia Cav., May 21, 1862. Resigned in ill health, Apr. 15, 1864. Merchant in Atlanta and Decatur. Living in Decatur in 1903. d. Eastman, Georgia, Sept. 3, 1910. bur. Woodlawn Cemetery.

MOSBY, JOHN SINGLETON. b. Powhatan Co., Virginia, Dec. 6, 1833. gr. U. Virginia. m. Pauline Clarke, 1856. Lawyer in Washington Co. Enlisted in 1st Virginia Cav. in 1861, and scouted for Stuart. Captain, P.A.C.S., Mar. 15, 1863. Major, P.A.C.S., Mar. 26, 1863. Lt. Col., 43rd Bn. Virginia Cav., Jan. 21, 1864. Colonel, Mosby's Virginia Cav. Regiment, Dec. 7, 1864. Lawyer in Warrenton and San Francisco. U.S. Consul in Hong Kong. d. May 30, 1916. A recent accession of further Mosby Papers reached the University of Virginia in 1988.

MOSBY, ROBERT GOODE. b. Powhatan Co., Feb. 21, 1838. att. Georgetown. U.S. Navy clerk. Lt., Co. I, 59th Virginia, May 20, 1862. Captain - immediately thereafter. Major - Nov. 1, 1862. POW at Dinwiddie C.H., Mar. 31, 1865, released July

25. Railroad conductor and carpenter in Richmond. 5′8″. d. Richmond, June 3, 1895.

MOSELEY, EDGAR FEARN. b. Feb. 16, 1837. att. Hampden-Sydney. Sgt., 3rd Co., Richmond Howitzers (Virginia), Apr. 21, 1861. Lt. - May 11, 1861. Capt. - Nov. 16, 1861. Major, 1st Virginia Artillery Regt., June 2, 1862. Lt. Col. - Mar. 22, 1863, although this promotion was not confirmed until nearly two years later—two weeks after Moseley's death. During much of his service as a field officer, Moseley was commanding an artillery bn. with the A.N.Va. The 1st Virginia Artillery Regt. and its later incarnation as the 1st Virginia Artillery Bn. represented an awkward and little used organization. Moseley was KIA at Petersburg, Dec. 16, 1864.

MOSELEY, HILLERY. b. Oct. 20, 1816. Physician in Panola Co., Mississippi, worth $94,000 in 1860. Lt. Col., 42nd Mississippi, May 14, 1862. Wded. at Gettysburg. Resigned Dec. 18, 1863 citing "family and business" reasons. Served in Mississippi legisl. later in the war. d. June 21, 1865. bur. Shiloh Cemetery, Panola Co.

MOSELEY, JOHN BAXTER. b. March 12, 1834, in Appomattox Co. gr. VMI. Capt., Co. A, 21st Virginia, June 20, 1861. Major - Apr. 21, 1862. Resigned June 10, 1863. Served in Co. B, 14th Virginia Cav. later in the war. Moseley's diary for 1864-65 is in the Virginia Historical Society. d. Aug. 27, 1897, in Buckingham Co.

MOSELEY, WILLIAM PERKINS. b. "Wheatland," Buckingham Co., Aug. 8, 1841. att. VMI. 5′7½″. Lt., Co. E, 21st Virginia, July 17, 1861. Captain - Apr. 21, 1862. Lt. Col. - June 10, 1863. Wded. shoulder, Sept. 19, 1864. POW near Petersburg, Mar. 25, 1865, released July 24. Teacher in Virginia, Georgia and Texas. d. Mexia, Texas, June 16, 1885. bur. Mexia Cemetery.

MOTT, CHRISTOPHER HAYNES. b. Livingston Co., Kentucky, June 22, 1826. att. Transylvania U. Lived in Holly Springs, Mississippi, and was law partner to L. Q. C. Lamar. Lt., 1st Mississippi, Mexican War. Colonel, 19th Mississippi, June 11, 1861. KIA at Williamsburg.

Museum of the Confederacy

EMMETT MASALON MORRISON
15th Virginia Infantry

MOUNGER, JOHN CLARK. b. 1813. Lawyer in Brooks Co. In Georgia legisl. Wife - Lucie H. Gartrell. Major, 9th Georgia, June 11, 1861. Lt. Col. - Apr. 15, 1862. Wded. four times at Sharpsburg. KIA at Gettysburg. bur. Laurel Hill Cemetery, Savannah. Mounger's papers are at the Georgia Archives.

MULLINS, JOHN BAILEY. b. Tennessee, Dec. 1829. gr. USMA, 1854. Lt., U.S. Army, 1854-61. Capt., C.S. Cavalry, Mar. 16, 1861. He was scheduled to be Major, 5th Virginia Cav., P.A.C.S., but the unit was never fully organized, and the 5th Virginia Cav. which served most of the war was a separate entity. Major, 19th Mississippi, Dec. 11, 1861. Lt. Col. - May 5, 1862. Colonel - Nov. 24, 1862. Wded. during the Seven Days. Resigned in July 1864 as the result of a "severe wound . . . abdomen." Lived in Norfolk Virginia, post-war. d. Oct. 3, 1891. bur. Elmwood Cemetery, Norfolk.

MUNFORD, JOHN DURBURROW. b. Richmond, 1810. att. U. Virginia. A "poet and scholar." Farmed in Amsterdam, Botecourt Co. Major, 1st Virginia Bn. Regulars ("Irish Battalion"), July 18, 1861. Dropped at re-org. in spring 1862. Munford was briefly transferred to the 15th Virginia on Mar. 28, 1862, in a trade for Thomas G. Peyton. Peyton promptly switched back to the 15th Virginia on May 2, 1862. One of the lieutenants in the 1st Bn. stated that Munford resigned when he found that "the officers of the battalion were not satisfied" with him. The same witness attributed fine courage to Munford, but declared him to be too much a gentleman—not enough a martinet. Lawyer in Richmond, in Ohio and in San Francisco. Died in Greenfield, Botetourt Co., Virginia, Oct. 10, 1876.

MUNFORD, THOMAS TAYLOR. b. Richmond, Mar. 28, 1831. gr. VMI, 1852. Lynchburg planter. Lt. Col., 2nd Virginia Cav., May 8, 1861. Colonel - Apr. 25, 1862. Although Munford frequently commanded his brigade, and was repeatedly recommended for promotion to Brigadier General by an impressive array of superiors, he never quite made the large star. He was a cotton planter in Uniontown, Alabama, post-war, and died there Feb. 27, 1918. Early described Munford as "a nice gentleman, but not remarkably brilliant intellectually."

MUNFORD, WILLIAM. b. Richmond, Aug. 16, 1829. att. U. Virginia and William & Mary. Brother of Thomas T. Munford. Lt. Col., 17th Virginia, June 13, 1861. Served at this rank with the 24th Virginia for awhile late in 1861. Early castigated him in writing, citing absence wthout leave while "laboring under the effects of intemperance," and urged his return to the 17th Virginia. Dropped at April 1862 re-org. "Sent to Canada by the Governor of Virginia." Late in the war he served as a private in the Otey Battery (Virginia). He was also listed as Major, "Munford's Bn. Va. LDT" in 1863, but that unit apparently never fully organized. Munford became an Episcopal minister in Dallas, Memphis and New Orleans. d. Annapolis, Maryland, Mar. 8, 1904. bur. Hollywood Cemetery, Richmond.

MUNFORD, WILLIAM PRESTON. b. Richmond, Nov. 9, 1818. att. U. Virginia. Secretary-Treasurer of the James River Canal Co. Clerk in the office of the Secretary of the Commonwealth. Major, 1st Virginia, Apr. 21, 1861 (state rank from Sept. 18, 1860). Promoted away from the regiment, May 17, 1861. Later served as a paymaster, and in the Richmond provost marshal office. d. Richmond, Feb. 21, 1887.

MURCHISON, JOHN REED. b. Holly Hill, North Carolina, Dec. 5, 1837. Cumberland Co. merchant. Brother of Kenneth M. Murchison. Lt., Co. E, 8th North Carolina, May 16, 1861. Captain - Jan. 1, 1862. Major - Oct. 1, 1863. Lt. Col. - Feb. 1, 1864. POW at Roanoke Island, Feb. 1862. MWIA in head at Cold Harbor, June 1, 1864, died at White House, Virginia, June 7.

MURCHISON, KENNETH McKENZIE. b. Fayetteville, North Carolina, Feb. 18, 1831. gr. UNC, 1853. 6′0″. Lt., Co. C, 8th North Carolina, May 1861. Capt., Co. F, 15th North Carolina, May 18, 1861. Capt., Co. C, 54th North Carolina, May 19, 1862. Major - May 16, 1862 (rank backdated). Lt. Col. - Sept. 3, 1862. Colonel - May 8, 1863. POW at Rappahannock Station, Nov. 7, 1863, released July 25, 1865. m. Katherine Williams. Financier in New York City and in Wilmington, North Carolina. Died in Baltimore, Maryland, June 3, 1904.

MURDEN, EDGAR O. b. South Carolina. Lt. in U.S. Revenue Service, 1845-1861. Capt., Co. D, 23rd South Carolina, Apr. 16,

1862. Major then Lt. Col., dates not found. Resigned Apr. 22, 1863, on surgeon's certificate. Wded. at 2nd Manassas. POW at Warrenton, Virginia, Sept. 29, 1862. Became Master of blockade runner *Victory*. Captured with her on June 21, 1863; exchanged Oct. 18, 1864, age 46.

MURFEE, JAMES THOMAS. b. Southampton Co., Virginia, Sept. 13, 1833. gr. VMI, 1853. Professor at U. Alabama. Lt. Col., 41st Alabama, June 2, 1862. Res. July 15, 1862. College educator post-war. On USMA Board of Visitors. d. Apr. 23, 1912.

MURRAY, EDWARD. b. Maryland, Aug. 12, 1819. Lt. and Capt., U.S. Infantry, 1841-55. Farmer in Fauquier Co., Virginia. gr. USMA, 1841. Capt., Co. C, 49th Virginia, May 1861. Lt. Col. - July 19, 1861. Dropped at May 1862 re-org. Lt. Col. and a.a.g. to R. E. Lee, 1862-64. d. West River, Maryland, July 3, 1874. bur. Anne Arundel Co.

MYERS, FRANKLIN McINTOSH. b. Waterford, Virginia, Oct. 16, 1840. m. Fannie Shawen. Capt., Co. A, 35th Virginia Cav. Bn., Jan. 11, 1862. Major - Feb. 17, 1865, "Valor & Skill." Paroled at Harpers Ferry, Apr. 24, 1865. Lincoln storekeeper and postmaster. 6'0". d. Lincoln, Virginia, Oct. 20, 1906, of heart disease. bur. Catoctin Free Church.

MYERS, SAMUEL B. b. Rochtsville, Pennsylvania, Aug. 1, 1830. gr. Jefferson College, Pennsylvania, 1851. Moved to Shenandoah Co., Virginia, 1852, and ran Columbia Iron Furnace. Lived near Woodstock. Also owned Union Forge. Capt., Co. C, 7th Virginia Cav., June 15, 1861. Major - 1863. Wded. at Orange C.H., Aug. 7, 1862. Resigned Aug. 5, 1863. Died of disease at Union Forge, Feb. 25, 1865.

NADENBOUSCH, JOHN QUINCY ADAMS. b. Hampshire Co., Virginia, Oct. 31, 1824. Mayor of Martinsburg. Capt., Co. D, 2nd Virginia, Apr. 18, 1861 (had commanded the company since Oct. 1859). Colonel - Sept. 16, 1862. Wded. (groin) at 2nd Manassas, and at Chancellorsville. Resigned, disability, Feb. 19, 1864. Commanded the post at Staunton, 1863-64. Ran a flour mill and distillery at Martinsburg post-war. d. 5 a.m., Sept. 13,

1892. bur. Old Norbourne Cemetery, Martinsburg. His papers are at Duke University and the University of Virginia.

NALL, DUKE. b. Alabama, 1830. Planter in Perry Co. m. Sarah A. Bennett. Capt., Co. K, 8th Alabama, May 16, 1861. Major - Nov. 2, 1864. Wded. at Frayser's Farm. MWIA at Wilderness, in the chest, d. in Perry Co., Alabama, early in 1865.

NANCE, JAMES DRAYTON. b. Newberry, South Carolina, Oct. 10, 1837. gr. SCMA. Lawyer. Never married. Capt., Co. E, 3rd South Carolina, Apr. 14, 1861. Colonel - May 14, 1862. KIA at Wilderness. bur. Newberry. Nance's fine papers are at the University of South Carolina. bur. Rosemont Cemetery, Newberry.

NASH, EDWIN ACTON. b. Troup Co., Apr. 30, 1835. m. Emaline A. Tharp. Farmer in Twiggs Co. Lt., Co. C, 4th Georgia, Apr. 25, 1861. Capt. - Oct. 22, 1861. Major - July 1, 1863. Lt. Col. - Aug. 5, 1864. POW at Wilderness, exchanged Aug. 1, 1864. Commanded Cook's Brigade at Appx. d. Baxley, Georgia, Oct. 21, 1913.

NASH, JESSE GENT. b. Blount Co., Alabama, Jan. 27, 1822. gr. Columbian U., D.C., 1849. m. Mary Louise Marsh, 1849. Pastor of Baptist Churches in Pickensville and Carrollton, Alabama. Capt., Co. C, 41st Alabama, Mar. 22, 1862. Major - June 27, 1863. Resigned Nov. 28, 1863, to return to his ministerial labors. Founded Mary Sharp College in Sherman, Texas, after the war. d. Sherman, 1897.

NEAL, JAMES HENRY. b. Macon, Oct. 1835. gr. U. Georgia. Lawyer in Zebulon, Georgia. Capt., Co. B, 19th Georgia, June 11, 1861. Major - June 26, 1862. Lt. Col. - Jan. 12, 1863. Colonel - Aug. 20, 1863. KIA at Bentonville. bur. Oakland Cemetery, Atlanta.

NEFF, JOHN FRANCIS. b. near Rude's Hill, Virginia, Sept. 5, 1834. Son of a Dunkard preacher. gr. VMI. Lawyer in New Orleans and Memphis. Lt. and Adj., 33rd Virginia, soon after the regiment's organization in 1861. Colonel, 33rd Virginia, Apr. 22, 1862. KIA at 2nd Manassas. Buried near Cedar Grove Church on Rude's Hill.

NELLIGAN, JAMES. b. Ireland. New Orleans auctioneer. Capt., Co. D, 1st Louisiana, Apr. 28, 1861. Major, 1st Louisiana, summer of 1862. Lt. Col. - July 1863. "Was court-martialed for leaving Regt. in fight at Fredericksburg and Gettysburg, but was whitewashed." Wded. at Seven Days, Chancellorsville (thigh) and Mine Run. POW at Winchester, Sept. 19, 1864, exchanged Nov. 15.

NELSON, ANDREW McCAMPBELL. b. Tennessee, Mar. 2, 1830. m. Laura Caldwell, 1850. 5′8″. Judge in Carroll Co., Mississippi. Capt., Co. A, 42nd Mississippi, May 14, 1862. Lt. Col. - Dec. 18, 1863. Colonel - May 5, 1864. Wded. at Wilderness. POW at Hatcher's Run, released June 18, 1865. Secretary to Governor John M. Stone of Mississippi. d. Winona, Mississippi, Oct. 2, 1883.

NELSON, PATRICK HENRY. b. 1824. Lived in Clarendon Dist., South Carolina. gr. South Carolina College. General of South Carolina State Troops at Ft. Sumter. Major, 7th South Carolina Bn., Feb. 24, 1862. Lt. Col. - July 10, 1862. KIA near Petersburg, June 24, 1864. According to some accounts, he was murdered by Negro troops while a prisoner.

NELSON, WILLIAM. b. Yorktown, Virginia, Dec. 14, 1808. In Virginia legisl. from Hanover Co. Captain, Hanover Light Artillery (Virginia), Apr. 1861. Dropped at re-org. Major of artillery, May 26, 1862. Lt. Col. - Mar. 3, 1863. Colonel - Feb. 18, 1865. His service is sometimes defined as being in command of the 31st Virginia Light Artillery Bn., but that artificially numbered unit was actually Nelson's Bn., which was a part of A.N.Va. Nelson never married, and died Apr. 17, 1892.

NESBITT, NILES. b. Sept. 23, 1828. Farmer in Spartanburg District in 1860, worth $16,200. Capt., Co. B, 1st South Carolina Cav. Bn., Aug. 22, 1861. The bn. was merged into the 1st South Carolina Cav. Regt. Nesbit was made Major, 1st South Carolina Cav., Sept. 15, 1864. d. Feb. 1, 1892. bur. Old Bethel (Westside) Church, somewhere in South Carolina.

NESMITH, SAMUEL PERRY. Lawyer at Haynesville in 1860, age 38, married. Pvt., Co. E, 6th Alabama, Apr. 17, 1861. He was promoted to Major, 6th Alabama, at some unknown date in 1861, and was killed at Seven Pines.

NETHERCUTT, JOHN H. b. 1824. Sheriff of Jones Co., North Carolina. Major, 8th North Carolina Bn., Aug. 23, 1862. Lt. Col., 66th North Carolina, Aug. 3, 1863. Colonel - June 3, 1864. Wded. in face and eye by a shell, June 18, 1864. Paroled at Greensboro. Nethercutt was murdered at his home on Dec. 8, 1867, in front of his family, by two Negroes at the instigation of a carpetbag sheriff. bur. Trenton, Jones Co.

NEWTON, JAMES MITCHELL. b. Jasper Co., Aug. 18, 1823. Teacher and postmaster at Indian Springs. Capt., Co. D, 6th Georgia, May 27, 1861. Lt. Col. - May 27, 1861. KIA at Sharpsburg.

NEWTON, JAMES W. b. Augusta Co., Mar. 8, 1838. att. Mossy Creek Academy. Merchant. 5'10". Capt., Co. E, 5th Virginia, Apr. 18, 1861 (had commanded this unit since Jan. 12, 1861). Major - Aug. 29, 1862. Wded. at 2nd Manassas. Lost a leg, Sept. 19, 1864. Paroled in the Shenandoah Valley, May 22, 1865. Farmer and builder. d. Jan. 6, 1896. bur. Thornrose Cemetery, Staunton.

NICHOLSON, BENJAMIN EDWARD. b. Mar. 10, 1841. Sgt., Co. B, Hampton Legion (South Carolina), June 12, 1861. Lt. - Aug. 15, 1861. Capt. - Sept. 17, 1862. Major - Sept. 3, 1864, for "Valor & Skill." Wded. at 1st Manassas and at Darbytown Road, in the arm, Oct. 13, 1864. Paroled at Augusta, Georgia, May 23, 1865. m. Elizabeth Juliett Hughes, 1865. Farmer and clerk of courts. Lived 7 miles from Edgefield, South Carolina. d. Mar. 20, 1885. bur. Blocker Family Cemetery.

NIEMEYER, WILLIAM FREDERICK. b. Portsmouth, Virginia, May 12, 1840. att. USMA. m. Sarah Campbell Smith, 1862. Lt. of artillery, P.A.C.S., Mar. 16, 1861. Lt. Col., 61st Virginia, May 22, 1862. Wded. at Bristoe Station. KIA at Spotsylvania, on his 24th birthday. bur. Cedar Grove Cemetery, Portsmouth.

NISBET, REUBEN BATTLE. b. Madison, Georgia, Feb. 6, 1830. att. Oglethorpe U. and Jefferson Medical College. Physician.

Capt., Co. B, 3rd Georgia, Apr. 26, 1861. Lt. Col. - July 1, 1862. Wded. at Malvern Hill. Wded. and POW at Sharpsburg. Retired due to wounds, May 16, 1864. d. Eatonton, Georgia, Apr. 10, 1901.

NOLAN, MICHAEL. b. Ireland. New Orleans grocer. Capt., Co. E, 1st Louisiana, Apr. 28, 1861, age 40. Lt. Col. - Apr. 30, 1862. Wded. at Sharpsburg. KIA at Gettysburg, July 3, 1863.

NORMENT, GEORGE M. b. Mecklenburg Co. Farmer. 6'0". Lt., Co. G, 34th North Carolina, Oct. 25, 1861, aged 27. Captain - Sept. 7, 1862. Major - Sept. 10, 1864. Lt. Col. - Nov. 25, 1864. Wded. at Gaines' Mill and Gettysburg (hip). Appx.

NORMENT, RICHARD M. b. Charlotte, North Carolina. Physician. 6'0". Capt., Co. A, 46th North Carolina, Feb. 8, 1862, aged 33. Major - Aug. 4, 1862. Resigned Sept. 30, 1862, due to bladder disease.

NORRIS, JOHN S. b. June 9, 1831. Lived in Clarksville, Georgia. 5'11". Lt., Co. C, Inf. Bn. of Phillips Legion (Georgia), June 11, 1861. Capt. - July 6, 1862. Major - Dec. 31, 1863. POW at Sayler's Creek, released July 25. Traveling salesman based in Atlanta. d. Apr. 11, 1884. bur. Oakland Cemetery.

NORTON, GEORGE FISHER. b. Richmond, May 1840. gr. VMI, 1860. 5'10". Sgt., Co. D, 1st Virginia, Apr. 21, 1861. Lt. - May 13, 1861. Captain - Apr. 26, 1862. Major - July 3, 1863. Wded. at Seven Pines and Gettysburg. POW at Sayler's Creek, released May 30. Druggist and Supt., Richmond Street Railway. d. July 12, 1883. bur. Hollywood Cemetery.

NORTON, JOSEPH JEPTHA. b. Pendleton Dist., South Carolina, June 13, 1835. gr. U. Georgia, 1855. m. Tabitha A. Campbell, 1860. Lawyer in Pickens, South Carolina. Capt., Co. C, 1st South Carolina Rifles, July 20, 1861. Major - Sept. 1, 1862. Lt. Col. - Nov. 12, 1862. Lost left arm at Fredericksburg. Resigned May 25, 1863. Judge and South Carolina legisl. d. Walhalla, South Carolina, June 20, 1896. bur. West View Cemetery. Norton's war papers are at the University of South Carolina and the South Carolina Historical Society.

Lawrence T. Jones

MICHAEL NOLAN
1st Louisiana

NORWOOD, ISAIAH THEOPHILUS. b. July 26, 1827. Major, 2nd Louisiana, May 1861. Colonel - May 2, 1862. KIA at Malvern Hill.

NOUNNAN, JAMES H. Lived in Salt Lake City prewar, and "served in Kansas against [John] Brown." Served in the 8th Virginia Cav. and the 22nd Virginia Inf. in 1861-1862. Capt., Co. K, 16th Virginia Cav., Oct. 7, 1862. Major - Jan. 15, 1863. Co. K was actually a part of Ferguson's Virginia Cav. Bn. (the "Guyandotte Bn.") in 1862. The 16th Virginia Cav. was formed on the date that Nounnan became its Major. A Confederate described Nounnan as handsome, but he "never washed, nor combed his hair nor put on clean garments . . . dirty, haggard and worn." But in battle "his eyes flashed and glistened . . . with fire that could scarcely be paralleled." Nounnan entered the Lee Camp Soldiers' Home in Richmond on May 10, 1895, from Salt Lake City, Utah, giving his age as 61 and citing rheumatism and war wounds. d. Oct. 1, 1900, at the home. bur. Hollywood Cemetery.

OATES, WILLIAM CALVIN. b. Pike Co., Alabama, Nov. 30, 1833. Capt., Co. G, 15th Alabama, July 1861. Colonel - to rank from Apr. 28, 1863, but the appt. was never confirmed, and Oates officially became a Major from that date. Lt. Col. - Dec. 7, 1864. Oates wrote a fine war memoir which supplies a plethora of detail on his life and career. He was Governor of Alabama, and a member of the U.S. Congress, 1880-94. d. Sept. 9, 1910.

O'BRIEN, ALFRED GEORGE. b. Tennessee, Dec. 25, 1839. 6'0". Lt., Co. D, 13th Mississippi, Mar. 15, 1861. Captain - Apr. 26, 1862. Major - July 3, 1863. Lt. Col. - July 29, 1863. POW at Knoxville, Nov. 29, 1863, never exchanged. m. Martha Ford, 1869. Newspaper publisher in Starkville, Mississippi. Alive in 1907.

O'CAIN, WATSON A. att. SCMA. Farmer in Orangeburg District in 1860, age 27, married, worth $14,500. Major, 1st South Carolina (Hagood's), Jan. 1861. Defeated at April 1862 re-org.

O'CONNELL, JAMES. Capt., Co. D, 22nd South Carolina, Jan.

10, 1862. Lt. Col. - Sept. 14, 1862. Wded. at Boonsboro, Sept. 14, 1862. Resigned Jan. 26, 1864.

O'DELL, LABAN. b. Nov. 8, 1836. Teacher in Randolph Co. Lt., Co. M, 22nd North Carolina, June 10, 1861. Captain - Apr. 27, 1862. Major - Mar. 16, 1863. KIA at Chancellorsville. bur. Gray's Chapel, Randolph Co., North Carolina.

O'FERRALL, CHARLES TRIPLETT. b. Frederick Co., Virginia, Oct. 21, 1840. att. Washington College. 5'11". Sgt., Co. A, 11th Virginia Cav., 1861. Lt., Co. I, 12th Virginia Cav., Apr. 1862. Captain - Aug. 1862. Lt. Col., O'Ferrall's Bn. Virginia Cav. - authority to raise this unit was granted Oct. 26, 1863, but organization was not successfully completed. Lt. Col., 23rd Virginia Cav., Apr. 28, 1864. Wded. at Poolesville, Maryland, Sept. 1862, and at Upperville, June 1863. Wrote a notable memoir, published by the Neale Co. In U.S. Congress, 1884-1894. Elected Governor of Virginia, 1894. d. Sept. 22, 1905.

OFFUTT, NATHANIEL G. b. Louisiana. gr. Georgetown U., 1860. Planter in St. Landry Parish. Capt., Co. C, 6th Louisiana, June 4, 1861, age 30. Major - May 25, 1862. Lt. Col. - summer of 1862. Resigned Nov. 7, 1862, "under charges of cowardice."

O'HARA, THEODORE. b. Danville, Kentucky, Feb. 11, 1820. gr. St. Joseph's College. Capt. and Major, Mexican War, 1846-48. Capt., 2nd U.S. Cavalry, 1855-56, and chased Comanches under R. E. Lee. Author of the famous poem, "The Bivouac of the Dead," and other pieces. Captain in a Cuban Filibustering Expedition, 1849-50. Capt. of Inf., P.A.C.S., Mar. 16, 1861. Lt. Col., 12th Alabama, July 17, 1861. Resigned Nov. 11, 1861. A.i.g. to A. S. Johnston, 1861. Capt. and a.a.g. in a long list of western staff billets the rest of the war. d. Guerryton, Alabama, June 6, 1867. bur. Frankfort, Kentucky.

OLD, CHARLES. b. Powhatan Co., July 10, 1823. att. William & Mary. Lt., Co. E, 4th Virginia Cav., Apr. 25, 1861. Captain - Apr. 25, 1862. Major - Oct. 14, 1864. Farmer in Powhatan Co. d. there Jan. 26, 1903.

OLIVER, JAMES McCARTHY. b. Elbert Co., Georgia, May 12, 1831. m. (1) Matilda Allen, 1850. Lawyer in Chambers Co.,

Alabama. Colonel, 47th Alabama, May 22, 1862. Resigned Aug. 11, 1862. m. (2) Kittie Carter, 1884. Lawyer in LaFayette, Alabama, in 1893. d. Perry, Georgia, Aug. 23, 1896, after striking his head on an outhouse while falling. bur. Evergreen Cemetery.

ORR, JAMES LAWRENCE. b. Craytonville, South Carolina, May 12, 1822. gr. U. Virginia. m. Mary Jane Marshall, 1844. Lawyer and in South Carolina legisl. Opposed nullification. In U.S. Congress, 1849-1859. Colonel, 1st South Carolina Rifles, July 20, 1861. Resigned Feb. 1, 1862, having been elected to C.S. Senate. U.S. Minister to Russia, 1872-73. d. Russia, May 5, 1873. bur. Anderson, South Carolina.

OSBORNE, EDWIN AUGUSTUS. b. Laurens Co., Alabama, May 6, 1837. Lived in Iredell Co., North Carolina. Lt., Co. C, 4th North Carolina, May 16, 1861. Captain - July 15, 1861, backdated to rank from May 16. Major - Dec. 23, 1862. Lt. Col. - May 19, 1864. Colonel - July 18, 1864. Wded. at Seven Pines and Spotsylvania (fingers amputated). Wded. and POW at Sharpsburg, exchanged Dec. 1862. Retired to Invalid Corps, Apr. 1, 1865. m. Fannie Moore, 1865. Lawyer, Episcopal minister, and orphanage superintendent in Charlotte. Chaplain during the Spanish-American War. Alive in Charlotte in 1900. d. Oct. 12, 1926. bur. Elmwood Cemetery, Charlotte.

OTEY, KIRKWOOD. b. Lynchburg, Oct. 19, 1829. gr. VMI, 1849. Officer of the Lynchburg Home Guard before and after the war. Lt., Co. G, 11th Virginia, Apr. 23, 1861. Captain - May 9, 1861. Major - May 23, 1862. Lt. Col. - Sept. 24, 1863. Colonel - 1864. Wded. at Gettysburg and Drewry's Bluff. Paroled at Lynchburg, Apr. 15, 1865. m. Lucy Dabney Norvell, 1862. Lynchburg official and insurance man. d. June 1, 1897.

OTEY, PETER JOHNSON. b. Lynchburg, Dec. 22, 1840. gr. VMI, 1860. 5′8″. Lt., CSA, Apr. 1861. Adjutant, 51st Virginia. Major, 30th Virginia Sharpshooters Bn., Oct. 5, 1862. POW at Waynesboro, Mar. 2, 1865, released May 30. m. Mollie Floyd. In U.S. Congress, 1895-1902. Railroad and banking executive in Lynchburg. d. there May 4, 1902. bur. Presbyterian Cemetery.

OWEN, MOSES TAGGART. b. Oct. 31, 1825. Jeweler in Abbeville in 1860, worth $25,400. Capt., Co. A, 1st South Carolina Cav. in 1861. Major, at organization of the regt., June 1862, but declined. Remained as Capt. until MWIA near Williamsport, Maryland, July 1863. An apparently minor heel wound developed tetanus, and Owen died at Abbeville, Aug. 4, 1863. bur. Long Cane Cemetery, Abbeville.

OWEN, THOMAS HOWERTON. b. Halifax Co., June 11, 1833. gr. VMI, 1856. Lived in South Boston, Virginia. Captain of an 1859 volunteer cavalry company. Lt., Co. C, 3rd Virginia Cav., Aug. 1861. Captain - Dec. 16, 1861. Lt. Col. - Oct. 21, 1862. Colonel - Nov. 18, 1862. Wounded in hand at Spotsylvania, May 7, 1864. Married Elizabeth Alice Williams, 1861. Civil engineer and farmer at South Boston. Died May 8, 1894.

OWEN, WILLIAM MILLER. b. Cincinnati, Ohio, 1840. Moved to New Orleans in 1858. Adj., Washington Artillery (Louisiana), May 26, 1861. Major of artillery - Aug. 10, 1863. Commanded the 13th Virginia Bn. Served in southwestern Virginia. Back with the Washington Artillery Bn. in the spring of 1864. Wded. at the Crater. Lt. Col. - early 1865. Commanded a bn. in the 3rd Corps, A.N.Va. Author of a famous Washington Artillery memoir. d. Jan. 10, 1893. bur. Metairie Cemetery.

OWENS, JOHN CROWDER. b. Mathews Co., Mar. 19, 1830. Pharmacist in Portsmouth. Capt., Co. G, 9th Virginia, Apr. 20, 1861. Major - May 24, 1862. Colonel on July 1, 1863, to rank from Oct. 30, 1862. MWIA in groin at Gettysburg, July 3, 1863. d. July 4. bur. Oakwood Cemetery, Portsmouth. A comparison of ranking dates suggests that Owens was doubtless promoted to Colonel in June 1863, on Godwin's departure. An unpublished letter by J. J. Phillips confirms the promotion.

OWENS, WILLIAM ALLISON. b. Charlotte, Sept. 19, 1833. gr. UNC, 1856. m. Alice Brandon Caldwell, 1857. Lt., Co. B, 1st North Carolina (Bethel), Apr. 16, 1861. Captain - Sept. 28, 1861. Major, 34th North Carolina, Nov. 1861. Lt. Col., 11th North Carolina, Mar. 31, 1862. Colonel, 53rd North Carolina, May 6, 1862. Wded. in hand and side at Spotsylvania. MWIA at Snicker's Ford, Virginia, July 19, 1864. bur. Presbyterian

Churchyard, Charlotte. He also has a marker in Old Chapel Cemetery, Clarke Co., Virginia.

PAGE, JOHN CARY, JR. b. Locust Grove, Cumberland Co., Feb. 22, 1830. gr. VMI, 1851. Major, 16th Virginia, May 17, 1861. Lt. Col. - Jan. 6, 1862. Dropped at May 1862 re-org. m. (1) Nellie Eppes, 1858. m. (2) Mrs. Julia Trent Gray, 1882. Cumberland Co. farmer. d. Feb. 12, 1897.

PAGE, POWHATAN ROBERTSON. b. New Quarter Farm, Gloucester Co., 1822. Lt. & QM, Mexican War. m. Elizabeth Scollay, 1853. Lt. Col., 26th Virginia, May 1861. Colonel - May 13, 1862. KIA at Taylor's Farm (near Petersburg), June 17, 1864. bur. Blandford Cemetery.

PAGE, RICHARD CHANNING MOORE. b. Albemarle Co., Virginia, Jan. 2, 1841. Pvt., Rockbridge Artillery (Virginia), July 14, 1861. Capt., Morris Artillery (Virginia), May 2, 1862. Major of artillery - Feb. 27, 1864. Served in southwestern Virginia with Echols in late 1864. gr. U. Virginia, 1868, as M.D. Physician in New York City. Wrote a history of his battery, and a Page genealogy. m. Mary Fitch Winslow, of Connecticut. d. June 19, 1898.

PAGE, THOMAS JEFFERSON, JR. b. New Jersey, Feb. 15, 1839. Lt. and Ordnance Officer, Sept. 25, 1861, at Williamsburg. A.d.c. to Genl. Magruder, Nov. 1861 to Jan. 1862. Capt., Magruder Light Artillery (Virginia), Mar. 1862. Major of artillery - Nov. 8, 1862, assigned to Hardaway's Bn. Page was on leave from Aug. 1863 until his death, which occurred in Florence, Italy, June 16, 1864.

PALMER, FRANCIS GENDRON. b. Pineville, South Carolina, Sept. 7, 1832. gr. SCMA. Captain of a volunteer company in the Kansas Wars. Planter near Charleston. Pvt., 2nd South Carolina Cavalry, 1861. Major, Holcombe Legion (South Carolina), Nov. 21, 1861. Lt. Col. - Oct. 8, 1862. MWIA at 2nd Manassas, died at Warrenton, Dec. 5, 1862. bur. Warrenton, Virginia. Palmer was a brother-in-law of Ellison Capers.

PALMER, WILLIAM HENRY. b. Richmond, Oct. 9, 1835. Merchant. Lt., Co. D, 1st Virginia, Apr. 21, 1861. Acting AQM, 1st

Jim Mayo

JOHN CROWDER OWENS
9th Virginia Infantry

Virginia, May to June 1861. Adj., 1st Virginia, Sept. 12, 1861. Major - Apr. 27, 1862. Wded. at Williamsburg and Chancellorsville. Ordered to A. P. Hill as a.a.g., May 2, 1863. m. Elizabeth Amiss. Richmond banker. d. July 14, 1926.

PARHAM, WILLIAM ALLEN. b. 1830. Planter in Sussex Co., owned 1062 acres. Lt., Co. A, 41st Virginia, May 24, 1861. Capt. - early 1862. Lt. Col. - May 3, 1862. Colonel - July 25, 1862. Wded. at Malvern Hill. Retired Mar. 31, 1865. "Died of wounds."

PARKER, FRANCIS MARION. b. Nash Co., Sept. 21, 1827. m. Sarah Phillips, 1851. Lt., Co. I, 1st North Carolina (Bethel), Apr. 19, 1861. Captain - Sept. 1, 1861. Colonel, 30th North Carolina, Oct. 7, 1861. Wded. at Sharpsburg, Gettysburg and Spotsylvania. Farmer at Enfield, South Carolina. d. Jan. 17, 1905.

PARKER, TULLY FRANCIS. b. June 14, 1823 in South Carolina. 5′6″. Carpenter in Itawamba Co., Mississippi. Capt., Co. G, 26th Mississippi, June 8, 1861. Major - Sept. 10, 1861. POW at Ft. Donelson; exchanged July 31, 1862. Wded. at Wilderness. Resigned, Mar. 7, 1865. d. Feb. 26, 1886 at Keeter, Texas.

PARKER, WILLIAM WATTS. b. Port Royal, Virginia, May 5, 1824. m. Ellen Jane Jordan, 1862. Lt., Co. B, 15th Virginia, May 1861. Capt., Parker's Battery (Virginia), Mar. 14, 1862. Major of artillery - Mar. 1865. Physician. d. Richmond, Aug. 4, 1899.

PARKS, MARCUS A. Of Wilkesboro. Aged 28 in 1861. Lt., Co. B, 1st North Carolina, May 16, 1861. Capt., Co. F, 52nd North Carolina, March 14, 1862. Lt. Col. - Apr. 25, 1862. Colonel - 1864. Wded. leg and POW at Gettysburg, exchanged Mar. 1865. m. Mary Lenoir Hickerson. Moved to California, then to Muskogee, Oklahoma.

PARR, LEWIS J. b. Atlanta, Oct. 5, 1830. Mexican War veteran. m. Lucy Patey Dickens. Capt., Co. M, 38th Georgia, Sept. 26, 1861. Major - Oct. 11, 1861. Lt. Col. - Feb. 14, 1862. Lost an arm at Gaines' Mill. Resigned Dec. 13, 1862. Hardware merchant in Atlanta. d. Ocala, Florida, Apr. 17, 1908.

PARRISH, HENRY TUCKER. b. Newington, Cumberland Co., Sept. 14, 1829. gr. VMI, 1851. gr. U. Virginia. Farmville lawyer.

Lt., Co. K, 3rd Virginia Cavalry, early 1861. Lt. Col., 16th Virginia, May 17, 1861. Colonel - Jan. 6, 1862. Dropped at May 1862 re-org.; reinstated after contesting the results, then dropped again eight days later. V.a.d.c. to R. E. Colston. Became Provost Marshal at Farmville. Lawyer and judge in Appomattox County. d. Feb. 15, 1913.

PARSLEY, WILLIAM MURDOCH. b. Wilmington, North Carolina, Oct. 6, 1840. m. Eliza Hall Nutt. Capt., Co. F, 3rd North Carolina, May 16, 1861. Major - Dec. 10, 1862. Lt. Col. - Oct. 3, 1863. Wded. at Malvern Hill. POW at Spotsylvania, exchanged Aug. 3, 1864. KIA at Sayler's Creek. bur. Oakdale Cemetery, Wilmington.

PATE, HENRY CLAY. b. Bedford Co., Apr. 21, 1832. att. U. Virginia. Lived in Louisville, Cincinnati and Westport, Missouri, before the war. Was in an 1856 skirmish with John Brown in Kansas. Editor of the Petersburg *Bulletin* in 1860. Capt., "Petersburg Rangers" (which eventually became Co. D, 5th Virginia Cav.), June 5, 1861. Lt. Col., 2nd Virginia Cavalry Battalion ("Pate's Bn."), May 1862. Lt. Col., 5th Virginia Cavalry, June 24, 1862, as his bn. was merged into that regiment. Wded. at Aldie. Colonel - Sept. 28, 1863. KIA at Yellow Tavern. Pate was involved in a bitter dispute with Rosser, who seems to have had an amazing number of such enemies, and less directly with Stuart.

PATE, JOHN HAYNES. b. Nov. 2, 1831. In Georgia legisl. Wife - Zilphia Ann. Lt., Co. K, 49th Georgia, Mar. 4, 1862. Captain - June 27, 1862. Major - July 28, 1863. Resigned Feb. 23, 1864. Businessman and farmer in Hawkinsville, Georgia. Killed in a train wreck near Blackshear, Georgia, Mar. 17, 1888. bur. Orange Hill Cemetery, Hawkinsville.

PATRICK, WILLIAM. b. Augusta Co., Dec. 12, 1822. Waynesboro merchant. m. Esther Massie. Deputy sheriff of Augusta Co. Capt., Co. E, 1st Virginia Cavalry, Apr. 1861. Major, 17th Virginia Cavalry Battalion, June 20, 1862. KIA at 2nd Manassas.

PATTON, GEORGE SMITH. b. Fredericksburg, June 26, 1833. Grandson of General Hugh Mercer of Revolutionary War fame, and great-grandfather of George Smith Patton III, of World War II fame. gr. VMI, 1852. Lawyer. m. Susan Thornton Glassell, 1855. Capt., Co. H, 22nd Virginia, May 22, 1861. Lt. Col. - July 1861. Colonel - Jan. 1863, to rank from Nov. 23, 1861. MWIA through both hips at Winchester, Sept. 19, 1864; d. Sept. 25. bur. Stonewall Cemetery.

PATTON, JOHN MERCER, JR. b. Spring Farm, Culpeper Co., May 9, 1826. Brother of George S. and Waller T. Patton. Lived in Richmond. gr. VMI, 1846. Lawyer. Major commanding at Jamestown Island, April 1861. Lt. Col., 21st Virginia, ca. June 1861. Colonel - Apr. 21, 1862. Resigned in "impaired health . . . stomach, bowels & liver," on Aug. 8, 1862. m. (1) Sarah Lindsay Taylor, 1858. m. (2) Lucy A. Crump, 1878. d. Oct. 9, 1898. Author of several legal books. Patton's papers are at the Virginia Historical Society.

PATTON, WALLER TAZEWELL. b. July 15, 1835 at Fredericksburg. gr. VMI, 1855. Never married. Lawyer in Culpeper. Capt., Co. B, 13th Virginia Inf., Apr. 17, 1861. Major, 7th Virginia, July 1, 1861. Lt. Col. - Apr. 27, 1862. Colonel - June 3, 1862. Wded. in the hand at 2nd Manassas. MWIA at Gettysburg (shot through jaws), d. July 21, 1863. bur. Stonewall Cemetery, Winchester.

PAUL, SAMUEL BUCKNER. b. Oct. 1826. att. U. Virginia. m. Sophronia W. Pickerell (1832-1908). Lived in Petersburg. Lt. Col., 28th Virginia, Sept. 6, 1861. Dropped at April 1862 re-org. Sought a position on a military court in 1864. Lawyer and insurance agent. d. Sept. 26, 1908. bur. Blandford Cemetery, Petersburg.

PEATROSS, ROBERT OLIN. b. June 8, 1837 in Caroline Co. Teacher and lawyer. gr. Emory & Henry. Lived at Flippo's Store, Caroline Co. m. Julia Archibald Samuel. Capt., Co. E, 30th Virginia, May 9, 1861. Major - Nov. 5, 1864. Wded. at Drewry's Bluff and Five Forks. Paroled at Richmond, May 9, 1865. Caroline Co. lawyer. In Virginia legisl. d. Nov. 29, 1905. bur. Lakewood Cemetery, Bowling Green.

PEEBLES, WILLIAM HUBBARD. b. May 4, 1837. Physician in Henry Co. 5′10″. m. Eliza Ann Weems, 1861. Capt., Co. A, 44th

Carl C. Rosen

ROBERT OLIN PEATROSS
30th Virginia

Georgia, Mar. 4, 1862. Surgeon, 44th Georgia, July 1862. Major - Mar. 4, 1863. Lt. Col. - May 26, 1863. Colonel - Sept. 11, 1863. POW at Spotsylvania, exchanged Aug. 3, 1864. Wded. at Winchester, Sept. 19, 1864. In Georgia legisl. d. Hampton, Georgia, Oct. 1, 1885. bur. Hampton City Cemetery.

PEGRAM, WILLIAM JOHNSON. b. Richmond, June 29, 1841. Brother of Genl. John Pegram and Major James West Pegram. att. U. Virginia. Member of Richmond's Co. "F" before the war. Entered Confederate service with that company (in the 21st Virginia), Apr. 1861. Lt., Purcell Artillery (Virginia), May 1861. Captain - Apr. 1862. Major of artillery - Mar. 2, 1863. Lt. Col. - Feb. 27, 1864. Colonel - Feb. 18, 1865. KIA at Five Forks. Pegram's excellent war letters are at the Virginia Historical Society.

PEGUES, CHRISTOPHER CLAUDIUS. b. Chesterfield Dist., South Carolina, Aug. 3, 1823. gr. South Carolina College. Lawyer in Cahaba, Alabama. m. Miss Coleman. Capt., Co. G, 5th Alabama, Apr. 10, 1861. Colonel - Apr. 27, 1862. MWIA at Gaines' Mill, d. July 15, 1862. Buried in Hollywood Cemetery, and apparently moved later to Live Oak Cemetery in Selma, where he has a marker.

PELHAM, JOHN. b. Calhoun Co., Alabama, Sept. 7, 1838. att. USMA. Lt. of artillery, P.A.C.S., Mar. 16, 1861. Served as Lt., Alburtis' Battery (Virginia) in 1861. Commanded the Beauregard Rifles (Virginia Artillery) as a Lt. in 1861. Capt., Pelham's Battery Horse Artillery - Mar. 23, 1862. Major - Aug. 9, 1862. Lt. Col. - Apr. 4, 1863 (three weeks after his death), backdated to Mar. 2, 1863. KIA at Kelly's Ford, Virginia, Mar. 17, 1863.

PENDLETON, ALBERT GALLATIN. b. Marion, Virginia, Feb. 20, 1836. Lived in Smyth Co. m. (1) Kate Blanks (d. 1862). m. (2) Miss Tinsley. Lawyer. Capt., Co. D, 4th Virginia, Apr. 18, 1861. Major - Jan. 31, 1862. Resigned in ill health late in 1862. Pendleton was serving as a commissary officer in Giles Co. in Oct. 1864. Smyth Co. Supt. of Schools, 1875-80. d. Roanoke, Mar. 2, 1901. bur. Marion. A member of the 4th Virginia wrote in Feb. 1862 that Pendleton was "the nastiest little squirt in the regiment."

PENDLETON, EDMUND. b. Amherst Co., Virginia, Sept. 29, 1823. gr. VMI, 1842. m. Cornelia M. Morgan. Lawyer. 5′9″. Major and Lt. Col., 3rd Louisiana Battalion, 1861-62. Lt. Col., 15th Louisiana (which was formed in part from the 3rd Louisiana Bn.), 1862. Colonel - 1862. POW in Seven Days, exchanged Aug. 5, 1862. Wded. hand at Chancellorsville. "Not highly considered" by the army high command. d. Lexington, Virginia, July 26, 1899.

PENDLETON, JOSEPH HENRY. b. Louisa Co., Jan. 16, 1827. Lawyer. gr. Bethany College. m. Margaret Campbell Ewing, 1848. Major, 23rd Virginia, May 1861. Wded. in head in the Laurel Hill campaign. Resigned, Sept. 14, 1861. QM of Colston's Brigade later in the war. In Virginia legisl. during the war. Wheeling lawyer. d. Wheeling, Feb. 2, 1881.

PENDLETON, PHILIP COLEMAN. b. Putnam Co., Sept. 17, 1812. m. Catherine Sarah Melissa Tebeau, 1841. Macon lawyer. Fought in Seminole War. Editor in Macon and Savannah. Capt., Co. B, 50th Georgia, Mar. 4, 1862. Major - Mar. 22, 1862. Resigned Oct. 8, 1862. d. June 19, 1869.

PENN, DAVIDSON BRADFUTE. b. Lynchburg, Virginia, May 13, 1836. att. Spring Hill College, Alabama. gr. VMI, 1856. gr. U. Virginia. 5′11½″. New Orleans businessman. Major, 7th Louisiana, Apr. 1861. Colonel - July 1862. WIA at Sharpsburg. POW at Chancellorsville and at Rappahannock Station (Nov. 7, 1863). Paroled at Athens, Georgia, May 12, 1865. Lt. Gov. of Louisiana, 1872. Adjutant General of Louisiana. Penn was instrumental in the overthrow of carpetbag government in Louisiana. d. Nov. 15, 1902, in New Orleans.

PENN, JOHN EDMUND. b. Patrick Co., July 3, 1837. att. Randolph-Macon and U. Virginia. Patrick Co. lawyer. Capt., Co. H, 42nd Virginia, May 1861. Penn was promoted Major, Lt. Col. and Colonel, each to rank from Aug. 9, 1862! This peculiar arrangement was not consummated until the next spring, at about the time that Penn resigned. He lost a leg at Sharpsburg and was captured there; exchanged Nov. 1862. Resigned ca. Apr. 1863. m. Alice Grant Hoge, 1866. Moved to Roanoke in 1882. d. Roanoke, Sept. 27, 1895.

PEPPER, RUFUS KERR. b. Germantown, July 25, 1832. Lawyer. Unmarried. Of Stokes Co. Capt., Co. F, 21st North Carolina, May 29, 1861. Lt. Col. - Apr. 26, 1862. MWIA in both hips at Winchester, May 25, 1862, d. June 10. bur. Winchester.

PERKINS, LYNVILLE J. Farmer in Grayson Co. in 1860, age 32, worth $125. Capt., Co. D, 50th Virginia, June 4, 1861. Major - Jan. 30, 1863. POW at Spotsylvania, May 10, 1864. No further record.

PERRIN, JAMES MONROE. b. Abbeville Dist., June 8, 1822. gr. South Carolina College. Sgt., Palmetto Regt., Dec. 1846. Lt., 12th U.S. Inf., May 1848. Abbeville lawyer. Capt., Co. B, 1st South Carolina Rifles, July 20, 1861. Absent in 1862 as a member of the South Carolina legisl. Lt. Col. - Sept. 1, 1862. Colonel - Nov. 12, 1862. MWIA at Chancellorsville, May 3, 1863. d. May 5. bur. Upper Long Cane Presbyterian Church, Abbeville.

PERRIN, WILLIAM KENNON. b. Nov. 6, 1834. Gloucester Co. planter. Capt., Co. F, 26th Virginia, May 12, 1861. Major - June 18, 1864. Appx. Gloucester Co. Treasurer. d. Gloucester Co., Nov. 29, 1904. bur. Ware Church, Gloucester C.H.

PETERS, WILLIAM ELISHA. b. Bedford Co., Aug. 18, 1829. gr. Emory & Henry. gr. U. Virginia, 1852. Studied in Berlin. m. (1) Margaret Sheffey, 1858. m. (2) Mary Sheffey, 1873. Lt. Col., 45th Virginia, Nov. 14, 1861. Colonel - Jan. 6, 1862. Dropped at spring 1862 re-org. Colonel, 2nd Virginia State Line, fall 1862. This unit was about one-third infantry, the remainder cavalry. The 2nd Virginia State Line became the 21st Virginia Cavalry in Aug. 1863, and Peters was commissioned as Colonel of the new regt. on Aug. 21, 1863. He fought a duel with John Blair Harvie at Bristol in Nov. 1863. Wded. at Moorefield, Aug. 7, 1864. On the faculty of U. Virginia and Emory & Henry. d. Mar. 22, 1906, at Charlottesville. An inspector called Peters "a gentleman, but ignorant of military duty."

PETTY, CHARLES Q. b. Spartanburg, South Carolina. Of Gaston Co., North Carolina. Farmer. 5′8″. Capt., Co. H, 49th North Carolina, Mar. 22, 1862, aged 31. Major - Aug. 5, 1864. Commanding the 49th North Carolina at Appx.

PETTY, ROBERT E. b. Chatham, North Carolina. Farmer. 5′11″. Lt., Co. D, 35th North Carolina, Oct. 17, 1861, aged 25. Captain - July 1, 1862. Major - June 18, 1864. Wded. at Fredericksburg, and in the shoulder on May 20, 1864. Appx. Merchant in Raleigh and Sanford. d. ca. 1900.

PETWAY, OLIVER CROMWELL. b. 1840. Of Edgecombe Co., North Carolina. att. VMI at the beginning of the war, and served with the cadets in drilling troops at Richmond. Major, 35th North Carolina, Nov. 8, 1861. Lt. Col. - Apr. 15, 1862. KIA at Malvern Hill.

PEYTON, CHARLES STEPHENS. b. Albermarle Co., Virginia, Jan. 21, 1841. Capt., Co. E, 19th Virginia, May 10, 1861. Major - Sept. 14, 1862. Lt. Col. - July 3, 1863. Lost an arm at 2nd Manassas. Wded. in legs at Gettysburg. Enrolling officer at Lynchburg and Staunton, beginning in summer of 1863. Retired to Invalid Corps, Oct. 24, 1864. m. Sallie E. Nimrod, 1867. Mayor of Ronceverte, West Virginia. High-ranking U.C.V. official. d. Charlottesville, Jan. 6, 1923.

PEYTON, THOMAS GREEN. b. Richmond, 1832. gr. U. Virginia. m. Cary Anne Carr, 1858. Richmond merchant. Major, 15th Virginia, July 1, 1861. Lt. Col. - Apr. 26, 1862. Briefly exchanged roles with Major Munford, 1st Virginia Battalion, in spring 1862. Resigned Aug. 19, 1862. Later served on staff of John C. Shields. Died at his home at 409 E. Franklin St., Richmond, on Sept. 18, 1900. bur. Hollywood Cemetery.

PFOHL, WILLIAM JACOB. b. Salem, North Carolina, July 11, 1837. Lived in Forsyth Co. Sgt., Co. D, 21st North Carolina, May 22, 1861. Sgt. Major of the regt., Nov. 21, 1861, Capt., Co. L, 21st North Carolina, Apr. 26, 1862. Major - Aug. 3, 1863. Wded. thigh at Gettysburg. KIA at Cedar Creek. bur. Moravian Cemetery, Winston-Salem.

PHILLIPS, JAMES JASPER. b. Nansemond Co., Jan. 23, 1832. gr. VMI, 1853. Teacher. m. Lou Emma Betts. Taught at VMI. 5′9″. Capt., Co. F, 9th Virginia, May 18, 1861. Major - June 1863. Lt. Col. - July 1, 1863. Colonel - July 4, 1863. POW at

Sayler's Creek, released July 25, 1865. Merchant in Norfolk and New York City. d. Feb. 11, 1908.

PHILLIPS, JEFFERSON CURLE. b. Elizabeth City Co., Sept. 30, 1821. m. Caroline Elizabeth Sinclair. Capt., Co. F, 3rd Virginia Cavalry, May 14, 1861. Major - Oct. 4, 1861. Lt. Col., 13th Virginia Cavalry, July 12, 1862. A court found Phillips guilty of AWOL in June 1863. Colonel - Dec. 19, 1863. Wded. in head "slightly" at Ashland, June 1, 1864. Resigned Feb. 11, 1865. Farmer in Hampton, Virginia. d. near Hampton, June 6, 1910. bur. on old Phillips Farm, near Ft. Worth St.

PHILLIPS, PLEASANT JACKSON. b. July 3, 1819. Occupation in 1860–"none," net worth $77,500. Colonel, 31st Georgia, Nov. 19, 1861. Resigned May 13, 1862. Became a Brigadier General of Georgia State Troops. Banker in Brunswick. d. Oct. 12, 1876, at Wynnton. bur. Linwood Cemetery, Columbus.

PHILLIPS, WILLIAM. b. Asheville, North Carolina, July 8, 1824. att. U. Georgia. Colonel, Phillips Legion (Georgia), Aug. 2, 1861. Resigned due to "paralysis," Feb. 13, 1863. Later was Major, 9th Battalion Cavalry, Georgia State Guard. Marietta lawyer. d. Marietta, Sept. 24, 1908. bur. Marietta City Cemetery.

PHIPPS, RICHARD WRIGHT. b. Marshall Co., Tennessee, Oct. 1, 1833. Moved to Oxford, Mississippi, in 1843. gr. U. Mississippi, 1852, as valedictorian. Lt., Co. F, 19th Mississippi, June 7, 1861. Captain - Jan. 1863. Major - Oct. 8, 1863. Lt. Col. - Jan. 20, 1864. Colonel - May 12, 1864. Appx. In Mississippi legisl. d. Terra Ceia, Florida, Oct. 21, 1912. bur. Myrtle Hill Cemetery, Tampa.

PICKENS, SAMUEL BONNEAU. b. July 13, 1839 in Pendleton, South Carolina. gr. SCMA. Lt. of Infantry, P.A.C.S., Mar. 16, 1861. Apptd. Lt. Col., 12th Alabama, June 1, 1862. Colonel - Sept. 14, 1862. Wded. at South Mountain and on May 10, 1864, at Spotsylvania. Wded. in hand, Sept. 19, 1864. Paroled at Farmville, Virginia. Railway employee post-war. d. Nov. 17, 1892. bur. St. Paul's Episcopal Church, Charleston.

PICKETT, JESSE HAVIS. b. Apr. 12, 1828, in North Carolina. Physician in Weston, Georgia. Capt., Co. K, 17th Georgia, Aug.

15, 1861. Major - June 9, 1862. Severely wded. at 2nd Manassas. Resigned Jan. 5, 1864. m. Lavina M. Harper. d. Dec. 15, 1903.

PIERSON, SCIPIO FRANCIS. Lt., DeGournay's Battery (Louisiana), Apr. 9, 1861. Major of artillery - Mar. 27, 1862. Commanded artillery bn. at Sharpsburg. Chief of Artillery, D. H. Hill's Division. Sent to Europe on ordnance duty, 1863-64. Reported to E. Kirby Smith in Texas, July 1864.

PINCKARD, LUCIUS. b. Aug. 4, 1841. att. U. Alabama. Lived in Tuskegee. Adj., 14th Alabama, Nov. 16, 1861. Lt. Col. - July 18, 1862. Colonel - Oct. 3, 1863. Wded. at Salem Church. Wded. and POW at Gettysburg, exchanged late in 1864. Macon Co. sheriff, 1884-88. m. Fannie L. Graves, 1865. Atlanta, Georgia, insurance man in 1900.

PINCKARD, WILLIAM E. b. Georgia. Farmer in Tuskegee in 1860, age 29. Capt., Co. A, 59th Alabama, May 21, 1863. Major, 61st Alabama, May 2, 1863 (actually done on Apr. 20, 1864, but backdated). POW at Petersburg, Apr. 2, 1865, aged 33, height 6'3"; released July 25.

PLAYER, SAMUEL THOMAS. Lawyer in Irwinton, Georgia. m. Nancy Ann Freeman. Capt., Co. A, 49th Georgia, Mar. 4, 1862. Major - Sept. 9, 1862. Lt. Col. - May 8, 1863. Colonel - June 9, 1863. Eelected to Georgia Senate and resigned, Mar. 24, 1864. Farmer in Wilkinson Co. in 1870.

POAGE, THOMAS. b. near Staunton, Jan. 1, 1825. Pulaski Co. lawyer. m. Mary A. Vermillion. Capt., Co. I, 50th Virginia, June 25, 1861. Colonel - May 25, 1862. KIA on the Blackwater River, Jan. 30, 1863.

POAGUE, WILLIAM THOMAS. b. Rockbridge Co., Dec. 20, 1835. gr. Washington College, 1857. Lawyer in St. Joseph, Missouri, pre-war. Lt., Rockbridge Artillery (Virginia), Apr. 1861. Captain - Apr. 22, 1862. Major - Mar. 2, 1863, assigned to McIntosh's Bn. Lt. Col. - Feb. 27, 1864. In Virginia legisl. Treasurer of VMI, 1885-1913. m. Sarah Josephine Moore, 1878. d. Lexington, Sept. 8, 1914. bur. near T. J. Jackson in Lexington.

POINDEXTER, PARKE. b. Sept. 5, 1826. Of Chesterfield Co. att. U. Virginia and Hampden-Sydney. Lt., Co. I, 14th Virginia,

May 11, 1861. Captain - May 5, 1862. Lt. Col. - July 3, 1863. MWIA in eight places, near Suffolk, Apr. 24, 1863. Died of his wounds, Oct. 28, 1863.

PONS, JOHN M. b. Florida. Living in Pensacola in 1860, age 21. Capt., Co. I, 8th Florida, May 14, 1862. Lt. Col. - July 5, 1862. Resigned Oct. 29, 1862.

POORE, ROBERT HENRY. b. May 31, 1823. Lived in Fluvanna Co. att. U. Virginia. m. Janetta Bankhead Magruder. Capt., Co. C, 14th Virginia, May 10, 1861 (he'd been commanding this volunteer unit since Apr. 1860). Major - Aug. 26, 1862. KIA at Gettysburg.

PORTERFIELD, GEORGE ALEXANDER. b. Berkeley Co., Nov. 24, 1822. gr. VMI, 1844. Mexican War officer. m. Emily Terrill. Colonel and Inspector General of a Virginia Division at Harpers Ferry, Apr. 24, 1861. Colonel, 25th Virginia, July 1861. Most of the regiment was captured, leaving Porterfield without a command. Colonel and "Chief of Ordnance" of Loring's army, Aug. 9, 1861. His home was looted by Federal sympathizers, his 12-year-old son was accidently shot by a playmate in 1862, and Porterfield was arrested and paroled by Banks in June 1862. Charlestown banker post-war. d. Charlestown, Feb. 27, 1919. bur. Martinsburg.

POWELL, RICHARD HOLMES. b. Monticello, Georgia, Nov. 2, 1821. att. Emory U. att. Randolph-Macon. Lawyer in Union Springs, Alabama. Capt., Co. D, 3rd Alabama, Apr. 26, 1861. Major - Aug. 20, 1863. Wded. at Malvern Hill, and in the calf at Spotsylvania. POW at Chancellorsville. Retired to Invalid Corps, Feb. 22, 1865. In Alabama legisl. Published a history of the 3rd Alabama in a Union Springs newspaper, 1866-67. d. Union Springs, 1884.

POWELL, ROBERT MICHAEL. b. Montgomery Co., Alabama, 1826. Moved to Texas in 1849. Lawyer. In Texas legisl. Capt., Co. D, 5th Texas, Aug. 2, 1861. Enrolled at Harrisburg. Major - Aug. 22, 1862. Lt. Col. - Aug. 30, 1862. Colonel - Nov. 1, 1862. Wded. through the body and POW at Gettysburg, released Feb.

2, 1865. Appx. Moved to St. Louis in 1882, lived at 4314 Maryland Avenue. Died of pneumonia, in St. Louis, on Jan. 15, 1916.

POWELL, THOMAS N. b. Donaldsonville, Louisiana, 1840. Planter near New Orleans. Lt., Co. C, 10th Louisiana, July 22, 1861. Captain - Jan. 17, 1862. Major - June 1863. Wounded at Spotsylvania. Killed in action at Petersburg, Apr. 2, 1865.

PRADOS, JOHN BAPTISTE EUGENE. b. New Orleans, Nov. 12, 1836. Bookkeeper in New Orleans. m. Emma Marie Icard, 1857. Major, 8th Louisiana, June 19, 1861. Defeated at April 1862 re-org. Later served as a brigade QM. Killed while pursuing a deserter aboard the schooner *Virtue*, on Lake Pontchartrain, Jan. 21, 1863. bur. St. Louis Cemetery, New Orleans.

PRESSLEY, JOHN GOTEA. b. Williamsburg Dist., South Carolina, May 24, 1833. gr. SCMA, 1851. Lawyer and in South Carolina legisl. Capt., Co. E, 1st South Carolina (Hagood's), Sept. 5, 1861. The company transferred to the 11th South Carolina Bn. (Eutaw Bn.) at the April 1862 re-org. When that bn. expanded into the 25th South Carolina, July 22, 1862, Pressley became Lt. Col. Lost an arm at Port Walthall. City attorney and judge in Suisun City and Santa Rosa, California. d. Santa Rosa, July 5, 1895. bur. there.

PRESTON, JAMES FRANCIS. b. Montgomery Co., Virginia, Nov. 8, 1813. att. USMA, resigned after 2½ years due to an extended illness. Capt. of a Virginia company during the Mexican War. Colonel, 4th Virginia, July 1861. Wded. at 1st Manassas. Died in Montgomery Co. of disease, said to have been induced by the Manassas wound, on Jan. 20, 1862. Wife - Sarah Ann Caperton.

PRESTON, JOHN THOMAS LEWIS. b. Lexington, Apr. 25, 1811. m. (1) Sara Lyle Caruthers, 1832. m. (2) Margaret Junkin Preston, the poetess, 1857. Preston was among the founders of VMI, and served on its staff, 1839-1882. Marched to Richmond with T. J. Jackson and the VMI cadets. Lt. Col., Army of Virginia, May 1, 1861. Lt. Col., 9th Virginia, July 7, 1861. After brief service with the 9th Virginia at Craney Island, Preston was assigned as a.a.g. to T. J. Jackson on Oct. 22, 1861. Ordered back to VMI, Dec. 27, 1861. Author of several books, and is well covered in his wife's literature. d. July 15, 1890. Preston's diary for 1861 is at the Library of Congress.

PRESTON, ROBERT TAYLOR. b. May 26, 1809. Colonel on duty at Lynchburg, May 1861. Colonel, 28th Virginia, July 1, 1861. Dropped at Apr. 1862 re-org. Became Colonel, 4th Virginia Reserves and Colonel, 5th Virginia State Line. He was distinguished by "snow white hair, a long white beard and flaming blue eyes." d. June 20, 1880.

PRICE, FELIX L. b. 1835. gr. Georgtetown, 1858. Lived in Jackson, Georgia. m. Mary Eugenia McCalla. Capt., Co. I, 14th Georgia, July 12, 1861. Major - July 17, 1861. Lt. Col. - Aug. 18, 1861. Colonel - Dec. 9, 1861. Lt. Patterson of the 14th Georgia wrote to his wife in Nov. 1861 that Price was on trial for "drunkness and improper conduct toward a lady." Wded. at Cedar Mountain. Resigned Oct. 23, 1862.

PRICE, WILLIAM J. b. 1804. Lived in New Hanover Co. Lt. Col., 8th North Carolina, May 16, 1861. POW at Roanoke Island, Feb. 1862. Resigned due to age and health, Oct. 25, 1862. d. June 26, 1868.

PRIDE, RODOLPHUS T. b. June 20, 1827. Capt., Co. B, 31st Georgia, Oct. 5, 1861. Major - July 1, 1863. Lt. Col. - Feb. 1864. Resigned Aug. 19, 1864. Wded. at Gaines' Mill, 2nd Manassas and Wilderness. d. Apr. 19, 1869, of pneumonia, leaving a childless widow. bur. Linwood Cemetery, Columbus, Georgia.

PRIDEMORE, AUBURN LORENZO. b. Scott Co., June 27, 1837. Capt., Co. C, 21st Virginia Bn., Aug. 1861. Major - 1862. Lt. Col. - Dec. 1862. Colonel, 64th Virginia, Oct. 1863. Lee Co. attorney. In Virginia legisl. In U.S. Congress. d. Lee Co., May 17, 1900. bur. Hill Cemetery, Jonesville.

PRITCHETT, J. WALTER. Lt. Col., 22nd Georgia, Aug. 31, 1861. Resigned June 2, 1862, because of drunkenness.

PROSKAUER, ADOLPH. b. Breslau, Germany, Nov. 11, 1838. Moved to U.S. in 1854. Cotton merchant in Mobile, Alabama. Corporal, Co. C, 12th Alabama, May 27, 1861. Major - Jan. 14,

1863. Wded. in abdomen at Sharpsburg, and at Chancellorsville and Spotsylvania. Retired to Invalid Corps, Jan. 12, 1865, and assigned to post duty at Mobile. "The best dressed man in the regiment . . . very handsome." Proskauer was sharply at odds with Col. Pickens. Wife - Julia. Served in Alabama legisl., 1869. Moved to St. Louis in 1895, where he was a leading businessman and president of a Hebrew congregation. d. St. Louis, Dec. 13, 1900. bur. Mt. Sinai Cemetery.

PRYOR, WILLIAM HAMLIN. b. Sept. 25, 1827. gr. VMI, 1848. Wife - Margaret H. Lt., Co. C, 3rd Virginia, Nov. 13, 1861. Adj. of regt., Jan. 1862. Captain - Apr. 27, 1862. Major - Sept. 24, 1862. Lt. Col. - July 3, 1863 (actually done on Aug. 20, 1864, and backdated). Paroled in Richmond, May 12, 1865. d. Feb. 28, 1912.

PUCKETT, WILLIAM B. C. b. South Carolina, Apr. 7, 1822. Farmer in Cherokee Co., Georgia. Capt., Co. C, Cav. Bn. of Phillips Legion (Georgia), June 22, 1861. Major - July 9, 1862. Ordered to Georgia with Genl. Young, Nov. 25, 1864. Member of the 1865 Georgia Constitutional Convention and in the state legisl. 1877-79.

PULLER, JOHN WILLIAM. b. Gloucester Co. Hotel keeper at Gloucester Court House in 1860, age 26. m. Emily Simcoe. Capt., Co. A, 5th Virginia Cav., May 7, 1861. Major - Dec. 18, 1862. KIA at Kelly's Ford, Virginia, Mar. 17, 1863. bur. near Ark, Gloucester Co. Grandfather of Lewis B. "Chesty" Puller, USMC.

PULLIAM, ANDREW J. b. Georgia. Merchant at Buena Vista, Mississippi in 1860, age 23, worth $5,000. Lt., Co. A, 17th Mississippi, Apr. 22, 1861. Captain - Aug. 26, 1861. Lt. Col. - Jan. 1, 1864. Colonel - Feb. 26, 1864. Wded. and POW at Gettysburg, exchanged Feb. 24, 1865.

PURDIE, THOMAS JAMES. b. Bladen Co., June 22, 1830. Farmer there. Lt., Co. K, 18th North Carolina, Apr. 26, 1861. Captain - July 26, 1861. Lt. Col. - Mar. 24, 1862. Colonel - Nov. 11, 1862. KIA at Chancellorsville.

PYLES, LEWIS G. b. Florida. Living in Newnansville in 1860, age 29, occupation - "Reg. Land Office." Major, 2nd Florida,

July 13, 1861. Lt. Col. - May 11, 1862. Colonel - Aug. 28, 1862. Retired to Invalid Corps, July 12, 1864. A bad wound at Seven Pines, from which he "never recovered," caused Pyles' death soon after the war.

QUATTLEBAUM, PAUL JONES. b. near Leesville, South Carolina, May 19, 1836. gr. USMA, 1857. Lt., U.S. Infantry, 1857-61. Lt. of infantry, P.A.C.S., appt. from South Carolina, Mar. 16, 1861. Major, 5th Texas, Oct. 2, 1861. Transferred to be a.a.g. to Genl. Wigfall, commanding the brigade, Nov. 2, 1861, and quite promptly resigned. Later in the war he was Lt. Col. and a.a.g. Engineer in Mobile post-war. Died Jan. 4, 1883, at Columbus, Georgia. bur. Covington, Kentucky.

RADCLIFFE, JAMES DILLARD. b. Columbia, Apr. 17, 1832. gr. SCMA, 1854. m. Elizabeth Drane Brown. Principal of a military school in Wilmington. Colonel, 18th North Carolina, July 18, 1861. Defeated at Apr. 1862 re-org. Colonel, 61st North Carolina, Aug. 30, 1862. POW at Kinston, Dec. 1862. Wded. by shell concussion, July 1864. Resigned Oct. 11, 1864, "under charges." Mercantile business in Georgia post-war. d. July 16, 1890, probably in New York City.

RADFORD, JOHN TAYLOR. b. Montgomery Co., July 4, 1838. gr. U. Virginia. Capt., Co. K, 24th Virginia, May 1861. Major, 4th Virginia State Line, 1862. A.d.c. to Genl. Wharton. Lt. Col., 22nd Virginia Cav., Nov. 9, 1863. KIA at Cedarville, Virginia, Nov. 12, 1864.

RADFORD, RICHARD CARLTON WALKER. b. Bedford Co., July 8, 1822. att. VMI. gr. USMA, 1845. Lt. and Capt., U.S. Cavalry, 1845-56. Colonel, 2nd Virginia Cav., May 8, 1861. Dropped at April 1862 re-org. Later was Colonel, 1st Virginia State Line. Bedford Co. planter. d. Bedford Co., Nov. 2, 1886. An old army comrade wrote of Radford: "a narrow, foolish Virginian, with little information but honest."

RAINEY, ALEXIS THEODORE. b. Tuscaloosa Co., Alabama, June 5, 1822. m. Anna Elizabeth Quarles, 1852. Moved to Palestine, Texas, 1854. Lawyer and Texas legisl. Capt., Co. H, 1st Texas, June 24, 1861. Major - Oct. 1, 1861. Lt. Col. - Oct. 21,

1861. Colonel - Jan. 3, 1862. Severely wounded at Gaines' Mill. Assigned to a command around Houston, Texas, Sept. 4, 1863. "Dropped" by order of the Secretary of War, July 15, 1864. Died in Elkhart, Texas, May 1891.

RAMSAY, WHITEFORD SMITH. b. Milledgeville, June 8, 1839. gr. Oglethorpe College. m. Henrietta Jane Guyton. Capt., Co. H, 14th Georgia, July 9, 1861. Lt. Col. - July 16, 1861. Resigned due to "ill health and extreme youth," Aug. 18, 1861. Baptist preacher and teacher in Dublin, Georgia. d. there, March 16, 1900. bur. Dublin.

RAMSEY, JAMES N. b. Newton Co., June 21, 1821. att. Randolph - Macon. Lawyer in Hamilton, Georgia. State legislator. In Secession Convention. Colonel, 1st Georgia, Apr. 3, 1861. Resigned Dec. 3, 1861. d. Nov. 10, 1869, in Columbus. bur. Linwood Cemetery.

RAMSEY, WILLIAM HENRY. b. April 10, 1831. m. Rebecca Ann Mahan. Pittsylvania Co. farmer. Capt., Co. E, 57th Virginia, June 29, 1861. Lt. Col. - July 5, 1863. Wded. shoulder at Gettysburg. Appx. On Pittsylvania Co. Board of Supervisors. d. Gretna, Virginia, Oct. 19, 1915. A photo of Ramsey is in the centennial booklet about Pittsylvania Co. soldiers.

RAND, OSCAR RIPLEY. b. Feb. 15, 1833. Of Raleigh. gr. UNC, 1854. m. Olivia Hall. Capt., Co. D, 26th North Carolina, May 29, 1861. Lt. Col. - Sept. 25, 1862, but the commission was "cancelled." POW at New Bern, Mar. 14, 1862. Lawyer and farmer. Died Jan. 29, 1904.

RANDOLPH, EDWARD GRAVES. b. Fairfield Dist., South Carolina, July 4, 1829. m. Mary Esther Thompson, 1854. Capt., Co. D, 9th Louisiana, June 17, 1861. Lt. Col. - July 7, 1861. Colonel - Aug. 1861. "Thrown out at re-organization," April 1862. One of his men described Randolph as an "excellent disciplinarian and drill-master . . . a rather reserved and studious man." d. Grant Parish, Louisiana, Sept. 16, 1893. bur. Rapides Cemetery, Pineville, Louisiana.

RANDOLPH, PEYTON. b. Sept. 23, 1833, Frederick Co., Virginia. gr. Columbian College. Lt. of Infantry, P.A.C.S., Jan. 7,

1862. A.a.g. to Rodes, 1862. Lt. and Provost Marshal with Armistead, Sept. 1862. Capt. and engineer officer on Armistead's staff, May 1863. Major, 1st Confederate Engineers, Apr. 1, 1864. Appx. m. Mary Elmslie Fisher. Railroad executive. d. Nov. 28, 1888. A lieutenant in the regiment called Randolph "a very nice gentleman and strict officer." (Two good sources use an 1891 death date.)

RANDOLPH, ROBERT. b. Nov. 18, 1835. Capt., Co. H, 4th Virginia Cavalry, Apr. 25, 1861. Major - Sept. 4, 1863. Lt. Col. - Sept. 1, 1863 (backdated from Feb. 11, 1864). KIA at Meadow Bridge, May 12, 1864. Several of the numerous sources available on Randolph attribute the middle name "Lee" to him, and give his birth year as 1837. Both of the most reliable sources, however, show name and birth as above. bur. "Eastern View," Fauquier Co. Randolph's war letters are in the Minor family papers at the Virginia Historical Society.

RANDOLPH, WILLIAM WELLFORD. b. Clarke Co., Feb. 20, 1837. att. Univ. Virginia. Occupation at enlistment - "laborer." m. Ada Stuart in 1863, and had one son. Pvt., Co. C, 2nd Virginia, June 1, 1861. Capt. - Apr. 20, 1862. In Virginia legisl., 1863-64. Lt. Col., 2nd Virginia, Apr. 26, 1864. KIA at Wilderness. bur. Old Chapel, Millwood.

RANKIN, NATHANIEL PATTERSON. Of Guilford Co. Capt., Co. F, 26th North Carolina, July 15, 1861, aged 33. Major - Mar. 25, 1862. Dropped at April 1862 re-org. Became Capt., Co. I, 5th North Carolina Cavalry.

RANKIN, RUFUS M. Major, 37th North Carolina, Apr. 1862. Present into 1865. (Although it cannot be positively proved, this man is probably William R. Rankin in garbled form. The CSR is very weak, and mixed in with that of WRR.) Further information developed for the third edition confirms the view that Rufus M. Rankin did *not* exist.

RANKIN, SAMUEL C. b. Guilford, North Carolina. Teacher. 5′11″. Lt., Co. B, 45th North Carolina, Feb. 24, 1862, aged 30. Captain - Sept. 1, 1862. Major - May 30, 1864, while a prisoner.

Wded. foot and POW at Gettysburg, paroled Mar. 14, 1865. m. Martha Thom. bur. Fayetteville, North Carolina.

RANKIN, WILLIAM RUFUS. b. Gaston, North Carolina, March 7, 1823. m. Sara E. Stowe, 1856. Farmer. 5′9″. Capt., Co. H, 37th North Carolina, Oct. 6, 1861. Major - March 27, 1862. Dropped at April 1862 re-org. Captain in the 87th North Carolina Militia, May 1862. Rankin was Sergeant-Major of the 28th North Carolina from Apr. 1863 to the end of the war. Inspector of whiskey distilleries in North Carolina. d. Belmont, North Carolina, Nov. 17, 1883. bur. Goshen graveyard. (See Rufus M. Rankin, above.)

RANKIN, WILLIAM S. b. Nov. 11, 1834. Of Guilford Co. Wife - Mildred. Lt., Co. M, 21st North Carolina, June 8, 1861. Captain - Feb. 1, 1862. Major - Aug. 28, 1862. Lt. Col. - Mar. 12, 1863. Wded. thigh and POW at Gettysburg, exchanged in Mar. 1865. Died Jan. 12, 1899. bur. Presbyterian Cemetery, Greensboro.

RAY, DUNCAN WILLIAM. b. Columbia, South Carolina, Mar. 11, 1812. gr. U. Pennsylvania, M.D., 1842. Capt., Co. B, 9th South Carolina, Apr. 8, 1861. Lt. Col. - July 12, 1861. The 9th South Carolina was dissolved at the April 1862 re-org. d. Richland Co., Oct. 18, 1868.

READ, JOHN HARLESTON, SR. b. Charleston, South Carolina, Oct. 14, 1815. gr. Harvard, 1836. m. Esther J. Lance. Lived in Georgetown, South Carolina. Capt., Co. A, 21st South Carolina, Dec. 20, 1861. Major - May 17, 1864. Retired to Invalid Corps, Oct. 10, 1864. Served in South Carolina legisl. for "25 years." d. Sept. 1, 1866. bur. St. Paul's Episcopal Church, Charleston. Read's son and namesake was an officer in the same company, and the two are easily confused. The son's dates were 7-25-1843 to 1-30-1912.

READ, JOHN POSTELL WILLIAMSON. b. Savannah, Georgia, Apr. 21, 1829. Savannah Chief of Police, 1856-1858. Capt., Co. K, 10th Georgia, 1861. This unit was transferred to artillery service and became Pulaski Artillery (Georgia), later known as Fraser's Georgia Battery. Major of artillery - Mar. 2, 1864, assigned to Hilary Jones' Bn. Lt. Col. - Nov. 5, 1864. d. Lynchburg, Virginia, Sept. 28, 1884.

READING, THOMAS R. b. Mississippi. Merchant in Vicksburg. Enlisted at Vicksburg as Lt., Co. C, 19th Mississippi, May 14, 1861. Lt. and a.d.c. to Genl. C. M. Wilcox, April to June, 1862, and briefly with Featherston. Captain, Co. C, 19th Mississippi, Jan. 1863. Major - July 14, 1863. Resigned Oct. 8, 1863. Reading's age at enlistment was given as 20 years. d. Oct. 25, 1876, age 36, in Vicksburg, of consumption.

READY, HORACE. Student in Murfreesboro in 1860, age 22, living at home. Lt., Co. K, 23rd Tennessee, Aug. 23, 1861. Adj. of regt., 1861. Major - 1862. Lt. Col. - Dec. 16, 1862. Colonel - June 30, 1864. Wded. at Chickamauga, and in the leg at Petersburg, Apr. 2, 1865. Appx.

REDDEN, RAYMOND DIAL. b. Lancaster Dist., South Carolina. m. Elizabeth Katherine Kirk. Attended medical school in New Orleans. Physician in Pickens, Lamar and Fayette counties, Alabama. Capt., Co. K, 26th Alabama, Dec. 7, 1861. Major - June 30, 1862. Res. Dec. 4, 1862. Moved to DeLeon, Texas, in 1873, and later died there.

REDWINE, MARTIN C. b. Mississippi. Merchant. Unmarried. Pvt., Co. F, 2nd Louisiana, May 9, 1861, age 26. Captain - May 1, 1862. Major - May 12, 1864. KIA at Winchester, Sept. 19, 1864.

REEDER, WILLIAM C. Major, 26th Alabama, Mar. 27, 1862. Lt. Col. - June 20, 1862. Dropped on Nov. 3, 1862, due to a prolonged absence.

REEDY, JOHN W. b. Alabama. Farmer in Union Co., Arkansas, in 1860, age 30, worth $8,900. Mexican War veteran. Enrolled at Three Creeks, Arkansas, on June 19, 1861, as Capt., Co. G, 3rd Arkansas. Major - Jan. 19, 1863. KIA at Chickamauga. bur. Marietta, Georgia, Confederate Cemetery. A member of the regiment called Reedy: "a good drill officer, but very wicked."

REEVES, RICHARD E. Of Surry Co. Capt., Co. A, 28th North Carolina, May 4, 1861, aged 40. Major - Sept. 21, 1861. Dropped at April 1862 re-org.

REGER, ALBERT G. b. Dec. 25, 1818. Lawyer in Barbour Co. In Va. Senate, 1850-1856. Major, 25th Virginia, during the first year of the war. An extremely inadequate service record shows Reger signing requisitions and other documents between Oct. 1861 and March 1862. He had been Capt., Co. H, 31st Virginia, in May 1861. Resigned March 25, 1862. Lawyer in Barbour Co. in 1880.

REID, JAMES SIDNEY. b. Oct. 25, 1830. m. Virginia Warren. Farmer in Morgan Co., worth $90,830 in 1860. Capt., Co. D, 3rd Georgia, Apr. 24, 1861. Lt. Col. - May 10, 1861. Resigned June 17, 1862. d. Sept. 25, 1896. bur. Madison City Cemetery.

REID, LEGH WILBER. b. Brentsville, Virginia, April 15, 1833. gr. VMI, 1858. Lt. Col., 36th Virginia, July 15, 1861. Wded. near Ft. Donelson, Feb. 23, 1862. Dropped at May 1862 re-org. Later served in the 17th Virginia Cavalry and was wounded, losing a leg, near Woodstock, Virginia, in Oct. 1864. m. Emma Catherine Jackson, daughter of William A. Jackson (q.v.), 1865. Railroad man and U. S. Treasury official. d. Alexandria, Nov. 26, 1908. bur. Ivy Hill Cemetery.

REILLY, JAMES. b. Athlone, County Westmeath, Ireland, on April 24, 1822. Lived in New Jersey and Maryland. Joined U. S. Army as enlisted artilleryman, fought in the ranks in Florida and Mexico, and stayed in the U. S. Army until 1861. m. Annie Quinn, 1848. Lt., Ellis Light Artillery (North Carolina), May 31, 1861. Capt., Rowan Artillery (North Carolina), June 28, 1861. Major of artillery - Sept. 7, 1863. POW at Ft. Fisher, early 1865, released May 15. d. Washington, North Carolina, Nov. 5, 1894. bur. Oakdale Cemetery. The soldiers called Reilly "Old Tarantula," and said he was "rough, gruff, grizzly, and brave."

RENTFRO, WILLIAM H. Lt., Co. E, 27th Georgia, Aug. 9, 1861. Captain - Dec. 20, 1861. Major - June 24, 1864. MWIA at Bentonville, died in Smithville, North Carolina, Apr. 6, 1865.

REYNOLDS, ARTHUR EXUM. b. Smith Co., Tennessee, Nov. 29, 1817. gr. Clinton College, Tennessee. m. Minerva Driver. Lawyer in Jacinto, Mississippi. Colonel, 26th Mississippi, Sept. 10, 1861. POW at Ft. Donelson. Absent on detail, Apr.-June

1864. Wded. at Weldon R.R., Aug. 1864. Paroled at Meridian, Mississippi, May 12, 1865. Judge and lawyer postwar. d. Corinth, Apr. 1882. bur. Jacinto Cemetery.

REYNOLDS, REUBEN OSCAR. b. Columbia Co., Georgia, Oct. 9, 1832. gr. U. Georgia and U. Virginia. Lawyer in Aberdeen, Mississippi. Lt., Co. I, 11th Mississippi, Feb. 20, 1861. Captain - May 1862. Major - Sept. 25, 1862. Colonel - Dec. 1, 1864. Wded. at Gaines' Mill and Gettysburg. Lost right arm on March 25, 1865. m. Sarah B. Young, 1865. In Mississippi legisl. Attorney General and Lt. Governor of Mississippi. d. Aberdeen, Sept. 4, 1887.

REYNOLDS, SAMUEL H. b. Virginia, June 1827. gr. USMA, 1849. Lt., U. S. Infantry, 1849-61. Colonel, 31st Virginia, apparently on Sept. 17, 1861. Resigned Nov. 28, 1861. At one point Reynolds was apptd. Lt. Col., 51st Virginia, but declined the commission. His record, as is that of most officers of the 25th and 31st Virginia Inf. Regiments, is very poorly preserved. d. Columbia, Tennessee, 1867.

RHETT, THOMAS SMITH. b. South Carolina, Feb. 25, 1827. gr. USMA, 1848. Lt., U. S. Artillery, 1848-55. Baltimore bank clerk, 1855-61. Capt. of artillery, P.A.C.S., Nov. 19, 1861, ordered to Charleston. Colonel of artillery (temporary rank) - May 10, 1862, and placed in charge of all batteries defending Richmond. Sent abroad to purchase arms in Oct. 1863. Lived in Baltimore post-war. d. Dec. 26, 1893.

RICE, EVAN. Farmer in Essex Co. in 1860, age 37. Capt., Co. A, 55th Virginia, Apr. 28, 1861. Major - June 30, 1862. Lt. Col. - May 2, 1863. POW at Falling Waters, July 14, 1863, exchanged Dec. 1864. Rice was among the "Immortal 600."

RICE, WILLIAM GEORGE. b. Union Dist., Dec. 9, 1831. gr. South Carolina College, 1851. Farmer in Laurens District, worth $28,000. Capt., Co. A, 3rd South Carolina Battalion, Nov. 5, 1861. Major - Jan. 31, 1862. Lt. Col. - Sept. 14, 1862. Retired Jan. 12, 1865, due to a gunshot wound in the thigh, which he had received at Knoxville. m. Sarah E. Sims. Living in Abbeville in 1899.

RICE, ZACHARIAH ARMISTEAD. b. Spartanburg, South Carolina, Sept. 22, 1822. Lt., Co. B, Cavalry Battalion of Cobb's Legion (Georgia), Aug. 14, 1861. Captain - Dec. 17, 1861. Major - Nov. 1, 1862. Resigned June 10, 1863, due to family and business considerations. Atlanta businessman, judge and City Councilman. d. Atlanta, July 2, 1890. bur. Oakland Cemetery, Atlanta.

RICH, WILLIAM W. Mexican War veteran. Capt., Co. B, Cavalry Battalion of Phillips Legion (Georgia), June 11, 1861, aged 38. Lt. Col. - July 9, 1862. Resigned Jan. 27, 1865, on disability. d. Apr. 26, 1892. bur. Oak Hill Cemetery, Cartersville.

RICHARDS, ADOLPHUS EDWARD. b. Loudoun Co., Virginia, May 26, 1844. att. Randolph-Macon. 5′10″. Entered Confederate service in the spring of 1862, as a Pvt. then Lt. in the 7th Virginia Cavalry. Lt. and v.a.d.c. to Genl. W. E. Jones, Feb. to May 1863. Pvt., Co. B, 43rd Virginia Cavalry Battalion, Oct. 1, 1863. Lt., Co. C, 43rd Virginia Cavalry Battalion, Dec. 7, 1863. Captain, Co. B, 43rd Virginia Cavalry Battalion, for "Valor & Skill," Apr. 6, 1864. Major, Mosby's Regiment Virginia Cavalry, Dec. 7, 1864. Paroled at Winchester, May 17, 1865. Lawyer and judge in Louisville, Kentucky, post-war. d. Louisville, Jan. 20, 1920.

RICHARDS, DANIEL T. b. July 9, 1836. Lt., Co. D, 6th Virginia Cavalry, Aug. 26, 1861. Captain - 1862. Lt. Col. - June 4, 1864. Wded. Sept. 25, 1864. Paroled Apr. 22, 1865. d. Aug. 3, 1872. bur. Presbyterian Cemetery, Gerrardstown, West Virginia.

RICHARDSON, ANDREW JACKSON. b. Louisa Co., Nov. 15, 1836. Fluvanna Co. lawyer. Pvt., Co. A, 23rd Virginia, May 15, 1861. Lt. - Nov. 5, 1861. Captain - Dec. 16, 1861. Major - Nov. 27, 1863. Wded. at Chancellorsville. In Virginia legisl., 1893-94. Louisa County Commissioner of Revenue for 37 years. d. Louisa, Apr. 13, 1912. bur. Bethpage Church of Disciples, near Frederickshall.

RICHARDSON, CHARLES b. 1835. Lived in Fredericksburg, Virginia. Lt. of artillery, P.A.C.S., Oct. 7, 1861. Major of artillery - March 1863. Lt. Col. - Feb. 27, 1864. Commanded A.N.

Va. Battalion. Badly wded. at Spotsylvania when a shell tore out a portion of his stomach. Paroled at Richmond, May 8, 1865. m. Charlotte Blaine, 1869. Owned a Fredericksburg pickle factory. d. Fredericksburg, Sept. 6, 1913, at his home, "Willis Hill." bur. Fredericksburg Confederate Cemetery, but has no grave marker. E. P. Alexander wrote that he "felt quite like preferring charges" against Richardson at Gettysburg.

RICHARDSON, GEORGE WILLIAM. b. Hanover Co., Sept. 23, 1819. att. William & Mary. Hanover Co. lawyer. In Virginia Secession Convention. Colonel, 47th Virginia, May 2, 1861. Dropped at May 1862 re-org., "because he was a disciplinarian." For the rest of the war, he steadily made application for a commission, but in vain.

RICHARDSON, JESSE MARTIN. b. Henry Co., Virginia, May 5, 1837. "Student" in 1860 census. Lt., Co. A, 42nd Virginia, June 15, 1861. Capt. - Apr. 21, 1862. Major - Nov. 29, 1863. Wded. at Gettysburg and Mine Run. MWIA in the side at Petersburg, Mar. 25, 1865.

RICHARDSON, JOHN HARVIE. b. Richmond, June 1828. Inaugurated street car firms in Cincinnati and St. Louis before the war. m. Catherine Churchill Hodges. Pre-war Virginia militia officer, and wrote an infantry manual which was issued as a Confederate imprint. Lt. Col., 46th Virginia, June 24, 1861. Colonel - May 17, 1862. Lost at May 1862 reorganization. Major, 39th Virginia Cavalry Battalion, Sept. 24, 1862. Present with this unit into 1865. Wded. at Gettysburg. Richmond city official and operator of a street car line. d. Richmond, Nov. 29, 1900.

RICHARDSON, JOHN MANLY. b. Sumter District, South Carolina, March 13, 1831. att. SCMA. att. U. Virginia. att. Harvard. On the staff of Hillsboro Military Academy in 1861. Major, 21st North Carolina, July 3, 1861. Resigned Jan. 28, 1862. Supt. of Georgia Military Institute, 1862-1863. Served later on Godwin's staff. Lost a leg at 3rd Winchester. Living in Texas in 1890. d. Feb. 4, 1898. This man is shown erroneously as *James* M. in most reference books.

RICHARDSON, JOHN QUINCY ADAMS. b. Portsmouth, Virginia, 1836. gr. VMI, 1857. Major, 52nd North Carolina, Apr. 29, 1862. KIA at Gettysburg.

RICHARDSON, WILLIAM JAMES. b. Portsmouth, Virginia, Feb. 29, 1828. Capt., Co. D, 9th Virginia, Apr. 27, 1861. Major - July 1, 1863, to rank from Oct. 30, 1862. Rank as Lt. Col. shows on two official documents, but the date of the commission was not discernible. POW at Gettysburg, paroled in early 1865. Portsmouth Police Commissioner post-war. d. Portsmouth, Feb. 5, 1902. bur. Oak Grove Cemetery, Portsmouth.

RICHMOND, JAMES BUCHANAN. b. Lee Co., Virginia, Feb. 27, 1842. att. Emory & Henry. Sgt., Co. A, 50th Virginia, 1861. Captain - 1862. Major, 64th Virginia, 1863. Lt. Col. - 1865. In Virginia legisl., 1874-75. County judge. In U. S. Congress, 1879-81. d. Baltimore, Maryland, Apr. 30, 1910. bur. Gate City, Virginia.

RIDDICK, RICHARD H. b. North Carolina. Lt., U. S. Cavalry, 1855-61. Of Gates Co. Lt. Col. and a.a.g. to Genl. Gatlin, June 1861. Adjutant General of North Carolina, July 1861. A.a.g. to Joseph R. Anderson, early 1862. Colonel, 34th North Carolina, Apr. 2, 1862. MWIA at Ox Hill, Sept. 1, 1862, d. Sept. 11.

RIERSON, JOHN W. b. Stokes Co., North Carolina. Farmer. 5′10″. Pvt., Co. G, 21st North Carolina, May 30, 1861, aged 24. Lt., Co. G, 53rd North Carolina, Apr. 30, 1862. Captain - May 15, 1862. Major - May 10, 1864. Wded. in the neck, Sept. 18, 1864. Detailed to the command of the 32nd North Carolina, Jan.-Feb. 1865. Wded. in the abdomen and POW near Petersburg, Mar. 25, 1865. Died near the end of the war and buried at Lynchburg, Virginia.

RIGHTOR, NICHOLAS H. b. Donaldsonville, Mar. 16, 1832. Capt., Co. E, 1st Louisiana Battalion, Apr. 16, 1861. Major - June 11, 1861. Resigned in June 1862. POW at Lafourche, July 15, 1863. m. Louise Scudday. Louisiana judge. d. New Orleans, Aug. 11, 1900.

RION, JAMES HENRY. b. Montreal, Canada, Apr. 17, 1828, son of an English army officer. gr. South Carolina College, 1850.

Winnsboro lawyer. Professor of mathematics. South Carolina militia colonel, 1858. m. Mary Catherine Weir. An address by Rion concerning South Carolina College was published in 1860. He was Colonel, 6th South Carolina, in early 1861, but lost the election when the regt. was put into Confederate service. Capt., Co. B, 7th South Carolina Battalion, Nov. 13, 1861. Major - Mar. 5, 1863. Lt. Col. - June 24, 1864. Rion was under arrest from Feb. 5 to May 21, 1862. In early 1863 he was detailed to command the 22nd South Carolina for a time. Wded. at Morris Island, 1863. d. Winnsboro, Dec. 12, 1886.

RIVERS, JONATHAN. b. Sept. 20, 1831. Justice of Inferior Court in Wilkinson Co. Lt., Co. F, 3rd Georgia, Apr. 26, 1861. Resigned Nov. 22, 1861. Pvt., Co. A, 49th Georgia, Mar. 4, 1862. Major - Mar. 22, 1862. Lt. Col. - Sept. 9, 1862. Wded. at Chantilly. Lost a leg at Chancellorsville and resigned on disability on June 9, 1863. d. Hawkinsville, March 31, 1875. bur. Orange Hill Cemetery.

ROBBINS, WILLIAM McKENDREE. b. Randolph Co., North Carolina, Oct. 26, 1828. gr. Randolph-Macon. Lawyer in Eufala, Alabama, Lt., Co. G, 4th Alabama, Apr. 24, 1861. Captain - Apr. 21, 1862. "Acting Major" - June 24, 1863. His actual commission seems to have been dated Oct. 3, 1863, although some confusion remains. Severely wded. in face at Wilderness. Appx. In Alabama legisl. In U. S. Congress, 1873-79. Served on the Gettysburg Battlefield Commission. d. Salisbury, North Carolina, May 5, 1905. bur. Statesville, North Carolina. His papers are at UNC.

ROBERTS, JOHN MILLER. b. June 24, 1813. m. Franky Mace. Farmer in Marion District in 1860, worth $25,000. Entered service on Nov. 10, 1861, as Capt., Co. H, 23rd South Carolina. Lt. Col. - Apr. 16, 1862. Wded. in knee at 2nd Manassas. Resigned for health reasons, Oct. 23, 1862, and died twelve days later.

ROBERTS, PHILETUS WOLCOTT. b. Feb. 2, 1828. Buncombe Co. lawyer. Lt., Co. F, 14th North Carolina, May 3, 1861. Captain - Sept. 20, 1861. Colonel - Apr. 27, 1862. Died of typhoid fever at 5 a.m. on July 5, 1862, at the residence of H. W. Tyler in Richmond. bur. Riverside Cemetery, Asheville, North Carolina.

ROBERTSON, JAMES EWEN. b. Appomattox Co., July 20, 1832. att. Washington College and Hampden-Sydney. Lived at Appomattox C. H. 6′1″. Capt., Co. A, 44th Virginia, Apr. 26, 1861. This unit became Co. A, 20th Bn. Virginia Heavy Artillery. Major, 20th Battalion Virginia Heavy Artillery, May 9, 1863. POW at Sayler's Creek, released July 25, 1865. Bedford Co. farmer post-war. d. Oklahoma City, June 12, 1907.

ROBERTSON, JAMES TOWNES. b. Abbeville, South Carolina, Aug. 19, 1832. Pvt., Co. D, 1st South Carolina, early 1861. Lt., Co. B, Orr's Rifles (1st South Carolina Rifles), July 1861. Captain - Aug. 29, 1862. Major - May 1864. Lt. Col. - July 28, 1864. Wded. at Fredericksburg. Claimed to have been in every battle and skirmish of the regiment. Appx. Abbeville farmer and merchant. m. Eugenia Ann Miller, 1872. In South Carolina legisl. d. Abbeville, Aug. 30, 1905. bur. Trinity Episcopal Church.

ROBERTSON, JOHN R. Captain of an independent company of Virginia Cavalry, the "Henry Rangers," Mar. 8, 1862. The company became Co. B, 32nd Virginia Cavalry Battalion, when that temporary bn. was organized Nov. 25, 1862. Robertson was made Major, 32nd Virginia Cavalry Battalion, at its organization. The bn. was merged with other units into the 42nd Virginia Cav. Bn. in Sept. 1863, Robertson being Major of the new bn. also. Further expansion in June 1864 resulted in the 24th Virginia Cav. Regt., of which Robertson became Major. He resigned Oct. 4, 1864. Lt. Col. T. G. Barham of the 24th wrote that Robertson "ran away with six companies" at Deep Bottom.

ROBINS, WILLIAM TODD. b. Gloucester Co., Virginia, Nov. 22, 1835. att. VMI. gr. Washington College. Wife - Sally M. Acting Sgt.-Major, 9th Virginia Cavalry, July 1861. Lt. and Adj., 9th Virginia Cavalry, Apr. 15, 1862. Capt., P.A.C.S., Oct. 30, 1862, ordered to report to W. H. F. Lee as a.a.g. Lt. Col., 40th Virginia Cavalry Battalion, July 15, 1863. Lt. Col., 42nd Virginia Cavalry Battalion (into which the 40th Bn. was merged), Sept. 24, 1863. Colonel, 24th Virginia Cavalry, June 14, 1864. Robins suffered an injured side from a falling tree in Feb. 1864 and was wded. in the arm Aug. 14, 1864, and again in the right foot ("very serious") on Oct. 26, 1864. Appx. Gloucester County lawyer. d. Richmond, Oct. 26, 1906. Buried in family cemetery, Gloucester Co.

ROBINSON, JOHN ARMSTEAD. b. Pruntytown, Taylor Co., Nov. 18, 1830. Merchant and postmaster at Fetterman. Capt., Co. A, 25th Virginia, May 13, 1861. Major - Oct. 8, 1862, Lt. Col. - between April and July 1863. Resigned Aug. 20, 1863, having been elected to the Virginia legisl. Paroled at Charlottesville, May 31, 1865. Farmer and merchant in Hampshire Co. In West Virginia legisl., 1877-79. d. Patterson's Creek, W. Va.

ROBINSON, WILLIAM GEORGE. b. Canada, Jan. 1836. Lived in Wake Co., North Carolina. gr. USMA, 1858. Lt., U. S. Army, 1858-61. Lt. Col., 2nd North Carolina Cavalry, Sept. 1, 1861. Colonel - Sept. 9, 1863. Wded. and POW at Gillett's Farm, April 13, 1862. Never rejoined the regiment. Dropped on May 25, 1864, having been detailed to the Navy Dept. by the Secretary of War. d. Feb. 1894.

ROGERS, ANDREW JACKSON. Lived in Warren and Granville Counties, North Carolina. Capt., Co. D, 8th North Carolina, May 16, 1861. POW at Roanoke Island. Major - June 7, 1864. Wded. at Morris Island. POW at Ft. Harrison, Sept. 30, 1864, released June 7, 1865.

ROGERS, ARTHUR LEE. b. Middleburg, Virginia, Oct. 21, 1831. att. VMI. Lawyer in Loudoun Co. Capt., Loudoun Artillery (Virginia), April 1861. Major of artillery - Sept. 26, 1862. Rogers was left out at the battalion re-organization in early 1863, but was present at Chancellorsville, where he was wounded and vacated his ambulance to give "Stonewall" Jackson a space. Rogers was "waiting orders" in Lexington, Virginia, for most of 1863-64. Rogers claimed to have designed one of the Confederate flags. d. Sept. 13, 1871. VMI has Rogers' uniform.

ROGERS, GEORGE THOMAS. b. Princess Anne Co., Virginia, Apr. 28, 1828. att. Kempsville Academy. He owned 11 slaves and a farm in 1860, but was impoverished by the war. Capt., Co. F, 6th Virginia, Apr. 22, 1861 (he had been commanding this volunteer unit since Dec. 1859). Major - Dec. 14, 1861. Colonel - May 3, 1862. Appx. m. (1) Louisa Green. m. (2) Sally C. Wise, 1870. City editor of a Norfolk newspaper. d. Princess Anne Co., Mar. 6, 1901. bur. family cemetery at Lynnhaven Farm.

ROGERS, HENRY A. b. 1833. Caswell Co. teacher. Lt., Co. D, 13th North Carolina, Apr. 17, 1861. Captain - Apr. 26, 1862. Major - Dec. 16, 1862. Lt. Col.- June 13, 1863. Wded. at Sharpsburg, Chancellorsville, and at Barnett's Ford, Virginia, Sept. 22, 1863. Retired to Invalid Corps, Oct. 19, 1864. d. 1884.

ROGERS, JAMES A. b. Northampton Co., Virginia, 1838. att. U. Virginia. Physician. 6′2″. Capt., Co. D, 54th North Carolina, June 3, 1862. Major - May 8, 1863. Applied for retirement in Aug. 1863, but was KIA at Drewry's Bluff, May 16, 1864.

ROGERS, JEFFERSON CARROLL. b. Lawrence Co., Tennessee, Mar. 24, 1824. Moved to Texas in 1852. m. Martha Reed. Capt., Co. G, 5th Texas, July 15, 1861. Major - Nov. 1, 1862. Wded. at Chickamauga and retired as a result on Oct. 25, 1864. Judge in Milam Co., Texas. d. Feb. 27, 1885. bur. Cameron, Texas.

ROGERS, JOHN VAN BUREN. b. Aug. 21, 1836, in Cherokee Co. Lt., Co. A, 2nd North Carolina Cavalry, June 18, 1861. Captain - Apr. 30, 1862. Major - June 23, 1864. Dropped on March 14, 1865, "desertion." Lived for a time in the Tennessee Soldiers' Home in Davidson Co. d. July 20, 1907.

ROGERS, LEONARD. Blacksmith in Pickens District in 1860, married, age 35. Lt., Co. C, 1st South Carolina Rifles, July 20, 1861. Captain - Sept. 1, 1863. Major - date unknown. POW at Spotsylvania, May 12, 1864, released June 16, 1865. bur. Moody family cemetery near Walhalla.

ROGERS, MATTHEW ROBERT. b. Assumption Paris, Louisiana, Oct. 23, 1836. Pvt., Co. C, 2nd Georgia Battalion, Apr. 20, 1861. Capt., Co. A, 45th Georgia, Feb. 1, 1862. Major - Oct. 13, 1862. Resigned May 6, 1863. m. Margaret Elizabeth Leyden. d. New Orleans, March 1911.

ROGERS, SAMUEL ST. GEORGE. b. Pulaski, Tennessee, June 30, 1832. Lawyer in Ocala, Florida, pre-war. In Florida legisl. Lt. Col., 2nd Florida, July 12, 1861. Defeated at May 1862 re-org. Later served in Marion Light Artillery (Florida) and as a Colonel on Beauregard's Military Court. In C. S. Congress, 1863-65. d. Sept. 11, 1880, while visiting in Terre Haute, Indiana.

ROGERS, SION HART. b. Raleigh, Sept. 30, 1825. gr. UNC, 1846. Wake Co. lawyer. Lt., Co. K, 14th North Carolina, May 21, 1861. Resigned Nov. 1861. Colonel, 47th North Carolina, Mar. 24, 1862. Resigned Jan. 5, 1863, having been elected Attorney General of North Carolina. In U. S. Congress, 1853-55 and 1871-73. d. Raleigh, Aug. 14, 1874.

RONALD, CHARLES ANDREW. b. Montgomery Co., Virginia, Jan. 18, 1827. Blacksburg lawyer. m. Sallie McCulloch, 1859. Pvt. in Preston's Co., Virginia Regt., Mexican War. Capt., Co. E, 4th Virginia, Apr. 18, 1861. Colonel - Apr. 23, 1862. Wded. in the thigh by a shell at Kearneysville, Virginia, Oct. 16, 1862. Resigned on Sept. 11, 1863, citing his wound and disease. In March 1865 he asked to be restored as a colonel. d. July 1, 1898. His grave marker in Blacksburg bears the enigmatic inscription: "I Have Suffered."

ROSS, ALBERT B. Corporal in "Macon Guards" during the Mexican War. Clerk of Court in 1860, age 34. Lt., Co. A, 20th Georgia, May 17, 1861. Captain - Sept. 14, 1861. Major - July 2, 1863. Resigned on May 8, 1864, to become Clerk of Courts in Bibb Co., Georgia. Ross still held that post in 1878. His diary is at the New York Historical Society.

ROSS, EGBERT A. b. Sept. 10, 1842. att. Hillsboro Military Academy. Lived in Mecklenburg Co. Capt., Co. C, 1st North Carolina (Bethel), Apr. 16, 1861. Mustered out - Nov. 13, 1861. Capt., Co. A, 11th North Carolina, Feb. 1, 1862. Major - May 6, 1862. KIA at Gettysburg, July 1, 1863. bur. Elmwood Cemetery, Charlotte, North Carolina.

ROSS, GEORGE W. b. Nov. 22, 1825, near Macon. Merchant in Bibb Co. in 1860, worth $65,000. Sgt., Co. C, 2nd Georgia Battalion, Apr. 20, 1861. Captain - May 17, 1861. Major - Apr. 20, 1862. MWIA at Gettysburg, July 2, 1863. d. Aug. 2. bur. Rose Hill Cemetery, Macon.

ROSS, JOHN DeHART. b. May 1, 1840, at "Bel Pre," Culpeper Co., Virginia. gr. VMI, 1859. Lived in Brandy Station. On the VMI staff, 1860-61. Lt. of engineers, on Loring's staff, July 1861. Major, 52nd Virginia, Aug. 1, 1862. Lt. Col. - June 6, 1863. Wded. at Cross Keys. Resigned Dec. 19, 1864. Enrolling officer at Staunton. m. Agnes J. Reid, 1862. Rockbridge Co. farmer. d. near Lexington, Dec. 12, 1912.

ROSSER, JOSEPH TRAVIS. b. Virginia, 1821. gr. U. Virginia. Petersburg lawyer. m. Mary Walker Armistead (1821-1857), a sister of Genl. L. A. Armistead. Territorial Secretary of Minnesota in 1853, and lawyer in Mankato, Minnesota, where a resident described him as "a kind, genial, courteous Virginia gentleman." Capt., Co. K, 10th Virginia Cavalry, June 1, 1861. Major - June 16, 1862. Resigned, due to health, Aug. 8, 1863. Rosser worked in the Treasury Dept. and the Conscript Bureau the rest of the war, despite his efforts to be reinstated in his commission. He died sometime prior to 1886.

ROWAN, WILLIAM SUMMERS. Clerk in a store at Gap Mills, Virginia in 1860, age 29. 5′10″. Lt., Co. A, 60th Virginia, May 16, 1861. This unit was actually Co. B, 59th Virginia, before it moved into the 60th Virginia. Captain - 1862. Major - May 9, 1864. Wded. in the mouth at Cloyd's Farm. POW at Winchester, Sept. 19, 1864, released June 20, 1865.

ROWE, DAVID PINKNEY. b. Newton, North Carolina, May 3, 1836. Catawba Co. carpenter. Lt., Co. A, 12th North Carolina, Apr. 27, 1861. Captain - Sept. 16, 1861. Major - July 1, 1862. Wded. at Gaines' Mill. MWIA at Chancellorsville, May 2, 1863, and died the next day - his 27th birthday.

ROWELL, CORNELIUS D. b. 1830 in Marion District. att. Jefferson Medical College, 1855. m. Martha Eliza Rowell, a cousin. Farmer in Marion District in 1860, worth $20,000. Capt., Co. C, 26th South Carolina, Mar. 22, 1862. Major - May 1, 1863. Wded. at Petersburg, July 1864. Resigned Oct. 29, 1864, due to chronic diarrhea. Preacher postwar. d. May 1, 1887, at Jonesville, South Carolina.

ROYSTON, YOUNG LEA. b. Perry Co., Alabama, June 22, 1819. gr. U. Alabama. 6'7½" tall! Selma lawyer. Capt., Co. A, 8th Alabama, May 2, 1861. Major - Mar. 20, 1862. Lt. Col. - May 5, 1862. Colonel - June 16, 1862. Wded. at Frayser's Farm and severely at Salem Church. Retired to post duty at Selma, Nov. 2, 1864. Selma lawyer and cotton dealer post-war. d. 1884.

RUFF, SOLON ZACKERY. b. 1837. gr. Georgia Military Institute, then taught math there. m. (1) Susan Volumia Varner. m. (2) Irene Arnold. Lt. Col., 18th Georgia, Apr. 25, 1861. WIA at 2nd Manassas. Colonel - Jan. 17, 1863. "Commanding in appearance, a fine tactician, and strict disciplinarian." KIA at Knoxville, Nov. 29, 1863. bur. Gibson family cemetery near Knoxville.

RUFFIN, THOMAS. b. Louisburg, North Carolina, Sept. 9, 1820. gr. UNC, 1841. Goldsboro lawyer. In U. S. Congress, 1853-61. Capt., Co. H, 1st North Carolina Cavalry, May 16, 1861. Major - June 29, 1863. Lt. Col. - July 23, 1863. Colonel - date not known. MWIA and POW at Auburn Mills, Virginia, Oct. 15, 1863. Died in a Yankee hospital in Alexandria, Oct. 18. bur. Louisburg, North Carolina.

RUFFIN, THOMAS, JR. b. Hillsboro, North Carolina, Sept. 21, 1824. Not directly related to the preceding officer. gr. UNC, 1844. Alamance Co. lawyer. Capt., Co. E, 13th North Carolina, April 26, 1861. Capt., Co. H, 6th North Carolina, Jan. to April 1862. Lt. Col., 13th North Carolina, May 1, 1862. Wded. at South Mountain. Resigned March 2, 1863, to become Judge of a military court in the Trans-Mississippi Dept. Served on the North Carolina Supreme Court, 1881-85. d. May 23, 1889. bur. St. Matthews Episcopal Churchyard, Hillsboro.

RUFFNER, HENRY DANIEL. b. Aug. 15, 1834. Farm manager in Charleston. m. Sarah Alethea Patrick, 1860. 5'11". Lt., Co. H, 22nd Virginia, May 8, 1861. Resigned Aug. 5, 1861. Capt., Co. G, 19th Virginia Cavalry, March 12, 1863. Major, 46th Virginia Cavalry Battalion, Feb. 26, 1864. Major, 26th Virginia Cavalry,

Kennesaw Mountain National Battlefield Park

SOLON Z. RUFF
18th Georgia

Jan. 1865. Paroled at Charleston, West Virginia, May 10, 1865. Lived in Charleston post-war. Also mined silver in Colorado. d. Roseland, Florida, July 25, 1925. bur. Spring Hill Cemetery, Charleston.

RUSSELL, W. LEE. (Russell normally did not use the first initial.) Of Montgomery Co. 5′9″. Pvt., Co. L, 22nd North Carolina, June 18, 1861, aged 25. Lt. - May 17, 1862. Captain - Aug. 28, 1862. Major - May 3, 1863. POW at Falling Waters, July 14, 1863, released June 11, 1865. Residence - Wind Hill, North Carolina.

RUSSELL, WHITEFORD DOUGHTY. b. June 13, 1839. Merchant's clerk in Augusta. Lt., Co. I, 1st Georgia, March 18, 1861. Mustered out with the regt., Mar. 18, 1862. Capt., Co. A, 21st Georgia Cavalry Bn., May 8, 1862. Transferred to Co. A, 7th Georgia Cav., Feb. 13, 1864. MWIA at Trevilian's, June 11, 1864, d. June 14. Russell's obituary refers to him as a Major, as do some other papers, but an official report shows him to have been only "acting as Major." bur. Magnolia Cemetery, Augusta.

RUST, ARMISTEAD THOMSON MASON. b. near Leesburg, Virginia, Jan. 18, 1820. att. Georgetown. gr. USMA, 1842. m. (1) Eliza Southgate Lawrence, 1849. m. (2) Ida Lee, 1860. Lt., U. S. Cavalry, 1842-45. Colonel, 19th Virginia, Nov. 20, 1861. Dropped at April 1862 re-org. Later in the war Rust was a Judge Advocate with Genl. Samuel Jones. Leesburg farmer post-war. d. there July 17, 1887. bur. Union Cemetery.

RUTHERFORD, WILLIAM DRAYTON. b. Newberry Dist., South Carolina, Sept. 21, 1837. m. Sallie H. Fair. Lawyer. Adj., 3rd South Carolina, April 14, 1861. Major - May 14, 1862. Coloney - May 6, 1864. Wded. at Fredericksburg. POW at South Mountain. KIA at Strasburg, Oct. 13, 1864.

RUTLEDGE, BENJAMIN HUGER. b. Stateburg, South Carolina, June 4, 1829. gr. Yale, 1848. Charleston lawyer. In South Carolina Secession Convention. Capt., Co. K, 4th South Carolina Cav., March 25, 1862. Colonel - Dec. 16, 1862. In South Carolina legisl. d. Charleston, April 30, 1893. bur. Magnolia Cemetery.

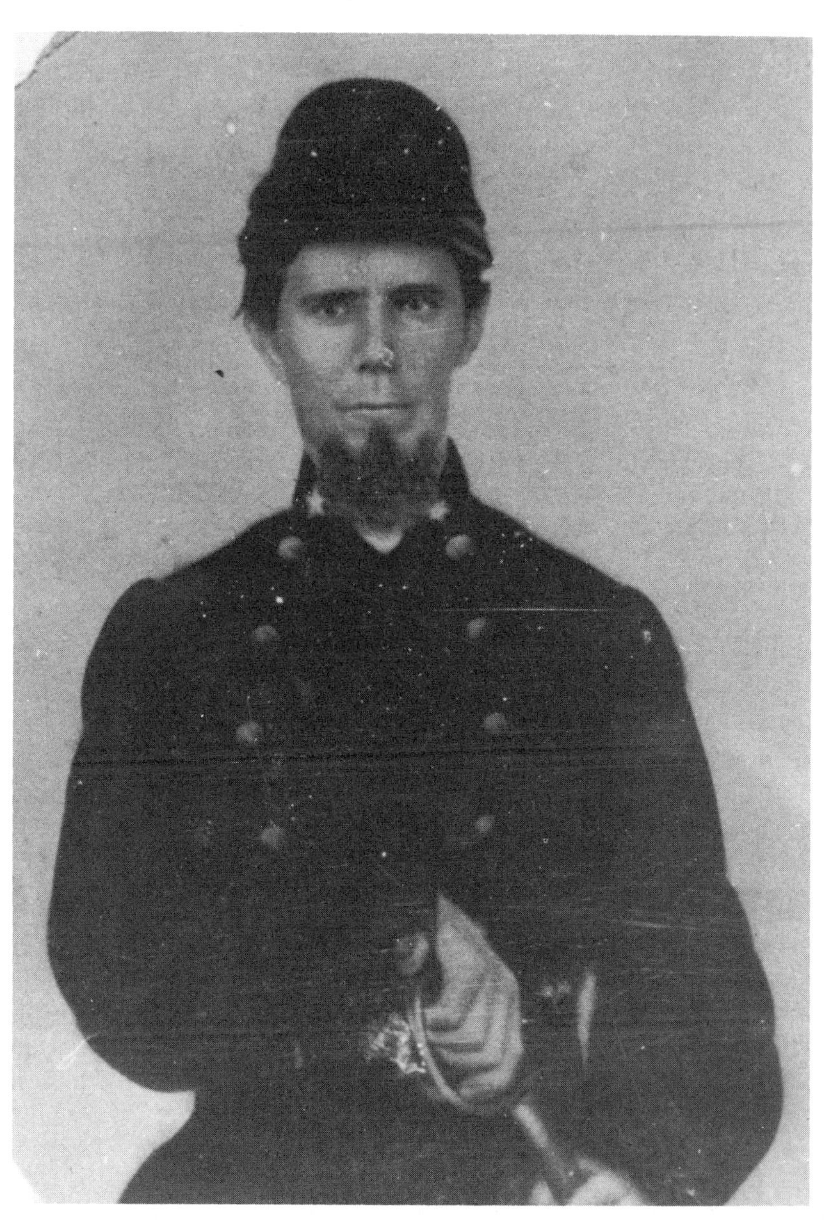

James Rylander

JOHN EMORY RYLANDER
10th Georgia Battalion

RUTLEDGE, HENRY MIDDLETON. b. South Carolina, Aug. 5, 1839. att. U. Virginia. Lt. of infantry, P.A.C.S., from South Carolina, May 21, 1861. Major, 25th North Carolina, Aug. 15, 1861. Lt. Col. - April 29, 1862. Colonel - May 17, 1862. Wded. at Petersburg, June 1864. Appx. Planter at Georgetown, South Carolina, post-war. m. Anne M. Blake. d. June 10, 1921. bur. St. John's in the Wilderness Cemetery, Flat Rock, North Carolina.

RYALS, HENRY J. b. Johnston Co. Farmer. Capt., Co. D, 50th North Carolina, April 21, 1862, aged 28. Major - April 11, 1864. Present into 1865.

RYLANDER, JOHN EMORY. b. Sept. 15, 1836, in Macon. gr. Emory. Teacher in Americus. Sgt., Co. A, 12th Georgia, June 15, 1861. Capt., Co. C, 10th Georgia Bn., March 4, 1862. Major - March 17, 1862. KIA at Cold Harbor, June 2, 1864. bur. Americus. There was some talk that Rylander had been killed by his own men.

ST. JOHN, COLUMBUS B., JR. Of Hillsboro, Alabama. Lt., Co. F, 48th Alabama, April 10, 1862, aged 18. Captain - 1862. Major - July 17, 1863. Wded. thigh at Gettysburg. Retired to Invalid Corp, Oct. 31, 1864. m. Harriet Emma Noble, 1867. d. Blount Co., Sept. 15, 1879.

ST. PAUL, HENRI. b. Antwerp, Belgium, Oct. 15, 1815. Lawyer and newspaper editor in Mobile. Capt., Co. A, 7th Louisiana Bn., April 22, 1861. Commanded the bn. as Acting Major in Dec. 1861. St. Paul had commanded a company around New Orleans as early as Jan. 1861. He was Major in the Mobile defenses in 1864, and Quarter Master there. Paroled at Mobile, May 12, 1865. Lawyer and editor, author of two Confederate imprints on foreign relations. d. New Orleans, Feb. 26, 1886.

SALYER, LOGAN HENRY NEIL. b. Copper Creek, Scott Co., Virginia, May 31, 1835. Lawyer. Capt., Co. H, 50th Virginia, June 3, 1861. Major - June 1862. Lt. Col. - Jan. 30, 1863. Wded. at Ft. Donelson and Chancellorsville (by a sword in the head). Appx. m. 4 times and produced 14 children. Kentucky judge post-war. d. Whitesburg, Letcher Co., Ky., May 3, 1916. bur.

Blair family cemetery. The middle name, revised from earlier editions, is on authority of two female descendants who still bear that family name themselves.

SANDERS, CHRISTOPHER COLUMBUS. b. Jackson Co., Georgia, May 8, 1840. gr. Georgia Military Institute, 1861. Lt. Col., 24th Georgia, Aug. 30, 1861. Colonel - Jan. 9, 1864. WIA May 15-18, 1864. POW at Sayler's Creek, paroled July 25, 1865. Gainesville banker. d. Gainesville, Aug. 3, 1908.

SANDERS, WILLIAM CAMPBELL. b. Wythe Co., Virginia, June 15, 1841. Pvt., Co. A, 4th Virginia, April 1861. Lt., Co. D, 45th Virginia, May 29, 1861. Captain - at spring 1862 re-org. Major - May 1864, but the appt. seems never to have been fully confirmed. Wded. at Piedmont, June 5, 1864, and incapacitated. m. Florence Alexander Peirce, 1864. Wythe Co. Treasurer. d. Richmond, Dec. 21, 1925. bur. East End Cemetery, Wytheville.

SANDS, ROBERT MARTIN. b. Tampa Bay, Fla., Oct. 12, 1825. Cotton merchant in Mobile, Alabama. Capt., "Mobile Cadets," 1845. gr. Spring Hill College. Capt., Co. A, 3rd Alabama, April 23, 1861. Major - May 31, 1862. Lt. Col. - Aug. 20, 1863. Wded. in the knee at Gettysburg. Retired Oct. 19, 1864. d. Mobile, Nov. 17, 1903. bur. Magnolia Cemetery.

SANFORD, JOHN WILLIAM AUGUSTINE. b. Georgia, Nov. 3, 1825. gr. U. Alabama. att. Harvard and Oglethorpe U. Lawyer. Pvt., 4th Georgia Inf., April 26, 1861; discharged Aug. 2, 1861. QM, 3rd Alabama, 1861. Lt. Col., 3rd Infantry Battalion, Hilliard's Legion (Alabama), June 25, 1862. Colonel, 60th Alabama, Nov. 25, 1863. Appx. Attorney General of Alabama. d. Montgomery, Aug. 1913. An article by Sanford appeared in *Confederate Veteran*, vol. XIII.

SAUNDERS, ANDREW D. Of Middlesex Co. Unmarried. Capt., Co. H, 55th Virginia, April 17, 1861. Major - June 30, 1862. KIA at Chancellorsville, May 2, 1863.

SAUNDERS, JOHN SELDEN. b. Norfolk, Virginia, Feb. 1836. gr. USMA, 1858. Lt. of ordnance, 1858-61. Saunders was seized by Florida State Troops in Jan. 1861, while still in the U. S.

Army, and paroled. Lt. of artillery, P.A.C.S., Mar. 16, 1861. Served in the Richmond Arsenal. Major and Judge Advocate by Jan. 1862. Commanded an artillery bn. at Sharpsburg. Acted as Chief of Artillery of R. H. Anderson's Division. Lt. Col. of artillery - Nov. 14, 1862. Saunders was assigned to the Ordnance Bureau in Dec. 1862 and served in various staff roles in Mississippi, Georgia, South Carolina and North Carolina. He was on Briscoe G. Baldwin's A.N. Va. staff for a time. Appx. m. Bierne Ellen Turner, 1863. Lived in Baltimore. Commanded the post-war 5th Maryland, and was a U.C.V. officer. d. Jan. 19, 1904.

SAUNDERS, JOSEPH HUBBARD. b. Oct. 23, 1839. Brother of Colonel William L. Pvt., Co. D, 1st North Carolina (Bethel), April 6, 1861. Capt., Co. A, 33rd North Carolina, April 25, 1862. Major - June 1, 1863. Lt. Col. - June 18, 1864. Wded. in the mouth and POW at Gettysburg. gr. UNC, 1866. Orange Co. and Pitt Co. planter. m. Fannie C. Neal, 1870. d. Sept. 24, 1885, in Pitt Co.

SAUNDERS, SAMUEL HYDE. Farmer in Franklin Co. in 1860, age 30. Lt., Co. K, 42nd Virginia, 1861. Captain - April 21, 1862. Lt. Col. - Nov. 29, 1863. Wded. at Chancellorsville. Wded. arm at Payne's Farm in Nov. 1863, and again in arm in Sept. 1864. Paroled at Franklin C.H., June 5, 1865. Alive in Franklin Co. in 1870.

SAUNDERS, WILLIAM ALEXANDER. b. Caroline Co., Virginia, Dec. 26, 1829. Insurance man, farmer and justice of the peace in King & Queen Co. m. Emiline Motley. Major, 21st Virginia Militia, 1861-62. This unit served with the A.N. Va. at Gloucester Point in early 1862. Also Major, 87th Virginia Militia. d. King & Queen Co., Aug. 8, 1896.

SAUNDERS, WILLIAM LAURENCE. b. Raleigh, North Carolina, July 30, 1835. Lawyer. gr. UNC. Brother of Joseph H., above. Capt., Co. B, 46th North Carolina, April 16, 1862. Major - Sept. 30, 1862. Lt. Col. - Jan. 21, 1863. Colonel - Dec. 31, 1863. Wded. at Fredericksburg (in the mouth) and Wilderness. Appx. m. Florida Cotten, 1864. Newspaper editor at Raleigh, Salisbury and Wilmington. Secretary of State of North

Carolina. Head of the Ku Klux Klan in the state. Author of *Colonial Records of North Carolina.* d. Raleigh, April 2, 1891. bur. Calvary Episcopal Church, Tarboro.

SAVAGE, ALEXANDER. b. Nansemond Co., Dec. 30, 1830. Sgt., Co. G, 5th Virginia Cavalry, April 1861. Captain - June 4, 1861. This unit became Co. I, 13th Virginia Cavalry, July 1862. Lt. Col., 13th Virginia Cavalry, Nov. 22, 1864. Wded. right hand, May 1864. Lost arm at Petersburg, 1865. Norfolk commission business. d. Norfolk, April 6, 1911. bur. Elmwood Cemetery.

SAVAGE, EDWARD. Of New Hanover Co. Capt., Co. D, 3rd North Carolina, May 16, 1861, aged 40. Major - April 26, 1862. Lt. Col. - July 1, 1862. Wded. at Mechanicsville. Resigned, "physical inability," Dec. 10, 1862. Living in New York in 1900.

SCAIFE, FERDINAND DUGROPHANEL. b. Chester District, 1805. m. Mary Wilkes before 1837. Planter at Union, South Carolina. In state legislature. Capt., Co. A, 18th South Carolina, Nov. 18, 1861. Lt. Col. - Jan. 2, 1862. Dropped at May 1862 re-org. Moved to Phillips Co., Arkansas. d. 1867 in Arkansas.

SCALES, JAMES TURNER. b. Henry Co., Virginia, Aug. 14, 1838. Lawyer. Lt., Co. E, 2nd North Carolina, May 16, 1861. Captain - June 21, 1862. Major - Aug. 30, 1864. Lt. Col. - Aug. 31, 1864. Wded. in head, Nov. 1863; at Spotsylvania, May 17, 1864; and near Petersburg in 1865. Appx. d. Jan. 26, 1904.

SCHENCK, HENRY FRANKLIN. b. Rutherford Co., Nov. 29, 1835. Merchant. 5′10″. Capt., Co. F, 56th North Carolina, May 10, 1862. Major - July 31, 1862. Resigned in ill health, Aug. 15, 1863 (chronic bronchitis). d. Shelby, North Carolina, Sept. 25, 1915.

SCOTT, ANDREW VAN BUREN. b. Amelia Co., Jan. 22, 1836. att. Hampden-Sydney. Capt., Co. C, 23rd Virginia, May 15, 1861 (had commanded the company since 1859). Major - Aug. 10, 1862. Wded. at 2nd Manassas, which caused him to resign on June 10, 1863. He became a tax assessor. Farmer. d. Amelia Co., April 18, 1895.

SCOTT, CHARLES LEWIS. b. Richmond, Virginia, Jan. 23, 1827. gr. William & Mary. Went to California in the 1849 gold rush. Lawyer in Sonora, California. In U. S. Congress from California, 1857-61. Major, 4th Alabama, May 7, 1861. Wded. in leg at Manassas. Resigned July 13, 1862, because the wound was unhealed and abscessed. Post-war farmer in Wilcox Co., Alabama. U. S. Minister to Venezuela. d. Monroe Co., Alabama, April 30, 1899. bur. Cedar Hill, Alabama.

SCOTT, JOHN. b. Fauquier Co., Virginia, April 23, 1820. gr. U. Virginia. m. Harriet Augusta Caskie, 1850. Editor of Richmond *Whig*. Organized the famous "Black Horse Cavalry" in Fauquier Co. in 1859. Capt. of cavalry, P.A.C.S., March 1861. Commanded a squadron of cavalry at 1st Manassas, shown as a major. Major, 24th Battalion Virginia Partisan Rangers, 1862-63. The bn. was disbanded in Jan. 1863. In April 1863, Scott was commanding some stray cavalry units in Arkansas, and signing as a colonel. Later in the war he returned to serve with partisan ranger units in Virginia. Fauquier Co. Commonwealth's Attorney for 21 years. Author of *Partisan Life with Mosby* and several other publications. d. Warrenton, May 7, 1907. Scott's Battalion was a rowdy and useless unit.

SCOTT, JOSEPH V. b. Petersburg, Aug. 17, 1822. Petersburg city official. Capt., Co. E, 3rd Virginia, April 20, 1861. Major - Nov. 6, 1861. Lt. Col. - April 27, 1862. KIA at Frayser's Farm, June 30, 1862. Scott had been extremely sick, but came out to lead the regiment in the fight and was killed. bur. Blandford Church, Petersburg.

SCOTT, THADDEUS B. b. 1833. Merchant in Columbus. Capt., Co. E, 12th Georgia, June 15, 1861. Lt. Col. - Nov. 5, 1862. Wded. at Gaines' Mill. KIA at Fredericksburg. bur. Linwood Cemetery, Columbus, Georgia.

SCOTT, WILLIAM CAMPBELL. b. Powhatan Co., Virginia, 1809. att. Hampden-Sydney. gr. U. Virginia. In Virginia legisl. Powhatan lawyer. Colonel, 102nd Virginia Militia, 1861. Brigadier General of Virginia Militia, 1861. Colonel, 44th Virginia Inf., June 14, 1861. Resigned on surgeon's certificate, Jan. 14, 1863. d. April 9, 1865, in Powhatan.

SCOTT, WILLIAM LAFAYETTE. b. 1828. Lawyer in Guilford County. gr. UNC. Capt., Co. M, 21st North Carolina, June 8, 1861. Lt. Col. - Feb. 1, 1862. Defeated at April 1862 re-org. d. 1872.

SCOTT, WILLIAM WASH. b. Liberty Co., Georgia, Sept. 6, 1824. Lived in Lake City, Florida. Capt., Co. F, 1st Florida Bn., Nov. 5, 1861. Major - May 15, 1862. The 1st and 2nd Florida Bns. were merged into the 10th Florida Inf. Regt. in June 1864. Scott became Lt. Col., 10th Florida, June 11, 1864. d. Nov. 17, 1891. bur. Newnanville Cemetery, Alachua County, Florida.

SCREVEN, JOHN. b. Savannah, Sept. 18, 1827. att. U. Georgia. In Georgia legisl. Planter. Capt., Co. A, 18th Georgia Bn., early 1861. Major - 1862. Detached for transportation duties, Dec. 1862. Commanded local troops in Savannah. Railroad president and Mayor of Savannah post-war. d. Savannah, Jan. 9, 1900.

SCREVEN, THOMAS EDWARD. b. April 5, 1830. Attorney at Grahamville in 1860, married, worth $50,200. Capt., Co. B, 2nd South Carolina Cav., 1862. Major - June 10, 1863. Lt. Col. - Sept. 1, 1863.

SCRUGGS, DANIEL EDWARD. b. Richmond, Virginia, 1833. Sgt., Co. H, Crescent Regt. Louisiana Inf., 1861. Transferred to QM duties, and became an employee of the QM Department in Richmond. Capt., Co. A, 2nd Virginia Bn. LDT ("Quartermaster Bn."), June 18, 1863. Major - May 10, 1864. Colonel, 2nd Virginia Regt. LDT, Aug. 29, 1864. d. Nov. 1, 1871. bur. New Orleans.

SCRUGGS, LAWRENCE HOUSTON. b. Jackson Co., Alabama, June 13, 1836. Cotton merchant in Huntsville. Pvt., Co. I, 4th Alabama, April 26, 1861. Commissary Sgt. soon thereafter, but resigned during 1861. Captain, Co. I, 4th Alabama, April 16, 1862. Major - Sept. 30, 1862. Lt. Col. - Oct. 3, 1862. Wded. at Malvern Hill and Chickamauga. Appx. Alive in Nashville, Tennessee, in 1902.

SEAGO, ELI M. b. 1822. Mexican War veteran. Produce and commission merchant in Atlanta. Capt., Co. F, 20th Georgia,

June 18, 1861. WIA in foot at 2nd Manassas. Major - May 29, 1863. Lt. Col. - July 2, 1863. Wded. at Chickamauga and Wilderness. Moved to Texas (probably Shelby Co.) and died there before 1890.

SEAWELL, WILLIAM H. b. Gloucester Co., Virginia. Lived in Tennessee pre-war. Lt., U. S. Infantry, 1847-48. Merchant at Gloucester Court House in 1860, age 48. Major, 21st Virginia Militia, Oct. 19, 1861. Lt. Col. - Dec. 31, 1861. Present into May 1862. d. May 29, 1875.

SECREST, ANDREW JACKSON. Clerk in Chester District in 1860, age 32, married. Lt. Col., 6th South Carolina, Feb. 19, 1861. Thrown out at the re-org. Later served as a private in the 4th South Carolina Bn., and as Colonel, 6th South Carolina Reserves. Lived in Chester Dist., South Carolina. d. May 1865.

SEDDON, JOHN. b. Oct. 8, 1826. Brother of C. S. Secretary of War James A. Seddon. m. Mary Alexander Little, 1848. Lt. of Inf. during Mexican War. Capt., Co. D, 1st Virginia Bn. ("Irish Bn."), May 14, 1861. Major - May 20, 1862. Resigned in ill health, Oct. 11, 1862. In Virginia legisl. during the war. d. Dec. 5, 1863. bur. Fredericksburg Confederate Cemetery.

SEIBELS, EMMETT. b. Lexington Dist., South Carolina, Oct. 3, 1821. gr. South Carolina College, 1844. Lawyer at Edgefield C. H. Brother of Colonel John J. Seibels. Married Anne Goldthwaite. Major, 7th South Carolina, April 15, 1861. Lt. Col. - May 9, 1862. Dropped at May 1862 re-org., when he lost election for Colonel. Seibels fought a duel with Capt. (later Lt. Col.) Bland near Manassas during the war's first winter over "a game of chess." Late in the war he was still seeking another field appointment. Served as volunteer on M. C. Butler's staff. d. Montgomery, Alabama, Dec. 1899.

SEIBELS, JOHN JACOB. b. Edgefield Dist., South Carolina, Dec. 8, 1816. Mexican War officer. U. S. Minister in Belgium. Brother of Emmett Seibels. A.d.c. to Gov. of Alabama, March 1861. Colonel, 6th Alabama, May 14, 1861. Dropped at April 1862 re-org. d. Aug. 8, 1865. bur. Oakwood Cemetery, Montgomery.

SETTLE, THOMAS. b. Rockingham Co., North Carolina, Jan. 23, 1831. gr. UNC, 1850. m. Mary Glenn, 1854. In North Carolina legisl. Capt., Co. I, 13th North Carolina, May 3, 1861. Colonel 21st North Carolina, April 27, 1862, but declined the appt. and "went home." Became a Republican post-war. U. S. Minister to Peru. U. S. District Judge in Florida. d. Dec. 1, 1888.

SEYMOUR, ISAAC GURDON b. Savannah, Georgia, Oct. 1804. Mayor of Macon, Georgia. Served in Indian and Mexican Wars. m. Caroline Whitlock. Moved to New Orleans in 1848, where he edited the *Bulletin*. Mayor of Macon, Georgia. Colonel, 6th Louisiana, June 4, 1861. KIA at Gaines' Mill. bur. Rose Hill Cemetery, Macon. "Beast" Butler sent Seymour's son to prison for publishing an obituary of the traitorous colonel in a New Orleans newspaper. Seymour was "a martial man with long, silvery locks." Some of Seymour's war papers and a good photo are in the Schoff collection at the U. of Michigan.

SHACKLEFORD, JOHN C. Merchant. Lt., Co. G, 1st Tennessee, April 29, 1861, at Fayetteville, aged 24. Lt. Col. - April 27, 1862. KIA at Gaines' Mill.

SHANNON, GEORGE W. Sgt., Co. C, 11th Mississippi, March 2, 1861, at Okolona, aged 21. Lt. - Jan. 7, 1862. Captain - May 1, 1862. Lt. Col. - Dec. 1, 1864. Wded. at Gaines' Mill. POW at Hatcher's Run, released July 25. 6′2″.

SHANNON, JAMES J. Lived in Jasper Co. Capt., Co. F, 16th Mississippi, May 31, 1861, aged 36. Lt. Col. - April 28, 1862. Res. Dec. 20, 1862, citing "diarrhea, neuralgia, hemorrhoids."

SHANNON, PETER J. b. July 23, 1825. Harness maker in Elberton. Mexican War veteran. Lt., Co. I, 15th Georgia, July 15, 1861. Adj. - Feb. 9, 1862. Major - Aug. 1, 1862. Appx. d. Nov. 3, 1876.

SHARP, JOHN JAMES AUGUSTUS. b. Pickens Dist., South Carolina, March 6, 1828. Teacher and merchant in Cherokee Co., Georgia. Capt., Co. G, 23rd Georgia, Aug. 31, 1861. Major - Dec. 15, 1863. Lt. Col. - Aug. 13, 1864. Wded. at Sharpsburg and Bentonville. m. Mary Jane Reinhardt, 1868. In Georgia legisl. d. Oct. 16, 1896.

SHARP, THOMAS HUNTER. b. Hertford Co., North Carolina, 1837. att. UNC and U. Virginia Physician. Capt., Co. D, 17th North Carolina, May 22, 1861. Capt., Co. C, 17th North Carolina, March 24, 1862. Major - May 16, 1862. Lt. Col. - May 27, 1864. Wded. at Petersburg, June 1864. Planter near Charleston, South Carolina, post-war. Died at Charleston.

SHARPE, GEORGE W. b. Alexander Co., North Carolina, Sept. 23, 1835. Mechanic. 6'1". Capt., Co. G, 38th North Carolina, Nov. 2, 1861. Major - Jan. 17, 1862. Dropped at April 1862 re-org. d. Oct. 11, 1893.

SHAW, ELIAS FAISON. b. Sampson Co., North Carolina, May 2, 1822. Farmer and physician. Capt., Co. C, 5th North Carolina Cav., May 16, 1862. Lt. Col. - Jan. 28, 1865. KIA at Chamberlain Run, March 31, 1865. Buried in Faison family cemetery near Elliott, North Carolina.

SHAW, HENRY MARCHMORE. b. Newport, Rhode Island, Nov. 20, 1819. gr. U. Pennsylvania, M. D. Physician in Camden and Currituck cos., North Carolina. In U. S. Congress, 1853-59. Colonel, 8th North Carolina, May 16, 1861. Paroled at Roanoke Island, Feb. 1862. KIA near New Bern, Feb. 1, 1864. bur. Shawboro, North Carolina.

SHEDD, JAMES NELSON. b. ca. 1827. Pvt., Co. D, 6th South Carolina Inf., April 1861. Lt., Co. E, 22nd South Carolina, May 18, 1864. Captain - June 7, 1864. Major - Dec. 2, 1864. Appx. d. Greensboro, North Carolina, April 26, 1865.

SHEFFIELD, JAMES LAWRENCE. b. Huntsville, Alabama, Dec. 5, 1819. Sheriff of Marshall Co. In Alabama legisl. In Alabama Secession Convention. Colonel, 48th Alabama, May 13, 1862. Sheffield "spent $60,000 of his own money outfitting the regiment." Wded. at Cedar Mountain. Resigned May 31, 1864. d. Montgomery, July 2, 1892.

SHEFFIELD, PLINY. b. Thomasville, Georgia, Feb. 15, 1839. att. U. Virginia. Capt., Co. K, 50th Georgia, March 4, 1862. Major - July 31, 1862. Lt. Col. - Dec. 21, 1863. Lost arm at Wilderness. Resigned Nov. 28, 1864. m. Mary Read Hunt, 1864. Planter in Quitman. d. Brooks Co., Georgia, Jan. 29, 1908.

SHELLEY, JAMES E. b. Sept. 2, 1831 in Tennessee. Brick maker in Talladega, Alabama. Lt., Co. E, 10th Alabama, June 4, 1861. Captain - May 21, 1863. Lt. Col. - July 9, 1863. Wded. at Gaines' Mill and Spotsylvania. KIA June 22, 1864. bur. Oak Hill Cemetery, Talladega.

SHELOR, WILLIAM BANKS. b. Montgomery Co., Virginia, Jan. 30, 1820. Sheriff of Floyd Co., 1851-56. m. Sarah Elizabeth Helms. Major, 54th Virginia, Sept. 4, 1861. Lt. Col. - May 13, 1862. Resigned Nov. 13, 1862, to become Clerk of Courts of Floyd Co. Floyd Co. farmer post-war. d. Roanoke Co., Jan. 10, 1916.

SHELTON, WILLIAM DOSCA. b. Buffalo Lithia Springs, Mecklenburg Co., Virginia, Nov. 12, 1836. att. VMI. Pvt., Co. E, 14th Virginia, May 12, 1861. Sgt. - Aug. 12, 1861. Lt. - May 6, 1862. Captain - Aug. 5, 1862. Major - Aug. 8, 1864. Appx. m. Martha Susan Crowder, 1867. Mecklenburg Co. farmer. d. July 21, 1913. bur. Shelton family cemetery, Rte. 699.

SHEPARD, SAMUEL G. b. Lebanon, Tennessee, Jan. 28, 1830. Capt., Co. G, 7th Tennessee, May 21, 1861. Major - July 9, 1862. Lt. Col. - April 8, 1863. Appx. m. Martha Major, 1865. Minister in Wilson Co., Tennessee. d. June 6, 1917. bur. Cedar Grove Cemetery, Wilson Co.

SHEPHERD, F. B. Lt. Col., 5th Alabama Bn., at the organization of that unit in Dec. 1861. Shepherd has no extant service record and his rank is shown as temporary on the battalion's field and staff card—which is the only place he is mentioned in the unit's compiled records.

SHEPHERD, WILLIAM SMYTHE. b. Stewart Co., Georgia, 1830. att. Georgia Military Institute, U. Georgia, and U. Virginia. Pvt., Co. G, 2nd Georgia, April 16, 1861. Captain - July 24, 1861. Major - Sept. 17, 1862. Lt. Col. - July 2, 1863. Wded. at Chickamauga (elbow) and Ft. Harrison by a shell fragment on Sept. 29, 1864. Stewart Co. planter. d. Columbus, June 24, 1924. bur. Linwood Cemetery. Never married.

SHERRARD, JOHN BROOME. b. Hampshire Co., Virginia, Dec. 13, 1822. gr. VMI, 1845. 5′6″. m. Susan A. Gibson in 1847.

Capt., Co. K, 13th Virginia, May 18, 1861. Major - April 25, 1862. Resigned Oct. 30, 1862. When James A. Walker left the 13th Virginia via promotion, Sherrard wanted to return to the unit again, but failed in this effort. POW at Wheeling, Oct. 24, 1863. Merchant in Canton, Mississippi. Cattleman in Sherman and Burnet, Texas. d. Burnet, Nov. 30, 1912.

SHINGLER, WILLIAM PINKNEY. b. Orangeburg Dist., South Carolina, Nov. 11, 1827. Charleston planter and banker. In South Carolina Secession Convention. m. Susan Ball Venning. Volunteer aide to Bee. Lt. Col., Holcombe Legion (South Carolina), Nov. 21, 1861. Colonel - Oct. 8, 1862. Transferred to the 7th South Carolina Cav. in 1864, having raised that regiment. Resigned May 30, 1864, after a running dispute with Jefferson Davis. In South Carolina legisl. post-war. d. Sept. 14, 1869. bur. near Mt. Pleasant at Myrtle Grove Plantation.

SHIPLEY, JAMES S. b. Mathews Co. Merchant there in 1860, age 29. Major, 61st Virginia Militia, Sept. 25, 1858. Present with the unit at Yorktown into 1862. The regt. was disbanded in May 1862.

SHIPP, SCOTT. b. Warrenton, Virginia, Aug. 2, 1839. gr. VMI, 1859. Major, 21st Virginia, June 1861. Detailed to VMI staff, Jan. 20, 1862 (left the 21st Virginia at Unger's Store on Jan. 11, 1862). Served briefly with Co. H, 4th Virginia Cav., as a private, while on leave from VMI during the summer of 1863. Commanded the VMI cadets at New Market. m. Anne Alexander Morson, 1869. On VMI staff for decades. d. Lexington, Dec. 4, 1917.

SHIVERS, WILLIAM R. b. Georgia. Merchant in South Port, Louisiana. Capt., Co. A, 1st Louisiana, April 28, 1861, aged 35. Major - May 1861. Lt. Col. - Oct. 10, 1861. Colonel - 1862. Severely wounded in right arm during Seven Days, and never returned to the regt. On duty at Shreveport later in the war.

SHOBER, CHARLES EUGENE. b. Salem, North Carolina. gr. UNC. Lawyer. 5′8″. Lived in Guilford Co. Capt., Co. B, 45th North Carolina, Feb. 15, 1862, aged 33. Major - Sept. 30, 1862. Resigned Jan. 30, 1863. Lt. Col., 2nd North Carolina Bn., rank backdated to Oct. 1, 1862. Resigned June 6, 1863, "asthma." Later became Colonel, 7th North Carolina Reserves. d. Sept. 27, 1877.

SHOFFNER, MARTIN. Major, 34th North Carolina, Oct. 25, 1861. Resigned Jan. 25, 1862, for "personal reasons," to the delight of his superiors.

SHOOTER, WASHINGTON PINCKNEY. b. Marion Dist., South Carolina, Jan. 1837. gr. SCMA, 1859. Lawyer in Marion and eidtor of the Marion *Star*. Capt., Co. E, 1st South Carolina (Gregg's), Aug. 1, 1861. Lt. Col. - Jan. 4, 1864. KIA at Spotsylvania, May 12, 1864. bur. Spotsylvania Confederate Cemetery. Shooter was "of short stature."

SHRIVER, DANIEL McELLERAN. Of Wheeling, Virginia. Capt., Co. G, 27th Virginia, May 16, 1861, aged 25. Major - May 27, 1862. Lt. Col. - Nov. 19, 1862. Resigned Sept. 4, 1863, having been elected to the Virginia Senate. Colonel - Feb. 6, 1864, but never accepted the commission. Wded. in shoulders at Port Republic. d. July 1865 near Wheeling. bur. Greenwood Cemetery.

SHULER, WILLIAM MURCHEY. b. Orangeburg District, May 4, 1824. gr. Charleston Medical College, 1845. Physician in Colleton District. In South Carolina legisl. Lt. Col., 11th South Carolina, 1861. The sole document in Shuler's service record is a requisition signed at that rank in Sept. 1861. d. Jan. 30, 1898. bur. Murray-Shuler Cemetery, Dorchester Co.

SHUMAKER, LINDSAY MAYO. b. Lynchburg. Lawyer in Danville in 1860, age 36. Capt., Danville Artillery (Virginia), April 1861. Not re-elected in April 1862 re-org. Major of artillery - July 5, 1862. Commanded an artillery bn. and served as Chief of Artillery of Taliaferro's Division at 2nd Manassas. Relieved from duty with A.N. Va. on Oct. 10, 1862, ordered to report to A.I.G.O. Served with S. G. French in North Carolina as Chief of Artillery later in the war. Judge and Danville *Register* editor postwar. d. Oct. 1884. bur. Green Hill Cemetery, Danville.

SILLERS, WILLIAM WALTER. b. April 10, 1838. gr. UNC, 1859. Lawyer in Clinton, North Carolina. Pvt., Co. A, 30th

North Carolina, April 20, 1861. Lt. - Aug. 13, 1861. Major - May 1, 1862. Lt. Col. - Sept. 3, 1863. Wded. at Malvern Hill. MWIA at Kelly's Ford, Virginia, Nov. 7, 1863, died at Gordonsville, Nov. 9.

SIMMONS, THOMAS JEFFERSON. b. Hickory Grove, Georgia, June 25, 1837. att. Brownwood Institute in LaGrange. Lt., Co. E, 6th Georgia, May 27, 1861. Lt. Col., 45th Georgia, March 15, 1862. Colonel - Oct. 13, 1862. Wded. at Gaines' Mill. Appx. In Georgia Senate. On Georgia Supreme Court, 1887-1905, as Chief Justice after 1894. Died September 12, 1905.

SIMMONS, WILLIAM EDWARD. b. Lawrenceville, Georgia, Feb. 10, 1839. Lawyer. Lt., Co. I, 16th Georgia, March 6, 1861. Captain, Co. I, 16th Georgia, April 1862. Transferred as Capt., Co. C, 3rd Georgia Sharpshooter Bn., June 8, 1863. Major - Sept. 18, 1863. POW at Front Royal, Virginia, Aug. 16, 1864, released July 24, 1865. Simmons' Ft. Delaware prison diary was printed in a history of Gwinnett Co., Georgia. m. Mary Lou Ambrose. Newspaper editor. d. Lawrenceville, Oct. 15, 1931.

SIMONTON, ABSALOM KNOX. b. July 23, 1835. Served in North Carolina legislature. Ran a brick yard in Iredell Co. Wife - Margaret Isabelle. Capt., Co. A, 4th North Carolina, May 16, 1861. Major - May 1, 1862. KIA at Seven Pines. bur. old Fourth Creek Cemetery, Statesboro.

SIMONTON, CHARLES HENRY. b. Charleston, South Carolina, July 11, 1829. gr. South Carolina College, 1849. Charleston lawyer. In South Carolina legisl. Major, 11th South Carolina Bn. ("Eutaw Bn."), 1861. Colonel, 25th South Carolina, July 22, 1862. Detached for duty in South Carolina, Aug. 1864. U. S. District Court Judge, apptd. by Cleveland. Died in Philadelphia, Pennsylvania, April 25, 1904. bur. Charleston.

SIMPSON, ROBERT HENRY. b. Front Royal, Virginia, July 26, 1826. gr. VMI, 1845. 5'8½". Teacher. Capt., Co. B, 17th Virginia, April 18, 1861. Major - Nov. 1, 1862. POW at Frayser's Farm, exchanged July 31, 1862. Wded. at 2nd Manassas. MWIA at Drewry's Bluff (leg amputated). d. June 9, 1864. bur. Prospect Hill Cemetery, Front Royal.

SIMPSON, WILLIAM DUNLAP. b. Laurens Dist., South Carolina, Oct. 27, 1823. gr. South Carolina College, 1843. att. Harvard Law School. In South Carolina legisl. Aide to Bonham at Ft. Sumter and in Virginia, 1861. Major, 14th South Carolina, Sept. 9, 1861. Lt. Col. - April 11, 1862. Resigned to enter the C. S. Congress, where he replaced Bonham. Lt. Gov. and Gov. of South Carolina post-war. Chief Justice of South Carolina Supreme Court. d. Columbia, Dec. 26, 1890.

SIMS, JOHN. b. Oct. 6, 1833. att. Yale. Lt., Co. D, 21st Mississippi, May 22, 1861. Captain - June 1861. Major - Aug. 12, 1863. Lt. Col. - Oct. 28, 1863. KIA at Cedar Creek, Oct. 19, 1864. bur. Stonewall Cemetery, Winchester.

SIMS, THOMAS W. b. Dec. 18, 1818, in South Carolina. Physician in Newton Co., Georgia, in 1860. Capt., Co. B, 53rd Georgia, May 1, 1862. Major - Oct. 27, 1862. Resigned, disability, Oct. 28, 1863. Lived in Jasper Co. after the war. Died after 1880.

SINCLAIR, JAMES. b. Tiree, Scotland, ca. 1823. gr. Western Theological Seminary, 1857. Presbyterian clergyman at Smyrna, North Carolina. Chaplain, 5th North Carolina, May 15, 1861. Colonel, 35th North Carolina, Nov. 8, 1861. Dropped at April 1862 re-org., due to cowardice at New Bern. He deserted and served in the Northern forces as a chaplain. Sinclair became an ardent Republican and served in the North Carolina legislature. "A notorious figure during Reconstruction." d. Monroe, North Carolina, Aug. 5, 1877. bur. Lumberton. The dates above, from a family history, conflict with Sinclair's sketch in a Presbyterian directory (1832-1883).

SINCLAIR, JEFFERSON. b. Elizabeth City Co., Virginia, March 14, 1825. A "gentleman farmer" there. m. Mary Frances Lowry. Sinclair was "a very heavy man . . . every saddle horse he owned was sway-backed." Capt., Co. D, 32nd Virginia, May 27, 1861. Major - May 21, 1862. Resigned Jan. 5, 1863. d. Nov. 9, 1899. Buried at "Sherwood," Gloucester Co.

SINCLAIR, PETER JOHN. b. Isle of Tiree Argyll, Scotland, Apr. 8, 1835. Brother of Col. James Sinclair. Lived in Pennsylvania until 1858, then in Cumberland Co., North Carolina. Pvt., Co.

F, 1st North Carolina, early 1861. Capt., Co. A, 5th North Carolina, May 15, 1861. Major - March 6, 1862. Lt. Col. - May 5, 1862. Wded. at Williamsburg and Gaines' Mill. Resigned on Dec. 30, 1862, due to "personal difficulties in regt." Published the *Daily North Carolinian* during the war. Lawyer post-war. m. (1) Ellen Arthur. m. (2) Margaret Cason, 1874. d. March 1, 1914. bur. Presbyterian Cemetery, Marion, McDowell Co.

SINGLETARY, ALFRED A. (This man and each of the other three officers of the same surname are sometimes spelled "Singeltary" without certainty as to which version is accurate. The weight of evidence is somewhat stronger for the spelling used here.) b. Louisiana. Farmer in Livingston Parish. Lt., Co. G, 9th Louisiana, July 7, 1861, aged 28. Captain - May 1, 1862. Major - Oct. 8, 1863.

SINGLETARY, GEORGE BADGER. Lawyer in Greenville. Mexican War veteran. In N.C. legislature. m. Cora Manly, daughter of the Gov. of North Carolina. Capt., Co. H, 27th North Carolina, Aug. 20, 1861. Colonel - Sept. 28, 1861. Suspended by a court-martial on D. H. Hill's charges of disobedience. Resigned, and became Colonel, 44th North Carolina, March 20, 1862. KIA at Tranter's Creek, North Carolina, June 5, 1862.

SINGLETARY, RICHARD WILLIAM. b. Beaufort Co., North Carolina, Feb. 10, 1837. gr. UNC, 1858. Lt., Co. H, 27th North Carolina, April 26, 1861. Captain - July 10, 1861. Lt. Col. - March 18, 1862. Colonel - Nov. 1, 1862. Resigned due to wounds, Dec. 4, 1862. In North Carolina legisl. Newspaper editor in Wilson, North Carolina. Later lived in Leasburg, Florida. d. 1892. bur. family cemetery near Lady Lake, Florida.

SINGLETARY, THOMAS CHAPPEAU. b. Aug. 9, 1840. gr. UNC. Lived in Pitt Co., North Carolina. Brother of Col. George B. Singletary. Lt., Co. E, 27th North Carolina, April 19, 1861. Major - Sept. 28, 1861. Lt. Col. - Jan. 6, 1862. Resigned, March 12, 1862. Colonel, 44th North Carolina, June 28, 1862. A general order dated Dec. 26, 1863, cashiered Singletary for drunkenness, but the sentence probably was suspended. Wded. in early May 1864. Paroled at Lynchburg, April 15, 1865. d.

Jan. 18, 1873. bur. Episcopal Churchyard, Washington, North Carolina.

SKELTON, JOHN HAMILTON. b. Elbert Co., Georgia, Nov. 10, 1827. Mayor of Hartwell. Capt., Co. C, 16th Georgia, July 13, 1861. POW at Fredericksburg, Dec. 13, 1862. Major - Oct. 1, 1863. POW at Front Royal, Virginia, Aug. 16, 1864, released July 24, 1865. In Georgia legisl. m. Mary Lavinia Richardson, 1867. d. Sept. 21, 1893. bur. Skelton family cemetery off Highway 77, Hart Co.

SKINNER, FREDERICK GUSTAVUS. b. Annapolis, Maryland, March 17, 1814. Educated in France, as a result of Skinner's father's friendship with Lafayette. m. Martha Stuart Thornton, 1841. Major, 1st Virginia, May 1861. Lt. Col. - Nov. 18, 1861. Wounded severely in the chest at 2nd Manassas, and never returned to full active duty, but was promoted Colonel nonetheless, effective July 3, 1863. Officially retired to the Invalid Corps, Feb. 6, 1865. Lived in Baltimore, Maryland, and Rappahannock Co., Virginia. d. Charlottesville, Virginia, May 22, 1894. bur. Westminster Churchyard, Baltimore. Skinner's war letters are at the Virginia Historical Society.

SKINNER, JAMES H. b. Norfolk, Jan. 18, 1826. att. U. Virginia. Augusta Co. lawyer. Capt., Co. A, 52nd Virginia, July 9, 1861. Lt. Col. - May 1, 1862. Colonel - June 6, 1863. Wded. at 2nd Manassas, Gettysburg and Spotsylvania (in the face on May 12). Retired to Invalid Corps, and assigned to command post at Staunton, March 4, 1865. d. May 19, 1898, at Staunton. bur. Cedar Grove Cemetery, Norfolk.

SKINNER, TRISTRIM LOWTHER. b. Edenton, North Carolina, May 11, 1820. att. UNC and William Mary. m. Eliza Fish Harwood. In North Carolina legisl. Chowan Co. planter. Capt., Co. A, 1st North Carolina, May 16, 1861. Major - April 21, 1862. KIA at Mechanicsville, June 26, 1862.

SLAUGHTER, PHILIP PEYTON. b. Orange Co., Virginia, Aug. 10, 1834. gr. VMI, 1857. Teacher in Baton Rouge, Louisiana. Lt. Col., 56th Virginia, May 3, 1862. Colonel - July 30, 1863. Applied for retirement, May 20, 1864, due to thigh wound at

Gaines' Mill. m. Emma Thompson, 1871. Orange railroad agent. Died in the Richmond Soldiers' Home, April 21, 1893.

SLAUGHTER, WILLIAM MARION. b. 1825. gr. William and Mary. Lawyer and planter near Albany, Georgia. m. Marcella Jane Tinsley. Capt., Co. K, 51st Georgia, March 4, 1862. Colonel - March 22, 1862. MWIA near Zoan Church at Chancellorsville on May 1, 1863, and died that evening. bur. Albany.

SLEMP, CAMPBELL. b. Lee Co., Virginia, Dec. 2, 1839. att. Emory & Henry. Capt., Co. A, 21st Virginia Battalion, Sept. 16, 1861. Lt. Col. - 1862. Colonel, 64th Virginia, Dec. 1862. m. Nannie B. Cawood, 1864. In U. S. Congress, 1903-1907. d. Wise Co., Oct. 13, 1907.

SLOAN, JOHN. Of Guilford Co. Capt., Co. B, 27th North Carolina, April 20, 1861. Lt. Col. - Sept. 28, 1861. Colonel - Dec. 23, 1861. Dropped at re-org. Died sometime before 1883.

SLOAN, JOHN BAYLIS EARLE. b. Franklin Co., Georgia, March 29, 1828. Merchant in Pendleton, South Carolina, in 1860, worth $17,000. m. Mary Earle Seaborn. Colonel, 4th South Carolina, April 14, 1861. The regiment ceased to exist at 1862 re-org. Sloan later was collector of the War Tax in Kind for South Carolina. m. Mollie Seaborne. In South Carolina legisl., 1880-82. d. Charleston, Feb. 23, 1906. bur. St. Paul's Episcopal Church, Pendleton.

SLOAN, THOMAS. Lawyer in Columbus in 1860, age 30. Lt., Co. D, 3rd Georgia Battalion, Nov. 18, 1861. Capt., Co. F, 53rd Georgia, May 2, 1862. Lt. Col. - June 4, 1862. MWIA at Sharpsburg, died Sept. 23, 1862. bur. Hagerstown Confederate Cemetery. A member of the regiment wrote on Aug. 25, 1862: "[Sloan] treats the boys very tyranically and has got the ill will of all the regt. I don't suppose he has a friend in the whole regt."

SLOUGH, NELSON. b. Cabarrus Co., North Carolina. Mexican War veteran, suffered a wounded leg in Mexico. Cabarrus Co. Clerk of Courts. Capt., Co. A, 20th North Carolina, April 19, 1861, aged 43. Major - June 27, 1862. Lt. Col. - Nov. 8, 1862.

POW at South Mountain, exchanged Nov. 1862. Wded. at Gettysburg. Resigned to become Cabarrus Co. Sheriff, Oct. 26, 1863. d. Anderson, South Carolina, 1900.

SMEAD, ABNER. b. Georgia, April 4, 1833. att. U. Virginia. gr. USMA, 1854. Lt., U. S. Army, 1854-61. Lt. of artillery, P.A.C.S., April 3, 1861. Major, 19th Mississippi, June 10, 1861. Major, 12th Georgia, June 15, 1861. Lt. Col., 12th Georgia, Dec. 13, 1861. Lt. Col. and a.a.g. to Genl. Edward Johnson, May 17, 1862. Colonel and a.i.g. to T. J. Jackson then to Ewell. Colonel of artillery - Aug. 11, 1862. Ordered to Wilmington, North Carolina, in Nov. 1864. Physician in Harrisonburg, Virginia, postwar. d. Salem, Virginia, July 24, 1904.

SMITH, ALEXANDER D. b. South Carolina, Nov. 23, 1839. Capt., Co. D, 26th South Carolina, Feb. 4, 1862. Lt. Col. - March 24, 1862. Colonel - Sept. 9, 1862. "Suspended by court-martial six months from Jan. 1, 1864." d. Dec. 1, 1867. bur. Smith family cemetery, Marlboro Co., South Carolina.

SMITH, ANDREW J. b. Mecklenburg Co., Virginia, June 28, 1821. Tobacconist in Pittsylvania Co. in 1860. Capt., Co. I, 57th Virginia, July 17, 1861. Major - May 7, 1862. Resigned due to a lung hemorrhage, May 23, 1862. Moved to Augusta, Georgia, fall of 1862. Ran a grocery and commission house there. d. Augusta, Jan. 10, 1895.

SMITH, AUGUSTUS MARSHALL. b. Abbeville Dist., Oct. 22, 1827. gr. South Carolina College, 1848. A very wealthy man. Major, 1st South Carolina (Gregg's), July 1861. Lt. Col. - Dec. 14, 1861. MWIA at Gaines' Mill, where he entered the fight despite being seriously ill. Died at the residence of Mrs. Allan, 5th & Main Streets, Richmond, on June 30, 1862. bur. Trinity Church, Abbeville.

SMITH, BENJAMIN BURGH, JR. b. May 15, 1835. gr. SCMA, 1855. Physician. Lt. of Engineers, Jan. 1861. Capt., Co. B, 11th South Carolina, June 18, 1861. Major - Sept. 19, 1861. Dropped at May 1862 re-org. Major, 2nd Battalion South Carolina Sharpshooters, June 22, 1862. Served as a.a.g. to Gist. Wded. at Franklin. Paroled at Greensboro, May 1, 1865, as commander of the 16th and 24th South Carolina combined. Civil engineer in Charleston. d. Charleston, Feb. 7, 1904. bur. St. Paul's Episcopal Cemetery, Summerville, South Carolina.

SMITH, CALEB. b. Petersburg, Virginia, Dec. 14, 1824. Nephew of Gov. "Extra Billy" Smith. Lt. of Artillery, U. S. Army, 1848-61. Capt. of infantry, P.A.C.S., June 26, 1861, to rank from March 16. Major, 49th Virginia, July 17, 1861. Wded. leg (broken near hip) at 1st Manassas. Dropped at May 1, 1862, re-org. Captain commanding Paroled & Exchanged Prisoners late in the war. Paroled at Richmond, May 17, 1865. Lawyer in Nelson Co. d. Dec. 22, 1874, at Lovingston Station, Nelson Co.

SMITH, EDWIN R. b. Washington Co., Virginia, Nov. 14, 1828. Bricklayer in Russell Co. Capt., Co. G, 29th Virginia, March 27, 1862. Major - April 10, 1863. Wded. in right arm and right leg near Bermuda Hundred, May 18, 1864. Lt. Col. - June 2, 1864. Bricklayer in Russell Co. post-war. d. Oct. 8, 1908.

SMITH, FRANCIS HENNEY. b. Norfolk, Oct. 18, 1812. gr. USMA, 1833. USMA faculty. m. Sara Henderson, 1835. Professor at Hampden-Sydney. On VMI staff, and its Supt., 1839-1889. Colonel, 9th Virginia, July 7, 1861 (had been Col. of Virginia State Troops in May). Dropped at re-org. Author of several educational and text books. d. Lexington, March 21, 1890. Evidence of hostility between Smith and "Stonewall" Jackson is in the Jed Hotchkiss Papers at the Library of Congress.

SMITH, FRANCIS WILLIAMSON. b. Norfolk, Nov. 12, 1838. Nephew of Francis Henney Smith. gr. VMI and U. Virginia. On VMI staff. Military Secretary to R. E. Lee in May 1861, while Lee was commanding Virginia forces. Served briefly as Major, 41st Virginia, during the summer of 1861. V.a.d.c. to Mahone at Seven Pines. Major of artillery - May 21, 1862, stationed at Drewry's Bluff. Commanded an artillery bn. during the retreat from Petersburg and was MWIA at Amelia Springs, April 5, 1865. d. April 6. bur. Baltimore. Smith also has a stone in Cedar Grove Cemetery, Norfolk.

SMITH, FREDERICK C. Pvt., Co. C, 24th Georgia, Aug. 24, 1861. Captain - Dec. 27, 1862. Major - Sept. 10, 1864. Wded.

slightly in face, May 1864. POW at Sayler's Creek, released July 25, 1865.

SMITH, FREDERICK FRELINGHUYSEN. b. Ripley, Virginia, April 1, 1840. Capt., Co. G, 17th Virginia Cavalry (originally in 33rd Virginia Cav. Bn.), Oct. 1, 1862. Major, 17th Virginia Cavalry, Jan. 28, 1863. KIA at Monocacy, July 9, 1864. bur. Zion Episcopal Church, but stone has been removed.

SMITH, GAYNES CHISLOM. b. Giles City, Tennessee, Feb. 23, 1827. Lawyer and teacher in Limestone Co., Alabama. Lt., Co. H, 9th Alabama, June 18, 1861. Captain - Oct. 1, 1861. Lt. Col. - March 19, 1863. POW at Gettysburg. d. April 28, 1910.

SMITH, GEORGE HUGH. b. Philadelphia, Pennsylvania, Feb. 3, 1834. gr. VMI, 1853. 5′8″. Capt., Co. E, 25th Virginia, June 11, 1861. Colonel - May 1, 1862. Wded. thigh at McDowell and arm at 2nd Manassas. POW at Rich Mountain. Colonel, 62nd Virginia, Jan. 28, 1863. Paroled at Amherst C. H., June 7, 1865. Married the widow of Col. George S. Patton, Susan Thornton Glassell Patton, and thus became the step-grandfather of General George S. Patton of 20th-century note. Judge and law author in Los Angeles. Died Feb. 6, 1915.

SMITH, ISAAC NOYES. b. Charleston, Virginia, April 6, 1831. gr. Washington College. In Virginia legisl. pre-war. Major, 22nd Virginia, July 16, 1861. Resigned Nov. 6, 1861. Early in 1862 Smith went through the Federal lines and reported to General Rosecrans, although it is not clear for what precise purpose. Owned the Kanawha Salt Co. In West Virginia legisl. postwar. d. Oct. 6, 1883. bur. Spring Hill Cemetery, Charleston.

SMITH, JAMES MILTON. b. Twiggs Co., Georgia, Oct. 24, 1823. Columbus lawyer. Capt., Co. D, 13th Georgia, July 8, 1861. Major - same date. Lt. Col. - Feb. 1, 1862. Colonel - Sept. 17, 1862. Severely wded. at Gaines' Mill. Resigned Dec. 14, 1863, having been elected to the C. S. Congress. Judge and Gov. of Georgia post-war. d. Nov. 26, 1890. bur. Gainesville.

SMITH, JOHN T. Of Randolph Co. Capt., Co. I, 13th Alabama, July 19, 1861. Major - Jan. 14, 1863. KIA at Chancellorsville.

SMITH, JOSEPH THOMAS. b. Elbert Co., Georgia, Sept. 19, 1824. m. Mary Elizabeth Alexander. Capt., Co. I, 15th Georgia, July 15, 1861. Major - Dec. 23, 1861. Major, 9th Georgia Battalion, March 19, 1862. Lt. Col., 37th Georgia, May 6, 1863. Smith had his name legally changed to Armand after the war. d. Waycross, May 16, 1885.

SMITH, LEVI BECK. b. Jones Co., May 5, 1819. m. Mary Margaret Gullet, 1841. Lawyer and planter in Talbotton. In Georgia legisl. and Secession Convention (voted yes). Capt., Co. K, 27th Georgia, Sept. 10, 1861. Colonel - Sept. 11, 1861. Wded. in thigh at Seven Pines. KIA at Sharpsburg.

SMITH, MAURICE THOMPSON. b. Granville, North Carolina, 1828. att. UNC. Planter. 5′11″. Capt., Co. K, 55th North Carolina, May 30, 1862. Lt. Col. - early 1863. KIA at Gettysburg.

SMITH, ROBERT A. b. Clinton, Georgia, Dec. 19, 1824. gr. Oglethorpe College, 1843. Macon lawyer. Capt., Co. B, 2nd Georgia Battalion, April 20, 1861. Colonel, 44th Georgia, March 15, 1862. MWIA at Mechanicsville, d. June 28, 1862. bur. Rose Hill Cemetery, Macon.

SMITH, ROBERT CARTER. b. Baltimore Co., Maryland, 1828. Baltimore merchant. Grandson of Baltimore's famous War of 1812 General, Samuel Smith. Lt., Co. C, 1st Maryland, May 1861. Capt., Co. C, 1st Maryland Cavalry Battalion, Aug. 4, 1862. Major - Aug. 25, 1863. Wded. at Greenland Gap, April 25, 1863. Retired to Invalid Corps, Dec. 2, 1864. Unmarried. d. Catonsville, Maryland, Feb. 13, 1900. bur. Loudon Park, Baltimore.

SMITH, ROBERT S. b. April 14, 1836. Lived in Troup Co., Georgia. Capt., Co. B, 4th Georgia, April 26, 1861. Major - May 8, 1862. KIA at Sharpsburg. bur. Hillview Cemetery, LaGrange.

SMITH, SAMUEL WEBB. b. Granville Co., North Carolina, Oct. 20, 1839. Lived in Tulip, Arkansas. Pvt., Co. I, 3rd Arkansas, June 25, 1861. Sgt. - July 5, 1861. Lt. - Feb. 11, 1862. Capt. - mid-1862. Major - May 6, 1864. Wded. in both legs at Gettysburg. Retired, due to wounds, Dec. 3, 1864. m. Hester Ann

Hargrove. Merchant and bank president in Malvern, Arkansas. d. June 5, 1903. bur. Oak Grove Cemetery, Malvern.

SMITH, THEOPHILUS JACKSON. b. Sparta, Georgia, Nov. 17, 1819. A large planter. m. Mary Salome Gardner. Capt., Co. E, 15th Georgia, July 15, 1861. Major - May 1, 1862. Lt. Col. - 1862. Resigned, disability, Jan. 14, 1863. d. Leesburg, Florida, Oct. 14, 1881. bur. Sparta.

SMITH, THOMAS. b. Culpeper C. H., Virginia, Aug. 25, 1836. Son of Gov. "Extra Billy" Smith. att. U. Virginia. gr. William & Mary. Lawyer in Charleston, Virginia. Pvt., Co. H, 22nd Virginia, briefly in early 1861. Major, 36th Virginia, July 16, 1861. Lt. Col. - March 30, 1864. Colonel - May 18, 1864. Wded. at Cloyd's Farm. Warrenton lawyer and in Virginia legisl. U. S. Attorney for New Mexico, then Chief Justice, New Mexico Territory. m. Elizabeth Fairfax Gaines. d. Warrenton, Virginia, June 29, 1918.

SMITH, THOMAS McGEHEE. b. 1834. gr. UNC, 1855. Caswell Co. lawyer. Capt., Co. I, 45th North Carolina, April 8, 1862. Major - June 26, 1863. KIA at Bethesda Church, May 30, 1864.

SMITH, TIMOLEON. b. Louisa Co. Master carpenter there in 1860, age 33. m. Mrs. Bettie V. Goodwin (nee Terrell), 1868. Capt., Co. C, 56th Virginia, July 9, 1861. Major - July 30, 1863. Lt. Col. - June 13, 1864. Wded. at Frayser's Farm. Paroled at Louisa C. H., May 22, 1865. Farmer. d. Louisa Co., April 30, 1903.

SMITH, WILLIAM RUSSELL. b. Russellville, Kentucky, March 27, 1815. att. U. Alabama. Lawyer and editor in Tuscaloosa, Alabama. In Alabama legisl. In U. S. Congress, 1851-57. Recruited the 26th Alabama, and was its Colonel in early 1861, but resigned before fighting began. In C. S. Congress, 1861-65. President, U. Alabama. Washington, D. C., lawyer. d. there Feb. 26, 1896. Wrote several books, including a personal memoir.

SMITH, WILLIAM THOMAS. b. Petersburg, Virginia, Jan. 4, 1844. Farm worker in St. Clair Co., Alabama. Lt., Co. F, 10th Alabama, Sept. 15, 1861. Captain - July 9, 1863. Lt. Col. - Nov.

26, 1864. In Alabama legisl. Shelby County merchant. d. Wilsonville, Alabama, April 23, 1915.

SNEAD, CLAIBORNE. b. Augusta, Georgia, March 31, 1836. att. U. Georgia. m. Cora Clayton. Lawyer and planter in Parnell, Georgia. Lt., Co. G, 3rd Georgia, April 26, 1861. Captain - April 28, 1862. Lt. Col. - July 13, 1864, for "Valor & Skill." Wded. at Malvern Hill. POW at Gettysburg, exchanged April 1864. Appx. Judge and Georgia legisl. d. Jan. 25, 1909.

SNOWDEN, ROBERT BOGARDUS. b. New York, May 24, 1836. Raised in Tennessee, attended military school under Bushrod Johnson. Lt., Co. C, 1st Tennessee, May 25, 1861. Dropped at re-org. Capt. and a.a.g. to Bushrod Johnson, 1862-63. Lt. Col., 25th Tennessee, June 24, 1863. Retired to Invalid Corps, March 8, 1865. Realtor in Memphis. Multi-millionaire New York City businessman. d. Atlantic City, New Jersey, Oct. 6, 1909. bur. Memphis, Tennessee.

SPALDING, JAMES WILLETT. b. Richmond, Virginia, 1827. m. Miss Fetterman. Sailed to Japan with Perry as a naval clerk, and wrote a book on the experience. Lived in Texas after leaving the navy, and in Philippi, West Virginia. Lt. Col., 60th Virginia, Aug. 20, 1861. KIA at Sewell Mountain, Virginia, Sept. 27, 1861. bur. Shockoe Cemetery, Richmond. According to one soldier, Spalding "got drunk and rode right into the pickets of the enemy and they shot him through the body, and he died in five minutes."

SPEER, WILLIAM HENRY ASBURY. b. July 6, 1826. Of Yadkin Co., North Carolina. 5'10". Capt., Co. I, 28th North Carolina, Aug. 13, 1861. POW at Hanover C.H., May 27, 1862. Major - Nov. 1, 1862. Lt. Col. - March 12, 1863. Colonel - July 8, 1864. Wded. at Chancellorsville and Gettysburg. MWIA by shell in the head at Reams' Station, August 24, 1864, d. August 29.

SPENCE, JOHN MIDDLETON. b. Appling Co., 1834. m. (1) Miss Hargraves, 1853. Capt., Co. C, 50th Georgia, Mar. 4, 1862. Major - Dec. 21, 1863. Present into 1864. Farmer post-war in Coffee Co. m. (2) Levinia S. Brett, 1866. In Georgia legisl. d. Ware Co., Nov. 22, 1896.

SPENCER, SAMUEL BACON. b. Liberty Co., Dec. 26, 1827. Lawyer and teacher. att. U. Georgia. Capt., Co. A, 20th Georgia Partisan Rangers, May 12, 1862. Major - Sept. 15, 1863. Lt. Col. - May 28, 1864. Unit was broken up in July 1864. Mayor of Atlanta, 1866. d. Atlanta, Oct. 16, 1901.

SPENCER, WILLIAM H. b. Kentucky, 1823. Opelousas, Louisiana, editor. Capt., Co. K, 10th Louisiana, July 22, 1861. Major - Jan. 16, 1862. Lt. Col. - July 1862. KIA at 2nd Manassas.

SPENGLER, ABRAHAM. b. Shenandoah Co., March 21, 1832. Moved to Moorefield in 1850. Carpenter. 5′4″. Capt., Co. F, 33rd Virginia, May 23, 1861. Lt. Col. - Feb. 1, 1863. Colonel - Mar. 21, 1864. Wded. at Cedar Mountain. Lived in Hardy Co., West Virginia, post-war. d. Hardy Co., Aug. 1880. bur. Olivet Cemetery, Moorefield.

SPESSARD, MICHAEL PETERS. b. Aug. 26, 1821. Lived in Craig Co., Virginia. Capt., Co. C, 28th Virginia, May 10, 1861. Major - July 3, 1863. Wded. at Gaines' Mill. Commanded Hunton's Brigade at Appomattox. m. 3 times. d. June 17, 1889, in Craig Co.

SPRUILL, SAMUEL B. Of Bertie Co. Member of North Carolina Secession Convention. Colonel, 2nd North Carolina Cavalry, June 21, 1861. Resigned March 29, 1862.

SQUIRES, CHARLES WINDER. b. New Orleans, Dec. 26, 1841. Lt., 1st Co., Washington Artillery (Louisiana), May 26, 1861. Capt. - Sept. 27, 1861. Wded. at Fredericksburg. POW at 2nd Fredericksburg, May 3, 1863. Major - Jan. 1864. Sent to the Trans-Mississippi Dept., 1864. Moved to St. Louis in 1872, where he developed mining interests. Died in St. Louis, Jan. 23, 1900.

STACKHOUSE, ELI THOMAS. b. Marion Dist., South Carolina, March 27, 1824. Planter. m. Anna Fore. Capt., Co. I, 8th South Carolina, April 13, 1861. Major - July 5, 1863. Lt. Col. - Sept. 18, 1863. Wded. in the chest by a shell, July 1864. In South Carolina legisl. A founder of Clemson U. In U. S. Congress, 1891-92. d. Washington, D. C., June 14, 1892.

STAKES, EDWARD THOMAS. b. Accomack Co., Virginia, Sept. 18, 1835. Brick mason in Northumberland County. Capt., Co. A, 40th Virginia, May 26, 1861. Major - Sept. 15, 1862. POW in Northumberland Co., June 2, 1863, exchanged Feb. 24, 1865. Paroled at Northumberland C. H., May 8, 1865. Went to Texas and served as a peace officer. d. Beverlyville, Northumberland Co., Virginia, Feb. 18, 1881. bur. Rehoboth Methodist Churchyard.

STALLINGS, WALTER SCOTT. Of Franklin Co., North Carolina. att. Yale, in the class of 1857. Capt., Co. D, 2nd North Carolina, July 16, 1861, age 27. Major - Sept. 17, 1862. Lt. Col. - Mar. 21, 1863. Wded. at Chancellorsville. KIA at Snicker's Gap, Virginia, July 18, 1864. bur. Stonewall Cemetery, Winchester.

STALLWORTH, NICHOLAS. b. Conecuh Co., Alabama, March 10, 1837. att. U. Alabama. Lived in Evergreen, Alabama. Pvt., Co. C, 1st Alabama, 1861. Capt., Co. F, Hilliard's Legion (Alabama), May 14, 1862. Major, 23rd Alabama Battalion Sharpshooters, March 14, 1864. Wded. Sept. 20, 1863. Appx. Farmer and tax assessor in Falls Co., Texas, post-war. d. Marlin, Texas, Feb. 28, 1909. In 1865, a North Carolina Captain called Stallworth "a real clever gentleman."

STANSEL, MARTIN LUTHER. b. Washington Co., Georgia, Apr. 23, 1822. gr. U. Alabama. Carrollton lawyer. Pvt., Co. C, 41st Alabama, March 25, 1862. Major - May 16, 1862. Lt. Col. - Oct. 15, 1862. Colonel - June 27, 1863. Wded. leg at Murfreesboro. Appx. In Alabama legisl. President, Alabama Bar Assoc., 1882-83. U.C.V. official. d. Carrollton, June 25, 1902.

STANSILL, JESSE F. Of Rowan Co. Lt., Co. B, 4th North Carolina, May 16, 1861, aged 27. Captain - Feb. 11, 1863. Major - summer 1864. Wded. at Chancellorsville, Gettysburg and Snicker's Gap (July 18, 1864). Paroled at Salisbury, May 19, 1865.

STARK, ALEXANDER WALLACE. b. Virginia, 1839. Lt., USMC, 1855-62. Stark was aboard the U.S. Sloop *St. Marys* at sea until she came to port in San Francisco many months after the war began. Major of artillery - June 18, 1862. Lt. Col. - Nov. 26,

1864. Served in the Richmond defenses most of the war. Appx. d. Norfolk, Virginia, April 5, 1898, aged 58.

STEDMAN, CHARLES MANLY. b. Pittsboro, North Carolina, Jan. 29, 1841. gr. UNC, 1861. 5′11″. Pvt., Co. H, 1st North Carolina (Bethel), April 17, 1861. Lt., Co. E, 44th North Carolina, Feb. 17, 1862. Captain - March 28, 1862. Major - July 28, 1862. Suffered a shell wound in the foot, May 1864. Appx. Lt. Gov. of North Carolina, 1884-88. In U. S. Congress, 1911-1930, where he was the last surviving CSA veteran. d. Washington, D. C., Sept. 23, 1930.

STEEDMAN, JOHN MARCELLUS. b. Sept. 18, 1833. Planter and merchant in Lexington District. gr. SCMA. Capt., Co. K, 9th South Carolina, July 8, 1861. Major - July 12, 1861. Lt. Col., 6th South Carolina, April 22, 1862. Colonel - May 6, 1864. Wded. at Seven Days and 2nd Manassas. Assassinated by Negroes at his residence on the Edisto in Lexington District, Jan. 7, 1867. bur. Batesburg, South Carolina.

STEPHENS, LINTON. b. Crawfordville, Georgia, July 1, 1823. gr. U. Georgia, 1843, with first honors. gr. U. Virginia, 1845. In Georgia legisl. Lt. Col., 15th Georgia, July 15, 1861. Resigned Dec. 19, 1861. Later became Capt. and Lt. Col., 7th Georgia Battalion States Guard Cavalry. d. July 14, 1872. bur. near Crawfordville.

STEVENS, PETER FAYSSOUX. b. Florida, June 22, 1830. Brother of Gen. C. H. Stevens and brother-in-law of Ellison Capers. Supt. of SCMA, and commanded that institution's cadets at Ft. Sumter. Ordained as an Episcopal minister in 1861. Colonel, Holcombe Legion (South Carolina), Nov. 21, 1861. Wded. at Sharpsburg. Resigned Oct. 8, 1862. Returned to clerical duties in South Carolina, primarily laboring amongst the Negroes of that state. Episcopal bishop post-war. d. Charleston, Jan. 9, 1910. bur. West Side Episcopal Church, Pendleton, South Carolina.

STEWART, CHARLES H. Clerk in Jefferson Co., Virginia. Lt., Co. K, 2nd Virginia, April 20, 1861, aged 29. Captain - April 20,

1862. Major - April 21, 1864. Paroled at Mt. Jackson, April 20, 1865. d. Oct. 18, 1866. bur. Edge Hill Cemetery, Jefferson Co.

STEWART, DAVID BOSTON. b. Nov. 4, 1826. Farmer in Monongalia Co., Virginia. 5′8½″. Major, 48th Virginia, 1861. Dropped at April 1862 re-org. POW in Highland Co., Virginia, Aug. 7, 1862. Stewart was authorized to raise a bn. of Partisan Rangers in 1862, but no record of success exists. He was commanding some miscellaneous cavalry forces under Genl. William L. Jackson at Beverly in the summer of 1863. In Virginia legisl., 1863-64. m. (1) Rhena Snider. m. (2) Sarah Jane Evans. d. Morgantown, West Virginia, March 21, 1915. bur. Oak Grove Cemetery, Monongalia Co.

STEWART, JAMES MADISON. b. Pickens Dist., South Carolina, May 16, 1839. Capt., Co. F, 22nd South Carolina, Jan. 18, 1862. Major - May 5, 1862. "Cashiered Oct. 16, 1862," obviously as the result of his performance at Sharpsburg (see Col. Stevens' report). Stewart went on to serve in the ranks in Virginia throughout the war. Pickens Co. Clerk of Courts. Baptist minister in North Carolina and South Carolina. d. Feb. 26, 1929. bur. Secona Church, Pickens, South Carolina.

STEWART, JOSEPH A. Physician in Newton Co. in 1860, age 37. m. Rebecca Starr. Capt., Co. B, 18th Georgia, April 30, 1861. Major - May 27, 1863. Wded. at Chancellorsville. Resigned to accept appt. of Surgeon from the Gov. of Georgia, Jan. 4, 1864.

STEWART, WILLIAM HENRY. b. Deep Creek, Virginia, Sept. 25, 1838. att. U. Virginia. Lt., "Wise Light Dragoons," April 22, 1861, but the unit never organized. Capt., Co. A, 61st Virginia, July 11, 1861. (The company did not become part of the 61st Virginia until May 1862.) Major - May 22, 1862. Lt. Col. - May 12, 1864. Wded. at Spotsylvania. Appx. Portsmouth lawyer. Wrote a history of Norfolk Co., Virginia, and two fine Confederate books. d. Feb. 9, 1912. bur. Maplewood Cemetery, Charlottesville.

STIKES, AUGUSTUS. b. South Carolina. Capt., Co. C, 12th Alabama, May 27, 1861. The very scanty service record supplies no further information, but Stikes is shown on some lists as Major of the 12th Alabama.

STILES, BENJAMIN EDWARD. b. Savannah, April 24, 1836. m. Clelia Stiles (1840-1887). Capt., Co. E, 16th Georgia, July 24, 1861. Major - May 18, 1863. Lt. Col. - Nov. 29, 1863. Wded. at Malvern Hill. KIA near Front Royal, Virginia, Aug. 16, 1864. bur. Winchester.

STILES, ROBERT AUGUSTUS. b. Woodford, Kentucky, June 27, 1836. gr. Yale U. and U. Virginia. Dropped his middle name after the war. Pvt., 1st Co., Richmond Howitzers, July 22, 1861. Adj., Cabell's Artillery Battalion, May 1863 until late 1864. Lt., 1st Confederate Engineers, to rank from Sept. 29, 1864. Major of artillery, Jan. 13, 1865, to rank from Nov. 29, 1864. Richmond lawyer. d. Oct. 5, 1905.

STILES, WILLIAM HENRY. b. Savannah, Jan. 1, 1810. att. Yale. In U. S. Congress and U. S. diplomatic service pre-war. Lt. Col., 4th Georgia Battalion, Sept. 19, 1861. Colonel, 60th Georgia, July 15, 1862. Wded. at Fredericksburg. Resigned Aug. 30, 1864. d. Savannah, Dec. 20, 1865. Stiles' papers are at Emory and UNC. He is buried in Laurel Grove Cemetery, Savannah.

STOCKDALE, THOMAS RINGLAND. b. Green Co., Pennsylvania, Feb. 28, 1828. gr. Washington & Jefferson College and U. Mississippi. Lt., Co. E, 16th Mississippi, April 23, 1861. Adj., 16th Mississippi, June 4, 1861. Major - June 17, 1861. Dropped at May 1862 re-org. Later became Major and Lt. Col., 4th Mississippi Cavalry; also was Major, Stockdale's Battalion Mississippi Cavalry. m. Fannie Wicker, 1867. In U. S. Congress, 1887-95. On Mississippi Supreme Court, 1896-99. Died in Summit, Mississippi, Jan. 9, 1899.

STOKES, MONTFORT SYDNEY. (given names are sometimes rendered Mumford Sidney) b. Oct. 6, 1810. Major in the Mexican War. U. S. Navy pre-war. Lived in Wilkes Co., North Carolina. Colonel, 1st North Carolina, May 16, 1861. MWIA at Mechanicsville, June 26, 1862, d. July 8.

STOKES, WILLIAM. b. Oct. 20, 1836. Lt. Col., 4th South Carolina Cavalry, Dec. 16, 1862, at org. Assigned command at Green

Pond, June 15, 1863, and at Coosawhatchie, Dec. 1863. Still Lt. Col., 4th South Carolina Cavalry, in Dec. 1864. m. Eliza Jane Boulware. Planter and lumberman. d. June 30, 1906. bur. Hampton Cemetery, Hampton, South Carolina.

STONE, JOHN MARSHALL. b. Gibson Co., Tennessee, April 30, 1830. Capt., Co. K, 2nd Mississippi, May 1, 1861. Colonel - April 16, 1862. POW at Salisbury, North Carolina, April 12, 1865. m. Mary Gillam Coman, 1872. Wrote that in battle "I almost always lost my bearings." Gov. of Mississippi. 6'0" d. Holly Springs, Mississippi, March 26, 1900.

STONE, WILLIAM MERK. b. Tennessee, March 20, 1834. Lived in Lamar Co., Alabama. m. Elizabeth M. Lloyd. Capt., Co. D, Jeff Davis Legion, June 29, 1861. Major - Feb. 13, 1862. Conscript officer in Alabama in 1864. d. Lamar Co., Dec. 18, 1916.

STOVER, JOSHUA. b. Strasburg, Virginia, April 29, 1824. Mexican War veteran. m. Mary Jane Crabill, 1853. Capt., Co. A, 10th Virginia, April 18, 1861. Major - May 8, 1862. KIA at Chancellorsville. bur. Fredericksburg Confederate Cemetery.

STOWE, SAMUEL NEEL. b. 1822. Physician in Gaston Co., North Carolina. 6'3". m. twice. Lt., Co. B, 28th North Carolina, July 30, 1861. Captain - Feb. 27, 1862. Major - April 16, 1863. Retired to Invalid Corps, Dec. 13, 1864. POW at Slash Church, May 27, 1862. Wded. at Gettysburg. Moved to Texas after the war. d. 1894. Brother of William A. Stowe (see next entry) and of Jasper and Leroy W. Stowe (see appendix).

STOWE, WILLIAM A. b. Jan. 31, 1832. Of Gaston Co., North Carolina. Sgt., Co. M, 16th North Carolina, May 1, 1861. Captain - June 17, 1861. Major - April 26, 1862. Lt. Col. - May 31, 1862. Colonel - Dec. 8, 1863. Wded. at Gaines' Mill and in the head at Chancellorsville. Appx. In North Carolina legisl. Planter. d. June 19, 1908.

STRANGE, JAMES MAGRUDER. b. Fluvanna Co., Virginia, Aug. 6, 1818. In Virginia legisl. Planter. Capt., Co. D, 1st Battalion Virginia Reserves, April 16, 1864. Major - May 31, 1864. Paroled at Richmond, May 5, 1865.

Ben Ritter

JOSHUA STOVER
10th Virginia Infantry

STRANGE, JOHN BOWIE. b. Fluvanna Co., Virginia, 1823. gr. VMI, 1842. Founded Albermarle Military Institute. President of Norfolk Academy. Staff officer of Virginia Volunteers pre-war. Lt. Col., 19th Virginia, May 2, 1861. Colonel - April 29, 1862. KIA at Boonsboro, Sept. 14, 1862.

STRATON, WILLIAM. b. Logan Co., Virginia, April 14, 1821. m. Mary Ann Perry, 1849. Lawyer and Clerk of Logan Co. Court. Capt., Co. B, 34th Virginia Cavalry Battalion, Jan. 18, 1862. Major - May 2, 1863. Wded. in arms and chest at Beech Creek, Logan Co., Virginia, Aug. 7, 1862. Dropped, June 28, 1864. In West Virginia legisl. post-war. d. Logan Co., June 29, 1903.

STRIBLING, ROBERT MACKEY. b. Markham, Virginia, Dec. 3, 1833. gr. U. Pennsylvania, M.D., 1854. 5′9″. Lived at Farrowsville, Fauquier Co. m. twice. Capt., Fauquier Artillery (Virginia), July 1861. Major of artillery - Feb. 27, 1864, assigned to Cutshaw's Bn. Lt. Col. - Feb. 18, 1865. Paroled at Winchester, April 20, 1865. d. Markham, March 27, 1914.

SPRINGFIELD, WILLIAM WILLIAMS. b. Nashville, Tennessee, May 7, 1837. Lived near Knoxville. Pvt., Co. F, 1st Tennesee Cavalry, 1861. Capt., Co. E, 31st Tennessee, Nov. 1861 - 1862. Major, Thomas' Legion (North Carolina), Sept. 27, 1862. Present into 1865. m. Maria M. Love. In North Carolina legisl. Asheville businessman; Waynesville surveyor and hotel proprietor. d. March 6, 1923 at Waynesville.

STRONG, HENRY B. b. Ireland. Clerk in New Orleans. Capt., Co. B, 6th Louisiana, June 5, 1861, aged 40. Lt. Col. - May 9, 1862. Colonel - 1862. KIA at Sharpsburg. Buried "in the hollow south of Dunkard Church." An 1872 paper reported the removal of Strong's body to Rosehill Cemetery, Hagerstown.

STUART, WILLIAM DABNEY. b. Staunton, Sept. 30, 1830. gr. VMI, 1850. Richmond teacher and school official. Lt. Col., 15th Virginia, July 1861. Colonel, 56th Virginia, Sept. 17, 1861. MWIA at Gettysburg, died at Staunton on July 30, 1863. bur. Thornrose Cemetery.

STUBBS, JOHN W. b. Oct. 23, 1828. Farmer in Bibb Co. Capt., Co. B, 27th Georgia, June 12, 1861. Major - Aug. 24, 1862. Lt. Col. - Sept. 17, 1862. Resigned, chronic nephritis, Jan. 10, 1863. d. Apr. 28, 1882.

STURGES, JOHN REYNOLDS. b. Dec. 31, 1827. gr. Yale, 1847. Lawyer. Never married. Lt., Co. A, 3rd Georgia, April 26, 1861. Major - April 28, 1862. Lt. Col. - June 15, 1862. Colonel - June 19, 1862. KIA at Malvern Hill. bur. Waynesboro, Georgia, Confederate Cemetery.

STYLES, CAREY WENTWORTH. b. Spartanburg, South Carolina, 1825. Mayor of Brunswick, Georgia. Lawyer and duelist; killed a man in a duel at Brunswick. Capt., Co. L, 26th Georgia, April 18, 1861. Colonel - Aug. 17, 1861. Resigned, May 10, 1862. Founded the Atlanta *Constitution*, and owned or was associated with 21 other papers in Georgia and Texas. In Georgia legisl. d. Stephenville, Texas, Feb. 25, 1897. bur. there.

SULAKOWSKI, VALERY. b. Poland. Colonel, 14th Louisiana, June 1861. "Cruel, despotic, and absolutely merciless." Resigned Feb. 15, 1862, suffering from offended pride. He expressed vivid anti-Confederate sentiments in correspondence with "Beast" Butler, but subsequently served on Magruder's staff as an engineer officer—until he resigned in yet another huff.

SUMMERS, JOHN CALHOUN. b. Monroe Co., Virginia, Feb. 1, 1839. att. Emory & Henry and U. Virginia. Capt., Co. A, 60th Virginia (had been Co. B, 59th Virginia), June 17, 1861. Major, 60th Virginia, April 27, 1862. Lt. Col. - Aug. 6, 1862. Convicted on Mar. 20, 1862, by a court-martial, of "Mutinous Conduct," and suspended for 30 days after a public reprimand. Resigned in July 1863 due to disagreements with the company officers. Elected to 1902 Virginia Constitutional Convention. d. Abingdon, June 19, 1907. bur. Walnut Grove Cemetery.

SUTHERLAND, ST. CLAIR F. Lived in Maryland. Civilian employee of the QM Dept. in Richmond. Capt., Co. E, 3rd Virginia LDT, June 16, 1863, aged 38. Major - May 26, 1864. Lt. Col. - Sept. 23, 1864. Cashiered, Dec. 20, 1864, and returned to the ranks as Pvt., Co. E.

SWAN, ROBERT. Of Alleghany Co., Maryland. Lt., Voltigeurs Regt., Mexican War. Distinguished himself there at Chapultepec, at the age of 19. Major, 1st Virginia Cavalry, July 16, 1861. Defeated at April 1862 re-org. Did volunteer service at Seven Pines. V.a.d.c. to Genl. Archer, Dec. 1862. His service record contains an impressive array of recommendations from Confederate generals, but he won no further appointment. Swan was under arrest by the Federals in Maryland in 1864 and 1865, for "being obnoxious to the Loyal citizens." W. W. Blackford's memoir contains a harshly critical comment on Swan. Lived in Alleghany Co. again post-war.

SWANK, WILLIAM A. Lawyer in Norfolk in 1860, age 30. Acting Lt. Col., 60th Virginia, 1861. His sparse service record contains only two items. One is a plaintive letter of Dec. 31, 1861, to General H. A. Wise, asking for clarification of his status. Living in Norfolk in 1870.

SWANN, SAMUEL AMERY. b. Caroline Co., Virginia, June 2, 1831. att. U. Virginia. Teacher in Caroline. Capt., Co. B, 9th Virginia Cavalry, May 6, 1861. Major - May 9, 1864. Paroled at Ashland, April 29, 1865. In Virginia legisl. Caroline Co. Sheriff. Supt. of Virginia State Penitentiary. d. Goochland Co., Feb. 18, 1880.

SWANN, THOMAS BELT. b. Powhatan County, Virginia, Sept. 12, 1825. Pvt., Co. E, 22nd Virginia, early 1861. Captain - June 8, 1861. Dropped at May 1862 re-org. V.a.d.c. to Genl. Heth, 1862. Lt. Col. and Colonel, 3rd Virginia Infantry State Line. Lt. Col., Swann's Battalion Virginia Cavalry, Dec. 1864. Lawyer in Charleston, West Virginia. d. May 14, 1897. bur. St. John's Episcopal Church.

SWANSON, WILLIAM G. b. Georgia. Farmer in Macon Co. in 1860, age 44, worth $75,000. The census taker called him "Dr. W. G. Swason." Colonel, 61st Alabama, Apr. 11, 1864. Paroled at Montgomery, Alabama, May 16, 1865.

SWEENEY, JAMES W. Of Wheeling, Virginia. Major, 60th Virginia, Oct. 14, 1861. Lt. Col. - Aug. 6, 1862. Major, 36th Virginia Cavalry Battalion, Feb. 5, 1863. Badly wounded in the right arm and left leg near Winchester, June 13, 1863. Absent most of the rest of the war. Paroled at Charleston, West Virginia, May 6, 1865, aged 28. 5′8″. Died before 1901.

SWINDLER, AYLETTE ANDREW. b. Aug. 27, 1833. m. Mary Ann Hamrick, 1854. Machinist in Sperryville. Lt., Co. B, 7th Virginia, April 20, 1861. Captain - April 26, 1861. Major - June 15, 1862. Wded. at Frayser's Farm and lost leg at 2nd Manassas. Recruiting officer in Rappahannock Co. POW at home on March 18, 1864, exchanged Dec. 13, 1864. Swindler was among the "Immortal 600" while a prisoner. d. Sept. 24, 1894. bur. Swindler family cemetery on Route 600 near Sperryville.

TABB, WILLIAM BARKSDALE. b. "The Forest," Amelia Co., Virginia, Sept. 11, 1840. gr. VMI, 1859. gr. U. Virginia. Capt. and a.a.g. to Genl. Wise, 1861-62. Major, 28th Battalion Virginia Heavy Artillery, Sept. 9, 1862. Colonel, 59th Virginia, Nov. 1, 1862. Wded. in thigh at Petersburg, June 15, 1864. Appx. m. Emily Rutherford, 1865. Lawyer. d. Amelia Co., Dec. 4, 1874. bur. Grub Hill Episcopal Church.

TAIT, GEORGE. b. Haddington, Scotland. Merchant in Bladen Co., North Carolina. Capt., Co. K, 18th North Carolina, April 26, 1861, aged 26. Major - July 20, 1861. Resigned Jan. 16, 1862, because of "an entire lack of good feeling" with his superiors. Later was Capt. and Lt. Col., 3rd North Carolina Artillery.

TALBIRD, HENRY. b. Beaufort Dist., South Carolina, Nov. 7, 1811. Baptist preacher in Montgomery and Tuscaloosa, Alabama. Colonel, 41st Alabama, May 16, 1862. Resigned, disability, June 27, 1863. Minister in Henderson, Kentucky, and Lexington, Missouri, post-war.

TALCOTT, THOMAS MANN RANDOLPH. b. Philadelphia, Pennsylvania, March 27, 1838. Capt. of engineers, P.A.C.S., 1861. Major and engineer, R. E. Lee's staff, April 26, 1862. Lt. Col. - July 25, 1863, still with Lee. Colonel, 1st Confederate Engineers, April 1, 1864. Appx. Civil engineer post-war, based in Richmond. d. Richmond, May 7, 1920. bur. Hollywood. Talcott's papers are at the Virginia Historical Society.

TALIAFERRO, ALEXANDER GALT. b. Gloucester Co., Virginia, Sept. 1808. gr. William & Mary, 1832. Culpeper lawyer.

m. Agnes Harwood Marshall (granddaughter of Chief Justice John Marshall) in 1836. Lt. Col. of Virginia Militia at the beginning of the war. Capt., Co. G, 13th Virginia, May 28, 1861. Lt. Col., 23rd Virginia, Sept. 12, 1861. Colonel - April 15, 1862. Wded. at Kernstown, Port Republic (shoulder) and 2nd Manassas (hand). Post commander at Charlottesville, Sept. 1863 to 1865. Retired, "debility," March 18, 1865. Paroled at Richmond, May 3, 1865. d. Culpeper Co., June 29, 1884.

TALIAFERRO, THOMAS SEDDON. b. Gloucester Co., Virginia, 1833. Major, 21st Virginia Militia, Dec. 1861. Present into May 1862 with the A.N.Va. on the Peninsula. Lawyer and Virginia legisl. m. Harriotte Hopkins Lee, a cousin of R. E. Lee. d. Richmond, Jan. 10, 1918. bur. Ware Episcopal Church, Gloucester Co.

TALIAFERRO, WARNER THROCKMORTON. b. Gloucester Co., 1833. Member of Virginia legisl. from Mathews Co. m. (1) Martha Paul. m. (2) Frances Hardy. Taliaferro was the nephew of Confederate Secretary of War Seddon. Major, 40th Virginia, July 1, 1861. Dropped at April 1862 re-organization, after much criticism from his fellow officers. Aide to his half brother, Wm. B. Taliaferro, and to Colston and D. H. Hill. Norfolk businessman in real estate and railroads. d. Norfolk, Jan. 12, 1881. (The first edition of *Lee's Colonels* called this man William Tell Taliaferro, 1826-1878, and cautioned against confusing him with Warner T. That was based on the usually unimpeachable files of VMI. Ample contemporary manuscript evidence has turned up, however, to make this revised identity certain.)

TANNER, WILLIAM E. b. Buckingham Co., Virginia, March 13, 1836. m. Mary Mildred Mallory, 1857. Employee of Tredegar Works in Richmond before and during the war. Lt., Letcher Artillery (Virginia), early 1862. Lt., Co. A, 6th Virginia Battalion LDT, Oct. 16, 1863. Major - same date. Lt. Col., 2nd Virginia Infantry Regiment LDT, Aug. 29, 1864. The 6th Battalion was merged into the 2nd Regt. d. Richmond, Aug. 6, 1898. bur. Hollywood.

TATE, SAMUEL McDOWELL. b. Morganton, North Carolina, Sept. 8, 1830. Merchant in Philadelphia, Pennsylvania, and Morganton. Capt., Co. D, 6th North Carolina, May 16, 1861. Major - June 11, 1862. Lt. Col. - July 3, 1863. Wded. at Sharpsburg, Cedar Creek and Ft. Stedman. Paroled at Morganton, May 16, 1865. m. Jennie Pearson, 1866. Railroad president. d. Morganton, June 25, 1897. bur. Forest Hills Cemetery.

TAVENNER, WILLIAM CABELL. b. May 11, 1841. Of Pocahontas Co., Virginia. Tavenner was in New Orleans at the outbreak of war, and enlisted as Lt., Co. F, 1st Louisiana, April 1861. Resigned, Aug. 10, 1861. Capt., Co. C, 17th Virginia Cavalry, Aug. 25, 1862. Lt. Col. - Jan. 28, 1863. Dropped in Feb. 1864 for "prolonged absence without leave," but restored to command the next month. MWIA at Monocacy, July 9, 1864. d. July 11. bu. Zion Episcopal Church, Frederick, but his grave stone was found in use as a splash block for an old house in 1983.

TAYLOE, EDWARD POINSETT. b. King George Co., Virginia, Nov. 3, 1831. gr. VMI, 1851. 5′10½″. Lived in Pittsylvania Co. Capt., Co. B, 47th Virginia, June 5, 1861. Major - May 1, 1862. Lt. Col., 22nd Virginia Battalion, Nov. 20, 1862. Wded. May 1864. POW at Sayler's Creek, released May 30, 1865. d. April 23, 1888, in Westmoreland Co.

TAYLOE, GEORGE EDWARD. b. June 26, 1838. Lived at Big Lick, Virginia. gr. VMI, 1858. Capt., Co. D, 11th Alabama, June 11, 1861. Lt. Col. - Sept. 11, 1862. Colonel - Aug. 21, 1864. Wded. in Seven Days. Commanded Sorrel's Brigade at Appx. m. Delia S. Willis, 1863. Planter. d. Orange Co., Virginia, 1879.

TAYLOR, BENNETT. b. Jefferson Co., Virginia, Aug. 15, 1836. att. U. Virginia. Lived in Albermarle Co. Capt., Co. F, 19th Virginia, May 25, 1861. Major - July 3, 1863. Lt. Col. - Oct. 24, 1864. Wded. at Williamsburg. Wded. and POW at Gettysburg, paroled March 14, 1865. m. Lucy Colston, 1866. Albermarle Co. lawyer and Clerk of Court. d. April 9, 1898. bur. at Monticello, being a descendant of Thomas Jefferson's family.

TAYLOR, FIELDING LEWIS. b. Norfolk, Virginia, April 10, 1825. att. Washington College. Lived in Gloucester Co. m. Elizabeth Farley Fauntleroy. Lt. Col., 21st Virginia Militia,

April 18, 1861. Lt. Col., 12th Virginia, May 2, 1861. MWIA at Crampton's Gap, died Oct. 3, 1862, at Charlestown, Virginia. bur. Hollywood Cemetery, Richmond.

TAYLOR, GEORGE W. Lived in Milltown, Alabama. Lt., Co. K, 14th Alabama, July 22, 1861, aged 24. Captain - May 12, 1862. Major - May 26, 1863. Wded. at Spotsylvania, May 12, 1864. Retired to Invalid Corps, Nov. 10, 1864.

TAYLOR, JACOB N. Capt., Co. E, 60th Virginia, June 19, 1861. Major - July 24, 1863. KIA at Cloyd's Mountain.

TAYLOR, JAMES CRAIG. b. Montgomery Co., Virginia, Sept. 23, 1826. Mexican War veteran. Montgomery Co. lawyer. Capt., Co. C, 54th Virginia, Sept. 10, 1861. Major - May 13, 1862. Resigned due to illness, Sept. 20, 1862. Sought in vain to have his resignation cancelled. In Virginia legisl. later in the war and after the war. Attorney General of Virginia, 1870-1874. d. Christiansburg, Oct. 25, 1887.

TAYLOR, JOHN GIBSON. b. Kentucky, March 1828. att. USMA. Lt., U. S. Army, 1855-61. Major, 21st Mississippi, July 17, 1861. Lt. Col., 2nd Mississippi Battalion, Nov. 2, 1861. KIA at White Oak Swamp, Virginia, June 30, 1862.

TAYLOR, ROBERT BARRAUD. b. Norfolk, Virginia, June 8, 1838. gr. VMI and U. Virginia. Physician. m. Lelia Baker. Lt., Co. G, 6th Virginia, April 29, 1861. Captain, Co. C, 6th Virginia, Aug. 25, 1861. Major - May 3, 1862. Appx. d. Norfolk, Aug. 20, 1896.

TAYLOR, ROBERT P. Of Pike Co., Georgia. Pvt., Co. A, 1st Georgia, March 1861. Capt., Co. G, 53rd Georgia, April 30, 1862. Lt. Col. - Oct. 14, 1863. KIA at Knoxville, Nov. 29, 1863.

TAYLOR, ROBERT SAMUEL. Lived at Selma, Arkansas. Capt., Co. D, 3rd Arkansas, June 20, 1861, aged 35. Major - April 23, 1862. Lt. Col. - Jan. 11, 1863. Wded. in the side at Wilderness. Appx.

TAYLOR, SIMON BRUTON. b. Mar. 16, 1834. Merchant. 5′8″. m. Nancy Murrell. Lt., Co. A, 35th North Carolina, Oct. 17,

1861. Captain - April 21, 1862. Major - June 15, 1863. Lt. Col. - June 18, 1864. Wded. arm at Ft. Stedman, March 25, 1865. Merchant in Onslow, North Carolina. d. Jan. 27, 1929.

TAYLOR, WILLIAM H. b. Virginia. Capt., Co. C, 12th Mississippi, at Raymond, March 13, 1861. Lt. Col. - May 16, 1861. Colonel - April 28, 1862. Elected to Mississippi legisl. in 1863. "Dropped" from 12th Mississippi rolls, March 19, 1864. d. 1897, age 88. bur. Greenwood Cemetery, Jackson.

TEBBS, CHARLES BINNS. b. Loudoun Co., Virginia, July 23, 1826. Loudoun Co. Commonwealth's Attorney. Capt., Co. C, 17th Virginia, April 1861. Lt. Col., 8th Virginia, June 28, 1861. Dropped at April 1862 re-org. Spent the rest of the war in Richmond civilian offices. d. Sept. 26, 1867.

TEBBS, WILLIAM HENRY. Enrolled at Portland, Ashley Co., Arkansas, as Capt., Co. A, 3rd Arkansas, May 20, 1861, aged 40. Lt. Col. - March 11, 1862. Resigned Jan. 19, 1863, for urgent private reasons which he refused to state.

TERRELL, LEIGH RICHMOND. b. 1835 in Virginia. Lawyer in Uniontown, Alabama, in 1860. Lt., 4th Alabama, 1861. Capt. and a.a.g. to Evander Law, Oct. 14, 1862. Lt. Col., 47th Alabama, June 15, 1864. Wded. shoulder, June 18, 1864. MWIA in side, Oct. 13, 1864, d. Oct. 22.

TERRY, JOHN F. b. Virginia. Resided at Bristol. Capt., Co. A, 37th Virginia, April 20, 1861. Lt. Col. - June 28, 1862. Wded. in both legs at McDowell. Wded. at Sharpsburg. Commanded post at Goodson, Virginia, in Nov. 1864.

TERRY, THOMAS M. b. St. Tammany, Louisiana, 1838. Farmer at Livingston, Louisiana. m. Ella F. Tucker. Capt., Co. K, 7th Louisiana, June 7, 1861, aged 23. Major - July 1862. Lt. Col. - July 25, 1862. POW at 2nd Fredericksburg, May 4, 1863. d. St. Jammian, Louisiana.

TEW, CHARLES COURTENAY. b. Charleston, South Carolina, Oct. 17, 1827. gr. SCMA, 1846, with first honors. Professor at SCMA for 11 years. Established Hillsboro Military Academy in

North Carolina in 1858. Colonel, 2nd North Carolina, May 8, 1861, assumed command on June 20. KIA at Sharpsburg.

THOMAS, GEORGE S. b. Aug. 14, 1834, in Columbus. m. Martha Owen Stark. Lt., Co. F, 20th Georgia, June 18, 1861. Capt., Co. C, 64th Georgia, Apr. 1, 1863. Major - date not found. POW at Deep Bottom, Virginia, Aug. 16, 1864, released June 17, 1865. Lawyer in Atlanta. d. May 25, 1896. bur. Griffin, Georgia.

THOMAS, HENRY PHILIP. b. Franklin Co., May 10, 1810. gr. U. Georgia, 1832. Officer in the 1836 Creek War. m. Ellen E. Burroughs, 1837. In Georgia legisl. Gwinnett Co. planter; Lawrenceville lawyer. Major, 16th Georgia, July 19, 1861. Lt. Col. - Feb. 15, 1862. Colonel - Aug. 31, 1863. KIA at Knoxville, Nov. 29, 1863.

THOMAS, ROBERT BRENHAM. b. Kentucky, Nov. 20, 1828. gr. USMA, 1852. Lt., U.S. Artillery, 1852-56. Lt., staff of Genl. Mercer, Dec. 1861. Major and a.i.g. to Genl. Finegan, Feb. 17, 1862. At some point, Thomas served as Colonel, 9th Florida, but he has no service record with that unit's files. The death of two of the field officers of the 9th Florida in 1864 may well have prompted Finegan to assign his long-time staffer to that duty. d. Jan. 25, 1901. bur. Oaklawn Cemetery, Tampa.

THOMAS, SAMUEL BEAUCHAMP. b. July 17, 1825. Mexican War veteran. Sheriff of Hinds Co., Mississippi. Pvt., Co. C, 12th Mississippi, Feb. 11, 1861. Captain - May 18, 1861. Major - April 2, 1863. Lt. Col. - March 19, 1864. Wded. at Frayser's Farm. Wded. in elbow and POW, Aug. 21, 1864, exchanged Feb. 27, 1865. d. June 13, 1907. bur. Terry, Mississippi.

THOMAS, THOMAS W. b. 1822. Lawyer and judge in Elbert Co. Colonel, 15th Georgia, July 15, 1861. Resigned, disability, Mar. 26, 1862. d. Apr. 24, 1864. bur. Elmhurst Cemetery, Elbert Co.

THOMAS, WILLIAM HOLLAND. b. Haywood Co., North Carolina, Feb. 5, 1805. Lived in Jackson Co., North Carolina. 5′8½″. In North Carolina legisl. Cherokee Indian agent and a leading proponent of Indian rights. In North Carolina Secession Convention. m. Sarah J. Love, 1858. Major of Infantry, July 19,

1862. Colonel, Thomas' Legion (North Carolina), Sept. 27, 1862. Surrendered at Waynesville, North Carolina, May 8, 1865. d. Morganton, North Carolina, May 10, 1893.

THOMPSON, GEORGE HARVEY. Capt. of the pre-war "Gate City Guards." Major, 1st Georgia, Apr. 3, 1861. Lt. Col. - Dec. 11, 1861. Mustered out with the regt., Mar. 18, 1862. d. Dec. 18, 1864, age 26. bur. Oakland Cemetery, Atlanta.

THOMPSON, ROBERT ANDERSON. b. Pickens Dist., June 13, 1828. In South Carolina Secession Convention. m. Valinda Rose Starritt. Capt., Co. B, 2nd South Carolina Rifles, Oct. 31, 1861. Major - July 6, 1862. Lt. Col. - Sept. 3, 1862. Resigned Sept. 13, 1863, because an act of Congress "exempts me as Commissioner in Equity of Pickens District." Walhalla lawyer. d. Walhalla, Aug. 7, 1914.

THOMPSON, WILLIAM P. b. Wheeling, Virginia, Jan. 7, 1837. att. Jefferson College, Pennsylvania. Lawyer in Fairmount, Virginia. Capt., Co. A, 31st Virginia, May 1861. Thompson apparently served briefly as Major, 25th Virginia Infantry. Some sources identify the 25th Virginia's ephemeral Major Thompson as being William T., but there is evidence that he was actually William P., and presumably this man. Lt. Col., 19th Virginia Cavalry, April 11, 1863. Paroled at Staunton, May 20, 1865. 6′0″ Millionaire businessman in the lead industry and with Standard Oil. d. Brookdale, New Jersey, Feb. 3, 1896.

THOMPSON, WILLIAM T. Major, 25th Virginia. See entry for William P. Thompson, above.

THOMSON, JAMES WALTON. b. Berryville, Virginia, Oct. 28, 1843. att. VMI. Lived at Summit Point, Virginia. V.a.d.c. to T. J. Jackson at 1st Manassas, for which service he received a letter of commendation. Lt., Chew's Battery Horse Artillery (Virginia), fall 1861. Captain - March 14, 1864. Major of artillery - Feb. 18, 1865. KIA at High Bridge, April 6, 1865. bur. Stonewall Cemetery, Winchester.

THOMSON, THOMAS. b. Tarbolton, Scotland, June 5, 1813. Lawyer in Charleston, South Carolina. In South Carolina legisl.

In South Carolina Secession Convention. m. twice. Capt., 1st South Carolina Rifles, 1861. Capt., Co. A, 2nd South Carolina Rifles, Oct. 22, 1861. Major - May 12, 1862. Lt. Col. - July 6, 1862. Colonel - Sept. 3, 1862. Resigned Dec. 3, 1863, having been elected to the South Carolina Senate. d. Abbeville, May 12, 1881. bur. Upper Long Cane Presbyterian Church, Abbeville.

THOMSON, WILLIAM GOULDING. b. Liberty Co., Georgia, April 6, 1822. att. U. Georgia. Capt., Co. B, 20th Georgia Cavalry Battalion, May 1862. The bn. was merged into the 8th Georgia Cav. Major - Feb. 1864. MWIA at Haw's Shop, Virginia, May 28, 1864, d. June 23 at Goldsboro, North Carolina.

THOMSON, WILLIAM T. b. 1829. Lived in Union District. Major, 5th South Carolina, Apr. 13, 1861. No further record. d. 1899. bur. Presbyterian Cemetery, Union Co.

THORBURN, CHARLES EDMONSTON. b. Norfolk, Virginia, Nov. 23, 1831. gr. U. S. Naval Academy, 1853. Lt., Virginia Navy, early 1861. Major, P.A.C.S., assigned to 50th Virginia, July 3, 1861. Dropped at May 1862 re-org. Lt. Col. of artillery, Aug. 1, 1862. Colonel and a.i.g. on Loring's staff, Sept. 20, 1862. Assigned as Colonel, 14th Virginia Cavalry, Sept. 5, 1862, but the order seems to have been revoked. Resigned Nov. 11, 1863. Went to London and Paris on Confederate business. Back with Lee near Petersburg. Thorburn was with the Jefferson Davis retreat party for awhile. d. New York City, Oct. 21, 1909. bur. Norfolk.

THORNTON, JOHN THRUSTON. b. Cumberland Co., Virginia, 1829. gr. Hampden-Sydney and U. Virginia. Lawyer. m. Martha Jane Riddle. Capt., Co. K, 3rd Virginia Cavalry, June 24, 1861. Lt. Col. - April 26, 1862. KIA at Sharpsburg. Thornton's papers are at U. Virginia.

THRIFT, JAMES. Farmer in Fairfax Co. in 1860, age 43. Officer in the 1st Virginia Inf. during the Mexican War. Capt., Co. G, 8th Virginia, June 22, 1861. Major - April 27, 1862. MWIA at Seven Pines, died in Richmond, June 2, 1862.

THRUSTON, STEPHEN DECATUR. b. Gloucester Co., Virginia, Nov. 28, 1833. att. U. Virginia. gr. U. Pennsylvania, M.D., 1854.

Physician in Brunswick Co., North Carolina. Capt., Co. B, 3rd North Carolina, May 18, 1861. Major - July 1, 1862. Lt. Col. - March 26, 1863, to rank from Dec. 10, 1862. Colonel - Oct. 3, 1863. Wounded at Sharpsburg, Chancellorsville, Spotsylvania and Winchester (Sept. 19, 1864). Moved to Dallas, Texas in 1870's. d. Dallas, Nov. 15, 1906.

TILLMAN, HENRY. b. Bulloch Co., Georgia, ca. 1821. Farmer. Capt., Co. D, 61st Georgia, Sept. 9, 1861. Major - Sept. 23, 1862. Lt. Col. - Jan. 1863. Resigned Jan. 25, 1863. Justice in Taylor Co., Florida. Died in Perry, Florida, Mar. 22, 1877.

TIMBERLAKE, JOHN CORBETT. b. 1829. Lived at New Kent Court House, Virginia. 5′8″. Capt., Co. E, 53rd Virginia, July 8, 1861. Major - March 5, 1863. Lt. Col. - Oct. 22, 1864. POW at Gettysburg, exchanged May 3, 1864. POW at Sayler's Creek, released July 25. d. 1888. bur. Cedar Grove Cemetery, Williamsburg.

TODD, RUTHERFORD PRESSLEY. b. Laurens Dist., South Carolina, Feb. 4, 1834. gr. South Carolina College, 1855. Capt., Co. G, 3rd South Carolina, April 14, 1861 (state appt. from Jan. 22). Major - May 6, 1864. Wded. at Fredericksburg, Chickamauga and Cedar Creek. Paroled at Greensboro, May 1865. Lawyer and South Carolina legislator. Married Mary Farley, 1866. Died Aug. 15, 1886. bur. Laurens City Cemetery.

TOLER, WILLIAM H. b. Virginia. Clerk in New Orleans. 5′8¾″. m. Susie Hickman. Lt., Co. C, 14th Louisiana, June 6, 1861, aged 30. Captain - Sept. 12, 1861. Major - Aug. 15, 1862. Wded. severely in thigh, Frayser's Farm. Paroled at Nashville, May 12, 1865.

TOMLIN, HARRISON BALL. b. Clifton, Hanover Co., Virginia, 1815. att. U. Virginia. Planter in King William County. Colonel, Tomlin's Battalion Virginia Infantry, Sept. 13, 1861. Colonel 53rd Virginia, Jan. 1862 at org. Resigned Jan. 7, 1863. Served in Virginia legisl. for 17 years, including during the war. Unmarried. d. Aug. 17, 1896.

TOMPKINS, CHRISTOPHER QUARLES. b. Virginia, Aug. 4, 1813. att. William & Mary. gr. USMA, 1836. Lt. and Capt.,

U.S. Artillery, 1836-47. m. Ellen Wilkins. Iron manufacturer in Richmond and Kanawha. Colonel, 22nd Virginia, Apr. 1861. Resigned Nov. 1861. According to a letter of his wife, Tompkins resigned because Confederate General Floyd fired on Tompkins' home during an engagement, despite Tompkins' protest. Coal mine operator. d. May 28, 1877. bur. Hollywood Cemetery.

TOON, WILLIAM H. b. Bladen Co., North Carolina, ca. 1832. Farmer. m. Miss Costin. Capt., Co. K, 20th North Carolina, April 23, 1861. Major - July 19, 1861. Lt. Col. - June 27, 1862. Resigned, Nov. 8, 1862, suffering from "conjestive chill" ailment. d. Whiteville, North Carolina, March 14, 1870. bur. Oakdale Cemetery, Wilmington.

TOWERS, JOHN R. b. Anderson Dist., South Carolina, July 2, 1824. Merchant in Rome, Georgia. Capt., Co. E, 8th Georgia, May 14, 1861. Lt. Col. - Nov. 16, 1861. Colonel - Dec. 16, 1862. POW on June 27, 1862. Wded. in hand at Gettysburg. Appx. In Georgia legislature. Supt., Georgia State Penitentiary. Sheriff of Floyd Co. A Georgia lieutenant called Towers "a very interesting man and an old soldier." A member of the 8th Georgia said of Towers: "All the regiment call him 'Grand-ma' and he seems to enjoy it finely. We all like him." d. Marietta, Sept. 29, 1903. bur. Citizen's Cemetery.

TOWNS, J. RANDOLPH. b. Jasper Co., Georgia. Planter in Albany in 1860, worth $333,150. m. Josephine Crook. Adj., 7th Georgia State Troops, Nov. 1861. Capt., Co. A, 62nd Georgia, May 29, 1862. Lt. Col. - Aug. 1, 1862. Resigned, "business affairs," July 24, 1863. Died of rheumatism "contracted in service," Nov. 16, 1867, age 37. bur. Oakland Cemetery, Atlanta.

TOWNSEND, WILLIAM PURNELL. b. Mississippi, Aug. 1822. Moved to Texas in 1852. m. Almira Rebekah Jennings. Enrolled in Robertson Co., Texas, July 15, 1861, as Capt., Co. C, 4th Texas. Major - July 10, 1862. Lost a foot at 2nd Manassas. Res. Dec. 29, 1862; later served on a military court in Bragg's army. d. Oct. 1882.

TRACY, PHILEMON. b. June 27, 1831. Brother of General E. D.

Tracy. gr. Yale. Macon editor. Major, 6th Georgia, May 27, 1861. Wounded at Gaines' Mill. MWIA in thigh at Sharpsburg, Sept. 17, 1862, died Sept. 18. Tracy's uncle, a judge in New York had the major buried in Batavia, New York. Tracy was very near-sighted.

TREUTLEN, JOHN FLETCHER. b. Cokesbury, South Carolina, 1828. Grandson of Georgia governor of the same surname. m. Carrie Agnes Smith. Lt., 1st Alabama, Jan. 1861. Lt. Col., 15th Alabama, July 27, 1861. Colonel - late 1862. Resigned, "bad lungs," April 28, 1863. Became Colonel of Barbour Co., Alabama, Militia. "Modest and affable." Planter in Clay Co., Georgia, then lived in South Carolina. Moved to Washington, D. C., and worked for the U. S. Congress, 1878. d. Feb. 27, 1908. bur. Fairview Cemetery, Eufala, Alabama.

TRIGG, ROBERT CRAIG. b. Christiansburg, Virginia, Dec. 12, 1830. gr. VMI. Lawyer in Christiansburg. Colonel, 54th Virginia, Sept. 4, 1861. Wded. near Suffolk on Jan. 30, 1863. Present until disbandment of the regt. in Montgomery Co., Apr. 1865. d. Christiansburg, Jan. 2, 1872.

TRIMMIER, THEODORE GAILLARD. b. Spartanburg Dist., South Carolina, April 11, 1825. m. Mary Letitia Thomson. Merchant in Spartanburg, in Anderson Dist., South Carolina, and in Tuscaloosa, Alabama. Capt., Co. A, 41st Alabama, March 13, 1862. Major - Oct. 15, 1862. Lt. Col. - Jan. 27, 1863. MWIA at White Oak Road, Virginia, March 31, 1865. d. April 7. bur. Blandford Cemetery, Petersburg.

TROY, DANIEL SHIPMAN. b. Oct. 9, 1832. Of Montgomery and Cahaba, Alabama. Lawyer. Major, Hilliard Legion (Alabama), fall 1862. Lt. Col., 60th Alabama, Oct. 18, 1863. Wded. in left arm at Drewry's Bluff. Wded. thorax and POW at Hatcher's Run, March 25, 1865. d. 1895.

TRUSS, JAMES DAVIS. Farmer in St. Clair Co., Alabama. m. Martha Cordelia Coleman. Capt., Co. F, 10th Alabama, June 4, 1861, aged 31. Major - July 9, 1863. Cashiered by court-martial, July 14, 1864, as the final result of a longstanding quarrel with Genl. J. C. C. Saunders. Truss was returned to the ranks. Lived in Nashville, Tennessee, post-war.

TUCKER, HENRY ST. GEORGE, JR. (he "rarely used" the first name) b. Winchester, Virginia, Jan. 5, 1828. att. William & Mary and Washington College. gr. U. Virginia. Clerk of the Virginia Senate. Capt., Co. E, 15th Virginia, April 23, 1861. Major - July 1, 1862. Lt. Col. - Aug. 19, 1862. Died of disease at Charlottesville, Jan. 24, 1863.

TURNER, JOHN McLEOD. b. Washington, D. C. Engineer in Rowan Co., North Carolina. Capt., Co. F, 7th North Carolina, May 16, 1861, aged 21. Major - May 3, 1863. Lt. Col. - Nov. 28, 1864. Wded. at Fredericksburg and 2nd Manassas. Wded. in abdomen and POW at Gettysburg, exchanged Sept. 1864. Paroled at Salisbury, North Carolina, May 1, 1865. bur. Oakwood Cemetery, Raleigh.

TURNER, WILLIAM J. Capt., Co. K, 8th Florida, Oct. 27, 1861. Major - July 5, 1862. Resigned, Sept. 1862.

TURNEY, PETER. b. Jasper, Tennessee, Sept. 22, 1827. Lawyer in Franklin Co. Colonel, 1st Tennessee, April 27, 1861. Suffered from the "unfriendliness of Jeff Davis." Under arrest in Feb. 1862. Wded. at Fredericksburg in the face and neck. Retired after a long absence, May 26, 1864. On Tennessee Supreme Court. Gov. of Tennessee, 1893-97. d. Oct. 19, 1903, at Winchester, Tennessee.

TURNISPEED, RICHARD AUGUSTUS. b. Richland Dist., South Carolina, June 12, 1830. Lawyer in Clay Co., Georgia. Lt. Col., 9th Georgia, June 11, 1861. Colonel - Apr. 15, 1862. Resigned, July 26, 1862. m. Sarah Marable, 1869. Judge and Georgia legislator. d. Nov. 21, 1900.

TWIGGS, HANSFORD DADE DUNCAN. b. Barnwell, South Carolina, March 25, 1837. att. U. Pennsylvania. gr. U. Georgia and Georgia Military Institute. Lt., Co. D, 1st Georgia, Feb. 1, 1861. Lt., Co. G, 1st Georgia, June 4, 1861. Capt., Co. D, 1st Georgia, Feb. 6, 1862. Wded. and POW at Sharpsburg. Capt. and a.i.g. on Wm. B. Taliaferro's staff, 1863 Wded. at Morris

Island. Returned to the 1st Georgia late in the war, and was said to have been made the regiment's Lt. Col. in early 1865, although there is no official confirmation. Paroled at Greensboro, North Carolina, April 26, 1865. In Georgia legisl. Augusta lawyer and judge. Died in Savannah, March 25, 1917.

TWIGGS, JOHN DAVID. b. Apr. 6, 1826 in Georgia. m. Sarah Eugenia Rambo, 1848. Physician in Hamburg, South Carolina. Capt., Co. C, 1st South Carolina Cavalry Battalion, Aug. 27, 1861. Major - May 26, 1862. Lt. Col., 1st South Carolina Cavalry Regiment, June 1862. Injured in a riding accident, Nov. 1863. Killed in a street fight while at home in Hamburg, South Carolina, Sept. 15, 1864.

TWITTY, FRANCIS LOGAN. b. Rutherford Co., North Carolina, May 11, 1840. att. North Carolina Military Inst. Farmer. 5′11″. Lt., Co. C, 34th North Carolina, Sept. 2, 1861. Captain - June 1862. Major - July 1, 1863. Wded. arm at Gettysburg. d. Sept. 10, 1864, at Petersburg, Virginia. Buried in family cemetery at Rutherfordton.

TYLER, GRAYSON. b. Prince William Co., Virginia, 1834. Farmer there. 5′11½″. Lt., Co. F, 17th Virginia, April 26, 1861. Captain - May 1, 1862. Major - June 30, 1864. Lt. Col. - July 8, 1864. POW at Sayler's Creek, released July 25, 1865. d. Alexandria, Virginia, Dec. 16, 1897. bur. family cemetery, Prince William County.

TYLER, NATHANIEL. b. Dumfries, Virginia, March 9, 1828. gr. VMI, 1848. gr. U. Virginia. Editor in Warrenton. Edited the Richmond *Enquirer* during and after the war. Tyler was half of the notable Confederate imprint firm of "Tyler and Allegre, Public Printers," which shows up on so many Confederate publications. Major, 20th Virginia, July 1861. Lt. Col. - fall 1861. Tyler's efforts to recruit the shattered regiment (which was only two companies strong for some time after its 1861 misfortunes) were all in vain, and the regiment was dissolved in spring 1862. Tyler was an editor in Baltimore, 1866-1882, then moved to Washington, D. C. Died in Washington, Dec. 4, 1917. bur. Hollywood Cemetery, Richmond.

UNDERWOOD, DAVIDSON ALEXANDER. b. Albemarle, North Carolina, Sept. 5, 1830. Lived in Stanly Co. m. Mary Elizabeth Locke. Capt., Co. C, 42nd North Carolina, Feb. 28, 1862. Major - April 22, 1862. Resigned, Nov. 21, 1862, due to "being drunk and absent . . . in the face of the enemy." d. Rockwall, Texas, June 7, 1898.

UPSHAW, EDWARD W. b. Virginia. Lawyer in Holly Springs, Mississippi. Pvt., Co. F, 17th Mississippi, May 25, 1861, aged 35. Capt., Co. I, 17th Mississippi, July 2, 1861. Major - April 26, 1862. Resigned, "deficient vision," Oct. 21, 1862. He was later assigned to duty at the same rank with Pillow. d. Sept. 13, 1878, age 53. bur. Hill Crest Cemetery, Holly Springs.

UPSHAW, THOMAS EDMUND. b. Caroline Co., Virginia, June 16, 1828. gr. VMI, 1851. Lt., "Spruill's Legion," a North Carolina Cav. company, July 13, 1861; resigned, Oct. 11, 1861. Capt., Co. C, 13th Virginia Cav., March 5, 1862. Major - Oct. 19, 1863. Lt. Col. - Dec. 19, 1863. Wded. at Upperville (June 21, 1863). POW at Spotsylvania, May 14, 1864. Res. Oct. 1, 1864. Civil engineer and railroad man. d. St. Louis, Aug. 28, 1906.

UPTON, JOHN CUNNINGHAM. b. Franklin Co., Tennessee, Jan. 22, 1823. Went to the gold fields of California in 1850. Moved to Fayette Co., Texas, in 1859. Enrolled in Colorado Co., Texas, on July 10, 1861, as Capt., Co. B, 5th Texas. Major - June 1, 1862. Lt. Col. - July 18, 1862. KIA at 2nd Manassas.

URQUHART, CHARLES FOX. b. Southampton Co., May 12, 1838. gr. VMI, 1860. Pvt., Co. D, 3rd Virginia, May 3, 1861. Lt. - July 1, 1861. Capt. - April 27, 1862. Major - late August 1862. KIA at Sharpsburg.

UTTERBACK, ROBERT EDWIN. b. Fauquier Co., Jan. 1, 1824. m. Annie Freeman. Physician. Capt., Co. D, 4th Virginia Cav., May 25, 1861. Major - June 8, 1862. Resigned due to typhoid fever, Sept. 4, 1863. Supt. of Schools in Culpeper Co. d. Culpeper Co., Sept. 3, 1881.

VAIDEN, VULOSKO. b. New Kent Co., 1835. att. William & Mary. m. Virginia Pickett. Baptist preacher. Major, 52nd Virginia Militia, early 1861. Also served as Pvt., Co. F, 3rd Virginia Cav.; orderly to R. S. Ewell; and Pvt., Co. H, 5th Virginia Cav. The 52nd Virginia Militia served around Williamsburg in 1861 and 1862. Vaiden was in the Virginia legisl. during and after the war. He was captured in Dec. 1863 and held until Jan. 1865. A prominent Readjustor post-war. d. Lanexa, Virginia, June 28, 1893, of "asthma."

VANCE, ZEBULON BAIRD. b. Buncombe Co., May 13, 1830. att. UNC. Capt., Co. F, 14th North Carolina, May 3, 1861. Colonel, 26th North Carolina, Aug. 31, 1861. Resigned to become governor of North Carolina, Aug. 19, 1862. He was governor again post-war, and in both houses of the U.S. Congress. d. Washington, D.C., Apr. 14, 1894. bur. Asheville, North Carolina.

VAN DE GRAAFF, ALBERT SEBASTIAN. b. June 27, 1832. att. Yale and U. Virginia. Lawyer in Sumter Co., Alabama. Capt., Co. A, 5th Alabama Bn., May 26, 1861. Major - June 26, 1862. Wded. at Fredericksburg. Died in California, May 28, 1868.

VANDEVENTER, ALEXANDER SPOTSWOOD. b. Lee County, Virginia, Nov. 9, 1840. Capt., Co. B, 50th Virginia, June 27, 1861. Lt. Col. - May 25, 1862. Colonel - Jan. 30, 1863. POW at Spotsylvania, May 10, 1864, exchanged Oct. 1864. Absent without leave into 1865, ordered to be dropped. m. Mollie Patton, 1866. Lawyer in Fayetteville, Arkansas, and died there on April 26, 1910.

VAN HOOK, JOHN CAMPBELL, JR. b. Caswell Co., North Carolina, July 10, 1831. Farmer in Person Co. Capt., Co. A, 50th North Carolina, April 21, 1862. Major - Dec. 1, 1862. Lt. Col. - Nov. 10, 1863. Methodist Sunday School teacher. d. April 18, 1910.

VAN VALKENBURGH, JAMES DUNBAR. b. New York City, 1828. Lived in Macon, Georgia. Colonel of Georgia Militia prewar. m. Mary E. K. Morgan. Capt., Co. I, 61st Georgia, Sept. 24, 1861. Major - July 1, 1863. Lt. Col. - May 12, 1864. KIA at Monocacy. bur. Rose Hill Cemetery, Macon.

VAUGHAN, JOHN BURFOOT. b. Richmond, April 29, 1829. Civilian foreman in the Richmond Arsenal. Lt., Co. C, 5th Virginia Bn. LDT ("Arsenal Bn."), June 24, 1863. Captain - Aug. 11, 1864. Major - Sept. 26, 1864. Paroled at Richmond, April 28, 1865. Carpenter and draughtsman for the Richmond and Danville R. R. post-war. d. Richmond, April 22, 1901. bur. Hollywood.

VAUGHAN, WARD G. Enlisted at Oxford, Mississippi, on May 15, 1861, as Capt., Co. F, 19th Mississippi, aged 37. Major - Nov. 24, 1862. Lt. Col. - April 2, 1863. Wded. at Williamsburg. Resigned July 17, 1863.

VENABLE, THOMAS BROWN. b. Dec. 9, 1824. Lived in Granville Co., North Carolina. Lt. Col., 24th North Carolina, July 16, 1861. Dropped at May 1862 re-org. d. June 24, 1893. bur. Elmwood Cemetery, Oxford, North Carolina.

VINCENT, WILLIAM G. b. Norfolk, Virginia, 1829. New Orleans auctioneer. Lt., 2nd New York, Mexican War. Lt. Col., 1st Louisiana, April 28, 1861. Colonel - Sept. 27, 1861. Dropped at re-org. Later was Colonel, 2nd Louisiana Cav. and Colonel, 33rd Louisiana Partisan Rangers. Active in New Orleans civic and veterans affairs. d. New Orleans, Oct. 28, 1916.

WADDELL, ALFRED MOORE. b. Hillsboro, North Carolina, Sept. 16, 1834. att. UNC. Wilmington lawyer and mayor. Adj., 3rd North Carolina Cav., Jan. 4, 1863. Lt. Col. - Aug. 18, 1863. Resigned, ill health, Aug. 10, 1864. In U. S. Congress, 1871-1879. d. Wilmington, March 17, 1912. Waddell wrote three books.

WADDELL, JAMES DANIEL. b. Abbeville Dist., South Carolina, Dec. 22, 1832. gr. U. Georgia, 1853. In Georgia legisl. Capt., Co. D, 20th Georgia, June 1, 1861. Major - June 14, 1862. Lt. Col. - May 29, 1863. Colonel - July 2, 1863. Paroled at Augusta, May 23, 1865. Marietta lawyer. Author of biography of Linton Stephens. d. Marietta, Dec. 15, 1881. bur. Citizen's Cemetery. Waddell's war letters and an unrecorded pamphlet sketching his life are at Emory U.

Kennesaw Mountain National Battlefield Park

JAMES D. WADDELL
20th Georgia

WADDILL, GEORGE MAJOR. b. Isle of Wight Co., Virginia, May 3, 1838. m. Margaret E. Cabell, 1861. Capt., Co. K, 53rd Virginia, May 9, 1861. Major - Nov. 9, 1861. Lt. Col. - May 22, 1862. Resigned, Aug. 29, 1862, complaining of asthma and liver problems. Paroled at Lynchburg, April 14, 1865. For a brief period in 1861 there existed an unformed two-company battalion known as "Waddill's Bn.," but it quickly merged into the newly forming 53rd Virginia. Waddill practiced law in Isle of Wight Co., and went to the Virginia legisl. d. Windsor, Virginia, March 14, 1885.

WADE, BENJAMIN H. Physician in Franklin Co. in 1860, age 30. Lt., Co. G, 57th Virginia, Aug. 5, 1861. Captain - Oct. 17, 1861. Major - Oct. 13, 1862. Lt. Col. - Feb. 2, 1863. MWIA at Gettysburg, July 3, 1863, d. July 5.

WADE, BENJAMIN O. Druggist in Warren Co., North Carolina. Capt., Co. F, 12th North Carolina, April 18, 1861, aged 22. Lt. Col. - May 1, 1862. Colonel - June 6, 1862. Resigned, Dec. 30, 1862.

WADE, JOHN JESSE. b. Montgomery Co., Virginia, Sept. 13, 1824. m. Mary A. Chapman. att. Washington College. Lawyer at Pearisburg. Capt., Co. E, 54th Virginia, Sept. 10, 1861. Major - May 1862. Lt. Col. - fall 1862. Present into 1865. Lawyer in Giles and Montgomery counties. Moved to Baltimore, Maryland, in 1875. d. Baltimore, Nov. 24, 1897.

WAGGAMAN, EUGENE. b. New Orleans, Sept. 18, 1826. gr. Mt. St. Mary's College, 1846. m. Felicie Sauve, 1851. In Louisiana legisl. Capt., Co. I, 10th Louisiana, July 22, 1861. Lt. Col. - Jan. 16, 1862. POW at Malvern Hill, exchanged Aug. 5, 1862. WIA at Winchester, Sept. 19, 1864. Appx. d. April 24, 1897, in New Orleans. bur. St. Louis Cemetery, New Orleans.

WALKER, EDWARD J. b. Dec. 19, 1830, in South Carolina. gr. SCMA, 1851, from Edgefield Dist., South Carolina. Lawyer in Georgia. Capt., Co. G, 3rd Georgia, April 26, 1861. Major - June 15, 1862. Lt. Col. - June 19, 1862. Colonel - July 1, 1862. Wded. at Sharpsburg. Wded. at Manassas Gap, Virginia, July 23, 1863.

He died in Richmond Co., Georgia, of wounds and disease on Aug. 21, 1864. bur. Magnolia Cemetery, Augusta, Georgia.

WALKER, EDWARD THOMAS. b. Feb. 5, 1835. att. Washington College. Farmer in Bedford Co. in 1860, worth $19,500. Capt., Co. A, 58th Virginia, July 25, 1861, aged 26. Major - Oct. 30, 1862. Suffered a severe thigh wound at 2nd Manassas, which resulted after much delay in Walker's retirement on Dec. 2, 1864. Bedford Co. Treasurer. d. there March 9, 1911. bur. Walker family cemetery.

WALKER, JOHN DAVID. b. 1825. Severely wded. at Churubusco in 1847. Filibusterer with William Walker in Nicaragua. Capt., Co. C, 1st Georgia, Feb. 1, 1861. Major - June 19, 1861. MWIA in the leg at 2nd Manassas, Aug. 29, 1862. d. Oct. 3 at Warrenton. bur. Augusta, in a family cemetery. Walker never married. He was a brother of General W. H. T. Walker.

WALKER, JOHN STEWART. b. Oct. 1827. att. Washington College and Harvard U. m. Lucy Wilhelmina Otey. Capt., Co. B, 15th Virginia, May 14, 1861. Major - April 29, 1862. KIA at Malvern Hill. Walker was brother-in-law of Col. Kirkwood Otey. bur. Hollywood Cemetery.

WALKER, JOSEPH. b. Spartanburg, South Carolina, May 18, 1835. Capt., Co. K, 5th South Carolina, April 13, 1861. Lt. Col., Palmetto Sharpshooters (South Carolina), April 15, 1862. Colonel - July 22, 1862. Commanded his brigade at South Mountain. In South Carolina legisl., 1864. Bank president and very wealthy businessman in Spartanburg. Six terms as mayor of the town. d. Jan. 27, 1902. bur. Spartanburg.

WALKER, NATHANIEL JEFFERSON. b. South Carolina. Farmer at Pine Ridge, Louisiana. m. Indiana Holman. Capt., Co. H, 9th Louisiana, June 25, 1861, age 58. Major - July 7, 1861. Lt. Col. - Aug. 1861. Walker was "fat, good-natured, short-winded and red-faced." "Thrown out" at April 1862 re-org.

WALKER, SAMUEL T. b. Emmittsburg, Maryland, March 30, 1830. m. Mary Regina Sommers. Editor in Harrisonburg in 1860. Major, 10th Virginia, May 17, 1861. Lt. Col. - May 8, 1862. KIA at Chancellorsville. Walker's home was in Shenandoah County. He has markers in both Woodbine Cemetery in Harrisonburg and the Lutheran Cemetery in New Market.

WALKER, THOMAS. Lived in Albany. Mexican War veteran. Major, 17th Georgia, Aug. 15, 1861. Resigned, May 1862.

WALKER, WILLIAM ALEXANDER. b. Chester, South Carolina, June 14, 1819. gr. South Carolina College, 1840. m. Catherine Eliza McLure. Chester lawyer and banker. Capt., Co. D, 1st South Carolina Cav. Bn., Sept. 10, 1861. Major, 1st South Carolina Cav. Regt., June 1862. Lt. Col. - Sept. 15, 1864. Wded. at Gettysburg. In South Carolina legisl., 1865-67 and 1877-82. d. Chester, Apr. 21, 1882. bur. Old Purity Presbyterian Church.

WALKUP, SAMUEL HOEY. b. Jan. 22, 1818. gr. UNC, 1841. Lived in Union and Mecklenburg Cos., North Carolina. Capt., Co. F, 48th North Carolina, March 4, 1862. Lt. Col. - April 9, 1862. Colonel - Dec. 4, 1863. Wded. at Fredericksburg in the hip. Appx. d. Oct. 26, 1876. Walkup's war memoir is at UNC.

WALL, EDWIN GIRARD. b. Winchester, Aug. 24, 1824. gr. VMI, 1848. Farmer and civil engineer, Supt. of Southside R.R. prewar. Capt., Co. D, 18th Virginia, Apr. 24, 1861. Major - July 21, 1864. Lost a leg at Gaines' Mill "while gallantly leading the regiment to storm a battery." Retired, Nov. 5, 1864. Died at the Soldiers' Home in Richmond, Aug. 21, 1899. bur. Mt. Hebron Cemetery, Winchester.

WALLACE, WILLIAM. b. Columbia, South Carolina, Nov. 16, 1824. gr. South Carolina College, 1844. Lawyer in Columbia and militia officer. Capt., Co. C, 2nd South Carolina, Apr. 8, 1861. Major - June 3, 1863. Lt. Col. - May 6, 1864. Wded. cheek at 2nd Manassas; wded. at Gettysburg and in Sept. 1864. Postmaster of Columbia. d. Columbia, Nov. 12, 1902. bur. 1st Presbyterian Churchyard.

WALLACE, WILLIAM SHARP. b. Georgia, Nov. 9, 1828. m. Jennette A. Leonard. In Georgia legisl. Lawyer in Butler, Georgia, worth $47,000 in 1860. Capt., Co. E, 45th Georgia, Mar. 4, 1862. Major - Mar. 17, 1864. Lt. Col. - June 22, 1864. Wded. in

Mrs. Felicia Parlier

THOMAS CONWAY WALLER
9th Virginia Cavalry

Seven Days and at Cedar Mountain. Retired to Invalid Corps, Dec. 2, 1864. Also served in Georgia legisl. during the war. d. 1901. bur. Butler City Cemetery.

WALLER, THOMAS CONWAY. b. Stafford Co., Dec. 9, 1832. Farmer and politician in Stafford Co., Virginia. m. Sarah Elizabeth Wickliffe (1837-1921). Capt., Co. A, 9th Virginia Cavalry, April 21, 1861. Major - Oct. 18, 1862. Lt. Col. - Sept. 16, 1864 (this rank was doubtless back-dated to May 1864, when Beale vacated the commission, but Waller's service record stubbornly uses the Sept. date). Colonel - Jan. 6, 1865. Wded. at Brandy Station, Oct. 11, 1863. Paroled at Ashland, April 25, 1865. d. Stafford Co., Dec. 23, 1895. Buried at "Grafton," near Garrisonville, Stafford Co.

WALSH, THOMAS VARDELL. b. Charleston, South Carolina, April 12, 1833. Capt., Co. A, Holcombe Legion (South Carolina), Nov. 18, 1861. Lt. Col. - Dec. 5, 1863. Retired, chronic bronchitis, Aug. 12, 1864. Became a conscript officer. Merchant and justice in Sumter County. d. Sumter, Dec. 25, 1906.

WALTON, JAMES BURDGE. b. Newark, New Jersey, Nov. 18, 1813. gr. Louisiana College. m. Amelia Sack, 1836. Colonel of Louisiana Regt., Mexican War. New Orleans wholesale grocer. Adj. of Washington Artillery (Louisiana) at its 1839 org. Major of the Washington Artillery Battalion at its acceptance into C. S. service, May 1861. Colonel - March 26, 1862. Assigned to duty as "Inspector-General of Field Artillery" in June 1864, but resigned out of pique over E. P. Alexander's assignment to command 1st Corps artillery, on July 18, 1864. d. Sept. 8, 1885.

WALTON, SIMEON TAYLOR. b. Prince Edward Co., 1825. Lived in Charlotte Co. gr. Jefferson Medical College. Capt., Co. K, 23rd Virginia, June 29, 1861. Major - April 21, 1862. Lt. Col. - Aug. 9, 1862. Wded. at Kernstown and Sharpsburg. KIA at Mine Run, Nov. 27, 1863, by a bullet in the head. bur. Ash Camp Memorial Cemetery, Keysville, Virginia.

WARD, GEORGE. Of Mississippi. Capt., Madison Light Artillery (Mississippi), April 1861. Major of artillery - Feb. 27, 1864, assigned to Poague's Battalion. KIA at Jericho Ford, Virginia, May 23, 1864, when a cannon ball took off his head.

WARD, GEORGE TALIAFERRO. b. Fayette Co., Kentucky, about 1800. gr. Transylvania U. Wealthy planter and banker in Leon Co., Florida. Colonel, 2nd Florida, July 12, 1861. KIA at Williamsburg. bur. Bruton Parish Church.

WARD, WILLIAM NORVELL. b. Lynchburg, Virginia, April 19, 1805. att. USMA. m. Mary Blincoe, 1836. Episcopal cleric in Spotsylvania Co. and on Virginia's Northern Neck. Major of a two-company bn., May 25, 1861. Major, 55th Virginia, Sept. 1861. Dropped at May 1862 re-org. Ward's wife and 12 children were stranded behind enemy lines on the Northern Neck while he stayed in Richmond seeking a position, with glowing referrals from several generals and from Rev. Charles Minnigerode. d. Feb. 25, 1881.

WARING, JOSEPH FREDERICK. b. 1832. Savannah alderman before the war. Capt., Co. F, Jeff Davis Legion (Mississippi), Sept. 17, 1861. Lt. Col. - Dec. 2, 1862. Colonel - early 1865. Wded. Dec. 4, 1861. d. Oct. 5, 1876. Waring's papers are at UNC.

WARREN, EDWARD TIFFIN HARRISON. b. Rockingham Co., Virginia, June 19, 1829. m. Virginia Magruder, 1855. Harrisonburg lawyer. Lt. Col., 10th Virginia, July 1, 1861. Colonel - Aug. 16, 1862, to rank from May 8, 1862. KIA at Wilderness. bur. Harrisonburg. Warren's papers are at the University of Virginia.

WARTHEN, THOMAS JEFFERSON, SR. b. Washington Co., Georgia, March 18, 1804. m. Sarah Wicker. Lived in Warthen then Sandersville. Judge and state legislator. Fought Creeks and and Seminoles in Georgia and Florida. Lt. Col., 8th Georgia Battalion, early 1861. Colonel, 28th Georgia, Sept. 10, 1861. MWIA at Malvern Hill, died July 3, 1862, at the residence of John M. Blakey on 20th Street in Richmond. bur. Forest Grove Cemetery, Washington County.

WARWICK, BRADFUTE. b. Richmond, Virginia, Nov. 24, 1839. gr. U. Virginia and Medical College of New York. Fought under Garibaldi. Capt. on Wise's staff, 1861. Major, 4th Texas, Oct. 2, 1861. Lt. Col. - March 3, 1862. Colonel - June 27, 1862 (posthumously). MWIA at Gaines' Mill, d. July 6, 1862.

WASDEN, JOSEPH. b. Glascock Co., 1828. Lawyer in Warrenton. Raised Co. H, 22nd Georgia. Major, 22nd Georgia, Aug. 31, 1861. Lt. Col. - June 2, 1862. Wded. at 2nd Manassas. Colonel - April 22, 1863. KIA at Gettysburg, by a canister round. "He was an infidel." bur. Laurel Hill Cemetery, Savannah.

WASHINGTON, JAMES AUGUSTUS. b. Wayne Co., North-Carolina, March 8, 1832. gr. UNC, 1851. att. Wake Forest. m. Virginia Pope. Capt., Co. H, 2nd North Carolina, May 16, 1861. Lt. Col., 50th North Carolina, April 15, 1862. Colonel - Dec. 1, 1862. Resigned on Nov. 9, 1863, after having been censured by a court for conduct during a Yankee raid on Tarboro. d. Feb. 17, 1911. bur. Goldsboro.

WATKINS, THOMAS C. Farmer at Pendleton in 1860, age 35, worth $8,000. Capt., Co. G, 22nd South Carolina, Jan. 1862. Lt. Col. - May 5, 1862. MWIA in head and POW at Boonsboro, Sept. 14, 1862, d. Sept. 20. bur. Mt. Olivet Cemetery, Frederick, Maryland.

WATKINS, THOMAS H. b. Rockbridge Co., Virginia. Railroad manager and ironmaster at Glenwood Furnace in 1860. 6′2″. Age 21 in 1860. Capt., Co. E, 52nd Virginia, July 31, 1861. Major - Oct. 24, 1863, to rank from June 6, 1863. Lt. Col. - Dec. 19, 1863. Wded. at McDowell and Gaines' Mill. KIA at Bethesda Church, May 30, 1864.

WATSON, DAVID. b. Louisa Co., Virginia, Nov. 25, 1834. att. U. Virginia. Lt., Albermarle Artillery (Virginia), July 3, 1861. Capt., 2nd Co., Richmond Howitzers, May 1, 1862. Major of artillery - Feb. 27, 1864, assigned to Nelson's Bn. MWIA at Spotsylvania, May 10, 1864. d. May 13. bur. Bracketts Farm, Louisa Co.

WATTS, JAMES WINSTON. b. Bedford Co., Virginia, April 19, 1833. Lt., Co. A, 2nd Virginia Cavalry, May 11, 1861. Captain - Sept. 1861. Lt. Col. - May 1862. Disabled at Aldie, July 17,

1863. Commanded post at Bedford late in the war. Farmer and merchant at Lynchburg. d. Lynchburg, Dec. 3, 1906.

WATTS, WILLIAM. b. Campbell Co., Virginia, Dec. 20, 1817. gr. U. Virginia. Roanoke Co. lawyer. Major, 19th Virginia, July 13, 1861. Transferred to 28th Virginia, Aug. 20, 1861. Lt. Col. - May 1, 1862. Colonel - July 3, 1863. Paroled at Lynchburg, May 24, 1865. In Virginia legisl. d. May 1, 1877. Eppa Hunton called Watts "not much of a tactician." A member of the 28th wrote that Watts was drunk "about three fourths of his time."

WAYNE, RICHARD ALEXANDER. b. South Carolina. Customs House officer in Savannah in 1860, age 26. Capt., Co. E, 1st Georgia Regulars, Feb. 1, 1861. Major - Oct. 3, 1862. Lt. Col. - Aug. 3, 1864. Colonel - Sept. 3, 1864. Surrendered at Greensboro. A member of the regiment described Wayne as "personally one of the most fearless men I have ever known. . . . a gruff man, short and peremptory in manner, in camp disliked by his . . . men, but . . . battle . . . commanding the respect of all."

WEBB, JOHN G. b. Georgia. Clerk at Ft. Gaines in 1860, age 23. Capt., Co. D, 9th Georgia, June 11, 1861. Major - Oct. 26, 1864. Lt. Col. - Feb. 23, 1865. Lost arm at Ream's Station, Aug. 25, 1864. m. Emma W. Jenkins, 1869. Capt. of post-war volunteers. Judge in Clay Co., 1880.

WEBB, JOSEPH CALDWELL. b. Greene Co., Alabama, Dec. 4, 1835. Lived in Orange Co., North Carolina. 5′8½″. Lt., Co. G, 27th North Carolina, April 20, 1861. Captain - Aug. 17, 1861. Major - Dec. 7, 1862. Lt. Col. - Jan. 11, 1865. WIA at Fredericksburg and Wilderness. Wded. leg at Spotsylvania. Appx. Some of Webb's war letters have recently been printed. He moved to Texas after the war, where he died in Madison Co. on June 16, 1915.

WEBB, ROBERT FULTON. (The middle name is once given as Frederick, with less authority.) b. Washington, D. C., April 25, 1825. Mexican War veteran. Farmer in Orange Co., North Carolina. Capt., Co. B, 6th North Carolina, May 20, 1861. Major - July 11, 1861. Lt. Col. - July 11, 1862. Colonel - July 3, 1863. Wded. at Sharpsburg. POW at Rappahannock Station,

Nov. 7, 1863, released July 25, 1865. Tobacco and furniture merchant in Durham. d. Durham, January 1891. Buried in Maplewood Cemetery.

WEEMS, JOHN B. b. Oct. 24, 1824. Merchant. Capt. of an Augusta volunteer company pre-war. Capt., Co. B, 10th Georgia, May 18, 1861. Major - July 4, 1861. Lt. Col. - Sept. 25, 1861. Colonel - Oct. 29, 1862. Wded. at Savage Station and Gettysburg. Retired to Invalid Corps, May 19, 1864. d. ca. 1876.

WEEMS, WALTER H. Lawyer in Russell Co., Alabama. Capt., Co. F, 6th Alabama, May 2, 1861. Major - Jan. 1, 1862. Major, 64th Georgia, May 26, 1863. Lt. Col. - Feb. 20, 1864. Colonel - July 30, 1864. Wded. at Sanderson, Florida, Feb. 22, 1864.

WELCH, WESTERN R. b. Waynesville, North Carolina, Aug. 7, 1829. Wife - Nannie C. Capt., Co. D, 11th Georgia, July 3, 1861. Major - May 26, 1862. Resigned, disability, July 5, 1862. In Georgia legisl. d. Gilmer Co., Georgia, June 19, 1904.

WERTH, WILLIAM H. Of Pittsylvania Co., Virginia. Capt., "Chatham Grays," Feb. 1860. He entered service with his company as Co. B, Montague's Battalion Virginia Infantry, but resigned on July 14, 1861. Major, 45th Virginia, Nov. 14, 1861. Lt. Col. - Jan. 6, 1862. Dropped at re-org. Repeatedly sought appt. to a military court, in vain. Age 40 in 1870 census. d. Feb. 10, 1872. bur. behind site of the old Patrick Springs Hotel, Patrick Co.

WESTCOTT, JOHN. b. New Jersey, July 1807. att. USMA. Physician in Florida. Surveyor-General of Florida. Capt., Co. I, 10th Florida, 1862. Major, 2nd Florida Battalion, June 24, 1863. Major, 10th Florida, June 11, 1864. Paroled at Madisonville, May 15, 1865. 5′4″. St. Augustine businessman. In Florida legisl. d. Jan. 1889.

WESTON, JAMES AUGUSTUS. b. Lake Comfort, North Carolina, May 6, 1838. att. Trinity College. Lived in Hyde Co. Lt., Co. B, 33rd North Carolina, Sept. 9, 1861. Captain - Aug. 5, 1862. Major - July 28, 1864. POW at New Bern, March 1862. Wded. at Jericho Ford, May 23, 1864. Appx. Episcopal rector in North Carolina. Wrote some Civil War history and another book. d. Hickory, North Carolina, 1905.

WHALEY, DAVID M. b. Pennsylvania. Moved to Texas in 1853. Druggist in Centerville. In Texas legisl. Capt., Co. C, 5th Texas, July 11, 1861. Major - July 17, 1862. KIA at Freeman's Ford, Virginia, Aug. 22, 1862.

WHARTON, RUFUS WATSON. b. Feb. 10, 1827. m. Mary Latham Perry. Lived in Beaufort Co., North Carolina. Capt., Co. E, 21st North Carolina, May 24, 1861. Major, 1st Battalion North Carolina Sharpshooters, April 26, 1862. POW near Port Royal, Virginia, Jan. 11, 1863; exchanged April 6, 1863. Lt. Col., 67th North Carolina, Jan. 18, 1864. Wharton had actually been acting as a.d.c. to Hoke during the first months of 1864; his commission as Lt. Col. was backdated. d. Nov. 15, 1915.

WHEAT, CHATHAM ROBERDEAU. b. Alexandria, Virginia, April 9, 1826. gr. U. Nashville, 1845. 6′4″. New Orleans lawyer and Louisiana legisl. Military adventurer of some note. Major, 1st Louisiana Special Battalion ("Wheat's Tigers"), May 25, 1861. KIA at Gaines' Mill. bur. Hollywood Cemetery. The colonel of the 38th Georgia described Wheat as "a wild, uncouth person [with] a passion for wild adventure." A member of Ewell's staff called Wheat "big, blackguard, good-natured. . . . A strange compound of some good & a great many bad qualities."

WHEELWRIGHT, WILLIAM HENRY. b. Westmoreland Co., July 23, 1824. gr. VMI. Clergyman in Warren Co. Married Margaret Kerfoot. Major, 26th Virginia, July 1, 1861. Dropped at May 1862 re-org. d. Warren County, Dec. 17, 1879.

WHILDEN, JOHN MARSHALL. b. July 20, 1839, in Charleston. gr. SCMA, 1861. Never married. Pvt., 5th South Carolina, 1861. Enrolled as Capt., Co. B, 23rd South Carolina, at Mt. Pleasant, Sept. 25, 1861. Major - Apr. 16, 1862. MWIA at 2nd Manassas, d. Sept. 6, 1862.

WHITAKER, JOHN HENRY. b. June 19, 1827. gr. UNC, 1847. Planter in Northampton Co., North Carolina. Capt., Co. B, 1st North Carolina Cavalry, May 16, 1861. Major - July 12, 1862. MWIA at Fairfax Station, Virginia, June 27, 1863. d. June 29.

WHITAKER, MACKERNESS HUDSON. b. Georgia. Lawyer in Lauderdale Co., Mississippi, in 1860, age 24. Lt., Co. H, 13th Mississippi, March 19, 1861. Lt. Col. - May 18, 1861. Not re-elected in April 1862 re-org. and "went home." Still in Lauderdale Co. in 1870 census, age 36.

WHITE, ELIJAH VIERS. b. Poolesville, Maryland, Aug. 29, 1832. att. Granville College, Ohio. Fought in the pre-war Kansas troubles. 5′11″. m. Sarah Elizabeth Gott, 1857. Enlisted in the "Loudoun Cavalry" (later Co. K, 6th Virginia Cavalry) in 1859. Pvt., Co. G, 7th Virginia Cavalry, 1861. Distinguished himself at Ball's Bluff in a volunteer capacity. Capt., "White's Rebels," an independent Virginia cavalry company, Jan. 11, 1862. Lt. Col., 35th Virginia Cavalry Battalion, Feb. 4, 1863. Paroled at Winchester, May 8, 1865. Leesburg banker. Loudoun Co. farmer and sheriff. d. Jan. 11, 1907. bur. Union Cemetery, Leesburg. White's chief subordinate accused him of "moral cowardice" in Apr. 1865 and called him "a stubborn fool." In Nov. 1862, A. P. Hill called White "a trump, and one of the best cavalry officers we have."

WHITE, ISAAC. b. Albermarle Co., Jan. 29, 1837. Physician. m. Mary Virginia Day. Surgeon, 31st Virginia, Sept. 2, 1861; resigned Dec. 6, 1861. Major, 29th Virginia, May 13, 1862. Resigned, Oct. 18, 1862, wanting to become a surgeon again. Surgeon, 62nd Virginia, March 24, 1863. POW on Dec. 10, 1864. d. Shawsville, Virginia, Aug. 3, 1889.

WHITE, JOHN M. b. April 10, 1833. Farmer near Fort Mill, m. Adeline Allison. Capt., Co. H, 6th South Carolina, June 22, 1861. Major - July 4, 1863. Lt. Col. - May 6, 1864. Wded. at Seven Pines. Appx. d. May 13, 1897. bur. Unity Church, Fort Mill.

WHITE, OSCAR. b. Tallahassee. Lived in Florida. Lt. of infantry, P.A.C.S., July 19, 1861. Lt. and Adj., 1st Virginia Battalion, 1861-62. Aide to J. R. Jones, June 1862. Major, 48th Virginia, Nov. 20, 1862. Lt. Col. - May 3, 1863. Wded. at Winchester, Sept. 19, 1864, and at 2nd Manassas. Appx. White arrived in San Francisco on July 10, 1865, and took up residence at 218 Bush St. At that time he was 29 years old, 5′9″ tall, with gray eyes and brown hair. bur. Mirage Cemetery, Moffat, Colorado.

WHITE, ROBERT. b. Romney, Virginia, Feb. 7, 1833. Lawyer in Romney. 5′6″. Capt., Co. I, 13th Virginia, May 1861. Major, 41st Virginia Cavalry Battalion, Sept. 18, 1863. Lt. Col. - Dec. 9, 1863. Colonel, 23rd Virginia Cavalry, April 28, 1864. Paroled at Patterson Creek, West Virginia, May 7, 1865. In West Virginia legisl., 1885-91. Lawyer in Wheeling. Attorney General of West Virginia. Grand Master of West Virginia Masons. d. near Wheeling, July 1916. White wrote the West Virginia volume of *Confederate Military History.*

WHITE, WILLIAM. b. Norfolk Co., Virginia, Jan. 7, 1820. att. Yale, Medical College of Virginia, and gr. U. Pennsylvania, M.D. m. Henrietta Kemp Turner. Physician at Deep Creek, Virginia. In Virginia Secession Convention. Major, 14th Virginia, May 17, 1861. Lt. Col. - Aug. 26, 1862. Colonel - July 3, 1863. Severely wded. in Pickett's Charge. Present into 1865. Active in Portsmouth veterans affairs. d. June 22, 1894. bur. Cedar Grove Cemetery, Portsmouth.

WHITE, WILLIAM CAPERS. b. Nov. 17, 1821. Overseer at Georgetown, South Carolina. Capt., Co. L, 7th South Carolina, June 26, 1861. Major - May 14, 1862. KIA at Sharpsburg.

WHITE, WILLIAM PARKER. Colonel, 7th Georgia Cavalry, Jan. 24, 1864. Died on April 6, 1864, from a wound received on Waccamaw Neck inflicted by Sgt. Grimes, at the instigation of Capt. C. C. Bowen.

WHITE, WILLIAM WILKINSON. Lawyer in Cobb Co., Georgia. m. Pauline Laphelia Kirkpatrick (1836-1868). Capt., Co. I, 7th Georgia, 1861. Lt. Col. - May 12, 1862. Colonel - Aug. 30, 1862. Retired - July 27, 1864, having been disabled by a throat wound at Garnett's Farm near Richmond. White died near the end of the war.

WHITEHEAD, CHARLES LOWNDES. b. Richmond Co., Georgia, June 29, 1835. In the Georgia Secession Convention (voted yes). Sgt., Co. E, 4th Georgia, April 28, 1861. Major - May 8, 1861. Resigned April 28, 1862, at re-org. Capt. and a.d.c. to Wright, June 1862. Wded. at Sharpsburg. d. Sept. 25, 1866.

WHITEHEAD, JAMES S. b. Pitt Co., North Carolina. Lawyer in Pitt Co. 6′2″. Capt., Co. E, 55th North Carolina, May 1862, aged 25. Major - May 1862. Died of disease in 1862.

WHITEHEAD, JOHN RANDOLPH. b. Burke Co., Georgia, 1829. att. Princeton and U. Georgia. Lt., Co. E, Cobb's Legion (Georgia), Aug. 8, 1861. Major, 48th Georgia, March 22, 1862. Resigned July 17, 1863, due to wounds. d. Miller Co., Georgia, June 5, 1877. bur. Laurel Grove Cemetery, Savannah.

WHITEHEAD, RICHARD OWEN. b. Suffolk, Virginia, Dec. 27, 1830. gr. VMI and U. Virginia. Lawyer. Capt., Co. A, 16th Virginia, April 17, 1861. Major - Aug. 30, 1862. Lt. Col. - March 16, 1863. Wded. at Burgess Mill, Oct. 27, 1864. Appx. In Virginia legisl., then removed to California and was a teacher, lawyer and civil engineer there. d. Oakland, California, March 4, 1911. Some of Whitehead's uniform items are at the Museum of the Confederacy.

WHITFIELD, GEORGE FRANKLIN. b. North Carolina. Lived in Lenoir Co. gr. UNC. Capt., Co. C, 27th North Carolina, April 17, 1861. Major - Nov. 1, 1862. Lt. Col. - Dec. 5, 1862. Colonel - Jan. 11, 1865. Wded. at Bristoe Station and Cold Harbor. d. 1881.

WHITFORD, EDWARD. b. March 18, 1840. Brother of Col. John N. Whitford. Of Craven Co., North Carolina. Farmer. Lt., Co. I, 1st North Carolina Artillery, Sept. 20, 1861. Capt., Co. A, 1st Battalion North Carolina LDT, March 28, 1863. Major, 67th North Carolina, Jan. 18, 1864. m. Nancy Moore, 1866. d. March 18, 1894.

WHITFORD, JOHN NATHANIEL. b. Craven Co., North Carolina, May 4, 1835. m. Mary Elizabeth Williamson. Capt., Co. I, 1st North Carolina Artillery, Sept. 20, 1861. Major, 1st Battalion North Carolina LDT, Jan. 1, 1863. Lt. Col. - July 21, 1863. Colonel, 67th North Carolina, Jan. 18, 1864. In North Carolina legisl. in 1882. d. near New Bern, June 26, 1890. bur. Cedar Grove Cemetery. Whitford's papers are at Duke.

WHITING, HENRY AUGUSTINE. b. Hanover Co., Virginia, Jan. 8, 1832. Lived at Old Church, Virginia. gr. VMI, 1852.

Library of Congress

ELIJAH VIERS WHITE
35th Battalion Virginia Cavalry

Capt. and a.a.g. to Rodes, Nov. 1861 to June 1862. Lt. Col., 41st Alabama, Aug. 5, 1862, but declined the appt. Major and a.a.g. to Rodes, 1863-64. Major and a.i.g. to Bryan Grimes, 1865. m. Mrs. Harriet Harriott Raoul Lumsden, 1869. Railroad civil engineer. d. Dec. 26, 1907.

WHITNER, JAMES HARRISON. b. Nov. 3, 1832. Lawyer at Pendleton. Major, 4th South Carolina, April 14, 1861. Became Pvt., Co. C, Palmetto Sharpshooters (South Carolina) after the 4th South Carolina failed to re-org. Volunteer aide to R. H. Anderson, 1862. Later Capt., 22nd South Carolina. Lawyer at Walhalla and Greenville. d. May 2, 1896. bur. Springwood Cemetery, Greenville.

WHITSON, JAMES MONROE. b. Currituck Co., Oct. 10, 1825. m. Susan Tipton. Capt., Co. B, 8th North Carolina, May 16, 1861. Major - April 22, 1863. Lt. Col. - July 8, 1863. Colonel - Feb. 1, 1864. Wded. at Morris Island. Wded. and POW while on furlough, April 1864, released July 24, 1865. d. Yancey Co., Nov. 30, 1902.

WHITTLE, POWHATAN BOLLING. b. Mecklenburg Co., Virginia, June 26, 1829. att. U. Virginia. 6′4″ tall. Lawyer in Macon, Georgia. Youngest brother of Wm. C. Whittle, CSN. Lt. Col., 38th Virginia, June 12, 1861. Colonel - July 1863. Wded. arm at Williamsburg. Lost arm at Malvern Hill. Suffered a bad thigh wound at Gettysburg, where he was also imprisoned. Retired in early 1864 to QM Dept. and military court service. Lawyer and judge in Valdosta, Georgia. d. Feb. 21, 1905. Whittle was his mother's fifteenth child. Among his brothers was Colonel Lewis Neal Whittle (see appendix).

WIATT, FRANCIS LATIMER. b. Fredericksburg, Virginia, Sept. 2, 1815. m. Lucy J. Brickey, in Mo., 1842. 6′0″. Lived in Union Co., North Carolina and listed his occupation as "miner." Capt., Co. A, 48th North Carolina, Feb. 17, 1862. Major - July 15, 1862. Wded. at Harpers Ferry, Sept. 14, 1862. Resigned Oct. 20, 1862.

WIGGINTON, JOHN W. b. Georgia. Justice of the peace and farmer in Calhoun Co., Alabama. Age 32 in 1860. Capt., Co. I,

H. George Carrison

POWHATAN BOLLING WHITTLE
38th Virgina

48th Alabama, Apr. 26, 1862. Major - June 17, 1863. Wded. at Sharpsburg and Fussell's Mill. Appx. d. Cleburne Co., Alabama, 1898.

WILCOXON, JOHN B. Lawyer in Newnan, Georgia, in 1860, age 36, worth $80,000. Capt., Co. D, Cav. Bn. of Phillips Legion (Georgia), June 11, 1861. Major - July 1, 1861. Resigned, disability, July 4, 1862. Colonel of state troops. Built a cotton factory in Coweta Co. in 1867. Elected to Georgia legislature in 1874.

WILDS, SAMUEL HUGH. b. Darlington, South Carolina, Oct. 20, 1819. m. Anna Rosa Ellison. In South Carolina legisl., 1856-57 and 1864. 6'2". Capt., Co. B, 21st South Carolina, Dec. 23, 1861. Major - Oct. 10, 1864. Wded. thigh at Petersburg, Aug. 21, 1864. POW on Feb. 20, 1865, released July 24. Died in Darlington of rheumatic problems contracted while a prisoner, Oct. 29, 1867.

WILKINS, WILLIAM K. b. Tennessee. Carpenter in Hamburg, Arkansas, in 1860, age 29. Enrolled at Hamburg on May 20, 1861, as Lt., Co. K, 3rd Arkansas. Captain - July 15, 1861. Major - Sept. 19, 1863. KIA at Wilderness.

WILKINSON, ROBERT ANDREWS. b. Natchez, Mississippi, Oct. 16, 1809. Planter in Plaquemine, Louisiana. m. Mary Farrar Gildart Stark. Capt., Co. B, 15th Louisiana, June 11, 1861. Major - June 5, 1862. Lt. Col. - 1862. KIA at 2nd Manassas. Buried Haymarket, Virginia, at St. Paul's Episcopal Church.

WILLETT, EDWARD D. b. Kentucky, Sept 6, 1835. Clerk. Lt., Co. G, 1st Louisiana, May 2, 1861. Major - 1864. Wded. at Wilderness. Paroled at Meridian, Mississippi, May 9, 1865. Author of a list of Confederate dead from Louisiana in Napier Bartlett's book. Alive in Long Beach, Mississippi, in 1907.

WILLIAMS, CHARLES JONES. b. ca. 1821. Major in Mexican War. In state legislature, 1859-60. att. USMA one year. m. Mary Ann Eliza Howard. Colonel, 1st Georgia, Mar. 15, 1861. Died at home of illness, Feb. 3, 1862.

WILLIAMS, HAZAEL JOSEPH. b. Bath Co., Virginia, April 28, 1830. Capt., Co. D, 5th Virginia, Apr. 17, 1861. Major - Apr. 21, 1862. Lt. Col. - Aug. 29, 1862. Wded. in thigh at Winchester, June 15, 1863; wded. Oct. 19, 1864 (shoulder). Contractor and farmer in Augusta Co. In Virginia legisl. d. July 18, 1911. bur. Mt. Tabor Lutheran Church, Augusta Co.

WILLIAMS, HENRY L. N. b. Alabama. Merchant in Mansfield, Louisiana. Capt., Co. F, 9th Louisiana, July 7, 1861, aged 25. Major - 1862. POW at 2nd Fredericksburg. MWIA at Gettysburg, d. July 5, 1863.

WILLIAMS, JAMES HENDERSON. b. Newberry Dist., South Carolina, Oct. 4, 1813. m. Jane W. Duckett, 1844. Served in Florida wars and as Capt. in Mexican War. Newberry lawyer. In South Carolina legisl., 1858-67. South Carolina Militia General before the war. Colonel, 3rd South Carolina, Feb. 6, 1861. Dropped at May 1862 re-org. Later was: Colonel, 9th South Carolina Reserves (90-days troops); Colonel, 5th South Carolina State Troops (6 mos.); Major and Lt. Col., 4th Bn. South Carolina Reserves. Moved to Arkansas in 1867 and planted there. d. Rocky Comfort, Arkansas, Aug. 21, 1892.

WILLIAMS, JEREMIAH HENRY JOHNSTON. b. Jackson Co., Mar. 28, 1829. m. Susan A. Arendale. Civil engineer at Pole Cat Hollow. Capt., Co. B, 9th Alabama, May 23, 1861. Major - Oct. 21, 1861. Wded. at Sharpsburg. When Williams resigned, Sept. 4, 1863, the resignation was accepted, with obvious relish on the part of his superiors, on Sept. 11. d. Mar. 6, 1912. bur. on his estate, "Bowling Green," near Bridgeport, Alabama.

WILLIAMS, JESSE MILTON. b. Jan. 11, 1831. att. U. Alabama. Lived in Mansfield, Louisiana. Capt., Co. D, 2nd Louisiana, May 11, 1861. Colonel - 1862. Wded. and POW at Sharpsburg. Commanded Nicholls' Brigade a lot in 1863-64. KIA at Spotsylvania, May 12, 1864.

WILLIAMS, LEE ANDREW JACKSON. b. October 1830. Farmer in Troup Co. Capt., Co. D, 35th Georgia, Sept. 23, 1861. Major - Dec. 21, 1863. MWIA May 12, 1864. d. May 19. bur. Williams Cemetery, Troup Co.

WILLIAMS, LEWIS BURWELL, JR. b. Sept. 13, 1833. gr. VMI, 1855. Lawyer and professor at VMI. Unmarried. Capt., Co. A, 13th Virginia, April 17, 1861. Lt. Col., 7th Virginia, May 15, 1861. Colonel, 1st Virginia, April 27, 1862. Wded. and POW at Williamsburg. MWIA at Gettysburg. Reburied in Hollywood Cemetery in 1896.

WILLIAMS, SOLOMON. b. North Carolina, July 1835. Lived in Nash Co. gr. USMA, 1858, after having been suspended for a time for "deficiency in conduct." Lt., U. S. Cavalry, 1858-61. Colonel, 12th North Carolina, May 14, 1861. Colonel, 2nd North Carolina Cav., June 6, 1862. KIA at Brandy Station. m. Maggie Pegram, 2 weeks before his death. bur. family cemetery, Hilliardston, Nash Co., North Carolina.

WILLIAMS, TITUS VESPASIAN. b. Tazewell Co., Virginia, June 2, 1835. gr. VMI, 1859. Major, 37th Virginia, April 21, 1862. Colonel - June 28, 1862. Wded. at Cedar Mountain. Appx. Physician in Edinburgh, Missouri. d. Valeria, Iowa, May 7, 1908. A contemporary called him "rather excitable."

WILLIAMS, WILEY JACKSON. b. Telfair Co., Georgia, Nov. 19, 1836. Pvt., Co. B, 49th Georgia, March 4, 1862. Lt. - July 26, 1862. Captain - Aug. 22, 1862. Major - Feb. 23, 1864. Lt. Col. - March 24, 1864. Merchant in Telfair Co. In Georgia legisl. d. Eastman, Georgia, 1915. bur. Woodlawn Cemetery.

WILLIAMS, WILLIAM T. b. June 25, 1840. Lived in Nash Co., North Carolina. Capt., Co. H, 12th North Carolina, May 1, 1861. Lt. Col., 1st North Carolina Bn. (which became 32nd North Carolina Regt.), Nov. 29, 1861. Resigned, June 18, 1863, saying that he wanted to pick a company and serve as a private. d. March 7, 1864. Buried in Arrington family cemetery, just off Highway 43, Nash Co., North Carolina.

WILLIAMSON, GEORGE. Of Caswell Co., North Carolina. Major, 8th North Carolina, May 16, 1861. Lt. Col. - Oct. 25, 1862. POW at Roanoke Island, Feb. 1862. Resigned, Feb. 20, 1863, citing asthma troubles.

WILLIAMSON, HENRY WATSON. b. Norfolk, Sept. 23, 1823. gr. VMI, 1845. m. Pattie S. Green. Lt. in Mexican War. Civil engineer. Lt., Co. G, 6th Virginia, April 19, 1861 (had held such rank since Dec. 1859). Captain - May 20, 1861. Sent on special duty as an engineer at Craney Island, 1861-1862. Lt. Col., 6th Virginia, May 3, 1862. Wded. thigh at Spotsylvania, lost an arm at the Crater. Retired, Dec. 21, 1864. Librarian at VMI, 1876-84. d. Oct. 10, 1884. bur. Lexington.

WILLIAMSON, WILLIAM HENRY. b. Oct. 29, 1828, at Greenville, Tennessee. Lawyer. Capt., Co. H, 7th Tennessee, May 20, 1861. Major - Apr. 8, 1863. Wded. at Gaines' Mill. POW at Gettysburg, released Feb. 16, 1865. m. Mrs. Martha Morgan, widow of Genl. John Hunt Morgan. d. March 16, 1887. bur. Cedar Grove Cemetery, Wilson Co., Tennessee.

WILLINGHAM, JAMES J. b. Feb. 14, 1839, in Alabama. Planter in Lowndes Co. in 1860, worth $24,750. Capt., Co. E, 6th Alabama, Apr. 17, 1861. Lt. Col. - Apr. 28, 1862. KIA at Seven Pines. bur. Taylor Cemetery, Montgomery Co., Alabama.

WILLIS, EDWARD (S.) USMA manuscripts show the middle initial, but Willis never used it. b. Aug. 10, 1840. att. USMA. Adj., 12th Georgia, July 5, 1861. Served on T. J. Jackson's staff in 1862. Lt. Col., 12th Georgia, Dec. 13, 1862. Colonel - Jan. 22, 1863. Wded. in thigh at Wilderness. MWIA at Bethesda Church, d. May 31, 1864. bur. Laurel Grove Cemetery, Savannah. A member of the regiment wrote: "In the death of Col. Willis the Regt. lost its best friend."

WILLIS, WILLIAM HENRY. b. Jones Co., Georgia, Feb. 10, 1829. Oglethorpe businessman. Lt., Co. I, 4th Georgia, April 29, 1861. Capt., Co. E, 4th Georgia, 1862. Major - May 30, 1863. Lt. Col. - Aug. 15, 1863. Col. - Aug. 5, 1864. m. Isabella C. Griffin, 1864. In Georgia legisl., 1873-77. d. Oglethorpe, 1889.

WILLIS, WILLIAM ROYALL. b. Sept. 1830. Lawyer. Capt., Co. A, 32nd Virginia, May 13, 1861. Lt. Col. - May 21, 1862. Present into 1865. Paroled at Richmond, April 18, 1865. Judge in Elizabeth City Co. d. Hampton, Feb. 1, 1881. bur. St. John's Cemetery, Hampton.

WILSON, J. MOORE. b. Ireland. New Orleans merchant. Capt., Co. C, 7th Louisiana, June 7, 1861, age 30. Major - prior to

1864. Wded. at Winchester, June 14, 1863. POW at Wilderness, held at Ft. Delaware. d. Jan. 3, 1894. bur. Metairie Cemetery, New Orleans.

WILSON, JOHN PARKE, JR. b. Cumberland Co., Virginia, Sept. 16, 1833. gr. VMI, 1855. m. Elizabeth Inskeep Gibson. Major, 5th Virginia Bn., April 29, 1861. Dropped at May 1862 re-organization. Volunteer aide to Jubal Early at Sharpsburg. Pvt., Co. I, 13th Virginia, Feb. 1863. Pvt., Co. B, 9th Virginia, Dec. 11, 1863. Captain, Co. B, 9th Virginia, April 9, 1864. Commanded the 9th Virgina, as a captain, in 1865. Farmer and civil engineer in North Carolna. d. Black Mountain, North Carolina, Feb. 13, 1922.

WILSON, JOHN THOMAS. b. Sampson Co., North Carolina. Farmer. 6′0″. Lt., Co. C, 38th North Carolina, Oct. 18, 1861. Captain - April 18, 1862. Major - June 18, 1864. Appx.

WILSON, NATHANIEL CLAIBORNE. b. Fincastle, Virginia, Sept. 12, 1839. att. VMI. gr. U. Virginia. Capt., Co. B, 28th Virginia, May 15, 1861. Major - May 1, 1862. Wded. in face at Seven Pines. KIA in Pickett's Charge at Gettysburg.

WILSON, SAMUEL M. Farmer in Norfolk Co. in 1860, age 42, worth $18,500. Lt. Col., 7th Virginia Bn., 1861. When this bn. was expanded into the 61st Virginia Regt., in May 1862, Wilson was elected Lt. Col., but declined the commission.

WILSON, WILLIAM SYDNEY. b. Snow Hill, Md., Nov. 7, 1816. gr. Princeton, 1835. Lawyer in Port Gibson, Mississippi. In Missippi legisl. Served in the C. S. Congress for a brief period in 1861. Capt., Co. F, 48th Mississippi, Aug. 13, 1861, at a time when that unit was still a part of the 2nd Mississippi Bn. (which later became the 48th). Major - 2nd Mississippi Bn., Nov. 2, 1861. Lt. Col., 48th Mississippi, June 30, 1862. MWIA at Sharpsburg, d. Nov. 3, 1862.

WILSON, WILLIAM TUNSTALL. b. Danville, Virginia, Dec. 15, 1815. Mexican War veteran. Moved to Georgia in 1853. Mayor of Oglethorpe. Farmer and judge in Houston County. Atlanta railroad agent and postmaster. m. Marion McHenry Lumpkin.

Commissary, 7th Georgia, May 31, 1861. Colonel - Feb. 13, 1862. KIA at 2nd Manassas.

WIMBISH, JOHN. Colonel, 54th North Carolina, May 16, 1862. Resigned, Sept. 3, 1862, "private business." Entered the Soldiers' Home in Richmond, Virginia, on Nov. 9, 1893, age 81, from Halifax Co. d. May 30, 1905. bur. Hollywood Cemetery.

WINFIELD, BENJAMIN F. b. Virginia. Physician and farmer in Sussex Co., in 1860, worth $27,000. Lived alone. Capt., Co. D, 13th Virginia Cav., March 9, 1862. Major - Dec. 19, 1863. Resigned on Nov. 22, 1864, after being relieved from duty by Lee on Nov. 5. Entered the Soldiers' Home in Richmond on Oct. 7, 1885, age 62, citing debility and old age. d. May 16, 1888.

WINGFIELD, WILLIAM LEWIS. b. Bedford Co., Virginia, April 12, 1837. gr. VMI, 1859. 5′11″. Capt., Co. D, 28th Virginia, May 20, 1861. Lt. Col. - July 3, 1863. Wded. and POW at Williamsburg, exchanged Aug. 5, 1862. POW at Sayler's Creek, released July 25, 1865. Bedford Co. farmer. Died in the Soldiers' Home in Richmond, March 23, 1911. bur. Bedford.

WINKLER, CLINTON McKAMY. b. Burke Co., North Carolina, Oct. 19, 1821. Moved to Indiana in 1835 and to Texas in 1840. Lawyer in Corsicana, Texas. In Texas legisl. Capt., Co. I, 4th Texas, July 17, 1861. Major - July 21, 1863. Lt. Col. - April 29, 1864. Appx. d. May 13, 1882. bur. Corsicana.

WINN, DAVID READ EVANS. b. Camden, South Carolina, July 5, 1831. gr. Jefferson Medical College. Physician in Americus. Married Frances Mary Dean. Lt., Co. K, 4th Georgia, April 27, 1861. Captain - April 28, 1862. Major - Sept. 24, 1862. Lt. Col. - Nov. 1, 1862. KIA at Gettysburg, July 1, 1863. Winn's papers are at Emory U. bur. Laurel Hill Cemetery, Savannah.

WINN, THOMAS ELISHA. b. Clarke Co., Georgia, May 21, 1839. gr. Emory & Henry. Lawyer in Milton Co. Lt., Co. F, 24th Georgia, Aug. 24, 1861. Captain - Aug. 19, 1862. Major - May 6, 1864. Lt. Col. - Sept. 10, 1864. Paroled at Atlanta, May 9, 1865. In U. S. Congress, 1891-1893. Died at Confederate Soldiers' Home in Atlanta, June 5, 1925. bur. Ridge Grove Cemetery, Greensboro, Georgia.

WINSTON, JOHN ANTHONY. b. Madison Co., Alabama, Sept. 4, 1812. Mobile merchant. In Alabama legisl., 1839-53. Gov. of Alabama. Colonel, 8th Alabama, June 11, 1861. Resigned, June 16, 1862, due to chronic rheumatism. Elected to U. S. Senate after the war, but denied his seat. d. Mobile, Dec. 21, 1871.

WINSTON, JOHN R. b. Rockingham Co., North Carolina, April 13, 1839. Lived at Reidsville. Teacher. 5'9". Capt., Co. F, 45th North Carolina, March 11, 1862. Major - Feb. 9, 1863. Lt. Col. - June 26, 1863. Colonel - May 19, 1864. Wded. and POW at Gettysburg, then escaped from Johnson's Island. Back on duty by May 1864. Wded. at Spotsylvania. Wded. in head at Sayler's Creek. Appx. d. March 7, 1888. bur. Red House Presbyterian Churchyard, Caswell Co.

WISE, JAMES CALVERT. b. St. Mary's Co., Maryland, Nov. 29, 1823. Civil engineer in Alexandria, Louisiana. Sheriff of Rapides Parish, 1848-60. Capt., Co. B, 1st Louisiana, Aug. 2, 1861. Major - 1861. Defeated at April 1862 re-org. QM General of Louisiana later in the war. In Louisiana legisl. Rapides planter. d. Alexandria, Louisiana, Feb. 4, 1904.

WISE, PEYTON. b. Accomack Co., Virginia, Feb. 9, 1838. Educated in Washington and Philadelphia. Pvt., Co. H, 46th Virginia, July 3, 1861. Lt. - May 19, 1862. Major - May 24, 1862. Lt. Col. - March 28, 1864. Wded., June 16, 1864 in the shoulder. POW, Oct. 26, 1864, to the end of the war. Richmond merchant and militia general post-war. m. Laura Chilton (daughter of General Robert Chilton). d. March 29, 1897.

WITCHER, VINCENT A. b. Pittsylvania Co., Virginia, Feb. 16, 1837. Lawyer in Wayne Co. Capt., Co. A, 34th Virginia Cav. Bn., Dec. 11, 1861. Major - June 1, 1862. Lt. Col. - May 2, 1863. Dropped during 1864, but the order was revoked later in the year. Lawyer in Utah and West Virginia post-war, before returning to Pittsylvania as a farmer. d. Riceville, Virginia, Dec. 7, 1912.

WITCHER, WILLIAM ADDISON. b. Pittsylvania Co., Virginia, 1820. Lawyer and journalist in Clay Co., Missouri, 1841-55, then returned to Virginia. Capt., Co. I, 21st Virginia, June 29, 1861. Lt. Col. - Dec. 1, 1862. Colonel - April 1863 (rank backdated to Dec. 1, 1862, also). Wded. at Chancellorsville and in May 1864. Appx. In Virginia legisl. d. Jan. 29, 1887. Witcher was the officer who brought charges of cowardice against Gen. J. R. Jones.

WITHERS, ELIJAH BENTON. b. Caswell Co., North Carolina, Dec. 31, 1836. gr. UNC, 1859. Capt., Co. A, 13th North Carolina, April 26, 1861. Major - June 13, 1863. Lt. Col. - Oct. 19, 1864. Wded. at Gettysburg. Appx. In North Carolina legisl. Lawyer. Moved to Danville, Virginia, in 1876. d. Danville, April 23, 1898. bur. Green Hill Cemetery.

WITHERS, ROBERT ENOCH. b. Campbell Co., Virginia, Sept. 18, 1821. gr. U. Virginia. Physician in Campbell Co. and Danville. Colonel, 18th Virginia, May 23, 1861. Badly wded. at Gaines' Mill. Retired, July 21, 1864. Commanded post at Danville. Newspaper editor post-war. Lt. Gov. of Virginia. U. S. Senator. U. S. Consul at Hong Kong. d. Wytheville, Sept. 21, 1907. bur. East End Cemetery.

WITHERS, ROBERT WOODSON. b. Campbell Co., Virginia, Jan. 18, 1835. Farmer. m. Blanche Thomas Payne. Lt., Co. I, 42nd Virginia, 1861. Captain - April 21, 1862. Lt. Col. - Nov. 30, 1862. Colonel - Nov. 29, 1863. Wded. in hand at North Anna. Wded. and POW at Shepherdstown, Aug. 25, 1864; exchanged Oct. 31, 1864. d. Rustburg, Virginia, 1896.

WITT, HORACE HILL. b. Feb. 25, 1830. Lt., Co. B, 7th Georgia, May 31, 1861. Captain - May 12, 1862. Major - Aug. 30, 1862. Resigned, Feb. 16, 1863. Wded. at 1st Manassas. Witt later became Captain of a George six-months unit. Commission merchant in Atlanta pre-war and post-war. d. Augusta, Aug. 29, 1901. bur. Oakland Cemetery, Atlanta.

WOFFORD, JOSEPH LEWELLYN. b. Spartanburg, Jan. 17, 1833. m. Letitia Elizabeth Petit. Physician. Capt., Co. E, 13th South Carolina, Aug. 27, 1861. Major - June 21, 1863. Wded. thigh at Fredericksburg, which caused him to resign, Nov. 4, 1863. In South Carolina legisl., 1870-72. d. Spartanburg, June 19, 1912.

WOLFE, JOHN P. Farmer. Capt., Co. A, 51st Virginia, July 16, 1861. Lt. Col. - July 8, 1863. KIA at Leetown, Virginia, Aug. 25, 1864. He is probably buried in Edgehill Cemetery, Charlestown, West Virginia, but that is uncertain because of errors on the gravestone.

WOOD, ALFRED CAMPBELL. b. Georgia. Merchant in Randolph Co., Alabama, in 1860, age 33. Capt., Co. K, 14th Alabama, July 22, 1861. Major - May 12, 1862. Lt. Col. - June 30, 1862. Colonel - July 8, 1862. Wded. at Frayser's Farm, Resigned, surgeon's certificate, Oct. 3, 1862. m. Emily Pate, 1863. bur. High Pines Church, Randolph Co., Alabama.

WOOD, HENRY CLINTON. b. Scott Co., Virginia, Feb. 15, 1836. Capt., Co. D, 37th Virginia, May 20, 1861. Major - June 28, 1862. Wded. at Sharpsburg. Suffered a broken arm, March 15, 1864. In Virginia legisl. Merchant, real estate investor, and ice plant owner. Unmarried. d. Dec. 8, 1909. b. East Hill Cemetery, Bristol.

WOOD, JAMES HALL. b. Aug. 26, 1840. Lived in Rowan County. Capt., Co. B, 4th North Carolina, May 16, 1861. Major - July 22, 1862. Lt. Col. - Dec. 23, 1862. Colonel - May 19, 1864. Wded. at Seven Pines and Gaines' Mill. KIA at Snicker's Gap, July 18, 1864. Buried in Third Creek Presbyterian Churchyard, Rowan County, North Carolina.

WOOD, WILLIAM WALTER. b. Amelia, Virginia, Nov. 18, 1838. att. Hampden-Sydney. Clarksville lawyer. Lt., Co. E, 14th Virginia, May 12, 1861 (actually held this position from Jan. 1861). Capt., Co. G, 14th Virginia, April 29, 1862. Major - July 3, 1863. Lt. Col. - Oct. 28, 1863. Present into 1865. In Virginia legisl., 1870. Moved to St. Louis in 1874. Dabbled in Mexican mineral investments. d. St. Louis, Jan. 1892.

WOODFIN, JOHN WOODS. b. 1818. Lived in Buncombe Co., North Carolina. m. Myra McDowell. Capt., Co. G, 1st North Carolina Cav., May 16, 1861. Major, 2nd North Carolina Cav., Sept. 23, 1861. Resigned, ill health, Sept. 6, 1862. Later commanded the 14th North Carolina Cav. Bn. and was KIA at Marshall, North Carolina, Oct. 22, 1863.

WOODHOUSE, JOHN THOMAS. b. Princess Anne Co., April 15, 1838. att. William & Mary. Capt., Co. G, 16th Virginia, June 11, 1861. Major - March 16, 1863. Wded. at Malvern Hill, Gettysburg and the Crater (foot and leg). Retired to Invalid Corps, Mar. 8, 1865. m. Virginia Elizabeth Whitehurst, 1871. Planter and County Treasurer of Princess Anne Co. d. May 22, 1917. bur. Eastern Shore Chapel, Oceans, Virginia.

WOODRUM, RICHARD. b. Sept. 5, 1833. Lived at Union, Virginia. 5′10″. m. Eliza Maddy. Lt., Co. F, 26th Virginia Bn., June 12, 1861. Captain - Dec. 1861. Major - Nov. 24, 1862. Wded. in hip and POW at Cold Harbor, released July 19, 1865. Woodrum was among the "Immortal 600" while a prisoner. A leading Republican (which predilection he had displayed before the war) in Monroe Co., West Virginia. d. Summers Co., West Virginia, Aug. 1906.

WOODSON, BLAKE LYNCH. b. Botetourt Co., Virginia, May 21, 1835. att. U. Virginia. gr. Lynchburg College. Lawyer. Lt., Beauregard Rifles (a Virginia artillery company from Lynchburg), 1861. Major, 45th Virginia Bn., Dec. 21, 1863. Wded. in left arm and paroled at Piedmont. In Virginia legisl. Lawyer, judge and prosecutor in Jackson Co., Missouri. d. Kansas City, March 16, 1902. bur. Forest Hill Cemetery.

WOODWARD, JOHN JEFFERSON. b. Fairfield Dist., South Carolina, Oct. 1808. Lawyer in Talladega, Alabama. In Alabama legisl. Capt., Co. E, 10th Alabama, June 4, 1861. Major - Sept. 4, 1861. Lt. Col. - Dec. 20, 1861. Colonel - March 14, 1862. KIA at Gaines' Mill.

WOODWARD, JOHN R. b. South Carolina, ca. 1832. Physician. Enrolled at Palestine, Texas, on June 23, 1862, as Capt., Co. G, 1st Texas. Acting Major in May 1863; actual promotion date is not shown in Woodward's service record. MWIA in the head by a piece of shell at Gettysburg, d. Aug. 26, 1863.

WOODWARD, THOMAS WILLIAM. b. Rockton, South Carolina, May 7, 1883. att. South Carolina College and Wake Forest. Major, 6th South Carolina, Feb. 19, 1861. Severely wded. thigh at Dranesville. Dropped at spring 1862 re-org. Later became

QM, 20th South Carolina and AQM with Kershaw's Brigade. In South Carolina legisl. Author of an interesting tract on the 6th South Carolina. d. Rockton, Sept. 4, 1902. Buried in Winnsboro.

WOOLDRIDGE, WILLIAM BEVERLEY. b. Chesterfield Co., 1827. att. U. Virginia. Chesterfield Co. planter. Lt., Co. B, 4th Virginia Cav., April 23, 1861. Captain - April 25, 1862. Major - Sept. 4, 1863. Lt. Col. - May 12, 1864. Colonel - Nov. 1, 1864. Wded. at Spotsylvania, May 9, 1864, leg amputated. m. Mrs. Martha Virginia Cowan Stanard, widow of Capt. Robert Conway Stanard (3rd Co., Richmond Howitzers). President of Midlothian Coal Co. d. Chesterfield Co., March 15, 1881. bur. Maury Cemetery.

WOOTEN, THOMAS JONES. b. Columbus Co., North Carolina, Oct. 16, 1840. Pvt., Co. K, 18th North Carolina, May 22, 1861. Lt. - April 24, 1862. Captain - Oct. 17, 1862. Major - May 3, 1863. Wded. at Chancellorsville. Appx. Wooten won considerable notice while commanding the sharpshooters of Lane's Brigade around Petersburg. m. Carrie McNair. d. Maxton, North Carolina, Nov. 26, 1923.

WORK, PHILLIP ALEXANDER. b. Breckinridge Co., Kentucky, Feb. 1832. m. Adeline F. Lea, 1855. In Texas Secession Convention. Capt., Co. F, 1st Texas, May 28, 1861. Lt. Col. - May 19, 1862. Resigned Jan. 5, 1864, because of syphilis. Later organized a company for service in Texas under Magruder. d. Kountze, Texas, March 17, 1911. bur. Old Hardin Cemetery.

WORTHAM, GEORGE W. b. 1828. Of Oxford, North Carolina. att. UNC. Lawyer. Capt., Co. D, 12th North Carolina, April 22, 1861. Major, 50th North Carolina, April 15, 1862. Lt. Col. - Dec. 1, 1862. Colonel - Nov. 10, 1863. Under arrest in Feb. 1864. Paroled at Greensboro. d. 1883.

WRAY, GEORGE. b. 1821. att. U. Virginia. Sheriff of Elizabeth City Co. Major, 115th Virginia Militia, 1861-62. The 115th served on the Peninsula under Magruder and Johnston. Wray did staff work for Magruder and B. S. Ewell during the same period. He also commanded the post at Savage Station. d. 1864.

WREN, JOHN F. b. Richmond. Merchant. m. Catherine Lee Kennon. Wren was an officer of Virginia volunteer cavalry years before the war. Capt., Co. A, 40th Virginia Cav. Bn., March 19, 1862 (at that date, the company was a local defense unit). Major, 40th Virginia Cav. Bn., Nov. 11, 1862. Res. Aug. 28, 1863.

WRIGHT, AUGUSTUS ROMALDUS. b. Wrightsboro, Georgia, June 16, 1813. gr. U. Georgia. m. (1) Elizabeth Richardson, 1832. m. (2) Miss Allman. In U. S. Congress, 1857-59. In Georgia Secession Convention. Colonel, 38th Georgia, Aug. 27, 1861. Resigned, Feb. 14, 1862, to enter the C. S. Congress. Lawyer and Baptist preacher in Rome, Georgia. d. near Rome, March 31, 1891. bur. Myrtle Hill Cemetery.

WRIGHT, CLEMENT GILLESPIE. b. Oct. 15, 1824. gr. UNC. Pvt., Co. A, 5th North Carolina Cav., 1861. Aide to Genl. Robertson. Major, 13th North Carolina Bn., May 19, 1863. Major, 66th North Carolina, Aug. 3, 1863. Lt. Col. - June 3, 1864. Wded. in June 1864. Died in service, March 14, 1865. bur. in Presbyterian Cemetery, Greensboro, North Carolina.

WRIGHT, GILBERT JEFFERSON. b. Gwinnett Co., Georgia, Feb. 18, 1825. Wded. as a private in the Mexican War. 6′4″. Lawyer, judge and mayor in Albany, Georgia. m. Dorothy Chandler, 1850. Killed a friend in a pre-war drunken brawl. Lt., Co. D, Cav. Bn. of Cobb's Legion (Georgia), Aug. 10, 1861. Captain - 1862. Major - June 10, 1863. Colonel - Oct. 9, 1863. Transferred to the 9th Georgia Cav., 1865. Surrendered at Greensboro. d. Forsyth, Georgia, June 3, 1895. bur. Oakland Cemetery.

WYLIE, JOHN DUNOVANT. b. Lancaster Dist., Dec. 14, 1833. gr. SCMA, 1855. m. Eliza Jane Witherspoon, 1857. Capt., Co. A, 9th South Carolina, 1861. Capt., Co. A, 5th South Carolina, April 1862. Major - Nov. 1, 1862. Lt. Col. - Dec. 24, 1862. Wylie was absent sick quite frequently. Lancaster Co. lawyer and South Carolina legisl. d. May 15, 1894. bur. First Presbyterian Old Cemetery, Lancaster, South Carolina.

YANCEY, BENJAMIN CUDWORTH. b. Charleston, South Carolina, March 27, 1817. gr. U. Georgia and Harvard. In South

Carolina legisl. Lived in Cherokee Co., Alabama, and served in Alabama Senate. Moved to Athens, Georgia. Minister to the Argentine Republic under Buchanan. Brother of William Lowndes Yancey. Capt., Co. B, Cav. Bn. of Cobb's Legion (Georgia), Aug. 14, 1861. Major - Nov. 15, 1861. d. Floyd Co., Georgia, Oct. 25, 1891. T. R. R. Cobb called Yancey "a slow coach," who "seeks to throw every obstacle in my way."

YARBOROUGH, WILLIAM HENRY. b. March 1, 1840. Lived in Franklin Co., North Carolina. Lt., Co. L, 15th North Carolina, May 20, 1861. Captain - May 2, 1862. Major - May 2, 1862. Lt. Col. - Feb. 27, 1863. Colonel - Nov. 4, 1864. Appx. Suffered "four slight wounds" during the war. m. Lula Davis. Merchant. Died in Louisburg, North Carolina, Aug. 3, 1914.

YEATES, JESSE JOHNSON. b. Murfreesboro, North Carolina, May 29, 1829. att. Emory & Henry. Major, 31st North Carolina, Sept. 19, 1861. Paroled at Roanoke Island, Feb. 1862. Resigned, illness, Dec. 15, 1862. In North Carolina legisl. during the war. In U. S. Congress, 1875-81. Washington, D. C., lawyer. d. Washington, D. C., Sept. 5, 1892. bur. there.

YELLOWLEY, EDWARD CLEMENTS. b. Martin Co., North Carolina, Oct. 22, 1821. Greenville lawyer. gr. UNC, 1844. Fought a fatal duel in the 1840's. Capt., Co. G, 8th North Carolina, May 16, 1861. Major - July 8, 1863. Lt. Col., 68th North Carolina, Oct. 1, 1863. In North Carolina legisl. d. 1885.

YONCE, WILLIAM AUGUSTA. b. Nov. 16, 1835. Lived in Wythe Co., Capt., Co. C, 51st Virginia, July 20, 1861. Major - April 23, 1864. MWIA in the chest, Sept. 19, 1864. d. Sept. 24 at Charlottesville. bur. St. John's Church, Wythe Co.

YORK, RICHARD WATSON. b. Randolph Co., North Carolina, Sept. 30, 1839. Son of Rev. Brantley York, a founder of Duke U. Richard York co-authored an 1873 textbook with his father. Capt., Co. I, 6th North Carolina, May 16, 1861. Major - July 3, 1863. Wded. at Gaines' Mill and Fisher's Hill, never returning after the latter wound. Planter, lawyer and teacher in Wake and Chatham counties. d. Chatham Co., Nov. 29, 1893.

YOUNG, JOHN AUGUSTUS. b. Iredell Co., North Carolina. Married Malvina Graham. In North Carolina legisl. Lt. Col., 4th North Carolina, May 16, 1861. Resigned, illness (and re-org.?), May 5, 1862. Milling and mercantile business in Charlotte. d. Charlotte at the age of 80.

YOUNG, JOHN SMITH. b. Raleigh, North Carolina, Nov. 4, 1834. Lived in Tennessee and Arkansas before gr. Centenary College, 1855. Lawyer in Claiborne Paris, Louisiana. Lt. Col., 2nd Louisiana, May 11, 1861. Dropped at spring 1862 re-org. In U. S. Congress, 1878-79. Died in Shreveport, Oct. 11, 1916.

YOUNG, ROBERT SIMONTON. b. Concord, North Carolina, Jan. 20, 1821. Cabarrus Co. farmer. Capt., Co. B, 7th North Carolina, May 16, 1861. Major - June 27, 1862. POW at Frederick, Maryland, Sept. 1862; exchanged Nov. 1862. Resigned, ill health, Jan. 6, 1863. Aide to R. F. Hoke. KIA at Petersburg, July 8, 1864. bur. Poplar Tent Presbyterian Churchyard, Cabarrus Co.

ZABLE, DAVID. b. New Orleans, 1832. Clerk. Capt., Co. K, 14th Louisiana, June 12, 1861. Major - Feb. 19, 1862. WIA at Williamsburg. Lt. Col. - Aug. 3, 1862. m. Alice Dalton, 1868. New Orleans businessman, state official and U.C.V. officer. d. Oct. 22, 1906. bur. Metairie Cemetery.

ZACHRY, CHARLES THORNTON. b. Covington, Georgia, Feb. 4, 1828. Capt., Co. H, 27th Georgia, Sept. 9, 1861. Major - same date. Lt. Col. - Dec. 24, 1861. Colonel - Sept. 17, 1862. Wded. at Sharpsburg. Surrendered at Greensboro. In Georgia legisl. Henry Co. farmer. Died in McDonough, Feb. 9, 1906. bur. there.

ZEIGLER, MARTIN GOVAN. Of Cokesbury, South Carolina. Capt., Co. F, Holcombe Legion (South Carolina), Dec. 28, 1861. Major - Dec. 5, 1862. Paroled at Kinston, North Carolina, Dec. 15, 1862. POW at Stoney Creek, Virginia, May 7, 1864; released July 24, 1865. 5′9½″. m. Lavinia Ann Frances Dunwody, who produced 10 children. Clerk of Courts in Abbeville Co. d. Sept. 13, 1888, aged 58. bur. Upper Long Care Presbyterian Church, Abbeville.

CLARK, MERIWETHER LEWIS. b. Jan. 16, 1809. Son of William Clark of Lewis and Clark fame. gr. USMA. Resigned U.S. Army in 1833. Major of Missouri arty. bn. in Mexican War. Commanded 500-man force that put down St. Louis riots in 1850. Architect. m. Abby Churchill (their grandson began Kentucky Derby, and named Churchill Downs for Abby). Brigadier General, Missouri State Guard, Oct. 1861. Major of CSA arty., Nov. 11, 1861. Colonel and chief of artillery to Van Dorn. Assigned to Ordnance Dept. at Richmond. Commanding Barton's Brigade, A.N.Va., as colonel, in Nov. 1864 and into 1865. POW at Amelia C.H., April 5, 1865. 5′9″ d. Oct. 29, 1881, in Frankfort, Kentucky. bur. Bellefontaine Cemetery, St. Louis.

Confederate Field Officers, other than Army of Northern Virginia

An Appendix

INTRODUCTION TO THE APPENDIX

The appendix is based on the list of Confederate field officers published by the Government Printing office late in the 19th century. A very large number of changes have been made from that starting point, as enumerated below.

1. All of the Army of Northern Virginia officers were deleted, since they are the subject of the much more extensive sketches in the main body of this book.

2. A number of field officers were added to the published list by General Marcus J. Wright, in holograph notes in the margin of a published copy. These notes are in the possession of Robert J. Younger, who made them available for addition to the appendix. Wright's additions are identified with a double asterisk throughout the appendix.

3. The present author has added a considerable number of field officers, most of them from irregular organizations, such as Virginia militia regiments.

4. Quite a number of errors in the published listing have been rectified. These included such things as errant spelling, wrong initials, multiple listings of the same man, and mis-identification of units.

The resulting list includes 3,524 entries. After extensive research in the same sorts of sources used for the main body of the book, I was able to add one or more given names to 1,066 of the officers listed, and one or more of the years of life to 1,390 of the officers listed. Pinning down the lives of one-third of the list is hardly a definitive performance, but it represents a substantial start. I will be eagerly in quest of the rest of them as long as life lasts, or until the government claps me in irons for general iconoclasm, inability to pay its odious taxes, or other crimes against our glorious republic.

Abbitt, Wyatt, Colonel 174th Virginia Militia.
Abbott, S. T., Major 1st Battn. Ark. Res. Cavy., 1864-65.
Abercrombie, Leonard Anderson, Lieutenant-Colonel 20th Texas Infantry. (1832-1891).
Abercrombie, Robert Haden, Major, Lieutenant-Colonel 45th Alabama Infantry. (1837-1891).
Abernathy, Alfred Harris, Colonel 53d Tennessee Infantry. (d. 1881).
Abert, George William, Lieutenant-Colonel, Colonel 14th Mississippi Infantry. (d. 1912).
Abington, Hardeman A., Major 38th (formerly 8th, Looney's) Tennessee Infantry.
Adair, John Alexander, Lieutenant-Colonel 4th Kentucky Infantry.
Adair, (**) Walter T., Surgeon 2d Cherokee Ark. Regt.
Adair, William Penn, Colonel 2d Cherokee Mounted Rifles. (b. 1830).
Adaire, Thomas N., Major, Lieutenant-Colonel, Colonel 4th Mississippi Infantry.
Adams, C., Major Rawlings' Infantry Battalion, 2d Div., Missouri State Guard.
Adams, Charles W., Colonel 23d (Adams') Arkansas Infantry; Major Adams' Battalion Arkansas Infantry. (1817-1878).
Adams, Daniel Weisiger, Lieutenant-Colonel, Colonel 1st Louisiana Regulars. (1821-1872).
Adams, Fleming W., Colonel 38th Mississippi Infantry.
Adams, James Pickett, Major 10th (also called 3d) Battalion South Carolina Cavalry. (1828-1904).
Adams, J. F., Lieutenant-Colonel Kentucky Partisan Rangers.
Adams, J. L., Major 7th Arkansas Cavalry.
Adams, Lysander, Colonel 33rd Tennessee Infantry.
Adams, Samuel, Colonel 33d Alabama Infantry. (1829-1864).
Adams, T. C., Major 156th Virginia Militia.
Adams, Warren, Major 3d South Carolina Artillery Regiment (1st South Carolina Regulars or Enlisted men). (1838-1880).
Adams, William C., Lieutenant-Colonel 38th Arkansas Infantry.
Adams, William Wirt, Colonel Wirt Adams' Mississippi Cavalry. (1819-1888).
Aderhold, Jacob Wilson, Lieutenant-Colonel 1st Confederate Infantry. (1826-1911).
Adrian, Thomas W., Major, Lieutenant-Colonel 12th Battalion Tennessee Cavalry. (k. 1863).
Aikin, James Houston, Major 9th Battalion Tennessee Cavalry. (1832-1911).
Albert, Henry St. George, Colonel 1st Virginia Militia, 7th Brigade.
Albright, William A., Colonel 48th North Carolina Militia.
Alcorn, Milton Stewart, Major 1st Mississippi Infantry. (1843-1879).
Alexander, Almerine M., Colonel 34th (also called 2d Partisans) Texas Cavalry.
Alexander, Charles McClung, Major 59th (afterward mounted) Tennessee Infantry. (1837-1863).
Alexander, David W., Lieutenant-Colonel 8th (Baxter Smith's, also called 4th) Tennessee Cavalry. (Cancelled).
Alexander, George L., Major 16th (also called 4th) Battalion Alabama Infantry. (d. 1862).
Alexander, J. T., Colonel 98th Virginia Militia.
Alexander, Thomas Williamson, Lieutenant-Colonel 29th Georgia Infantry; Major Floyd Legion, Georgia State Guard. (1826-1915).
Alexander, W. J., Major Frontier Cavalry Regiment, Texas.
Allen, Alexander C., Major 1st and 2d Tennessee Consolidated; Major 27th Tennessee Infantry.
Allen, Augustus C., Major 19th Texas Infantry.
Allen, Henry Watkins, Lieutenant-Colonel, Colonel 4th Louisiana Infantry. (1820-1866).
Allen, Jack, Lieutenant-Colonel 3d Kentucky Cavalry.
Allen, John K., Major 30th Mississippi Infantry.
Allen, Joseph V. H., Major 63d Georgia Infantry. (1830-1883).
Allen, Lawrence Marion, Colonel 64th North Carolina Infantry; Lieutenant-Colonel 11th Battalion North Carolina Infantry. (d. 1903).
Allen, Robert Dickinson, Major 17th Texas Infantry.
Allen, Robert Thomas Pritchard, Colonel 17th Texas Infantry. (1813-1888).

Allen, William Wirt, Major, Lieutenant-Colonel, Colonel 1st Alabama Cavalry. (1835-1894).
Alley, Alexander K., Colonel 36th Tennessee Infantry.
Allin, John, Major 14th (Mitchell's) Arkansas Infantry.
Allin, Phillip T., Major 26th Battalion Tennessee Cavalry. (d. 1869).
Allison, Robert D., Colonel 24th Tennessee Infantry; Colonel Allison's Squadron Tennessee Cavalry. (1810-1900).
Alston, Charles, Jr., Major 18th South Carolina Battalion Artillery (Siege Train). (1826-1869).
Alston, Robert A., Major, Lieutenant-Colonel 9th Tennessee Cavalry; Lieutenant-Colonel 1st Special Battalion Kentucky Cavalry.
Amacker, Obediah P., Lieutenant-Colonel 3d Louisiana Cavalry, 1865. (1838-1880).
Amerine, John Porter Warner, Major 37th Alabama Infantry; Colonel 57th (also called 54th) Alabama Infantry.
Amis, James Sanders, Colonel 42d North Carolina Militia. (1825-1903).
Anderson, Benjamin M., Major 1st Kentucky Infantry; Major, Lieutenant-Colonel 3d Kentucky Infantry. (d. 1865).
Anderson, Charles D., Colonel 21st Alabama Infantry; Major, Colonel 20th Alabama Infantry. (1829-1901).
Anderson, (**) G. H., Colonel 2d Georgia Reserves.
Anderson, James Boys, Major 1st Louisiana Regular Artillery Regiment. (d. 1863).
Anderson, James Patton, Colonel 1st Florida Infantry. (1822-1872).
Anderson, J. B., Major 1st Infantry Battalion Texas State Troops.
Anderson, J. J., Major 3d South Carolina State Troops.
Anderson, John H., Lieutenant-Colonel 2d North Carolina Battalion Reserves; Major 2d (Anderson's) Battalion Junior Reserves; Colonel 2d Regiment North Carolina Junior Reserves.
Anderson, John H., Lieutenant-Colonel, Colonel 8th (Fulton's) Tennessee Infantry. (d. 1902).
Anderson, Joseph, Major 19th (Dawson's) Arkansas Infantry.
Anderson, Paul F., Lieutenant-Colonel 8th (Baxter Smith's, also called 4th) Tennessee Cavalry. (d. 1878).
Anderson, Robert Houstoun, Major 1st Battalion Georgia Sharpshooters; Colonel 5th Georgia Cavalry. (1835-1888).
Anderson, Thomas Scott, Lieutenant-Colonel 6th Texas Infantry; Colonel Anderson's Regiment Texas Cavalry. (d. 1868).
Anderson, (**) William, Colonel 160th Virginia Militia.
Andrews, Garnett, Major, Lieutenant-Colonel 8th Confederate Battalion Infantry. (1837-1903).
Andrews, John Frederick, Major 66th Georgia Infantry (declined appointment). (1830-1892).
Andrews, Julius A., Colonel 32d (also called 15th) Texas Cavalry.
Anglade, J. G., Colonel 1st Tennessee Zouaves.
Ansley, David Henry, Major 5th Georgia Infantry. (1828-1887).
Antrim, C. W., Major 88th Virginia Militia.
Anvil, Daniel M. (**) Colonel 139th Virginia Militia.
Apperson, (**) John H., Major 5th Virginia Militia, Lt. Colonel 3d Virginia Infantry (?).
Appleby, Morgan Thomas, Major 24th South Carolina Infantry. (1814-1867).
Armant, Leopold L., Major, Colonel 18th Louisiana Infantry. (1835-1864).
Armistead, Charles G., Colonel 12th Mississippi Cavalry.
Armistead, Edward Herbert, Major, Lieutenant Colonel 22d Alabama Infantry. (1839-1864).
Armistead, Frank Stanley, Colonel 1st North Carolina Junior Reserves. (1835-1889).
Armistead, Robert Burbage, Major 22d Alabama Infantry. (1826-1862).
Armstrong, D. F., Lieutenant Colonel Williamson's Arkansas Infantry Battalion.
Armstrong, Frank Crawford, Colonel 3d Louisiana Infantry. (1835-1909).
Armstrong, ..., Colonel 2d Division Georgia State Militia.

Arnold, George Weeden, Lieutenant-Colonel 50th (Coltart's, also known as 26th) Alabama Infantry. (1840-1864).
Arnold, John W., Major 9th South Carolina Reserves.
Arnold, Mark, Colonel 25th Virginia Militia.
Arnold, P. M., Lieutenant-Colonel 25th Virginia Militia.
Arnold, Reuben, Lieutenant-Colonel 29th Tennessee Infantry.
Arnold, William E., Colonel, 8th Division, Missouri State Guard. (1830-1902).
Arnot, Zachariah P., Lieutenant-Colonel, 166th Virginia Militia.
Arrington, John A., Major Gordon's Regiment Arkansas Cavalry.
Arrington, Thomas Mann, Lieutenant-Colonel 31st (Hundley's) Alabama Infantry.
Ashby, Henry Marshall, Colonel 2d (Ashby's) Tennessee Cavalry. (1836-1868).
Ashcraft, Thomas C., Lieutenant-Colonel Ashcraft's Regiment Mississippi Cavalry; Lieutenant-Colonel 3d Battalion Mississippi State Cavalry; Colonel Ashcraft's, Ham's, and Lowry's Consolidated Mississippi Cavalry Regiments.
Ashe, Thomas Porter, Major 32d Alabama Infantry. (1830-1891).
Ashford, Alva Elgin, Major 35th Alabama Infantry. (1834-1904).
Ashford, Frederick A., Major, Lieutenant-Colonel, Colonel 16th Alabama Infantry. (1830-1864).
Ashford, James A., Lieutenant-Colonel 2d Tennessee Volunteers.
Ashley, William Percy Mortimer, Lieutenant-Colonel 25th Georgia Infantry.
Atkins, John DeWitt Clinton, Lieutenant-Colonel 5th Tennessee Infantry. (1825-1908).
Atkins, Thomas Morris, Lieutenant-Colonel, 49th Tennessee Infantry. (1827-1897).
Aunspaugh, Charles, Major Botetourt Regiment, Virginia Home Guards.
Austin, (**) A. J., Lieutenant-Colonel 1st Missouri Cavalry, 4th Division, Missouri State Guard. (d. 1861).
Austin, John E., Major 14th Battalion Louisiana Sharpshooters. (d. 1876).
Austin, John P., Major 9th Kentucky Cavalry. (1829-1911).
Autry, James Lockhart, Lieutenant-Colonel, Colonel 9th Mississippi Infantry; Lieutenant-Colonel 27th Mississippi Infantry. (1840-1862).
Avegno, Anatole P., Major 13th (Gibson's) Louisiana Infantry. (d. 1862).
Avery, Isaac Wheeler, Colonel 4th (Avery's) Georgia Cavalry; Lieutenant-Colonel 23d Battalion Georgia Cavalry. (1837-1897).
Avery, William Tecomsah, Lieutenant-Colonel 1st Alabama, Tennessee, and Mississippi Infantry. (1819-1880).
Aymett, Hans H., Major 53d Tennessee Infantry.
Baber, Milton D., Major, Lieutenant-Colonel 38th (Shaver's) Arkansas Infantry; Colonel 45th Arkansas Infantry.
Backus, William F., Lieutenant-Colonel 7th Virginia Militia.
Bacon, Edwin Henry, Jr., Major, Lieutenant-Colonel 32d Georgia Infantry. (b. 1839).
Badger, Edward, Major, Lieutenant-Colonel 4th Florida Infantry. (b. 1840).
Bagby, Arthur Pendleton, Major, Colonel 7th Texas Cavalry. (1833-1921).
Bagley, William H., Major, 68th North Carolina Infantry.
Bailey, Benjamin, Colonel 72d North Carolina Militia.
Bailey, David, Lieutenant-Colonel Camden County Georgia Militia.
Bailey, David Jackson, Colonel 30th Georgia Infantry. (1812-1897).
Bailey, (**) George H., Major 15th Virginia Militia.
Bailey, James Edmund, Colonel 49th Tennessee Infantry. (1820-1885).
Baird, Alfred Hunter, Lieutenant-Colonel 65th North Carolina Volunteers (6th North Carolina Cavalry); Major 5th Battalion North Carolina Cavalry.
Baird, Spruce McCoy, Colonel 4th Texas Cavalry Regiment, Arizona Brigade. (1814-1872).
Baker, Alpheus, Colonel 4th Confederate Infantry (after 54th Alabama); Colonel 54th Alabama Infantry; Colonel 1st Alabama, Tennessee, and Mississippi Infantry; Lieutenant-Colonel 7th Battalion Alabama Infantry. (1828-1891).
Baker, Thomas Henry, Major, Lieutenant-Colonel, Colonel 55th Tennessee Infantry. (b. 1836).
Baker, Thomas McDonald, Major, Lieutenant-Colonel 3d South Carolina Artillery (1st South Carolina Regulars).

Baker, William N., Major 53d Tennessee Infantry.
Baker, William Y., Major 18th (Newsom's, also called 19th) Tennessee Cavalry.
Balch, Robert Langdon, Major 3d (N. B. Forrest's) Tennessee Cavalry; Lieutenant-Colonel 18th Battalion Tennessee Cavalry.
Baldwin, Gaston W., Lieutenant-Colonel 30th (McNeill's) Arkansas Infantry.
Baldwin, William Edwin, Colonel 14th Mississippi Infantry. (1827-1864).
Baldwin, W. W., Major Ordnance Battalion, Columbus, Ga.
Bale, Alfred F., Major 6th Georgia Cavalry. (1839-1863).
Ball, Charles P., Colonel 8th (Hatch's, also called 9th) Alabama Cavalry.
Ball, Glover Alling, Major 1st Florida Infantry.
Ball, Lewis, Major, Colonel 41st Mississippi Infantry. (1820-1896).
Ball, Martin V., Major 2d Infantry Regiment, Virginia State Line.
Ballentine, John Goff, Colonel Ballentine's (also called 2d Mississippi Partisan Rangers) Mississippi Cavalry. (1825-1915).
Banks, James Oliver, Major, Lieutenant-Colonel 43d Mississippi Infantry. (b. 1829).
Baptiste, Francis, Lt. Col. . . . . Indian Regt.
Barber, Flavel C., Major 3d Tennessee Volunteers. (1830-1864).
Barbiere, Joseph, Major 4th Confederate Infantry (after 54th Alabama); Major Barbiere's Cavalry Battalion Alabama Reserves. (d. 1895).
Barclay, Hugh W., Lieutenant-Colonel 11th Georgia Cavalry; Major 30th Battalion Georgia Cavalry.
Barker, J. J. A., Major 3d Texas Cavalry.
Barksdale, Hickerson Hartwell, Lieutenant-Colonel 3d Mississippi Cavalry. (1825-1903).
Barksdale, James Armistead, Lieutenant-Colonel 5th Mississippi Cavalry; Lieutenant-Colonel 3d Mississippi Cavalry State Troops. (1835-1864).
Barksdale, (**) John H., Lieutenant-Colonel 47th Virginia Militia.
Barkuloo, William, Colonel 57th Georgia Infantry. (d. 1873).
Barnes, James William, Lieutenant-Colonel 4th Texas Infantry State Troops; Colonel Texas Reserve Corps. (1815-1892).
Barnes, William Deans, Lieutenant-Colonel 1st Regiment Florida Reserves.
Barnett, Timothy, Major, Colonel 2d Creek Regiment.
Barnett, T. T., Major, Lieutenant-Colonel 3d Kentucky Infantry. (1838-1899).
Barnett, W. D., Major 2d Battalion Arkansas Cavalry.
Barnette, D. J. (**)?, Major 2d Battalion South Carolina Reserves.
Barnhardt, Jacob Columbus, Colonel 84th North Carolina Militia.
Barr, James, Jr., Major, Lieutenant-Colonel, Colonel 10th Mississippi Infantry. (1830-1864).
Barrow, Robert Hilliard, Lieutenant-Colonel 11th Louisiana Infantry. (1824-1878).
Barrow, Robert J., Colonel 4th Louisiana Infantry (b. 1817).
Barry, James Buckner, Major 1st (McCulloch's) Texas Mounted Riflemen; Lieutenant-Colonel Frontier Regiment, Texas Cavalry.
Barry, William Taylor Sullivan, Colonel 35th Mississippi Infantry. (1821-1868).
Barteau, Clark Russell, Lieutenant-Colonel, Colonel 2d (Barteau's, afterward 22d) Tennessee Cavalry; Lieutenant-Colonel Barteau's Tennessee Cavalry Battalion. (1835-1900).
Bartlett, (**) A. W., Colonel 2d Regt. Alcorn's Brigade, Army of Miss. 10,000.
Bartlett, Frank A., Colonel Beauregard Regiment, Louisiana Militia.
Barton, James M., Lieutenant-Colonel 10th Texas Cavalry.
Basham, Oliver, Lieutenant-Colonel 7th Arkansas Cavalry. (d. 1864).
Baskerville, Charles, Lieutenant-Colonel 4th (also called 2d) Battalion Mississippi Cavalry.
Bass, Thomas Coke, Colonel 20th Texas Cavalry. (1825-1870).
Batchelor, S. S., Major, Lieutenant-Colonel 1st Louisiana Regulars.
Bate, Henry C., Major 1st (also called 12th) Confederate Cavalry.
Bate, William Brimage, Colonel 2d Tennessee Infantry (Provisional Army). (1826-1905).
Bateman, Mannah Wheaton, Major 26th Louisiana Infantry. (1831-1894).
Bateman, Thomas P., Lieutenant-Colonel 11th Tennessee Infantry.
Bates, James Campbell, Major 9th Texas Cavalry.

Bates, Joseph, Colonel 13th Texas Infantry; Lieutenant-Colonel Bates' Battalion Texas Infantry.

Battice, Franceway, Lieutenant-Colonel 1st (Battice's) Choctaw Cavalry Battalion.

Battle, Joel Allen, Colonel 20th Tennessee Infantry. (1811-1872).

Battle, Nicholas Williams, Lieutenant-Colonel 30th Texas Cavalry (also called 1st Partisan Rangers). (1820-1905).

Baucum, George F., Major, Lieutenant-Colonel, Colonel 8th Arkansas Infantry.

Baxter, Eli Harris, Jr., Lieutenant-Colonel 28th Texas Cavalry. (b. 1837).

Baxter, George Lewis, Major, Baxter's Confederate Cavalry Battalion; merged into Jeffrey Forrest's Alabama Cavalry.

Baylor, George Wythe, Colonel 2d Texas Cavalry Regiment, Arizona Brigade; Lieutenant-Colonel 2d Texas Cavalry Battalion, Arizona Brigade. (1832-1916).

Baylor, John Robert, Lieutenant-Colonel 2d Texas Cavalry (or Mounted Rifles). (1822-1894).

Baylor, (**) Robert W., Colonel 3d Virginia Militia Cavalry.

Beall, Thaddeus Solon, Major Beall's Battalion Alabama Cavalry. (1833-1903).

Bean, Elwood M., Major Texas Reserve Corps.

Bean, Onslow, Major 3d (also called 14th) Battalion Tennessee Cavalry; Lieutenant-Colonel 1st (Carter's) Tennessee Cavalry. (d. 1864).

Beard, William Kelly, Lieutenant-Colonel 1st Florida Infantry. (1830-1882).

Beasley, William Fessenden, Major 2d (Anderson's) North Carolina Battalion Reserves; Lieutenant-Colonel 2d Regiment North Carolina Junior Reserves. (1845-1923).

Beasley, William Park, Lieutenant-Colonel 2d Cavalry Georgia State Guard. (1812-1894).

Beaty, Charles Roambrose, Major, Lieutenant-Colonel 13th Texas Cavalry.

Beaumont, Thomas W., Lieutenant-Colonel 50th (old) Tennessee Infantry. (d. 1863).

Beck, Franklin King, Colonel 23d Alabama Infantry. (1814-1864).

Beckett, Newton J., Acting Major 1st Battalion Mississippi Infantry (60 days).

Bedford, Henry Hale, Major 2d Missouri Cavalry, 1st Division, Missouri State Guard.

Beeson, William E., Lieutenant-Colonel 9th (Maxey's, also called 8th) Texas Infantry.

Bell, Charles J. Major, Lieutenant-Colonel 30th Louisiana Infantry. (d. 1864).

Bell, Hiram Parks, Lieutenant-Colonel, Colonel 43d Georgia Infantry. (1827-1907).

Bell, James Madison, Lieutenant-Colonel 2d Cherokee Mounted Rifles; Lieutenant-Colonel, Colonel 1st Cherokee Mounted Rifles. (1826-1915).

Bell, Madison, Major 11th Georgia Cavalry. (1836-1896).

Bell, Robert Eagleton, Major 20th Texas Infantry. (1832-1910).

Bell, Samuel Slade, Colonel 37th (Bell's) Arkansas Infantry; Major 29th (afterward 37th) Arkansas Infantry. (1828-1877).

Bell, Tyree Harris, Lieutenant-Colonel, Colonel 12th Tennessee Infantry; Colonel 12th and 22d Tennessee Infantry Consolidated. (1815-1902).

Beltzhoover, (**) .... Batt'n. Inf., supposed Miss. State Troops, see Forrest's Campaigns, page 506, Battle Harrisburg.

Beltzhoover, Daniel M., Major, Lieutenant-Colonel 1st Louisiana Artillery. (1826-1870).

Benavides, Santos, Major 33d Texas Cavalry; Colonel Benavides' Texas Cavalry. (1823-1891).

Bennett, Albert Gallatin, Major 12th Battalion Alabama Partisan Rangers. (d. 1882).

Bennett, Enoch R., Lieutenant-Colonel 6th (also called 7th) Mississippi Infantry. (d. 1862).

Bennett, George W. C., Major MacDonald's Missouri Cavalry; Major 10th Missouri Cavalry; Major 11th Battalion Missouri Cavalry.

Bennett, George W., Major 12th (also called 1st Partisan Rangers) Tennessee Cavalry.

Bennett, James Dearing, Lieutenant-Colonel 7th Battalion Tennessee Cavalry; Colonel 9th Tennessee Cavalry. (1816-1863).
Bennett, Thomas F., Colonel 156th Virginia Militia.
Benson, Berry B., Major 12th (also called 1st Partisan Rangers) Tennessee Cavalry. (d. 1863).
Benton, Nat., Lieutenant-Colonel 36th (Wood's, also called 32d) Texas Cavalry.
Benton, Samuel, Colonel 34th (also called 37th) Mississippi Infantry. (1820-1864).
Beraud, Desire, Major 10th (Yellow Jackets) Battalion Louisiana Infantry.
Berry, (**) A. L., Col. 7th Ark. Mil.
Berry, Thomas G., Lieutenant-Colonel 9th Texas Cavalry. (k. 1864).
Berryman, Richard C., Major 12th Missouri Infantry.
Bethune, William C., Lieutenant-Colonel 57th (also called 54th) Alabama Infantry.
Bevier, Robert S., Lieutenant-Colonel 5th Missouri Infantry; Major 2d Battalion Missouri Infantry; Colonel 5th Missouri Infantry, 3d Division, Missouri State Guard. (d. 1892).
Bibb, Joseph Banajah, Lieutenant-Colonel, Colonel 23d Alabama Infantry. (1822-1869).
Bidwell, Bell G., Major 30th Tennessee Infantry.
Biffle, Jacob Barnett, Lieutenant-Colonel 2d Battalion Tennessee Cavalry; Colonel 9th (Biffle's also called 19th) Tennessee Cavalry. (1828-1877).
Bilbrey, Josiah H., Major 25th Tennessee Infantry.
Billopp, W. W., Major, Lieutenant-Colonel 29th Georgia Infantry. (d. 1864).
Billups, Lafayette Washington, Major 33d Virginia Militia. (1824-1893).
Binford, James Robert, Major, Lieutenant-Colonel 15th Mississippi Infantry. (d. 1918).
Bingham, Jabez, Major 8th Kentucky Infantry.
Bingham, William, Colonel 46th North Carolina Militia. (1835-1873).
Binns, John Esselman, Major 11th Tennessee Infantry; Major 11th and 29th Tennessee Infantry Consolidated. (d. 1914).
Bird, Edward, Lieutenant-Colonel, Colonel 5th Georgia Cavalry; Lieutenant-Colonel 2d Battalion Georgia Cavalry. (1825-1893).
Bird, Thompson J., Major 1st Battalion Trans-Mississippi Cavalry, Louisiana.
Birthright, C. E., Major 1st Missouri Infantry, 1st Division, Missouri State Guard.
Bishop, J. W., Major Harrell's Battalion Arkansas Cavalry.
Bishop, Samuel L., Major, Lieutenant-Colonel 20th Louisiana Infantry.
Bishop, William Harrison, Colonel 7th Mississippi Infantry. (d. 1864).
Bishop, William P., Colonel 29th Tennessee Infantry.
Bisland, John R., Colonel Terre Bonne Regiment, Louisiana Militia.
Bitzer, (**) John, Major 132d Virginia Militia.
Bivins, James Monroe, Major 19th (Thompson's) Battalion Georgia State Guard. (1818-1876).
Black, Erastus L., Major, Lieutenant-Colonel 23d (Lyles') Arkansas Infantry.
Black, George Robison, Lieutenant-Colonel 63d Georgia Infantry. (1835-1886).
Black, Gideon B., Lieutenant-Colonel 55th Tennessee Infantry.
Black, John, Major 1st Arkansas Militia (30-days' men).
Black, (**), Samuel L., Lieutenant-Colonel 15th Arkansas Infantry Regiment (Cleburne's).
Black, William Thomas, Colonel 5th Georgia Infantry. (1833-1862).
Blacknall, T. H., Major 37th (Bell's) Arkansas Infantry. (1833-1918).
Blackwell, John Lindsay, Major 5th Tennessee Cavalry. (1817-1895).
Blackwell, William H., Major 3d Arkansas Cavalry.
Blackwell, Y. H., Major, Lieutenant-Colonel 5th Missouri Cavalry.
Blair, James Douglas, Colonel 2d Louisiana Cavalry. (1828-1874).
Blakey, David Taliaferro, Major, Lieutenant-Colonel, Colonel 1st Alabama Cavalry. (1833-1902).
Blanding, Ormsby, Major 1st South Carolina Artillery. (1823-1889).
Blankenbeker, Elliott Finks, Major 82d Virginia Militia.
Blanton, James C., Major 3d (N. B. Forrest's) Tennessee Cavalry. (d. 1908).
Blanton, William C., Lieutenant-Colonel 1st Northeast Missouri Cavalry.

Bledsoe, Hiram Miller, Lieutenant-Colonel 6th Missouri Infantry, 8th Division, Missouri State Guard. (1826-1899).
Bledsoe, Willis Scott, Major 8th (Baxter Smith's, also called 4th) Tennessee Cavalry, and Murray's Regiment Tennessee Cavalry (1837-1877).
Blevins, Absalom K., Major 29 Tennessee Infantry. (d.1864).
Blount, James Henderson, Lieutenant-Colonel 1st Cavalry Battalion Georgia Reserves. (1837-1903).
Blount, Nathan Snow, Major 7th Florida Infantry. (1832-1880).
Blount, Robert P., Lieutenant-Colonel 9th Battalion Alabama Infantry. (b. 1819).
Blythe, Andrew K., Colonel 44th Mississippi Infantry; Lieutenant-Colonel 1st (Blythe's) Battalion Mississippi Infantry. (1818-1862).
Blythe, Green L., Major 1st Mississippi Cavalry Battalion (or Minute Men) State Troops; Colonel 2d Mississippi State Partisan Rangers. (1826-1879).
Bocage, Joseph W., Lieutenant-Colonel 2d Arkansas Infantry. (b. 1819).
Bogart, E. G., Lieutenant-Colonel 6th Missouri Cavalry, 8th Division Missouri State Guard.
Boggess, Abijah F., Major, Lieutenant-Colonel 26th Tennessee Infantry. (d. 1865).
Boggess, Jiles S., Major, Lieutenant-Colonel 3d Texas Cavalry.
Bohannan, Lewis, Lieutenant-Colonel 1st Missouri Cavalry, 4th Division, Missouri State Guard.
Bohannon, L. C., Colonel, ordered to North Missouri to recruit cavalry regiment for State service.
Bolling, Eugene S., Major Waul's Texas Legion.
Bolton, George W., Major 7th Missouri Cavalry, 8th Division, Missouri State Guard.
Bone, Henry F., Major 11th Texas Cavalry.
Bonham, D. W. C., Colonel 22d Mississippi Infantry. (d. 1861).
Bonneau, Peter, Colonel 19th South Carolina Militia.
Bonner, Thomas Reuben, Major, Lieutenant-Colonel, Colonel 18th Texas Infantry. (1838-1891).
Boone, Hannibal Honostus, Major 13th Battalion Texas Cavalry. (1834-1897).
Boone, Lafayette, Major 1st (Stirman's) Regiment Arkansas Sharpshooters.
Boone, Squire, Lieutenant-Colonel 15th (Hobb's) Arkansas Infantry; Colonel 15th (Boone's) Arkansas Infantry.
Booton, Daniel F., Major 3d Georgia Cavalry. (1834-1900).
Borden, Thomas J., Major, Lieutenant-Colonel 6th (also called 7th) Mississippi Infantry.
Border, John Pelham, Colonel Border's Regiment Texas Cavalry; Lieutenant-Colonel Anderson's Regiment Texas Cavalry; Lieutenant-Colonel Border's Texas Cavalry Battalion. (1821-1873).
Borland, Solon, Colonel 3d Arkansas Cavalry, Borland's Regiment Arkansas Militia; Lieutenant-Colonel 1st (Borland's) Battalion Arkansas Cavalry. (1808-1864).
Bosang, William H., Major 11th Battalion Virginia Reserves.
Bostick, Joseph, Major 34th (formerly 4th Tennessee, Provisional Army) Tennessee Infantry. (1832-1886).
Bostick, Nay, Major 1st Missouri Cavalry, 5th Division, Missouri State Guard.
Bosworth, Abel W., Major, Colonel Crescent Regiment Louisiana Infantry.
Bottles, James L., Lieutenant-Colonel 26th Tennessee Infantry. (c. 1825-1863).
Botts, William H., Major 8th (Fulton's) Tennessee Infantry.
Bouchelle, Thomas Sleighter, Colonel 2d Regiment North Carolina Detailed Men.
Boudinot, Elias Cornelius, Major 1st Cherokee Mounted Rifles. (1835-1890).
Boughan, Richard A., Lieutenant-Colonel 7th Missouri Cavalry, 1st Division, Missouri State Guard.
Bounds, Joseph Murphy, Lieutenant-Colonel, Colonel 11th Texas Cavalry. (d. 1863).
Bourland, James, Colonel Bourland's Regiment Texas Cavalry. (1801-1868).
Bowdre, Albert R., Major 9th Mississippi Infantry.
Bowen, C. W., Major 2d Mississippi State Partisan Rangers.
Bowen, John Stevens, Colonel 1st Missouri Infantry. (1830-1863).

Bowen, Wiles Lyde Lasham, Major, Lieutenant-Colonel, Colonel 4th Florida Infantry. (1838-1905).
Bowie, James W., Major Wright's Battalion Arkansas Cavalry; Lieutenant-Colonel Wright's Regiment Arkansas Cavalry.
Bowles, James W., Major, Lieutenant-Colonel 2d (Morgan's) Kentucky Cavalry. (1837-1921).
Bowman, Henry Farrar, Major 15th (Russell's, also called 20th) Tennessee Cavalry. (1830-1893).
Bowman, James H., Major 3d Kentucky Infantry.
Bowman, John Parker, Major 6th Missouri Infantry, 8th Division, Missouri State Guard. (d. 1862).
Bowman, Samuel, Major 12th Missouri Cavalry. (d. 1863).
Bowyer, Thomas Mickie, Major Artillery, P.A.C.S. (1830-1900).
Boyce, ..., Major 1st Missouri Infantry, 3d Division, Missouri State Guard.
Boyd, James A., Lieutenant-Colonel 12th Louisiana Infantry.
Boyd, John R., Lieutenant-Colonel 1st Missouri Infantry Battalion, 5th Division, Missouri State Guard. (d. 1862).
Boyd, Joseph C., Major 3d Tennessee Infantry (Provisional Army). (d. 1863).
Boyd, Samuel, Lieutenant-Colonel 20th Louisiana Infantry; Lieutenant-Colonel 9th (also called 17th) Battalion Louisiana Infantry (temporary commander).
Boyd, Thomas, Major 98th Virginia Militia.
Boyd, Wier, Colonel 52d Georgia Infantry. (1820-1893).
Boyles, William, Colonel 56th Alabama Partisan Rangers; Major 15th Battalion Alabama Partisan Rangers. (1818-1882).
Boynton, James Stoddard, Major, Lieutenant-Colonel, Colonel 30th Georgia Infantry. (1833-1902).
Brackenridge, John Thomas, Major 33d Texas Cavalry. (1828-1906).
Bradford, Alsey H., Colonel 31st (A. H. Bradford's) Tennessee Infantry.
Bradford, Henry, Major, 1st Florida Cavalry.
Bradford, Henry Clay, Lieutenant-Colonel 2d Alabama Infantry. (1829-1879).
Bradford, J. D., Major Battalion Mississippi Scouts.
Bradford, James Andrew John, Colonel 10th North Carolina Volunteers (1st North Carolina Artillery). (1804-1863).
Bradford, James C., Jr., Major 3d (also called 14th) Battalion Tennessee Cavalry.
Bradford, Jesse J., Major 37th Georgia Infantry. (1838-1878).
Bradford, William M., Colonel 31st (W. M. Bradford's, after 39th) Tennessee Infantry. (1832-1912).
Bradley, Benjamin Franklin, Major 1st Battalion Kentucky Mounted Rifles. (1825-1897).
Bradley, John A., Lieutenant-Colonel 5th South Carolina State Troops.
Bradley, John M., Colonel 9th Arkansas Infantry.
Bradley, Joseph W., Lieutenant-Colonel 34th Georgia Infantry.
Bradshaw, A. C., Major Bradshaw's Battalion Georgia Cavalry.
Bradshaw, John Anderson, Colonel 70th North Carolina Militia. (b. 1826).
Bradshaw, Oliver Anderson, Major, Lieutenant-Colonel 34th (formerly 4th Tennessee, Provisional Army) Tennessee Infantry; Lieutenant-Colonel 50th (new) Tennessee Infantry. (1832-1873).
Branch, John Luther, Colonel, 1st South Carolina Militia Rifles.
Brand, Frederick B., Lieutenant-Colonel Miles Legion, Louisiana.
Brandon, Stephen O. W., Major 10th Tennessee Infantry.
Branner, Benjamin M., Lieutenant-Colonel 4th Battalion Tennessee Cavalry.
Brantley, William Felix, Major 15th Mississippi Infantry; Lieutenant-Colonel, Colonel 29th Mississippi Infantry. (1830-1870).
Brashear, Elbridge Geary, Major, Lieutenant-Colonel 2d Arkansas Infantry.
Brashear, Ezra M., Major 2d Missouri Infantry, 8th Division, Missouri State Guard.
Brasher, Seymour C., Major 10th Texas Infantry. (1832-1864).
Bratton, Hugh Lawson White, Major, Lieutenant-Colonel, Colonel 24th Tennessee Infantry. (1837-1862).
Bratton, John C., Major 9th Arkansas Infantry. (b. 1830).
Brawner, William Gardner, Colonel 36th Virginia Militia. (1829-1863).

Brazelton, William, Jr., Lieutenant-Colonel 2d (also called 14th) Battalion Tennessee Cavalry; Colonel 1st (Carter's) Tennessee Cavalry.
Breaux, Gustavus A., Colonel 30th Louisiana Infantry; Colonel Sumter Regiment, Louisiana Militia. (1828-1910).
Breazeale, Winter W., Lieutenant-Colonel 2d Louisiana Cavalry; Major 33d Louisiana Partisan Rangers; Major Breazeale's Battalion Louisiana Partisan Rangers.
Breckinridge, Peachy Gilmer, Major 3d Infantry Regiment Virginia State Line.
Breckinridge, William Campbell Preston, Colonel 9th (also called 4th Mounted Rifles) Kentucky Cavalry; Major Breckinridge's Battalion Kentucky Cavalry. (1837-1904).
Breedlove, Ephraim B., Major, Lieutenant-Colonel, Colonel 45th Alabama Infantry.
Brenizer, Addison Gorgas, Colonel 1st Regiment North Carolina Detailed Men.
Brent, Preston, Lieutenant-Colonel, Colonel 38th Mississippi Infantry. (1833-1884).
Brent, Thomas Y., Jr., Major 5th Kentucky Cavalry. (1835-1863).
Brewer, George E., Major 46th Alabama Infantry.
Brewer, (**) James Fielding, Lieutenant-Colonel Carter's 1st Tennessee Cavalry. (Cancelled). (1836-1864).
Brewer, Oliver Hazard Perry, Lieutenant-Colonel 2d Cherokee Mounted Rifles.
Brewer, Richard Henry, Major Brewer's Battalion Alabama Cavalry; Colonel 8th Confederate Cavalry Regiment (also called 2d Alabama and Mississippi Cavalry Regiment). (d. 1864).
Brewer, (**) S. L., Colonel Georgia Militia.
Brewster, James Pendleton, Major 56th (also called 55th) Georgia Infantry. (b. 1840).
Bridgers, John Luther, Lieutenant-Colonel 10th North Carolina Volunteers (1st North Carolina Artillery). (1821-1884).
Bridges, Henry W., Lieutenant-Colonel 1st (Stirman's) Regiment Arkansas Sharpshooters; Major Bridges' Battalion Arkansas Sharpshooters; Major, commanding troops under S. D. Lee in Mississippi. (d. 1864).
Bridgman, John M., Major 4th Battalion Tennessee Cavalry.
Bringier, Louis Amedee, Lieutenant-Colonel 7th Louisiana Cavalry. (1829-1897).
Brittain, (**) Marcus L., Major "Cherokee Home Guards" N. C.
Broadfoot, Charles Wetmore, Lieutenant-Colonel 1st North Carolina Junior Reserves; Major 1st Battalion North Carolina Junior Reserves. (1842-1919).
Broke Arm, Major Osage Battalion.
Bromley, W. C., Colonel 4th Mississippi Infantry (or Minute Men) State Troops.
Broocks, John H., Major, Lieutenant-Colonel 27th Texas Cavalry (1st Texas [Whitfield's] Legion). (1827-1901).
Brooks, A. G., Colonel 33d North Carolina Militia.
Brooks, Iverson Lea, Lieutenant-Colonel, Colonel 26th Arkansas Infantry.
Brooks, (**) Samuel H., Lieutenant-Colonel Terry's Texas Cavalry. (b. 1833).
Brooks, Terrell, Major 6th Regiment North Carolina Senior Reserves.
Brooks, Thorndyke, Lieutenant-Colonel 15th Tennessee Infantry.
Brooks, T., Lieutenant-Colonel 1st Regiment Local Defense Troops, Macon, Georgia.
Brooks, William H., Colonel 34th (also called 2d) Arkansas Infantry; Major 1st (Brooks') Battalion Arkansas Cavalry.
Brooks, William McLin, Colonel 3d Alabama Reserves.
Broughton, Dempsey W., Major 20th Texas Cavalry.
Browder, Bartlett M., Colonel 51st Tennessee Infantry.
Brown, A. D., acting Major Brown's Mississippi (?) Battalion Infantry (found in Featherston's Brigade, return Army of Tennessee, July 31, 1864).
Brown, Alexander H., Colonel 1st Charleston Reserves, South Carolina. (1809-1879).
Brown, Alexander Jackson, Colonel 55th Tennessee Infantry.
Brown, A. R., Lieutenant-Colonel 13th Arkansas Infantry.
Brown, Benjamin F., Lieutenant-Colonel 6th Georgia Cavalry; Major Cavalry Battalion, Smith's Georgia Legion. (1821-1908).

Brown, Benjamin Johnson, Colonel 1st Missouri Cavalry, 6th Division, Missouri State Guard. (d. 1861).
Brown, Blackburn H., Lieutenant-Colonel, Colonel 27th Tennessee Infantry.
Brown, Daniel T., Lieutenant-Colonel 16th Tennessee Infantry.
Brown, Drury J., Colonel 36th Mississippi Infantry.
Brown, Edward, Lieutenant-Colonel 36th Mississippi Infantry.
Brown, Henry K., Major, Lieutenant-Colonel 2d Arkansas Mounted Rifles.
Brown, James P., Major, Lieutenant-Colonel 59th Tennessee Infantry.
Brown, James S., Major 46th Tennessee Infantry.
Brown, John Calvin, Colonel 3d Tennessee Volunteers. (1827-1889).
Brown, Joseph, Major 35th (formerly 5th Tennessee, Provisional Army) Tennessee Infantry.
Brown, J. Welsman, Major, Lieutenant-Colonel 2d South Carolina Artillery.
Brown, Robert G., Major 6th Mississippi Cavalry.
Brown, Reuben R., Lieutenant-Colonel 13th Texas Infantry; Colonel 35th (Brown's) Texas Cavalry; Lieutenant-Colonel 12th Battalion Texas Cavalry. (b. 1808).
Brown, Thomas, Major, Lieutenant-Colonel 1st Missouri Infantry Battalion, 1st Division, Missouri State Guard.
Brown, Thomas B., Lieutenant-Colonel 1st Alabama Cavalry. (d. 1862).
Brown, Thomas R., Lieutenant-Colonel 5th Battalion South Carolina Reserves.
Brown, Uriah T., Lieutenant-Colonel, Colonel 28th Tennessee Infantry.
Brown, William N., Major, Lieutenant-Colonel, Colonel 20th Mississippi Infantry.
Brown, ..., Lieutenant-Colonel 1st Georgia State Troops.
Browning, A. F., Lieutenant-Colonel 18th South Carolina Militia.
Brownlow, William W. J., Major 32d Tennessee Infantry; Major, temporarily attached to 35th (formerly 5th Tennessee, Provisional Army) Tennessee Infantry.
Broyles, Charles Edward, Major, Colonel 36th (Glenn's) Georgia Infantry. (1826-1906).
Bruce, Thomas, Colonel Bruce's Missouri Cavalry, 2d Division, Missouri State Guard.
Bryan, Joel Mayes, Major 1st (Bryan's) Cherokee Cavalry Battalion. (1809-1899).
Bryan, Moses Austin, Major 4th Texas Infantry State Troops. (1817-1895).
Buchanan, (**) M. B., Lieutenant-Colonel 2d Regiment Army of 10,000 Mississippi.
Buchel, Augustus, Colonel 1st (Buchel's) Texas Cavalry; Lieutenant-Colonel Texas Infantry. (1811-1864).
Buck, John A., Major 22d (also called 1st Indian Texas Regiment) Texas Cavalry.
Buck, William Amos, Colonel 24th Alabama Infantry; Colonel 4th Alabama Militia (90 days). (1830-1892).
Buckner, G. W., Acting Major 1st Arkansas and Louisiana Battalion Cavalry.
Buford, John W., Lieutenant-Colonel 9th Tennessee Infantry; Lieutenant-Colonel 6th and 9th Tennessee Infantry Consolidated. (1836-1897).
Buie, Duncan, Major 4th Battalion Louisiana Infantry.
Bulger, William Douglass, Major, Lieutenant-Colonel 3d Alabama Reserves. (1843-1894).
Bull, John Payne, Major, Lieutenant-Colonel Morgan's (also called 2d) Arkansas Cavalry; Lieutenant-Colonel 5th Arkansas Cavalry. (b. 1840).
Bullard, James G., Lieutenant-Colonel 10th Mississippi Infantry. (d. 1862).
Bullitt, William G., Major 6th Kentucky Cavalry; Major Bullitt's Battalion Kentucky Cavalry.
Bullock, Edward Courtney, Colonel 18th Alabama Infantry. (1822-1861).
Bullock, Robert, Lieutenant-Colonel, Colonel 7th Florida Infantry. (1828-1905).
Bullock, Robert S., Major 8th Kentucky Cavalry.
Bunch, Bryan B., Jr., Major 5th Tennessee Infantry.
Bunn, Henry Gaston, Lieutenant-Colonel and Colonel 4th (McNair's) Arkansas Infantry; Colonel 31st Arkansas Infantry (temporary command). (1838-1908).
Burbridge, John Q., Colonel 2d (also called 1st) Missouri Infantry; Colonel 4th Missouri Cavalry; Colonel 1st Missouri Infantry, 3rd Division Missouri State

Guard; Colonel Burbridge's Missouri Cavalry, 2d Division, Missouri State Guard. (b. 1830).
Burford, Nathaniel Macon, Colonel 19th Texas Cavalry. (1824-1898).
Burford, William G., Major 8th (Fulton's) Tennessee Infantry.
Burgin, Thomas A., Lieutenant-Colonel 3d Battalion (or Minute Men) Mississippi State Troops.
Burke, Joseph K., Major Stowe's Battalion North Carolina Reserves; Major 5th Regiment North Carolina Senior Reserves.
Burke, Martin, Major, Lieutenant-Colonel 1st Missouri Infantry.
Burks, John C., Colonel 11th Texas Cavalry.
Burks, Joseph Hinton, Major 4th Georgia Reserves. (d. 1899).
Burks, Robert Skillen, Lieutenant-Colonel Botetourt Regiment Virginia Home Guards. (1828-1886).
Burleson, Andrew Bell, Lieutenant-Colonel 12th Texas Cavalry.
Burleson, Edward, Major 1st (McCulloch's) Texas Mounted Riflemen. (1826-1877).
Burnet, James, Major 9th (Maxey's, also called 8th) Texas Infantry; Major 1st Battalion Texas Sharpshooters. (k. 1864).
Burnett, Henry Cornelius, Colonel 8th Kentucky Infantry. (1825-1866).
Burnett, John H., Colonel 13th Texas Cavalry. (b. 1830).
Burnett, Thomas Jefferson, Major 17th Alabama Infantry. (1826-1888).
Burns, A. D., Major 1st Texas Partisan Rangers.
Burns, James Randolph, Lieutenant-Colonel 35th (Likens') Texas Cavalry; Lieutenant-Colonel Burns' Texas Cavalry Battalion.
Burns, John T., Major 6th Georgia Cavalry. (b. 1837).
Burns, Simon P., Lieutenant-Colonel 2d (Hunter's, changed to 8th) Missouri Infantry; Colonel 8th (Burns', changed to 11th) Missouri Infantry; Colonel 11th Missouri Infantry.
Burr, James G., Colonel Masonborough Home Guards, North Carolina Battalion. (d. 1898).
Burr, William Hughson, Major 30th Alabama Infantry. (b. 1836).
Burrow, Reuben, Major 12th (also called 1st Partisan Rangers) Tennessee Cavalry.
Burtwell, John Robertson Bedford, Colonel 11th (also called 10th) Alabama Cavalry; Major 21st Battalion Tennessee Cavalry. (1835-1873).
Burwell, William P., Major 2d Virginia Heavy Artillery. (b. 1828).
Bush, Louis, Major, Lieutenant-Colonel 18th Louisiana Infantry (last commission declined); Colonel 7th Louisiana Cavalry. (b. 1820).
Bush, William M., Major, Lieutenant-Colonel 34th (also called 2d Partisans) Texas Cavalry. (1827-1900).
Buster, Michael Woods, Lieutenant-Colonel 9th (Clark's) Missouri Infantry; Lieutenant-Colonel Buster's Battalion Arkansas Cavalry; Major, Lieutenant-Colonel of J. J. Clarkson's Missouri Infantry Battalion. (1823-1915).
Buswell, Thomas, Lieutenant-Colonel 2d Virginia Militia.
Butler, Edward George Washington, Jr., Major 11th Louisiana Infantry. (1829-1861).
Butler, John Andrew, Lieutenant-Colonel 2d Tennessee Infantry (Provisional Army). (d. 1862).
Butler, John Russell, Colonel 3d Kentucky Cavalry.
Butler, Loudon, Major, Lieutenant-Colonel 19th Louisiana Infantry. (d. 1863).
Butler, William, Lieutenant-Colonel, Colonel 3d South Carolina Artillery (1st South Carolina Regulars).
Butler, William Lavelle, Major, Lieutenant-Colonel 28th Alabama Infantry.
Butler, William R., Lieutenant-Colonel 18th Tennessee Infantry.
Butts, (**) H. G., Major 10th Arkansas Militia.
Bynum, George Washington, Major Ham's Mississippi Cavalry. (1839-1920).
Bynum, Thomas, Major 9th (also called 17th) Battalion Louisiana Infantry.
Byrd, William, Lieutenant-Colonel 14th Texas Infantry. (1828-1898).
Byrd, William M., Colonel 1st Alabama Militia.
Byrd, William Wallace, Major 10th Battalion Virginia Reserves. (1821-1901).
Cage, Duncan S., Lieutenant-Colonel 26th Louisiana Infantry.

Cage, John B., Major, Lieutenant-Colonel 14th Confederate Cavalry. (d. 1864).
Cain, W. R., Lieutenant-Colonel 7th Arkansas Infantry.
Caldwell, Alexander W., Lieutenant-Colonel, Colonel 27th Tennessee Infantry.
Caldwell, John William, Major 1st Kentucky Cavalry; Major, Lieutenant-Colonel, Colonel 9th (also called 5th) Kentucky Infantry; Major, Lieutenant-Colonel 5th Kentucky Infantry (latter appointment cancelled). (1837-1903).
Caldwell, Josiah H., Lieutenant-Colonel, Colonel 7th (Jackman's, afterward 16th) Missouri Infantry.
Caldwell, Otis, Major Battalion Virginia Cavalry (to 16th Virginia Cavalry).
Caldwell, Robert Porter, Major 12th Tennessee Infantry. (1821-1885).
Caldwell, (**) Thomas Jefferson, Major 1st Battalion Louisiana State Cavalry (North Louisiana Cavalry). (d. 1865).
Calhoon, Solomon Saladin, Lieutenant-Colonel 9th Mississippi Infantry. (b. 1838).
Calhoun, William Ransom, Lieutenant-Colonel 1st South Carolina Artillery Battalion; Colonel 1st South Carolina Artillery Regiment. (1827-1862).
Cameron, Allen, Major Waul's Texas Legion. (d. 1863).
Cameron, F. J., Major, Lieutenant-Colonel 6th Arkansas Infantry.
Cameron, John Fraser, Major, Lieutenant-Colonel 3d (formerly 18th Arkansas) Confederate Infantry. (d. 1882).
Camfield, Caleb Halsted, Major 29th Battalion Georgia Cavalry.
Camp, John Lafayette, Colonel 14th Texas Cavalry. (1828-1891).
Camp, Raleigh Spinks, Major 40th Georgia Infantry. (1829-1867).
Camp, Thompson, Major 14th Texas Cavalry; Colonel 2d Texas Infantry State Troops.
Camp, William Addison, Major 36th Tennessee Infantry. (1818-1884).
Campbell, Alexander William, Colonel 33d Tennessee Infantry. (1828-1893).
Campbell, Andrew Jackson, Major, 48th (Voorhies') Tennessee Infantry. (1834-1863).
Campbell, Charles Carroll, Major 1st Missouri Infantry. (1838-1912).
Campbell, Churchill Gibbs, Lieutenant-Colonel 5th Kentucky Cavalry. (b. 1824).
Campbell, Francis Lee, Major, Lieutenant-Colonel, Colonel 13th (Gibson's) Louisiana Infantry.
Campbell, James A., Major, Lieutenant-Colonel, Colonel 27th Mississippi Infantry. (d. 1864).
Campbell, Josiah Adams Patterson, Lieutenant-Colonel 40th Mississippi Infantry. (1830-1917).
Campbell, L. A., Major, Lieutenant-Colonel 3d Missouri Cavalry.
Campbell, Leonidas Cardwell, Lieutenant-Colonel 3d Battalion Missouri Cavalry; Lieutenant-Colonel 6th Battalion Missouri Cavalry; Lieutenant-Colonel 3d Missouri Cavalry. (1827-1863).
Campbell, (**) S. W., Major 1st Louisiana Cavalry.
Campbell, Thomas J., Major 5th Battalion Tennessee Cavalry.
Campbell, William Hans, Major, Lieutenant-Colonel 3d Battalion South Carolina Light Artillery. (1823-1901).
Campbell, William Peyton, Major 1st Arkansas Mounted Rifles. (d. 1896).
Camron, Orville G., Major 1st Battalion Kentucky Mounted Rifles.
Candler, Allen Daniel, Lieutenant-Colonel 4th Georgia Reserves. (1834-1910).
Canfield, Mercer, Major Crescent Regiment, Louisiana Infantry. (k. 1864).
Canon, John Job, Major, Lieutenant-Colonel 22d Texas Infantry.
Cansler, Adolphus Philip, Major 1st Alabama, Tennessee, and Mississippi Regiment.
Cantrell, Robert, Lieutenant-Colonel 23d Tennessee Infantry. (1823-1903).
Capers, Ellison, Lieutenant-Colonel, Colonel 24th South Carolina Infantry. (1837-1908).
Capers, James H., Major 13th Battalion Louisiana Partisan Rangers.
Capers, Richard L., Major 3d (Pargoud's) Louisiana Cavalry; Major, Lieutenant-Colonel 13th Batallion Louisiana Partisan Rangers; Colonel 5th Louisiana Cavalry.
Capers, William, Major 1st Louisiana Artillery.
Caraway, Nathaniel Jackson, Major 11th Texas Infantry.
Carden, Albert G., Lieutenant-Colonel 18th Tennessee Infantry.

Carew, John Edward, Colonel 3d South Carolina State Troops; Colonel 18th South Carolina Militia. (1808-1877).
Cargile, C. M., Major 10th Arkansas Infantry.
Carlton, Charles H., Major 15th (Polk's) Arkansas Infantry; Colonel Carlton's Regiment Arkansas Cavalry.
Carpenter, John N., Major, Lieutenant-Colonel, Colonel 2d Alabama Cavalry.
Carpenter, Simeon, Lieutenant-Colonel 82d Virginia Militia.
Carr, John S., Colonel 151st Virginia Militia.
Carroll, Charles A., Colonel Carroll's Regiment Arkansas Cavalry.
Carroll, Charles Montgomery, Colonel 15th Tennessee Infantry. (b. 1821).
Carroll, De Rosey, Colonel 1st Arkansas Cavalry State Troops, 1861.
Carroll, D. W., Colonel 18th (Carroll's) Arkansas Infantry.
Carroll, Joseph Alexander, Major 29th Texas Cavalry. (b. 1832).
Carroll, William Henry, Colonel 37th (formerly 7th Tennessee, Provisional Army) Tennessee Infantry; Colonel 1st East Tennessee Rifles. (d. 1868).
Carruth, (**) R. H., Colonel Regiment Louisiana Militia.
Carswell, Nathaniel Alexander, Lieutenant-Colonel 22d Infantry Battalion Georgia State Guard. (1823-1868).
Carter, Dabney C., Colonel 188th Virginia Militia.
Carter, George Washington, Colonel 21st Texas Cavalry, Colonel 1st Texas Lancers. (1826-1901).
Carter, Haley M., Lieutenant-Colonel 18th (also called 10th) Battalion Louisiana Cavalry. (1837-1883).
Carter, James E., Lieutenant-Colonel 3d (also called 14th) Battalion Tennessee Cavalry; Colonel 1st (Carter's) Tennessee Cavalry. (1828-1905).
Carter, J. C., Lieutenant-Colonel 2d Texas Cavalry State Troops; Major 2d Cavalry Battalion Texas State Troops.
Carter, John C., Lieutenant-Colonel 34th Alabama Infantry.
Carter, John Carpenter, Colonel 38th (formerly 8th, Looney's) Tennessee Infantry. (1837-1864).
Carter, John W., Major, Lieutenant-Colonel 2d Virginia Infantry Battalion Local Defense (Quartermaster's).
Carter, Mosco B., Lieutenant-Colonel 20th Tennessee Infantry.
Carter, Nathan W., Colonel 21st (N. W. Carter's) Tennessee Cavalry (unofficial). (1818-1886).
Carter, Richard W., Major 2d Alabama Cavalry.
Carter, R. S., Major, Lieutenant-Colonel 7th Mississippi Infantry.
Carter, Samuel A., Major 45th Tennessee Infantry.
Carter, Thomas Miller, Major, Lieutenant-Colonel 2d (Burbridge's, also called 1st) Missouri Infantry. (1830-1910).
Carter, William Farley, Major 2d (Burbridge's, also called 1st) Missouri Infantry. (1843-1930).
Caruthers, Camillus Kotzebue, Acting Major Caruthers' Battalion Mississippi Sharpshooters.
Carver, D. C., Lieutenant-Colonel 88th Virginia Militia.
Cason, Caleb McKnight, Lieutenant-Colonel 31st (A. H. Bradford's) Tennessee Infantry.
Casseday, Alexander, Lieutenant-Colonel 9th Kentucky Infantry.
Cassell, Jacob T., Major 2d Special Battalion Kentucky Cavalry.
Castleman, John Breckinridge, Major Dukes 2d Kentucky.
Caswell, Theodore D., Major 4th Battalion Georgia Sharpshooters.
Cathey, William H., Major 15th Texas Cavalry.
Cato, William W., Lieutenant-Colonel 37th Regular (Militia District) Georgia.
Caton, William R., Major 23d Texas Cavalry.
Caudill, Benjamin Everett, Colonel 13th Kentucky Cavalry (also called 10th Kentucky Mounted Rifles and 11th Kentucky Mounted Rifles).
Caudill, David J., Lieutenant-Colonel 13th Kentucky Cavalry (also called 10th Kentucky Mounted Rifles and 11th Kentucky Mounted Rifles). (1830-1889).
Caudle, John Hiram, Lieutenant-Colonel, Colonel 34th Texas Cavalry (also called 2d Partisans). (1835-1895).

Cawthorn, James, Colonel 4th Missouri Cavalry, 8th Division, Missouri State Guard.
Cayce, Henry P., Lieutenant-Colonel 13th Texas Infantry; Major of Bates' Battalion Texas Infantry.
Cayce, Stewart W., Lieutenant-Colonel 21st Alabama Infantry; Lieutenant-Colonel 1st Mobile Volunteers, Local Defense Troops.
Cearnal, James T., Colonel 1st Missouri Cavalry, 5th Division, Missouri State Guard.
Chadick, William Davidson, Lieutenant-Colonel 50th (also known as 26th, Coltart's) Alabama Infantry; Major 2d (also called 8th) Battalion Alabama Infantry. (1817-1878).
Chalmers, A. H., Major of Major's Missouri Cavalry Regiment, 3d Division, Missouri State Guard.
Chalmers, Alexander H., Major, Lieutenant-Colonel 18th Battalion Mississippi Cavalry; Colonel 18th Mississippi Cavalry Regiment; Colonel Chalmers' Consolidated Mississippi Cavalry Regiment.
Chalmers, James Ronald, Colonel 9th Mississippi Infantry. (1831-1898).
Chamblin, (**) John, Major 132d Virginia Militia.
Chambliss, Nathaniel Rives, Major 1st Kentucky Cavalry. (1835-1897).
Chambliss, Samuel L., Lieutenant-Colonel 3d (Pargoud's) Louisiana Cavalry; Lieutenant-Colonel 13th Battalion Louisiana Partisan Rangers.
Chancellor, (**) John L., Lieutenant-Colonel 8th Alabama Cavalry.
Chancellor, Lorman, Colonel 132d Virginia Militia. (1817-1894).
Chandler, Greene C., Colonel 8th Mississippi Infantry. (1829-1905).
Chandler, (**) John L., ... 8th Alabama Cavalry.
Chandler, Joseph Benson, Major 2nd South Carolina Reserves. (1827-1897).
Chapin, William P., Major 8th (Dibrell's, also called 13th) Tennessee Cavalry.
Charlton, (**) Rice D. M., Major 75th Virginia Militia.
Charlton, Richard, Lieutenant-Colonel 33d (Hardcastle's) Mississippi Infantry; Lieutenant-Colonel 45th Mississippi Infantry. (b. 1825).
Chatfield, William M., Major 20th Mississippi Infantry. (d. 1864).
Cheairs, Nathaniel F., Major 3d Tennessee Volunteers.
Chekote, Samuel, Lieutenant-Colonel 1st Creek Regiment.
Chenault, David Waller, Colonel 11th Kentucky Cavalry. (1826-1863).
Cheney, W. F., Lieutenant-Colonel Avoyelles Regiment, Louisiana Militia.
Chenoweth, Benjamin D., Major 21st Texas Cavalry.
Chenoweth, John Thomas, Major 13th Kentucky Cavalry (also called 10th Kentucky Mounted Rifles and 11th Kentucky Mounted Rifles). (b. 1834).
Chenoweth, James Q., Major 3d Kentucky Cavalry. (1841-1909).
Cherry, D. H., Colonel 15th North Carolina Militia.
Chester, John, Lieutenant-Colonel, Colonel 51st Tennessee Infantry.
Childress, James R., Lieutenant-Colonel 40th Mississippi Infantry.
Childs, Frederick Lynn, Major, Lieutenant-Colonel 2d Battalion North Carolina Local Defense Troops. (d. 1894).
Chiles, Elijah, Lieutenant-Colonel 1st Missouri Cavalry, 8th Division Missouri State Guard.
Chiles, Richard B., Lieutenant-Colonel 1st Missouri Cavalry; Lieutenant-Colonel Extra Cavalry Battalion, 4th Division, Missouri State Guard.
Chiles, W. P., Lieutenant-Colonel 2d Missouri Infantry, 5th Division, Missouri State Guard.
Chilton, George W., Major 3d Texas Cavalry. (1828-1883).
Chism, Howard, Major 1st Missouri Cavalry, 8th Division, Missouri State Guard.
Chisum, Isham, Lieutenant-Colonel, Colonel 2d Texas Partisan Rangers (originally Stone's Regiment).
Chrisman, Francis M., Major Chrisman's Battalion Arkansas Cavalry.
Chrisman, George, Major 7th (3d?) Battalion Virginia Reserves. (1832-1915).
Christian, Samuel Patterson, Major, Lieutenant-Colonel 8th Texas Cavalry. (1835-1913).
Church, Lucius A., Major, Lieutenant-Colonel 3d Florida Infantry.
Churchill, Thomas James, Colonel 1st Arkansas Mounted Rifles. (1824-1905).
Churchwell, William Montgomery, Colonel 4th (Churchwell's, afterward 34th)

Tennessee, Provisional Army; Colonel 34th (formerly 4th Provisional Army) Tennessee Infantry. (1826-1862).

Clack, Calvin Jones, Lieutenant-Colonel, Colonel 3d Tennessee Volunteers. (b. 1829).

Clack, Franklin Hulse, Major 16th (should be 12th) Battalion Louisiana Infantry; Lieutenant-Colonel Crescent Regiment Louisiana Infantry; Colonel 33d Regiment Louisiana Infantry; Lieutenant-Colonel 4th Battalion Confederate Infantry. (1828-1864).

Claiborne, Thomas, Captain, P.A.C.S., temporary commander as Colonel 6th Confederate Cavalry. (1823-1911).

Claiborne, Thomas Doddridge, Major, Lieutenant-Colonel 7th Confederate Cavalry; Lieutenant-Colonel 10th Georgia Cavalry. (1836-1864).

Claiborne, William C., Colonel 7th Confederate Cavalry; Lieutenant-Colonel 4th Battalion North Carolina Partisan Rangers.

Clanton, James Holt, Colonel 1st Alabama Cavalry. (1827-1871).

Clanton, Turner, Jr., Major, Lieutenant-Colonel 7th Alabama Cavalry. (b. 1838).

Clark, Ben. W., Lieutenant-Colonel 1st Battalion Louisiana State Cavalry; Colonel 1st Regiment State Cavalry.

Clark, Edward, Colonel 14th Texas Infantry. (1815-1880).

Clark, Edward A., Major 51st Tennessee Infantry.

Clark, George, Colonel Continental Regiment, Louisiana Militia.

Clark, Henry E., Colonel Clark's Missouri Cavalry.

Clark, John Bullock, Jr., Colonel 9th (Clark's) Missouri Infantry; Major, Colonel 1st Missouri Infantry, 3d Division Missouri State Guard.

Clark, John M., Colonel 46th Tennessee Infantry. (1832-1905).

Clark, J. W., Major 31st Arkansas Infantry.

Clark, Walter McKenzie, Major 1st North Carolina Junior Reserves; Major 4th Battalion North Carolina Reserves. (1846-1912).

Clark, Whitfield, Major, Lieutenant-Colonel, Colonel 39th Alabama Infantry.

Clark, William, Major, Lieutenant-Colonel 12th (also called 8th) Texas Infantry.

Clark, William Henry, Major, Lieutenant-Colonel, Colonel 46th Mississippi Infantry. (1836-1864).

Clarke, Edward Y., Major 16th Battalion Georgia Cavalry.

Clarke, William Logan, Major, Lieutenant-Colonel 6th Kentucky Infantry. (1839-1895).

Clark's Battalion Missouri Infantry, Series I, Vol. X, pt. II.

Clarkson, (**) J. A., Lieutenant-Colonel 179th Virginia Militia.

Clarkson, James J., Colonel Clarkson's Battalion Missouri Cavalry; Colonel 5th Missouri Infantry, 8th Division, Missouri State Guard.

Clarkson, John Nicholas, Colonel 3d Infantry Regiment Virginia State Line. (1816-1906).

Clay, Charles C. Major 1st (Jackson's afterward 7th) Tennessee Cavalry.

Clay, Ezekiel Field, Lieutenant-Colonel 3d Battalion Kentucky Mounted Rifles. (b. 1841).

Claybrooke, Frederick, Major 20th Tennessee Infantry. (1837-1863).

Clayton, George Wesley, Lieutenant-Colonel, Colonel 62d North Carolina Infantry. (1841-1900).

Clayton, Henry DeLamar, Colonel 39th Alabama Infantry; Colonel 1st Alabama Infantry. (1827-1889).

Cleburne, Patrick Ronayne, Colonel 1st (Cleburne's) Arkansas Infantry; Colonel 15th (Cleburne's) Arkansas Infantry and 5th Arkansas Militia. (1828-1864).

Clements, Newton Nash, Lieutenant-Colonel 50th (also known as 26th, Coltart's) Alabama Infantry. (1837-1900).

Cleveland, (**) C. B., Lieutenant-Colonel 1st Missouri Cavalry.

Cleveland, L. G., Major 1st Infantry Texas State Troops.

Cleveland, Stephen Black, Major Wirt Adams' Mississippi Cavalry. (b. 1827).

Clifton, James M., Major 10th (also called 4th) Battalion Alabama Infantry.

Clifton, William C., Lieutenant-Colonel, Colonel 39th Alabama Infantry.

Clinch, Duncan Lamont, Jr., Colonel 4th (Clinch's) Georgia Cavalry; Major, Lieutenant-Colonel 3d Battalion Georgia Cavalry.

Clinch, Henry A., Major 1st Louisiana Artillery. (1829-1895).

Cloud, George, Major 1st Seminole Cavalry Battalion. (d. 1864).
Clough, Jeremiah M., Lieutenant-Colonel 7th Texas Infantry. (d. 1862).
Cluke, Roy S., Colonel 8th Kentucky Cavalry. (1824-1864).
Coarser, John W., Lieutenant-Colonel Morgan's Regiment Arkansas Cavalry (also called 2d).
Cobb, Pharaoh A., Major 2d (Ashby's) Tennessee Cavalry.
Cobb, Robert, Major commanding artillery battalion, Army of Tennessee.
Cobbs, Paul M., Major, Lieutenant-Colonel 30th (Rogan's, also called 39th) Arkansas Infantry.
Coble, (**) D., Colonel 68th North Carolina Militia.
Cochran, Thomas M., Lieutenant-Colonel 2d Arkansas Cavalry.
Cocke, Cary C., Colonel 12th Virginia Militia.
Cocke, John B., Colonel Hawthorn's Arkansas Infantry.
Cockrell, Francis Marion, Lieutenant-Colonel, Colonel 2d (Burbridge's, also called 1st) Missouri Infantry. (1834-1915).
Cofer, Martin Hardin, Lieutenant-Colonel, Colonel 6th Kentucky Infantry; Lieutenant-Colonel 1st (Cofer's) Battalion Kentucky Infantry. (1832-1881).
Coffee, Chatham, Acting Major 11th Tennessee Cavalry.
Coffee, John T., Colonel 6th Missouri Cavalry; Colonel 6th Missouri Cavalry, 8th Division, Missouri State Guard. (1816-1890).
Coffee, Patrick H., Major 16th Tennessee Infantry.
Cohoon, John Thomas Philip Couper, Lieutenant-Colonel 6th Battalion North Carolina Infantry; Lieutenant-Colonel Cohoon's Battalion Virginia Infantry. (1838-1869).
Coiner, David W., Lieutenant-Colonel 32d Virginia Militia.
Coit, John T., Lieutenant-Colonel 18th Texas Cavalry. (d. 1872).
Colbert, Wallace Bruce, Colonel 40th Mississippi Infantry. (1834-1865).
Colbert, (**) W. T., Major Georgia Militia.
Colcock, Charles Jones, Colonel 3d South Carolina Cavalry; Lieutenant-Colonel 8th (also called 2d) Battalion South Carolina Cavalry. (1820-1891).
Cole, James C., Lieutenant-Colonel 3d Confederate Infantry; Lieutenant-Colonel 5th (Smith's also called 9th) Confederate Infantry; Major 21st Tennessee Infantry.
Cole, Peter H., Major 13th Tennessee Infantry. (k. 1862).
Coleman, Augustus Aurelius, Colonel 40th Alabama Infantry. (1825-1910).
Coleman, Cicero, Lieutenant-Colonel 8th Kentucky Cavalry.
Coleman, David, Colonel 39th North Carolina Infantry. (1824-1883).
Coleman, James T., Major Miles Legion, Louisiana Volunteers.
Coleman, J. G., Major 1st Texas Cavalry State Troops.
Coleman, W. O., Colonel 46th Arkansas Infantry. (1836-1921).
Coles, Thomas R., Major 37th Virginia Militia.
Collins, Joseph, Lieutenant-Colonel 18th Louisiana Infantry.
Collins, Nathaniel Dixon, Colonel Collins' Tennessee Cavalry Regiment.
Colms, Stephen H., Major 1st (Colms', also called 20th) Battalion Tennessee Infantry; Colonel 50th (new) Tennessee Infantry.
Colquitt, John W., Major, Colonel 1st (Colquitt's) Arkansas Infantry; Major 1st (Fagan's) Arkansas Infantry. (1840-1903).
Colquitt, Peyton H., Colonel 46th Georgia Infantry. (1832-1863).
Coltart, John Gordon, Lieutenant-Colonel 7th Alabama Infantry (12 months); Colonel 50th (also known as 26th, Coltart's) Alabama Infantry; Lieutenant-Colonel 3d (Coltart's) Battalion Alabama Infantry.
Colton, John F., Colonel 62d North Carolina Militia.
Colvin, Charles H., Colonel 6th Alabama Cavalry.
Compton, John R., Colonel 198th Virginia Militia.
Cone, James G., Major 47th Georgia Infantry.
Cone, Joseph S., Major, Lieutenant-Colonel 47th Georgia Infantry.
Conerly, James M., Lieutenant-Colonel 2d Regiment Mississippi Infantry (or Minute Men) State Troops.
Conn, (**) Raphael Morgan, Colonel 43d Virginia Militia.
Conner, (**) L. P., Lieutenant-Colonel A.D.C. Louisiana State Guard.
Connor, George W., Major, Lieutenant-Colonel 5th Kentucky Infantry. (1830-1894).

Conoley, John Francis, Lieutenant-Colonel, Colonel 29th Alabama Infantry; Lieutenant-Colonel 4th Battalion Alabama Infantry. (1811-1883).
Cook, Edmund C., Colonel 32d Tennessee Infantry. (d. 1864).
Cook, F. W. C., Major 23d Infantry Battalion Georgia State Guard.
Cook, Gustave, Major, Lieutenant-Colonel, Colonel 8th Texas Cavalry. (1835-1897).
Cook, Henry F., Major 2d Mississippi Infantry Battalion (or Minute Men) State Troops.
Cook, (**) John H., Colonel 33d North Carolina Militia.
Cook, Joseph H., Major, Lieutenant-Colonel 3d Battalion Texas Artillery; Colonel 1st Regiment Texas Artillery.
Cook, W. D. S., Lieutenant-Colonel 12th Arkansas Infantry.
Cook, William L., Lieutenant-Colonel 4th (Avery's) Georgia Cavalry; Major 23d Battalion Georgia Cavalry.
Cooke, H. W., Major 4th Cavalry Texas State Troops.
Cooke, James Burch, Colonel 59th Tennessee Infantry.
Cooper, Albert G., Lieutenant-Colonel 9th (Biffle's, also called 19th) Tennessee Cavalry.
Cooper, Douglas Hancock, Colonel 1st Choctaw and Chickasaw Mounted Rifles. (1815-1879).
Cooper, (**) James W., Major Cooper's Battalion, 1st Indian Brigade District Indian Territory, C.S.A. May 30, 1865.
Cooper, John, Major 11th Infantry Battalion Georgia State Guard.
Cooper, Stephen B., Major, Lieutenant-Colonel 6th Missouri Infantry. (1836-1903).
Cooper, Sylvester C., Major 46th Tennessee Infantry.
Copeland, John R., Colonel 59th Virginia Militia.
Corbett, (**) E. C., Colonel 2d Georgia Militia.
Cording, Jerome B., Lieutenant-Colonel 49th Tennessee Infantry.
Corley, John A., Major, Lieutenant-Colonel 23d Texas Cavalry.
Corley, Samuel M., Major Dobbin's Arkansas Cavalry (also called 1st). (d. 1863).
Corn, F. M., Major, Lieutenant-Colonel 3d (also called 11th) Confederate Cavalry.
Corner, John B., Major 1st Missouri Cavalry, 4th Division Missouri State Guard.
Corpening, David J., Colonel 5th North Carolina Regiment Senior Reserves.
Cotter, Hamilton W., Major 38th (formerly 8th, Looney's) Tennessee Infantry (1833-1899).
Couch, Henry M., Lieutenant-Colonel 8th Arkansas Infantry.
Council, J. M., (**) Colonel 58th Arkansas Militia.
Counselman, Lawrence W., Lieutenant-Colonel 2d Missouri Infantry, 8th Division, Missouri State Guard.
Coupland, A. J., Lieutenant-Colonel 11th Texas Infantry.
Couzens, William H., Major 2d Missouri Cavalry; Major 1st Missouri Cavalry Battalion, 1st Division, Missouri State Guard.
Covedo, John S., Major Camden County Georgia Militia.
Cox, J. J., Major 2d Battalion Georgia Sharpshooters.
Cox, John T., Colonel 1st (also called 12th) Confederate Cavalry.
Cox, Nicholas Nichols, Colonel 10th Tennessee Cavalry; Major 2d Battalion Tennessee Cavalry; Major Cox's Battalion Tennessee Cavalry. (1837-1912).
Craig, Washington De La Fayette, Major, Lieutenant-Colonel 10th Texas Cavalry.
Crandall, Lee, Colonel 47th Arkansas Infantry.
Cravens, Jeremiah C., Major 11th Missouri Cavalry. (1838-1899).
Cravens, Jesse L., Colonel 5th Missouri Cavalry, 8th Division, Missouri State Guard.
Cravens, Jordan Edgar, Colonel 21st (Cravens') Arkansas Infantry. (1830-1914).
Crawford, Anderson Floyd, Lieutenant-Colonel, Colonel 13th Texas Cavalry. (1829-1867).
Crawford, James, Colonel 21st Alabama Infantry. (1807-1881).
Crawford, (**) John H., Lieutenant-Colonel 160th Virginia Militia.
Crawford, John H., Colonel 60th (also called 79th) Tennessee Infantry.
Crawford, Martin Jenkins, Colonel 3d Georgia Cavalry. (1820-1883).
Crawford, Robert W., Lieutenant-Colonel 13th Missouri Cavalry, 8th Division

Missouri State Guard; Lieutenant-Colonel 5th Missouri Infantry, 8th Division, Missouri State Guard.

Crawford, William Ayers, Lieutenant-Colonel Crawford's Battalion Arkansas Infantry; Colonel 1st (Crawford's) Arkansas Cavalry; Lieutenant-Colonel 1st (Fagan's) Arkansas Infantry.

Crawford, William L., Major, Lieutenant-Colonel 19th Texas Infantry. (b. 1839).

Creasman, William B., Major, Lieutenant-Colonel, Colonel 29th North Carolina Infantry.

Crenshaw, John B., Major 91st Virginia Militia.

Crenshaw, W. L., Major 33d Arkansas Infantry.

Crews, Charles Constantine, Colonel 2d Georgia Cavalry. (c.1830-c.1894).

Crews, James M., Colonel 58th Tennessee Infantry; Lieutenant-Colonel Crews' Battalion Tennessee Infantry; Lieutenant-Colonel McDonald's 18th Battalion (formerly Balch's Tennessee Cavalry); Major Nixon's Tennessee Cavalry Regiment.

Crisp, John T., Lieutenant-Colonel Coffee's Regiment Missouri Cavalry. (d. 1903).

Crittenden, Robert Flournoy, Major, Lieutenant-Colonel, Colonel 33d Alabama Infantry. (1837-1914).

Crittenden, Stephen Stanley, Lieutenant-Colonel 3d South Carolina Reserves. (1829-1911).

Crockett, (**) Robert Hamilton, Captain Company H 1st Arkansas Regiment; Major, Lieutenant-Colonel, Colonel 18th (Carroll's) Arkansas Infantry. (b. 1832).

Crook, David C., Major 28th Tennessee Infantry; Lieutenant-Colonel, Colonel 28th and 84th Tennessee Infantry Consolidated.

Crook, James, Major 27th Battalion Tennessee Cavalry.

Crook, (**) W. B., Major 7th Arkansas Militia.

Crook, William J., Major 13th Tennessee Infantry.

Cross, David C., Colonel 5th Arkansas Infantry. (1818-1874).

Crossland, Edward, Major, Lieutenant-Colonel 1st Kentucky Infantry; Colonel 7th Kentucky Infantry. (1827-1881).

Crow, William C., Lieutenant-Colonel, Colonel 26th Louisiana Infantry.

Crowder, John A., Major 19th South Carolina Infantry.

Crump, R. P., Major, Lieutenant-Colonel 1st Battalion Texas Cavalry; Lieutenant-Colonel 1st Texas Partisan Rangers.

Crump, William N., Lieutenant-Colonel 49th Alabama Infantry.

Culberson, Augustus B., Lieutenant-Colonel 6th Battalion Cavalry, Georgia State Guard.

Culberson, David Browning, Lieutenant-Colonel, Colonel 18th Texas Infantry. (1830-1900).

Cumby, Robert H., Colonel 3d Texas Cavalry.

Cumming, Montgomery, Lieutenant-Colonel 2d Battalion Georgia Cavalry.

Cumming, Pleasant W. H., Major, Lieutenant-Colonel 7th (Jackman's, afterward 16th) Missouri Infantry; Lieutenant-Colonel 16th (formerly 7th) Missouri Infantry.

Cummings, David H., Colonel 19th Tennessee Infantry.

Cummings, Thomas B., Lieutenant-Colonel 9th Missouri Cavalry, 8th Division, Missouri State Guard.

Cundiff, W. H. Lieutenant-Colonel 1st Missouri Infantry, 5th Division Missouri State Guard.

Cunningham, Charles J. L., Major, Colonel 57th (also called 54th) Alabama Infantry.

Cunningham, James, Lieutenant-Colonel 2d Alabama Cavalry. (1834-1874).

Cunningham, John, Major 1st (Symons') Regiment Georgia Reserves.

Cunningham, John, Major Cunningham's Battalion South Carolina Reserves.

Cunningham, John F., Major 67th Virginia Militia.

Cunningham, Preston Davidson, Lieutenant-Colonel, Colonel 28th Tennessee Infantry. (d. 1863).

Cunningham, Robert, Lieutenant-Colonel 10th Missouri Cavalry, 8th Division, Missouri State Guard.

Curlee, William P., Lieutenant-Colonel Ham's Mississippi Cavalry; Lieutenant-

Colonel Ashcraft's, Ham's, and Lowry's Consolidated Mississippi Cavalry Regiment.
Curley, Barnard, Major 5th Infantry Georgia State Guard; Colonel 65th Georgia Militia. (d. 1898).
Curry, (**) John G. M., Colonel .... Georgia Militia.
Curtis, William Ezra, Lieutenant-Colonel, Colonel 41st Georgia Infantry. (d. 1864).
Curtis, (**) William P., Lieutenant-Colonel 3d Virginia Militia.
Cypert, Jesse N., Major 7th Battalion Arkansas Cavalry. (b. 1823).
Dabney, William Harris, Colonel 1st Infantry Georgia State Guard. (1817-1899).
Daly, Andrew, Lieutenant-Colonel Daly's Battalion Texas Cavalry.
Daly, John N., Lieutenant-Colonel, Colonel 18th (Carroll's) Arkansas Infantry. (d. 1862).
Dancy, Clifton, Lieutenant Colonel 24th Mississippi Infantry. (1833-1898).
Danforth, John B., Colonel 1st Virginia State Reserves, Second Class Militia.
Daniel, Charles P., Major, Colonel 5th Georgia Infantry.
Daniel, James E., Lieutenant-Colonel 27th Battalion Tennessee Cavalry.
Daniel, James Jacquelin, Colonel 1st Regiment Florida Reserves. (1832-1888).
Daniel, John Warwick, Major, Lieutenant-Colonel 15th Texas Infantry. (1830-1905).
Daniel, William Augustus, Lieutenant-Colonel 46th Georgia Infantry. (1824-1897).
Daniel, (**) William P., Colonel 56th Georgia Militia.
Danley, Benjamin F., Lieutenant-Colonel 3d Arkansas Cavalry.
Darden, Stephen Heard, Colonel 5th Infantry Texas State Troops. (1816-1902).
Dark, Joseph N., Major 25th Texas Cavalry.
Darnell, Nicholas Henry, Colonel 18th Texas Cavalry. (1807-1885).
Darst, James H., Major 185th Virginia Militia. (d. 1907).
Daugherty, Davis G., Major 31st Arkansas Infantry.
Daugherty, Ferdinand H., Lieutenant-Colonel 8th (Dibrell's, also called 13th) Tennessee Cavalry.
Davant, Richard James, Jr., Major, Lieutenant-Colonel 5th Georgia Cavalry; Major, 2d Battalion Georgia Cavalry. (1833-1899).
Davenport, John H., Major 30th Texas Cavalry (also called 1st Partisan Rangers).
Davenport, John M., Lieutenant-Colonel, Colonel 39th Virginia Militia.
Davenport, Stephen, Major Davenport's Battalion Mississippi State Cavalry.
Daves, Joel Thomas, Major 19th Texas Cavalry.
Davidson, A. H., Major, Lieutenant-Colonel 1st Texas Battalion (also called 4th) Arizona Brigade.
Davidson, Hugh Harvey, Lieutenant-Colonel 39th North Carolina Infantry. (b. c. 1814).
Davidson, James Lafayette, Major, Lieutenant-Colonel 1st Alabama Reserves. (1837-1896).
Davidson, Robert Hamilton McWhorter, Major, Lieutenant-Colonel, 6th Florida Infantry. (1832-1908).
Davidson, Thomas J., Colonel 23d (also called 2d and 3d) Mississippi Infantry. (d. 1862).
Davie, James Madison, Major, Colonel 36th Arkansas Infantry. (b. 1830).
Davies, (**) J. F., Lieutenant-Colonel 7th Missouri Cavalry; Lieutenant-Colonel Battalion Missouri Cavalry.
Davies, Thomas W. W., Major, Lieutenant-Colonel 28th Alabama Infantry.
Davis, Benjamin Thadeus, Major 22d Tennessee Infantry.
Davis, C. M., Colonel 10th Georgia State Troops.
Davis, (**) George W., Major 98 Virginia Militia.
Davis, Henry C., Lieutenant-Colonel 1st Mississippi and Tennessee Battalion (retired March 17, 1865).
Davis, James Ward, Lieutenant-Colonel Virginia Cavalry Battalion, 1861. (1819-1903).
Davis, (**) J. F., Lieutenant-Colonel Davis' Battalion, attached to Kitchen's Regiment (Vol. 41 part 1).
Davis, John R., Major of Davis' Battalion Tennessee Cavalry; Major 8th (Baxter Smith's, also called 4th) Tennessee Cavalry (cancelled).

Davis, John W., Major, Lieutenant-Colonel 20th Alabama Infantry. (1828-1870).
Davis, Joseph Robert, Lieutenant-Colonel 10th Mississippi Infantry. (1825-1896).
Davis, (**) Jesse S., Colonel .... Georgia Militia.
Davis, M. D., Major 1st (Fagan's and Monroe's) Arkansas Cavalry.
Davis, Newton Nimrod, Major, Lieutenant-Colonel, Colonel 24th Alabama Infantry. (1829-1887).
Davis, Nicholas, Lieutenant-Colonel 2d (5th?) (also called 8th) Battalion Alabama Infantry (temporarily commanding 19th Alabama Infantry, declined appointment). (1825-1874).
Davis, Samuel, Lieutenant-Colonel 25th Tennessee Infantry.
Davis, Samuel Boyer, Major 7th Battalion Texas Infantry; Major of Debray's Battalion Texas Cavalry.
Davis, Samuel W., Major 18th Tennessee Infantry.
Davis, Thomas Sturgis, Battalion Missouri Cavalry, disbanded, Co. attached to 23d Virginia Cavalry as Co. M.
Davis, William George Mackey, Lieutenant Colonel, Colonel 1st Florida Cavalry. (1812-1898).
Davis, W. L., Major 7th Mississippi Cavalry (also called 1st Mississippi Partisan Rangers).
Davison, Samuel, Major 89th Virginia Militia.
Davitte, Samuel W., Major, Lieutenant-Colonel, Colonel 1st Georgia Cavalry.
Dawson, Charles L., Colonel 19th (Dawson's) Arkansas Infantry; Colonel Dawson's Arkansas Infantry Regiment.
Dawson, John W., Major, Lieutenant-Colonel 154th Senior Tennessee Infantry; Major 13th and 154th Tennessee Infantry Consolidated. (1844-1892).
Dawson, Jonathan S., Colonel 46th Tennessee Infantry.
Dawson, Martin, Major 30th (Rogan's, also called 39th) Arkansas Infantry.
Dawson, William Azariah, Lieutenant-Colonel 15th (Stewart's, also called 14th) Tennessee Cavalry. (d. 1864).
Day, Charles B., Lieutenant-Colonel 5th Georgia Infantry; Major 18th Battalion Georgia State Guard.
Day, George W., Major, Lieutenant-Colonel 12th Battalion Tennessee Cavalry.
Deadrick, James Gallitzine, Major, Lieutenant-Colonel 19th Tennessee Infantry. (b. 1838).
Deakins, George S., Major 35th (formerly 5th Tennessee, Prov. Army) Tennessee Infantry.
Dean, John Mills, Major, Lieutenant-Colonel 7th Arkansas Infantry. (1835-1862).
Dearing, William, Colonel 54th Tennessee Infantry.
Dearmont, Washington, Colonel 122d Virginia Militia.
Deas, Zachariah Cantey, Colonel 22d Alabama Infantry. (1819-1882).
Deason, John B., Colonel 3d Mississippi Infantry.
Deatherage, William W., Colonel 34th Virginia Militia.
Deavenport, M. W., Major 34th (also called 2d Partisans) Texas Cavalry.
Deaver, (**) George, Major 114th Virginia Militia.
Deaver, William H., Major, Lieutenant-Colonel 60th North Carolina Infantry.
DeBardeleben, Arthur Warren, Major, Lieutenant-Colonel 56th Alabama Partisan Rangers. (1823-1880).
DeBaun, James, Major 9th Battalion Louisiana Cavalry.
De Bow, William A., Major 2d (Barteau's, afterwards 22d) Tennessee Cavalry.
Debray, Xavier Blanchard, Major 2d Texas Infantry; Colonel 26th Texas Cavalry; Lieutenant-Colonel of Debray's Battalion Texas Cavalry. (1819-1895).
De Clouet, Alexander Etienne, Colonel 26th Louisiana Infantry. (1812-1890).
Dedman, James M., Lieutenant-Colonel, Colonel 20th Alabama Infantry. (1822-1886).
De Gournay, Paul Francis, Major, Lieutenant-Colonel 12th Battalion Louisiana Artillery. (d. 1904).
DeJarnett, John, Colonel 129th Virginia Militia.
De Morse, Charles, Colonel 29th Texas Cavalry. (1816-1887).
De Moss, Wm. E., Major, Lieutenant-Colonel, Colonel 10th Tennessee Cavalry; Lieutenant-Colonel 10th and 11th Tennessee Cavalry Consolidated.
Dempsey, William A., Lieutenant-Colonel 129th Virginia Militia.

Deneale, (**) George E., Lieutenant-Colonel .... Battalion, Choctaw Warriors.
Dennett, William Bibb, Lieutenant-Colonel 24th Alabama Infantry. (b. 1822).
Denny, William Ritenour, Lieutenant-Colonel 31st Virginia Militia. (1833-1904).
Dennis, James B., Major 15th Mississippi Infantry.
Dennis, Thomas C., Colonel 84th Virginia Militia.
Desha, Benjamin, Major 9th Kentucky Infantry.
Desha, Franklin W., Major, Lieutenant-Colonel 7th Battalion Arkansas Infantry. (d. 1869).
Desha, Joseph, Acting Major Desha's Battalion Kentucky Infantry.
De Treville, (**) Richard, Colonel 1st South Carolina Reserves.
De Treville, Robert, Major, Lieutenant-Colonel 3d South Carolina Artillery (1st South Carolina Regulars); Colonel 17th South Carolina Militia. (1833-1865).
De Venne, (**) Henry, Colonel "Planters Life Guards" Louisiana Volunteers.
De Walt, Kerr B., Colonel 1st Infantry Texas State Troops; Major Texas Reserve Corps.
De Witt, Christopher Columbus, Major Texas Reserve Corps. (1820-1890).
Dial, (**) Hamilton C., Major 9th Texas Cavalry.
Dial, William Henry, Major 1st Regiment Florida Reserves. (1831-1913).
Diamond, George R., Lieutenant-Colonel, Colonel 10th (May's) Kentucky Cavalry). (1837-1919).
Diamond, James J., Lieutenant-Colonel, Colonel 11th Texas Cavalry.
Diamond, John R., Lieutenant-Colonel Bourland's Regiment Texas Cavalry.
Diamond, William W., Major, Lieutenant-Colonel 16th Texas Cavalry.
Dibrell, George Gibbs, Lieutenant-Colonel 25th Tennessee Infantry; Colonel 8th (Dibrell's, also called 13th) Tennessee Cavalry. (1822-1888).
Dickey, James B., Major 55th Alabama Infantry.
Dickins, John R., Colonel 5th Mississippi Infantry; Major 12th Mississippi Infantry.
Dillard, James P., Colonel 70th North Carolina Militia.
Dillard, John James, Major 35th Arkansas Infantry. (1820-1865).
Dillard, John L., Colonel 64th Virginia Militia.
Dillard, Miles A., Lieutenant-Colonel 9th (Maxey's, also called 8th) Texas Infantry.
Dillard, (**) Terisha W., Colonel 90th Virginia Militia.
Dillon, Edward, Colonel 2d (also called 4th) Mississippi Cavalry. (1834-1897).
Dills, ..., Major Dills' Missouri Infantry Battalion, 6th Division, Missouri State Guard.
Dilworth, William Scott, Colonel 3d Florida Infantry.
Dismukes, William H., Lieutenant-Colonel 19th (Smead's and Dockery's) Arkansas Infantry. (d. 1863).
Dixon, (**) L. V., Colonel Memphis (Tennessee) Legion.
Doak, William R., Major 2d Tennessee Infantry (Provisional Army). (d. 1862).
Doan, John F., Lieutenant-Colonel 11th Alabama Cavalry.
Dobbin, Archibald S., Colonel Dobbin's Regiment Arkansas Cavalry. (1836-c. 1872).
Dobbins, Joseph J., Major 1st (Wheeler's, afterward 6th) Tennessee Cavalry.
Dockery, Thomas C., Major 22d Mississippi Infantry.
Dockery, Thomas Pleasant, Colonel 19th (Smead's and Dockery's) Arkansas Infantry; Colonel 5th Arkansas Infantry State Troops, 1861. (1833-1898).
Dodd, Nathan, Major 61st (also called 81st) Tennessee Infantry.
Dodson, Eli, Lieutenant-Colonel, Colonel 14th (Mitchell's) Arkansas Infantry.
Dodson, Elijah Mosely, Major 1st Confederate Infantry. (1835-1904).
Dodson, J. N., Major, Lieutenant-Colonel 9th Texas Cavalry.
Donelson, John, Major 2d Texas Cavalry (or Mounted Rifles). (1829-1864).
Donnell, David M., Lieutenant-Colonel, Colonel 16th Tennessee Infantry.
Donnell, Robert, Major 22d Alabama Infantry. (b. 1842).
Dorman, James Baldwin, Major 3d Virginia Artillery, Local Defense Troops. (1823-1893).
Dorough, Thomas Travis, Major 34th Georgia Infantry. (d. 1877).
Dorsey, Caleb W., Lieutenant-Colonel Slayback's Missouri Regiment.
Dorsey, (**) S. D., Colonel 53d Georgia Militia.

Dortch, John Basket, Captain, commanding 2d Consolidated Kentucky Battalion.
Doss, Washington LaFayette, Major, Lieutenant-Colonel, Colonel 14th Mississippi Infantry. (1825-1900).
Dotson, James M., Major 10th Mississippi Infantry.
Dotson, Josephus, Lieutenant-Colonel 17th (Rector's) Arkansas Infantry; Lieutenant-Colonel Rector's Arkansas Regiment (12 months).
Douglas, Hugh Thomas, Lieutenant-Colonel 1st Battalion Engineers; Colonel 4th Regiment Engineer Troops.
Douglass, De Witt Clinton, Major Douglass' Battalion Tennessee Cavalry.
Douglass, Henry L., Colonel 9th Tennessee Infantry.
Douglass, William F., Major 6th Arkansas Infantry.
Douthat, Robert, Major of Cavalry Virginia forces; formerly Captain Cos. C and D, 3d Virginia Cavalry.
Dovel, (**) John E., Colonel 116th Virginia Militia.
Dowd, William Francis, Colonel 24th Mississippi Infantry. (1820-1878).
Dowdell, James Ferguson, Colonel 37th Alabama Infantry. (1818-1871).
Dowdle, William M., Major 21st (Cravens') Arkansas Infantry. (d. 1862).
Downing, Joseph, Major 37th Virginia Militia.
Downing, Lewis, Lieutenant-Colonel Drew's Cherokees. (d. 1872).
Downing, Samuel, Colonel 92nd Virginia Militia. (1808-1891).
Drake, Jabez L., Major, Lieutenant-Colonel, Colonel 33d (Hurst's) Mississippi Infantry. (d. 1864).
Drake, Joseph, Colonel 4th Mississippi Infantry. (d. 1878).
Drane, James W., Major, Lieut. Col. 31st Mississippi Infanrty. (b. 1833).
Draughton, James Walker, Major 31st Louisiana Infantry.
Drew, John, Colonel Drew's Cherokee Mounted Rifles (also called 1st and 2d Cherokee Mounted Rifles). (d. 1865).
Driver, William T., Major 2d Tennessee Infantry (Provisional Army). (1840-1864).
Dubroca, Edgar Martin, Major, Lieutenant-Colonel 13th (Gibson's) Louisiana Infantry.
Duckworth, William Lafayette, Major, Lieutenant-Colonel, Colonel 1st (Jackson's afterward 7th) Tennessee Cavalry. (1834-1915).
Dudley, Richard Houston, Major 21st (N. W. Carter's) Tenn. Cavalry (unofficial). (1836-1914).
Duff, James, Colonel 33d Texas Cavalry; Major, Lieutenant-Colonel 14th Battalion Texas Cavalry.
Duffy, Patrick, Major 20th Tennessee Infantry.
Duffy, Robert J., Major 1st Missouri Infantry.
Dugan, (**) P. B., Maj. 14th Miss. Inf., S. O. 37 Dept. Ala., Miss. & E. La., Feb. 7, 1865.
Duke, Basil Wilson, Lieutenant-Colonel, Colonel 2d (Morgan's) Kentucky Cavalry. (1838-1916).
Dula, Thomas J., Major, Lieutenant-Colonel 58th North Carolina Infantry.
Dunaway, George O., Lieutenant-Colonel 3d Cavalry Texas State Troops.
Duncan, Blanton, Lieutenant-Colonel 1st (Duncan's) Battalion Kentucky Infantry. (d. 1902).
Duncan, Jeptha, Major 6th Missouri Infantry. (1828-1911).
Duncan, Johnson Kelly, Major, Colonel 1st Louisiana Artillery. (1827-1862).
Duncan, Robert Alexander, Major, Lieutenant-Colonel 13th Arkansas Infantry.
Duncan, William A., Major 25th Tennessee Infantry.
Dunklin, James Hilliard, Major, Lieutenant-Colonel 33d Alabama Infantry. (1834-1877).
Dunlop, Isaac L., Colonel 9th Arkansas Infantry.
Dunlop, James E., Lieutenant-Colonel 2d Georgia Cavalry. (b. 1831).
Dunlop, Samuel John Calhoun, Major, Colonel 46th Georgia Infantry. (b. 1833).
Dunn, David Campbell, Lieutenant-Colonel 63d Virginia Infantry. (1829-1905).
Dunn, John N., Lieutenant-Colonel 36th Tennessee Infantry.
Dupeire, St. L., Major Dupeire's Louisiana Zouave Battalion.
Durr, R. J., Major 39th Mississippi Infantry.
Dwyer, Robert D. A., Major, Lieutenant-Colonel 2d (Burbridge's, also called 1st)

Missouri Infantry; Major Burbridge's Missouri Cavalry, 2d Division, Missouri State Guard. (1834-1864).
Dye, James T., Major 51st Alabama Partisan Rangers.
Dyer, Beverly L., Major, Lieutenant-Colonel 13th Tennessee Infantry.
Dyer, Samuel M., Major, Lieutenant-Colonel 3d Mississippi Infantry.
Eager, Robert, Lieutenant-Colonel 3d Mississippi Infantry.
Eagle, James Phillip, Major 2d Arkansas Mounted Rifles. (1837-1904).
Eaker, Jonas, Lieutenant-Colonel 3d Missouri Infantry, 1st Division, Missouri State Guard.
Eakin, William L., Lieutenant-Colonel, Colonel 59th Tennessee Infantry; Major 1st (Eakin's) Battalion Tennessee Infantry.
Earle, Fontaine Richard, Major 34th (also called 2d) Arkansas Infantry, Brooks' Regiment. (d. 1908).
Earle, Josiah Francis, Major 3d Arkansas Cavalry. (1824-1884).
Earle, Richard Gordon, Colonel 2d Alabama Cavalry. (d. 1864).
Earle, Samuel Girard, Colonel 3d Arkansas Cavalry. (1833-1863).
Earp, C. R., Lieutenant-Colonel, Colonel 10th Texas Cavalry.
Easley, Samuel A., Lieutenant-Colonel 4th Cavalry Texas State Troops.
Easterling, William K., Lieutenant-Colonel 46th Mississippi Infantry.
Easton, Thomas S., Major 32d Alabama Infantry.
Eatherly, Jonathan, Lieutenant-Colonel 28th Tennessee Infantry.
Echols, James Walter, Lieutenant-Colonel 34th Alabama Infantry. (d. 1869).
Echols, John H., Major 2d Alabama Reserves.
Echols, Philip H., Lieutenant-Colonel 5th Mississippi Cavalry.
Ector, Matthew Duncan, Colonel 14th Texas Cavalry. (1822-1879).
Ector, Wiley B., Major 10th Texas Cavalry. (b. 1829).
Edmondson, A. C., Lieutenant-Colonel 2d Mississippi State Partisan Rangers.
Edmondson, James Howard, Colonel 11th Tennessee Cavalry. (1831-1885).
Edmonston, J., Lieutenant-Colonel Edmonston's Louisiana Battalion.
Edwards, Aaron Coon, Lieutenant-Colonel, Colonel 47th Georgia Infantry. (1833-1868).
Edwards, David, Major 2d Regiment North Carolina Detailed Men.
Edwards, Jeptha, Colonel 49th (also called 31st, Hale's) Alabama Infantry.
Edwards, Joseph J., Major 68th North Carolina Infantry.
Egbert, Daniel, Major Border's Regiment Texas Cavalry.
Elford, Charles James, Colonel 16th South Carolina Infantry; Colonel 3d South Carolina Reserves. (1820-1867).
Elgin, (**) Charles G., Major 47th Virginia Militia.
Ellington, A. B., Major 3d Regiment North Carolina Junior Reserves.
Ellington, James B., Major 8th Battalion North Carolina Reserves.
Elliott, Benjamin, Lieutenant-Colonel, Colonel 1st (Elliott's, also called 10th) Missouri Cavalry Battalion; Colonel 2d Missouri Infantry Regiment, 8th Division, Missouri State Guard. (1830-1911).
Elliott, James Kelly, Major, Lieutenant-Colonel 30th Alabama Infantry. (1837-1908).
Ellison, Jesse, Lieutenant-Colonel 7th (also called 10th) Missouri Cavalry.
Ellsberry, Thomas Wright, Major 5th Arkansas Infantry.
Elmore, Henry Marshall, Colonel 20th Texas Infantry. (1816-1879).
Embry, Benjamin T., Lieutenant-Colonel, Colonel 2d Arkansas Mounted Rifles. (1820-1892).
English, James W., Colonel 86th Virginia Militia.
Erwin, Engene, Colonel 6th Missouri Infantry; Lieutenant-Colonel 3d (also called 5th) Battalion Missouri Infantry; Major 1st Missouri Infantry Regiment, 8th Division, Missouri State Guard. (d. 1863).
Erwin, (**) William D., Colonel 81st Virginia Militia.
Erwin, William Hugh, Lieutenant-Colonel 12th Missouri Cavalry; Colonel 10th Missouri Cavalry Regiment, 8th Division, Missouri State Guard.
Estes, John W., Lieutenant-Colonel 52d Tennessee Infantry.
Estes, William E., Major 32d (also called 15th) Texas Cavalry.
Estes, William N., Lieutenant-Colonel, Colonel 3d (also called 11th) Confederate Cavalry; Major 11th Battalion Alabama Cavalry. (d. 1863).

Euliss, Alfred E., Major 48th North Carolina Militia.
Evans, Beverly Daniel, Lieutenant-Colonel 2nd Georgia State Line. (1826-1897).
Evans, Henry G., Lieutenant-Colonel 48th (Nixon's) Tennessee Infantry. (1842-1914).
Evans, J. A., Major Crews' Battalion Tennessee Infantry.
Evans, (**) J. M., Major Terry's Regiment, Texas Cavalry.
Evans, John C., Major 4th South Carolina State Troops.
Evans, Marcus Lagrand, Major, Lieutenant-Colonel 8th Texas Cavalry.
Evans, Thomas J., Colonel 19th Virginia Militia (afterwards 2d State Reserves). (1822-1889).
Everett, Peter M., Major 3d Battalion Kentucky Mounted Rifles.
Ewin, Henry Clayton, Major 44th Tennessee Infantry. (1839-1863).
Ewing, Albert G., Lieutenant-Colonel 8th (Fulton's) Tennessee Infantry.
Fagan, James Fleming, Colonel 1st (Fagan's and Monroe's) Arkansas Infantry; Colonel 1st (Fagan's) Arkansas Cavalry. (1828-1893).
Fain, Joel Caesar, Major, Lieutenant-Colonel 6th Georgia Cavalry. (1839-1895).
Fain, John Simpson, Lieutenant-Colonel 8th Georgia State Troops, Colonel 65th Georgia Infantry; Lieutenant-Colonel Infantry Battalion, Smith's Georgia Legion.
Falconer, Thomas A., Major 34th (also called 37th) Mississippi Infantry.
Falconnet, Eugene F., Major 9th Alabama Cavalry; Major 14th Battalion Alabama Cavalry.
Falkner, Jefferson, Lieutenant-Colonel 8th Confederate Cavalry. (1810-1895).
Fannin, James Henry, Colonel 1st (Fannin's) Georgia Reserves. (1835-1909).
Fant, Albert E., Colonel 5th Mississippi Infantry.
Farish, John D., Major 3d Alabama Cavalry.
Fariss, Robert Clement, Lieutenant-Colonel 17th Alabama Infantry. (1830-1905).
Farley, John D., Major 4th Mississippi Infantry Battalion (or Minute Men) State Troops.
Farmer, Benjamin James, Major, Lieutenant-Colonel 2d Missouri Infantry, 1st Division, Missouri State Guard.
Farmer, Samuel, Major 16th Arkansas Infantry.
Farquharson, Robert, Colonel 41st Tennessee Infantry. (1814-1869).
Farrar, Frederick H., Jr., Major, Lieutenant-Colonel 1st Louisiana Regular Infantry; Colonel Pointe Coupee Regiment, Louisiana Militia. (d. 1863).
Farrar, Lochlin Johnson, Major 12th Texas Cavalry.
Farrell, Michael, Lieutenant-Colonel, Colonel 15th Mississippi Infantry. (d. 1864).
Farrington, Samuel, Lieutenant-Colonel 1st Missouri Infantry Regiment, 3d Division Missouri State Guard.
Farris, Oliver B., Major 2d (Barteau's) Tennessee Cavalry. (d. 1909).
Faucett, Samuel F. M., Major, Lieutenant-Colonel 5th Mississippi Infantry.
Faulkner, Henry H., Major 16th Tennessee Infantry.
Faulkner, Thomas L., Lieutenant-Colonel 8th (Livingston's) Alabama Cavalry.
Faulkner, William Wallace, Colonel 12th Kentucky Cavalry. (d. 1864).
Favrot, Henry Mortimer, Lieutenant-Colonel 2d Battalion Louisiana State Cavalry.
Fayth, William H., Major Gordon's Regiment Arkansas Cavalry. (d. 1864).
Feaster, Elbert S., Major 4th Missouri Infantry Regiment, 8th Division, Missouri State Guard.
Featherston, Lucius, Colonel 5th Arkansas Infantry; Colonel 13th Arkansas Infantry; Colonel 5th and 13th Arkansas Infantry Consolidated. (d. 1863).
Feild, Hume R., Major, Colonel 1st Tennessee Volunteers. Colonel 1st and 2d Tennessee Consolidated. (1834-1921).
Felton, L. M., Major 12th Cavalry Georgia State Guard.
Fergus, W. C., Major 42d Alabama Infantry.
Ferguson, Samuel Wragg, appointed Colonel 5th South Carolina Cavalry, but commission not issued; Lieutenant-Colonel 28th Mississippi Cavalry. (1834-1917).
Ferguson, Thomas B., Major of Artillery. (d. 1922).
Ferrill, Stephen C., Major, Lieutenant-Colonel 8th Texas Cavalry.
Ficklin, (**) John, Colonel Ficklin's Kentucky Battalion. (b. 1822).
Field, Joseph H., Colonel 8th Confederate Cavalry.
Fielding, William C., Major 24th Tennessee Infantry. (d. 1864).

Findlay, C. D., Lieutenant-Colonel 5th Battalion, Georgia Reserves. (d. 1910).
Findley, James J., Major 52d Georgia Infantry.
Finlay, Luke William, Major, Lieutenant-Colonel 4th Tennessee Vols. (1831-1908).
Finley, Jesse Johnson, Colonel 6th Florida Infantry. (1812-1904).
Finney, Louis C. H., Lieutenant-Colonel 39th Virginia Infantry (disbanded).
Finter, Cullin W., Major 2d Virginia Militia 7th Brigade.
Fisher, Rhoades, Major 6th Texas Infantry.
Fisk, Stuart Wilkins, Colonel 25th Louisiana Infantry. (1820-1862).
Fitzgerald, Edward, Major, Colonel 154th Senior Tennessee Infantry.
Fitzhugh, William, Colonel 16th Texas Cavalry. (d. 1883).
Flagg, John S., Lieutenant-Colonel 89th Virginia Militia.
Flanagin, Harris, Colonel 2d Arkansas Mounted Rifles. (1817-1874).
Fleisher, Henry H., Lieutenant-Colonel 162d Virginia Militia.
Fleming, David P., Major 10th Missouri Cavalry Regiment, 8th Division, Missouri State Guard.
Fletcher, James Henry, Major, Lieutenant-Colonel 20th Arkansas Infantry. (1839-1906).
Flewellen, James Thweat, Lieutenant-Colonel 39th Alabama Infantry. (1828-1889).
Flippen, (**) ...., Colonel 1st Battalion Arkansas Reserve Cavalry. 1864-5).
Flippen, William S., Major 1st Tennessee Zouaves.
Florence, ..., Major 5th Missouri Infantry Regiment (mounted), 5th Division, Missouri State Guard.
Flournoy, Camp, Major 19th Louisiana Infantry.
Flournoy, George, Colonel 16th Texas Infantry. (1832-1889).
Flournoy, Peter C., Colonel 2d (Burbridge's, also called 1st) Missouri Infantry. (b. 1828).
Flournoy, R. W., Colonel 1st Division Georgia State Militia.
Flournoy, (**) T. C., Colonel Desha County Militia (Arkansas).
Floyd, Henry Hamilton, Colonel Camden County Georgia Militia. (1814-1873).
Floyd, John Julius, Colonel 10th Cavalry Georgia State Guard. (1803-1883).
Floyd, William J., Major Chalmers' Consolidated Regiment Mississippi Cavalry. (b. 1829).
Fly, George Washington Lafayette, Major 2d Texas Infantry. (1835-1905).
Flynt, Guilford G., Colonel 8th Mississippi Infantry.
Foard, Robert L., Major 13th Texas Infantry.
Folk, George Nathaniel, Colonel 65th North Carolina Volunteers (6th North Carolina Cavalry); Lieutenant-Colonel 7th Battalion North Carolina Cavalry. (d. 1896).
Folsom, Simpson N., Major 1st (Battice's) Choctaw Cavalry Battalion; Colonel 1st Choctaw War Regiment, 2d Choctaw. (d. 1900).
Fontaine, Sydney Thurston, Major 7th Battalion Texas Artillery. (b. 1840).
Footman, William, Major Commissary Battalion, Florida Cavalry (temporary).
Ford, Barney, Lieutenant-Colonel Ford's Battalion Arkansas Cavalry.
Ford, John Salmon, Colonel 2d Texas Cavalry (or Mounted Rifles). (1815-1897).
Ford, Martin J., Major, Lieutenant-Colonel 1st Volunteers Georgia.
Ford, S. S., Lieutenant-Colonel 10th Arkansas Infantry.
Ford, William H., Major Ballentine's (also called 2d Mississippi Partisan Rangers) Mississippi Cavalry.
Forkner, Samuel, Colonel 73d North Carolina Militia.
Forney, Daniel P., Major 2d Alabama Infantry.
Forney, George Hoke, Major, Lieutenant-Colonel 1st Battalion Confederate Infantry. (d. 1864).
Forrest, Jeffrey E., Colonel Forrest's Regiment Alabama Cavalry; Major 8th (Dibrell's, also called 13th) Tennessee Cavalry. (1837-1864).
Forrest, Jesse Anderson, Colonel 16th (Wilson's, also called 21st) Tennessee Cavalry. (d. 1890).
Forrest, Nathan Bedford, Lieutenant-Colonel, Colonel 3d (Forrest's) Tennessee Cavalry. (1821-1877).

Forsyth, John, Colonel 3d Alabama Militia.
Forsyth, Robert Charles, Lieutenant-Colonel 1st Battalion Alabama Artillery.
Fort, William, Colonel 2d South Carolina State Troops (6 months). (d. 1875).
Fort, ..., Lieutenant-Colonel 6th Missouri Infantry Regiment, 3d Division, Missouri State Guard.
Foster, Thomas Jefferson, Colonel Foster's Regiment Alabama Volunteers. (1809-1887).
Foster, William Green, Colonel 65th Georgia Infantry. (1831-1892).
Fouche, R. T., Major 8th Confederate Infantry Battalion.
Fournet, Gabriel Antoine, Major 33d Louisiana Infantry.
Fournet, Valsin Antoine, Lieutenant-Colonel 10th Battalion Louisiana Infantry; Lieutenant-Colonel 33d Louisiana Infantry.
Foute, Auguste M., Lieutenant-Colonel Memphis Battalion Infantry (also called 3d Battalion).
Fowler, Andrew J., Lieutenant-Colonel 20th Texas Cavalry.
Fowler, John W., Lieutenant-Colonel 8th Infantry George State Guard.
Fowler, Pleasant, Lieutenant-Colonel 14th (Mitchell's) Arkansas Infantry.
Foxworth, Franklin W., Major 38th Mississippi Infantry.
Francis, John C., Lieutenant-Colonel 30th Alabama Infantry. (d. 1864).
Franklin, B. H., Colonel Franklin's Cavalry Regiment 2d Division, Missouri State Guard.
Franklin, Cyrus, Colonel 7th (Franklin's) Missouri Infantry Regiment; Colonel 2d Northeast Cavalry Regiment.
Franklin, James J., Major 25th (also called 30th) Arkansas Infantry.
Frayser, Robert Dudley, Lieutenant-Colonel 37th (formerly 7th Tennessee, Provisional Army) Tennessee Infantry; Lieutenant-Colonel 15th and 37th Tennessee Infantry Consolidated. (1840-1893).
Frazer, George M., Major P. T. Herbert's Texas Battalion, Arizona Brigade.
Frazer, John Wesley, Lieutenant-Colonel 8th Alabama Infantry; Colonel 28th Alabama Infantry. (1827-1906).
Frazier, W. L. H., Major of Frazier's Battalion Missouri Infantry.
Frederick, Andrew David, Lieutenant-Colonel, Colonel 2d South Carolina Artillery. (1818-1888).
Freeman, Dandridge Claiborne, Major Freeman's Battalion Kentucky Infantry.
Freeman, George Charles, Major 45th Alabama Infantry. (1825-1866).
Freeman, John M., Major 3d Cavalry Georgia State Guard.
Freeman, John R., Lieutenant-Colonel Floyd Legion, Georgia State Guard. (c. 1813-1896).
Freeman, Thomas Jones, Colonel 22d Tennessee Infantry. (1827-1891).
Freeman, Thomas Roe, Colonel Freeman's Missouri Cavalry.
French, James Milton, Major, Colonel 63d Virginia Infantry. (1834-1916).
French, William Foster, Lieutenant-Colonel 3d Regiment North Carolina Junior Reserves; Major 7th North Carolina Battalion Reserves.
Frierson, William, Lieutenant-Colonel 27th Tennessee Infantry. (1839-1882).
Fristoe, Edward T., Colonel Fristoe's Regiment Missouri Cavalry. (1829-1892).
Frost, Thomas C., Lieutenant-Colonel 1st (McCulloch's) Mounted Riflemen.
Frye, Moses C., Major Cherokee Battalion.
Fulcrod, Philip, Lieutenant-Colonel Border's Regiment Texas Cavalry; Lieutenant-Colonel Fulcrod's Cadets, Battalion Texas Cavalry.
Fuller, Anthony Cook, Lieutenant-Colonel 9th South Carolina Reserves. (1825-1917).
Fuller, Charles Alexander, Lieutenant-Colonel, Colonel 1st Louisiana Artillery. (1814-1890).
Fuller, Haley G., Major 6th Battalion Cavalry Georgia State Guard.
Fulton, Alfred S., Colonel 8th (Fulton's) Tennessee Infantry.
Fulton, Winston, Lieutenant-Colonel 2d Regiment North Carolina Detailed Men.
Gadsden, Christopher Schulz, Major, 1st Rifle Regiment, South Carolina Militia. (1834-1915).
Gaines, Frank Young, Major 3d Alabama Cavalry. (1825-1873).
Gaines, John F., Lieutenant-Colonel 53d Alabama Partisan Rangers.

Gaines, Richard, Major 9th (Clark's) Missouri Infantry; Major 8th Battalion Missouri Infantry. (1834-1881).
Gaither, Beal, Major, Colonel 27th Arkansas Infantry.
Gallie, John B., Major 22d Battalion Georgia Siege Artillery. (1806-1863).
Galloway, Morton G., Lieutenant-Colonel, Colonel 1st Arkansas Mounted Rifles.
Galt, Edward Machen, Colonel 1st Regiment Georgia State Troops. (1819-1866).
Gano, Richard Montgomery, Colonel 7th Kentucky Cavalry; Lieutenant-Colonel Gano's Battalion Texas Cavalry. (1830-1913).
Gant, ..., Colonel 4th Regiment, 2d Brigade, Georgia Militia.
Gantt, George, Lieutenant-Colonel 9th Battalion Tennessee Cavalry. (1824-1897).
Gardner, Thomas F., Major, Lieutenant-Colonel 29th North Carolina Infantry.
Garland, Hugh A., Major, Lieutenant-Colonel, Colonel 1st Missouri Infantry; Major, Lieutenant-Colonel 1st and 4th Missouri Infantry Consolidated. (1837-1864).
Garland, (**) Landon C., Colonel Alabama Tuscaloosa Cadets.
Garland, Robert R., Colonel 6th Texas Infantry. (1821-1870).
Garland, William Daniel, Lieutenant-Colonel 41st Virginia Militia. (1822-1898).
Garland, William H., Lieutenant-Colonel 14th Confederate Cavalry; Major Garland's Battalion Mississippi Cavalry.
Garr, (**) Presley N., Major Sypert's Kentucky Cavalry. (d. 1864).
Garrett, George Washington Brooks, Major 23d Mississippi Infantry.
Garrett, William N., Major, Lieutenant-Colonel 64th North Carolina Infantry.
Garrison, Fleming Hodges, Major 14th Texas Cavalry. (1824-1887).
Garrison, (**) George W., Colonel P. A. Virginia. Formerly C.S. Navy.
Garrott, Isham Warren, Colonel 20th Alabama Infantry. (1816-1863).
Gaston, (**) Joseph H., Lieutenant-Colonel Georgia Militia.
Gaston, Matthew A., Major 18th Texas Infantry.
Gates, Elijah, Colonel 1st Missouri Cavalry; Lieutenant-Colonel 1st Missouri Cavalry, 5th Division, Missouri State Guard. (b. 1829).
Gates, James T., Lieutenant-Colonel 8th Mississippi Infantry.
Gaulden, William B., Colonel Coast Guard Battalion, Georgia Militia. (1817-1873).
Gause, Lucian Coatsworth, Major, Colonel 32d Arkansas Infantry. (1836-1880).
Gause, William R., Lieutenant-Colonel, Colonel 3d (also called 2d) Missouri Infantry; Major 2d Missouri Infantry, 4th Division, Missouri State Guard.
Gay, William, Major of R. M. Russell's Tennessee Cavalry, organized February, 1864. (1827-1901).
Gee, James M., Lieutenant-Colonel 3d Arkansas Cavalry; Colonel 15th (Gee's) Arkansas Infantry.
Gee, James Thomas, Major, Lieutenant-Colonel 1st Battalion Alabama Artillery.
Gee, Joseph James, Major, Lieutenant-Colonel 4th Mississippi Infantry. (1834-1914).
Genette, Jones, Major 154th Senior Tennessee Infantry.
Geoghegan, John A., Major, Lieutenant-Colonel 29th Arkansas Infantry.
George, James, Lieutenant-Colonel 1st (Rector's War Regiment) Arkansas Volunteers.
George, James Zachariah, Colonel 5th Mississippi Cavalry; Lieutenant-Colonel 19th (George's) Battalion Mississippi Cavalry. (1826-1897).
George, J. N., Major Moreland's Regiment Alabama Cavalry.
Gerard, Aristides, Lieutenant-Colonel, Colonel 13th (Gibson's Louisiana Infantry).
Gibbons, William McD., Major 40th Mississippi Infantry. (d. 1864).
Gibbs, J. G., Major North Carolina Prison Guard Battalion.
Gibson, (**) Howard, Colonel 44th Virginia Militia.
Gibson, John H., Major 18th Alabama Battalion Partisan Rangers; Major 16th (also called 4th) Battalion Alabama Infantry. (d. 1863).
Gibson, (**) John Thomas, Colonel 55th Virginia Militia. (1825-1904).
Gibson, (**) R. F., Major 5th Alabama Cavalry.
Gibson, Randall Lee, Colonel 13th (Gibson's) Louisiana Infantry. (1832-1892).
Gibson, Samuel, Major 26th Arkansas Infantry.
Gibson, ..., Major 21st Battalion Alabama Infantry.
Giddings, De Witt Clinton, Lieutenant-Colonel 21st Texas Cavalry. (1827-1903).

Giddings, George H., Lieutenant-Colonel Texas Battalion Cavalry. (b. 1823).
Gilbert, Thomas H., Major 50th (Coltart's, formerly known as 26th) Alabama Infantry.
Gilbert, Calvin, Major 20th (Nixon's) Tennessee Cavalry.
Gilbreath, Montgomery, Lieutenant-Colonel 31st (Hale's) Alabama Infantry. (1814-1885).
Gilchrist, James Graham, Lieutenant-Colonel, Colonel 45th Alabama Infantry. (b. 1814).
Giles, John R., Major 63d Georgia Infantry. (d. 1865).
Gilhurst, (**) ...., Colonel 10 Kentucky C. S. Regiment, surrendered at Louisa, Kentucky, April 27, 1865.
Gilkey, Charles A., Major, Lieutenant-Colonel, Jackson County (afterward 12th) Missouri Cavalry.
Gill, William Perry, Major, Lieutenant-Colonel 3d Battalion South Carolina Reserves.
Gillenland, (**) D. C., Commanding Battalion Mississippi State Troops.
Gillespie, Clayton Crawford, Colonel 25th Texas Cavalry; 3d Texas Lancers.
Gillespie, D. A., Colonel 7th Arkansas Infantry. (d. 1863).
Gillespie, Francis M., Major 31st Mississippi Infantry (d. 1864).
Gillespie, Henry Clay, Lieutenant-Colonel 2d (Ashby's) Tennessee Cavalry.
Gillespie, James Wendell, Colonel 43d Tennessee (afterward Mounted Infantry). (1819-1874).
Gillett, L. E., Major Wells' (also called 34th) Regiment Texas Cavalry.
Gilmore, Jerome B., Lieutenant-Colonel, Colonel 3d Louisiana Infantry.
Gitner, Henry Liter, Colonel 4th Kentucky Cavalry. (1829-1892).
Ginevan, (**) Mathias, Major, 114th Virginia Militia.
Gipson, William, Major 2d Arkansas Mounted Rifles; Major Gipson's Battalion Arkansas Cavalry.
Girardey, (**) Isadore P., Major 1st Regiment L. D. Troops Augusta, Georgia. (1828-1898).
Girault, J. F., Colonel Confederate Guards, Louisiana Militia.
Gladden, Adley Hogan, Colonel 1st Louisiana Regulars. (1810-1862).
Glass, (**) W. H., Lieutenant-Colonel 1st Virginia Militia.
Glass, William Wood, Major, Lieutenant-Colonel 51st Virginia Militia. (1835-1911).
Glenn, Jesse A., Colonel 36th (Glenn's) Georgia Infantry. (1833-1904).
Glenn, J. N., Lieutenant-Colonel 10th Cavalry Georgia State Guard.
Glenn, John E., Major 1st (Cleburne's) Arkansas Infantry; Colonel 36th Arkansas Infantry; Lieutenant-Colonel 28th Arkansas Infantry.
Gober, Daniel C., Major, Colonel 16th Louisiana Infantry; Colonel 16th and 25th Louisiana Consolidated; temporarily commanding Mounted Infantry Regiment in East Louisiana in 1864.
Godfrey, William, Lieutenant-Colonel 11th Infantry George State Guard.
Godwin, Aaron S., Lieutenant-Colonel 48th (Voorhies') Tennessee Infantry.
Goforth, Alexander McF., Major 1st (Carter's) Tennessee Cavalry. (1834-1864).
Golladay, Edward Isaac, Lieutenant-Colonel 38th (formerly 8th, Looney's) Tennessee Infantry; Lieutenant-Colonel 5th (Golladay's) Battalion Alabama Infantry. (1830-1897).
Gooch, John Saunders, Lieutenant-Colonel 20th Tennessee Infantry. (1842-1915).
Good, Chaplin, Lieutenant-Colonel Wells' (also called 34th) Regiment Texas Cavalry.
Goodall, David L., Lieutenant-Colonel 2d Tennessee Infantry (Provisional Army).
Goodbar, Joseph H., Major 16th Tennessee Infantry. (d. 1862).
Goode, Enos J., Colonel 7th Mississippi Infantry.
Goode, (**) William O., Colonel 22d Virginia Militia.
Goodwin, Edward, Lieutenant-Colonel, Colonel 35th Alabama Infantry. (d. 1863).
Goodwyn, William Sabb, Colonel 45th Alabama Infantry. (1825-1868).
Gordon, Anderson, Colonel Gordon's Regiment Arkansas Cavalry.
Gordon, Benjamin Franklin, Major, Lieutenant-Colonel, Colonel 5th Missouri Cavalry. (c. 1827-1866).
Gordon, Eugene Cornelius, Major 25th Battalion Alabama Cavalry. (d. 1913).

Gordon, George Anderson, Colonel 63d Georgia Infantry; Major 13th Battalion Georgia Infantry. (1830-1872).
Gordon, George Pemberton, Major 5th Missouri Cavalry. (1828-1909).
Gordon, George Washington, Lieutenant-Colonel, Colonel 11th Tennessee Infantry. (1836-1911).
Gordon, James, Lieutenant-Colonel 2d (also called 4th) Mississippi Cavalry. (1833-1912).
Gordon, James Clark, Major, Lieutenant-Colonel 1st Confederate Infantry.
Gordon, J. B., Major 6th Arkansas Infantry.
Gordon, Thomas Martin, Lieutenant-Colonel 3d Tennessee Volunteers. (d. 1901).
Gordon, William Wallace, Lieutenant-Colonel 11th Battalion Tennessee Cavalry.
Gore, Mounce Lauderdale, Colonel 8th (Dibrell's, also called 13th) Tennessee Cavalry. (1840-1908).
Gould, Nicholas C., Colonel 23rd Texas Cavalry.
Gould, Robert Simonton, Major 6th Battalion Texas Cavalry. (b. 1826).
Gourdain, Joseph Kleber, Major 18th Louisiana Infantry.
Gourdin, Robert Newman, Lieutenant-Colonel 1st Charleston Reserves, South Carolina. (1812-1894).
Govan, Daniel Chevilette, Lieutenant-Colonel, Colonel 2d Arkansas Infantry. (1829-1911).
Govan, George Morgan, Major 24th Mississippi Infantry.
Grace, William, Major, Lieutenant-Colonel, Colonel 10th Tennessee Infantry. (1839-1864).
Graham, Neill Smith, Lieutenant-Colonel 55th Alabama Infantry; Lieutenant-Colonel 59th-61st Alabama Infantry. (1818-1886).
Graham, Robert H., Lieutenant-Colonel 19th Texas Infantry.
Graham, Thomas B., Major 20th Mississippi Infantry.
Grambling, Enoch G., Major Cherokee Legion, Georgia State Guard.
Granbery, Joseph G., Colonel 4th North Carolina Militia.
Granbury, Hiram Bronson, Major, Lieutenant-Colonel, Colonel 7th Texas Infantry; Colonel Bailey's Consolidated Tennessee Regiment (temporary command). (1831-1864).
Grant, Isaac A., Lieutenant-Colonel 23d Texas Cavalry.
Gratiot, John R., Colonel 3d Arkansas Infantry State Troops, 1861.
Graves, (**) Isaac L., Lieutenant-Colonel 3d Virginia Militia.
Graves, John Robinson, Colonel 2d Missouri Infantry, 8th Division, Missouri State Guard. (1832-1908).
Gray, Edward Fairfax, Major, Lieutenant-Colonel 3d Texas Infantry. (d. 1884).
Gray, Henry, Colonel 28th Louisiana Infantry. (1816-1892).
Gray, John F., Major 48th (Voorhies') Tennessee Infantry. (b. 1836).
Gray, John William, Major 8th Battalion Georgia Infantry. (1829-1911).
Grayson, A. D., Lieutenant-Colonel 13th Arkansas Infantry. (d. 1862).
Green, James A., Major 172d Virginia Militia.
Green, John Uriah, Lieutenant-Colonel, Colonel 12th (also called 1st Partisan Rangers) Tennessee Cavalry.
Green, John W., Major 3d Engineer Regiment. (1827-1914).
Green, Martin Edwin, Colonel Green's Missouri Cavalry Regiment, 2d Division Missouri State Guard. (1815-1863).
Green, Peter V., Major, Lieutenant-Colonel, Colonel 5th Arkansas Infantry; Major 13th Arkansas Infantry; Major, Lieutenant-Colonel 5th and 13th Arkansas Infantry Consolidated.
Green, Thomas, Colonel 5th Texas Cavalry. (1814-1864).
Green, William, Major 11th Tennessee Infantry.
Greene, Alexander A., Lieutenant-Colonel 37th Alabama Infantry. (d. 1864).
Greene, Colton, Colonel 3d Missouri Cavalry. (c. 1838-1900).
Greenwood, A. G., first Colonel 26th Arkansas Infantry.
Greer, Elkanah Brackin, Colonel 3d Texas Cavalry. (1825-1877).
Greer, Henry Clay, Lieutenant-Colonel 15th (Russell's, also called 20th) Tennessee Cavalry.
Greer, Hugh Dunlap, Lieutenant-Colonel 38th (formerly 8th, Looney's) Tennessee Infantry. (b. 1836).

Gregg, Edward Pearsall, Lieutenant-Colonel, Colonel 16th Texas Cavalry.
Gregg, John, Colonel 7th Texas Infantry. (1828-1864).
Gregg, Nathan, Lieutenant-Colonel, Colonel 60th (also called 79th) Tennessee Infantry. (1835-1894).
Gregory, Edward H., Major 10th Mississippi Infantry.
Gregory, Nathaniel A., Major 2d Regiment North Carolina Junior Reserves.
Gregory, Roger, Lieutenant-Colonel 87th Virginia Militia. (b. 1833).
Grice, Daniel, Major 3d South Carolina Reserves.
Grider, Jesse S., Lieutenant-Colonel McGehee's Arkansas Regiment.
Griffin, J. B., Major 3d Georgia Reserves.
Griffin, Sidney H., Lieutenant-Colonel 31st Louisiana Infantry.
Griffin, William Henry, Lieutenant-Colonel 21st Texas Infantry; Major, Lieutenant-Colonel Griffin's Battalion Texas Infantry. (1816-1871).
Griffith, Jacob Wark, Lieutenant-Colonel 1st Kentucky Cavalry; Lieutenant-Colonel 3d Kentucky Cavalry. (1819-1881).
Griffith, John, Lieutenant-Colonel, Colonel 17th (Rector's) Arkansas Infantry; Lieutenant-Colonel, Colonel Rector's Arkansas Regiment (12 months).
Griffith, John Summerfield, Lieutenant-Colonel 6th Texas Cavalry. (1829-1901).
Grigsby, John Warren, Colonel 6th Kentucky Cavalry. (d. 1877).
Grigsby, Thomas Kenley, Lieutenant-Colonel 49th Tennessee Infantry. (1823-1896).
Grimsley, William Cage, Major 4th Missouri Infantry, 1st Division, Missouri State Guard. (1813-1887).
Grindle, (**) James T., Major 330 Battalion Georgia Militia.
Grinsted, Hiram L., Colonel 33d Arkansas Infantry. (1829-1864).
Groves, John F., Major 1st Infantry Georgia State Guard.
Guerrant, (**) William G., Lieutenant-Colonel 75th Virginia Militia.
Guess, George W., Lieutenant-Colonel 31st Texas Cavalry.
Guillet, Charles, Major, Lieutenant-Colonel 20th Louisiana Infantry.
Guilmartin, Lawrence J., Major 22d Battalion Georgia Siege Artillery.
Guion, Henry T., Major, Lieutenant-Colonel 10th North Carolina Volunteers (1st North Carolina Artillery).
Gulley, Ezekiah Slocum, Major, Lieutenant-Colonel 40th Alabama Infantry. (1831-1896).
Gunter, (**) Benjamin T., Colonel 3d Regiment Accomack Virginia Militia.
Gunter, Thomas Montague, Lieutenant-Colonel 34th (also called 2d) Arkansas Infantry; Lieutenant-Colonel Gunter's Arkansas Battalion Cavalry. (1826-1904).
Gunter, William T., Major 1st Battalion Alabama Partisan Rangers.
Gurley, B., Major 5th Infantry Georgia State Guard.
Gurley, Edwards Jeremiah, Colonel 30th Texas Cavalry (also called 1st Partisan Rangers). (d. 1914).
Guthrie, John F., Major 20th Tennessee Infantry. (1833-1864).
Guthrie, Lawson, Major 43d Tennessee Infantry (after Mounted Infantry).
Guyton, Cincinnatus Saxon, Lieutenant-Colonel 57th Georgia Infantry. (1834-1884).
Gwynne, Andrew Dunn, Major 50th (also known as 26th, Coltart's) Alabama Infantry; Lieutenant-Colonel 38th (formerly 8th, Looney's) Tennessee Infantry. (b. 1839).
Haddox, Clinton B., Major 34th Virginia Militia. (b. c. 1831).
Hagan, James, Major Wirt Adams' Mississippi Cavalry; Colonel 3d Alabama Cavalry. (1821-1901).
Hale, Henry Stephenson, Major 7th Kentucky Infantry. (1836-1922).
Hale, Smith D., Colonel 31st (Hale's, afterwards 49th) Alabama Infantry (never took command). (b. 1827).
Hale, Stephen F., Colonel 4th Missouri Infantry, 8th Division, Missouri State Guard.
Hale, William J., Lieutenant-Colonel 2d Tennessee Infantry (Prov. Army). (1836-1923).
Hall, Alexander, Lieutenant-Colonel 45th Tennessee Infantry.
Hall, Henry Gerard, Major, Lieutenant-Colonel 28th Texas Cavalry. (1833-1873).
Hall, John Gracey, Lieutenant-Colonel 51st Tennessee Infantry. (d. 1880).

Hall, (**) N. B., Lieutenant-Colonel .... Georgia Militia.
Hall, Robert J., Major 33d (Hurst's) Mississippi Infantry.
Hall, Winchester, Major, Colonel 26th Louisiana Infantry. (1819-1909).
Hallonquist, James Henry, Major, Lieutenant-Colonel, 2d Battalion Alabama Artillery. (1836-1883).
Ham, Thomas Wiley, Major 16th Battalion Mississippi Cavalry State Troops; Colonel Ham's Mississippi Cavalry. (d. 1864).
Hambleton, John W., Major 15th Tennessee Infantry. (b. 1834).
Hambrick, Joseph M., Lieutenant-Colonel 4th (Russell's) Alabama Cavalry.
Hamilton, Algernon Sydney, Lieutenant-Colonel 66th (also called 65th) Georgia Infantry. (b. 1833).
Hamilton, Alexander Samuel, Lieutenant-Colonel 1st Mississippi Infantry. (1830-1864).
Hamilton, John S., Major 1st Missouri Cavalry, 8th Division, Missouri State Guard.
Hamilton, Oliver Perry, Major, Lieutenant-Colonel Hamilton's Battalion Tennessee Cavalry; Lieutenant-Colonel R. C. Morgan's Kentucky Cavalry. (1825-1864).
Hamiter, David H., Major 19th (Dawson's) Arkansas Infantry.
Hammock, Porter, Major 2d Cherokee Mounted Rifles.
Hammond, Andrew J., Major 24th South Carolina Infantry. (1814-1882).
Hamner, H. A., Major of Griffin's Battalion Texas Infantry.
Hampton, Ezekiel H., Major 29th North Carolina Infantry.
Hampton, George James, Major, Lieutenant-Colonel 4th Texas Cavalry.
Hampton, (**) G. W., Colonel .... Kentucky Volunteers.
Hampton, Henry, Major 4th Tennessee Volunteers.
Hancock, Abram Booth, Major, 195th Virginia Militia.
Hancock, Ezekiel Wheeler, Lieutenant-Colonel, Colonel 7th Regiment North Carolina Reserves.
Hand, Moses Henry, Colonel 87th North Carolina Militia. (1812-1887).
Handley, James M., Major 46th Alabama Infantry.
Handly, Robert W., Lieutenant-Colonel 135th Virginia Militia.
Hankins, E. L., Major Ashcraft's Regiment Mississippi Cavalry; Major 3d Battalion Mississippi State Cavalry.
Hanna, W. S., Lieutenant-Colonel 36th Arkansas Infantry; Major 28th Arkansas Infantry.
Hannah, John Harvey, Major 19th Tennessee Infantry. (1838-1880).
Hannon, Moses Wright, Lieutenant-Colonel 1st Alabama Cavalry; Colonel 53d Alabama Partisan Rangers. (b. 1827).
Hanson, Roger Weightman, Colonel 2d Kentucky Infantry. (1827-1863).
Haptenstall, D. S., Major 135th Virginia Militia.
Haralson, (**) T. J., Colonel 96th Georgia Militia.
Harbin, (**) A. A., Colonel Harbin's Regiment North Carolina Home Guards.
Hardcastle, Aaron Bascom, Colonel 33d (Hardcastle's) Mississippi Infantry; Colonel 45th Mississippi Infantry; Major 3d (Hardcastle's) Battalion Mississippi Infantry. (1836-1915).
Hardeman, Peter, Lieutenant-Colonel, Colonel 1st Texas Cavalry Regiment, Arizona Brigade; Lieutenant-Colonel Hardeman's Battalion Texas Cavalry, Arizona Brigade; Colonel 31st Texas Cavalry. (1831-1882).
Hardeman, William Polk, Colonel 1st Texas Cavalry Regiment, Arizona Brigade; Lieutenant Colonel, Colonel 4th Texas Cavalry. (1816-1898).
Harden, J. R., Major 2d Cherokee Mounted Rifles.
Hardie, Joseph, Major Hardie's Cavalry Battalion Alabama Reserves. (b. 1833).
Hardy, Washington Morris, Major, Colonel 60th North Carolina Infantry.
Hardy, William Richard, Lieutenant-Colonel Dawson's Arkansas Infantry; Major, Lieutenant-Colonel 24th Arkansas Infantry.
Hargett, Flynn, Lieutenant-Colonel 5th Infantry Georgia State Guard. (1811-1896).
Hargrove, Lemuel, Major, Lieutenant-Colonel 39th Alabama Infantry.
Harkie, C. B., Colonel 55th Georgia Infantry.
Harkins, David F., Lieutenant-Colonel 1st Choctaw Cavalry Regiment.
Harlin, J. A., Lieutenant-Colonel 3d Regiment Mississippi Infantry (or Minute Men) State Troops.

Harllee, William Wallace, General Harllee's Legion South Carolina Militia. (1812-1897).
Harman, Bledsoe Desha, Colonel Harman's Confederate Cavalry Regiment; (also called Harman's Mississippi Cavalry Regiment).
Harper, Armistead Richardson, Lieutenant-Colonel 1st Georgia Cavalry. (1835-1863).
Harper, Alfred Yarborough, Lieutenant-Colonel 6th (also called 7th) Mississippi Infantry.
Harper, (**) George B., elected Lieutenant-Colonel 2d Missouri Cavalry (did not accept).
Harper, N. B., Major 13th Battalion Mississippi Infantry.
Harper, Robert W., Major, Colonel 1st Arkansas Mounted Rifles.
Harper, S. G., Lieutenant-Colonel 36th Mississippi Infantry.
Harper, W. B., Major 1st Battalion Mississippi Infantry (or Minute Men) State Troops.
Harrell, John Mortimer, Lieutenant-Colonel Harrell's Battalion Arkansas Cavalry. (b. 1831).
Harrell, William Virgil, Major Lewis' Battalion Alabama Cavalry.
Harrington, Pinkney C., Major, Lieutenant-Colonel 14th Confederate Cavalry.
Harris, Abraham, Lieutenant-Colonel 14th Texas Cavalry. (b. 1825).
Harris, Benjamin J., Major 47th Virginia Militia.
Harris, (**) H., Colonel 40th North Carolina Militia.
Harris, James L., Major 2d Mississippi Cavalry.
Harris, James Thomas, Major 15th (Cleburne's, also called 1st) Arkansas Infantry. (1836-1884).
Harris, John Gideon, Major 20th Alabama Infantry. (1834-1908).
Harris, John L., Major 3d Battalion Georgia Cavalry; Lieutenant-Colonel 4th (Clinch's) Georgia Cavalry.
Harris, John Lewis, Major, Lieutenant-Colonel 6th Tennessee Infantry. (1832-1892).
Harris, John Wyatte, Lieutenant-Colonel 16th Alabama Infantry. (1831-1899).
Harris, Joseph D., Lieutenant-Colonel 1st Chickasaw Cavalry Battalion.
Harris, Nicholas Cobbs, Lieutenant-Colonel Harris' Battalion Virginia Heavy Artillery. (1837-1898).
Harris, Simon, Major, Lieutenant-Colonel 10th (also called 12th) Missouri Infantry.
Harris, Thomas Walton, Major 2d (Harris') Battalion Mississippi State Cavalry; Lieutenant-Colonel Ashcraft's Regiment Mississippi Cavalry. (1825-1890).
Harrison, (**) D. S., Lieutenant-Colonel 99th Georgia Militia.
Harrison, George Paul, Jr., Colonel 32d Georgia Infantry. (1841-1922).
Harrison, Isaac F., Major Wirt Adams' Mississippi Cavalry; Major, Lieutenant-Colonel 15th Battalion Louisiana Cavalry; Colonel 3d (Harrison's) Louisiana Cavalry. (b. 1818).
Harrison, James, Lieutenant-Colonel 2d Infantry Regiment Virginia State Line.
Harrison, James Edward, Lieutenant-Colonel, Colonel 15th Texas Infantry; Major 1st (Speight's) Battalion Texas Infantry. (1815-1875).
Harrison, Richard, Major, Lieutenant-Colonel, Colonel 43d Mississippi Infantry. (1821-1876).
Harrison, Robert D., Major 2d Florida Cavalry. (1842-1916).
Harrison, Thomas, Major, Lieutenant-Colonel, Colonel 8th Texas Cavalry. (1823-1891).
Harrison, William, Colonel 6th Louisiana Cavalry. (b. 1829).
Harrison, William M., Major 9th (Maxey's, also called 8th) Texas Infantry.
Harriss, (**) Robert Y., Colonel 9th Georgia State Troops.
Harrod, John, Major, Lieutenant-Colonel 33d (Hurst's) Mississippi Infantry.
Hart, Benjamin R., Major, Lieutenant-Colonel, Colonel 22d Alabama Infantry. (d. 1864).
Hart, John R., Colonel 6th Georgia Cavalry; Lieutenant-Colonel Cavalry Battalion, Smith's Georgia Legion. (d. 1886).
Hart, Robert A., Colonel 30th (Hart's) Arkansas Infantry; Lieutenant-Colonel 30th (McNeill's) Arkansas Infantry.

Hartley, Henry K., Lieutenant-Colonel 4th Missouri Cavalry, 8th Division, Missouri State Guard.
Hartley, Thomas J., Major 4th Missouri Cavalry, 8th Division, Missouri State Guard.
Hartridge, Alfred L., Major 27th Battalion Georgia Infantry.
Hartwell, William, Major 1st Mobile Volunteers, Local Defense Troops.
Harvey, Reuben F., Major, Lieutenant-Colonel 2d Arkansas Infantry.
Harwood, (**) Thomas M., Major Cavalry Battalion Ward's Texas Legion.
Hash, John J., Major 1st Missouri Infantry Battalion, 5th Division, Missouri State Guard.
Haskell, Alexander McDonald, Major 6th Texas Infantry.
Haskins, David Calvin, Major, Lieutenant-Colonel 3d Tennessee Infantry (Provincial Army). (1821-1888).
Hatch, Lemuel Durant, Major, Lieutenant-Colonel, Colonel 8th (Hatch's, also called 9th) Alabama Cavalry. (1841-1905).
Hathaway, Joseph F., Major 36th Arkansas Infantry.
Haven, William Stuart, Major 20th Arkansas Infantry. (d. 1911).
Hawes, James Morrison, Colonel 2d Kentucky Infantry. (1824-1889).
Hawes, Richard, Major 5th Kentucky Infantry. (1797-1877).
Hawkins, A. T., Major 15th Battalion Mississippi Sharpshooters. (d. 1863).
Hawkins, B. W., Lieutenant-Colonel Hawkins' Missouri Cavalry Regiment, 2d Division, Missouri State Guard.
Hawkins, Edwin R., Lieutenant-Colonel, Colonel 27th Texas Cavalry (1st Texas Legion). (b. 1831).
Hawkins, Hiram, Lieutenant-Colonel, Colonel 5th Kentucky Infantry. (b. 1826).
Hawkins, James Marion, Major Nashville Battalion Infantry.
Hawkins, Pink., Lieutenant-Colonel 2d Creek Regiment.
Hawkins, William Stewart, Major 11th Battalion Tennessee Cavalry. (1837-1865).
Hawpe, Trezevant C., Colonel 31st Texas Cavalry. (1820-1863).
Hawthorne, Alexander Travis, Lieutenant-Colonel, Colonel 6th Arkansas Infantry; Colonel Hawthorne's Arkansas Infantry. (1825-1899).
Haynes, Milton A., Lieutenant-Colonel Tennessee Artillery Corps; Lieutenant-Colonel 1st Tennessee Light Artillery. (1814-1867).
Haynes, Peril C., Lieutenant-Colonel 4th (Starnes', also called 3d) Tennessee Cavalry.
Haynes, Robert P., Major 166th Virginia Militia.
Hays, Abram B., Major 1st Chickasaw Cavalry Regiment.
Hays, Andrew Jackson, Lieutenant-Colonel 27th Mississippi Infantry. (d. 1896).
Hays, Jesse L., Lieutenant-Colonel 31st Arkansas Infantry.
Hays, Thomas Hercules, Major 6th Kentucky Infantry; Major 1st (Cofer's) Battalion Kentucky Infantry. (1837-1909).
Hays, Upton, Colonel Jackson County (after 12th) Missouri Cavalry; Lieutenant-Colonel 1st Missouri Cavalry, 8th Division, Missouri State Guard. (1832-1863).
Head, John W., Colonel 30th Tennessee Infantry. (1822-1878).
Heard, (**) Benjamin W., Brigadier General Georgia Militia. (1821-1893).
Heard, S. S., Colonel 17th Louisiana Infantry.
Hearin, William Jefferson, Major, Lieutenant-Colonel 38th Alabama Infantry. (1823-1898).
Hearn, John Foster, Major 15th Tennessee Infantry.
Hearn, William C., Lieutenant-Colonel 41st Mississippi Infantry.
Heath, A. J., Colonel 41st North Carolina Militia.
Hébert, Louis, Colonel 3d Louisiana Infantry. (1820-1901).
Hébert, Paul Octave, Colonel 1st Louisiana Artillery. (1818-1880).
Hedgpeth, Isaac N., Lieutenant-Colonel, Colonel 6th Missouri Infantry; Lieutenant-Colonel 3d Missouri Infantry, 1st Division, Missouri State Guard; Major Hedgpeth's Battalion Missouri Infantry.
Hedrick, John J., Colonel 40th North Carolina Volunteers (3d North Carolina Artillery).
Heilig, (**) Lawson Gilbert, Major 84th North Carolina Militia. (1831-1889).
Heiman, Adolphus, Colonel 10th Tennessee Infantry. (1816-1862).

Heiskell, Carrick White, Major, Lieutenant-Colonel, Colonel 19th Tennessee Infantry. (1836-1923).
Helm, Benjamin Hardin, Colonel 1st Kentucky Cavalry. (1831-1863).
Helvenston, Alexander H., Major, Lieutenant-Colonel, Colonel 16th Alabama Infantry.
Hemphill, J. W., Lieutenant-Colonel 15th Mississippi Infantry.
Henderson, Charles C., Lieutenant-Colonel, Colonel 40th Tennessee Infantry; Lieutenant-Colonel, Colonel 5th (Walker's) Confederate Infantry Regiment.
Henderson, John T., Colonel 8th Infantry Georgia State Guard.
Henderson, Marzarine J., Major, Lieutenant-Colonel 3d Arkansas Cavalry.
Henderson, Robert Johnson, Colonel 42d Georgia Infantry. (1822-1894).
Henderson, William N., Colonel 190th Virginia Militia.
Hendon, William Thomas, Major 6th (also called 7th) Mississippi Infantry. (d. 1917).
Hendrick, Henry, Major 30th Georgia Infantry. (1821-1887).
Hendricks, Sterling B., Lieutenant-Colonel 17th Texas Cavalry.
Henagan, Charles S., Major 36th Alabama Infantry.
Henry, George F., Colonel 79th Virginia Militia.
Henry, James L., Lieutenant-Colonel 14th Battalion North Carolina Cavalry.
Henry, John F., Major 4th Tennessee Volunteers. (1837-1862).
Henry, Patrick, Major 28th Texas Cavalry.
Henry, R. R., Major 38th Arkansas Infantry.
Henry, Robert William, Major 8th Kentucky Infantry. (d. 1862).
Henry's Battalion Tennessee Infantry, Series 1, Vol. VII.
Henshaw, (**) Thomas, Major 3d Virginia Militia.
Henson, (**) Bartlett A., Colonel 40th Virginia Militia. (1817-1882).
Herbert, Philemon Thomas, Lieutenant-Colonel 7th Texas Cavalry; Lieutenant-Colonel of Herbert's Texas Battalion, Arizona Brigade. (1825-1864).
Herndon, DeWitt Clinton, Major 1st Battalion Mississippi Cavalry.
Herndon, Thomas Hord, Major, Lieutenant-Colonel, Colonel 36th Alabama Infantry. (1828-1883).
Herr, B. F., Major 1st Missouri Infantry Battalion, 1st Division, Missouri State Guard.
Herrell, Jesse P., Major, Lieutenant-Colonel 7th (Jackman's, afterward 16th) Missouri Infantry.
Herrick, Charles H., Colonel 22d (formerly 23d) Louisiana Infantry. (d. 1863).
Herring, John Bannister, Major, Lieutenant-Colonel 5th Mississippi Infantry.
Hester, James T., Major 23d Alabama Infantry.
Hester, (**) Nathaniel, Lieutenant-Colonel .... Georgia Militia.
Hewitt, James W., Major, Lieutenant-Colonel 2d Kentucky Infantry. (1827-1863).
Hewitt, Robert A., Lieutenant-Colonel 2d Missouri Infantry, 4th Division, Missouri State Guard.
Hewlett, William A., Lieutenant-Colonel 56th Alabama Partisan Rangers; Major 13th Alabama Partisan Rangers.
Hicks, J. M., Major 9th Mississippi Infantry.
Hicks, William, Lieutenant-Colonel 32d Arkansas Infantry.
Higgins, Edward, Lieutenant-Colonel, Colonel 21st (Patton's) Louisiana Infantry. (1821-1875).
Higgins, Hiram Harrison, Major 40th Tennessee Infantry; Major 5th (Walker's) Confederate Infantry.
Higley, John H., Lieutenant-Colonel, Colonel 40th Alabama Infantry; Colonel 2d Alabama Militia.
Hill, (**) ...., Colonel Hill's Regiment Arkansas Militia.
Hill, Andrew A., Major Hill's Battalion North Carolina Reserves.
Hill, Benjamin, Lieutenant-Colonel Cherokee Legion, Georgia State Guard.
Hill, Benjamin Jefferson, Colonel 35th (formerly 5th Tennessee, Provincial Army) Tennessee Infantry. (1825-1880).
Hill, Charles Henry, Major 6th Battalion Tennessee Cavalry.
Hill, D. F., Major 24th South Carolina Infantry.
Hill, J. M., Colonel 9th Regiment, 3d Brigade Georgia State Troops Militia.
Hill, James D., Major Orleans (Louisiana) Fire Regiment.

Hill, John A., Major 7th Arkansas Infantry.
Hill, John F., Colonel 16th Arkansas Infantry; Colonel 7th Arkansas Cavalry. (b. 1822).
Hill, (**) John J., Lieutenant-Colonel 172nd Virginia Militia.
Hill, John W., Major 8th (Mitchell's) Missouri Infantry.
Hill, Munson R., Colonel 47th Tennessee Infantry. (1821-1867).
Hill, ..., Major 4th (Peel's) Arkansas Infantry.
Hilliard, Henry Washington, Colonel Hilliard's Alabama Legion. (1808-1892).
Hillsman, John Hines, Major 55th Tennessee Infantry. (1821-1892).
Hinchman, (**) John, Major 166th Virginia Militia.
Hindman, Thomas Carmichael, Colonel 2d Arkansas Infantry. (1828-1868).
Hinsdale, John Wetmore, Colonel 3d Regiment North Carolina Junior Reserves. 1843-1921).
Hoadley, Frederick W., Major 1st Tennessee Heavy Artillery. (d. 1863).
Hobbs, James H., Lieutenant-Colonel, Colonel 15th (McRae's) Arkansas Infantry; Colonel 15th (Hobbs') Arkansas Infantry.
Hobbs, (**) R. W., Colonel 62d Virginia Militia.
Hobby, Alfred Marmaduke, Colonel 8th (Hobby's) Texas Infantry; Major 8th Battalion Texas Infantry. (1836-1881).
Hobson, Anson W., Lieutenant-Colonel, Colonel, 3d Arkansas Cavalry. (c. 1824-1882).
Hobson, Joseph A., Lieutenant-Colonel Henry's Regiment Virginia Reserves.
Hodge, Benjamin L., Colonel 19th Louisiana Infantry.
Hodges, Lafayette, Major, Lieutenant-Colonel 41st Mississippi Infantry. (1831-1864).
Hodges, W. Ludlow, Lieutenant-Colonel 1st South Carolina State Troops (6 months).
Hodgson, Joseph, Colonel 7th Alabama Cavalry. (1838-1913).
Hoffman, Gustave, Major 7th Texas Cavalry. (1817-1889).
Holcombe, Edward Paddleford, Lieutenant-Colonel 17th Alabama Infantry. (1833-1880).
Holden, William Boye, Major, Lieutenant-Colonel, Colonel 53d Tennessee Infantry.
Holladay, John B., Major 3d Battalion Kentucky Mounted Rifles.
Holland, Daniel P., Lieutenant-Colonel 1st Special Battalion Florida Infantry.
Holland, D. D., Lieutenant-Colonel 1st Battalion Cavalry Texas State Troops.
Holland, Orlando S., Lieutenant-Colonel, Colonel 37th Mississippi Infantry.
Holland, William A., Major 40th North Carolina Volunteers (3d North Carolina Artillery).
Holland, Washington Thomas, Major 32d Georgia Infantry.
Holliday, Jesse Gray, Major 15th North Carolina Cavalry Battalion. (1830-1874).
Hollingsworth, James M., Lieutenant-Colonel 19th Louisiana Infantry.
Holloway, Edmond B., Colonel 1st Missouri Infantry, 8th Division, Missouri State Guard.
Holman, Cyrus Kirkham, Major 27th Texas Cavalry (1st Texas Legion). (b. 1819).
Holman, John B., Major 28th and 84th Tennessee Infantry Consolidated.
Holmes, Benjamin, Lieutenant-Colonel 12th Missouri Infantry; Major 9th (White's, also called 12th) Missouri Infantry.
Holmes, Benjamin R., Major 1st Mississippi Artillery.
Holmes, John M., Lieutenant-Colonel 45th Virginia Militia. (b. c. 1818).
Holmes, Stokely M., Major 36th (Woods', also called 32d) Texas Cavalry.
Holmes, Thomas F., Major 35th Mississippi Infantry.
Holmes, W. E., Lieutenant-Colonel 47th Tennessee Infantry.
Holsey, (**) Julius H., Major Holsey's Battalion, Georgia S. G. (Geneva Squadron).
Holt, Gustavus A. C., Lieutenant-Colonel 3d Kentucky Infantry. (1840-1910).
Holt, John Hackett, Major, Lieutenant-Colonel 1st Battalion, Hilliard's Alabama Legion.
Holtzclaw, James Thadeus, Major, Lieutenant-Colonel, Colonel 18th Al[illegible] Infantry. (1833-1893).

Hood, Arthur, Lieutenant-Colonel 29th Battalion Georgia Cavalry; Lieutenant-Colonel 2d Georgia Cavalry. (1827-1886).
Hooks, Boaz F., Major 3d Battalion North Carolina Senior Reserves; Major 8th Regiment North Carolina Reserves.
Hooks, Robert Warren, Lieutenant-Colonel 11th Texas Cavalry. (1838-1868).
Hooper, James C., Lieutenant-Colonel, Colonel 6th (after 11th) Missouri Cavalry; Lieutenant-Colonel 11th Missouri Cavalry.
Hopkins, Edward D., Colonel 4th Florida Infantry. (1810-1887).
Hopkins, (**) Wade, Major 1st Regiment Army of 10,000, Mississippi.
Horn, Daniel Hilliard, Lieutenant-Colonel 33d Alabama Infantry. (1822-1912).
Horn, Oliver P., Major 4th Virginia Militia, 7th Brigade.
Hoskins, ..., Lieutenant-Colonel Major's Missouri Cavalry Regiment, 3d Division, Missouri State Guard.
Hottel, J. A., Lieutenant-Colonel 3d Virginia Militia, 7th Brigade, or 136th Virginia Militia.
Hough, Wade H., Lieutenant-Colonel 12th Louisiana Infantry.
House, John L., Major, Lieutenant-Colonel 1st Tennessee Volunteers; Lieutenant-Colonel 1st and 27th Tennessee Consolidated.
Housand, C. B., Major Extra Battalion Missouri Infantry, 4th Division, Missouri State Guard.
Hovis, Lawson Berry, Lieutenant-Colonel 7th (also called 1st Mississippi Partisan Rangers) Mississippi Cavalry. (1826-1864).
Howard, James Ross, Colonel 3d Confederate Cavalry (also called 11th); Lieutenant-Colonel 11th Battalion Alabama Cavalry. (1822-1892).
Howard, Joseph David, Major 48th (Voorhies') Tennessee Infantry. (1830-1912).
Howard, (**) P. C., Colonel 117th Virginia Militia.
Howard, Thacker Brock, Jr., Major Howard's (also called 27th) Battalion Georgia Infantry.
Howell, Albert, Lieutenant-Colonel 1st Georgia State Line. (d. 1927).
Howell, E. A., Major, Lieutenant-Colonel 5th Arkansas Infantry; Major 5th and 13th Arkansas Infantry Consolidated; Major 13th Arkansas Infantry.
Howland, E. J., Major 1st Cherokee Mounted Rifles.
Hoxey, Thomas R., Major of Bradford's Regiment Texas Cavalry. (d. 1864).
Hubbard, Josiah R., Major 42d Tennessee Infantry.
Hubbard, Richard Bennett, Lieutenant-Colonel 5th (Hubbard's) Battalion Texas Infantry; Colonel 22d Texas Infantry. (1832-1901).
Hubbell, Finley L., Major, Lieutenant-Colonel 3d (also called 2d) Missouri Infantry. (1830-1863).
Hudson, Samuel H., Major 31st (A. H. Bradford's) Tennessee Infantry.
Huey, (**) James K., Commanding Kentucky Battalion.
Huff, (**) Isaac B., Colonel 12th Georgia Militia.
Huff, James Thomas, Major 60th North Carolina Infantry. (1839-1919).
Huffman, J. M., Lieutenant-Colonel 7th Kentucky Cavalry.
Hufstedler, Eli, Lieutenant-Colonel 25th (also called 30th) Arkansas Infantry. (1830-1864).
Huger, Daniel Elliott, Colonel 1st Alabama Reserves; Major 25th Alabama Infantry (temporarily commanding); Lieutenant-Colonel Thomas' Regiment Alabama Cavalry. (b. 1836).
Hughes, Adolphus Alexander, Colonel 27th Alabama Infantry. (1818-1877).
Hughes, Daniel G., Major 22d Infantry Battalion Georgia State Guard.
Hughes, (**) Edward, Lieutenant-Colonel 117th Virginia Militia.
Hughes, Harry H., Major 9th (Clark's) Missouri Infantry.
Hughes, John T., Colonel 1st Missouri Infantry, 4th Division Missouri State Guard. (k. 1863).
Hughes, Simon P., Lieutenant-Colonel 23d (Adams') Arkansas Infantry. (1830-1906).
Hughs, Thomas R., Lieutenant-Colonel 48th (Nixon's) Tennessee Infantry; Lieutenant-Colonel 20th (Nixon's) Tennessee Cavalry.
Huguenin, Thomas Abraham, Major 3d South Carolina Artillery (1st South Carolina Regulars). (1839-1897).
Hull, Edward B., Lieutenant-Colonel 2d (Burbridge's, also called 1st) Missouri

Infantry; Lieutenant-Colonel Burbridge's Cavalry Regiment, 2d Division, Missouri State Guard.
Hull, George W., Colonel 162d Virginia Militia. (d. 1862).
Hull, Robert Newton, Major 66th (also called 65th) Georgia Infantry. (d. 1865).
Hulme, Isaac Newton, Lieutenant-Colonel, Colonel 42d Tennessee Infantry. (1826-1873).
Hulsey, William Henry, Major, Lieutenant-Colonel 42d Georgia Infantry. (b. 1838).
Humble, Thomas C., Major 31st Louisiana Infantry.
Humes, James White, Lieutenant-Colonel 31st (W. M. Bradford's, after 39th) Tennessee Infantry. (d. 1871).
Humphreys, (**) Frederick Clifton, Major .... Georgia Militia.
Hundley, Daniel Robinson, Colonel 31st (Hundley's) Alabama Infantry. (1832-1899).
Hundley, William B., Major 5th Georgia Infantry.
Hundley, William H., Major, Lieutenant-Colonel 12th Battalion Alabama Partisan Rangers; Lieutenant-Colonel 1st Alabama Cavalry.
Hunley, Peter Forney, Major, Lieutenant-Colonel 18th Alabama Infantry. (1829-1882).
Hunsucker, (**) James, Major 194th Virginia Militia.
Hunt, Archibald Anderson, Colonel 2d Georgia Partisan Rangers, formerly 1st Battalion Partisan Rangers.
Hunt, Benjamin Franklin, Major 8th Battalion Georgia Infantry.
Hunt, Edward F., Major 37th (formerly 7th Tennessee Provisional Army) Tennessee Infantry.
Hunt, George B., Major 13th Arkansas Infantry.
Hunt, James P., Colonel 4th Florida Infantry. (d. 1862).
Hunt, John W., Colonel 44th North Carolina Militia.
Hunt, Thomas Hart, Colonel 9th Kentucky Infantry. (1815-1884).
Hunt, (**) ...., Lieutenant Colonel 1st Regiment L. D. Troops, Augusta, Virginia.
Hunter, Bushrod Washington, Major of Artillery. (1807-1888).
Hunter, De Witt C., Colonel 2d (Hunter's, afterward 8th) Missouri Infantry; Colonel Hunter's Missouri Cavalry, 1864; Colonel 7th Missouri Cavalry, 8th Division Missouri, State Guard.
Hunter, Fountain Winston, Colonel 2d Alabama Cavalry. (1819-1887).
Hunter, Jason H., Major 2d Missouri Cavalry Battalion, 1st Division, Missouri State Guard; Lieutenant-Colonel 4th Missouri Infantry, 1st Division, Missouri State Guard.
Hunter, Samuel E., Major, Lieutenant-Colonel, Colonel 4th Louisiana Infantry.
Hunter, Sherod, Major 2d Texas Cavalry Regiment, Arizona Brigade.
Hunter, William LeGrand, Colonel 1st Chickasaw Cavalry Regiment (rejected). (1847-1937).
Hurst, David Wiley, Colonel 33d (Hurst's) Mississippi Infantry.
Hurst, Edgar V., Colonel 3d Missouri Infantry, 8th Division, Missouri State Guard.
Hurt, Charles Stuart, Lieutenant-Colonel, Colonel 9th Tennessee Infantry; Colonel 6th and 9th Tennessee Consolidated. (1836-1886).
Hutcheson, John B., Lieutenant-Colonel 2d (Morgan's) Kentucky Cavalry. (d. 1863).
Hutchison, Augustus Simpson, Lieutenant-Colonel, Colonel 19th (Dawson's) Arkansas Infantry (commanding 19th and 24th, temporarily attached). (1837-1912).
Hutchison, William Oscar, Major, Lieutenant-Colonel 36th (Woods', also called 32d) Texas Cavalry.
Hutson, William F., Lieutenant-Colonel 11th South Carolina Reserves.
Hutt, (**) J. Warren, Colonel 111th Virginia Militia. (1827-1907).
Hutto, John C., Major 50th (also known as 26th, Coltart's) Alabama Infantry.
Hyams, Samuel M., Jr., Colonel 7th (also called 1st Mississippi Partisan Rangers) Mississippi Cavalry (temporary command); Lieutenant-Colonel 2d Missouri Cavalry.

Hyams, (°°) Samuel Myers, Sr., Lieutenant-Colonel 3d Louisiana Infantry. (1840-1882).
Hyatt, Arthur W., Lieutenant-Colonel Crescent Regiment Louisiana Infantry; Lieutenant-Colonel Confederate Guard Response Battalion Louisiana.
Hyde, ..., Lieutenant-Colonel 3d Missouri Infantry, 3d Division, Missouri State Guard.
Hydrick, (°°) J. H., Major, 15th South Carolina Militia.
Hynes, Andrew R., Lieutenant-Colonel 4th Kentucky Infantry.
Inge, Richard Freer, Lieutenant-Colonel 18th Alabama Infantry. (1830-1863).
Inge, William Murphy, Major 12th Battalion Mississippi Partisan Rangers; Colonel 10th (also known as 12th) Mississippi Cavalry. (1832-1900).
Inger, (°°) John W., Major, 5/9 Battalion Alabama Infantry.
Ingersoll, Andrew J., Lieutenant-Colonel 21st Alabama Infantry.
Ingram, Augustus John, Major 12th Alabama Cavalry. (c. 1829-1901).
Ingram, Tillman, Major, Lieutenant-Colonel 7th Florida Infantry.
Inzer, John Washington, Lieutenant-Colonel 58th Alabama Infantry. (1834-1928).
Ireland, John, Major, Lieutenant-Colonel 8th (Hobby's) Texas Infantry. (1827-1896).
Irvine, J. S., Major 11th Battalion Texas Cavalry and Infantry.
Irwin, Thomas Kilshaw, Major 3d Alabama Militia. (1835-1911).
Isom, Newton A., Major 29th Mississippi Infantry.
Ison, Francis M., Major, Lieutenant-Colonel 2d Georgia Cavalry.
Iverson, John F., Lieutenant-Colonel 5th Georgia Infantry. (d. 1887).
Ives, Samuel Spencer, Major, Lieutenant-Colonel, Colonel 35th Alabama Infantry (b. 1835).
Ivor, W. B., Major, Lieutenant-Colonel 16th South Carolina Infantry.
Ivy, Edward, Major, Lieutenant-Colonel 21st (Patton's) Louisiana Infantry.
Jackman, Sidney D., Colonel 7th (Jackman's, afterward 16th) Missouri Infantry Colonel .... Regiment Missouri Cavalry. (c. 1825-1886).
Jackson, Andrew, Jr., Colonel 1st Tennessee Heavy Artillery. (1834-1906).
Jackson, Congreve, Colonel 2d Missouri Infantry, 3d Division, Missouri State Guard.
Jackson, James, Lieutenant-Colonel, Colonel 27th Alabama Infantry. (1822-1879)
Jackson, J. F. B., Lieutenant-Colonel 39th Georgia Infantry. (b. 1832).
Jackson, John King, Colonel 5th Georgia Infantry. (1828-1866).
Jackson, John M., Major 34th Georgia Infantry. (d. 1864).
Jackson, Thomas E., Colonel Virginia State Line Artillery.
Jackson, William Hicks, Colonel 1st (Jackson's, afterward 7th) Tennessee Cavalry (1835-1903).
Jacoway, John A., Lieutenant-Colonel 31st Arkansas Infantry.
Jamison, Thomas E., Major 48th (Voorhies') Tennessee Infantry. (1835-1914).
Jaques, J., Major Jaques' Battalion Mississippi (?) Infantry (found in Ector's Brigade, Return Army of Tennessee, July 31, 1864).
Jaques, Samuel R., Major 1st City Battalion, Columbus, Georgia.
Jaquess, John A., Major, Lieutenant-Colonel, Colonel 1st Louisiana Regulars.
Jarmon, William R., Major 8th Texas Cavalry.
Jarnigan, Rufus A., Major 19th Tennessee Infantry. (k. 1862).
Jarrett, J. M., Colonel 109th North Carolina Militia.
Jeans, Beal Green, Lieutenant-Colonel, Colonel Jackson County (after 12th) Missouri Cavalry.
Jeffers, William L., Colonel 8th Missouri Cavalry; Lieutenant-Colonel 2nd Missouri Cavalry, 1st Division, Missouri State Guard.
Jenkins, John, Major 3d South Carolina Cavalry. (1824-1905).
Jenkins, Thomas Farewell, Major 53d Alabama Partisan Rangers. (b. 1827).
Jennings, D. L., Major 2d Missouri Infantry Battalion, 1st Division, Missouri State Guard.
Jessee, George M., Lieutenant-Colonel 6th Confederate Battalion Cavalry; Major Jessee's Battalion Kentucky Mounted Rifles. (b. 1818).
Jett, Benjamin P., Major 17th (Rector's) Arkansas Infantry; Major Rector Arkansas Regiment (12 months).
Jett, William G., Lieutenant-Colonel 5th Infantry Texas State Troops.

Jewett, Origen Sibley, Major 38th Alabama Infantry. (1820-1863).
Jinkins, Mansfield D., Lieutenant-Colonel 31st (A. H. Bradford's) Tennessee Infantry.
Johns, Benjamin F., Major, Lieutenant-Colonel 7th Mississippi Infantry.
Johns, William M. R., Lieutenant-Colonel 6th Tennessee Infantry.
Johnson, Abda, Colonel 40th Georgia Infantry. (1826-1881).
Johnson, Adam Rankin, Colonel 10th (Johnson's) Kentucky Partisan Rangers. (1834-1922).
Johnson, Augustus H., Major 1st Alabama Cavalry.
Johnson, Alfred W., Colonel Johnson's Regiment Arkansas Infantry.
Johnson, B. C., Major 31st (Hale's) Alabama Infantry.
Johnson, Benjamin Whitfield, Colonel 15th (Johnson's) Arkansas Infantry. (b. 1825).
Johnson, B. G., Lieutenant-Colonel Johnson's Arkansas Infantry Battalion.
Johnson, Henry Poston, Colonel 20th Arkansas Infantry. (1826-1862).
Johnson, Hiram H., Major 3d Georgia Cavalry.
Johnson, James A. W., Colonel 34th Georgia Infantry; Colonel 10th Georgia State Troops.
Johnson, James B., Lieutenant-Colonel 3d Confederate Infantry; Major 1st Battalion Arkansas Infantry.
Johnson, James F., Lieutenant-Colonel 31st Arkansas Infantry.
Johnson, James M., Major, Lieutenant-Colonel 30th Mississippi Infantry.
Johnson, James Matthew, Major 44th Tennessee Infantry. (1817-1885).
Johnson, J. B., Colonel 4th Cavalry Texas State Troops.
Johnson, Jeptha C., Lieutenant-Colonel 37th (Bell's) Arkansas Infantry.
Johnson, John B., Major, Lieutenant-Colonel 29th Tennessee Infantry. (d. 1864).
Johnson, John H., Colonel 46th Virginia Militia.
Johnson, (**) John J., Colonel 12th Virginia Militia.
Johnson, John R., Major 20th Texas Cavalry.
Johnson, John William, Lieutenant-Colonel 46th Tennessee Infantry. (1827-1866).
Johnson, Joseph A., Lieutenant-Colonel 2d Mississippi State Cavalry.
Johnson, Middleton Tait, Colonel 14th Texas Cavalry. (1810-1866).
Johnson, R. P., Lieutenant-Colonel 62d Arkansas Militia.
Johnson, Richard W., Major 4th (Roddey's) Alabama Cavalry. (d. 1864).
Johnson, Thomas, Major, Lieutenant-Colonel 2d Battalion Kentucky Mounted Rifles. (1812-1906).
Johnson, Thomas Hewlett, Lieutenant-Colonel 3d South Carolina Cavalry; Major 8th (also called 2d) Battalion South Carolina Cavalry. (b. 1825).
Johnson, (**) W. G., Major Johnson's Battalion Georgia S. G.
Johnson, Waldo Porter, Major 1st Battalion Missouri Infantry; Lieutenant-Colonel 4th Missouri Infantry. (1817-1885).
Johnson, William Arthur, Major, Lieutenant-Colonel, Colonel 4th (Roddey's) Alabama Cavalry. (1828-1891).
Johnson, William B., Lieutenant-Colonel 33d (Hurst's) Mississippi Infantry.
Johnson, William H., Lieutenant-Colonel 22d Texas Cavalry (also called 1st Indian Texas Cavalry).
Johnson, W. W., Colonel Johnson's Special Battalion, Louisiana.
Johnson, ..., Colonel 3d Regiment, 1st Brigade, Georgia State Troops.
Johnston, Alfred, Major, Lieutenant-Colonel 3d Kentucky Infantry.
Johnston, Charles B., Major 21st Alabama Infantry.
Johnston, George Doherty, Major, Lieutenant-Colonel, Colonel 25th Alabama Infantry. (1832-1910).
Johnston, J. A., Lieutenant-Colonel Carroll's Regiment Arkansas Cavalry.
Johnston, Miles Eddings, Lieutenant-Colonel 25th Battalion Alabama Cavalry. (1823-1915).
Johnston, Robert A., Lieutenant-Colonel, Colonel 2d Kentucky Infantry; Lieutenant-Colonel 9th (also called 5th, Hunt's) Kentucky Infantry.
Johnston, Samuel, Colonel 89th Virginia Militia.
Johnston, Thomas Henry, Major, Colonel 1st Mississippi Infantry. (b. 1836).
Johnston, William Preston, Lieutenant-Colonel 1st Kentucky Infantry; Major 3d Kentucky Infantry; Major 2d Kentucky Infantry. (1831-1899).

Jones, Abraham, Major, Lieutenant-Colonel 19th South Carolina Infantry.
Jones, Andrew F., Colonel 1st Missouri Cavalry, 1st Division, Missouri State Guard.
Jones, Andrew J., Major, Lieutenant-Colonel 27th Mississippi Infantry. (d. 1864).
Jones, Bart., Lieutenant-Colonel 8th (also designated as 1st) Battalion Arkansas Infantry.
Jones, Bushrod, Lieutenant-Colonel 9th (also called 5th) Battalion Alabama Infantry; Colonel 58th Alabama Infantry. (1836-1872).
Jones, Charles, Lieutenant-Colonel 17th Louisiana Infantry.
Jones, Charles Melton, Lieutenant-Colonel 2d Georgia Reserves. (1829-1910).
Jones, Daniel Webster, Major, Colonel 20th Arkansas Infantry. (1839-1918).
Jones, Dudley William, Lieutenant-Colonel, Colonel 9th Texas Cavalry. (1842-1868).
Jones, Edward P., Major, Lieutenant-Colonel 28th Mississippi Cavalry.
Jones, Elliotte Pope, Colonel 109th Virginia Militia. (d. 1864).
Jones, Edwin Thomas, Lieutenant-Colonel 15th Battalion Cavalry Georgia State Guard.
Jones, George W., Major 3d Tennessee Volunteers.
Jones, George Washington, Lieutenant-Colonel, Colonel 17th Texas Infantry. (1828-1903).
Jones, James F., Colonel 1st Virginia Infantry Local Defense Troops. (1821-1866).
Jones, James Henry, Lieutenant-Colonel, Colonel 11th Texas Infantry. (1830-1904).
Jones, Jesse Stancel, Major, Lieutenant-Colonel 24th South Carolina Infantry. (1833-1864).
Jones, John Elliott, Major 14th Battalion Infantry Georgia State Guard. (1839-1900).
Jones, John W., Major 6th (Balfour's) Battalion Mississippi Infantry.
Jones, Joseph H., Major 55th Alabama Infantry. (d. 1864).
Jones, J. P., Colonel 17th Alabama Infantry (signs as J. Jones, temporary appointment).
Jones, Malcolm D., Major 9th Georgia Cavalry.
Jones, O. R., Lieutenant-Colonel 109th North Carolina Militia.
Jones, Richard W., Lieutenant-Colonel 1st Infantry Georgia State Guard.
Jones, Robert B., Major 17th Louisiana Infantry.
Jones, Samuel, Major, Lieutenant-Colonel 22d (formerly 23d) Louisiana Infantry.
Jones, Samuel Barksdale, Colonel, 6th South Carolina Militia. (1828-1894).
Jones, Samuel H., Lieutenant-Colonel 2d Battalion Tennessee Cavalry.
Jones, Theodore Allan, Major 33d (Hardcastle's) Mississippi Infantry. (1832-1872).
Jones, Thomas M., Colonel 27th Mississippi Infantry. (c. 1832-1913).
Jones, Thomas P., Major 64th North Carolina Infantry.
Jones, (**) Thomas T., Colonel 110th Virginia Militia.
Jones, Tignal W., Colonel 1st Texas Cavalry State Troops. (b. 1820).
Jones, Timothy Pickering, Lieutenant-Colonel 6th Tennessee Infantry. (1814-1904).
Jones, Warner P., Lieutenant-Colonel, Colonel 33d Tennessee Infantry.
Jones, William A., Lieutenant-Colonel 55th Tennessee Infantry (formerly Jones' Battalion).
Jones, William E., Major 9th Kentucky Cavalry.
Jones, Willis J., Major 1st Choctaw and Chickasaw Mounted Rifles.
Jordan, Charles R., Lieutenant-Colonel 35th Mississippi Infantry.
Jordan, E. C., Lieutenant-Colonel 12th Arkansas Infantry.
Jordan, Powhatan, Maj., Lieutenant-Colonel 7th Texas Cavalry. (1827-1906).
Josey, John E., Major, Lieutenant-Colonel, Colonel 15th (Polk's) Arkansas Infantry.
Joyner, William H., Major 18th Tennessee Infantry. (1833-1897).
Julian, William Reese, Lieutenant-Colonel Julian's Alabama Cavalry Battalion.
Jumper, John, Lieutenant-Colonel 1st Seminole Cavalry Battalion.

Kalfus, Columbus C., Major 1st Missouri Cavalry, 1st Division, Missouri State Guard.
Kamey, Sanford J., Colonel 57th Virginia Militia.
Kampmann, John H., Major 3d Texas Infantry.
Karr, F. C., Major 32d Mississippi Infantry. (d. 1863).
Keener, John C., Major, Lieutenant-Colonel 58th North Carolina Infantry.
Keep, Henry V., Major, Lieutenant-Colonel 3d Confederate Infantry.
Keirn, Walter Leake, Major, Lieutenant-Colonel 38th Mississippi Infantry. (d. 1901).
Keith, Bradford, Major 1st Missouri Infantry.
Keith, James A., Lieutenant-Colonel 64th North Carolina Infantry. (d. 1895).
Kellar, Andrew J., Lieutenant-Colonel, Colonel 4th Tennessee Infantry; Colonel 4th and 5th Tennessee Infantry Consolidated.
Kelley, David Campbell, Major, Lieutenant-Colonel, Colonel 3d (Forrest's) Tennessee Cavalry; Lieutenant-Colonel 26th Battalion Tennessee Cavalry. (1833-1909).
Kelley, W. R., Lieutenant-Colonel 20th Arkansas Infantry.
Kellogg, Henry Clay, Major, Lieutenant-Colonel, Colonel 43d Georgia Infantry. (1829-1889).
Kelly, J. H., Colonel 1st Louisiana Infantry.
Kelly, John Herbert, Colonel 8th Arkansas Infantry; Major 9th Battalion Arkansas Infantry; Major 14th (McCarver's) Regiment Arkansas Infantry; Colonel, temporarily commanding 44th Tennessee Infantry. (1840-1864).
Kelly, ..., Colonel Kelly's Missouri Infantry Regiment, 6th Division, Missouri State Guard.
Kelsey, Robert G., Major, Lieutenant-Colonel 44th Mississippi Infantry. (1832-1864).
Kelso, George W., Major 9th Tennessee Infantry.
Kenan, Daniel L. Major, Lieutenant-Colonel, Colonel 6th Florida Infantry.
Kendrick, Meredith, Major 37th Georgia Infantry. (d. 1864).
Kenedy, James B., Major 21st Battalion Infantry Georgia State Guard; Major Wright's Cavalry Regiment (also called 12th) Georgia State Guard.
Kennard, John R., Major 10th Texas Infantry.
Kennedy, Hyder A., Major, Lieutenant-Colonel 19th Louisiana Infantry.
Kennedy, John B. G., Lieutenant-Colonel 5th Battalion Louisiana Infantry; Lieutenant-Colonel, Colonel 21st (Kennedy's) Louisiana Infantry.
Kennedy, Julius B., Major 27th Mississippi Infantry. (d. 1864).
Kennon, Richard E., Lieutenant-Colonel, Colonel 3d Georgia Cavalry (1840-1894).
Kent, Frederick M., Major, Lieutenant-Colonel 1st Louisiana Regulars. (d. 1864).
Ketchum, Charles Thomas, Colonel 38th Alabama Infantry. (1815-1876).
Key, David McKendree, Lieutenant-Colonel 43d Tennessee Infantry (afterward mounted infantry). (1824-1900).
Key, Pierce Columbus, Lieutenant-Colonel 4th Cavalry Georgia State Guard. (k. 1864).
Kiddoo, John F., Major 5th Georgia Infantry.
Kilgore, Benjamin M., Major 3d Mississippi Cavalry State Troops; Major 4th Mississippi Infantry (or Minute Men) State Troops. (d. 1863).
Kilgore, Dawson L., Major 6th Arkansas Infantry; Lieutenant-Colonel 1st (Crawford's) Regiment Arkansas Cavalry. (b. 1822).
Kilpatrick, William H., Major 5th Battalion Mississippi Infantry.
Kimbell, John C., Major 32d Alabama Infantry.
Kimbrough, George R., Lieutenant-Colonel 19th Alabama Infantry.
King, A. D., Lieutenant-Colonel 10th Arkansas Militia.
King, Benjamin, Colonel 1st Mississippi Infantry (or Minute Men) State Troops. (1822-1884).
King, George W., Colonel 22d Regiment Arkansas Infantry.
King, Henry Clay, Major King's Battalion Kentucky Cavalry; Colonel 1st (also called 12th) Confederate Cavalry; Major 6th Confederate Cavalry. (d. 1903).
King, H. W., Major 14th Missouri Cavalry, 8th Division, Missouri State Guard.

King, James P., Major 1st (Rector's War Regiment) Arkansas Volunteers; Colonel 35th Arkansas Infantry.
King, James Roswell, Acting Major Roswell Battalion Cavalry, Georgia Local Defense. (1827-1897).
King, John B., Major 1st (Carter's) Tennessee Cavalry. (d. 1864).
King, (**) John E., Lieutenant-Colonel King's Special Battalion Louisiana Infantry.
King, Wilburn Hill, Major, Lieutenant-Colonel, Colonel 18th Texas Infantry. (1839-1910).
Kinsey, Benjamin F., Lieutenant-Colonel 34th Virginia Militia.
Kirby, Edmund, Lieutenant-Colonel 58th North Carolina Infantry. (d. 1863).
Kirby, Jared E., Major 3d Battalion Texas Infantry.
Kirk, Elijah P., Major 15th (Stewart's, also called 14th) Tennessee Cavalry.
Kirkpatrick, (**) J. D., Captain Commanding Kirkpatrick's Battalion Kentucky Cavalry.
Kirkpatrick, Milton L., Lieutenant-Colonel 51st Alabama Partisan Rangers.
Kirtley, Cave J., Lieutenant-Colonel 2d Missouri Infantry, 8th Division, Missouri State Guard.
Kirtley, George R., Major 5th Missouri Cavalry. (1824-1863).
Kitchen, Solomon G., Colonel 7th (also called 10th) Missouri Cavalry; Lieutenant-Colonel Kitchen's Battalion Missouri Infantry; Major, Lieutenant-Colonel 2d Missouri Cavalry, 1st Division, Missouri State Guard. (d. 1891).
Knight, John, Major 41st Georgia Infantry.
Knight, Levi J., Major 29th Georgia Infantry.
Knott, John C., Major 12th Louisiana Infantry.
Knox, Samuel Luckie, Major 1st Alabama Infantry. (1840-1864).
Kuhn, John Hendrix, Major, Lieutenant-Colonel 2nd (Ashby's) Tenn. Cavalry. (1818-1895).
Kyle, Osceola, Lieutenant-Colonel 46th Alabama Infantry. (1837-1888).
Labuzan, Augustin S., Major 3d Battalion Texas Artillery.
Lamar, Thomas G., Major 2d Battalion South Carolina Artillery; Colonel 2d South Carolina Artillery. (1826-1862).
Lamb, John C., Major 29th Georgia Infantry. (d. 1863).
Lamb, Jonathan J., Major, Colonel 5th Tennessee Infantry; Colonel 4th and 5th Tennessee Infantry Consolidated. (1814-1864).
Lamb, William, Colonel 36th North Carolina Volunteers (2d N.C. Artillery). (1835-1909).
Lampkin, Alexander W., Major 2d Alabama Militia; Col. 1st Mobile Volunteers.
Lampley, Harris D., Major, Lieut. Col., Col. 45th Alabama Infantry. (d. 1864).
Landis, John C., Major 1st Missouri Artillery Battalion, 5th Division, Missouri State Guard.
Landry, Joseph O., Lieutenant-Colonel 22nd Louisiana Infantry Consolidated; Lieutenant-Colonel 29th (also called 28th) Louisiana Infantry.
Lane, J. M., Major 2d Cavalry Georgia State Guard.
Lane, (**) T. N., Lieutenant-Colonel 7th Arkansas Militia.
Lane, Walter Paye, Lieutenant-Colonel 3d Texas Cavalry; Colonel 1st Texas Partisan Rangers. (1817-1892).
Langston, William C., Major 5th Missouri Cavalry, 8th Division Missouri State Guard.
Lanier, Thomas C., Lieutenant-Colonel, Colonel 42d Alabama Infantry. (1824-1891).
Lankford, Augustus R., Lieutenant-Colonel, Colonel 38th Alabama Infantry. (b. 1823).
Lannom, William D., Lieutenant-Colonel 7th Kentucky Infantry; Lieutenant-Colonel 12th Kentucky Cavalry.
Larey, Peter H., Major 1st Battalion Georgia Infantry.
Lary, Washington T., Lieutenant-Colonel 6th Alabama Cavalry. (d. 1890).
Lash, Jacob A., Major 4th Florida Infantry. (d. 1865).
Laswell, George S., Major, Lieutenant-Colonel 1st Arkansas Mounted Rifles.
Latham, (**) J. B., Colonel 51st Arkansas Militia.
Latimer, Reuben, Major 7th Infantry Georgia State Guard. (1809-1879).

Lavender, Frank M., Major, Lieutenant-Colonel 20th Tennessee Infantry.
Lavender, Joseph G., Major 110th Virginia Militia. (b. 1833).
Law, George W., Major, Lieutenant-Colonel 1st Missouri Cavalry.
Law, Junius Augustus, Lieutenant-Colonel 2d Alabama Reserves. (d. 1881).
Lawhon, J., Lieutenant-Colonel 1st Mississippi Infantry (or Minute Men) State Troops.
Lawrence, Robert J., Major, Lieutenant-Colonel 14th Mississippi Infantry.
Lawther, Robert R., Major 1st Missouri Cavalry; Colonel Lawther's Temporary Regiment of Dismounted Missouri Cavalry; Colonel 10th Missouri Cavalry.
Lawton, William John, Colonel 2d Georgia Cavalry. (1824-1912).
Lay, Benjamin D., Colonel Lay's Regiment Mississippi Cavalry.
Lay, (**) John T., Colonel 6th Confederate.
Layton, Pierre S., Lieutenant-Colonel, Colonel 4th Mississippi Infantry. (b. 1839).
Lea, Allen, Major 2d (also known as 19th) Battalion Alabama Cavalry.
Lea, Benjamin James, Colonel 52d Tennessee Infantry. (1833-1894).
Leavell, H. C., Lieutenant-Colonel 1st Kentucky Cavalry. (d. 1862).
Le Baron, William A., Lieutenant-Colonel 3d Alabama Militia. (b. 1827).
Lee, Philip Lightfoot, Major, Lieutenant-Colonel 2d Kentucky Infantry. (1832-1875).
Lee, P. Lynch, Lieutenant-Colonel 15th (Johnson's) Arkansas Infantry; Major 15th (Gee's) Arkansas Infantry. (1838-1911).
Lee, William R., Major 10th (May's) Kentucky Cavalry.
Leeds, Paul B., Major 18th Louisiana Infantry.
Le Flore, Mitchell, Major 1st Choctaw and Chickasaw Mounted Rifles.
Leigh, Richard Watson, Lieutenant-Colonel 43d Mississippi Infantry. (1831-1862).
Lemmon, Alexander C., Major 5th Missouri Infantry, 8th Division, Missouri State Guard.
Lemoyne, George W., Colonel 17th (Lemoyne's) Arkansas Infantry.
Lesley, John Thomas, Major 4th Florida Infantry. (1839-1913).
Leslie, (**) Sam., Colonel 45th Arkansas Militia.
Lester, George Nelson, Colonel 7th Infantry Georgia State Guard, Lieutenant-Colonel Battalion State Guard. (1824-1892).
Lester, James D., Colonel 22d Mississippi Infantry.
Lester, William Cicero, Major 43d Georgia Infantry. (b. 1835).
Lesueur, Charles Marion, Major 4th Texas Cavalry. (1824-1889).
Lewelling, Thomas, Lieutenant-Colonel 22d Texas Cavalry.
Lewers, Thomas, Lieutenant-Colonel, Major Wirt Adams' Mississippi Cavalry.
Lewie, G. A., Lieutenant-Colonel 2d South Carolina State Troops (6 months).
Lewis, Edward A., Lieutenant-Colonel 1st Missouri Cavalry, 1st Division, Missouri State Guard.
Lewis, Henry Byrd, Major 25th Virginia Militia. (1826-1917).
Lewis, James H., Lieutenant-Colonel 1st (Wheeler's, afterward 6th) Tennessee Cavalry.
Lewis, Joseph C., Lieutenant-Colonel, Colonel 25th Louisiana Infantry.
Lewis, Joseph Horace, Colonel 6th Kentucky Infantry. (1824-1904).
Lewis, Levin M., Lieutenant-Colonel 7th (Jackman's, afterward 16th) Missouri Infantry; Colonel 16th (formerly 7th) Missouri Infantry; Colonel 3d Missouri Infantry, 5th Division, Missouri State Guard. (1832-1887).
Lewis, Robert N., Major, Lieutenant-Colonel, Colonel 34th Tennessee Infantry.
Lewis, Thomas Hall, Major Lewis' Battalion Alabama Cavalry. (1832-1864).
Lewis, Tom, Acting Lieutenant-Colonel 3d Choctaw Regiment.
Lewis, Thomas Wilson, Major 2d (Woodward's) Kentucky Cavalry. (1840-1915).
Lewis, (**) ...., Major Thomas' Regiment Alabama Cavalry.
Liggin, ..., Lieutenant-Colonel 1st Arkansas Militia (30 days).
Likens, James B., Major 6th (Likens') Battalion Texas Infantry; Colonel 35th (Likens') Texas Cavalry.
Lillard, John Mason, Colonel 26th Tennessee Infantry. (1827-1863).
Lillard, Newton Jackson, Lieutenant-Colonel 3d Tennessee Infantry (Prov. Army). (1832-1905).

Lindsay, Andrew Jackson, Colonel Lindsay's Regiment Mississippi Cavalry. (1820-1895).
Lindsay, Robert Hume, Major, Lieutenant-Colonel 16th Louisiana Infantry. (1833-1910).
Lipscomb, George H., Major 27th Mississippi Infantry. (k. 1862).
Lipscomb, Thomas C., Major, Lieutenant-Colonel 6th Mississippi Cavalry. (1834-1901).
Little, Stinson, Major 1st (Colquitt's) Arkansas Infantry.
Littlefield, Asahel, Lieutenant-Colonel 8th Battalion Georgia Infantry; Colonel 33d Georgia Infantry.
Littrell, Leroy Newyear, Colonel 37th Virginia Militia. (1817-1880).
Livingston, Henry James, Lieutenant-Colonel 7th Alabama Cavalry; Colonel 8th (Livingston's) Alabama Cavalry. (1833-1907).
Livingston, Thomas R., Major 1st Missouri Cavalry Battalion, 1st Indian Brigade.
Lloyd, William David Clinton, Major 9th (also called 5th) Battalion Alabama Infantry.
Locke, (**) M. A., Colonel 120th North Carolina Militia.
Locke, Matthew F., Colonel 10th Texas Cavalry. (1824-1911).
Locke, Michael B., Lieutenant-Colonel 1st Alabama Infantry.
Lockhart, Harrison C., Major, Lieutenant-Colonel 50th (old) Tennessee Infantry, Lieutenant-Colonel Lockhart's Battalion Alabama Exempts.
Lockridge, Samuel A., Major 5th Texas Cavalry. (1829-1862).
Loering, Sampson, Major 1st Choctaw and Chickasaw Mounted Rifles.
Lofland, (**) H. O., Major Memphis (Tennessee) Legion.
Lofton, William Alpheus, Colonel 6th Infantry Georgia State Guard, formerly Major Battalion State Guard (aft. 6th Regiment). (d. 1896).
Logan, George William, Lieutenant-Colonel Chalmette Regiment Louisiana Militia; Lieutenant-Colonel 2d Louisiana Battalion Heavy Artillery. (1828-1896).
Logan, John Leroy, Colonel 11th Arkansas Infantry.
Logwood, Thomas H., Lieutenant-Colonel 6th Battalion Tennessee Cavalry; Lieutenant-Colonel, Colonel 15th and 16th Tennessee Cavalry Consolidated and known as 16th; Colonel 16th (Logwood's) Tennessee Cavalry; Lieutenant-Colonel of Nixon's Tennessee Cavalry Regiment.
Long, James A., Major, Lieutenant-Colonel, Colonel 11th Tennessee Infantry. (d. 1864).
Long, J. W., Major 20th Arkansas Infantry.
Longmire, John J., Major 23d Alabama Infantry.
Longstreet, Anderson P., Lieutenant-Colonel Wright's Cavalry Regiment (also called 12th) Georgia State Guard.
Loomis, John Q., Colonel 25th Alabama Infantry; Lieutenant-Colonel 1st Battalion Alabama Infantry.
Looney, Abraham McClellan, Major 1st Tennessee Volunteers. (1820-1904).
Looney, Robert Fain, Colonel 38th (formerly 8th, Looney's) Tennessee Infantry. (1824-1899).
Looscan, Michael, Major 1st Texas Cavalry Regiment, Arizona Brigade; Major 1st Texas Battalion (also called 4th) Cavalry Regiment Arizona Brigade and 31st Texas Cavalry. (1840-1897).
Lott, Elias Everett, Lieutenant-Colonel 22d Texas Infantry; Major 5th (Hubbard's) Battalion Texas Infantry.
Loudermilk, John, Major 36th (Glenn's) Georgia Infantry. (1829-1864).
Love, Andrew Pickens, Major (acting) 4th Battalion Alabama Cavalry. (1818-1896).
Love, James Flavius, Major 59th Tennessee Infantry. (1841-1902).
Love, Joseph B., Lieutenant-Colonel Freeman's Regiment Missouri Cavalry.
Love, Samuel T., Major 27th Tennessee Infantry. (d. 1862).
Lovell, William Storrow, Major 1st Battalion Georgia Infantry; Major 36th (Villepigue's) Georgia Infantry; Major 1st Confederate Infantry (formerly 36th Georgia Infantry). (1829-1900).
Lovell, William S., Lieutenant-Colonel 23d (after 22d) Louisiana Infantry.
Lovern, James, Major 5th Missouri Infantry, 3d Division, Missouri State Guard. (1822-1908).

Lowe, Aden, Colonel 3d Missouri Infantry, 1st Division, Missouri State Guard.
Lowe, (**) William M., Colonel Alabama Burr Tailed Regiment October 1864, 39 (3) Page 435.
Lowrey, Mark Perrin, Colonel 32d Mississippi Infantry; Colonel 4th Mississippi State Troops. (1828-1885).
Lowry, James Marion, Lieutenant-Colonel 29th North Carolina Infantry.
Lowry, Robert, Major, Colonel 6th (also called 7th) Mississippi Infantry. (1830-1910).
Lowry, William L., Lieutenant-Colonel, Colonel 2d Mississippi State Cavalry.
Lubbock, Thomas Saltus, Lieutenant-Colonel, Colonel 8th Texas Cavalry. (1817-1862).
Lucas, Henry Clay, Major 20th Tennessee Infantry. (1834-1874).
Lucas, Hugh R., Major 11th Tennessee Infantry.
Lucas, James Jonathan, Major 15th Battalion South Carolina Artillery. (1831-1914).
Luckett, Philip N., Colonel 3d Texas Infantry.
Lupton, (**) Isaiah, Lieutenant-Colonel 114th Virginia Militia.
Lutz, Levi P., Major 1st Virginia Militia.
Lybrook, (**) Samuel E., Major 86th Virginia Militia.
Lyles, Oliver P., Colonel 23d (Lyles') Arkansas Infantry. (1829-1893).
Lyles, William L., Lieutenant-Colonel 24th Mississippi Infantry. (d. 1900).
Lynam, Thomas H., Major, Lieutenant-Colonel 9th Mississippi Infantry.
Lynch, Connally H., Lieutenant-Colonel 63d Virginia Infantry.
Lynn, David Andrew, Major, Colonel 49th Tennessee Infantry.
Lyon, Hylan Benton, Lieutenant-Colonel, Colonel 8th Kentucky Infantry. (1836-1907).
Lyon, Richard, Colonel 6th Arkansas Infantry.
Lyon, (**) Robert P., Lieutenant-Colonel 28th Virginia Militia.
Lythgoe, Augustus Jackson, Lieutenant-Colonel, Colonel 19th South Carolina Infantry. (1830-1862).
Lytle, Ephraim Foster, Lieutenant-Colonel 45th Tennessee Infantry.
McAfee, Allen Lawrence, Major 6th Battalion Confederate Cavalry. (1833-1870).
McAlexander, Edward, Major, Lieutenant-Colonel 27th Alabama Infantry.
McBee, Joshua T., Major 28th Mississippi Cavalry.
McCain, Henry V., Major 12th Louisiana Infantry.
McCaleb, James H., Colonel 1st Arkansas Militia (30 days).
McCall, James K., Major Atlanta Arsenal Battalion, Georgia.
McCammon, William Young, Lieutenant-Colonel 9th Arkansas Infantry. (1831-1863).
McCann, (**) James Richard, Major 15th Tennessee Cavalry; Major 9th Tennessee Cavalry. (d. 1880).
McCarley, Moses, Lieutenant-Colonel 23d Mississippi Infantry. (1829-1882).
McCarty, J. L., Colonel 2d (also called 4th) Mississippi Cavalry.
McCarver, John Stanhope, Colonel 14th (McCarver's) Arkansas Infantry. (1820-1895).
McCaskill, John, Lieutenant-Colonel 3d Confederate Cavalry.
McCauley, John C., Major 7th Arkansas Infantry.
McCay, Robert C., Major 38th Mississippi Infantry. (k. 1864).
McClanahan, Meredith M., Major 41st Virginia Militia.
McClarty, John, Major, Lieutenant-Colonel 17th Texas Cavalry.
McClellan, George R., Lieutenant-Colonel 5th Battalion Tennessee Cavalry. (1816-1904).
McClellan, William B., Lieutenant-Colonel 25th Alabama Infantry; Lieutenant-Colonel 6th (McClellan's) Battalion Alabama Infantry. (b. 1797).
McClelland, Robert H., Major 49th Tennessee Infantry.
McClung, Francis Barclay, Major, Lieutenant-Colonel 1st Confederate Infantry Battalion. (b. 1841).
McClure, (**) R. J., Major 1st Battalion Georgia Militia.
McClure, Robert G., Lieutenant-Colonel 41st Tennessee Infantry.
McCollum, Levi, Major, Lieutenant-Colonel 42d Tennessee Infantry.
McConnell, Joseph T., Colonel 39th Georgia Infantry.

McConnell, Thomas M., Major 26th Tennessee Infantry.
McCoole, Thomas E., Lieutenant-Colonel 31st Virginia Militia.
McCord, Henry J., Lieutenant-Colonel, Colonel 35th Arkansas Infantry.
McCord, James Ebenezer, Colonel Frontier Regiment Texas Cavalry. (b. 1834).
McCorkle, Matthew L., Major McCorkle's Battalion North Carolina Senior Reserves.
McCormick, Abner H., Lieutenant-Colonel 2d Florida Cavalry.
McCown, James, Colonel 5th Missouri Infantry; Lieutenant-Colonel, Colonel 2d Missouri Cavalry, 8th Division, Missouri State Guard; Lieutenant-Colonel 2d Battalion Missouri Infantry.
McCown, John Porter, Colonel Tennessee Artillery Corps; Colonel 1st Tennessee Light Artillery. (1815-1879).
McCoy, Franklin J., Major 21st Alabama Infantry.
McCoy, Henry R., Major 34th Alabama Infantry.
McCray, Thomas H., Colonel 31st Arkansas Infantry; Major McCray's Battalion Arkansas Infantry.
McCreary, James Bennett, Major, Lieutenant-Colonel 11th Kentucky Cavalry. (1838-1918).
McCulloch, Henry Eustace, Colonel 1st (McCulloch's) Texas Mounted Riflemen. (1816-1895).
McCulloch, Joseph B., Major 4th (McNair's) Arkansas Infantry. (b. 1827).
McCulloch, Robert, Lieutenant-Colonel 4th Battalion Missouri Cavalry; Colonel 2d Missouri Cavalry. (b. 1820).
McCulloch, Robert A., Major, Lieutenant-Colonel 2d Missouri Cavalry. (1820-1905).
McCullough, Frisby H., Lieutenant-Colonel Franklin's Northeast Missouri Regiment; Lieutenant-Colonel 2d Northeast Missouri Cavalry.
McCullough, James, Lieutenant-Colonel, Colonel 16th South Carolina Infantry. (1824-1892).
McCune, Samuel Houston, Colonel 32d Virginia Militia; Major 3d Battalion Valley Reserves. (1819-1889).
McCurtain, Jackson, Lieutenant-Colonel 1st (McCurtain's) Choctaw Battalion: Colonel 3d Choctaw Regiment.
McCutcheon, (**) Samuel, Major 2d Battalion Louisiana State Guard Cavalry.
McDaniel, Charles Addison, Colonel 41st Georgia Infantry. (1830-1862).
McDaniel, Coleman A., Colonel 44th Tennessee Infantry. (1823-1896).
McDaniel, Washington, Major 1st (Elliott's) Missouri Battalion Cavalry.
McDonald, Charles, Major 18th Battalion Tennessee Cavalry; Major 26th Battalion Tennessee Cavalry.
McDonald, Emmett, Colonel McDonald's Missouri Cavalry.
McDonald, Enoch, Major 40th Mississippi Infantry.
McDonald, Jesse Campbell, Major 4th (Clinch's) Georgia Cavalry. (1832-1918).
McDonald, Joseph E., Major 55th Tennessee Infantry.
McDonell, Thaddeus A., Major, Lieutenant-Colonel 1st Florida Infantry.
McDougall, Myford, Major Crescent Regiment Louisiana Infantry.
McDowell, Byron G., Major 62d North Carolina Infantry.
McDowell, Harvey, Major 2d Kentucky Infantry. (1835-1901).
McDowell, James K., Major, Lieutenant-Colonel 3d (also called 2d) Missouri Infantry.
McDowell, Joseph A., Colonel 60th North Carolina Infantry.
McDowell, William Wallis, Major 60th North Carolina Infantry. (1826-1905).
McEnery, John, Major, Lieutenant-Colonel 4th Battalion Louisiana Infantry.
McFarland, Robert, Major 31st (W. M. Bradford's, after 39th) Tennessee Infantry. (b. 1836).
Macfarlane, Archibald, Colonel 1st and 4th Missouri Infantry Consolidated; Colonel 4th Missouri Infantry; Major Macfarlane's Missouri Infantry Battalion.
McGaughy, John H., Major, Lieutenant-Colonel 16th Alabama Infantry. (d. 1863).
MacGavock, Randall William, Lieutenant-Colonel, Colonel 10th Tennessee Infantry. (1826-1863).
McGee, John, Major 37th Mississippi Infantry. (b. 1831).
McGee, J. W., Major 17th Battalion Infantry Georgia State Guard.

McGehee, Edward F., Lieutenant-Colonel 25th Mississippi Infantry; Lieutenant Colonel 2d Confederate Infantry. (1816-1867).
McGhee, James, Colonel McGhee's Arkansas Regiment.
McGinnis, Noble L., Major, Lieutenant-Colonel, Colonel 2d Texas Infantry.
McGoodwin, Al., Major 3d Kentucky Infantry.
McGregor, Charles E., Major 5th Georgia Reserves.
McGregor, Donelson, Lieutenant-Colonel 1st (Colquitt's) Arkansas Infantry. (d 1862).
McGriff, Patrick A., Major 11th Infantry Georgia State Guard; Major 75th Georgia Militia.
McGuire, John P., Major, Colonel 32d Tennessee Infantry.
McHenry, James, Major 1st Creek Regiment.
McIntosh, Chilly, Colonel 2d Creek Regiment; Lieutenant-Colonel 1st Creek Cavalry Battalion.
McIntosh, Daniel Newman, Lieutenant-Colonel 1st Creek Regiment.
McIntosh, James McQueen, Colonel 2d Arkansas Mounted Rifles. (1828-1862).
McIntosh, William R., Lieutenant-Colonel 1st Creek Regiment.
MacIntyre, Archibald Thompson, Colonel 11th Infantry Georgia State Guard; Major MacIntyre's Battalion Georgia State Guard. (1822-1900).
McJunkin, W. S., Major 7th South Carolina Reserves.
McKamy, James A., Major, Lieutenant-Colonel Cavalry Battalion, Thomas' North Carolina Legion. (d. 1898).
McKamy, Samuel L., Major 29th Tennessee Infantry.
McKamy, William H., Major 43d Tennessee Infantry (afterward Mounted Infantry). (1827-1894).
McKay, John, Major 4th Battalion Arkansas Infantry.
McKean, John G., Major 19th (Dawson's) Arkansas Infantry.
McKelvaine, Robert Public, Lieutenant-Colonel, Colonel 24th Mississippi Infantry.
McKennie, Marcellus, Colonel 88th Virginia Militia.
McKenzie, George Washington, Lieutenant-Colonel 13th Battalion Tennessee Cavalry; Lieutenant-Colonel, Colonel 5th Tennessee Cavalry. (1818-1906).
McKinney, Christopher Columbus, Major, Lieutenant-Colonel 8th (Fulton's) Tennessee Infantry. (1824-1902).
McKinney, ..., Colonel 4th Missouri Infantry, 3d Division, Missouri State Guard.
McKinstry, Alexander, Colonel 32d Alabama Infantry. (1822-1879).
McKoin, James L., Colonel 55th Tennessee Infantry.
McKowen, John C., Lieutenant-Colonel Powers' Regiment Louisiana and Mississippi Cavalry.
McKoy, Almond A., Colonel 8th Regiment North Carolina Reserves. (1825-1886).
McLain, Robert, Colonel 37th Mississippi Infantry.
McLaurin, Cornelius, Lieutenant-Colonel 4th Mississippi Cavalry; Major McLaurin's Battalion Mississippi Cavalry.
McLaurin, Laurin L., Lieutenant-Colonel 27th Louisiana Infantry. (k. 1863).
McLean, Angus D., Lieutenant-Colonel, Colonel 6th Florida Infantry. (d. 1864).
McLean, James B., Major 2d Cavalry Texas State Troops.
McLean, James R., Major 7th Regiment North Carolina Reserves; Major Camp Stokes Light Duty Battalion.
McLean, Nathaniel, Lieutenant-Colonel 8th Regiment North Carolina Reserves.
McLemore, Amos, Major 27th Mississippi Infantry. (1829-1863).
McLemore, William Sugars, Colonel 4th (Starnes', also called 3d) Tennessee Cavalry. (1830-1908).
McLin, John B., Major 1st East Tennessee Cavalry; Colonel 5th Tennessee Cavalry.
McLucas, (**) Daniel A., Major .... Georgia Militia.
McMackin, Andrew J., Major 54th Tennessee Infantry.
McMahon, John J., Colonel 63d Virginia Infantry.
McManus, (**) J. A., Major 3d Georgia Reserves.
McMillan, H. W., Lieutenant-Colonel 33d Arkansas Infantry.
McMullan, Mark J., Major 22d Battalion Georgia Siege Artillery.
McMurray, Francis, Major 23d Alabama Infantry.

McMurry, James A., Colonel 34th Tennessee Infantry. (c. 1825-1863).
McMurry, Lipscomb P., Major, Colonel 22d Tennessee Infantry; Lieutenant-Colonel 12th and 22d Tennessee Infantry Consolidated.
McMurtrey, Elisha L., Lieutenant-Colonel McMurtrey's Battalion Arkansas Cavalry.
McNair, Evander, Lieutenant-Colonel, Colonel 4th (McNair's) Arkansas Infantry. (1820-1902).
McNairy, Frank Nathaniel, Lieutenant-Colonel 1st Battalion Tennessee Cavalry. (1825-1863).
McNeely, James A., Major, Colonel 13th Arkansas Infantry.
McNeill, Aden, Lieutenant-Colonel 8th Mississippi Infantry. (d. 1863).
McNeill, Archibald J., Colonel 30th (McNeill's) Arkansas Infantry; Major 6th Battalion Cavalry; Colonel 4th Louisiana Cavalry; Major McNeill's Battalion Louisiana Cavalry.
McNeill, Henry C., Lieutenant-Colonel, Colonel 5th Texas Cavalry. (b. 1835).
McNeill, Henry C., Major, Lieutenant-Colonel 33d Tennessee Infantry. (d. 1864).
McPhaill, Hugh A., Major 5th Texas Cavalry. (1830-1865).
McPheeters, George P., Lieutenant-Colonel, Colonel Crescent Regiment Louisiana Infantry. (1831-1862).
McQuiddy, Thomas J., Major 3d Battalion Missouri Cavalry.
MacRae, Alexander, Major 1st Battalion North Carolina Heavy Artillery. (1796-1868).
McRae, Dandridge, Major 3d Battalion Arkansas Infantry; Colonel 15th (McRae's) Arkansas Infantry; Colonel 28th (McRae's Emergency) Arkansas Infantry. 1829-1899).
McRae, James B., Lieutenant-Colonel 3d Mississippi Infantry.
McRae, James Cameron, Major McRae's North Carolina Battalion. (1838-1909).
McReynolds, Felix C., Major 21st Texas Infantry (1835-1912).
McReynolds, James H., Major 9th (Maxey's, also called 8th) Texas Infantry.
McReynolds, Joseph T., Major 37th (formerly 7th Tennessee, Provisional Army) Tennessee Infantry.
McSpadden, Samuel King, Major, Lieutenant-Colonel, Colonel 19th Alabama Infantry. (1823-1896).
McSwean, Colin, Major 39th Alabama Infantry.
McWaters, James A., Lieutenant-Colonel 33d Louisiana Partisan Rangers.
McWhorter, Eliphalet Ariel, Major 6th Alabama Cavalry. (1830-1898).
Mabrey, James Walton, Lieutenant-Colonel 57th Alabama Infantry.
Mabry, Hinchie Parham, Lieutenant-Colonel, Colonel 3d Texas Cavalry. (1829-1885).
Maddox, Robert Flournoy, Lieutenant-Colonel 42d Georgia Infantry; Colonel 2d Georgia Reserves. (1829-1899).
Maddox, William A., Major 17th Louisiana Infantry.
Madison, George T., Lieutenant-Colonel 3d Texas Cavalry Regiment, Arizona Brigade; Lieutenant-Colonel 3d Battalion Texas Cavalry, Arizona Brigade.
Magee, Jacob O., Major 2d Regiment Mississippi Infantry (or Minute Men) State Troops.
Magee, (**) Turpin Dixon, Major 46th Mississippi Infantry.
Magenis, Arthur J., Lieutenant-Colonel 27th Arkansas Infantry.
Magevney, Michael, Jr., Lieutenant-Colonel, Colonel 154th Senior Tennessee Infantry.
Magoffin, Elijah, Major 10th (also called 12th) Missouri Infantry.
Magrath, Edward, Colonel 1st Regiment Charleston Guards, South Carolina.
Mains, Samuel F., Lieutenant-Colonel 14th Texas Cavalry.
Major, Elliott D., Major 1st Northeast Missouri Cavalry; Major 7th (Franklin's) Regiment Missouri Infantry.
Major, James Patrick, Colonel Major's Missouri Cavalry Regiment, 3d Division, Missouri State Guard. (1836-1877).
Malcolm, Green, Major 1st Battalion Tennessee Cavalry.
Mallett, Peter, Colonel Mallett's Battalion North Carolina Infantry. (1825-1907).
Malone, Frederick J., Major, Colonel 31st Texas Cavalry. (d. 1891).
Malone, James C., Jr., Colonel 9th Alabama Cavalry; Lieutenant-Colonel 14th Battalion Alabama Cavalry, Major 2d Battalion Confederate Infantry.
Malone, John M., Major 12th Kentucky Cavalry.

Maney, Frank, Major 24th Battalion Tennessee Sharpshooters.
Mangham, Samuel Watson, Colonel 5th Georgia Infantry; Lieutenant-Colonel 6th Infantry Georgia State Guard; Commanding Battalion State Guard aft. 6th Georgia State Guard. (1830-1888).
Mangham, Thomas Woodward, Lieutenant-Colonel, Colonel 30th Georgia Infantry. (1836-1873).
Mangum, Thomas H., Major 25th Mississippi Infantry; Major 2d Confederate Infantry. (1834-1903).
Manigault, Arthur Middleton, Colonel 10th South Carolina Infantry. (1824-1886).
Manigault, Edward, Major 6th Battalion South Carolina Infantry; Major 18th Battalion South Carolina Artillery. (1817-1874).
Manly, John H., Lieutenant-Colonel 1st Regiment Texas Artillery.
Mann, Walter L., Colonel Mann's Regiment Texas Cavalry; Lieutenant-Colonel Bradford's Regiment Texas Cavalry.
Mann, William Henry, Major 54th Georgia Infantry. (1812-1864).
Mann, ..., Colonel 5th Regiment Georgia Militia.
Marks, Albert Smith, Major, Colonel 17th Tennessee Infantry. (1836-1891).
Marks, Leon D., Colonel 27th Louisiana Infantry. (k. 1863).
Marks, Matthew Robinson, Major 2d Alabama Cavalry. (1834-1911).
Marks, Samuel F., Colonel 11th Louisiana Infantry.
Marks, Washington, Major 22d (formerly 23d) Louisiana Infantry; Major 22d Louisiana Consolidated.
Marmaduke, John Sappington, Colonel 3d Confederate Infantry; Lieutenant-Colonel 1st Battalion Arkansas Infantry. (1833-1887).
Marrast, John Calhoun, Lieutenant-Colonel, Colonel 22d Alabama Infantry. (1825-1863).
Marshall, John W., Colonel 17th Tennessee Cavalry.
Marshall, L. L., Major 2d Mississippi State Cavalry; Major Ashcraft's, Ham's and Lowry's Consolidated Mississippi Cavalry Regiment.
Marshall, L. M., Lieutenant-Colonel 15th (Stewart's) Tennessee Cavalry.
Martin, Barclay, Major 9th (Biffle's, also called 19th) Tennessee Cavalry.
Martin, (**) D. B., Colonel Commanding Conscripts, Rusk Texas.
Martin, Jacob T., Acting Lieutenant-Colonel 11th Tennessee Cavalry. (1829-1897).
Martin, James T., Major 7th Arkansas Infantry. (d. 1876).
Martin, John D., Major 154th Senior Tennessee Infantry.
Martin, John D., Colonel 25th Mississippi Infantry; Colonel 2d Confederate Infantry.
Martin, John W., Lieutenant-Colonel, Colonel 1st Missouri Cavalry, 8th Division, Missouri State Guard.
Martin, Joseph C., Major 30th (McNeill's) Arkansas Infantry; Major 30th (Hart's) Arkansas Infantry. (d. 1863).
Martin, Leonidas M., Colonel 5th Texas Partisan Rangers; Major 10th Battalion Texas Cavalry.
Martin, Luther H. O., Lieutenant-Colonel 3d Cavalry Georgia State Guard.
Martin, Mathias, Colonel 23d Tennessee Infantry. (1812-1892).
Martin, Robert Maxwell, Lieutenant-Colonel 10th (Johnson's) Kentucky Partisan Rangers. (1840-1901).
Martin, Samuel H., Lieutenant-Colonel 1st Chickasaw Cavalry Regiment (rejected).
Martin, William, Major, Lieutenant-Colonel 56th Alabama Partisan Rangers.
Martin, William E., Colonel 1st South Carolina Mounted Militia.
Martin, William H., Major, Lieutenant-Colonel 1st (Colquitt's) Arkansas Infantry.
Martin, William Whitnell, Major 26th Louisiana Infantry. (1840-1863).
Martin, ..., Major 2d Battalion Texas Infantry.
Mashburn, Elisha, Major, Lieutenant-Colonel 3d Florida Infantry.
Mason, Alexander, Major 11th Louisiana Infantry.
Mason, A. P., Colonel (not confirmed) 2d Mississippi Cavalry.
Mason, Armistead T., Major 34th (also called 37th) Mississippi Infantry.
Mason, Enoch, Lieutenant-Colonel 16th Louisiana Infantry.

Mason, Samuel J., Lieutenant-Colonel 14th (McCarver's) Regiment Arkansas Infantry; Lieutenant-Colonel 9th Battalion Arkansas Infantry.
Massey, Conrad K., Major 20th Mississippi Infantry. (d. 1864).
Massie, Josiah C., Lieutenant-Colonel 9th (Nichols', also called 5th) Texas Infantry (6 months).
Masten, William K., Lieutenant-Colonel 15th Texas Cavalry.
Mastin, J., Colonel 71st North Carolina Militia.
Matheny, William G., Lieutenant-Colonel, Colonel 21st (Cravens') Arkansas Infantry.
Matheson, Walter H., Major 17th (Rector's) Arkansas Infantry.
Matlock, Charles H., Lieutenant-Colonel 1st Arkansas Mounted Rifles; Lieutenant-Colonel, Colonel 32d Arkansas Infantry; Lieutenant-Colonel Matlock's Battalion Arkansas Cavalry. (d. 1864).
Mattison, George W., Major 31st (Hundley's) Alabama Infantry.
Mattison, H. S., Major 13th Battalion South Carolina Infantry.
Mauldin, Tyirie Harris, Lieutenant-Colonel 3d Alabama Cavalry.
Maupin, William Allen, Colonel 4th Virginia Militia. (1815-1882).
Maupin, William D., Lieutenant-Colonel 1st Missouri Cavalry.
Maury, Henry, Colonel 2d Alabama Infantry; Lieutenant-Colonel 32d Alabama Infantry; Colonel 15th Confederate Cavalry. (1827-1869).
Maxey, Samuel Bell, Colonel 9th (Maxey's, also called 8th) Texas Infantry. (1825-1895).
Maxson, George W., Major 6th Kentucky Infantry.
Maxwell, George Troup, Major, Lieutenant-Colonel, Colonel 1st Florida Cavalry.
Maxwell, William L., Major, Lieutenant-Colonel Ballentine's (also called 2d Mississippi Partisan Rangers) Mississippi Cavalry.
May, Andrew J., Lieutenant-Colonel, Colonel 5th Kentucky Infantry; Major May's Battalion Kentucky Mounted Rifles; Colonel 10th (May's) Kentucky Cavalry. (1829-1903).
May, James H., Major, Lieutenant-Colonel 4th (McNair's) Arkansas Infantry. (Found also on Confederate Register as Major 7th Arkansas Battalion). (b. 1816).
May, Joseph J., Major, Lieutenant-Colonel 16th Alabama Infantry.
May, (**) J. W., Colonel 10th Arkansas Militia.
Mayo, James W., Major, 2d Georgia Cavalry.
Mayrant, John W., Major 11th Texas Cavalry.
Mayrant, William N., Major 5th Texas Partisan Rangers.
Mayson, James Hamilton, Lieutenant-Colonel, Colonel 7th Mississippi Infantry.
Mead, Lemuel G., Major 25th Battalion Alabama Cavalry. (1827-1879).
Mecaslin, John H., Major 3d Battalion Cavalry Georgia State Guard (Atlanta Fire Battalion).
Meek, A. T., Major 2d Arkansas Infantry.
Meek, (**) Samuel M., Lieutenant-Colonel 1st Regiment Army of 10,000, Mississippi.
Mell, Patrick Hues, Colonel 9th Infantry Georgia State Guard; Lieutenant-Colonel Battalion State Guard. (1814-1888).
Mellett, F. M., Lieutenant-Colonel 4th South Carolina State Troops.
Mellon, Thomas A., Major, Lieutenant-Colonel, Colonel 3d Mississippi Infantry.
Menard, Medard, Major, Lieutenant-Colonel 26th Texas Cavalry.
Mercer, Fleet C., Major 3d Regiment Mississippi Infantry (or Minute Men) State Troops.
Mercer, Hugh Weedon, Colonel 1st Volunteers Georgia. (1808-1877).
Mercer, (**) W. N., Major Brewer's 2d Battalion, Mississippi and Alabama Cavalry (aft. 8th Confederate).
Merriam, (**) Albert W., Lieutenant-Colonel Continental Regiment Louisiana Militia.
Merrick, George W., Major, Lieutenant-Colonel 22d Texas Cavalry.
Merrick, Thomas D., Colonel 10th Arkansas Infantry.
Merriwether's Battalion South Carolina Reserves.
Messick, E. H., Major 14th (Mitchell's) Arkansas Infantry.
Messick, J. H., Major 14th (Mitchell's) Arkansas Infantry.

Messick, Otis M., Major, Lieutenant-Colonel, Colonel 11th Texas Cavalry.
Messick, W. R., Acting Major 4th Special Battalion Kentucky Cavalry.
Mesten, J. F., Major 1st Cavalry Mississippi Reserves.
Metts, David W., Lieutenant-Colonel 5th Mississippi Infantry (or Minute Men) State Troops; Lieutenant-Colonel 1st Cavalry Mississippi Reserves.
Meyer, Benjamin W., Major 1st (Meyer's) Battalion Cherokee Cavalry.
Miangolarra, (**) Juan, Major 7th Battalion Louisiana Infantry (30th Regiment).
Miles, William Raphael, Colonel Miles Louisiana Legion. (1817-1900).
Millard, David T., Major Millard's (also called 1st, 8th, and 9th) North Carolina Battalion Junior Reserves.
Miller, C. C., Colonel 21st (Kennedy's) Louisiana Infantry (notified of appointment, but failed to obtain commission).
Miller, Carillaus ("Crill"), Lieutenant-Colonel 2d Texas Partisan Rangers. (d. 1892).
Miller, Horace H., Lieutenant-Colonel 20th Mississippi Infantry; Colonel 9th Mississippi Cavalry.
Miller, John, Major 8th Battalion Arkansas Infantry.
Miller, John H., Major, Lieutenant-Colonel 1st Battalion Mississippi Cavalry. (1812-1863).
Miller, Joseph Zachariah, Major, Lieutenant-Colonel 17th Texas Infantry. (b. 1834).
Miller, Mark S., Lieutenant-Colonel 11th Arkansas Infantry.
Miller, T. C. H., Lieutenant-Colonel, Colonel 17th Tennessee Infantry.
Miller, Thomas G., Major, Lieutenant-Colonel 41st Tennessee Infantry.
Miller, William, Colonel 1st Florida Infantry, Lieutenant-Colonel Battalion Florida Infantry. (1820-1909).
Miller, William A. J., Major 8th Battalion Virginia Reserves. (b. ca. 1818).
Millett, Joseph H., Major 4th Kentucky Infantry. (d. 1864).
Mills, Andrew G., Lieutenant-Colonel 7th Mississippi Infantry; Major 9th Mississippi Infantry. (d. 1894).
Mills, Roger Quarles, Lieutenant-Colonel, Colonel 10th Texas Infantry. (1832-1911).
Millsaps, Reuben Webster, Lieutenant-Colonel 9th Arkansas Infantry. (1837-1916).
Milton, G. B., Major Bruce's Missouri Cavalry Regiment, 2d Division Missouri State Guard.
Milton, William Henry, Major 5th Battalion Florida Cavalry. (1829-1900).
Milton, William P., Lieutenant-Colonel 39th Georgia Infantry.
Minor, John, Major 10th Tennessee Cavalry; Major 10th and 11th Tennessee Cavalry Consolidated. (b. 1837).
Minter, John A., Lieutenant-Colonel, Colonel 54th Alabama Infantry; Lieutenant-Colonel 4th Confederate Infantry; Major, Lieutenant-Colonel 40th Tennessee Infantry; Major, Lieutenant-Colonel 5th (Walker's) Confederate Infantry Regiment. (1835-1909).
Mirick, William, Major 1st Missouri Infantry, 4th Division, Missouri State Guard.
Mitchell, Addison, Colonel 45th Tennessee Infantry.
Mitchell, Charles Samuel, Colonel 8th (Mitchell's) Missouri Infantry; Lieutenant-Colonel 7th Battalion Missouri Infantry. (1840-1910).
Mitchell, (**) R. G., Colonel 66th Georgia Militia.
Mitchell, Thomas A., Major 8th Mississippi Cavalry.
Mitchell, W. C., Colonel 14th (Mitchell's) Arkansas Infantry.
Mitchell, William Dickey, Lieutenant-Colonel, Colonel 29th Georgia Infantry. (1839-1892).
Mitchell, William R., Major 18th Battalion Mississippi Cavalry.
Moffett, (**) Gabriel, Major, Lieutenant-Colonel 37th Tennessee Infantry.
Moffett, Hunter P., Major, Lieutenant-Colonel 37th Tennessee Infantry.
Monroe, James C., Lieutenant-Colonel 1st (Fagan's) Arkansas Infantry; Colonel 1st (Fagan's and Monroe's) Arkansas Cavalry.
Monroe, Thomas Bell, Jr., Major 4th Kentucky Infantry. (d. 1862).
Montaigne, Raymond, Major 1st Louisiana Artillery. (d. 1864).

Montgomery, Franklin Alexander, Lieutenant-Colonel 1st Mississippi Cavalry. (1830-1903).
Montgomery, (**) Hugh W., Major Consolidated Crescent Louisiana Infantry.
Montgomery, John G. M., Major 13th Battalion Tennessee Cavalry; Lieutenant-Colonel 5th Tennessee Cavalry. (1833-1904).
Montgomery, Joseph Terrell Monroe, Major, Lieutenant-Colonel 14th Battalion Georgia Artillery. (1819-1872).
Montgomery, W. E., Major Montgomery's Battalion Cavalry Mississippi State Troops.
Moody, Andrew E., Major 8th Mississippi Infantry.
Moody, William Lewis, Major, Lieutenant-Colonel, Colonel 7th Texas Infantry. (b. 1828).
Moore, Benjamin B., Major 3d Battalion Mississippi Infantry (or Minute Men) State Troops.
Moore, Beriah F., Lieutenant-Colonel 19th Tennessee Infantry. (d. 1864).
Moore, Calvin H., Major, Lieutenant-Colonel 25th Louisiana Infantry.
Moore, George Fleming, Colonel 17th Texas Cavalry. (1822-1883).
Moore, Harrison, Major 21st (Cravens') Arkansas Infantry.
Moore, James, Lieutenant-Colonel 44th Mississippi Infantry. (d. 1862).
Moore, James Butler, Major 45th Tennessee Infantry. (1831-1883).
Moore, James R., Major 5th Mississippi Infantry.
Moore, John Creed, Colonel 2d Texas Infantry; Lieutenant-Colonel 1st Regiment Local Defense Troops, Augusta, Georgia; Major 48th Battalion Georgia Militia. (1824-1910).
Moore, John Jay, Major 52d Georgia Infantry. (1833-1894).
Moore, Robert Hughes, Major Infantry Battalion, Smith's Georgia Legion; Lieutenant-Colonel, Colonel 65th Georgia Infantry. (1809-1890).
Moore, William L., Lieutenant-Colonel, Colonel 8th (Fulton's) Tennessee Infantry.
Moore, William M., Lieutenant-Colonel, Colonel 10th (also called 12th) Missouri Infantry. (b. 1837).
Moore, William P., Lieutenant-Colonel 32d Tennessee Infantry. (k. 1862).
Moorman, George, Lieutenant-Colonel Moorman's Mississippi Cavalry Battalion.
Moragne, William Cain, Colonel 19th South Carolina Infantry.
Morehead, Joseph C., Colonel Morehead's Kentucky Partisan Rangers. (d. 1864).
Moreland, J. S., Major Moreland's Battalion Alabama Sharpshooters.
Moreland, M. D., Colonel Moreland's Alabama Cavalry.
Moreland, William S., Major Fire Battalion (Exempts), Alabama.
Morelock, William C., Major 3d Tennessee Infantry (Provisional Army).
Moreno, Stephen A., Major 17th Alabama Infantry (temporary appointment). (1839-1900).
Morgan, Asa S., Colonel 26th Arkansas Infantry. (d. 1909).
Morgan, Charles C., Major 18th Texas Cavalry.
Morgan, Charles Leroy, Major Morgan's Texas Cavalry Battalion. (1840-1924).
Morgan, Edward Ford, Major 8th Battalion Georgia Infantry. (1843-1869).
Morgan, George Washington, Major 3d Tennessee Infantry (Provisional Army); Major 2d (Morgan's) Kentucky Cavalry. (1817-1862).
Morgan, Hiram S., Major Terrell's Texas Regiment Cavalry.
Morgan, James Bright, Major, Lieutenant-Colonel 29th Mississippi Infantry. (1833-1892).
Morgan, James M., Major 31st Arkansas Infantry.
Morgan, John Hunt, Colonel 2d (Morgan's) Kentucky Cavalry. (1825-1864).
Morgan, Richard C., Colonel Morgan's Regiment Kentucky Cavalry; Colonel 2d Special Battalion Kentucky Cavalry. (b. 1836).
Morgan, Robert Jarrel, Colonel 36th Tennessee Infantry. (1826-1899).
Morgan, Thomas Jefferson, Colonel Morgan's Arkansas Cavalry.
Morgan, William E., Lieutenant-Colonel 13th Tennessee Infantry. (1831-1863).
Morgan, William Henry, Major 3d Mississippi Infantry. (d. 1905).
Morgan, ..., Colonel 57th Tennessee Infantry.
Morin, John M., Lieutenant-Colonel 3d Battalion Cavalry Texas State Troops.
Morris, Benjamin, Major 4th Battalion Alabama Infantry; Major, Lieutenant-Colonel 29th Alabama Infantry. (1829-1913).

Morris, (**) John Dabney, Colonel Kentucky Mounted Rifles. (b. 1816).
Morris, Robert F., Colonel 179th Virginia Militia.
Morris, Z. Fenton, Acting Major Morris' Independent Battalion Virginia Infantry.
Morrison, Charles H., Colonel 31st Louisiana Infantry; Lieutenant-Colonel 6th Battalion Louisiana Infantry.
Morton, George Huddleston, Major, Lieutenant-Colonel 2d (Barteau's, afterward 22d) Tennessee Cavalry. (1836-1902).
Morton, J. Quin, Major 9th (Clark's) Missouri Infantry; Major Clarkson's Battalion Missouri Cavalry.
Morton, Robert C., Major 7th Battalion Virginia Infantry, Local Defense Troops.
Morton, Tignal Jones, Lieutenant-Colonel 53d Tennessee Infantry. (1843-1871).
Moses, George C., Lieutenant-Colonel 1st Battalion North Carolina Home Guard.
Moses, Sidney A., Major 8th (Livingston's) Alabama Cavalry.
Moss, Adolphus A., Lieutenant-Colonel Moss' Battalion North Carolina Reserves; Colonel 6th Regiment North Carolina Senior Reserves.
Moss, James W., Major, Lieutenant-Colonel, Colonel 2d Kentucky Infantry. (1822-1864).
Mouton, Alfred, Colonel 18th Louisiana Infantry (1829-1864).
Mouton, William, Major 18th Louisiana Infantry; Major 7th Louisiana Cavalry.
Moxley, William M., Major 18th Alabama Infantry.
Muldrow, Henry Lowndes, Lieutenant-Colonel 11th Mississippi Cavalry. (1837-1905).
Mullen, John W., Lieutenant-Colonel 2d Texas Cavalry Regiment, Arizona Brigade; Lieutenant-Colonel 12th Texas Cavalry; Lieutenant-Colonel Mullen's Texas Cavalry Battalion, Arizona Brigade.
Munnerlyn, Charles James, Lieutenant-Colonel Commissary Battalion Florida Cavalry (temporary).
Murphey, Virgil S., Major, Colonel 17th Alabama Infantry.
Murphy, (**) George W., Colonel 13th Virginia Militia.
Murphy, J., Major 2d Missouri Infantry, 5th Division, Missouri State Guard.
Murphy, Robert H., Lieutenant-Colonel 30th Tennessee Infantry. (1814-1881).
Murphy, Samuel Jennings, Lieutenant-Colonel Murphy's Independent Alabama Cavalry Battalion. (d. 1893).
Murray, George M., Lieutenant-Colonel 15th (Polk's) Arkansas Infantry.
Murray, James Harvey, Lieutenant-Colonel 16th (Logwood's) Tennessee Cavalry.
Murray, John Ed., Lieutenant-Colonel, Colonel 5th Arkansas Infantry; Colonel 5th and 13th Arkansas Infantry Consolidated; Lieutenant-Colonel 13th Arkansas Infantry. (c. 1843-1864).
Murray, John Porry, Colonel 28th Tennessee Infantry; Colonel Murray's regiment (also called 4th) Tennessee Cavalry. (1830-1895).
Murray, Thomas B., Lieutenant-Colonel 22d Battalion Tennessee Infantry Sharpshooters; Lieutenant-Colonel 16th Tennessee Infantry.
Murray, Thomas H., Major 2d (Hunter's, afterwards 8th) Missouri Infantry; Major, Lieutenant-Colonel 8th (Burns', changed to 11th) Missouri Infantry; Major 4th Missouri Infantry, 8th Division, Missouri State Guard.
Murrell, R. K., Lieutenant-Colonel 2d Missouri Cavalry, 8th Division, Missouri State Guard; Major 8th Missouri Cavalry, 8th Division, Missouri State Guard.
Musgrove, Francis Asbury, Major Musgrove's Battalion Alabama Cavalry. (1827-1865).
Musgrove, James, Major 4th Missouri Cavalry, 8th Division, Missouri State Guard.
Musser, Richard H., Lieutenant-Colonel 8th Battalion Missouri Infantry; Lieutenant-Colonel 9th (Clark's) Missouri Infantry.
Myers, George Boggan, Lieutenant-Colonel 10th Mississippi Infantry. (1831-1897).
Myers, John Jacob, Lieutenant-Colonel, Colonel 26th Texas Cavalry; Major of Debrays' Battalion Texas Cavalry. (1817-1874).
Myers, Robert A., Major 1st (Buchel's) Texas Cavalry. (b. 1840).
Myers, Thomas J., Major 3d Battalion Florida Cavalry; Lieutenant-Colonel 15th Confederate Cavalry.
Mynheir, William, Major, Acting Colonel, 5th Kentucky Infantry. (d. 1892).
Nail, Jonathan, Major Chickasaw Cavalry Battalion.

Nall, Marcus S., Major 41st Georgia Infantry. (d. 1864).
Nalle, (**) Benjamin F., Colonel 3d Virginia Militia.
Napier, Leroy, Jr., Lieutenant-Colonel 8th Battalion Georgia Infantry. (1832-1866).
Napier, LeRoy, Major 2d Alabama Cavalry (temporary command).
Napier, Thomas Alonzo, Colonel Napier's Battalion Tennessee Cavalry. (1837-1862).
Napier, Thomas W., Lieutenant-Colonel 6th Kentucky Cavalry. (d. 1864).
Nathusius, Otto, Major Waul's Texas Legion.
Neal, J. M., Lieutenant-Colonel 47th North Carolina Militia.
Neal, John Randolph, Lieutenant-Colonel 16th Battalion Tennessee Cavalry. (1836-1889).
Neal, Joseph L., Lieutenant-Colonel 5th Arkansas Infantry State Troops, 1861. (d. 1861).
Neal, William T., Lieutenant-Colonel 16th Arkansas Infantry.
Neely, James J., Lieutenant-Colonel 7th Infantry Georgia State Guard; Lieutenant-Colonel 1st (Fannin's) Regiment Georgia Reserves; Colonel 4 State Troops, Major Lester's Battalion Georgia State Guard.
Neely, James Jackson, Colonel 14th (also called 13th) Tennessee Cavalry. (b. 1827).
Neely, Rufus Polk, Colonel 4th Tennessee Volunteers. (1805-1900).
Neill, George Gilbreath Falls, Colonel 30th Mississippi Infantry. (1810-1877).
Neill, James F., Lieutenant-Colonel, Colonel 23d Tennessee Infantry.
Neilson, Charles P., Lieutenant-Colonel 33d Mississippi Infantry. (1839-1894).
Nelms, Charles G., Major, Lieutenant-Colonel 22d Mississippi Infantry. (d. 1862).
Nelson, Allison, Colonel 10th Texas Infantry. (1822-1862).
Nelson, Noel L., Major, Lieutenant-Colonel 12th Louisiana Infantry.
Nelson, Thomas Mauduit, Lieutenant-Colonel 6th Mississippi Cavalry. (d. 1864).
Nelson, Thomas Pleasant, Major 4th Mississippi Infantry. (1824-1910).
Nesbit, Ralph, Lieutenant-Colonel Nesbit's Infantry Battalion South Carolina State Troops. (1840-1912).
Nesbit, (**) William T., Lieutenant-Colonel 5th Mississippi Cavalry, 44th Mississippi Infantry.
Newell, John Henry, Major 3d Virginia Militia, 7th Brigade 136th Virginia Militia.
Newman, Tazewell W., Colonel 17th Tennessee Infantry; Colonel 23d Battalion Tennessee Infantry; Major 45th Tennessee Infantry (supernumerary during consolidation). (1827-1867).
Newsom, John E., Major 4th (Roddey's) Alabama Cavalry. (b. 1838).
Newsom, John F., Colonel 18th (Newsom's) Tennessee Cavalry.
Newton, (**) G. W., Major Jackman's Missouri Cavalry Regiment, 1864.
Newton, Robert Crittenden, Colonel 5th Arkansas Cavalry. (1840-1887).
Neyland, (**) Robert, Lieutenant-Colonel 1st Texas Lancers.
Neyland, Robert Reese, Lieutenant-Colonel 24th Texas Cavalry.
Neyland, William Madison, Lieutenant-Colonel 25th Texas Cavalry.
Nichols, (**) C. H., Lieutenant-Colonel Jackman's Regiment Missouri Cavalry, 1864.
Nichols, Ebenezer B., Colonel 9th (Nichols', also called 5th) Texas Infantry (6 months). (1814-1872).
Nichols, George W., Major 6th (after 11th) Missouri Cavalry.
Nichols, Isaac B., Acting Major Nichols' Florida Battalion Reserves, Series 1, Volume XXXV, pt. II.
Nicholson, Andrew Jackson, Lieutenant-Colonel 11th Texas Cavalry.
Nickell, George W. H., Lieutenant-Colonel 108th Virginia Militia.
Nighbert, James A., Major 1st Infantry Regiment Virginia State Line.
Nisbet, James Cooper, Colonel 66th Georgia Infantry. (1839-1917).
Nisbet, John Wingfield, Major 26th Battalion Georgia Infantry. (b. 1833).
Nix, F. M., Lieutenant-Colonel 16th Battalion Georgia Cavalry, formerly Lieutenant-Colonel 1st Battalion aft. 54th Tennessee.
Nixon, George Henry, Major 23d Tennessee Infantry; Colonel 48th (Nixon's) Tennessee Infantry; Colonel 20th (Nixon's) Tennessee Cavalry; Colonel of Nixon's Tennessee Cavalry Regiment. (1822-1887).

Nixon, James O., Lieutenant-Colonel 1st Louisiana Cavalry.
Noble, John I., Major Confederate Guards, Louisiana Militia.
Noble, Sebron M., Major, Lieutenant-Colonel 17th Texas Cavalry.
Nolan, Matthew, Major 2d Texas Cavalry.
Noles, L. L., Major 25th (also called 30th) Arkansas Infantry.
Norman, James M., Major 4th Mississippi Cavalry.
Norman, Matthew J., Major Fristoe's Regiment Missouri Cavalry. (d. 1907).
Norris, Marion E., Lieutenant-Colonel 14th Mississippi Infantry.
Norsworthy, (**) B. H., Major 27th Texas Cavalry.
Norwood, Alexander S., Major, Colonel 27th Louisiana Infantry.
Norwood, John H., Lieutenant-Colonel 55th Alabama Infantry; Major 6th Battalion Alabama Infantry.
Norwood, John Henry, Lieutenant-Colonel 43d Tennessee Infantry. (1828-1891).
Nuckols, Joseph Preyer, Major, Lieutenant-Colonel, Colonel 4th Kentucky Infantry. (1828-1896).
Nunn, Elisha F., Major 45th Mississippi Infantry; Major 3d (Williams') Battalion Mississippi Infantry.
Nunnally, Aaron D., Major 6th Infantry Georgia State Guard.
Oatis, Martin Augustus, Major 22d Mississippi Infantry.
O'Bannon, Lawrence W., Major 1st Battalion Confederate Infantry and 20th Regiment Infantry. (d. 1882).
Ochiltree, William Beck, Colonel 18th Texas Infantry. (1811-1867).
Odell, James J., Lieutenant-Colonel 26th Tennessee Infantry. (b. c. 1827).
Offield, (**) James F., Colonel 155th Virginia Militia.
Ogden, Frederick Nash, Major 8th Battalion Louisiana Artillery.
Ogden, Samuel, Lieutenant-Colonel 4th (McNair's) Arkansas Infantry.
Oglesby, L. W., Colonel 8th (Fulton's) Tennessee Infantry.
O'Kane, Walter S., Lieutenant-Colonel 4th Missouri Infantry, 8th Division, Missouri State Guard.
Oldham, Thomas, Colonel 41st Virginia Militia.
O'Leary, Stephen, Major 13th Louisiana Infantry.
Oliver, H. L., Lieutenant-Colonel 52d Tennessee Infantry.
Oliver, John E., Major of Mann's Regiment Texas Cavalry.
Oliver, Robert P., Major 16th Louisiana Infantry.
Oliveros, J. B., Lieutenant-Colonel Ordnance Battalion, Columbus, Georgia.
Olmstead, Charles Hart, Major, Colonel 1st Volunteers Georgia. (1837-1926).
O'Neal, William P., Lieutenant-Colonel 32d Tennessee Infantry.
O'Neil, James M., Lieutenant-Colonel 1st (Fagan's and Monroe's) Arkansas Cavalry.
O'Neill, Charles C., Major 16th South Carolina Infantry. (k. 1864).
O'Neill, John, Major, Lieutenant-Colonel, Colonel 10th Tennessee Infantry.
Orr, Jehu Amaziah, Lieutenant-Colonel 5th (Orr's) Battalion Mississippi Infantry; Colonel 31st Mississippi Infantry. (1828-1921).
Osborn, N. C., Major 1st Cavalry Battalion Georgia Reserves.
Oswald, Theodore, Major 4th Battalion Texas Infantry (6 months).
Outlaw, Drew A., Major, Lieutenant-Colonel 12th Tennessee Infantry; Major Outlaw's Battalion Tennessee Partisan Rangers.
Owen, D. Jackson, Major 4th (Avery's) Georgia Cavalry.
Owen, John J., Major 29th Georgia Infantry.
Owen, John L., Major Hawkins' Missouri Cavalry Regiment, 2d Division, Missouri State Guard.
Owen, (**) Joshua, Colonel .... Georgia Militia.
Owen, T. E., Lieutenant-Colonel 8th Missouri Cavalry, 8th Division, Missouri State Guard. (b. 1826).
Owen, Washington G., Major 10th (Johnson's) Kentucky Partisan Rangers.
Owens, George W., Major 26th Texas Cavalry; Major of Terrell's Regiment Texas Cavalry.
Owens, Robert A., Lieutenant-Colonel, Colonel 46th Tennessee Infantry.
Owens, Winfrey J., Colonel 3d Mississippi Infantry (or Minute Men) State Troops.
Ownbey, R. L., Major 109th North Carolina Militia.

Owsley, (**) C. B., Major 3d Kentucky Cavalry Battalion, 1863.
Ozier, Joseph D., Lieutenant-Colonel 18th (Newsom's) Tennessee Cavalry.
Page, John, Major 1st (McCurtain's) Choctaw Battalion.
Paine, F. J., Major 16th Battalion Tennessee Cavalry.
Palmer, John B., Colonel 58th North Carolina Infantry; Lieutenant-Colonel 5th Battalion North Carolina Partisan Rangers.
Palmer, Joseph, Major 14th Battalion Georgia Artillery. (1835-1898).
Palmer, Joseph Benjamin, Colonel 18th Tennessee Infantry. (1825-1890).
Palmer, Solomon, Major 19th Alabama Infantry. (1839-1896).
Panky, David Young, Lieutenant-Colonel 1st Missouri Infantry, 1st Division, Missouri State Guard. (1832-1910).
Pannill, Joseph, Lieutenant-Colonel 2d Virginia Heavy Artillery.
Pardue, L. B., Lieutenant-Colonel 7th Battalion Mississippi Infantry. (d. 1864).
Pargoud, John Frank, Colonel 3d (Pargoud's) Louisiana Cavalry.
Parham, William Thomas, Major 16th (Wilson's, also called 21st) Tennessee Cavalry; Major 18th (Newsom's) Tennessee Cavalry. (1832-1905).
Parish, W. N., Lieutenant-Colonel 18th (Carroll's) Arkansas Infantry.
Park, James M., Major, Lieutenant-Colonel 7th Mississippi Cavalry (also called 1st Mississippi Partisan Rangers).
Park, John Wesley, Major 1st (Fannin's) Georgia Reserves.
Parker, H. S., Major Cavalry Battalion, Waul's Texas Legion.
Parker, James P., Lieutenant-Colonel 1st Mississippi Artillery. (b. 1839).
Parker, Nathan, Major 4th Kentucky Cavalry. (1825-1864).
Parker, William, Lieutenant-Colonel 62d (also called 80th) Tennessee Infantry. (1837-1864).
Parker, William C., Major 1st Missouri Cavalry.
Parkes, Benjamin F., Major 22d Texas Infantry.
Parks, Robert Calvin, Lieutenant-Colonel 1st Cherokee Mounted Rifles.
Parks, William H., Major 2d Infantry Texas State Troops.
Parrish, William, Major 2d (Barteau's, afterwards 22d) Tennessee Cavalry. (d. 1908).
Parrott, James, Major 8th Missouri Cavalry; Lieutenant-Colonel 4th Missouri Infantry, 1st Division, Missouri State Guard.
Parsons, William H., Colonel 12th Texas Cavalry.
Partin, Charles Perry, Major 36th Mississippi Infantry. (1825-1893).
Partlow, John M., Major 20th South Carolina Infantry.
Partridge, Robert H., Major 15th Confederate Cavalry.
Pate, A. C., Colonel 2nd Georgia Militia. (1836-1916).
Patrick, Marsh M., Major 154th Senior Tennessee Infantry.
Patterson, Charles E., Lieutenant-Colonel 2d Arkansas Infantry. (d. 1862).
Patterson, John, Lieutenant-Colonel 1st Tennessee Volunteers.
Patterson, Josiah, Colonel 5th Alabama Cavalry. (1837-1903).
Patterson, Thomas H., Major, Lieutenant-Colonel 30th Alabama Infantry. (d. 1864).
Patterson, William C., Major, Lieutenant-Colonel 30th Alabama Infantry.
Patterson, William K., Colonel 8th Arkansas Infantry.
Patton, Archibald K., Lieutenant-Colonel 15th (Cleburne's) Arkansas Infantry; Lieutenant-Colonel 1st (Cleburne's) Arkansas Infantry. (d. 1862).
Patton, Isaac Williams, Colonel 21st (Patton's) Louisiana Infantry; Colonel 22d Louisiana Infantry Consolidated; Major 23d (after 22d) Louisiana Infantry. (d. 1890).
Patton, John, Major Extra Cavalry Battalion, 4th Division, Missouri State Guard.
Patton, Oliver A., Lieutenant-Colonel Patton's Kentucky Partisan Rangers.
Patton, Thomas, Colonel 2d Missouri Infantry, 4th Division, Missouri State Guard.
Patton, William S., Lieutenant-Colonel 37th Mississippi Infantry; Colonel 1st Regiment Army 10,000.
Patton, (**) William T., Lieutenant-Colonel Botetourt Battalion, Conscripts & Reserves.
Patty, Obed., Major 10th Arkansas Infantry.
Payne, John W., Lieutenant-Colonel 6th Missouri Cavalry, 8th Division, Missouri State Guard. (b. 1823).

Payne, Robert N., Major, Colonel 33d Tennessee Infantry; Major 31st (A. H. Bradford's) and 33d Tennessee Infantry Consolidated.
Peacher, L., Major 4th Missouri Infantry, 3d Division, Missouri State Guard.
Peacock, Thomas P., Major 9th Infantry Georgia State Guard.
Peak, William Wallace, Major 31st Texas Cavalry.
Pearcy, Jacob Wilton, Major, Lieutenant-Colonel 65th Georgia Infantry. (1830?-1873).
Pease, George W., Major, Lieutenant-Colonel 50th (new) Tennessee Infantry.
Peay, Gordon N., Lieutenant-Colonel 6th Arkansas Infantry.
Peebles, Thomas Henry, Lieutenant-Colonel 24th Tennessee Infantry. (d. 1868).
Peek, George F., Major 8th Mississippi Infantry.
Peel, Samuel West, Colonel 4th (Peel's) Arkansas Infantry. (1831-1924).
Peery, William B., Major 5th Mississippi Cavalry.
Peery, William F., Colonel, recruiting Missouri Cavalry Regiment.
Pegg, Thomas, Major Drew's Cherokee Mounted Rifles (also called 1st and 2d Cherokee Mounted Rifles). (b. 1808).
Pegram, William G., Major 34th (also called 37th) Mississippi Infantry.
Pegues, C. M., Major 29th (also called 28th) Louisiana Infantry.
Pegues, Josiah James, Major, Lieutenant-Colonel 2d Alabama Cavalry. (1825-1906).
Peirce, Thomas W., Major 39th North Carolina Infantry.
Pell, James A., Lieutenant-Colonel 6th Confederate Cavalry.
Pemberton, John S., Lieutenant-Colonel 12th Cavalry Georgia State Guard.
Pendleton, Stephen Taylor, Major 19th Virginia Militia (afterward 2d State Reserves). (1828-1915).
Pennington, A. A., Major, Lieutenant-Colonel 23d Arkansas Infantry.
Pennington, William F., Major, Lieutenant-Colonel 4th Louisiana Infantry.
Peoples, S. J., Major Carlton's Regiment Arkansas Cavalry.
Percy, William Alexander, Lieutenant-Colonel 24th Battalion Mississippi Cavalry; Colonel 1st Regiment Alcorn's Brigade, Army of Mississippi 10,000. (d. 1888).
Perkins, Samuel William, Lieutenant-Colonel 35th (Brown's) Texas Cavalry; Major 12th Battalion Texas Cavalry.
Perkins, ..., Major 6th Missouri Infantry, 3d Division, Missouri State Guard.
Perrin, Robert O., Colonel 11th Mississippi Cavalry; Lieutenant-Colonel Perrin's Battalion Mississippi State Cavalry.
Perry, John J., Major 2d (also called 4th) Mississippi Cavalry. (d. 1885).
Perry, Madison Starke, Colonel 7th Florida Infantry. (1814-1865).
Perry, Stephen S., Major 13th Texas Infantry.
Person, Richard J., Major 5th (Smith's) Confederate Infantry. (1843-1909).
Persons, Alexander W., Lieutenant-Colonel, Colonel 55th Georgia Infantry.
Pettigrew, James R., Major, Lieutenant-Colonel 34th (also called 2d) Arkansas Infantry. (1829-1886).
Pettus' (Allen T.) Battalion Infantry Arkansas State Troops, Series 1, Vol. XXXIV, pt. 1. (k. 1864).
Pettus, Edmund Winston, Major, Lieutenant-Colonel, Colonel 20th Alabama Infantry. (1821-1907).
Pettus, (**) Thomas, Lieutenant-Colonel 22d Militia.
Peyton, E. A., Major, Lieutenant-Colonel 3d Mississippi Infantry; Major Peyton's Battalion Cavalry, Mississippi State Troops.
Peyton, Robert Ludwell Yates, Colonel 3d Missouri Cavalry, 8th Division, Missouri State Guard. (1822-1863).
Pheelan, William G., Colonel 2d Missouri Infantry, 1st Division, Missouri State Guard.
Phifer, Charles W., Major Phifer's Battalion Arkansas Cavalry. (b. 1834).
Phillips, Alexander Hamilton, Jr., Major 6th Texas Infantry. (d. 1863).
Phillips, Charles Duval, Lieutenant-Colonel, Colonel 52d Georgia Infantry. (1829-1912).
Phillips, James, Major 8th (Burns', changed to 11th) Missouri Infantry.
Phillips, John Lott, Major 3d Florida Infantry.
Phillips, Joseph, Colonel 3d Texas Cavalry Regiment, Arizona Brigade. (d. 1876).
Phillips, Seaborne Moses, Colonel 10th Mississippi Infantry. (d. 1861).

Phillips, William S., Lieutenant-Colonel 47th Georgia Infantry.
Philpott, Benjamin A., Lieutenant-Colonel 12th (also called 8th) Texas Infantry.
Phipps, Frank L., Major 12th Battalion Tennessee Cavalry.
Pickering, Alfred S., Major 20th Alabama Infantry. (d. 1863).
Pickett, Alexander Corbin, Colonel 10th (also called 12th) Missouri Infantry; Major Stearn's Battalion Missouri Infantry. (1821-1883).
Pickett, Edward, Jr., Colonel 21st Tennessee Infantry. (1828-1876).
Pickett, Edward Bradford, Major 25th Texas Cavalry.
Pickett, Richard Orrick, Colonel 10th Alabama Cavalry, Major Battalion Alabama Cavalry. (1814-1898).
Pickler, J. F., Major 1st Missouri Cavalry Battalion, 1st Indian Brigade.
Picolet, Arthur, Major 30th Louisiana Infantry.
Pierce, J. W., Major 1st Choctaw Battalion Cavalry, Mississippi.
Pierce, Junius J., Major 24th Alabama Infantry.
Piercey, Andrew J., Lieutenant-Colonel 11th Missouri Cavalry, 8th Division, Missouri State Guard.
Piercy, Andrew Jackson, Major 1st Missouri Cavalry Battalion, 1st Indian Brigade. (1828-1913).
Pierson, David, Major, Lieutenant-Colonel 3d Louisiana Infantry. (b. 1837).
Pilgrim, (**) Thomas J., Colonel 1st Georgia Militia.
Pillans, Job Palmer, Lieutenant-Colonel 2d Alabama Militia. (1816-1898).
Pinckard, James S., Major 8th Infantry Georgia State Guard.
Pinkney, William Elder, Major, Lieutenant-Colonel 8th Battalion Louisiana Artillery.
Pindall, Lebbeus Ashby, Major 9th Battalion Missouri Sharpshooters. (b. 1834).
Pindall, Xenophen J., Lieutenant-Colonel 5th Missouri Infantry, 3d Division, Missouri State Guard. (b. 1835).
Pinson, Richard Alexander, Colonel 1st Mississippi Cavalry. (1829-1873).
Pirtle, M. H., Lieutenant-Colonel 22d Tennessee Infantry.
Pitman, Robert William, Lieutenant-Colonel, Colonel 13th Tennessee Infantry; Lieutenant-Colonel 13th and 154th Tennessee Infantry Consolidated. (d. 1900).
Pitner, Tilmon Howard, Major 39th Georgia Infantry. (b. 1831).
Pitts, Fountain E., Colonel 61st (also called 81st) Tennessee Infantry.
Pitzer, (**) A. L., Major 2d Louisiana Cavalry.
Pixlee, Benjamin T., Lieutenant Colonel 16th Arkansas Infantry (d. 1863).
Platt, Charles A., Lieutenant-Colonel 18th Battalion Infantry Georgia State Guard. (d. 1887).
Plattsmier, John T., Lieutenant-Colonel 21st (Patton's) Louisiana Infantry.
Pleasants, J. C., Colonel 29th Arkansas Infantry.
Plummer, (**) Kemp, Major .... Infantry.
Poage, Alpheus Wilson, Major, Lieutenant-Colonel 4th (also called 5th) Virginia Reserves.
Poe, James T., Major 11th Arkansas Infantry; Major Poe's Battalion Arkansas Cavalry. (1829-1913).
Poe, William T., Major 8th (also called 9th) Alabama Cavalry.
Poe, Wilson W., Acting Major Poe's Battalion Florida Reserves, Series 1, Vol. XXXV, pt. II.
Pogue, (**) Robert, Major 160th Virginia Militia.
Poindexter, ..., Colonel 6th Missouri Infantry, 3d Division, Missouri State Guard.
Pointer, Marcellus, Lieutenant-Colonel 12th Alabama Cavalry. (d. 1909).
Polk, Cadwallader, Lieutenant-Colonel Hawthorn's Arkansas Infantry.
Polk, Lucius Eugene, Colonel 15th (Polk's) Arkansas Infantry. (1833-1892).
Pollard, (**) J. M., Lieutenant-Colonel 13th Arkansas Infantry.
Pond, Preston, Jr., Colonel 16th Louisiana Infantry. (d. 1864).
Ponder, Willis M., Colonel 12th Missouri Infantry; Lieutenant-Colonel 9th (White's, also called 12th) Missouri Infantry; Major 3d Missouri Infantry, 1st Division, Missouri State Guard.
Pool, M. L., Major 56th (also called 55th) Georgia Infantry.
Pool, Stephen Decatur, Major, Lieutenant-Colonel, Colonel 10th North Carolina Volunteers (1st North Carolina Artillery).

Pool, Stephen Decatur, Major, Lieutenant-Colonel, Colonel 10th North Carolina Volunteers (1st North Carolina Artillery).
Pool, Thomas W., Major, Colonel 28th Louisiana Infantry.
Pope, Henry, Major 7th Mississippi Infantry.
Pope, Riddick, Major 5th Arkansas Infantry.
Pope's Kentucky Battalion, Series 1, Vol. II, Captain John D. Pope.
Porcher, Julius Theodore, Major, Lieutenant-Colonel 10th South Carolina Infantry. (1829-1863).
Porter, Bradshaw W., Major 9th Battalion Tennessee Cavalry.
Porter, Edward E., Lieutenant-Colonel 3d (Forrest's) Tennessee Cavalry.
Porter, George Camp, Major, Colonel 6th Tennessee Infantry; Colonel 6th and 9th Tennessee Infantry Consolidated. (1835-1919).
Porter, J. M., Colonel Saint Landry Regiment, Louisiana Militia.
Porter, John Crump, Colonel 3d Virginia Artillery. (1828-1903).
Porter, Joseph C., Colonel 1st Northeast Missouri Cavalry; Lieutenant-Colonel Green's Cavalry Regiment, 2d Division, Missouri State Guard.
Porter, Mitchell Thomas, Major, Lieutenant-Colonel 20th Alabama Infantry. (b. 1825).
Portis, John Wesley, Colonel 42d Alabama Infantry.
Portis, William N., Major Morgan's (also called 2d) Regiment Arkansas Cavalry.
Portlock, Edward Edwards, Jr., Colonel 24th Arkansas Infantry. (1840-1887).
Postlethwaite, A. J., Lieutenant-Colonel 4th Battalion Mississippi Infantry (or Minute Men) State Troops.
Pound, William M., Lieutenant-Colonel 12th Battalion Mississippi Partisan Rangers.
Powel, Samuel, Colonel 29th Tennessee Infantry. (1821-1902).
Powell, Daniel Lee, Lieutenant-Colonel 19th Virginia Militia (afterward 2d State Reserves). (1826-1871).
Powell, John R., Lieutenant-Colonel 10th Alabama Cavalry; Major Battalion Alabama Cavalry.
Powell, William Alfred, Major 2d Georgia Reserves. (1825-1906).
Powell, (**) William L., Colonel 2d Battalion Alabama Artillery. (d. 1863).
Powers, Frank P., Colonel 14th (Mitchell's) Arkansas Infantry; Colonel Powers' Regiment Louisiana and Mississippi Cavalry.
Powers, Thomas, Major 2d Missouri Infantry, 1st Division, Missouri State Guard.
Prather, John Smith, Major, Lieutenant-Colonel 8th Confederate Cavalry. (d. 1920).
Prator, (**) William G., Colonel 51st Georgia Militia.
Prentice, Clarence J., Lieutenant-Colonel 7th Confederate Cavalry Battalion; Major 2d Battalion Kentucky Cavalry. (1840-1873).
Pressley, James Fowler, Lieutenant-Colonel, Colonel 10th South Carolina Infantry; Colonel 19th South Carolina Infantry (temporary command). (1835-1877).
Presstman, Stephen Wilson, Lieutenant-Colonel 3d Engineer Regiment; Major Presstman's Battalion Engineer Troops.
Prestidge, James S., Major, Lieutenant-Colonel 22d Mississippi Infantry.
Preston, C. H., Major 5th Infantry Regiment Virginia State Line.
Preston, William I. ("Ike"), Lieutenant-Colonel 4th Missouri Cavalry; Major Preston's Missouri Cavalry Battalion. (1832-1882).
Prewitt, Russell G., Major 15th Mississippi Infantry.
Price, Edwin, Lieutenant-Colonel 1st Missouri Infantry, 3d Division, Missouri State Guard; Colonel 3d Missouri Infantry, 3d Division, Missouri State Guard.
Price, Hawkins F., Major 10th Battalion Mounted Rifles Georgia State Guard (also called 9th Battalion Cavalry Georgia State Guard).
Price, John A., Major 8th Arkansas Infantry. (c. 1831-1862).
Price, John Valentine, Colonel 11th Regiment Georgia State Troops. (d. 1873).
Priest, John W., Lieutenant-Colonel 5th Missouri Infantry Battalion, Missouri State Guard.
Prince, (**) John, Lieutenant-Colonel 15th Virginia Militia.
Prince, Thomas McCarroll, Major 22d Alabama Infantry. (1842-1869).
Printup, Daniel S., Major 55th Georgia Infantry. (1823-1887).
Prior, John N., Major 4th North Carolina Senior Reserves. (d. 1913).
Pritchard, James A., Lieutenant-Colonel, Colonel 3d (also called 2d) Missouri

Infantry; Lieutenant-Colonel 1st Missouri Infantry, 4th Division, Missouri State Guard. (d. 1862).
Pritchard, (**) Paul, Major 1st South Carolina Mounted Militia.
Pritchard, Solomon S., Lieutenant-Colonel 51st Virginia Militia. (d. 1861).
Pritchard, William R., Lieutenant-Colonel 22d Battalion Georgia Siege Artillery.
Proffitt, Bacchus S., Major, Lieutenant-Colonel 29th North Carolina Infantry. (d. 1865).
Proffitt, William W., Lieutenant-Colonel 58th North Carolina Infantry.
Provence, David, Colonel 16th Arkansas Infantry; Lieutenant-Colonel 3d Arkansas Infantry State Troops, 1861.
Pruden, William H., Lieutenant-Colonel 32d Georgia Infantry.
Pryor, Moses Tandy, Lieutenant-Colonel 4th Kentucky Cavalry. (1832-1873).
Pullen, E. J., Major 4th Louisiana Infantry.
Pulliam, Thomas J., Major, 31st Mississippi (b. 1838).
Purdy, Lem., Major 14th Texas Cavalry.
Purl, James, Major 12th Tennessee Infantry.
Purves, George, Major 21st (Patton's) Louisiana Infantry.
Puryear, John B., Major 11th Texas Cavalry
Pyron, Charles Lynn, Major, Colonel 2d Texas Cavalry. (1819-1869).
Quarles, William Andrew, Colonel 42d Tennessee Infantry. (1825-1893).
Quattlebaum, Walter, Major 2d South Carolina State Troops (6 months).
Quayle, William, Lieutenant-Colonel 9th Texas Cavalry, Major State Troops. (1825-1901).
Query, (**) Robert, Colonel 21st Arkansas Militia.
Quin, W. Monroe, Major 39th Mississippi Infantry.
Quinn, D. H., Colonel 2d Mississippi Infantry (or Minute Men) State Troops.
Ragsdale, Samuel G., Major of Ragsdale's Battalion Texas Cavalry; Major of Daly's Battalion Texas Cavalry.
Raguet, Henry W., Major 4th Texas Cavalry. (k. 1862).
Railey, Charles R., Lieutenant-Colonel Confederate Guards, Louisiana Militia.
Raine, James W., Major 12th (also called 8th) Texas Infantry.
Rains, George Washington, Colonel 1st Regiment Local Defense Troops, Augusta, Georgia. (1817-1898).
Rains, James Edwards, Colonel 11th Tennessee Infantry. (1833-1862).
Rains, William W., Major 41st Virginia Militia.
Ramey, (**) Sanford J., Colonel 57th Virginia Militia.
Ramsaur, Leander Marcus, Major, Lieutenant-Colonel, Colonel 1st Arkansas Mounted Rifles. (1829-1881).
Ramsay, David, Major 1st Battalion South Carolina Infantry. (k. 1863).
Randal, Horace, Colonel 28th Texas Cavalry. (1833-1864).
Randall, Samuel J., Major 5th Mississippi Infantry (or Minute Men) State Troops.
Randals, Benjamin, Major 16th Tennessee Infantry.
Randell, Gabriel H., Major 39th Georgia Infantry.
Randle, James A., Major of Anderson's Cavalry Texas State Troops.
Randle, Thomas Green, Major 52d Tennessee Infantry.
Randolph, Francis Corbin, Major, Lieutenant-Colonel, Colonel 7th Alabama Cavalry. (1841-1905).
Randolph, John L., Major 9th Battalion Texas Partisan Rangers.
Rankin, Peter Turney, Major 4th (Starnes', also called 3d) Tennessee Cavalry. (1828-1901).
Rankin, William A., Lieutenant-Colonel 9th Mississippi Infantry. (d. 1862).
Rapley, W. F., Major 3d Battalion Missouri Infantry, 1st Division, Missouri State Guard.
Rapley, William Field, Major 12th Battalion Arkansas Sharpshooters. (b. 1838).
Rawlings, S. A., Lieutenant-Colonel Rawlings' Battalion Missouri Infantry, 2nd Division, Missouri State Guard.
Rawls, Morgan, Lieutenant-Colonel 54th Georgia Infantry. (1829-1906).
Raxsdale, Frank M., Major 16th Louisiana Infantry.
Ray, James Mitchel, Lieutenant-Colonel 60th North Carolina Infantry. (1838-1923).
Rayburn, Leander M., Major 8th Texas Cavalry.

Rayburn, William A., Major 1st (also called 10th and 20th) Battalion Mississippi Sharpshooters.
Rea, Constantine, Major 46th Mississippi Infantry; Major Rea's Battalion Mississippi Sharpshooters. (d. 1864).
Read, Alpheus LaFayette, Major 72nd Battalion Georgia Militia. (1826-1864).
Rector, Frank A., Colonel 1st (Rector's War Regiment) Arkansas Volunteers; Colonel 17th (Rector's) Arkansas Infantry; Colonel Rector's Arkansas Infantry (12 months).
Redding, A. F., Colonel 7th Regiment Georgia State Militia.
Redditt, William Antoine, Major 17th Louisiana Infantry.
Redwine, Hullum Duke Erasmus, Major 10th Texas Cavalry.
Redwood, Richard H., Major 8th (Hatch's, also called 9th) Alabama Cavalry. (d. 1864).
Redwood, William H., Major, Lieutenant-Colonel 16th Texas Infantry.
Reece, John M., Major 3d Battalion North Carolina Junior Reserves, 4th Battalion Junior Reserves.
Reed, Absalom, Major Perrin's Battalion Mississippi State Cavalry; Major 11th Mississippi Cavalry. (1828-1885).
Reed, (**) Eugene W., Major 3d Virginia Militia.
Reed, Wiley M., Lieutenant-Colonel 5th Mississippi Cavalry.
Reed, Wiley Martin, Lieutenant-Colonel 55th Tennessee Infantry. (1827-1864).
Reese, John J., Lieutenant-Colonel 3d Tennessee Infantry (Prov. Army).
Reese, Warren Stone, Colonel 12th Alabama Cavalry. (1842-1898).
Reeves, George R., Colonel 11th Texas Cavalry. (1826-1882).
Reeves, William N., Major 4th Battalion Artillery, Hilliard's Alabama Legion.
Reichard, Augustus, Colonel 20th Louisiana Infantry.
Reid, H. J., Lieutenant-Colonel 22d Mississippi Infantry. (1827-1906).
Reid, John Coleman, Lieutenant-Colonel, Colonel 28th Alabama Infantry. (b. 1824).
Reid, J. T., Lieutenant-Colonel 8th Battalion Georgia Infantry.
Reid, Peter C., Major 2d Virginia Militia.
Reid, Thomas Jefferson, Jr., Major, Colonel 12th Arkansas Infantry; Major 2d Arkansas Cavalry. (1837-1907).
Reiff, A. V., Major, Lieutenant-Colonel 1st (Fagan's and Monroe's) Arkansas Cavalry. (1836-1914).
Reily, James, Colonel 4th Texas Cavalry. (1811-1863).
Repass, W. G., Major 7th Confederate Battalion.
Reves, Timothy, Major Reves' Missouri Cavalry Battalion.
Reynolds, Abram David, Major Henry's Regiment Virginia Reserves. (1848-1925).
Reynolds, Daniel Harris, Major, Lieutenant-Colonel, Colonel 1st Arkansas Mounted Rifles. (1832-1902).
Reynolds, Francis A., Major, Lieutenant-Colonel 39th North Carolina Infantry. (1841-1875).
Reynolds, George Washington, Major 29th Mississippi Infantry. (d. 1864).
Reynolds, Hugh A., Major, Lieutenant-Colonel 30th Mississippi Infantry; Major 34/37 Mississippi Infantry (temporary) December 31, 1862. (d. 1863).
Reynolds, Lemuel M., Lieutenant-Colonel, 1st Chickasaw Cavalry Battalion.
Reynolds, Simon D., Major 62d (also called 80th) Tennessee Infantry.
Reynolds, William W., Lieutenant-Colonel 15th (Boone's) Arkansas Infantry; Lieutenant-Colonel 15th (Hobb's) Arkansas Infantry.
Rhea, James Alexander, Major, Lieutenant-Colonel 60th (also called 79th) Tennessee Infantry. (1840-1871).
Rhett, Alfred Moore, Major, Lieutenant-Colonel, Colonel 1st South Carolina Artillery. (1829-1889).
Rice, Horace, Major, Lieutenant-Colonel, Colonel 29th Tennessee Infantry; Colonel 11th and 29th Tennessee Infantry Consolidated. (d. 1871).
Rice, Olin F., Colonel 2d Alabama Reserves. (1839-1882).
Rice, P. H., Colonel 3d Confederate Cavalry. (1836-1895).
Rich, Lucius Loomis, Lieutenant-Colonel, Colonel 1st Missouri Infantry. (1831-1862).
Richards, John S., Major 3d Louisiana Infantry.

Richards, William Coolidge, Major 9th Battalion Mississippi Sharpshooters; Colonel 9th Mississippi Infantry. (1828-1916).
Richardson, John A., Lieutenant-Colonel 36th North Carolina Volunteers (2d North Carolina Artillery).
Richardson, Robert, Colonel 17th Louisiana Infantry.
Richardson, Robert Vinkler, Colonel 12th (also called 1st Partisan Rangers) Tennessee Cavalry. (1820-1870).
Richardson, Thomas J. M., Colonel 3d Cavalry Texas State Troops.
Richardson, William C., Major 53d Tennessee Infantry. (d. 1864).
Rider, E. C., Major 89th Virginia Militia.
Ridley, Alonzo, Major 3d Texas Cavalry Regiment, Arizona Brigade.
Riely, J. C., Major 31st Virginia Militia.
Riggs, James M., Lieutenant-Colonel 27th Arkansas Infantry.
Riley, Amos Camden, Lieutenant-Colonel, Colonel 1st Missouri Infantry; Lieutenant Colonel, Colonel 1st and 4th Missouri Consolidated. (k. 1864).
Riley, James, Lieutenant-Colonel 1st Choctaw and Chickasaw Mounted Rifles.
Rines, (**) Timothy, Colonel 15th Missouri Regiment.
Ringo, D. W., Lieutenant-Colonel Johnson's Regiment Arkansas Infantry.
Riordan, Edward, Major 4th Texas Cavalry Regiment, Arizona Brigade; Lieutenant-Colonel 1st Texas Cavalry Regiment, Arizona Brigade and 31st Texas Cavalry.
Ripley, Roswell Sabine, Lieutenant-Colonel 1st South Carolina Artillery Battalion. (1823-1887).
Rives, Benjamin Allen, Colonel 3d (also called 2d) Missouri Infantry; Colonel 13th Missouri Infantry; Colonel 1st Missouri Cavalry, 4th Division, Missouri State Guard. (1822-1862).
Roach, (**) E. M., Major 15th Arkansas Militia (afterwards Williamson's Battalion Arkansas Infantry).
Robb, Alfred, Lieutenant-Colonel 49th Tennessee Infantry. (1818-1862).
Roberts, Calvit, Major Moorman's Battalion Mississippi Cavalry.
Roberts, Charles McKinney, Major 14th Battalion North Carolina Cavalry. (1827-1864).
Roberts, E., Major 24th Battalion Mississippi Cavalry.
Roberts, Oran Milo, Colonel 11th Texas Infantry. (1815-1898).
Roberts, Riley B., Lieutenant-Colonel 35th (formerly 5th Tennessee, Prov. Army) Tennessee Infantry. (b. c. 1822).
Roberts, Thomas B., Colonel 1st South Carolina State Troops (6 months).
Robertson, A. T., Lieutenant-Colonel 22d Tennessee Infantry.
Robertson, Charles S., Lieutenant-Colonel 1st (also called 12th) Confederate Cavalry.
Robertson, Christopher Willis, Major 50th (old) Tennessee Infantry. (k. 1863).
Robertson, Francis Marion, Colonel 1st Charleston Reserves, South Carolina. (1806-1892).
Robertson, H. G., Lieutenant-Colonel 20th Arkansas Infantry.
Robertson, James Walthall, Colonel 35th Alabama Infantry. (1830-1911).
Robertson, (**) J. L., Major Squadron Arkansas Cavalry.
Robertson, John C., Lieutenant-Colonel Terrell's Regiment Texas Cavalry. (1824-1895).
Robertson, Richard J., Major 12th Missouri Cavalry, 8th Division, Missouri State Guard.
Robertson, Richard L., Major 21st (Patton's) Louisiana Infantry.
Robins, Josiah, Major 3d Alabama Cavalry. (1825-1901).
Robinson, E. C., Colonel 54th Virginia Militia.
Robinson, Henry C., Colonel 5th Mississippi Infantry (or Minute Men) State Troops.
Robinson, Israel, Lieutenant-Colonel 67th Virginia Militia. (1819-1863).
Robinson, James Forbes, Major 23d (Adams') Arkansas Infantry. (1830-1909).
Robinson, (**) John L., Major 33d Texas Cavalry.
Robinson, J. W., Major Robinson's Missouri Infantry Battalion, 2d Division, Missouri State Guard.
Robinson, Walter Calvin, Lieutenant-Colonel 36th Arkansas Infantry.

Robinson, William H., Colonel 12th Georgia Cavalry, Georgia State Guard.
Robison, William D., Colonel 2d Tennessee Infantry (Provisional Army). (1840-1891).
Rockwell, William S., Lieutenant-Colonel 1st Volunteers Georgia.
Roddey, Philip Dale, Colonel 4th (Roddey's) Alabama Cavalry. (1826-1897).
Roff, Charles L., Major Bourland's Regiment Texas Cavalry.
Rogan, James W., Colonel 30th (Rogan's, also called 39th) Arkansas Infantry; Major and Lieutenant-Colonel 30th (McNeill's) Arkansas Infantry; Lieutenant-Colonel 30th (Hart's) Arkansas Infantry.
Rogers, (**) Asa, Major General of Virginia Militia. (1802-1887).
Rogers, Augustus H., Major 14th Texas Infantry.
Rogers, E. W., Major 12th Texas Cavalry.
Rogers, Henry Ashe, Major 9th Tennessee Infantry.
Rogers, (**) Henry C., Colonel Georgia Militia.
Rogers, (**) Hugh, Lieutenant-Colonel 132d Virginia Militia.
Rogers, Jefferson W., Lieutenant-Colonel 9th Arkansas Infantry.
Rogers, John Byrd, Major 4th Kentucky Infantry. (1835-1864).
Rogers, John F., Colonel 1st East Tennessee (afterward 5th) Cavalry.
Rogers, L. M., Major 3d Cavalry Texas State Troops.
Rogers, Madison, Lieutenant-Colonel 17th Louisiana Infantry.
Rogers, W. E., Major 23d Mississippi Infantry.
Rogers, William Peleg, Lieutenant-Colonel, Colonel 2d Texas Infantry. (1817-1862).
Rollins, Richard D. F., Major 9th Battalion South Carolina Infantry; Major Nesbit's South Carolina Infantry Battalion State Troops.
Roman, Alfred, Lieutenant-Colonel 18th Louisiana Infantry. (b. 1824).
Roper, James Turner, Colonel 60th North Carolina Militia.
Rorer, Walter A., Major, Lieutenant-Colonel 20th Mississippi Infantry. (d. 1864).
Rose, James G., Lieutenant-Colonel, Colonel 61st (also called 81st) Tennessee Infantry.
Ross, David Lee, Lieutenant-Colonel 156th Virginia Militia. (1831-1927).
Ross, Jesse A., Major 4th Arkansas Battalion Infantry. (d. 1913).
Ross, Lawrence Sullivan, Major, Colonel 6th Texas Cavalry. (1838-1898).
Ross, Peter F., Major, Lieutenant-Colonel 6th Texas Cavalry. (1836-1909).
Ross, William B., Major, Lieutenant-Colonel 2d Tennessee Volunteers. (1831-1863).
Ross, William E., Lieutenant-Colonel 39th Mississippi Infantry.
Ross, William Potter, Lieutenant-Colonel Drew's Cherokee Mounted Rifles (also called 1st and 2d Mounted Rifles). (1820-1891).
Rosser, Thomas H., Lieutenant-Colonel, Colonel 1st Missouri Infantry, 8th Division, Missouri State Guard. (1818-1897).
Rountree, Charles N., Colonel 8th Georgia Militia. (b. 1827).
Rountree, Lee C., Major 13th Texas Infantry; Major 35th (Brown's) Texas Cavalry.
Rountree, Thomas H., Major 11th Texas Infantry.
Rouse, Napoleon B., Lieutenant-Colonel 22d Alabama Infantry.
Rouse, R. A., Lieutenant-Colonel 3d South Carolina State Troops.
Rowan, John A., Colonel 62d (also called 80th) Tennessee Infantry. (1820-1864).
Rowan, John Madison, Colonel 108th Virginia Militia; Colonel 189th Virginia Militia. (1829-1910).
Rowland, Alexander M., Major 1st Georgia Light Duty Men, Macon, Georgia; Major Battalion Consolidated Macon, Georgia. (1837-1871).
Rowley, R. P., Major 1st Battalion Engineers. (d. 1894).
Rozell, (**) B. L., Colonel 3d Regiment Alcorn's Brigade Army Mississippi 10,000.
Rucker, Edmund Winchester, Major 16th Battalion Tennessee Cavalry; Colonel Rucker's (1st Tennessee) Legion Cavalry. (1836-1924).
Rudler, Anthony F., Major 3d Battalion Georgia Infantry; Colonel 37th Georgia Infantry.
Rudolph, John Barrett, Major 10th Confederate Cavalry. (1835-1910).
Ruffin, Shep., Major 18th Alabama Infantry.

Runnels, Hal. G., Major 2d Texas Infantry.
Rusk, James E., Colonel Cherokee Legion Georgia State Guard.
Russell, Alfred A., Colonel 4th (Russell's) Alabama Cavalry; Major 7th Alabama Infantry (12 months); Lieutenant-Colonel 15th Battalion Tennessee Cavalry.
Russell, Daniel R., Colonel 20th Mississippi Infantry.
Russell, John R., Major, Lieutenant-Colonel 34th (also called 2d Partisans) Texas Cavalry. (b. 1822).
Russell, Robert Milton, Colonel 12th Tennessee Infantry; Colonel 15th (Russell's, also called 20th) Tennessee Cavalry. (1826-1894).
Russell, Samuel D., Major, Lieutenant-Colonel, Colonel 3d Louisiana Infantry.
Rust, (**) George, Lieutenant-Colonel 57th Virginia Militia.
Ruth, Ferdinand, Major 3d Missouri Infantry, 8th Division, Missouri State Guard.
Rutherford, James, Lieutenant-Colonel 7th Arkansas Infantry. (b. 1825).
Ryan, John, Lieutenant-Colonel 17th Alabama Infantry (temporary appointment).
Ryan, John J., Colonel 11th South Carolina Reserves. (1817-1869).
Ryan, William A., Major 18th Texas Cavalry.
Sadler, Lucian P., Major 5th South Carolina State Troops.
Sadler, (**) Thomas J., Major .... Army of 10,000 Mississippi.
Saffell, Richard Meredith, Major, Colonel 26th Tennessee Infantry.
Sale, Melville W., Major 11th (also called 10th) Alabama Cavalry.
Salisbury, William Lewis, Colonel 5th Infantry Georgia State Guard; Major 5th Georgia Infantry. (1830-1878).
Samuel, D. Todd, Major, Lieutenant-Colonel 3d Battalion Missouri Cavalry; Major 1st Missouri Infantry, 5th Division Missouri State Guard. (d. 1864).
Sanderlin, Willis Burgess, Major 68th North Carolina Infantry. (1829-1900).
Sanders, Edward J., Major 9th Mississippi Cavalry; Major 17th Battalion Tennessee Cavalry.
Sanders, Richard Casey, Lieutenant-Colonel 25th Tennessee Infantry. (1826-1889).
Sanders, Valerius P., Major 15th Texas Cavalry.
Sanford, Thomas B., Major 9th (White's, also called 3d and 12th) Missouri Infantry.
Sandusky, (**) G. C., Major 3/11 Confederate Cavalry.
Saufley, William Patton, Major of Saufley's Scouting Battalion, Texas. (1823-1878).
Saunders, James P., Colonel 1st Missouri Infantry, 5th Division, Missouri State Guard.
Saunders, Xenophon Boone, Major 16th Texas Infantry. (1828-1909).
Savage, James H., Major 19th Alabama Infantry.
Savage, John Houston, Colonel 16th Tennessee Infantry. (1815-1904).
Sawyer, Benjamin Franklin, Major, Lieutenant-Colonel 24th Alabama Infantry. (1833-1901).
Sayers, A., Major 2d Missouri Cavalry, 8th Division, Missouri State Guard.
Sayles, John, Colonel 4th Infantry Texas State Troops. (1825-1897).
Scaife, James W., Major, Lieutenant-Colonel, Colonel 2d Arkansas Infantry.
Scales, Joseph Absalom, Major Cherokee Battalion.
Scales, Junius Irving, Lieutenant-Colonel, Colonel 30th Mississippi Infantry. (d. 1880).
Schaller, Frank, Lieutenant-Colonel, Colonel 22d Mississippi Infantry.
Schlater, Gervais, Major 1st Louisiana Cavalry.
Schnable, J. A., Lieutenant-Colonel Battalion Missouri Cavalry; Colonel in Shelby's Division 1864.
Scoggins, L. G., Major 3d Battalion Cavalry Texas State Troops.
Scott, George Washington, Major, Lieutenant-Colonel 5th Battalion Florida Cavalry. (d. 1903).
Scott Henry C., Major Jackson Hospital Battalion, Virginia Infantry.
Scott, (**) John G., Colonel Commanding 3d Regiment State Corps.
Scott, John S., Colonel 1st Louisiana Cavalry.
Scott, R., Lieutenant-Colonel 10th Battalion Arkansas Infantry.
Scott, Thomas Moore, Colonel 12th Louisiana Infantry. (1829-1876).
Scott, Winfrey Bond, Major 19th Louisiana Infantry.

Scott, ..., Colonel 8th Regiment, 3d Brigade, Georgia State Troops.
Scruggs, (**) John Emmett, Colonel 85th Virginia Militia. (d. 1864).
Scurry, William Read, Lieutenant-Colonel 4th Texas Cavalry. (1821-1864).
Seale, Elias T., Major 13th Texas Cavalry.
Searcy, Anderson, Colonel 45th Tennessee Infantry.
Sears, Claudius Wistar, Colonel 46th Mississippi Infantry. (1817-1891).
Self, David W., Major 17th Louisiana Infantry.
Sencendiver, Jacob Morgan, Colonel 67th Virginia Militia. (d. 1914).
Senteny, Pembroke S., Major, Lieutenant-Colonel 2d (Burbridge's, also called 1st) Missouri Infantry. (d. 1863).
Settle, Marcus George, Lieutenant-Colonel 1st Battalion Infantry Texas State Troops.
Sevier, Theodore Francis, Lieutenant-Colonel 1st Tennessee Volunteers.
Shaaff, Arthur, Major 1st Battalion Georgia Sharpshooters.
Shackelford, Thaddeus H., Major 4th Confederate Infantry; Major, Lieutenant-Colonel 54th Alabama Infantry.
Shacklett, Absalom R., Lieutenant-Colonel 8th Kentucky Infantry equals Colonel.
Shacklett, ..., Major Green's Missouri Cavalry Regiment, 2d Division, Missouri State Guard.
Shaler, James R., Colonel 27th Arkansas Infantry.
Shall, David F., Major 3d Arkansas Cavalry.
Shanks, David, Major, Lieutenant-Colonel Jackson County Cavalry (afterwards 12th), Missouri; Colonel 12th Missouri Cavalry. (d. 1864).
Shannon, Denman William, Major, Lieutenant-Colonel 5th Texas Cavalry. (1835-1879).
Shannon, Samuel E., Major, Lieutenant-Colonel 24th Tennessee Infantry. (1838-1921).
Sharp, (**) A. B., Major 2d Missouri Cavalry, Dept. Alabama, Mississippi & East Louisiana, 1865.
Sharp, Jacob Hunter, Colonel 44th Mississippi Infantry. (1833-1907).
Sharp, Samuel, Major 31st (A. H. Bradford's) Tennessee Infantry. (1838-1907).
Shaver, Michael Van Buren, Major Freeman's Cavalry Regiment. (d. 1876).
Shaver, Robert Glenn, Colonel 7th Arkansas Infantry; Colonel 38th Arkansas Infantry. (1831-1915).
Shaw, Archibald James, Major 10th South Carolina Infantry. (1826-1878).
Shaw, Joseph, Major of Hamilton's Battalion Tennessee Cavalry.
Shaw, Thomas Pickens, Lieutenant-Colonel, Colonel 19th South Carolina Infantry. (b. 1828).
Shaw, William A., Lieutenant-Colonel 49th Tennessee Infantry.
Shawhan, John, Major 1st Battalion Kentucky Cavalry. (1810-1862).
Shea, Daniel D., Lieutenant-Colonel 8th (Hobby's) Texas Infantry.
Shearon, Thomas R., Major 47th Tennessee Infantry. (1825-1887).
Sheco, Martin, Lieutenant-Colonel Chickasaw Cavalry Battalion.
Shelby, Joseph Orville, Colonel 5th Missouri Cavalry. (1830-1897).
Shelby, William B., Colonel 39th Mississippi Infantry.
Shelley, Charles Miller, Colonel 30th Alabama Infantry. (1833-1907).
Shelley, Jacob D., Lieutenant-Colonel 11th Battalion Louisiana Infantry.
Shelton, Edward O., Lieutenant-Colonel 51st Tennessee Infantry. (d. 1862).
Shepard, James E., Lieutenant-Colonel 16th Texas Infantry.
Sherburne, Henry Newton, Major 18th (also called 10th) Battalion Louisiana Cavalry.
Sherfey, (**) Reuben M., 145th Regiment Virginia Militia.
Sherrill, L. J., Lieutenant-Colonel 7th Kentucky Infantry. (d. 1864).
Shied, Henry S., Lieutenant-Colonel 44th Tennessee Infantry.
Shields, John Camden, Lieutenant-Colonel 3d Virginia Artillery, Local Defense Troops. (1820-1904).
Shields, Thomas, Lieutenant-Colonel 3d Battalion Louisiana Infantry; Lieutenant-Colonel 30th Louisiana Infantry.
Shinholser, John W., Major 57th (also called 54th) Georgia Infantry. (d. 1864).
Shivers, James A., Major 7th Battalion Cavalry Georgia State Guard.

Shorter, Eli Sims, Lieutenant-Colonel, Colonel 18th Alabama Infantry. (1823-1879).
Shotwell, Reuben Henley, Lieutenant-Colonel 35th Mississippi Infantry. (b. 1830).
Shoup, Francis Asbury, Major Shoup's Battalion Arkansas Artillery. (1834-1896).
Showalter, Daniel, Lieutenant-Colonel 4th Texas Cavalry Regiment, Arizona Brigade.
Shropshire, John Samuel, Major, 5th Texas Cavalry. (1833-1862).
Shryock, Charles Edward, Colonel 51st Virginia Militia.
Shuler, Alfred, Major 18th South Carolina Militia. (1812-1879).
Shy, William M., Major, Lieutenant-Colonel, Colonel 20th Tennessee Infantry. (1838-1864).
Sibert, James H., Colonel 3d Virginia Militia, 7th Brigade, 136th Virginia Militia.
Sibert, John W., Major 136th Virginia Militia.
Sigwald, Christopher B., Major 24th South Carolina Infantry. (1827-1889).
Sikes, Jesse Hodges, Major 10th Georgia Cavalry; Major 7th Confederate Cavalry. (1825-1872).
Siler, Thaddeus P., Major 7th North Carolina Cavalry Battalion; Lieutenant-Colonel 65th North Carolina Volunteers (6th North Carolina Cavalry). (1823-1890).
Silver, Samuel M., Lieutenant-Colonel 58th North Carolina Infantry.
Simington, Thomas S., Lieutenant-Colonel 25th (also called 30th) Arkansas Infantry.
Simkins, John Calhoun, Major, Lieutenant-Colonel 3d South Carolina Artillery (1st South Carolina Regulars or Enlisted Men). (1827-1863).
Simmons, John Samuel, Major 1st Mississippi Cavalry. (1836-1913).
Simmons, (**) Thomas S., Colonel 15th Virginia Militia.
Simms, Gilmore F., Lieutenant-Colonel 77th Virginia Militia.
Simms, William Emmett, Lieutenant-Colonel 1st Kentucky Cavalry Battalion. (1822-1898).
Simonton, John M., Colonel 1st Mississippi Infantry.
Simrell, Eli D., Major 28th Tennessee Infantry.
Sims, Richard, Colonel 12th Cavalry Georgia State Troops.
Sims, William B., Colonel 9th Texas Cavalry.
Sims, (**) William H., Lieutenant-Colonel 44th Mississippi Infantry.
Sinclair, (**) B. W., Colonel 81st Georgia Militia.
Singleton, M. G., Lieutenant-Colonel 4th Missouri Infantry, 3d Division, Missouri State Guard.
Sipe, Emanuel, Lieutenant-Colonel 1st Virginia Militia, 7th Brigade. (b. 1830).
Skillern, David S., Lieutenant-Colonel 54th Tennessee Infantry.
Slaton, William Franklin, Major 37th Alabama Infantry. (1831-1916).
Slaughter, John Nicholson, Major 34th Alabama Infantry. (1828-1909).
Slaughter, John Thomas, Lieutenant-Colonel 56th (also called 55th) Georgia Infantry.
Slaughter, Miles M., Major 5th Battalion Cavalry, Hilliard's Alabama Legion; Lieutenant-Colonel 10th Confederate Cavalry.
Slayback, Alonzo William, Colonel 5th Missouri Infantry (Mounted), 5th Division, Missouri State Guard; Slayback's Command, Price Raid October 1864. (1838-1882).
Slemons, William Ferguson, Colonel 2d Arkansas Cavalry. (1830-1918).
Slover, Thomas Henderson, Lieutenant-Colonel, Colonel 5th Missouri Cavalry, 8th Division, Missouri State Guard.
Smead, Hamilton P., Colonel 19th (Smead's and Dockery's) Arkansas Infantry.
Smith, Abraham, Major 77th Virginia Militia.
Smith, Albert W., Major 25th Georgia Infantry.
Smith, (**) Alexander, Colonel Jefferson Davis Louisiana Regiment.
Smith, Ashbel, Lieutenant-Colonel, Colonel 2d Texas Infantry. (1805-1886).
Smith, Baxter, Major 7th Battalion Tennessee Cavalry; Colonel 8th (Baxter Smith's also called 4th) Tennessee Cavalry; Major Spiller's Battalion Tennessee Cavalry. (1832-1919).
Smith, Caraway, Colonel 2d Florida Cavalry.
Smith, Charles, Colonel 39th Virginia Infantry. (1832-1907).

Smith, Dennis, Major 4th Missouri Cavalry.
Smith, Dabney Howard, Colonel 5th Kentucky Cavalry. (1821-1889).
Smith, Drewry H., Major 39th Alabama Infantry. (d. 1864).
Smith, Erastus W., Major 12th (also called 8th) Texas Infantry. (1843-1929).
Smith, E. S., Major, Lieutenant-Colonel 10th (also called 11th) Battalion Tennessee Cavalry; Colonel Smith's 2d Tennessee Cavalry.
Smith, George A., Lieutenant-Colonel, Colonel 1st Confederate Infantry; Lieutenant-Colonel 36th (Villepigue's) Georgia Infantry. (1824-1864).
Smith, Gideon, Colonel 2d Cavalry Texas State Troops.
Smith, Henry H., Major 3d Battalion Georgia Sharpshooters.
Smith, J. Alexander, Major 9th Missouri Cavalry, 8th Division, Missouri State Guard.
Smith, Jabez Mitchell, Colonel 11th Arkansas Infantry. (b. 1826).
Smith, James Argyle, Colonel 5th (Smith's, also called 9th) Confederate Infantry; Lieutenant-Colonel 2d Tennessee Volunteers. (1831-1901).
Smith, James T., Major, Lieutenant-Colonel 2d Arkansas Mounted Rifles. (k. 1864).
Smith, James Waverly, Lieutenant-Colonel 18th Mississippi Cavalry; Lieutenant-Colonel Chalmers' Consolidated Regiment Mississippi Cavalry.
Smith, J. F., Colonel 2d Cavalry Mississippi State Troops. (b. 1834).
Smith, John, Major 5th Arkansas Cavalry.
Smith, John A., Lieutenant-Colonel 36th Tennessee Infantry.
Smith, John Bass, Major 30th Alabama Infantry. (d. 1863).
Smith, John F., Major 31st (A. H. Bradford's) Tennessee Infantry.
Smith, John F., Major, Lieutenant-Colonel 8th Mississippi Infantry. (d. 1864).
Smith, John H. A., Major 6th (also called 13th) Battalion Virginia Reserves.
Smith, John J., Major 2d Missouri Cavalry; Major 4th Battalion Missouri Cavalry; Colonel 2d Missouri Cavalry, 1st Division, Missouri State Guard.
Smith, John Rufus, Major Cavalry Battalion, Waul's Texas Legion. (1823-1864).
Smith, Joseph A., Lieutenant-Colonel 35th Tennessee Infantry.
Smith, Marshall Joseph, Colonel Crescent Regiment Louisiana Infantry. (1824-1904).
Smith, Martin Luther, Colonel 21st (Patton's) Louisiana Infantry. (1819-1866).
Smith, M. B., Major 115th Virginia Militia.
Smith, Moses W., Major 6th (after 11th) Missouri Cavalry; Colonel 11th Missouri Cavalry; Major 2d Missouri Cavalry, 8th Division, Missouri State Guard; Major 6th Missouri Cavalry, 8th Division, Missouri State Guard.
Smith, M. Whitt, Lieutenant-Colonel 4th Florida Infantry.
Smith, P. R., Lieutenant-Colonel 19th (Dawson's) Arkansas Infantry.
Smith, Preston, Colonel 154th Senior Tennessee Infantry. (1823-1863).
Smith, Raphael, Major Franklin's Northeast Missouri Regiment; Major 3d Northeast Cavalry.
Smith, Robert, Lieutenant-Colonel 6th (also called 13th) Virginia Reserves. (1819-1899).
Smith, Robert Alexander, Colonel 10th Mississippi Infantry. (d. 1862, age 26).
Smith, Robert Hardy, Colonel 36th Alabama Infantry. (b. 1814).
Smith, Samuel G., Major, Colonel 6th Arkansas Infantry.
Smith, Sumner J., Colonel Smith's Georgia Legion; Colonel Smith's Regiment (also called 1st Georgia Partisan Rangers).
Smith, Thomas Benton, Colonel 20th Tennessee Infantry. (1838-1923).
Smith, William Gooch, Major, Lieutenant-Colonel 28th and 84th Tennessee Infantry Consolidated; Major 84th Tennessee Infantry. (b. 1828).
Smith, William McPheeters, Major 2d (Ashby's) Tennessee Cavalry.
Smith, William R., Major 62d (also called 80th) Tennessee Infantry.
Smith, W. R., Lieutenant-Colonel 3d (Smith's) Alabama Battalion.
Smitheal, Green W., Major 51st Tennessee Infantry (declined).
Smizer, John W., Lieutenant-Colonel 8th (Mitchell's) Missouri Infantry; Major 7th Battalion Missouri Infantry.
Smyth, J. S., Acting Major Smyth's Mississippi Cavalry Battalion.
Snapp, James P., Major, Lieutenant-Colonel 61st (also called 81st) Tennessee Infantry. (1823-1901).
Snider, Henry G., Major Snider's Battalion Missouri Cavalry.

Snidow, (**) John C., Major 86th Virginia Militia.
Snodgrass, John, Lieutenant-Colonel 16th (also called 4th) Battalion Alabama Infantry; Colonel 55th Alabama Infantry. (1836-1888).
Snodgrass, Robert B., Major 24th Battalion Alabama Cavalry.
Snyder, John, Colonel, 135th Virginia Militia.
Snyder, Peter, Lieutenant-Colonel 6th Arkansas Infantry; Lieutenant-Colonel, Colonel 7th Arkansas Infantry.
Somervell, William Jones, Major 2d Arkansas Cavalry. (1839-1869).
Sorcy, William F., Major 1st Regiment North Carolina Detailed Men.
Soual, (**) Eugene, Major Chalmette Regiment, Louisiana.
Soule, George, Lieutenant-Colonel Crescent Regiment Louisiana Infantry. (1834-1926).
Southerland, Samuel H., Major 18th (Carroll's) Arkansas Infantry.
Sowell, William James, Lieutenant-Colonel 48th (Voorhies') Tennessee Infantry. (1824-1884).
Spaight, Ashley Wood, Lieutenant-Colonel 11th Battalion Texas Cavalry and Infantry; Colonel 21st Texas Infantry. (1821-1911).
Spalding, Charles Harris, Lieutenant-Colonel 1st Battalion Georgia Cavalry. (1808-1887).
Spalding, Randolph, Colonel 29th Georgia Infantry. (1822-1862).
Spann, John James, Major 65th North Carolina Volunteers (6th North Carolina Cavalry). (1834-1919).
Sparrow, Thomas, Major 10th North Carolina Volunteers (1st North Carolina Artillery). (1819-1884).
Spears, John A., Colonel 52d North Carolina Militia.
Speer, Alexander Middleton, Major 46th Georgia Infantry. (1821-1887).
Speight, Joseph W., Colonel 15th Texas Infantry; Lieutenant-Colonel 1st (Speight's) Battalion Texas Infantry.
Spence, Philip Brent, Lieutenant-Colonel 12th (Armistead's, also called 16th Confederate Cavalry) Mississippi Cavalry. (1836-1915).
Spencer, Thomas J., Lieutenant-Colonel 1st Virginia State Reserves, Second-Class Militia.
Spencer, William A., Major 2d Texas Cavalry (or Mounted Rifles).
Sperry, Jacob G., Colonel 121st Virginia Militia. (1820-1904).
Spiller, C. C., Lieutenant-Colonel Spiller's Battalion Tennessee Cavalry.
Spitler, Mann, Colonel 2d Virginia Militia, 7th Brigade. (b. ca. 1825).
Splaun, W. C., Lieutenant-Colonel Bruce's Missouri Cavalry Regiment, 2d Division, Missouri State Guard.
Spotswood, Edwin A., Major 3d (Forrest's) Tennessee Cavalry.
Sproule, (**) William S., Colonel 93d Virginia Militia.
Spurlock, John L., Lieutenant-Colonel 35th (formerly 5th Tennessee, Provisional Army) Tennessee Infantry.
Stacker, George W., Colonel 50th (old) Tennessee Infantry.
Stafford, Fountain E. P., Major, Lieutenant-Colonel, Colonel 31st (A. H. Bradford's) Tennessee Infantry; Lieutenant-Colonel 31st (A. H. Bradford's) and 3d Tennessee Infantry Consolidated.
Standifer, Thomas Cunningham, Major, Lieutenant-Colonel 12th Louisiana Infantry. (b. 1827).
Stanley, James Philip, Major, Lieutenant-Colonel 26th Arkansas Infantry.
Stanley, Wright A., Major, Colonel 9th (Maxey's, also called 8th) Texas Infantry.
Stansell, William Nelson, Major 7th Mississippi Cavalry (also called 1st Mississippi Partisan Rangers). (1835-1882).
Stanton, Sidney Smith, Col. 25th Tennessee Infantry; Colonel 28th and 84th Tennessee Infantry Consolidated; Colonel 84th Tennessee Infantry. (1829-1864).
Staples, (**) Thomas E., Major Missouri State Guard, W. D. (1817-1861).
Staples, William Carroll, Major 24th Mississippi Infantry. (1822-1884).
Stapleton, James, Colonel 2d (Stapleton's) Regiment Georgia State Troops.
Starke, (**) James, Lieutenant-Colonel 5th Virginia Militia.
Starke, Lucien Douglas, Colonel 4th North Carolina Militia. (1826-1902).
Starke, Peter Burwell, Colonel 28th Mississippi Cavalry. (1815-1888).

Starnes, James W., Colonel 4th (Starnes', also called 3d) Tennessee Cavalry; Lieutenant-Colonel 8th Battalion Tennessee Cavalry. (d. 1863).
Starr, Joseph Blake, Lieutenant-Colonel 1st North Carolina Infantry (6 months); Lieutenant-Colonel 13th Battalion North Carolina Light Artillery. (d. 1913).
Statham, Winfield S., Colonel 15th Mississippi Infantry. (1832-1862).
Steede, Abner C., Lieutenant-Colonel 9th Mississippi Cavalry; Major 17th Battalion Mississippi Cavalry.
Steedman, Isaiah George Washington, Lieutenant-Colonel, Colonel 1st Alabama Infantry. (1835-1917).
Steele, Milos William, Lieutenant-Colonel Williamson's Battalion Arkansas Infantry. (1830-1886).
Steele, Oliver, Major, Lieutenant-Colonel Waul's Texas Legion.
Steele, Theophilus, Major 7th Kentucky Cavalry. (1835-1911).
Steele, William, Colonel 7th Texas Cavalry. (1819-1885).
Steele, William T., Major 33d Arkansas Infantry.
Steen, Alexander Early, Colonel 10th (also called 12th) Missouri Infantry; Colonel Battalion Missouri Infantry. (c. 1825-1862).
Steever, West, Lieutenant-Colonel, P.A.C.S., temporarily assigned to 5th (Walker's) Confederate Infantry; Lieutenant-Colonel Battalion Artillery. (d. 1907).
Stennis, Adam T., Major, Lieutenant-Colonel 5th Mississippi Infantry.
Stephens, (**) George S., Major 27th Virginia Militia; Major 28th Virginia Militia.
Stephens, John H., Colonel 57th North Carolina Militia.
Stephens, John T., Major 8th Battalion Cavalry Georgia State Guard.
Stephens, Marcus D. L., Lieutenant-Colonel, Colonel 31st Mississippi Infantry.
Stephens, Samuel, Major 4th Cavalry Georgia State Guard.
Stephens, William H., Colonel 6th Tennessee Infantry.
Stephenson, Arthur Franklin, Major 32d Arkansas Infantry.
Stephenson, L. D., Colonel 39th North Carolina Militia.
Sterling, Robert, Lieutenant-Colonel 1st Tennessee Heavy Artillery. (1829-1864).
Stevens, Clement Hoffman, Colonel 24th South Carolina Infantry; Colonel 16th South Carolina Infantry. (1821-1864).
Stevens, James G., Major, Colonel 22d Texas Cavalry (also called 1st Indian Texas Cavalry). (d. 1888).
Stevens, J. R., Major 6th (also called 7th) Mississippi Infantry.
Stevenson, James Martin, Major 36th North Carolina Volunteers (2d North Carolina Artillery). (1824-1865).
Stewart, Alexander Peter, Major Tennessee Artillery Corps; Major 1st Tennessee Light Artillery. (1821-1908).
Stewart, Alfred T., Major 58th North Carolina Infantry.
Stewart, Augustus R., Major 4th (Avery's) Georgia Cavalry.
Stewart, Charles Somerville, Major, Lieutenant-Colonel 21st Alabama Infantry. (1828-1863).
Stewart, Francis M., Major, Lieutenant-Colonel 22d Tennessee Infantry; Colonel 15th (Stewart's, also called 14th) Tennessee Cavalry; Colonel 15th (Stewart's) and 16th (Logwood's) Tennessee Cavalry, Consolidated and known as 15th.
Stewart, Frederick, Major 21st Alabama Infantry.
Stewart, R. A., Colonel Stewart's Louisiana Legion.
Stewart, Thomas R., Major 12th Battalion Cavalry Georgia State Guard.
Stewart, William E., Major 15th (Johnson's) Arkansas Infantry.
Stuart, James H., Major Stuart's Battalion Alabama Cavalry.
Stidham, G. W., Lieutenant-Colonel 1st Cavalry Regiment Texas State Troops.
Stigler, James M., Major 1st (also called 19th and 20th) Battalion Mississippi Sharpshooters.
Stirman, Erasmus J., Lieutenant-Colonel Stirman's Battalion Arkansas Cavalry; Colonel 1st (Stirman's) Regiment Arkansas Sharpshooters. (1839-1914).
Stocks, John G., Lieutenant-Colonel, Colonel 1st (Jackson's, afterward 7th) Tennessee Cavalry. (1828-1913).
Stockton, William Tennent, Major, Lieutenant-Colonel 1st Florida Cavalry. (1812-1869).
Stokely, Royal G., Major 2d Missouri Cavalry, 8th Division, Missouri State Guard.
Stone, Absalom B., Major 3d Texas Cavalry.

Stone, Barton Warren, Colonel 6th Texas Cavalry; Colonel 2d Texas Partisan Rangers. (1817-1881).
Stone, J. J., Lieutenant-Colonel 4th Mississippi Infantry (or Minute Men) State Troops.
Stone, (**) John S., Colonel 60th Virginia Militia.
Stone, Robert D., Major, Lieutenant-Colonel 22d Texas Cavalry (also called 1st Indian Texas Cavalry). (k. 1864).
Stone, Thomas Oswald, Major, Lieutenant-Coloinel 40th Alabama Infantry. (1834-1864).
Stoner, Robert Gatewood, Lieutenant-Colonel 9th (also called 4th Mounted Rifles) Kentucky Cavalry; Major Stoner's Kentucky Cavalry Battalion. (1838-1898).
Storey, Richard Lawson, Colonel 2d (Storey's) Regiment Georgia State Troops. (1823-1892).
Storey, (**) Robert B., Lieutenant-Colonel Sypert's Kentucky Cavalry.
Stovall, Marcellus Augustus, Lieutenant-Colonel 3d Battalion Georgia Infantry. (1818-1895).
Stowe, George C., Lieutenant-Colonel Stowe's Battalion North Carolina Reserves; Lieutenant-Colonel 5th Regiment North Carolina Senior Reserves.
Stowe, Jasper, Lieutenant-Colonel 1st Regiment North Carolina Detailed Men. (1821-1902).
Stowe, Leroy Winchester, Lieutenant-Colonel 4th Regiment North Carolina Senior Reserves. (1830-1867).
Strahl, Otho French, Lieutenant-Colonel, Colonel 5th Tennessee Volunteers (1831-1864).
Straughan, Samuel Lamkin, Colonel 37th Virginia Militia. (1819-1874).
Strawbridge, James, Major, Lieutenant-Colonel, Colonel 1st Louisiana Regulars; temporarily assigned to 18th Alabama Infantry.
Street, Thomas Atkins, Major 49th Alabama Infantry. (1838-1904).
Street, Solomon G., Major 15th (Stewart's) and 16th (Logwood's) Tennessee Cavalry, consolidated and known as 15th; Major Street's Mississippi Cavalry Battalion. (d. 1864).
Strickland, James H., Major, Lieutenant-Colonel 1st Georgia Cavalry.
Strocky, F. A., Major 2d Tennessee Infantry.
Stuart, David A., Major 15th (Boone's) Arkansas Infantry.
Stuart, (**) James H., Major Stuart's Battalion Alabama Cavalry.
Stubblefield, William Thomas, Major 2d Battalion Infantry, Hilliard's Alabama Legion.
Stubbs, George W., Major Stubbs' Battalion Cavalry Mississippi State Troops.
Stubbs, (**) G. W., Lieutenant-Colonel 6th Mississippi State Troops.
Stubbs, Thomas B., Lieutenant-Colonel 1st Infantry Texas State Troops.
Stubbs, William Baradall, Major 27th Battalion Georgia Infantry. (1840-1864).
Stubles, (**) John M., Colonel 7th Georgia State Troops aft. 59th Infantry.
Sublett, Franklin Bolivar, Lieutenant-Colonel 2d Infantry Texas State Troops.
Sugg, Cyrus A., Lieutenant-Colonel, Colonel 50th (old) Tennessee Infantry.
Surridge, James, Major 3d Missouri Cavalry.
Sutton, B. F., Major 1st Mississippi Infantry (or Minute Men) State Troops.
Sutton, John Schuyler, Lieutenant-Colonel 7th Texas Cavalry. (1821-1862).
Swearingen, Patrick H., Major, Lieutenant-Colonel 24th Texas Cavalry.
Sweeney, Benjamin F., Lieutenant-Colonel 5th Arkansas Infantry.
Sweet, George Henry, Colonel 15th Texas Cavalry.
Sweet, James R., Lieutenant-Colonel 33d Texas Cavalry; Major 14th Texas Cavalry Battalion.
Swinney, James W., Major 32d Mississippi Infantry. (d. 1864).
Swor, William C., Major, Lieutenant-Colonel 5th Tennessee Infantry.
Sykes, Columbus, Major, Lieutenant-Colonel 43d Mississippi Infantry.
Sykes, W. L., Lieutenant-Colonel 5th Mississippi Infantry. (d. 1863).
Symons, James V., Lieutenant-Colonel 6th Regiment North Carolina Senior Reserves.
Symons, William R., Major 1st Infantry Battalion Georgia Reserves; Colonel 1st (Symons') Regiment Georgia Reserves.
Sypert, Leonidas Armistead, Colonel Kentucky Cavalry Regiment. (b. 1832).

Szymanski, Ignatius, Colonel Chalmette Regiment Louisiana Militia; Lieutenant-Colonel Chalmette Battalion Louisiana Militia.
Tabor, John Washington, Major 17th Texas Infantry. (1822-1901).
Tackett, Sevier, Major 34th (also called 2d Partisans) Texas Cavalry.
Tait, Charles William, Lieutenant-Colonel 4th Battalion Texas State Troops. (1815-1878).
Tait, Felix, Major 23d Alabama Infantry. (1822-1899).
Talbert, James R., Major 28th Tennessee Infantry. (d. 1862).
Talbot, Sanford J., Colonel 11th Missouri Cavalry, 8th Division, Missouri State Guard.
Taliaferro, Thomas Darcy, Lieutenant-Colonel 20th Texas Cavalry. (1831-1909).
Taliaferro, Valentine H., Lieutenant-Colonel, Colonel 7th Confederate Cavalry; Colonel 10th Georgia Cavalry.
Tankesley, Rufus M., Major 37th (formerly 7th Tennessee, Provisional Army) Tennessee Infantry.
Tansil, Egbert Erasmus, Colonel 31st (A. H. Bradford's) Tennessee Infantry. (1840-1919).
Tansill, Robert, Colonel 2d Virginia Heavy Artillery. (1812-1890).
Tappan, James Camp, Colonel 13th Arkansas Infantry. (1825-1906).
Tate, Frederick, Major 9th (Nichols', also called 5th) Texas Infantry.
Tate, Thomas S., Jr., Major 12th Kentucky Cavalry.
Tate, William, Major 1st Georgia State Line.
Tattnall, John Roger Fenwick, Colonel 29th Alabama Infantry. (1828-1907).
Tatum, Mark Thaddeus, Major 35th Arkansas Infantry. (1836-1910).
Taylor, Archibald, Major 9th Battalion Virginia Reserves.
Taylor, Algernon Sidney, Lieutenant-Colonel Light Infantry Provisional Army of Virginia 1861. (1817-1899).
Taylor, Ennis Ward, Major, Lieutenant-Colonel, Colonel 19th Texas Infantry. (b. 1839).
Taylor, (**) F. M., Major Russell's 4th Alabama Cavalry.
Taylor, James A., Major 156th Virginia Militia.
Taylor, James H. R., Lieutenant-Colonel 15th Tennessee Infantry.
Taylor, James R., Colonel 17th Texas Cavalry.
Taylor, John Douglas, Major, Lieutenant-Colonel 36th North Carolina Volunteers (2d North Carolina Artillery). (1831-1912).
Taylor, John M., Major 1st Louisiana Cavalry.
Taylor, John May, Major 27th Tennessee Infantry. (1838-1911).
Taylor, Joseph, Major 8th Battalion Texas Cavalry; Major 1st Battalion Cavalry Texas State Troops.
Taylor, Matthew P., Major 2d Battalion North Carolina Local Defense.
Taylor, Richard S., Colonel 4th Georgia Reserves.
Taylor, Robert H., Colonel 22d Texas Cavalry (also called 1st Indian Texas Cavalry). (b. 1825).
Taylor, Samuel F., Major 2d Missouri Infantry, 8th Division, Missouri State Guard.
Taylor, Thomas, Colonel 38th Virginia Militia.
Taylor, Thomas Fox, Lieutenant-Colonel 1st Cherokee Mounted Rifles.
Taylor, Thomas Hart, Lieutenant-Colonel, Colonel 1st Kentucky Infantry. (1825-1901).
Taylor, William A., Major, Colonel 24th Texas Cavalry.
Taylor, William F., Lieutenant-Colonel 1st (Jackson's 7th) Tennessee Cavalry. (b. 1835).
Tenbrink, William, Major Lewis' Infantry Battalion Louisiana Militia.
Tench, John Walter, Major 1st Georgia Cavalry.
Tenney, Otis S., Major 2d Battalion Kentucky Mounted Rifles. (b. 1822).
Templeton, (**) Samuel M., Major 93d Virginia Militia.
Terral, James Stephens, Lieutenant-Colonel 7th Battalion Mississippi Infantry. (d. 1862).
Terral, Samuel H., Major, Lieutenant-Colonel 37th Mississippi Infantry. (d. 1903).
Terrell, Alexander Watkins, Colonel Terrell's Texas Regiment Cavalry; Major 1st Regiment Texas Cavalry, Arizona Brigade; Lieutenant-Colonel Terrell's Texas Cavalry Battalion. (1827-1912).

Terrett, George Hunter, Colonel Marine Battalion. (1807-1875).
Terrill, George Parker, Colonel 157th Virginia Militia. (d. 1884).
Terry, Benjamin Franklin, Colonel 8th Texas Cavalry. (1821-1861).
Terry, (**) David Sloan, Colonel ...... Regiment Texas Cavalry. (1823-1889).
Terry, Francis A., Lieutenant-Colonel 4th Battalion Arkansas Infantry.
Terry, Joseph S., Major 23d Battalion Mississippi Cavalry.
Terry, Lamkin Straughn, Major 15th Mississippi Infantry. (1828-1893).
Tharpe, Cicero A., Major 30th Georgia Infantry. (1819-1896).
Theard, Paul Emile, Colonel 23d (after 22d) Louisiana Infantry. (1828-1892).
Thedford, William, Major, Lieutenant-Colonel 11th Tennessee Infantry.
Thomas, A., Colonel 40th North Carolina Militia.
Thomas, Allen, Colonel 29th (also called 28th) Louisiana Infantry. (1830-1907).
Thomas, Bryan Morel, Major, P.A.C.S., temporarily assigned to 18th Alabama Infantry; Colonel Thomas' Regiment Alabama Cavalry. (1836-1905).
Thomas, John Peyre, Major, Thomas' Battalion South Carolina Infantry. (1833-1912).
Thomas, Lovick Pierce, Major 42d Georgia Infantry. (1835-1910).
Thomason, (**) J. M., Major 5/9 Battalion Alabama Infantry.
Thomason, Zachariah, Major 10th (also called 11th) Battalion Tennessee Cavalry.
Thomason, Zachariah, Lieutenant-Colonel 2d (also known as 19th) Battalion Alabama Cavalry; Lieutenant-Colonel 9th Alabama Cavalry.
Thompson, Albert P., Lieutennt-Colonel, Colonel 3d Kentucky Infantry. (d. 1864).
Thompson, Dexter B., Lieutenant-Colonel 19th Battalion Infantry Georgia State Guard. (d. 1869).
Thompson, Gideon W., Colonel 6th (after 11th) Missouri Cavalry; Major 3d Missouri Infantry, 5th Division, Missouri State Guard. (b. 1823).
Thompson, Henry Bradford, Major 51st Alabama Partisan Rangers.
Thompson, James M., Major 2d Louisiana Cavalry.
Thompson, John B., Major Pound Gap Battalion Virginia Infantry.
Thompson, John Baker, Major, Lieutenant-Colonel 1st (Fagan's) Arkansas Infantry. (1834-1862).
Thompson, John C., Major 44th Mississippi Infantry. (d. 1863).
Thompson, Joseph Franklin, Major, Lieutenant-Colonel 1st Cherokee Mounted Rifles.
Thompson, Meriwether Jefferson, Lieutenant-Colonel 3d Missouri Infantry, 1st Division, Missouri State Guard. (1826-1876).
Thompson, Preston, Lieutenant-Colonel 5th Kentucky Cavalry. (b. 1815).
Thompson, Reginald Huber, Lieutenant-Colonel Carlton's Regiment Arkansas Cavalry.
Thompson, Robert, Colonel 3d Georgia Cavalry. (1833-1880).
Thompson, Samuel M., Major, Lieutenant-Colonel 10th Tennessee Infantry.
Thompson, Thomas Williams, Major, Lieutenant-Colonel 4th Kentucky Infantry. (1840-1882).
Thompson, William, Major 15th (McRae's) Arkansas Infantry.
Thompson, William B., Major 10th North Carolina Volunteers (1st North Carolina Artillery).
Thompson, ..., Colonel 6th Regiment Georgia State Troops.
Thomson, Lee L., Lieutenant-Colonel, Colonel Carroll's Regiment Arkansas Cavalry.
Thomson, Thomas D., Lieutenant-Colonel 33d Arkansas Infantry. (d. 1900).
Thorington, Jack, Lieutenant-Colonel 1st Battalion, Hilliard's Alabama Legion; Colonel Hilliard's Alabama Legion.
Thornton, C. C., Lieutenant-Colonel 3d Missouri Infantry, 5th Division, Missouri State Guard.
Thornton, Harry Innes, Major 58th Alabama Infantry.
Thornton, James T., Lieutenant-Colonel 3d Georgia Cavalry.
Thornton, J. C., Major Thornton's Battalion Missouri Infantry, 4th Division Missouri State Guard.
Thornton, John James, Colonel 6th (also called 7th) Mississippi Infantry. (1826-1886).
Thorpe, Cicero A., Major 30th Georgia Infantry. (see Tharpe).

Thrasher, David H., Major 38th (formerly 8th, Looney's) Tennessee Infantry.
Thrasher, (**) John O., Major, ... Georgia Militia.
Thurmond, James Gwynn, Major 14th (Neely's, also called 13th) Tennessee Cavalry. (1838-1864).
Thurston, A. J. D., Lieutenant-Colonel 1st Tennessee Zouaves.
Tidwell, Miles M., Lieutenant-Colonel 30th Georgia Infantry. (b. 1819).
Tilghman, Lloyd, Colonel 3d Kentucky Infantry. (1816-1863).
Tillman, James Davidson, Lieutenant-Colonel, Colonel 41st Tennessee Infantry. (b. 1841).
Tilman, Henry, Lieutenant-Colonel 21st Tennessee Infantry.
Timmons, Barnard, Lieutenant-Colonel, Colonel Waul's Texas Legion.
Timmons, William C., Major, Lieutenant-Colonel 2d Texas Infantry.
Tippen, William, Colonel 2d Missouri Infantry, 1st Division, Missouri State Guard.
Tison, William Henry Haywood, Lieutenant-Colonel, Colonel 32d Mississippi Infantry.
Tissot, Aristee L., Lieutenant-Colonel 22d (formerly 23d) Louisiana Infantry.
Tolleson, J. B., Lieutenant-Colonel 7th South Carolina Reserves.
Tool, Samuel, Lieutenant-Colonel 3d Tennessee Infantry (Provisional Army).
Toombs, Robert, Colonel 3d Cavalry Georgia State Guard. (1810-1885).
Topp, Harvey Everett, Major 31st Mississippi Infantry. (1837-1863).
Toulmin, Harry Theophilus, Major, Lieutenant-Colonel, Colonel 22d Alabama Infantry. (1838-1916).
Townes, Eggleston Dick, Major 4th Battalion Cavalry Texas State Troops. (1818-1864).
Townes, Nathan W., Major, Colonel 9th Texas Cavalry.
Townes, (**) William, Lieutenant-Colonel 98th Virginia Militia.
Trabue, Robert Paxton, Colonel 4th Kentucky Infantry. (1824-1863).
Tracey, Jesse Harrison, Lieutenant-Colonel Fristoe's Regiment Missouri Cavalry. (1840-1915).
Tracy, John C., Lieutenant-Colonel 3d Missouri Infantry, 8th Division, Missouri State Guard.
Tracy, Michael O., Major 13th (Gibson's) Louisiana Infantry.
Trader's (William H.) Battalion Infantry Arkansas State Troops, Series 1, Vol. XXXIV, pt. I.
Travis, William Edward, Colonel 5th Tennessee Infantry. (1824-1903).
Trenholm, William Lee, Lieutenant-Colonel 19th Battalion South Carolina Cavalry.
Trezevant, Edward Butler, Lieutenant-Colonel 10th Tennessee Cavalry; Major 3d (Forrest's) Tennessee Cavalry. (1838-1864).
Trimble, Edwin, Lieutenant-Colonel, Colonel 10th (May's) Kentucky Cavalry. (1838-1864).
Troyman, James W., Colonel 82d Virginia Militia.
Truehart, Daniel, Major Truehart's Battalion Alabama Artillery. (b. 1831).
Tucker, Caloway G., Major 32d Tennessee Infantry.
Tucker, George, Major 27th Louisiana Infantry.
Tucker, Joseph Thomas, Lieutenant-Colonel, Colonel 11th Kentucky Cavalry; Colonel 3d Special Battalion Kentucky Cavalry. (b. 1833).
Tucker, Julius G., Lieutenant-Colonel, Colonel Tucker's Confederate Infantry.
Tucker, Stephen S., Major of Alabama Artillery, 1861. (1807-1861).
Tucker, Thomas F., Major, Colonel 17th Texas Cavalry.
Tucker, Thomas M., Major 3d Tennessee Volunteers.
Tucker, William Feimster, Colonel 41st Mississippi Infantry. (1827-1881).
Tufts, Orrin, Major 1st Cavalry Battalion Georgia Reserves.
Tunnard, William Frederick, Major 3d Louisiana Infantry. (1809-1871).
Turnbull, Charles J., Colonel 25th (also called 30th) Arkansas Infantry; Lieutenant-Colonel 11th Arkansas Battalion Infantry.
Turner, Henry Blount, Major 29th Alabama Infantry. (1819-1901).
Turner, James J., Major, Lieutenant-Colonel, Colonel 30th Tennessee Infantry. (1831-1901).
Turner, Richard W., Major, Lieutenant-Colonel, Colonel 19th Louisiana Infantry.
Tuscaloosa Cadets, Infantry Battalion, Series 1, Vol. XXVI, pt. II. (Commander not known).

Twyman, James W., Colonel 82d Virginia Militia.
Tyler, Nathan L., Major 3d Missouri Cavalry, 8th Division, Missouri State Guard.
Tyler, Robert Charles, Lieutenant-Colonel, Colonel 15th Tennessee Infantry; Colonel 15th and 37th Tennessee Infantry Consolidated. (k. 1865).
Underhill, (**) Edward M., Lieutenant-Colonel 3d Battalion Alabama Reserves; Colonel 65th Alabama. (1842-1904).
Upshaw, (**) George W., Colonel 6th Virginia Militia.
Upton, J. D., Major 1st Tennessee Heavy Artillery.
Upton, William Felton, Lieutenant-Colonel of Mann's Regiment Texas Cavalry. (1832-1887).
Vance, James G., Major 2d Texas Partisan Rangers.
Vance, McDuff, Lieutenant-Colonel 11th Arkansas Infantry. (1845-1942).
Vance, Robert Brank, Colonel 29th North Carolina Infantry. (1828-1899).
Van Diviere, Solomon H., Lieutenant-Colonel 52d Georgia Infantry.
Vandiver, Joseph L., Major 77th Virginia Militia.
Vandyke, Richard Smith, Major 1st (Carter's) Tennessee Cavalry. (d. 1864).
Vann, Clement Neeley, Lieutenant-Colonel 1st Cherokee Mounted Rifles.
Vann, John, Major 2d Cherokee Mounted Rifles.
Van Pelt, (**) A. J., Lieutenant-Colonel 58th Virginia Militia; Lieutenant-Colonel 145th Virginia Militia.
Van Zandt, Khleber Miller, Major 7th Texas Infantry. (1836-1930).
Vason, William Isaac, Lieutenant-Colonel, Colonel 10th Confederate Cavalry. (1838-1913).
Vaughan, Alfred Jefferson, Jr., Colonel 13th Tennessee Infantry; Colonel 13th and 154th Tennessee Infantry Consolidated. (1830-1899).
Vaughan, Joseph P., Major 6th Missouri Infantry; Major 3d (also called 5th) Missouri Infantry Battalion.
Vaughn, Joe, Major 2d Missouri Infantry, 3d Division, Missouri State Guard.
Vaughn, John Crawford, Colonel 3d Tennessee Infantry (Provisional Army). (1824-1875).
Veal, Jesse Turnbull, Colonel 3d Texas Infantry State Troops.
Veitch, Daniel, Major 6th Missouri Infantry, 8th Division, Missouri State Guard.
Venable, Calvin D., Lieutenant-Colonel, Colonel 5th Tennessee Infantry. (d. 1862).
Venable, Luther R., Lieutenant-Colonel 10th Arkansas Infantry.
Ventress, James A., Jr., Major 11th Louisiana Infantry. (1831-1872).
Vernon, John A., Major 8th (Hobby's) Texas Infantry.
Vick, Thomas Eugene, Major 4th Louisiana Infantry; Colonel La Fourche Regiment, Louisiana Militia. (1831-1866).
Villepigue, John Bordenave, Colonel 1st Confederate Infantry; Major, Lieutenant-Colonel 1st Battalion Georgia Infantry; Colonel 36th (Villepigue's) Georgia Infantry. (1830-1862).
Vivien, H. J., Major 12th Missouri Cavalry.
Von Harten, Edward, Major 1st Regiment Texas Artillery.
Von Zinken, Leon, Major, Lieutenant-Colonel, Colonel 20th Louisiana Infantry.
Voorhies, William Milton, Colonel 48th (Voorhies') Tennessee Infantry.
Waddell, James Fleming, Major, Lieutenant-Colonel, Colonel 20th Battalion Alabama Artillery. (1828-1892).
Waddell, Owen A., Major 5th Missouri Infantry. (1837-1864).
Waddill, George Clarence, Major 4th Battalion Louisiana Infantry. (1831-1910).
Wade, James M., Colonel of Wade's Regiment Virginia Reserves.
Wade, William B., Colonel 8th Confederate Cavalry. (b. 1827).
Wadley, Caswell H., Major 45th Tennessee Infantry.
Wagener, Johann Andreas, Colonel 1st South Carolina Artillery Regiment Militia. (1816-1876).
Wager, (**) Charles H., Colonel 5th Virginia Militia. (1819-1904).
Wagner, Thomas Martin, Lieutenant-Colonel 1st South Carolina Artillery; Major 1st South Carolina Artillery Battalion. (1825-1862).
Walker, B. F., Lieutenant-Colonel, Colonel 4th Missouri Cavalry, 8th Division, Missouri State Guard.
Walker, Calvin H., Colonel 3d Tennessee Volunteers.

Walker, Cornelius Irvine, Lieutenant-Colonel 10th South Carolina Infantry. (1842-1927).
Walker, Dickerson Holliday, Lieutenant-Colonel 9th Infantry Georgia State Guard; Colonel 42d Georgia Militia. (1825-1893).
Walker, E. W., Acting Major 2d Battalion Local Defense Troops, Macon, Georgia.
Walker, Francis Marion, Lieutenant-Colonel, Colonel 19th Tennessee Infantry. (1827-1864).
Walker, James, Lieutenant-Colonel 2d Texas Cavalry. (1812-1886).
Walker, James A., Major 7th (also called 10th) Missouri Cavalry; Colonel 1st Missouri Infantry, 1st Division, Missouri State Guard.
Walker, James David, Colonel 4th Arkansas Infantry State Troops, 1861. (1830-1906).
Walker, James Madison, Lieutenant-Colonel, Colonel 10th Mississippi Infantry. (1821-1899).
Walker, John George, Lieutenant-Colonel 8th Texas Cavalry. (1822-1893).
Walker, John S., Major 12th Arkansas Infantry.
Walker, John W., Major 1st (Crawford's) Arkansas Cavalry.
Walker, Joseph Knox, Colonel 2d Tennessee Volunteers. (1818-1863).
Walker, Lucius Marshall, Lieutenant-Colonel, Colonel 40th Tennessee Infantry; Colonel 5th (Walker's) Confederate Infantry. (1829-1863).
Walker, Tandy, Lieutenant-Colonel, Colonel 1st Choctaw and Chickasaw Mounted Rifles.
Walker, Whitfield, Major 3d Alabama Reserves. (1815-1890).
Walker, William, Lieutenant-Colonel 28th Louisiana Infantry. (k. 1864).
Walker, William C., Lieutenant-Colonel 29th North Carolina Infantry; Lieutenant-Colonel Cavalry Battalion, Thomas' North Carolina Legion (1820-1864).
Walker, William E., Lieutenant-Colonel 16th Louisiana Infantry.
Walker, (**) William H. T., Colonel 2d Georgia Militia.
Walker, William L., Major, Lieutenant-Colonel 8th Mississippi Cavalry; Major 19th (Duff's) Battalion Mississippi Cavalry.
Wall, John M., Major 15th Tennessee Infantry; Major 15th and 37th Tennessee Infantry Consolidated.
Wallace, Alexander McGhee, Lieutenant-Colonel 36th (Glenn's) Georgia Infantry. (1822-1901).
Wallace, George P., Lieutenant-Colonel, Colonel 40th Mississippi Infantry.
Wallace, John W., Lieutenant-Colonel 35th Arkansas Infantry.
Wallace, (**) R. M., Major 9th Arkansas Infantry.
Wallace, Samuel M., Major, Lieutenant-Colonel 11th Battalion Virginia Reserves.
Wallace, William J., Major 9th Arkansas Infantry.
Waller, Edward Jr., Major 2d Texas Cavalry; Major, Lieutenant-Colonel 13th Battalion Texas Cavalry. (1825-1875).
Waller, John M., Colonel 16th Virginia Militia. (b. ca. 1814).
Waller, Richard P., Major 2d Virginia Battalion Local Defense (Quartermaster's).
Walthall, Edward Cary, Colonel 29th Mississippi Infantry; Lieutenant-Colonel 15th Mississippi Infantry. (1831-1898).
Walthersdorff, Albert, Major 5th Infantry Texas State Troops.
Walton, Isaac B., Lieutenant-Colonel 42d Tennessee Infantry.
Walton, Thomas Henry, Major 1st (Elliott's) Missouri Battalion Cavalry. (1826-1910).
Ward, H., Major 3d Arkansas Infantry State Troops, 1861.
Ward, J. C., Major 7th Arkansas Cavalry.
Ward, J. F., Lieutenant-Colonel 2d Texas Infantry.
Ward, James Washington, Major Ward's Battalion South Carolina Reserves, 7th Battalion.
Ward, Matthew S., Major 14th Battalion Mississippi Artillery.
Ward, Samuel J., Lieutenant-Colonel 8th Missouri Cavalry.
Ward, William W., Lieutenant-Colonel, Colonel 9th Tennessee Cavalry; Colonel 1st Special Battalion Kentucky Cavalry. (1825-1871).
Wardlaw, (**) William Alfred, Major 1st South Carolina Reserves. (1816-1876).
Ware, Josiah William, Colonel 34th Virginia Militia.

Warfield, Elisha, Major, Lieutenant-Colonel, Colonel 2d Arkansas Infantry; Colonel 24th Arkansas Infantry. (1838-1894).
Waring, (**) S. B., Major 4th Alabama Regiment Reserves.
Warley, Frederick Fraser, Major 2d South Carolina Artillery. (1831-1878).
Warner, William, Major 11th Missouri Cavalry, 8th Division, Missouri State Guard.
Warren, James Monroe, Major 22d Battalion Alabama Cavalry; Lieutenant-Colonel 5th Alabama Cavalry.
Warren, (**) Thomas, Colonel .... Georgia Militia.
Warren, William H., Captain Warren's Battalion Alabama Cavalry.
Washington, Burwell Bassett, Major 31st Virginia Militia. (1830-1868).
Waterhouse, Richard, Jr., Colonel 19th Texas Infantry. (1832-1876).
Watie, Stand, Colonel 1st Cherokee Mounted Rifles. (1806-1871).
Watkins, Anderson, Major, Lieutenant-Colonel 8th Arkansas Infantry.
Watkins, Elisha Pinson, Colonel 56th (also called 55th) Georgia Infantry. (d. 1868).
Watkins, William, Major 8th Mississippi Infantry. (c. 1821-1864).
Watkins, William M., Colonel 47th Tennessee Infantry; Colonel 12th and 47th Tennessee Consolidated.
Watson, Benjamin W., Lieutenant-Colonel 19th Texas Cavalry.
Watson, John R., Major, Lieutenant-Colonel, Colonel 18th Texas Infantry.
Watson, Oliver C., Major 35th Mississippi Infantry.
Watson, Tillman, Major 19th South Carolina Infantry. (1803-1910).
Watters, Zachariah L., Major, Lieutenant-Colonel 8th Battalion Georgia Infantry.
Watts, George Troup, Lieutenant-Colonel 1st Georgia Cavalry. (1827-1880).
Watts, S. W., Colonel 10th North Carolina Militia.
Watts, Thomas Hill, Colonel 17th Alabama Infantry. (1819-1892).
Waugh, Alexander, Major, Colonel 4th Missouri Infantry, 1st Division, Missouri State Guard.
Waul, Thomas Neville, Colonel Waul's Texas Legion. (1813-1903).
Way, Charlton H., Colonel 54th Georgia Infantry. (b. 1834).
Weaver, James A., Lieutenant-Colonel 32d (also called 15th) Texas Cavalry.
Weaver, James Thomas, Major, Lieutenant-Colonel 60th North Carolina Infantry. (1828-1864).
Weaver, William M., Lieutenant-Colonel 5th Texas Partisan Rangers.
Webb, James Daniel, Lieutenant-Colonel 51st Alabama Partisan Rangers. (1818-1863).
Webb, Robert Howell, Lieutenant-Colonel 11th Tennessee Infantry. (d. 1872).
Webb, Thomas Shepard, Major 16th (Logwood's) Tennessee Cavalry. (1840-1930).
Webb, Thomas W., Major 3d Mississippi Cavalry.
Webber, Thomas B., Major 2d (Morgan's) Kentucky Cavalry.
Weeden, John David, Major, Lieutenant-Colonel 49th Alabama Infantry; Lieutenant-Colonel Exchange Battalion, Alabama. (1840-1908).
Weedon, John, Major, Lieutenant-Colonel 22d Alabama Infantry. (d. 1863).
Weeks, Benjamin F., Major Cavalry Battalion, Waul's Texas Legion.
Weems, Philip Van Horn, Major 11th Tennessee Infantry.
Weightman, Richard Hanson, Colonel 1st Missouri Cavalry, 8th Division, Missouri State Guard. (1818-1861).
Weir, John, Major, Colonel 5th Mississippi Infantry.
Welborn, Joel E., Major 7th Battalion Mississippi Infantry.
Welborn, William Elbert, Major 1st South Carolina State Troops (6 months). (1817-1902).
Welborn, W. J. N., Major 7th Kentucky Infantry. (d. 1862).
Welch, Otis G., Lieutenant-Colonel 29th Texas Cavalry. (b. 1825).
Welcker, Benjamin F., Major Battalion Tennessee State Troops.
Welfrey, ..., Lieutenant-Colonel 5th Missouri Infantry (Mounted) 5th Division, Missouri State Guard.
Wells, George W., Major, Lieutenant-Colonel 1st Arkansas Mounted Rifles.
Wells, John W., Colonel Wells' (also called 34th) Regiment Texas Cavalry; Lieutenant-Colonel Wells' Battalion Texas Cavalry.

Wells, Joseph Moorehead, Lieutenant-Colonel, Colonel 23d (also called 2d and 3d) Mississippi Infantry. (1811-1896).
West, Doctor M., Major 16th Battalion Cavalry Georgia State Guard; Colonel 87th Georgia Militia.
West, Douglas, Major 1st Louisiana Regulars. (1826-1901).
West, John Porter, Lieutenant-Colonel 2d Alabama Cavalry.
Wetmore, William H., Major 36th Tennessee Infantry.
Whaley, C. A., Major 2d Georgia Cavalry.
Wharton, Jack, Major, Lieutenant-Colonel, Colonel 6th Texas Cavalry. (b. 1832).
Wharton, John Austin, Colonel 8th Texas Cavalry. (1828-1865).
Wheeler, E. G., Major 1st Mississippi Cavalry.
Wheeler, Joseph, Colonel 19th Alabama Infantry. (1836-1906).
Wheeler, James T., Colonel 1st (Wheeler's, afterward 6th) Tennessee Cavalry.
Wheeler, Samuel J., Major, Lieutenant-Colonel 12th Battalion North Carolina Partisan Rangers.
White, (**) Amenate B., Lieutenant-Colonel 168th Virginia Militia. (b. ca. 1831).
White, David G., Major 6th Battalion Arkansas Cavalry.
White, (**) D. M., Lieutenant-Colonel Battalion Kentucky Volunteers.
White, Edward Brickell, Major, Lieutenant-Colonel, Colonel 3d Battalion South Carolina Artillery. (1806-1882).
White, James Benjamin, Major State Cadets, South Carolina. (1828-1906).
White, James D., Colonel 9th (White's, also called 3d and 12th) Missouri Infantry; Lieutenant-Colonel 1st Battalion Missouri Cavalry, 1st Division, Missouri State Guard.
White, James Leonard, Major 19th South Carolina Infantry. (1833-1915).
White, Jesse E., Major 9th Mississippi Infantry.
White, John Fletcher, Lieutenant-Colonel 1st East Tennessee Cavalry. (1824-1901).
White, John R., Major, Lieutenant-Colonel, Colonel 53d Tennessee Infantry. (d. 1864).
White, J. R., Lieutenant-Colonel 2d Missouri Infantry, 3d Division, Missouri State Guard.
White, Martin, Lieutenant-Colonel 3d Missouri Cavalry, 8th Division, Missouri State Guard.
White, Moses, Lieutenant-Colonel, Colonel 37th (formerly 7th Tennessee, Provisional Army) Tennessee Infantry. (1829-1907).
White, Raleigh R., Lieutenant-Colonel 14th (Neely's, also called 13th) Tennessee Cavalry.
White, Richard Green, Major, 10th South Carolina Infantry. (1826-1875).
White, Robert, Colonel 4th Cavalry Georgia State Guard.
White, Robert M., Major 6th Texas Cavalry.
White, Samuel H., Major 9th Tennessee Infantry.
White, Thomas W., Colonel 9th Mississippi Infantry.
Whitehead, Archer, Major 4th Battalion Georgia State Guard.
Whiteley, Richard Henry, Major 2d Battalion Georgia Sharpshooters. (1830-1890).
Whiteside, (**) Samuel G., Major Naval Battalion.
Whitfield, Francis Eugene, Major, Lieutenant-Colonel 9th Mississippi Infantry.
Whitfield, John T., Major 27th Texas Cavalry (1st Texas Legion).
Whitfield, John Wilkins, Major 4th Battalion Texas Cavalry; Colonel 27th Texas Cavalry (1st Texas Legion). (1818-1879).
Whiting, (**) Manley T., Colonel 149th Virginia Militia.
Whittington, Thomas Monroe, Lieutenant-Colonel 24th Arkansas Infantry. (1828-1900).
Whittle, (**) Lewis Neal, Colonel .... Georgia Militia. (1818-1886).
Wicker, David Lambert, Major Wicker's Battalion Georgia State Guard. (1822-1868).
Wickliffe, Charles, Colonel 7th Kentucky Infantry. (1819-1862).
Wickliffe, John Cripps, Major, Lieutenant-Colonel 9th (also called 5th) Kentucky Infantry. (1830-1913).
Wickliffe, Nathaniel, Lieutenant-Colonel 5th Mississippi Cavalry.
Wicks, Moses J., Major 6th Confederate Cavalry.

Wier, William W., Major, Lieutenant-Colonel 37th Mississippi Infantry.
Wight, (**) S. B., Lieutenant-Colonel .... Georgia Militia.
Wilbourn, Christopher C., Colonel 4th Mississippi Cavalry; Lieutenant-Colonel Hughes' Mississippi Cavalry Battalion. (1835-1895).
Wilder, James A., Major 6th Tennessee Infantry; Major 6th and 9th Tennessee Infantry Consolidated.
Wiley, James Horatio, Major 57th (also called 54th) Alabama Infantry.
Wiley, John S., Colonel 85th North Carolina Militia.
Wilkes, Francis Collett, Colonel 24th Texas Cavalry. (d. 1882).
Wilkes, (**) John D., Lieutenant-Colonel .... Georgia Militia.
Wilkes, William Henderson, Lieutenant-Colonel, Colonel 53d Tennessee Infantry. (b. 1833).
Wilkins, Francis Gordon, Major City Battalion, Provost Guard, Columbus, Georgia. (1823-1897).
Wilkinson, John C., Colonel 8th Mississippi Infantry. (d. 1864).
Willey, William J., Colonel 31st Virginia Militia.
Williams, Andrew J., Lieutenant-Colonel 25th Georgia Infantry. (d. 1863).
Williams, Christopher Harris, Colonel 27th Tennessee Infantry. (1830-1862).
Williams, D. A., commanding regiment with Price in Missouri, 1864.
Williams, Danile, Major 6th South Carolina Reserves; Major 1st Battalion South Carolina Reserves.
Williams, Gilbert William Martin, Colonel 47th Georgia Infantry; Lieutenant-Colonel 11th Battalion Georgia Infantry. (d. 1863).
Williams, H. G. P., Major 19th (Smead's and Dockery's) Arkansas Infantry.
Williams, James H., Lieutenant-Colonel 4th (Peel's) Arkansas Infantry.
Williams, James Madison, Major, Lieutenant-Colonel 21st Alabama Infantry. (1837-1903).
Williams, J. Byrd, Major, Lieutenant-Colonel, Colonel 41st Mississippi Infantry. (d. 1864).
Williams, Jeremiah Norman, Major 1st Alabama Infantry. (1829-1915).
Williams, John D., Lieutenant-Colonel 3d (Williams') Mississippi Battalion Infantry.
Williams, John James, Major, Lieutenant-Colonel 24th Tennessee Infantry. (1829-1891).
Williams, John Stuart, Colonel 5th Kentucky Infantry. (1818-1898).
Williams, J. T., Major Williams' Battalion Alabama Cavalry.
Williams, Robert J., Major 3d (also called 2d) Missouri Infantry. (1825-1902).
Williams, Samuel Coleman, Major 18th Battalion Alabama Cavalry. (b. 1839).
Williams, Samuel F., Major 65th Georgia Infantry.
Williams, Timothy H., Major 25th Tennessee Infantry.
Williamson, George M. P., Major Williamson's Battalion Arkansas Infantry; Lieutenant-Colonel 15th Arkansas Militia.
Williamson, James Adamson, Lieutenant-Colonel, Colonel 2d Arkansas Mounted Rifles. (1826-1906).
Williamson, John L., Colonel 15th Arkansas Militia (afterward Williamson's Battalion Arkansas Infantry). (1811-1862).
Williamson, John T., Major 51st Tennessee Infantry.
Williamson, Robert C., Major 6th Tennessee Infantry. (1836-1886).
Williamson, R. W., Colonel 24th Mississippi Infantry.
Willis, Leonidas, Major, Lieutenant-Colonel Cavalry Battalion, Waul's Texas Legion.
Wilmeth, J. B., Colonel 3d Texas Infantry State Troops.
Wilson, Andrew Neal, Major, Lieutenant-Colonel, Colonel 51st Tennessee Infantry; Colonel 16th (Wilson's, also called 21st) Tennessee Cavalry.
Wilson, Claudius Charles, Colonel 25th Georgia Infantry. (1831-1863).
Wilson, Ewing A., Major 8th Battalion Tennessee Cavalry.
Wilson, James, Colonel 2d Georgia State Line.
Wilson, James Hamilton, Lieutenant-Colonel 8th Arkansas Infantry. (1828-1890).
Wilson, John A., Major, Lieutenant-Colonel, Colonel 24th Tennessee Infantry.
Wilson, John F., Major 6th Battalion Virginia Infantry.

Wilson, Joseph Dillard, Major, Lieutenant-Colonel 46th Tennessee Infantry. (1824-1911).
Wilson, (**) M. R., Major 1st (8th) Arkansas Infantry Battalion.
Wilson, Robert E., Major 37th Georgia Infantry.
Wilson, Stephen B., Major 6th Texas Cavalry.
Wilson, William A., Major 5th Battalion Infantry Georgia State Guard.
Wilson, William Blackburn, Colonel 7th South Carolina Reserves. (1827-1894).
Wilson, William M., Major 32d Virginia Militia.
Wiltberger, William H., Major 5th Georgia Cavalry. (1825-1872).
Winans, Wesley P., Major, Lieutenant-Colonel, Colonel 19th Louisiana Infantry.
Windes, F. M., Lieutenant-Colonel 4th (Roddey's) Alabama Cavalry.
Winfield, William Edward, Major, Lieutenant-Colonel 13th Tennessee Infantry.
Winfree, Christopher Valentine, Major Winfree's Battalion Virginia Militia. (1826-1902).
Winfree, John Bell Tilden, Major Winfree's Battalion Virginia Militia. (d. 1918).
Wingfield, James H., Lieutenant-Colonel 9th Battalion Louisiana Cavalry; Colonel 3d (Wingfield's) Louisiana Cavalry.
Winn, Samuel James, Major, Lieutenant-Colonel 16th Battalion Georgia Cavalry; Lieutenant-Colonel 13th Georgia Cavalry. (b. 1837).
Winn, William John, Major, Colonel 25th Georgia Infantry. (1838-1906).
Winn, (**) William R., Major 74th Virginia Militia.
Winstead, C. S., Lieutenant-Colonel 44th North Carolina Militia.
Winston, John H., Colonel 2d Missouri Infantry, 5th Division, Missouri State Guard.
Winston, Thomas F., Lieutenant-Colonel 53d Tennessee Infantry.
Wintter, D., Major 2d Engineer Regiment.
Wisdom, Dew Moore, Lieutenant-Colonel, Colonel 18th (Newsom's) Tennessee Cavalry; Major of Julian's Battalion Alabama Cavalry; Lieutenant-Colonel J. E. Forrest's Regiment Alabama Cavalry. (1836-1906).
Withers, H. R., Lieutenant-Colonel 2d Arkansas Cavalry.
Withers, Robert, Lieutenant-Colonel 21st (Carter's) Tennessee Cavalry (unofficial).
Withers, William Temple, Colonel 1st Mississippi Artillery.
Witherspoon, James H., Colonel 4th South Carolina State Troops; Colonel 8th South Carolina Reserves.
Witherspoon, James L., Major 13th Battalion Arkansas Cavalry.
Witherspoon, William Wallace, Major, Colonel 36th Mississippi Infantry. (d. 1865).
Witt, (**) Asa A., Colonel 28th Virginia Militia.
Witt, Allen Rufus, Colonel 10th Arkansas Infantry. (1830-1903).
Witt, W. P., Major 8th Arkansas Infantry.
Wofford, Jefferson Llewellyn, Major 1st Mississippi Artillery. (1834-1911).
Wolf, E. O., Major Ford's Battalion Arkansas Cavalry. (d. 1910).
Womble, D. W., Major 2nd Georgia State Line. (b. 1826).
Wood, Charles W., Lieutenant-Colonel 4th North Carolina Militia.
Wood, Francis H., Major Dawson's Regiment Arkansas Infantry; Major 24th Arkansas Infantry.
Wood, Joseph G. W., Major, Lieutenant-Colonel, Colonel 18th Texas Infantry.
Wood, Robert C., Major 14th Battalion Missouri Cavalry.
Wood, Robert Crooke, Jr., Lieutenant-Colonel, Colonel in Wirt Adams' Mississippi Cavalry. (1832-1900).
Wood, Stephen W., Major 4th Missouri Infantry.
Wood, Sterling Alexander Martin, Colonel 7th Alabama Infantry. (1823-1891).
Wood, William Basil, Colonel 16th Alabama Infantry. (b. 1820).
Woodruff, Lewis T., Lieutenant-Colonel, Colonel 36th Alabama Infantry. (1816-1869).
Woods, Michael Leonard, Colonel 46th Alabama Infantry. (b. 1833).
Woods, Peter Cavanaugh, Colonel 36th (also called 32d) Texas Cavalry. (b. 1820).
Woods, (**) Samuel B., Colonel 142d Virginia Militia.

Woodward, Thomas G., Lieutenant-Colonel 1st Kentucky Cavalry; Colonel 2d (Woodward's) Kentucky Cavalry; Lieutenant-Colonel Woodward's Battalion Kentucky Cavalry.
Woosley, James, Major Gunter's Battalion Arkansas Cavalry. (1827-1898).
Wooten, Council B., Major 15th Battalion South Carolina Cavalry.
Wooten, George H., Lieutenant-Colonel 34th Texas Cavalry (also called 2d Partisans).
Wootten, (**) J. C., Major 10th Georgia State Guard Cavalry.
Worsham, (**) J. J., Lieutenant-Colonel Memphis (Tennessee) Legion.
Worsham, (**) William W., Major 49th Virginia Militia. (b. ca. 1820).
Wortham, William A., Major 35th (Likens') Texas Cavalry. (1830-1910).
Wotring, Daniel E., Major 51st Virginia Militia. (b. ca. 1830).
Wrenn, W. P., Major 10th Alabama Cavalry.
Wright, Arthur J. T., Lieutenant-Colonel 3d Florida Infantry. (1826-1872).
Wright, Daniel Boone, Lieutenant-Colonel 34th (also called 37th) Mississippi Infantry. (1812-1887).
Wright, George M., Major Wright's Arkansas Cavalry.
Wright, Henry G., Major 20th Battalion Infantry Georgia State Guard; Colonel Wright's Cavalry Regiment (also called 12th) Georgia State Guard.
Wright, John A., Lieutenant-Colonel 43d Virginia Militia.
Wright, John Crowell, Lieutenant-Colonel 26th Arkansas Infantry; Colonel Wright's Arkansas Cavalry; Lieutenant-Colonel Wright's Battalion Arkansas Cavalry. (1835-1915).
Wright, John T., Major 8th Confederate Cavalry.
Wright, John Vines, Colonel 13th Tennessee Infantry. (1828-1908).
Wright, Marcus Joseph, Lieutenant-Colonel 154th Senior Tennessee Infantry. (1831-1922).
Wright, R. G., Major 27th Alabama Infantry.
Wright, (**) Robert, Brigadier General Virginia Militia.
Wright, (**) Woodson, Colonel 30th Virginia Militia.
Wrigley, James, Lieutenant-Colonel Waul's Texas Legion.
Wyatt, Josiah N., Major, Lieutenant-Colonel 12th Tennessee Infantry; Major 12th and 22d Tennessee Consolidated.
Wyche, Robert Emmett, Major 1st Battalion Louisiana State Cavalry. (1829-1889).
Wylly, William Henry, Major, Lieutenant-Colonel 25th Georgia Infantry.
Wynn, James Madison, Lieutenant-Colonel 15th Battalion North Carolina Cavalry. (1834-1906).
Wynne, Vincent G., Lieutenant-Colonel 47th Tennessee Infantry.
Yager, William Overall, Lieutenant-Colonel 1st (Buchel's) Texas Cavalry; Major 3d Battalion Texas Cavalry. (1833-1904).
Yancey, Benjamin Cunningham, Lieutenant-Colonel 17th Battalion Alabama Sharpshooters. (1836-1909).
Yarborough, Christopher C., Major 13th Battalion Infantry Georgia State Guard.
Yates, Alexander, Major 36th Mississippi Infantry. (d. 1863).
Yates, Joseph Atkinson, Major, Lieutenant-Colonel 1st South Carolina Artillery. (1829-1888).
Yeiser, James Garrad, Colonel Floyd Legion Georgia State Guard; Major 3d Battalion Confederate Infantry. (1826-1895).
Yell, F. P., Major, Lieutenant-Colonel, Colonel 26th Arkansas Infantry.
Yerger, William, Jr., Major 12th (Armistead's) Mississippi Cavalry.
Yniestra, Bruno F., Major 1st Alabama Reserves.
Young, Andrew, Lieutenant-Colonel 30th Battalion Georgia Cavalry; Colonel 11th Georgia Cavalry.
Young, Charles L., Major, Lieutenant-Colonel 32d Arkansas Infantry.
Young, Merritt L., Lieutenant-Colonel MacDonald's Missouri Cavalry; Lieutenant-Colonel 11th Battalion Missouri Cavalry; Lieutenant-Colonel 10th Missouri Cavalry.
Young, (**) M. J. B., Major Coffee's Regiment Missouri Cavalry.
Young, Overton Stephen, Colonel 12th (also called 8th) Texas Infantry. (1826-1877).

Young, Robert B., Major, Lieutenant-Colonel 10th Texas Infantry. (k. 1864).
Young, Robert Maxwell, Lieutenant-Colonel 40th Georgia Infantry. (1819-1878).
Young, William Cocke, Colonel 11th Texas Cavalry. (1812-1862).
Young, William F., Colonel 49th Tennessee Infantry. (1831-1899).
Young, William Hugh, Colonel 9th (Maxey's) (also called 8th) Texas Infantry. (1838-1901).
Young, William Joshua, Colonel 29th Georgia Infantry. (1828-1883).
Young, Wilton L., Major 10th Battalion North Carolina Artillery.
Young, (**) W. T., Colonel .... Georgia Militia.
Youngblood, E. H., Major Youngblood's Battalion Government Mechanics, Columbus, Georgia.
Younger, Joseph Thomas, Major 48th (Nixon's) Tennessee Infantry.
Zacharie, Francis Charles, Major, Lieutenant-Colonel, Colonel 25th Louisiana Infantry.

List of Regiments and Battalions in the Army of Northern Virginia, 1861-1865

ALABAMA

3rd Infantry Regiment
Battle, Cullen A., Col.
Forsyth, Charles, Col.
Lomax, Tennent, Col.
Powell, Richard H., Major
Sands, Robert M., Lt. Col.
Withers, Jones M., Col.

4th Infantry Regiment
Allston, Benjamin, Major
Bowles, Pinckney D., Col.
Coleman, Thomas K., Major
Goldsby, Thomas J., Lt. Col.
Jones, Egbert J., Lt. Col.
Law, Evander M., Col.
McLemore, Owen K., Lt. Col.
Robbins, William M., Major
Scott, Charles L., Major
Scruggs, Lawrence H., Lt. Col.

5th Infantry Battalion
(Prior to Oct. 1862, known as 8th Battalion.)
Shepherd, F. B., Lt. Col.
Van de Graaff, Albert S., Major
Walker, Henry H., Lt. Col.

5th Infantry Regiment
Blackford, Eugene, Major
Hall, Josephus M., Col.
Hobson, Edwin L., Col.
Jones, Allen C., Col.
Morgan, John T., Lt. Col.
Pegues, Christopher C., Col.
Rodes, Robert E., Col.

6th Infantry Regiment
Baker, Benjamin H., Lt. Col.
Culver, Isaac F., Major
Gordon, Augustus M., Lt. Col.
Gordon, John B., Col.
Hooper, George W., Lt. Col.
Lightfoot, James N., Col.
Nesmith, Samuel P., Major
Seibels, John J., Col.
Weems, Walter H., Major
Willingham, James J., Lt. Col.

8th Infantry Regiment
Emrich, John P., Lt. Col.
Frazer, John W., Lt. Col.
Herbert, Hilary A., Col.
Irby, Thomas E., Lt. Col.
Nall, Duke, Major
Royston, Young L., Col.
Winston, John A., Col.

9th Infantry Regiment
Crow, James M., Major
Hale, Stephen F., Lt. Col.
Henry, Samuel, Col.
King, J. Horace, Col.
O'Neal, Edward A., Lt. Col.
Smith, Gaynes C., Lt. Col.
Wilcox, Cadmus M., Col.
Williams, Jere H. J., Major

10th Infantry Regiment
Bradford, Taul, Major
Caldwell, John H., Lt. Col.
Cunningham, Arthur S., Lt. Col.
Forney, John H., Col.
Forney, William H., Col.
Johnson, Lewis W., Major
Martin, James B., Lt. Col.
Shelley, James E., Lt. Col.
Smith, William T., Lt. Col.
Truss, James D., Major
Woodward, John J., Col.

11th Infantry Regiment
Field, George, Major
Fletcher, Richard J., Major
Gracie, Archibald, Jr., Major
Hale, Stephen F., Lt. Col.
Moore, Sydenham, Col.
Sanders, John C. C., Col.
Tayloe, George E., Col.

12th Infantry Regiment
Brown, John C., Major
Gayle, Bristor B., Col.
Goodgame, John C., Col.
Jones, Robert T., Col.
O'Hara, Theodore, Lt. Col.
Pickens, Samuel B., Col.
Proskauer, Adolph, Major
Stikes, Augustus, Major
Tracy, Edward D., Lt. Col.

13th Infantry Regiment
Aiken, James, Col.
Betts, William H., Lt. Col.
Dawson, Reginald H., Lt. Col.
Fry, Birkett D., Col.
Marks, Samuel B., Lt. Col.
Mitchell, Julius C. B., Lt. Col.
Smith, John T., Major

14th Infantry Regiment
Baine, David W., Lt. Col.
Broome, James A., Lt. Col.
Ferrell, Mickleberry P., Major

Judge, Thomas J., Col.
McCord, Robert A., Major
McLemore, Owen K., Major
Pinckard, Lucius, Col.
Taylor, George W., Major
Wood, Alfred C., Col.

15th Infantry Regiment
Cantey, James, Col.
Daniel, John W. L., Major
Feagin, Isaac B., Lt. Col.
Lowther, Alexander A., Col.
Oates, William C., Lt. Col.
Treutlen, John F., Col.

23rd Battalion Sharpshooters
Stallworth, Nicholas, Major

26th Infantry Regiment
Bryan, David F., Major
Garvin, John S., Lt. Col.
Hunt, William H., Lt. Col.
O'Neal, Edward A., Col.
Redden, Raymond D., Major
Reeder, William C., Lt. Col.
Smith, William R., Col.

41st Infantry Regiment
Hudgings, Lemuel T., Major
Jeffries, John M., Major
King, Porter, Lt. Col.
Murfee, James T., Lt. Col.
Nash, Jesse G., Major
Stansel, Martin L., Col.
Talbird, Henry, Col.
Trimmier, Theodore G., Lt. Col.
Whiting, Henry A., Lt. Col.

43rd Infantry Regiment
Barbour, Thomas M., Major
Gracie, Archibald, Jr., Col.
Hart, Robert D., Major
Jolly, John J., Lt. Col.
Mims, William J., Major
Moody, Young M., Col.

44th Infantry Regiment
Cary, George W., Major
Derby, Charles A., Col.
Jones, John A., Lt. Col.
Kent, James, Col.
Perry, William F., Col.

47th Infantry Regiment
Bulger, Michael J., Col.
Campbell, James M., Major
Jackson, James W., Col.
Johnston, John Y., Major
Oliver, James M., Col.
Terrell, Leigh R., Lt. Col.

48th Infantry Regiment
Alldredge, Enoch, Major
Alldredge, Jesse J., Lt. Col.
Hardwick, William M., Lt. Col.
Hughes, Abner A., Lt. Col.
Sheffield, James L., Col.
St. John, Columbus B., Major
Wigginton, John W., Major

59th Infantry Regiment
Crumpler, Lewis H., Major
Hall, Bolling, Jr., Col.
Huguley, George W., Lt. Col.
McLennan, John D., Lt. Col.

60th Infantry Regiment
Cook, Hatch, Major
Sanford, John W. A., Col.
Troy, Daniel S., Lt. Col.

61st Infantry Regiment
Hill, Lewis H., Lt. Col.
Pinckard, William E., Major
Swanson, William G., Col.

ARKANSAS

2nd Infantry Battalion
Bronaugh, William N., Major

3rd Infantry Regiment
(Includes 2nd Battalion)
Barton, Seth M., Lt. Col.
Capers, J. Hickson, Major
Manning, Vannoy H., Col.
Reedy, Jno. W., Major
Rust, Albert, Col.
Smith, Samuel W., Major
Taylor, Robert S., Lt. Col.
Tebbs, William H., Lt. Col.
Wilkins, William K., Major

CONFEDERATE

1st Engineer Regiment
Blackford, William W., Lt. Col.
Randolph, Peyton, Major
Talcott, Thomas M. R., Col.

FLORIDA

2nd Infantry Regiment
Ballentine, William D., Major
Call, George W., Major
Moore, Walter R., Col.
Perry, Edward A., Col.
Pyles, Lewis G., Col.
Rogers, S. St. George, Lt. Col.
Ward, George T., Col.

5th Infantry Regiment
Davis, Benjamin F., Major
Hately, John C., Col.
Lamar, Thompson B., Col.

8th Infantry Regiment
Baya, William, Lt. Col.
Clarke, Thomas Erskine, Major
Floyd, Richard F., Col.
Lang, David, Col.
Pons, John M., Lt. Col.
Turner, William J., Major

9th Infantry Regiment
(Formed from 6th Florida Battalion.)
Bird, Pickens B., Major
Martin, John M., Col.
Thomas, Robert B., Col.

10th Infantry Regiment
(Formed from 1st and 2nd Battalions.)
Hopkins, Charles F., Col.
Scott, William W., Lt. Col.
Westcott, John, Major

11th Infantry Regiment
(Formed from 4th and part of 2nd Battalions.)
Brevard, Theodore W., Col.
Gee, John H., Major
McClellan, James F., Lt. Col.

GEORGIA

1st Georgia Regulars Infantry
Chastain, Elijah W., Lt. Col.
Grieve, Miller, Jr., Lt. Col.
Harden, Edward R., Major
Hill, Alonzo A. F., Major
Magill, William J., Col.
Martin, William, Lt. Col.
Smith, William D., Major
Walker, John D., Major
Wayne, Richard A., Col.
Williams, Charles J., Col.

1st Georgia Volunteers Infantry (Disbanded)
Anderson, James W., Major
Clarke, James O., Col.
Ramsey, James N., Col.
Thompson, George H., Lt. Col.

2nd Infantry Battalion
Hardeman, Thomas, Jr., Major
Moffett, Charles J., Major
Ross, George W., Major

2nd Infantry Regiment
Butt, Edgar M., Col.
Charlton, William W., Major
Harris, Skidmore, Lt. Col.
Harris, William T., Lt. Col.
Holmes, William R., Lt. Col.
Lewis, Abner McC., Major
Semmes, Paul J., Col.
Shepherd, William S., Lt. Col.

3rd Battalion Sharpshooters
Davant, Phillip E., Major
Hutchins, Nathan L., Jr., Lt. Col.
Simmons, William E., Major

3rd Infantry Regiment
Hayes, George E., Major
Jones, John F., Major
Lee, Augustus H., Major
Montgomery, Alexander B., Lt. Col.
Nisbet, Reuben B., Lt. Col.
Reid, James S., Lt. Col.
Snead, Claiborne, Lt. Col.
Sturges, John R., Col.
Walker, Edward J., Col.
Wright, Ambrose R., Col.

4th Infantry Regiment
Cook, Philip, Col.
DeGraffenried, Francis H., Major
Doles, George, Col.
Jordan, William F., Lt. Col.
Mathews, John J., Lt. Col.
Nash, Edwin A., Lt. Col.
Smith, Robert S., Major
Whitehead, Charles L., Major
Willis, William H., Col.
Winn, David R. E., Lt. Col.

6th Infantry Regiment
Anderson, Charles D., Lt. Col.
Arnold, William M., Lt. Col.
Cleveland, Wilde C., Lt. Col.
Colquitt, Alfred H., Col.
Culpepper, James M., Major
Harris, Sampson W., Lt. Col.
Lofton, John T., Col.
Newton, James M., Lt. Col.
Tracy, Phil., Major

7th Cavalry Regiment
Anderson, Edward C., Jr., Col.
Davies, John N., Major
McAllister, Joseph L., Lt. Col.
Russell, Whiteford D., Major
White, William P., Col.

7th Infantry Regiment
Alman, Moses T., Lt. Col.
Anderson, Lemuel B., Major
Carmical, George H., Col.
Cooper, James F., Lt. Col.
Dunwody, John, Lt. Col.
Gartrell, Lucius J., Col.
Hoyle, Eli W., Major
Kiser, John F., Major
White, William W., Col.
Wilson, William T., Col.
Witt, Horace H., Major

8th Cavalry Regiment
(Formed from 62nd Regiment and 20th Battalion.)
Griffin, Joel R., Col.
Millen, John M., Lt. Col.
Thomson, William G., Major

8th Infantry Regiment
Bartow, Francis S., Col.
Cooper, John F., Major
Cooper, Thomas L., Lt. Col.
Dawson, George O., Major
Gardner, William M., Col.
Lamar, Lucius M., Col.
Magruder, Edward J., Lt. Col.
Towers, John R., Col.

9th Artillery Battalion
Leyden, Austin, Major

9th Infantry Regiment
Arnold, John W., Major
Beck, Benjamin, Col.
Goulding, Edwin R., Col.
Hoge, Edward F., Col.
Jones, William M., Major
Mounger, John C., Lt. Col.
Turnipseed, Richard A., Col.
Webb, John G., Lt. Col.

10th Infantry Battalion
Frederick, James D., Major
Rylander, John E., Major

10th Infantry Regiment
Cumming, Alfred, Col.
Hawes, Richard R., Major
Holt, Willis C., Col.
Kibbee, Charles C., Lt. Col.
Loud, Philologus H., Major
McBride, Andrew J., Col.
McLaws, Lafayette, Col.
Weems, John B., Col.

11th Artillery Battalion
(Sumter Battalion)
Cutts, Allen S., Col.
Lane, John, Lt. Col.

11th Infantry Regiment
Anderson, George T., Col.
Goode, Charles T., Major
Guerry, Theodore L., Lt. Col.
Little, Francis H., Col.
Luffman, William, Lt. Col.
McDaniel, Henry D., Major
Welch, Western R., Major

12th Artillery Battalion
Capers, Henry D., Lt. Col.
Hanvey, George M., Major

12th Infantry Regiment
Blandford, Mark H., Lt. Col.
Carson, John T., Major
Conner, Zephaniah T., Col.
Hardeman, Isaac, Lt. Col.
Hawkins, Willis A., Lt. Col.
Johnson, Edward, Col.
Scott, Thaddeus B., Lt. Col.
Smead, Abner, Lt. Col.
Willis, Edward, Col.

13th Infantry Regiment
Baker, John H., Col.
Douglass, Marcellus, Col.
Ector, Walton, Col.
Jones, Samuel W., Lt. Col.
Long, James A., Major
Maltbie, Richard, Lt. Col.
Moore, John L., Major
Smith, James M., Col.

14th Infantry Regiment
Brumby, Arnoldus V., Col.
Fielder, James M., Lt. Col.
Folsom, Robert W., Col.
Goldsmith, Washington L., Lt. Col.
Harris, William A., Lt. Col.
Kelly, Charles C., Major
Lester, Richard P., Col.
Price, Felix L., Col.
Ramsay, Whiteford S., Lt. Col.

15th Infantry Regiment
Du Bose, Dudley M., Col.
Hearnsberger, Stephen Z., Lt. Col
McIntosh, William M., Col.
Millican, William T., Col.
Shannon, Peter J., Major
Smith, Joseph T., Major
Smith, Theophilus J., Lt. Col.
Stephens, Linton, Lt. Col.
Thomas, Thomas W., Col.

16th Infantry Regiment
Bryan, Goode, Col.
Cobb, Howell, Col.
Gholston, James S., Lt. Col.
McRae, John H. D., Col.
Skelton, John H., Major
Stiles, Benjamin E., Lt. Col.
Thomas, Henry P., Col.

17th Infantry Regiment
Barden, William A., Lt. Col.
Benning, Henry L., Col.
Hodges, Wesley C., Col.
Mathews, Charles W., Lt. Col.
Moore, James B., Major
Pickett, Jesse H., Major
Walker, Thomas, Major

18th Infantry Battalion
Basinger, William S., Major
Screven, John, Major

18th Infantry Regiment
Armstrong, Joseph, Col.
Calahan, W. G., Major
Ford, Francis M., Lt. Col.
Griffis, John C., Major
Johnson, Jefferson, Major
Ruff, Solon Z., Col.

Stewart, Joseph A., Major
Wofford, William T., Col.

19th Infantry Regiment
Boyd, William W., Col.
Flynt, Tilghman W., Lt. Col.
Hamilton, William F., Major
Hogan, Ridgeway B., Lt. Col.
Hooper, John W., Major
Hutchins, Andrew J., Col.
Johnson, Thomas C., Lt. Col.
Mabry, Charles W., Major
Neal, James H., Col.

20th Infantry Regiment
Coffee, John A., Major
Craig, William, Major
Cumming, John B., Col.
Gamble, Roger L., Major
Jones, John A., Col.
Ross, Albert B., Major
Seago, Eli M., Lt. Col.
Smith, William Duncan, Col.
Waddell, James D., Col.

21st Infantry Regiment
Glover, Thomas C., Lt. Col.
Hooper, Thomas W., Col.
Lynch, Michael, Major
Mercer, John T., Col.
Morrison, James J., Lt. Col.

22nd Infantry Regiment
Jones, George H., Col.
Jones, Robert H., Col.
Lallerstedt, Lawrence D., Major
McCurry, Benjamin C., Lt. Col.
Pritchett, J. Walter, Lt. Col.
Wasden, Joseph, Col.

23rd Infantry Regiment
Ballenger, Marcus R., Col.
Barclay, William P., Col.
Best, Emory F., Col.
Boston, William J., Major
Huggins, James H., Col.
Hutcherson, Thomas, Col.
Sharp, John J. A., Lt. Col.

24th Infantry Regiment
Chandler, Joseph N., Lt. Col.
McMillan, Robert, Col.
McMillan, Robert E., Major
Sanders, C. C., Col.
Smith, Frederick C., Major
Winn, Thomas E., Lt. Col.

26th Infantry Regiment
Atkinson, Edmund N., Col.
Blain, James S., Lt. Col.
Gardner, Thomas N., Major
Grace, Benjamin F., Major
Griffin, Eli S., Lt. Col.
Lane, William A., Lt. Col.
McDonald, William A., Lt. Col.
Styles, Carey W., Col.

26th (Lamar's) Infantry Regt.
(Afterward known as 7th Infantry Battalion, which was merged into 61st Infantry.)
Lamar, Charles A. L., Col.
Lamar, John H., Major
McDonald, James, Lt. Col.

27th Infantry Regiment
Brewer, Septimus L., Lt. Col.
Bussey, Hezekiah, Lt. Col.
Dennis, Charles J., Major
Dorsey, Jasper N., Lt. Col.
Edwards, William P., Lt. Col.
Gardner, James, Lt. Col.
Holliday, Henry B., Major
Rentfro, William H., Major
Smith, Levi B., Col.
Stubbs, John W., Lt. Col.
Zachry, Charles T., Col.

28th Artillery Battalion
Bonaud, A., Major

28th Infantry Regiment
Banning, James W., Major
Cain, James G., Lt. Col.
Crawford, William P., Lt. Col.
Graybill, Tully, Col.
Hall, George A., Lt. Col.
Warthen, Thomas J., Col.

31st Infantry Regiment
Crowder, John T., Lt. Col.
Evans, Clement A., Col.
Hill, Daniel P., Lt. Col.
Lowe, John H., Col.
Phillips, Pleasant J., Col.
Pride, Rodolphus T., Lt. Col.

35th Infantry Regiment
Bull, Gustavus A., Lt. Col.
Groves, William L., Major
Holt, Bolling H., Col.
McCullohs, William H., Lt. Col.
McElvany, James T., Major
Thomas, Edward L., Col.
Williams, Lee A. J., Major

38th Infantry Regiment
(Wright's Legion)
Bomar, Thomas H., Major
Davant, Phillip E., Lt. Col.
Flowers, John Y., Major
Lee, George W., Col.
Mathews, James D., Col.
Parr, Lewis J., Lt. Col.
Wright, Augustus R., Col.

44th Infantry Regiment
Adams, Joseph W., Major
Banks, Richard O., Major
Beck, James W., Lt. Col.
Estes, John B., Col.
Key, John C., Major
Lumpkin, Samuel P., Col.
Peebles, William H., Col.
Smith, Robert A., Col.

45th Infantry Regiment
Carter, James W., Lt. Col.
Conn, Charles A., Lt. Col.
Gibson, Aurelius W., Major
Grice, Washington L., Lt. Col.
Hardeman, Thomas, Jr., Col.
Rogers, Matthew R., Major
Simmons, Thomas J., Col.
Wallace, William S., Lt. Col.

48th Infantry Regiment
Carswell, Reuben W., Lt. Col.
Gibson, William, Col.
Hall, Matthew R., Col.
Whitehead, John R., Major

49th Infantry Regiment
Cooke, Oliver H., Lt. Col.
Duggan, James B., Major
Durham, John A., Major
Jordan, John T., Col.
Lane, Andrew J., Col.
Manning, Seaborn M., Lt. Col.
Pate, John H., Major
Player, Samuel T., Col.
Rivers, Jonathan, Lt. Col.
Williams, Wiley J., Lt. Col.

50th Infantry Regiment
Curry, Duncan, Major
Fleming, William O., Lt. Col.
Kearse, Francis, Lt. Col.
McGlashan, Peter A. S., Col.
Manning, William R., Col.
Pendleton, Philip C., Major
Sheffield, Pliny, Lt. Col.
Spence, John M., Major

51st Infantry Regiment
Anthony, Oliver P., Lt. Col.
Ball, Edward, Col.
Crawford, John P., Lt. Col.
Dickey, James, Col.
Dunwody, Henry M., Major
Slaughter, William M., Col.

53rd Infantry Regiment
Brown, Sheridan R., Major
Doyal, Leonard T., Col.
Hance, James W., Lt. Col.
Hartsfield, Wiley F., Lt. Col.
Simms, James P., Col.
Sims, Thomas W., Major
Sloan, Thomas, Lt. Col.
Taylor, Robert P., Lt. Col.

59th Infantry Regiment
Bass, Maston G., Major
Brown, William A. J., Col.
Fickling, William H., Major
Gee, Bolivar H., Lt. Col.
Harris, Charles J., Lt. Col.
Hunter, George R., Lt. Col.

60th Infantry Regiment
Berry, Thomas J., Lt. Col.
Jones, Waters B., Col.
Stiles, William H., Sr., Col.

61st Infantry Regiment
Brenan, Peter, Major
Lamar, John Hill, Col.
McArthur, Charles W., Lt. Col.
McDuffie, James Y., Lt. Col.
MacRae, Archibald P., Major
Tillman, Henry, Lt. Col.
Van Valkenburg, James D., Lt. Col.

62nd Regiment
Ellis, William L. A., Major
Griffin, Joel R., Col.
Kennedy, John T., Lt. Col.
Towns, J. Randolph, Lt. Col.

64th Infantry Regiment
Barrow, James, Lt. Col.
Evans, John W., Col.
Jenkins, Charles S., Lt. Col.
Thomas, George S., Major
Weems, Walter H., Col.

Cobb's Legion, Cavalry Battalion
Delony, William G., Lt. Col.
King, Barrington S., Lt. Col.
Rice, Zachariah A., Major
Yancey, Benjamin C., Major
Young, Pierce M. B., Col.
Wright, Gilbert J., Col.

Cobb's Legion, Infantry Battalion
Bagley, Edward F., Major
Camak, Thomas, Major
Cobb, Thomas R. R., Col.
Conyers, William D., Major
Garnett, Richard B., Lt. Col.
Glenn, Luther J., Lt. Col.
Knight, Gazaway B., Lt. Col.
Lamar, Jefferson M., Lt. Col.
McDaniel, William W., Major

Phillips' Legion, Cavalry Batn.
Puckett, William B. C., Major
Rich, William W., Lt. Col.
Wilcoxon, John B., Major

Phillips' Legion, Infantry Batn.
Barclay, E. Sandy, Lt. Col.
Cook, Robert T., Lt. Col.
Hamilton, Joseph, Lt. Col.
Jones, Seaborn, Jr., Lt. Col.
Norris, John S., Major
Phillips, William, Col.

LOUISIANA

1st Zouave Battalion
Coppens, Marie Alfred, Lt. Col.
Coppens, Georges A. G., Lt. Col.
De Bordenave, Fulgence, Major
Hyllested, Waldemar, Major

1st Infantry Battalion
Beard, James H., Major
Dreux, Charles D., Lt. Col.
Rightor, Nicholas H., Major

1st Volunteer Infantry Regiment
Blanchard, Albert G., Col.
Cormier, Charles E., Major
Harrison, Samuel R., Major
Nelligan, James, Lt. Col.
Nolan, Michael, Lt. Col.
Shivers, William R., Col.
Vincent, William G., Col.
Willett, Edward D., Major
Wise, James C., Major

2nd Infantry Battalion
(Wheat's Tigers)
Harris, Robert A., Major
Wheat, Chatham R., Major

2nd Infantry Regiment
Ashton, Richard W., Major
Burke, Ross E., Col.
De Russy, Lewis G., Col.
Grogan, Michael A., Lt. Col.
Levy, William M., Col.
Norwood, Isaiah T., Col.
Redwine, Martin C., Major
Williams, Jesse M., Col.
Young, John S., Lt. Col.

5th Infantry Regiment
Dean, William T., Major
Forno, Henry, Col.
Hart, Alexander, Major
Hunt, Theodore G., Col.
Menger, Bruce, Lt. Col.

6th Infantry Regiment
Christy, George W., Major
Hanlon, Joseph, Lt. Col.
James, Samuel L., Major
Lay, Louis, Lt. Col.
McArthur, Arthur, Jr., Major
Manning, William H., Major
Monaghan, William, Col.
Offutt, Nathaniel G., Lt. Col.
Seymour, Isaac G., Col.
Strong, Henry B., Col.

7th Infantry Battalion
Goodwyn, McGavock, Major (acting)
St. Paul, Henri, Major

7th Infantry Regiment
De Choiseul, Charles, Lt. Col.
Hays, Harry T., Col.
Penn, Davidson B., Col.
Terry, Thomas M., Lt. Col.
Wilson, J. Moore, Major

8th Infantry Regiment
De Blanc, Alcibiades, Col.
Kelly, Henry B., Col.
Lester, German A., Lt. Col.
Lewis, Trevanion D., Col.
Nicholls, Francis T., Lt. Col.
Prados, John B. E., Major

9th Infantry Regiment
Hodges, John J., Lt. Col.
Kavanaugh, James R., Major
Peck, William R., Col.
Randolph, Edward G., Col.
Singletary, Alfred A., Major
Stafford, Leroy A., Col.
Taylor, Richard, Col.
Walker, Nathaniel J., Lt. Col.
Williams, Henry L. N., Major

10th Infantry Regiment
De Marigny, Antoine James, Col.
Denis, Jules C., Lt. Col.
Dumonteil, Felix, Major
Legett, John M., Lt. Col.
Monier, Henry D., Col.
Powell, Thomas N., Major
Spencer, William H., Lt. Col.
Waggaman, Eugene, Lt. Col.

14th Infantry Regiment
Jones, Richard W., Lt. Col.
Sulakowski, Valery, Col.
Toler, William H., Lt. Col.
York, Zebulon, Col.
Zable, David, Lt. Col.

15th Infantry Regiment
Bradford, Charles M., Col.
Brady, Andrew, Major
Goodwyn, McGavock, Lt. Col.
Nicholls, Francis T., Col.
Pendleton, Edmund, Col.
Wilkinson, Robert A., Lt. Col.

Washington Artillery
Eshleman, Benjamin F., Lt. Col.
Miller, Merritt B., Major
Owen, William M., Lt. Col.
Walton, James B., Col.

MARYLAND

1st Cavalry Battalion
Brown, Ridgely, Lt. Col.
Smith, Robert C., Major

2nd Cavalry Battalion
Gilmor, Harry W., Major

1st Cavalry Regiment
Dorsey, Gustavus W., Lt. Col.

1st Infantry Battalion
Goldsborough, William W., Major
Herbert, James R., Lt. Col.

1st Infantry Regiment
Dorsey, Edward R., Lt. Col.
Elzey, Arnold, Col.
Johnson, Bradley T., Col.
Steuart, George H., Col.

2nd Infantry Battalion
Crane, James P., Major

MISSISSIPPI

2nd Infantry Battalion
Manlove, Thomas B., Lt. Col.
Taylor, John G., Lt. Col.
Wilson, William S., Lt. Col.

2nd Infantry Regiment
Blair, John A., Lt. Col.
Boone, Bartley B., Lt. Col.
Buchanan, John H., Major
Falkner, William C., Col.
Humphreys, David W., Lt. Col.
Stone, John M., Col.

11th Infantry Regiment
Butler, Samuel F., Lt. Col.
Evans, Taliaferro S., Major
Franklin, Alexander H., Lt. Col.
Green, Francis M., Col.
Liddell, Philip F., Col.
Lowry, William B., Lt. Col.
Moore, William H., Col.
Reynolds, Reuben O., Col.
Shannon, George W., Lt. Col.

12th Infantry Regiment
Bell, James R., Major
Dickins, John R., Major
Griffith, Richard, Col.
Harris, Merrie B., Col.
Hughes, Henry, Col.
Lilly, William H., Major
Taylor, William H., Col.
Thomas, Samuel B., Lt. Col.

13th Infantry Regiment
Barksdale, William, Col.
Bradley, John M., Lt. Col.
Carter, James W., Col.
Donald, George L., Major
Harrison, Isham, Major
McElroy, Kennon, Col.
O'Brien, Alfred G., Lt. Col.
Whitaker, Mackerness H., Lt. Col.

16th Infantry Regiment
Bain, Seneca M., Lt. Col.
Baker, Samuel E., Col.
Bankston, Thomas J., Major
Clarke, Robert, Lt. Col.
Councell, Edward C., Col.
Feltus, Abram M., Lt. Col.
Posey, Carnot, Col.
Shannon, James J., Lt. Col.
Stockdale, Thomas R., Major

17th Infantry Regiment
Cherry, Gwen R., Lt. Col.
Duff, William L., Major
Featherston, Winfield S., Col.
Fizer, John C., Col.
Holder, William D., Col.
Knox, Robert L., Major
Lyles, John M., Major
McGuirk, John, Lt. Col.
Pulliam, Andrew J., Col.
Upshaw, Edward W., Major

18th Infantry Regiment
Balfour, John W., Major
Burt, Erasmus R., Col.
Campbell, James C., Major
Gerald, George B., Major
Griffin, Thomas M., Col.
Henry, Eli G., Major
Kearney, Walter G., Lt. Col.
Luse, William H., Lt. Col.

19th Infantry Regiment
Allston, Benjamin, Major
Dean, Robert A., Major
Duncan, James H., Lt. Col.
Harris, Nathaniel H., Col.
Hardin, Thomas J., Col.
Lamar, Lucius Q. C., Col.
Mott, Christopher H., Col.
Mullins, John, Col.
Phipps, Richard W., Col.
Reading, Thomas R., Major
Smead, Abner, Major
Vaughan, Ward G., Lt. Col.

21st Infantry Regiment
Brandon, William L., Col.
Fitzgerald, William H., Lt. Col.
Humphreys, Benjamin G., Col.
Moody, Daniel N., Col.
Sims, John, Lt. Col.
Taylor, John G., Major

26th Infantry Regiment
Boone, Francis M., Lt. Col.
Parker, Tully F., Major
Reynolds, Arthur E., Col.

42nd Infantry Regiment
Feeney, William A., Col.
Locke, Robert W., Major
Miller, Hugh R., Col.
Moseley, Hillery, Lt. Col.
Nelson, Andrew M., Col.

48th Infantry Regiment
Jayne, Joseph M., Col.
Lee, Levi C., Major
Manlove, Thomas B., Lt. Col.
Wilson, William S., Lt. Col.

Jeff. Davis Legion
Avery, Richard M., Major
Conner, William G., Major
Henderson, William G., Major
Lewis, Ivey F., Major
Martin, William T., Col.
Stone, William M., Major
Waring, Joseph F., Col.

NORTH CAROLINA

1st Cavalry Regiment
Baker, Laurence S., Col.
Barringer, Rufus, Lt. Col.
Barringer, Victor C., Major
Cheek, William H., Col.
Cowles, William H. H., Lt. Col.
Crumpler, Thomas N., Major
Dewey, George S., Major
Gordon, James B., Col.
McLeod, Marcus D. L., Major
Ransom, Robert, Jr., Col.
Ruffin, Thomas, Col.
Whitaker, John H., Major

1st Battalion Sharpshooters
Wharton Rufus W., Major

1st Infantry Battalion
(Merged into 32nd Infantry)
Brabble, Edmund C., Major
Williams, William T., Lt. Col.

1st Infantry Regiment
(Bethel) (6-Months)
Hill, Daniel H.. Col.
Hoke, Robert F., Major
Lane, James H., Major
Lee, Charles C., Col.
Starr, Joseph Blake, Lt. Col.

1st Infantry Regiment
Brown, Hamilton A., Col.
Harrell, Jarrette N., Lt. Col.
Hines, James S., Major
Latham, Louis C., Major
McDowell, John A., Col.
Ransom, Matthew W., Lt. Col.
Skinner, Tristrim L., Major
Stokes, Montfort S., Col.

2nd Cavalry Regiment
Andrews, Clinton M., Col.
Davis, Matthew L., Jr., Col.
Gaines, James L., Lt. Col.
Roberts, William P., Col.
Robinson, William G., Col.
Rogers, John V. B., Major
Spruill, Samuel B., Col.
Williams, Solomon, Col.
Woodfin, John W., Major

2nd Infantry Battalion
Andrews, Hezekiah L., Lt. Col.
Erwin, Marcus, Major
Green, Wharton J., Lt. Col.
Hancock, John M., Major
Iredell, James J., Major
Shober, Charles E., Lt. Col.

2nd Infantry Regiment
Bynum, William P., Col.
Cobb, John P., Col.
Cox, William R., Col.
Cunningham, John W., Major
Howard, John, Major
Hurtt, Daniel W., Major
Scales, James T., Lt. Col.
Stallings, Walter S., Lt. Col.
Tew, Charles C., Col.

3rd Cavalry Regiment
Baker, John A., Col.
McClammy, Charles W., Jr., Major
Moore, Roger, Lt. Col.
Waddell, Alfred M., Lt. Col.

3rd Inf. Regiment State Troops
Cowan, Robert H., Lt. Col.
De Rosset, William L., Col.
Ennett, William T., Major
Meares, W. Gaston, Col.
Parsley, William M., Lt. Col.
Savage, Edward, Lt. Col.
Thruston, Stephen D., Col.

4th Cavalry Regiment
Barringer, Rufus, Lt. Col.
(temporarily attached)
Cantwell, Edward P., Lt. Col.
Ferebee, Dennis D., Col.
Groner, Virginius D., Lt. Col.
Mayo, James M., Major

4th Infantry Regiment
Anderson, George B., Col.
Carter, David M., Lt. Col.
Dunham, John W., Major
Grimes, Bryan, Col.
Marsh, Edward S., Major
Osborne, Edwin A., Col.
Simonton, Absalom K., Major

Stansill, Jesse F., Major
Wood, James H., Col.
Young, John A., Lt. Col.

5th Cavalry Regiment
Evans, Peter G., Col.
Evans, Stephen B., Lt. Col.
Gallaway, John M., Major
McNeill, James H., Col.
Shaw, Elias F., Lt. Col.

5th Infantry Regiment
Badham, John C., Lt. Col.
Garrett, Thomas M., Col.
Hill, William J., Lt. Col.
Jones, Joseph P., Lt. Col.
Lea, John W., Col.
McRae, Duncan K., Col.
Sinclair, Peter J., Lt. Col.

6th Infantry Regiment
Avery, Isaac E., Col.
Dortch, William T., Lt. Col.
Fisher, Charles F., Col.
Lightfoot, Charles E., Lt. Col.
Pender, William D., Col.
Tate, Samuel M., Lt. Col.
Webb, Robert F., Col.
York, Richard W., Major

7th Infantry Regiment
Campbell, Reuben P., Col.
Davidson, William L., Col.
Hall, Edward D., Major
Harris, James G., Major
Haywood, Edward, Col.
Hill, Junius L., Lt. Col.
McRae, Robert B., Major
Turner, John M., Lt. Col.
Young, Robert S., Major

8th Infantry Regiment
Barrier, Rufus A., Lt. Col.
Hinton, James W., Lt. Col.
McRae, Henry, Major
Murchison, John R., Lt. Col.
Price, William J., Lt. Col.
Rogers, Andrew J., Major
Shaw, Henry M., Col.
Whitson, James M., Col.
Williamson, George, Lt. Col.
Yellowley, Edward C., Major

11th Infantry Regiment
Bird, Francis W., Lt. Col.
Leventhorpe, Collett, Col.
Martin, William J., Col.
Owens, William A., Lt. Col.
Ross, Egbert A., Major

12th Infantry Regiment
Alston, Robert W., Major
Burton, Augustus W., Major
Cantwell, Edward P., Lt. Col.
Coleman, Henry E., Col.
Davis, William S., Lt. Col.
Jones, Thomas L., Lt. Col.
Rowe, David P., Major
Wade, Benjamin O., Col.
Williams, Solomon, Col.

13th Infantry Battalion
Wright, Clement G., Major

13th Infantry Regiment
Guy, William S., Lt. Col.
Hambrick, John T., Major
Hamilton, Daniel H., Jr., Major
Hyman, Joseph H., Col.
Martin, Thomas A., Major
Pender, William D., Col.
Rogers, Henry A., Lt. Col.
Ruffin, Thomas, Jr., Lt. Col.
Scales, Alfred M., Col.
Withers, E. Benton, Lt. Col.

14th Infantry Regiment
Bennett, R. Tyler, Col.
Daniel, Junius, Col.
Dixon, Edward, Major
Faison, Paul F., Major
Johnston, William A., Lt. Col.
Lambeth, Joseph H., Major
Lovejoy, George S., Lt. Col.
Roberts, Philetus W., Col.

15th Infantry Regiment
Dowd, Henry A., Col.
Green, William F., Major
Hammond, Gray W., Lt. Col.
Ihrie, Ross R., Lt. Col.
Jerome, Robert P., Major
McKinney, Robert M., Col.
MacRae, William, Col.
Yarborough, William H., Col.

16th Cavalry Battalion
Kennedy, John T., Lt. Col.

16th Infantry Regiment
Briggs, Benjamin F., Major
Cloud, Abel S., Lt. Col.
Davis, Champion T. N., Col.
Lee, Herbert D., Major
Lee, Stephen, Col.
Love, Robert G. A., Lt. Col.
McElroy, John S., Col.
Stowe, William A., Col.

17th Infantry Regiment
Gilliam, Henry A., Major
Johnson, Lucius J., Major
Johnston, George W., Lt. Col.
Lamb, John C., Lt. Col.
Martin, William F., Col.
Sharp, Thomas H., Lt. Col.

18th Infantry Regiment
Barry, John D., Col.
Cowan, Robert H., Col.
George, Forney, Lt. Col.
McGill, John W., Lt. Col.
Meares, Oliver P., Lt. Col.
Purdie, Thomas J., Col.

Radcliffe, James D., Col.
Tait, George, Major
Wooten, Thomas J., Major

20th Infantry Regiment
Brooks, John S., Lt. Col.
Devane, Duncan J., Major
Faison, Franklin J., Lt. Col.
Iverson, Alfred, Col.
Slough, Nelson, Lt. Col.
Toon, Thomas F., Col.
Toon, William H., Lt. Col.

21st Infantry Regiment
Beall, James F., Major
Fulton, Saunders F., Lt. Col.
Graves, Bazillia Y., Lt. Col.
Hoke, Robert F., Col.
Kirkland, William W., Col.
Leach, James M., Lt. Col.
Miller, Alexander, Major
Pepper, Rufus K., Lt. Col.
Pfohl, William J., Major
Rankin, William S., Lt. Col.
Richardson, James M., Major
Scott, William L., Lt. Col.
Settle, Thomas, Col.

22nd Infantry Regiment
Cole, Christopher C., Lt. Col.
Conner, James, Col.
Galloway, Thomas S., Jr., Col.
Graves, George A., Lt. Col.
Gray, Robert N., Lt. Col.
Lightfoot, Charles E., Col.
Long, John O., Lt. Col.
Mitchell, William L., Lt. Col.
Odell, Laban, Major
Pettigrew, James J., Col.
Russell, W. Lee, Major

23rd Infantry Regiment
Blacknall, Charles G., Col.
Christian, Edmund J., Major
Christie, Daniel H., Col.
Davis, William S., Lt. Col.
Hoke, John F., Col.
Johnston, Robert D., Col.
Leak, John W., Lt. Col.

24th Infantry Regiment
Clarke, William J., Col.
Evans, Jonathan, Major
Harris, John L., Lt. Col.
Love, Thaddeus D., Major
Venable, Thomas B., Lt. Col.

25th Infantry Regiment
Bryson, Samuel C., Lt. Col.
Clingman, Thomas L., Col.
Dearing, St. Clair, Lt. Col.
Francis, John W., Major
Grady, William S., Major
Love, Matthew N., Lt. Col.
Morgan, William Y., Major
Rutledge, Henry M., Col.

26th Infantry Regiment
Adams, James T., Lt. Col.
Burgwyn, Henry K., Jr., Col.
Carmichael, Abner B., Major
Jones, John T., Lt. Col.
Kendall, James S., Major
Lane, John R., Col.
Rand, Oscar R., Lt. Col.
Rankin, Nathaniel P., Major
Vance, Zebulon B., Col.

27th Infantry Regiment
Cooke, John R., Col.
Gilmer, John A., Jr., Col.
Herring, Calvin, Major
Singeltary, George B., Col.
Singeltary, Richard W., Col.
Singeltary, Thomas C., Lt. Col.
Sloan, John, Col.
Webb, Joseph C., Lt. Col.
Whitfield, George F., Col.

28th Infantry Regiment
Barringer, William D., Lt. Col.
Lane, James H., Col.
Lowe, Samuel D., Col.
Lowe, Thomas L., Lt. Col.
Montgomery, William J., Major
Reeves, Richard E., Major
Speer, William H. A., Col.
Stowe, Samuel N., Major

30th Infantry Regiment
Draughan, Walter, Lt. Col.
Holmes, James C., Major
Kell, James T., Lt. Col.
Parker, Francis M., Col.
Sillers, William W., Lt. Col.

31st Infantry Regiment
Fowle, Daniel G., Lt. Col.
Jordan, John V., Col.
Knight, Charles W., Lt. Col.
Liles, Edward R., Lt. Col.
McKay, John A. D., Major
Yeates, Jesse J., Major

32nd Infantry Regiment
Brabble, Edmund C., Col.
Cowand, David G., Col.
Lewis, Henry G., Lt. Col.
Williams, William T., Lt. Col.

33rd Infantry Regiment
Avery, Clark M., Col.
Branch, Lawrence O'B., Col.
Cowan, Robert V., Col.
Hoke, Robert F., Lt. Col.
Lewis, William G., Major
Mayhew, Thomas W., Major
Saunders, Joseph H., Major
Weston, James A., Major

34th Infantry Regiment
Clark, George M., Major
Gordon, George T., Lt. Col.

Hammerskold, Charles J., Lt. Col.
Houck, William A., Lt. Col.
Leventhorpe, Collett, Col.
Lowrance, William Lee J., Col.
McDowell, John L., Lt. Col.
McGee, Joseph B., Major
Miller, Eli H., Major
Norment, George M., Lt. Col.
Owens, William A., Major
Riddick, Richard H., Col.
Shoffner, Martin, Major
Twitty, Francis L., Major

35th Infantry Regiment
Craton, Marshall D., Lt. Col.
Johnson, James T., Col.
Jones, John G., Col.
Kelly, John M., Major
Petty, Robert E., Major
Petway, Oliver C., Lt. Col.
Ransom, Matthew W., Col.
Sinclair, James, Col.
Taylor, Simon B., Lt. Col.

37th Infantry Regiment
Ashcraft, John B., Lt. Col.
Barbour, William M., Col.
Bost, Jackson L., Major
Brown, Owen N., Major
Bryan, John G., Major
Hickerson, Charles N., Lt. Col.
Lee, Charles C., Col.
Morris, William G., Lt. Col.
Rankin, Rufus M., Major
Rankin, William R., Major

38th Infantry Regiment
Andrews, Lorenzo D., Major
Armfield, Robert F., Lt. Col.
Ashford, John, Col.
Dockery, Oliver H., Lt. Col.
Flowers, George W., Lt. Col.
Hoke, William J., Col.
McLauchlin, Murdock M., Major
Sharpe, George W., Major
Wilson, John T., Major

42nd Infantry Regiment
Bradshaw, Charles W., Lt. Col.
Brown, John E., Col.
Brown, Thomas J., Major
Gibbs, George C., Col.
Underwood, Davidson A., Major

43rd Infantry Regiment
Boggan, Walter J., Major
Kenan, Thomas S., Col.
Lewis, William G., Lt. Col.

44th Infantry Regiment
Cotton, Richard C., Lt. Col.
Cromwell, Elisha, Lt. Col.
Hargrove, Tazewell L., Lt. Col.
Singeltary, George B., Col.
Singeltary, Thomas C., Col.
Stedman, Charles M., Major

45th Infantry Regiment
Boyd, Andrew J., Lt. Col.
Boyd, Samuel H., Col.
Dalton, James S., Lt. Col.
Daniel, Junius, Col.
Morehead, John H., Col.
Rankin, Samuel C., Major
Shober, Charles E., Major
Smith, Thomas M., Major
Winston, John R., Col.

46th Infantry Regiment
Hall, Edward D., Col.
Jenkins, William A., Lt. Col.
McAlister, Alexander C., Lt. Col.
McNeill, Neill M., Major
Mitchell, Rush J., Major
Norment, Richard M., Major
Saunders, William L., Col.

47th Infantry Regiment
Crudup, Archibald D., Lt. Col.
Faribault, George H., Col.
Graves, John A., Lt. Col.
Lankford, William C., Major
Rogers, Sion H., Col.

48th Infantry Regiment
Hill, Albert A., Lt. Col.
Hill, Robert C., Col.
Huske, Benjamin R., Major
Jones, William H., Major
Walkup, Samuel H., Col.
Wiatt, Francis L., Major

49th Infantry Regiment
Chambers, Pinckney B., Major
Davis, James T., Lt. Col.
Eliason, William A., Lt. Col.
Flemming, John A., Lt. Col.
McAfee, Leroy M., Col.
Petty, Charles Q., Major
Ramseur, Stephen D., Col.

50th Infantry Regiment
Craton, Marshall D., Col.
Ryals, Henry J., Major
Van Hook, John C., Lt. Col.
Washington, James A., Col.
Wortham, George W., Col.

51st Infantry Regiment
Allen, William A., Lt. Col.
Cantwell, John L., Col.
Hobson, Caleb B., Lt. Col.
McDonald, James R., Major
McKethan, Hector M., Col.

52nd Infantry Regiment
Erson, Eric, Lt. Col.
Little, Benjamin F., Lt. Col.
Marshall, James K., Col.
Parks, Marcus A., Col.
Richardson, John Q. A., Major

53rd Infantry Regiment
Iredell, James J., Major
Morehead, James T., Col.
Owens, William A., Col.
Rierson, John W., Major

54th Infantry Regiment
Ellis, Anderson, Lt. Col.
McDowell, James C. S., Col.
Murchison, Kenneth M., Col.
Rogers, James A., Major
Wimbish, John, Col.

55th Infantry Regiment
Belo, Alfred H., Lt. Col.
Calloway, Abner S., Lt. Col.
Connally, John K., Col.
Smith, Maurice T., Lt. Col.
Whitehead, James S., Major

56th Infantry Regiment
Faison, Paul F., Col.
Graham, John W., Major
Luke, G. Gratiott, Lt. Col.
Schenck, Henry F., Major

57th Infantry Regiment
Craige, James A., Major
Godwin, Archibald C., Col.
Jones, Hamilton C., Jr., Col.

61st Infantry Regiment
Devane, William S., Col.
Harding, Henry, Major
Mallett, Edward, Lt. Col.
Radcliffe, James D., Col.

66th Infantry Regiment
Davis, David S., Major
Latta, Joseph W., Major
Moore, Alexander D., Col.
Nethercutt, John H., Col.
Wright, Clement G., Col.

67th Infantry Regiment
Wharton, Rufus W., Lt. Col.
Whitford, Edward, Major
Whitford, John N., Col.

Thomas' Legion
Love, James R., Jr., Lt. Col.
Stringfield, William W., Major
Thomas, William H., Col.

SOUTH CAROLINA

1st Cavalry Regiment
Black, John L., Col.
Nesbitt, Niles, Major
Owen, Moses T., Major
Twiggs, John D., Lt. Col.
Walker, William A., Lt. Col.

1st Regiment Volunteers
Duncan, William H., Col.
Glover, Thomas J., Col.
Grimes, George M., Major
Hagood, James R., Col.
Hagood, Johnson, Col.
Kilpatrick, Franklin W., Col.
Kirkland, Benjamin B., Lt. Col.
Livingston, Daniel, Lt. Col.
O'Cain, Watson A., Major

1st Regiment Rifles
(Orr's Rifles)
Hadden, William M., Lt. Col.
Harrison, Francis E., Col.
Ledbetter, Daniel A., Col.
Livingston, James W., Col.
Marshall, J. Foster, Col.
Miller, George M., Col.
Moore, John B., Major
Norton, Joseph J., Lt. Col.
Orr, James L., Col.
Perrin, James M., Col.
Robertson, James T., Lt. Col.
Rogers, Leonard, Major

1st Infantry Regiment
(Provisional Army)
Alston, Thomas P., Lt. Col.
Brailsford, Edward D., Major
Butler, Andrew P., Lt. Col.
Gregg, Maxcy, Col.
Hamilton, Daniel H., Col.
McCrady, Edward, Jr., Lt. Col.
McCreary, C. W., Col.
Shooter, Washington P., Lt. Col.
Smith, Augustus M., Lt. Col.

2nd Cavalry Regiment
Butler, Mttthew C., Col.
Easley, William K., Lt. Col.
Hampton, Frank, Lt. Col.
Lipscomb, Thomas J., Col.
Screven, Thomas E., Lt. Col.

2nd Infantry Regiment
Clyburn, Benjamin R., Major
Gaillard, Franklin, Lt. Col.
Goodwyn, Artemas D., Lt. Col.
Jones, Ervine P., Lt. Col.
Kennedy, John D., Col.
Kershaw, Joseph B., Col.
Wallace, William, Lt. Col.

2nd Regiment Rifles
Boggs, Thomas H., Lt. Col.
Bowen, Robert E., Col.
Cox, Daniel L., Major
Dendy, Stiles P., Major
Donald, David L., Lt. Col.
Moore, John V., Col.
Thompson, Robert A., Lt. Col.
Thomson, Thomas, Col.

3rd Infantry Battalion
Gunnels, George M., Major
James, George S., Lt. Col.
Miller, Daniel B., Major
Rice, William G., Lt. Col.

3rd Infantry Regiment
Baxter, James M., Lt. Col.
Foster, Barham B., Lt. Col.
Garlington, Benjamin C., Lt. Col.
Maffett, Robert C., Lt. Col.
Nance, James D., Col.
Rutherford, William D., Col.
Todd, Rutherford P., Major
Williams, James H., Col.

4th Cavalry Regiment
Emanuel, William P., Major
Rutledge, Benjamin H., Col.
Stokes, William, Lt. Col.

4th Infantry Regiment
(Reorganized as 4th Battalion)
Mattison, Charles S., Lt. Col.
Sloan, John B. E., Col.
Whitner, James H., Major

5th Cavalry Regiment
(Formed from 14th and 17th Bns.)
Davis, Zimerman, Col.
Dunovant, John, Col.
Edwards, J. C., Col.
Ferguson, Samuel W., Col.
Jeffords, Robert J., Lt. Col.
Morgan, Joseph H., Major

5th Infantry Regiment
Beckham, Thomas C., Major
Coward, Asbury, Col.
Foster, William M., Major
Giles, John R. R., Col.
Jackson, Andrew, Lt. Col.
Jenkins, Micah, Col.
Legg, George W. H., Lt. Col.
Thomson, William T., Major
Wylie, John D., Lt. Col.

6th Cavalry Regiment
Aiken, Hugh K., Col.
Ferguson, Thomas B., Major
Miller, Lovick P., Lt. Col.

6th Infantry Regiment
Bratton, John, Col.
Coker, James L., Major
McLure, Edward C., Major
Secrest, Andrew J., Lt. Col.
Steedman, John M., Col.
White, John M., Lt. Col.
Winder, Charles S., Col.
Woodward, Thomas W., Major

7th Cavalry Regiment
Boykin, Edward M., Major
Haskell, Alexander C., Col.
McKissick, Isaac G., Lt. Col.
Shingler, William P., Col.

7th Infantry Battalion
Blair, Lovick W. R., Major
Nelson, Patrick H., Lt. Col.
Rion, James H., Lt. Col.

7th Infantry Regiment
Aiken, David W., Col.
Bacon, Thomas G., Col.
Bland, Elbert, Lt. Col.
Fair, Robert A., Lt. Col.
Goggans, Elijah J., Lt. Col.
Hard, John S., Major
Seibels, Emmett, Lt. Col.
White, William C., Major

8th Infantry Regiment
Cash, Ellerbee B. C., Col.
Henagan, John W., Col.
Hoole, Axalla J., Lt. Col.
Lucas, Thomas E., Major
McLeod, Donald, Major
Stackhouse, Eli T., Lt. Col.

9th Infantry Regiment
Blanding, James D., Col.
Ray, Duncan W., Lt. Col.
Steedman, John M., Major

11th Infantry Battalion
Simonton, Charles H., Major

11th Infantry Regiment
Campbell, Robert, Lt. Col.
Ellis, Daniel H., Col.
Gantt, Frederick H., Col.
Gooding, John J., Major
Harrison, John J., Major
Heyward, William C., Col.
Izard, Allen C., Lt. Col.
Shuler, William, Lt. Col.
Smith, Benjamin B., Major

12th Infantry Regiment
Barnes, Dixon, Col.
Bookter, Edwin F., Col.
Clyburn, Thomas F., Lt. Col.
Davis, Henry C., Lt. Col.
Dunovant, Richard G. M., Col.
Jones, Cadwallader, Col.
McCorkle, William H., Lt. Col.
Miller, John L., Col.

13th Infantry Regiment
Brockman, Benjamin T., Col.
Calhoun, Patrick L., Lt. Col.
Duncan, David R., Major
Edwards, Oliver E., Col.
Farrow, Thomas S., Lt. Col.
Hunt, Isaac F., Col.
Lester, William, Lt. Col.
Wofford, Joseph L., Major

14th Infantry Regiment
Brown, Joseph N., Col.
Carter, William J., Major
Croft, Edward, Lt. Col.
Harper, Henry H., Major

Jones, James, Col.
McGowan, Samuel, Col.
Perrin, Abner, Col.
Simpson, William D., Lt. Col.

15th Infantry Regiment

Anderson, Richard, Lt. Col.
Davis, John B., Col.
De Saussure, William D., Col.
Gist, Joseph F., Col.
Gist, William M., Major
Lewie, Frederick S., Lt. Col.

17th Infantry Regiment

Avery, John W., Major
Culp, John R., Lt. Col.
McMaster, Fitz William, Col.
Means, John H., Col.
Means, Robert S., Lt. Col.
Mills, Julius, Major

18th Infantry Regiment

Allison, William B., Lt. Col.
Betsill, Robert J., Major
Gadberry, James M., Col.
Scaife, Ferdinand, Lt. Col.
Wallace, William H., Col.

20th Infantry Regiment

Boykin, Stephen M., Col.
Dantzler, Olin M., Lt. Col.
Keitt, Laurence M., Col.
McMichael, Paul A., Lt. Col.
Mimms, A., Major

21st Infantry Regiment

Dargan, Alonzo T., Lt. Col.
Graham, Robert F., Col.
McIver, George W., Lt. Col.
Read, John H., Major
Wilds, Samuel H., Major

22nd Infantry Regiment

Abney, Joseph, Col.
Adams, Cicero, Major
Burt, William G., Col.
Dantzler, Olin M., Col.
Fleming, David G., Col.
Goodlet, Spartan D., Col.
Hilton, Miel, Major
O'Connell, James, Lt. Col.
Shedd, James N., Major
Stewart, James M., Major
Watkins, Thomas C., Lt. Col.

23rd Infantry Regiment

Bancroft, Matthew V., Major
Benbow, Henry L., Col.
Green, Allen J., Lt. Col.
Hatch, Lewis M., Col.
Kinloch, John M., Lt. Col.
Lesesne, Henry H., Major
Miller, Lovick P., Major
Murden, Edgar O., Lt. Col.
Roberts, John, Lt. Col.
Whilden, John M., Major

25th Infantry Regiment

Glover, John V., Major
Pressley, John G., Lt. Col.
Simonton, Charles H., Col.

26th Infantry Regiment

Byrd, Stephen D. M., Lt. Col.
Hudson, Joshua H., Lt. Col.
Land, Ceth S., Major
Rowell, Cornelius D., Major
Smith, Alexander D., Col.

27th Infantry Regiment

Abney, Joseph, Major
Blake, Julius A., Lt. Col.
Gaillard, Peter C., Col.

Hampton Legion

Arnold, Robert B., Lt. Col.
Butler, Matthew C., Major
Conner, James, Major
Dingle, J. Hervey, Jr., Major
Gary, Martin W., Col.
Griffin, James B., Lt. Col.
Hampton, Wade, Col.
Johnson, Benjamin J., Lt. Col.
Lee, Stephen D., Major
Logan, Thomas M., Col.
Nicholson, Benjamin E., Major

Holcombe Legion

Crawley, William J., Col.
Elliott, Stephen, Jr., Col.
Garlington, Albert C., Major
Palmer, Francis G., Lt. Col.
Shingler, William P., Col.
Stevens, Peter F., Col.
Walsh, Thomas V., Lt. Col.
Zeigler, Martin G., Major

Palmetto Sharpshooters

Anderson, William, Major
Goss, John W., Lt. Col.
Humphreys, William W., Major
Jenkins, Micah, Col.
Kilpatrick, Franklin W., Col.
Walker, Joseph, Col.

TENNESSEE

1st Infantry Regiment
(Provisional Army)

Buchanan, Felix G., Major
George, Newton J., Lt. Col.
Holman, Daniel W., Major
Holman, James H., Lt. Col.
McLaughlin, Martin V., Major
Shackleford, John C., Lt. Col.
Turney, Peter, Col.

7th Infantry Regiment
Fite, John A., Col.
Goodner, John F., Col.
Hatton, Robert, Col.
Howard, John K., Lt. Col.
Shepard, Samuel G., Lt. Col.
Williamson, William H., Major

14th Infantry Regiment
Brandon, Nathan, Lt. Col.
Forbes, William A., Col.
Gholson, Milton G., Lt. Col.
Harrell, George A., Lt. Col.
Johnson, James H., Major
Lockert, James W., Lt. Col.
McComb, William, Col.
Morris, Nathaniel M., Major

17th Infantry Regiment
Davis, James C., Major
Floyd, Watt W., Lt. Col.
Landis, Absalom L., Major

23rd Infantry Regiment
Keeble, Richard H., Col.
Lowe, John G., Major
Ready, Horace, Col.

25th Infantry Regiment
Hughes, John M., Col.
McCarver, Samuel H., Major
Sanders, Richard C., Lt. Col.
Snowden, Robert B., Lt. Col.

44th Infantry Regiment
Crawford, Gibson M., Major
Fulton, John S., Col.
McEwen, John L., Jr., Lt. Col.

63rd Infantry Regiment
Aiken, John A., Lt. Col.
Fain, Richard G., Col.
Fulkerson, Abraham, Col.
Fulkerson, William H., Lt. Col.

TEXAS

1st Infantry Regiment
Bass, Frederick S., Col.
Black, Harvey H., Lt. Col.
Clopton, Albert G., Lt. Col.
Dale, Matt., Major
Harding, Richard J., Lt. Col.
McLeod, Hugh, Col.
Rainey, Alexis T., Col.
Wigfall, Louis T., Col.
Woodward, John R., Major
Work, Phillip A., Lt. Col.

4th Infantry Regiment
Bane, John P., Col.
Carter, Benjamin F., Lt. Col.
Hood, John B., Col.
Key, John C. G., Col.
Marshall, John, Col.
Martin, William H., Major
Townsend, William P., Major
Warwick, Bradfute, Col.
Winkler, Clinton M., Lt. Col.

5th Infantry Regiment
Archer, James J., Col.
Botts, Walter B., Lt. Col.
Bryan, King, Lt. Col.
Powell, Robert M., Col.
Quattlebaum, Paul J., Major
Robertson, Jerome B., Col.
Rogers, Jefferson C., Major
Upton, John C., Lt. Col.
Whaley, David M., Major

VIRGINIA

1st Artillery Regiment
Brown, John Thompson, Col.
Cabell, Henry Coalter, Col.
Coleman, Lewis M., Lt. Col.
Hardaway, Robert A., Lt. Col.
Moseley, Edgar F., Lt. Col.
Randolph, George W., Col.
Stribling, Robert M., Lt. Col.
Watson, David, Major

1st Cavalry Regiment
Brien, Luke T., Lt. Col.
Carter, R. Welby, Col.
Drake, James H., Col.
Irving, Charles R., Major
Jones, William E., Col.
Lee, Fitzhugh, Col.
Morgan, William A., Col.
Stuart, James E. B., Col.
Swan, Robert, Major

1st Infantry Battalion Regulars
(Irish Battalion)
Bridgford, David B., Major
Munford, John D., Major
Seddon, John, Major

1st Infantry Battalion
Local Defense Troops
(Armory Battalion)
Ayres, Thomas H., Major
Downer, William S., Major
Ford, Charles H., Major

1st Battalion Reserves
Duke, Richard T. W., Lt. Col.
Strange, James M., Major

1st Infantry Regiment
Dooley, John, Major
Fry, William H., Lt. Col.
Langley, Francis H., Lt. Col.

Moore, Patrick T., Col
Munford, William P., Major
Norton, George F., Major
Palmer, William H., Major
Skinner, Frederick G., Lt. Col.
Williams, Lewis B., Jr., Col.

1st Regiment Reserves
Averett, C. E., Major
Boswell, Thomas T., Lt. Col.
Farinholt, Benjamin L., Col.

2nd Cavalry Battalion
Pate, Henry Clay, Lt. Col.

2nd Cavalry Regiment
Breckinridge, Cary, Lt. Col.
Graves, William F., Major
Langhorne, John S., Major
Munford, Thomas T., Col.
Radford, Richard C. W., Col.
Watts, James W., Lt. Col.

2nd Battalion Reserves
Cook, Edward B., Major
Guy, John H., Lt. Col.

2nd Infantry Regiment
Allen, James W., Col.
Botts, Lawson, Col.
Colston, Raleigh T., Lt. Col.
Jones, Francis B., Major
Lackland, Francis, Lt. Col.
Moore, Edwin L., Major
Nadenbousch, John Q. A., Col.
Randolph, William W., Lt. Col.
Stewart, Charles H., Major

2nd Infantry Regiment
Local Defense Troops
Scruggs, Daniel E., Col.
Tanner, William E., Lt. Col.

3rd Cavalry Regiment
Carrington, Henry, Major
Carter, William R., Lt. Col.
Feild, William M., Lt. Col.
Goode, Thomas F., Col.
Johnston, Robert, Col.
Owen, Thomas H., Col.
Phillips, Jefferson C., Major
Thornton, John T., Lt. Col.

3rd Battalion Reserves
Archer, Fletcher H., Lt. Col.
Bond, Thomas H., Major
Hood, William H., Lt. Col.
Jarvis, William H., Major

3rd Infantry Regiment
Callcote, Alexander D., Lt. Col.
Mayo, Joseph, Jr., Col.
Pryor, Roger A., Col.
Pryor, William H., Lt. Col.
Scott, Joseph V., Lt. Col.
Urquhart, Charles F., Major

3rd Infantry Regiment
Local Defense Troops
(Departmental)
Baker, Bolling, Major
Henley, John A., Major
Jamison, Sanders G., Major
McAnerney, John, Jr., Col.
Sutherland, St. Clair F., Lt. Col.

3rd Regiment Reserves
Booker, Richard A., Col.
Ewers, William M., Major
Leftwich, Joel B., Lt. Col.

4th Heavy Artillery Regiment
(Became 34th Virginia Infantry)
Bagby, John R., Major
Goode, John Thomas, Col.
Harrison, Randolph, Lt. Col.
Leigh, J. Wickham, Major

4th Cavalry Regiment
Hobson, Alexander M., Major
Lee, Stephen D., Col.
Old, Charles, Major
Payne, William H., Col.
Randolph, Robert, Lt. Col.
Robertson, Beverly H., Col.
Utterback, Robert E., Major
Wickham, Williams C., Col.
Wooldridge, William B., Col.

4th Infantry Battalion
Local Defense Troops
(Naval Battalion)
Curlin, Martin W., Major
Minor, Robert D., Major

4th Battalion Reserves
Godwin, David E., Major

4th Infantry Regiment
Bennett, Matthew D., Major
Gardner, Robert D., Lt. Col.
Kent, Joseph F., Major
Moore, Lewis T., Lt. Col.
Preston, James F., Col.
Pendleton, Albert G., Major
Ronald, Charles A., Col.
Terry, William, Col.

5th Cavalry Regiment
(Provisional Army)
Allston, Benjamin, Major
Mullins, John, Major

5th Cavalry Regiment
Allen, James H., Lt. Col.
Boston, Reuben B., Col.
Douglas, Beverly B., Major
Eells, John, Major
Harding, Cyrus, Jr., Major
Pate, H. Clay, Col.
Puller, John W., Major
Rosser, Thomas L., Col.

5th Battalion Reserves
Henry, Patrick M., Lt. Col.
5th Infantry Battalion
Local Defense Troops
(Arsenal Battalion)
Broun, William L., Lt. Col.
Ennis, Phillip J., Lt. Col.
Vaughan, John B., Major
5th Infantry Battalion
Archer, Fletcher H., Lt. Col.
Foster, William R., Major
Wilson, John P., Jr., Major
5th Infantry Regiment
Baylor, William S. H., Col.
Funk, John H. S., Col.
Harman, William H., Col.
Harper, Kenton, Col.
Koiner, Absalom, Major
Newton, James W., Major
Williams, Hazael J., Lt. Col.
6th Cavalry Regiment
Cabell, John G., Lt. Col.
Field, Charles W., Col.
Flournoy, Cabell E., Major
Flournoy, Thomas S., Col.
Green, John S., Lt. Col.
Grimsley, Daniel A., Major
Harrison, Julien, Col.
Richards, Daniel T., Lt. Col.
6th Infantry Battalion
Local Defense Troops
(Tredegar Battalion)
Tanner, William E., Major
6th Infantry Regiment
Corprew, Thomas J., Col.
Lundy, William T., Lt. Col.
Mahone, William, Col.
Rogers, George T., Col.
Taylor, Robert B., Major
Williamson, Henry W., Lt. Col.
7th Cavalry Regiment
Ashby, Turner, Col.
Berry, Thomas J., Col.
Dulany, Richard H., Col.
Funsten, Oliver R., Major
Hatcher, Daniel C., Major
Jones, William E., Col.
Marshall, Thomas, Lt. Col.
McDonald, Angus W., Col.
Myers, Samuel B., Major
7th Infantry Battalion
(Merged into 61st Regiment)
Wilson, Samuel M., Lt. Col.
7th Infantry Regiment
Flowerree, Charles C., Col.
Kemper, James L., Col.
Patton, Waller T., Col.
Swindler, Aylett A., Major
Williams, Lewis B., Jr., Lt. Col.

8th Cavalry Battalion
Davis, J. Lucius, Lt. Col.
Duffield, Charles B., Major

8th Cavalry Regiment
Bowen, Thomas P., Major
Cook, Alphonso F., Lt. Col.
Corns, James M., Col.
Edmondston, Patrick M., Lt. Col.
Fitzhugh, Henry, Lt. Col.
Jenifer, Walter H., Col.
Jenkins, Albert G., Lt. Col.

8th Infantry Regiment
Berkeley, Edmund, Lt. Col.
Berkeley, Norborne, Col.
Berkeley, William N., Major
Hunton, Eppa, Col.
Tebbs, Charles B., Lt. Col.
Thrift, James, Major

9th Cavalry Regiment
Beale, Richard L. T., Col.
Johnson, John E., Col.
Lee, William H. F., Col.
Lewis, Meriwether, Lt. Col.
Swann, Samuel A., Major
Waller, Thomas C., Col.

9th Infantry Battalion
Camden, Gideon D., Jr., Major
Hansbrough, George W., Lt. Col.

9th Infantry Regiment
Crutchfield, Stapleton, Major
Gilliam, James S., Lt. Col.
Godwin, David J., Col.
Hardin, Mark B., Major
Owens, John C., Col.
Phillips, James J., Col.
Preston, John T. L., Lt. Col.
Richardson, William J., Lt. Col.
Smith, Francis H., Col.

9th Militia Regiment
Gresham, Thomas R., Lt. Col.
Saunders, William A., Major

10th Heavy Artillery Battalion
Allen, William, Major
Hensley, James O., Major

10th Cavalry Regiment
Caskie, Robert A., Col.
Clement, William B., Lt. Col.
Davis, J. Lucius, Col.
McGruder, Zachariah S., Lt. Col.
Rosser, Joseph T., Major

10th Infantry Regiment
Coffman, Isaac G., Major
Gibbons, Simeon B., Col.
Martz, Dorilas H. L., Lt. Col.
Stover, Joshua, Major
Walker, Samuel T., Lt. Col.
Warren, Edward T. H., Col.

11th Cavalry Regiment
Ball, Mottrom D., Lt. Col.
Funsten, Oliver R., Col.
Harness, William H., Major
Lomax, Lunsford L., Col.
McDonald, Edward H., Major

11th Infantry Regiment
Clement, Adam, Major
Funsten, David, Col.
Garland, Samuel, Jr., Col.
Harrison, Carter H., Major
Hutter, James R., Major
Langhorne, Maurice S., Col.
Otey, Kirkwood, Col.

12th Artillery Battalion
Boggs, Francis J., Major

12th Cavalry Regiment
Burks, Richard H., Lt. Col.
Harman, Asher W., Col.
Knott, John L., Major
Massie, Thomas B., Lt. Col.

12th Infantry Regiment
Brockett, Edgar L., Major
Feild, Everard M., Col.
Jones, Richard W., Major
Lewellen, John R., Lt. Col.
May, John P., Major
Taylor, Fielding L., Lt. Col.
Weisiger, David A., Col.

13th Artillery Battalion
Gibbes, Wade H., Major
King, J. Floyd, Lt. Col.
Owen, William M., Major

13th Cavalry Regiment
Belsches, Benjamin W., Major
Chambliss, John R., Jr., Col.
Gillette, Joseph E., Major
Phillips, Jefferson C., Col.
Savage, Alexander, Lt. Col.
Upshaw, Thomas E., Lt. Col.
Winfield, Benjamin F., Major

13th Infantry Regiment
Crittenden, Charles T., Major
Goodman, George A., Lt. Col.
Hill, Ambrose P., Col.
Sherrard, John B., Major
Terrill, Jamesc B., Col.
Walker, James A., Col.

14th Cavalry Battalion
Burroughs, Edgar, Major

14th Cavalry Regiment
Bailey, Robert A., Col.
Cochran, James, Col.
Eakle, Benjamin F., Major
Gibson, John A., Lt. Col.
Jackson, George, Major
Thorburn, Charles E., Col.

14th Infantry Regiment
Evans, Moses F. T., Lt. Col.
Godwin, David J., Col.
Hodges, James G., Col.
Poindexter, Parke, Lt. Col.
Poore, Robert H., Major
Shelton, William D., Major
White, William, Col.
Wood, William W., Lt. Col.

15th Cavalry Battalion
Critcher, John, Lt. Col.

15th Cavalry Regiment
Ball, William B., Col.
Burroughs, Edgar, Major
Collins, Charles R., Col.
Critcher, John, Lt. Col.

15th Infantry Regiment
August, Thomas P., Col.
Clarke, Charles H., Major
Crenshaw, James R., Lt. Col.
Morrison, Emmett M., Lt. Col.
Peyton, Thomas G., Lt. Col.
Tucker, Henry St. G., Lt. Col.
Walker, John S., Major

16th Cavalry Battalion
Belsches, Benjamin W., Major

16th Cavalry Regiment
Ferguson, Milton J., Col.
Graham, William L., Lt. Col.
Nounnan, James H., Major

16th Infantry Regiment
Colston, Raleigh E., Col.
Crump, Charles A., Col.
Crutchfield, Stapleton, Col.
Ham, Joseph H., Col.
Holladay, Francis D., Major
Page, John C., Lt. Col.
Parrish, Henry T., Col.
Whitehead, Richard O., Lt. Col.
Woodhouse, John T., Major

17th Cavalry Battalion
(Transferred to 11th Cavalry)
Funsten, Oliver R., Lt. Col.
Patrick, William, Major

17th Cavalry Regiment
French, William H., Col.
Smith, Frederick F., Major
Tavenner, William C., Lt. Col.

17th Infantry Regiment
Brent, George W., Major
Corse, Montgomery D., Col.
Herbert, Arthur, Col.
Marye, Morton, Col.
Munford, William, Lt. Col.
Simpson, Robert H., Major
Tyler, Grayson, Lt. Col.

18th Heavy Artillery Battalion
Hardin, Mark B., Major
Howard, James, Lt. Col.

18th Cavalry Regiment
Beall, David E., Lt. Col.
Imboden, George W., Col.
Monroe, Alexander, Major

18th Infantry Regiment
Cabell, George C., Lt. Col.
Carrington, Henry A., Col.
Wall, Edwin G., Major
Withers, Robert E., Col.

19th Heavy Artillery Battalion
Atkinson, John W., Lt. Col.
Cary, Nathaniel R., Major

19th Cavalry Regiment
Downs, George, Major
Jackson, William L., Col.
Thompson, William P., Lt. Col.

19th Infantry Regiment
Boyd, Waller M., Major
Cocke, P. St. George, Col.
Ellis, John T., Lt. Col.
Gantt, Henry, Col.
Peyton, Charles S., Lt. Col.
Rust, Armistead T. M., Col.
Strange, John B., Col.
Taylor, Bennett, Lt. Col.
Watts, William, Major

20th Artillery Battalion
DeLagnel, Johnston, Major
Robertson, James E., Major

20th Cavalry Regiment
Arnett, William W., Col.
Evans, Dudley, Lt. Col.
Hutton, Elihu, Major
Lady, John B., Lt. Col.

20th Infantry Regiment
Crenshaw, James R., Lt. Col.
Pegram, John, Lt. Col.
Tyler, Nathaniel, Lt. Col.

21st Cavalry Regiment
Edmundson, David, Lt. Col.
Halsey, Stephen P., Major
Peters, William E., Col.

21st Infantry Regiment
Berkeley, William R., Major
Cunningham, Richard H., Jr., Lt. Col.
Gilham, William, Col.
Kelley, Alfred, Major
Moseley, John B., Major
Moseley, William P., Lt. Col.
Patton, John M., Jr., Col.
Shipp, Scott, Major
Witcher, William A., Col.

21st Militia Regiment
Jones, Warner T., Col.
Seawell, William H., Lt. Col.
Taliaferro, Thomas S., Major
Taylor, Fielding L., Lt. Col.

22nd Cavalry Regiment
Bowen, Henry S., Col.
Kendrick, Henry F., Major
Radford, John T., Lt. Col.

22nd Infantry Battalion
Bowles, John S., Major
Johnson, James C., Lt. Col.
Tayloe, Edward P., Lt. Col.

22nd Infantry Regiment
Bailey, Robert A., Major
Barbee, Andrew R., Lt. Col.
Jackson, William A., Lt. Col.
McDonald, John C., Lt. Col.
Moore, Patrick H., Major
Patton, George S., Col.
Smith, Isaac N., Major
Tompkins, Christopher Q., Col.

23rd Cavalry Regiment
Calmese, Fielding H., Major
O'Ferrall, Charles T., Lt. Col.
White, Robert, Col.

23rd Infantry Battalion
Blessing, William, Major
Cecil, William P., Major
Derrick, Clarence, Lt. Col.
Hounshell, David S., Major

23rd Infantry Regiment
Camden, J. D., Major
Coleman, Clayton G., Jr., Lt. Col.
Crenshaw, James H., Lt. Col.
Curtis, George W., Lt. Col.
Fitzgerald, John P., Lt. Col.
Pendleton, Joseph H., Major
Richardson, Andrew J., Major
Scott, Andrew V., Major
Taliaferro, Alexander G., Col.
Taliaferro, William B., Col.
Walton, Simeon T., Lt. Col.

24th Battalion Partisan Rangers
Scott, John, Major

24th Cavalry Regiment
Barham, Theophilus G., Lt. Col.
Robertson, John R., Major
Robins, William T., Col.

24th Infantry Regiment
Bentley, William W., Major
Early, Jubal A., Col.
Hairston, Peter, Jr., Lt. Col.
Hambrick, Joseph A., Major
Hammet, James P., Major
Maury, Richard L., Lt. Col.
Terry, William R., Col.

25th Cavalry Regiment
Edmundson, Henry A., Lt. Col.
Hopkins, Warren M., Col.
McConnell, Sylvester P., Major

25th Infantry Battalion
Local Defense Troops
Bossieux, Louis J., Major
Elliott, Wyatt M., Lt. Col.
25th Infantry Regiment
Duffy, Patrick B., Lt. Col.
Harper, Wilson, Major
Heck, Jonathan M., Lt. Col.
Higginbotham, John C., Col.
Lilley, Robert D., Lt. Col.
Porterfield, George A., Col.
Reger, Albert G., Major
Robinson, John A., Lt. Col.
Smith, George H., Col.
Thompson, William P., Major
26th Cavalry Regiment
Kessler, Joseph R., Lt. Col.
Ruffner, Henry D., Major
26th Infantry Battalion
Edgar, George M., Lt. Col.
Woodrum, Richard, Major
26th Infantry Regiment
Councill, James C., Lt. Col.
Crump, Charles A., Col.
Fitzhugh, Patrick H., Major
Garrett, Joshua L., Major
Page, Powhatan R., Col.
Perrin, William K., Major
Wheelwright, William H., Major
27th Cavalry Bn. Partisan Rangers
Edmundson, Henry A., Lt. Col.
27th Infantry Regiment
Carpenter, Joseph H., Lt. Col.
Echols, John, Col.
Edmondson, James K., Col.
Frazer, Philip F., Major
Gordon, William W., Col.
Grigsby, Andrew J., Col.
Haynes, Charles L., Lt. Col.
Paxton, Elisha F., Major
Shriver, Daniel M., Lt. Col.
28th Artillery Battalion
Tabb, William B., Major
28th Infantry Regiment
Allen, Robert C., Col.
Paul, Samuel B., Lt. Col.
Preston, Robert T., Col.
Spessard, Michael P., Major
Watts, William, Col.
Wilson, Nathaniel C., Major
Wingfield, William L., Lt. Col.
29th Infantry Regiment
Bruster, Ebenezer, Major
Giles, James, Col.
Haynes, Alexander, Major
Horne, William R. B., Major
Leigh, William, Lt. Col.
Moore, Alfred C., Col.
Smith, Edwin R., Lt. Col.
White, Isaac, Major
30th Battalion Sharpshooters
Clarke, J. Lyle, Lt. Col.
Otey, Peter, Major
30th Infantry Regiment
Barton, William S., Major
Carry, R. Milton, Col.
Chew, Robert S., Col.
Gouldin, John M., Lt. Col.
Harrison, Archibald T., Col.
Peatross, Robert O., Major
31st Infantry Regiment
Arbogast, James C., Major
Boykin, Francis M., Lt. Col.
Chenoweth, Joseph H., Major
Cooper, William P., Major
Hoffman, John S., Col.
Jackson, Alfred H., Lt. Col.
Jackson, William L., Col.
McCutchen, James S. K., Lt. Col.
Reynolds, Samuel H., Col.
32nd Cavalry Battalion
Robertson, John R., Major
32nd Infantry Regiment
Cary, John B., Lt. Col.
Ewell, Benjamin S., Col.
Goggin, James M., Major
Lee, Baker P., Jr., Major
Montague, Edgar B., Col.
Sinclair, Jefferson, Major
Willis, William R., Lt. Col.
33rd Infantry Regiment
Cummings, Arthur C., Col.
Golladay, Jacob B., Major
Grace, Philip T., Major
Holliday, Frederick W. M., Col.
Huston, George, Lt. Col.
Jones, John R., Lt. Col.
Lee, Edwin G., Col.
Lee, William F., Lt. Col.
Neff, John F., Col.
Spengler, Abraham, Col.
34th Cavalry Battalion
McFarlane, John A., Major
Straton, William, Major
Witcher, Vinson A., Lt. Col.
34th Infantry Regiment
(Had been 4th Heavy Artillery)
Bagby, John R., Major
Goode, John T., Col.
Harrison, Randolph, Lt. Col.
35th Cavalry Battalion
Ferneyhough, George M., Major
Myers, Franklin M., Major
White, Elijah V., Lt. Col.
36th Cavalry Battalion
Sweeney, James W., Major

36th Infantry Regiment
Fife, William E., Lt. Col.
Linkous, Benjamin R., Lt. Col.
McCausland, John A., Col.
Reid, Legh W., Lt. Col.
Smith, Thomas, Col.

37th Cavalry Battalion
Claiborne, James R., Major
Dunn, Ambrose C., Lt. Col.

37th Infantry Regiment
Carson, Robert P., Lt. Col.
Fulkerson, Samuel V., Col.
Terry, John F., Lt. Col.
Williams, Titus V., Col.
Wood, Henry C., Major

38th Infantry Regiment
Cabell, Joseph R., Col.
Carrington, Isaac H., Major
Edmonds, Edward C., Col.
Griggs, George K., Col.
Lee, Henderson L., Major
Martin, George A., Lt. Col.
Whittle, Powhatan B., Col.

39th Cavalry Battalion
Richardson, John H., Major

40th Cavalry Battalion
Robins, William T., Lt. Col.
Wren, John F., Major

40th Infantry Regiment
Brockenbrough, John M., Col.
Claybrook, Richard A., Lt. Col.
Cox, Fleet W., Lt. Col.
Cunningham, Arthur S., Lt. Col.
Stakes, Edward T., Major
Taliaferro, Warner T., Major
Walker, Henry H., Lt. Col.

41st Cavalry Battalion
White, Robert, Lt. Col.

41st Infantry Regiment
Blow, George, Jr., Lt. Col.
Chambliss, John R., Jr., Col.
Etheridge, William H., Major
Minetree, Joseph P., Lt. Col.
Parham, William A., Col.
Smith, Francis W., Major

42nd Cavalry Battalion
Robertson, John R., Major
Robins, William T., Lt. Col.

42nd Infantry Regiment
Adams, Pearson B., Major
Burks, Jesse S., Col.
Deyerle, Andrew J., Col.
Lane, Henry, Major
Langhorne, Daniel A., Lt. Col.
Martin, William, Lt. Col.
Penn, John E., Col.
Richardson, Jesse M., Major
Saunders, Samuel H., Lt. Col.
Withers, Robert W., Col.

43rd Cavalry Battalion
Chapman, William H., Major
Mosby, John S., Lt. Col.

44th Infantry Battalion
Batte, Peter V., Major

44th Infantry Regiment
Anderson, David W., Major
Buckner, Thomas R., Lt. Col.
Cobb, Norvell, Col.
Hubard, James L., Lt. Col.
Jones, Alexander C., Lt. Col.
Scott, William C., Col.

45th Infantry Battalion
Beckley, Henry M., Lt. Col.
Woodson, Blake L., Major

45th Infantry Regiment
Browne, William H., Col.
Davis, Alexander M., Lt. Col.
Ficklin, Benjamin F., Lt. Col.
Harman, Edwin H., Lt. Col.
Heth, Henry, Col.
Logan, Robert H., Lt. Col.
Peters, William E., Col.
Sanders, William C., Major
Werth, William H., Lt. Col.
Wharton, Gabriel C., Major

46th Cavalry Battalion
Kessler, Joseph R., Lt. Col.
Ruffner, Henry D., Major

46th Infantry Regiment
Davis, James L., Col.
Duke, Richard T. W., Col.
Fry, Hugh W., Jr., Major
Harrison, Randolph, Col.
Hill, James C., Major
Richardson, John H., Col.
Wise, Peyton, Lt. Col.

47th Cavalry Battalion
Harman, William N., Major

47th Infantry Regiment
Bruce, James D., Lt. Col.
Green, Charles J., Major
Green, William J., Lt. Col.
Lyell, John W., Lt. Col.
Mayo, Robert M., Col.
Richardson, George W., Col.
Tayloe, Edward P., Major

48th Infantry Regiment
Campbell, James C., Major
Campbell, John A., Col.
Dungan, Robert H., Col.
Faris, Wilson, Major
Garnett, Thomas S., Col.
Stewart, David B., Major
White, Oscar, Lt. Col.

49th Infantry Regiment
Christian, Charles B., Lt. Col.
Gibson, Jonathan C., Col.
Murray, Edward, Lt. Col.
Smith, Caleb, Major
Smith, William, Col.

50th Infantry Regiment
Finney, William W., Lt. Col.
Perkins, Lynville J., Major
Poage, Thomas, Col.
Reynolds, Alexander W., Col.
Salyer, Logan H. N., Lt. Col.
Thorburn, Charles E., Major
Vandeventer, Alexander S., Col.

51st Infantry Regiment
Akers, William T., Major
Cunningham, George A., Lt. Col.
Dickey, Stephen M., Major
Forsberg, Augustus, Col.
Graham, David P., Major
Massie, James W., Lt. Col.
Reynolds, Samuel H., Lt. Col.
Wharton, Gabriel C., Col.
Wolfe, John P., Lt. Col.
Yonce, William A., Major

52nd Infantry Regiment
Baldwin, John B., Col.
Harman, Michael G., Col.
Lilley, John D., Lt. Col.
Ross, John D., Lt. Col.
Skinner, James H., Col.
Watkins, Thomas H., Lt. Col.

52nd Militia Regiment
Carter, Hill, Col.
Christian, Bartholomew D., Major
Vaiden, Vulosko, Major

53rd Infantry Regiment
Aylett, William R., Col.
Edmondson, Henry A., Major
Grammer, John, Jr., Col.
Leigh, William, Major
Martin, Rawley W., Lt. Col.
Montague, Edgar B., Lt. Col.
Stevenson, Carter L., Col.
Timberlake, John C., Lt. Col.
Tomlin, Harrison B., Col.
Waddill, George M., Lt. Col.

53rd Militia Regiment
Adams, Henry W., Col.

54th Infantry Regiment
Deyerle, John S., Major
Edmundson, Henry A., Lt. Col.
Harman, Austin, Major
Shelor, William B., Lt. Col.
Taylor, James C., Major
Trigg, Robert C., Col.
Wade, John J., Lt. Col.

55th Infantry Regiment
Archer, Robert H., Lt. Col.
Burke, Thomas M., Major
Christian, William S., Col.
Fauntleroy, Robert B., Major
Lawson, Charles N., Major
Mallory, Francis, Col.
Rice, Evan, Lt. Col.
Saunders, Andrew D., Major
Ward, William N., Major

56th Infantry Regiment
Green, William E., Col.
McPhail, John B., Major
Slaughter, Philip P., Col.
Smith, Timoleon, Lt. Col.
Stuart, William D., Col.

57th Infantry Regiment
Armistead, Lewis A., Col.
Carr, George W., Col.
Dyer, David, Col.
Fontaine, Clement R., Col.
Hanes, Garland B., Major
Heckman, David P., Major
James, Waddy T., Lt. Col.
Keen, Elisha F., Col.
Magruder, John B., Col.
Ramsey, William H., Lt. Col.
Smith, Andrew J., Major
Wade, Benjamin H., Lt. Col.

58th Infantry Regiment
Board, Francis H., Col.
Booker, George E., Major
Crutchfield, Stapleton, Lt. Col.
Goode, Edmund, Col.
Kasey, John G., Lt. Col.
Letcher, Samuel H., Col.
Walker, Edward T., Major

59th Infantry Regiment
Anderson, Frank P., Lt. Col.
Henningsen, Charles F., Col.
Jones, Joseph, Lt. Col.
Lawson, John, Major
Mosby, Robert G., Major
Tabb, William B., Col.

60th Infantry Regiment
Broun, Thomas L., Major
Corley, James L., Lt. Col.
Gilliam, William A., Lt. Col.
Hammond, George W., Lt. Col.
Jones, Buehring H., Col.
Rowan, William S., Major
Spalding, James W., Lt. Col.
Starke, William E., Col.
Summers, John C., Lt. Col.
Swank, William A., Lt. Col.
Sweeney, James W., Lt. Col.
Taylor, Jacob N., Major

61st Militia Regiment
Billups, Robert S., Major
Bohannan, John G., Col.
James, Lemuel, Lt. Col.
Shipley, James S., Major

61st Infantry Regiment
Groner, Virginus D., Col.
McAlpine, Charles R., Major
Niemeyer, William F., Lt. Col.
Stewart, William H., Lt. Col.
Wilson, Samuel M., Col.

62nd Mounted Infantry Regiment
Doyle, Robert L., Lt. Col.
Hall, Samuel Houston, Major
Imboden, George W., Major
Imboden, John D., Col.
Lang, David B., Lt. Col.
Smith, George H., Col.

64th Mounted Infantry Regiment
Gray, Harvey, Major
Pridemore, Auburn L., Col.
Richmond, James B., Lt. Col.
Slemp, Campbell, Col.

87th Militia Regiment
Gresham, Thomas R., Col.
Saunders, William A., Major

115th Militia Regiment
Mallory, Charles K., Col.
Wray, George, Major

Mosby's Rgt. Partisan Rangers
Chapman, William H., Lt. Col.
Mosby, John S., Col.
Richards, Adolphus E., Major